The Language of Law and the Foundations
of American Constitutionalism

For much of its history, the interpretation of the United States Constitution presupposed judges seeking the meaning of the text and the original intentions behind that text, a process that was deemed by Chief Justice John Marshall to be "the most sacred rule of interpretation." Since the end of the nineteenth century, a radically new understanding has developed in which the moral intuition of the judges is allowed to supplant the Constitution's original meaning as the foundation of interpretation. The Founders' Constitution of fixed and permanent meaning has been replaced by the idea of a "living" or evolving constitution. Gary L. McDowell refutes this new understanding, recovering the theoretical grounds of the original Constitution as understood by those who framed and ratified it. It was, he argues, the intention of the Founders that the judiciary must be bound by the original meaning of the Constitution when interpreting it.

Begs the question [handwritten]

Gary L. McDowell is a professor in the Jepson School of Leadership Studies at the University of Richmond, where he holds the Tyler Haynes Interdisciplinary Chair of Leadership Studies, Political Science, and Law. He is the author or editor of ten books, including *Equity and the Constitution: The Supreme Court, Equitable Relief and Public Policy*; *Curbing the Courts: The Constitution and the Limits of Judicial Power*; *Justice vs. Law: Courts and Politics in American Society* (with Eugene W. Hickok, Jr.); and *Friends of the Constitution: Writings of the "Other" Federalists* (edited with Colleen Sheehan). In addition to his teaching appointments, he has served as the director of the Office of the Bicentennial of the Constitution at the National Endowment for the Humanities; associate director of public affairs at the United States Department of Justice and chief speechwriter to United States Attorney General Edwin Meese III; and director of the Institute of United States Studies in the University of London.

Re McD's fairness to contrary thinkers, he seems to say that not only is the question whether to interpret the Constitution, but also whether to get at the intention of the document. By definition, then, those who disagree with McD. aren't interpreting the Const., because they're not looking for an intention, rather than coming up with a different meaning and intention. Yet his own discussion of Jeffersonian vs. Federalist const. interp. refutes the argument.

McD doesn't deal with language in any sophisticated sense, uncritically accepting Hobbes & Locke on language w/o any attention to or evident awareness of 20th-century work in the phil. of language.

The best part of the book is the chapters on the founding period, but they undermine McD's claim that recurrence to original intention suffices. He shows, but does not see the implications thereof, that the founders themselves were divided about the original intention.

McD. maintains a crude, early modern theory of private language, unaware of 20thC century critiques like Wittgenstein. Orphalis as a private-lang. argument

McD's point may be that under either a Federalist or a Jeffersonian view of the Const., there are strong limits on judicial power

The Language of Law and the Foundations of American Constitutionalism

Is McD. fair to the original intention of those thinkers he critiques?

No extended — and unnecessary — treatment of Locke and early modern pol. theory serves to justify the notion of pop. sovereignty and critique that of higher law.

GARY L. McDOWELL

University of Richmond

Why is this book necessary? Preaching to the choir? 1762 footnotes

McD. may be an advocate of "original meaning," but if his historical accounts correct, there was no unified original meaning — only a Federalist original meaning and a Jeffersonian original meaning.

McD. is so opposed to judicial power that he appears to endorse the compact theory of the union — the theory relied only the secessionists — as the best or only way of undercutting the interpretive claims of the fed. judiciary over state courts.

P. 302: Taylor says (McD. quotes approvingly?) that the Convention created a federal and not a national govt. That rejects not only Madison's claim (and he changed his mind, so which was Madison the founder?) that the new govt. was a mixture of both, but the more persuasive claim that it was a distinctly new kind of govt (no fed nat. zero-sum game).

CAMBRIDGE UNIVERSITY PRESS

CAMBRIDGE UNIVERSITY PRESS
Cambridge, New York, Melbourne, Madrid, Cape Town, Singapore,
São Paulo, Delhi, Dubai, Tokyo, Mexico City

Cambridge University Press
32 Avenue of the Americas, New York, NY 10013-2473, USA

www.cambridge.org
Information on this title: www.cambridge.org/9780521140911

First published 2010

Printed in the United States of America

A *catalog record for this publication is available from the British Library.*

Library of Congress Cataloging in Publication data

McDowell, Gary L., 1949–
The language of law and the foundations of American
constitutionalism / Gary L. McDowell.
p.   cm.
Includes bibliographical references and index.
ISBN 978-0-521-19289-7 (hardback) – ISBN 978-0-521-14091-1 (pbk.)
1. Constitutional law – United States.   2. Law – United States – Language.
3. Constitutional law – Interpretation and construction.   I. Title.
KF4550.M33   2010
342.73–dc22   2009039190

ISBN 978-0-521-19289-7 Hardback
ISBN 978-0-521-14091-1 Paperback

To
Walter Berns, Robert H. Bork, and Edwin Meese III;
and to the memory of
Raoul Berger, James McClellan, and Herbert J. Storing;
but, above all,
to
Brenda

And when a strict interpretation of the Constitution, according to the fixed rules which govern the interpretation of laws, is abandoned, and the theoretical opinions of individuals are allowed to control its meaning, we have no longer a Constitution; we are under the government of individual men, who, for the time being, have power to declare what the Constitution is, according to their own views of what it ought to mean.

Justice Benjamin Robbins Curtis,
Dred Scott v. Sandford (dissenting)

Contents

Preface and Acknowledgments   *page* ix

    Introduction: The Politics of Original Intention   1

1   The Constitution and the Scholarly Tradition: Recovering the
    Founders' Constitution   9

2   Nature and the Language of Law: Thomas Hobbes and the
    Foundations of Modern Constitutionalism   55

3   Language, Law, and Liberty: John Locke and the Structures of
    Modern Constitutionalism   82

4   The Limits of Natural Law: Modern Constitutionalism and
    the Science of Interpretation   169

5   The Greatest Improvement on Political Institutions: Natural
    Rights, the Intentions of the People, and Written Constitutions   225

6   Chains of the Constitution: Thomas Jefferson, James Madison,
    and the "Political Metaphysics" of Strict Construction   252

7   The Most Sacred Rule of Interpretation: John Marshall,
    Originalism, and the Limits of Judicial Power   311

8   The Same Yesterday, Today, and Forever: Joseph Story and
    the Permanence of Constitutional Meaning   343

    Epilogue: The Moral Foundations of Originalism   379

Index of Cases   401
General Index   403

Preface and Acknowledgments

The debate over the proper role of judges in the Anglo-American legal system is as old as the system itself. Long ago, Thomas More summed it up in a way that could have been clipped from yesterday's news, making clear there was no doubt in his mind about what Sir John Baker has called simply the "evil of judicial arbitrariness."[1] More was unambiguous: "If you take away laws and leave everything free to the judges," he argued, "... they will rule as their own nature leads and order whatever pleases them, in which case the people will in no wise be more free but worse off and in a condition of slavery, since instead of settled and certain laws they will have to submit to uncertain whims changing from day to day." This is not a matter of regrettable personal excess, but of inevitable institutional inclination; without restraint, More concluded, "this is bound to happen even under the best judges."[2]

Two and a half centuries later, Sir William Blackstone would make largely the same argument in his *Commentaries on the Laws of England*, arguing that "the liberty of considering all cases in an equitable light must not be indulged too far, lest thereby we destroy all law, and leave the decision of every question entirely in the breast of the judge." Blackstone knew, as More had known before him, that "law, without equity, though hard and disagreeable, is much more desirable for the public good, than equity without law: which would make every judge a legislator, and introduce a most infinite confusion; as there would be almost as many different rules

[1] Sir John Baker, *The Oxford History of the Laws of England* (Oxford: Oxford University Press, 2003), VI (1483–1558): 177.
[2] Thomas More, *Responsio ad Lutherum*, ed. J. M. Headley (1969), pp. 276–279, volume five of *The Complete Works of St. Thomas More*, 15 vols. (New Haven, CT: Yale University Press, 1963–1997), as retranslated and quoted in Baker, *Oxford History of the Laws of England*, p. 177.

of action laid down in our courts, as there are differences of capacity and sentiment in the human mind."[3]

In the United States, Justice Joseph Story, in his capacity as Dane Professor of Law at Harvard University, reemphasized that early learning to his fellow citizens in their still relatively young republic. To assume that judicial power "embraced a jurisdiction so wide and extensive as ... the principles of natural justice," Story argued, would be a "great mistake."[4] Were any court ever to possess such an "unbounded jurisdiction" as that of "enforcing all the rights ... arising from natural law and justice ... it would be ... the most formidable instrument of arbitrary power, that could well be devised."[5] Its arbitrariness would be completely at odds with the most basic premises of the Anglo-American legal system itself. This would be especially true under a written constitution of limited and enumerated powers, the meaning of which was to be deemed "the same yesterday, to-day, and forever."[6] Eventually, in American constitutional terms, the battle lines would come to be drawn over what would come to be called "originalism," the belief that the only legitimate way to interpret the fundamental law is by recourse to the original and binding intentions of those who framed and ratified it.[7]

The literature on this question grew dramatically after the publication in 1977 of Raoul Berger's *Government by Judiciary: The Transformation of the Fourteenth Amendment*.[8] A decade later, after the vote against the nomination of Judge Robert Bork to the Supreme Court of the Untied States, writing on both sides of the divide simply exploded.[9] There are those among the historians who insist that the compromises and concessions demanded of the Constitution's framers and ratifiers mean that there is no easily

---

[3] Sir William Blackstone, *Commentaries on the Laws of England*, 4 vols. (8th ed.; Oxford: Clarendon Press, 1778), I: 91, 62, 62.

[4] Joseph Story, *Commentaries on Equity Jurisprudence*, 2 vols. (12th ed.; Boston: Little, Brown and Co., 1877), I.2.2. Citation indicates volume, section, and page number.

[5] Ibid., I.19.15.

[6] Joseph Story, *Commentaries on the Constitution of the United States*, 2 vols. (Boston; 3rd ed.; Little, Brown and Co., 1858), I.426.303. Citation indicates volume, section, and page number.

[7] A masterful history of this debate is to be found in Johnathan O'Neill, *Originalism in American Law and Politics: A Constitutional History* (Baltimore: The Johns Hopkins University Press, 2005). See also Christopher Wolfe, *The Rise of Modern Judicial Review: From Constitutional Interpretation to Judge-Made Law* (New York: Basic Books, 1986); and Matthew J. Franck, *Against the Imperial Judiciary: The Supreme Court vs. the Sovereignty of the People* (Lawrence: University Press of Kansas, 1996).

[8] (Cambridge: Harvard University Press, 1977); the second edition contains a helpful bibliography of Berger's many essays defending his views on originalism (Indianapolis: Liberty Fund, 1997). For a brief sketch of Berger's contributions and the controversies he spawned, see Gary L. McDowell, "The True Constitutionalist: Raoul Berger, 1901–2000," *Times Literary Supplement* (25 May 2001), p. 15.

[9] Not least among the most important books is Robert H. Bork's own *The Tempting of America: The Political Seduction of the Law* (New York: The Free Press, 1989).

discernible original meaning or intention to be found.[10] So, too, are there those who argue that language itself presents barriers to ever being able to know the original intention behind the words.[11] There are also those who are generally sympathetic to the idea of turning to original intention but who believe it is an approach less historical than analytical.[12] And then there are those with real power who insist that originalism, properly understood, is a judicial recourse to the original meaning of the text, thus avoiding any confusions about intentions that might be more subjective than objective.[13]

What follows makes no effort to review comprehensively that sprawling literature, not even, as is often the case, in seemingly endless discursive footnotes designed to smuggle in a book within a book. Rather, the objective here is to take account of the origins and fate of originalism as a primary interpretive method with roots not only in the common law tradition but also in the philosophic sources of modern liberalism, in particular the theories of language and meaning and the abuse of words to be found in the works of Thomas Hobbes and John Locke.[14] These are then traced through the influential writings of such thinkers as Jean Jacques Burlamaqui, Thomas Rutherforth, John Trenchard and Thomas Gordon, William Blackstone, Montesquieu, and the American Founders, and then through the constitutional jurisprudence of Chief Justice John Marshall and Justice Story. The

[10] See, for example, Jack N. Rakove, *Original Meanings: Politics and Ideas in the Making of the Constitution* (New York: Knopf, 1997); and Joseph M. Lynch, *Negotiating the Constitution: The Earliest Debates over Original Intent* (Ithaca, NY: Cornell University Press, 1999).

[11] See, for example, Dennis J. Goldford, *The American Constitution and the Debate over Originalism* (Cambridge: Cambridge University Press, 2005).

[12] See, for example, Keith Whittington, *Constitutional Interpretation: Textual Meaning, Original Intent and Judicial Review* (Lawrence: University Press of Kansas, 1999); and see also the same author's *Constitutional Construction: Divided Powers and Constitutional Meaning* (Cambridge, MA: Harvard University Press, 1999).

[13] Antonin Scalia, *A Matter of Interpretation: Federal Courts and the Law*, ed. A. Gutmann (Princeton, NJ: Princeton University Press, 1997). For a careful assessment of Scalia's constitutional jurisprudence, see Ralph A. Rossum, *Antonin Scalia's Jurisprudence: Text and Tradition* (Lawrence: University Press of Kansas, 2006).

[14] For an important survey of the common law tradition and its principle that the duty of a judge is to follow the law of the land, see Philip Hamburger, *Law and Judicial Duty* (Cambridge, MA: Harvard University Press, 2008).

For critical consideration of some of the literature, see Gary L. McDowell, "Great Collaboration," *Times Literary Supplement* (9 June 1995); "Madison's Filter," *Times Literary Supplement* (24 May 1996); "Reading the Letter of the Law,' *Times Literary Supplement* (6 June 1997); "No Room for Plato," *Times Literary Supplement* (12 June 1998); "Liberty's Vestal Flame," *Times Literary Supplement* (30 April 1999); "Blessings of Liberty," *Times Literary Supplement* (31 August 2001); "A Few Good Men," *Times Literary Supplement* (12 December 2003); "Behind the Words," *Times Literary Supplement* (18 March 2005); "Highly Original," *Times Literary Supplement* (22 September 2006); and "Age of Reason," *Times Literary Supplement* (4 May 2007).

thesis of the book is that there is a moral foundation to originalism when it comes to the interpretation of a written constitution, the natural rights legitimacy of which rests upon the consent of the governed.

As a matter of style, archaic spelling, punctuation, capitalization, and italicization have been changed to conform to contemporary conventions, in most cases.

This book has been a long time in the making and, as a result, the debts I have incurred are many. At various times along the way the research was financially supported by the Smith Richardson Foundation, the Earhart Foundation (on several occasions, in fact), the Lynde and Harry Bradley Foundation, the John M. Olin Foundation, and by a fellowship from the National Endowment for the Humanities. Institutions that provided homes away from home to carry out the research and writing include the Woodrow Wilson International Center for Scholars at the Smithsonian Institution, the Center for Judicial Studies, the Institute of Advanced Legal Studies in the University of London, and a generous three-year stint as a visiting scholar at Harvard Law School. Among the individuals who made this support possible, I owe special thanks to Michael Greve, Hillel Fradkin, James Piereson, William Voegeli, Antony Sullivan, Richard Ware, David Kennedy, Terence Daintith, Robert Clark, and the late James McClellan. My time at Harvard was made even more rewarding by the opportunity to teach in the Department of Government, an opportunity made possible by the limitless generosity of Harvey Mansfield.

Over the years, a team of research assistants contributed much to the project. I am especially grateful to Bill Mikhail at the Wilson Center; Eric Jaso at the Center for Judicial Studies; Curtis Gannon and Roger Fairfax at the University of London; and, at the University of Richmond, Sean Roche, Ellis Baggs, Brian Johnson, John O'Herron, Alison Smith, Joseph Harrington, and Stinson Lindenzweig. Other essential assistance was provided by Anna Brooke, Lucy Pratt Kihlstrom, and Lucy Rainbow.

I am also grateful to the students through the years who have patiently allowed me to work out these arguments in my classes on American constitutional law and history at Harvard, the Institute of United States Studies in the University of London, and the University of Richmond. So, too, is my debt great to my remarkable colleagues who make Richmond the most collegial and supportive university one can imagine.

A veritable army of friends and colleagues generously read and commented on the various chapters as they emerged. This is a much better book than it would otherwise have been thanks to the suggestions and criticism of Raoul Berger, Walter Berns, Robert H. Bork, John Douglass, Terry Eastland, Robert Faulkner, Curtis Gannon, Robert George, Mary Ann Glendon, Robert Goldwin, Lino Graglia, Eugene Hickok, Charles F. Hobson, A. E. Dick Howard, Eric Jaso, Stephen Macedo, James McClellan,

Robert McGeehan, Michael McGiffert, Noel Malcolm, Harvey C. Mansfield, Jr., Kenneth Minogue, Walter Murphy, R. Kent Newmyer, David K. Nichols, Johnathan O'Neill, Thomas Pangle, Stephen Presser, Ralph Rossum, William A. Schambra, Jeffrey Sedgwick, James Stoner, C. Bradley Thompson, Gordon S. Wood, and Michael Zuckert.

I am also deeply appreciative of ideas, suggestions, and words of encouragement offered through the years by Henry J. Abraham, John Agresto, John Bolton, Clement Brown Jr., Hamilton Bryson, J. H. Burns, Sir David Cannadine, Charles J. Cooper, Kenneth Cribb, William Curran, Charles Donahue, Alexander Ercklentz, Charles Fried, Ben Grigsby, Daniel Walker Howe, Mark Levin, Sanford Levinson, Harvey C. Mansfield Jr., Edwin Meese III, John E. A. Morgan, Sandra Peart, James Piereson, J. R. Pole, Terry L. Price, Paul Rahe, Wm. Bradford Reynolds, Sir Christopher Ricks, Robert C. Ritchie, Fred Rosen, Kenneth Ruscio, Rodney Smolla, Kenneth W. Starr, Stephan and Abigail Thernstrom, Herbert W. Vaughan, William Voegeli, and John Wood. I am especially indebted to two colleagues at the University of Richmond, my then-dean J. Thomas Wren and then-provost June Aprille, for making the necessary arrangements for an early sabbatical that enabled me to accept the fellowship from the National Endowment for the Humanities, support that allowed the project to be brought to completion. I am also deeply grateful to my editor at Cambridge University Press, Lewis Bateman, whose interest in the project for more than two decades kept it very much alive.

Scholarship is simply impossible without the assistance of dedicated librarians and the gifted members of their staffs. Special thanks are here owed to the library of American University in Washington, D.C., where I often surreptitiously found Saturday morning asylum from the vicissitudes of government service in order to make my way through Sir William S. Holdsworth's magnificent *History of English Law*; to the Library of Congress for the assistance offered to Fellows at the Wilson Center; to the libraries of Senate House, the Institute of Historical Research, and the Institute of Advanced Legal Studies in the University of London; to the splendid collections of Harvard University generally and especially the rare books room of the library of Harvard Law School; to the libraries of the University of Richmond; and to the incomparable British Library. I owe personal words of thanks to David Warrington of the Harvard Law School, Lucretia McCulley of the University of Richmond's Boatwright Memorial Library, and Jules Winterton of the library of the University of London's Institute of Advanced Legal Studies.

Alongside the great libraries and the attentive librarians in providing assistance have been three notable booksellers. Jordan Luttrell of Meyer Boswell Books, Robert Rubin of Robert Rubin Books, and Herb Tandree of Herb Tandree Philosophy Books have assisted me in various bibliographic queries – as well as supplying shelves of books to feed an undiminishing habit of collection. Their knowledge of the literature of the law is extraordinary.

This book draws freely from articles and essays that have been published along the way. I wish to thank the publishers and editors for their permission to incorporate material from the following here: "The Politics of Original Intention," in Robert A. Goldwin and William A. Schambra, eds., *The Constitution, the Courts, and the Quest for Justice* (Washington, DC: American Enterprise Institute, 1989), pp. 1–24; "The Corrosive Constitutionalism of Edward S. Corwin," *Law & Social Inquiry* 14 (1989): 603–614; "The Limits of Natural Law: Thomas Rutherforth and the American Legal Tradition," *American Journal of Jurisprudence* 37 (1992): 57–81; "Coke, Corwin and the Constitution: The 'Higher Law Background' Reconsidered," *The Review of Politics* 55 (1993): 393–420; "Giles Jacob's *Conduct of Life*," *Notes and Queries* 242 (1997): 190–193; "Leviathan Harpooned," *National Review* (30 June 1997); "The Language of Law and the Foundations of American Constitutionalism," *The William and Mary Quarterly* 55 (1998): 375–398; "The Politics of Meaning: Law Dictionaries and the Liberal Tradition of Interpretation," *American Journal of Legal History* 44 (2000): 257–283; "Bork Was the Beginning: Constitutional Moralism and the Politics of Federal Judicial Selection," *University of Richmond Law Review* 39 (2004–05): 809–818; "The Perverse Paradox of Privacy," in Robert H. Bork, ed., *"A Country I Do Not Recognize": The Legal Assault on American Values* (Stanford, CA: Hoover Institution Press, 2005), pp. 57–84; and "The War for the Constitution," *Wall Street Journal* (23 October 2007), p. A19.

Books often have distant beginnings, and this one began on a cold Tuesday morning in January 1977 in room 302 in the old Social Science Building at the University of Chicago. It was there and then that Professor Herbert J. Storing convened his graduate course on "The American Founding" for the final time. I was blessed to be among those who would be led through the moral, political, and legal intricacies of the creation of the American republic by that most masterful of teachers before his untimely death later that year; like all the others, I would leave his class with an abiding appreciation not only for the American founders but especially for their magnificent Constitution – an appreciation, like that of so many of those who were fortunate enough to have learned from Professor Storing, that has never waned. That is not to say that he would necessarily have agreed with all or even any of what follows. But it is to say that I hope that he might at least have appreciated this effort as a small, if inadequate, token of gratitude for the ways in which he touched and transformed my life.

Nearly a decade later I was privileged to serve in the United States Department of Justice under Attorney General Edwin Meese III. For anyone with an interest in the American Founding, it was a magnificent time to be in government service as the nation prepared to celebrate the bicentennial of the Constitution. No one contributed more to that celebration than did Attorney General Meese with his call for a return by the courts and the nation to "a jurisprudence of original intention," a call that echoes still in our national politics. It is an honor to have been part of his administration, and his friendship has continued to be a constant source of support.

President Reagan's commitment to the Constitution was made manifest by three of his nominees to the Supreme Court of the United States, each of whom subscribed to originalism. Not only was he able in 1986 to elevate Justice William H. Rehnquist to the chief justiceship of the United States, and to appoint federal judge Antonin Scalia as Rehnquist's replacement as an associate justice, but when the retirement of Justice Lewis Powell was announced in 1987, the president turned to Judge Robert H. Bork to fill Powell's seat. Judge Bork was, of all the jurists, the one most committed to the idea of originalism. Although he was denied confirmation to the highest court, his jurisprudential views have not faded, his intellectual followers have not vanished. His principled stand in defense of the Constitution continues to inspire.

In addition to Professor Storing, Attorney General Meese, and Judge Bork, my scholarly debts in the first instance include three others. Over the years my learning about constitutional matters has always been deepened by the writings of, and by conversations with, Walter Berns. It was, in fact, one of his most impressive scholarly efforts that first gave rise to the idea that has come to fruition in this book.[15] During the early years of researching and writing this book, I was – it is not too much to say – adopted by Raoul Berger. Not only did he share with me his office at Harvard Law School, and meet me for a weekly luncheon to discuss my work (nearly always at the splendidly scruffy Three Aces restaurant), but he read and commented upon every word I presumed to write on the subject of originalism in constitutional interpretation until his passing at the age of ninety-nine in 2000. So, too, was my thinking deepened and directed by the sturdy friendship and constant scholarly attention and encouragement of James McClellan. His encyclopedic knowledge of legal literature generally and the American constitutional tradition in particular was both an inspiration and a guide. And on more than one occasion he fearlessly undertook to protect me from myself. Had he lived, this book would have been far better than it is. To say that Jim, like Raoul, is missed daily is to sorely understate the case. The scholarly world is a lesser place without them.

This book is dedicated to these six men with gratitude for the ways in which they have enriched my life, both personally and professionally. This book simply would not have been possible without them – gentlemen all, constitutionalists all.

---

[15] Walter Berns, "Judicial Review and the Rights and Laws of Nature," *Supreme Court Review: 1982* (Chicago: University of Chicago Press, 1983), pp. 49–83.

There are two final debts to acknowledge. The first is to my best friend, Travis McDowell. His patience on our early morning walks in listening to the arguments of this book unfold was remarkable. I never doubted his support, in his own quiet way, even as he often tried to tug me in new and unfamiliar directions.

Finally, my most abiding gratitude is due to my beloved wife, Brenda Evans McDowell. Not only has she lived with this book since she met me, but it was by her enthusiastic encouragement that I returned to it as a full-time project, prompting our move back to the United States after a most spirited decade in London. Her confidence that it would appear never wavered, and for this alone every writer knows how grateful I must be. As with this book, she makes all things possible.

Richmond, Virginia

The Language of Law and the Foundations
of American Constitutionalism

Introduction

The Politics of Original Intention

At 2:00 PM, on Friday, October 23, 1987, the United States Senate committed what many considered then – and what many still consider today – to be an unforgivable political and constitutional sin. Wielding their power to advise and consent on presidential nominations to the federal courts, the members of the upper house voted 58–42 not to confirm Judge Robert H. Bork to the Supreme Court of the United States, the post for which President Ronald Reagan had nominated him nearly four months earlier. The vote, which was the largest margin of defeat in history for a nominee to the Supreme Court, concluded one of the most tumultuous political battles in the history of the republic.[1]

The Senators perhaps had every reason to believe that that would be the end of the story. However ugly it had been, however much time it had taken, Judge Bork's defeat was only one more routine sacrifice to partisan politics. But time would prove wrong anyone who actually thought that. The unprecedented vote against his confirmation reflected something far more fundamental than an ordinary partisan standoff. The battle over Bork was politically transformative, its constitutional lessons enduring.

Bork, of course, was not the first or the only nominee to the high court to be denied confirmation. From the days of President Washington, twenty-nine others had been rejected.[2] But the Bork confirmation fight was historic, and what made it so was that the Senate had chosen to deny confirmation

---

[1] 133 Cong. Rec. 14,985, 15,011 (1987). For accounts of the Bork hearings and their political implications, see Robert H. Bork, *The Tempting of America: The Political Seduction of the Law* (New York: The Free Press, 1990), pp. 269–355; Ethan Bronner, *Battle for Justice: How the Bork Nomination Shook America* (New York: W. W. Norton, 1989), pp. 208–327; and Eugene W. Hickok, Jr., and Gary L. McDowell, *Justice vs. Law: Courts and Politics in American Society* (New York: The Free Press, 1993), pp. 148–162.

[2] Henry J. Abraham, *Justices, Presidents, and Senators: A History of the U.S. Supreme Court Appointments from Washington to Clinton* (Lanham, MD.: Rowman and Littlefield, 1999), p. 13.

to a nominee whose professional qualifications, legal abilities, and personal integrity were never in question.[3] Instead, the Senate rejected his judicial philosophy, even though that philosophy had been the received tradition in the Anglo-American legal system for hundreds of years. His jurisprudence was what has come to be called originalism, the belief that judges and justices in their interpretations of the Constitution must be bound by the original intentions of its framers.

In the end, Bork was rejected on the basis of his beliefs about the limited nature and circumscribed extent of the judicial power he would wield as a justice on the Supreme Court. The issue that united the judge's critics in their scorched-earth opposition to his nomination was the fact that in his sober constitutional jurisprudence there was no room for any airy talk about a general right to privacy, allegedly unwritten constitutions, vague notions of unenumerated rights, or what the progressive Justice Hugo Black once derided as "any mysterious and uncertain natural law concept."[4] In particular, Bork was denied a seat on the highest court because of his unfaltering belief in what Chief Justice John Marshall once called "the most sacred rule of interpretation," the idea that it is "the great duty of a judge who construes an instrument . . . to find the intention of its makers."[5]

For Bork, originalism was the only, or at least the primary, means of interpretation that can accord with a written and ratified constitution of

---

[3] During the Senate confirmation hearings on the nomination, it was repeatedly recalled that former Chief Justice Warren Burger had recently described Judge Bork as being without question the most highly qualified candidate to have been nominated to the Supreme Court in Burger's professional lifetime – a lifetime, it is worth noting, that would have included the appointments of some of the giants of the Supreme Court such as Benjamin Cardozo (1932–38), Hugo Black (1937–71), Felix Frankfurter (1939–62), and Robert H. Jackson (1941–54). For years, Bork had been a formidable intellectual presence in American legal circles, both public and scholarly. He had been solicitor general of the United States, a Yale Law School professor, a scholar whose groundbreaking work in the field of antitrust law was widely acclaimed, and, most recently, a judge on the United States Court of Appeals for the District of Columbia Circuit, where none of his opinions had ever been overturned by the Supreme Court and where, on several occasions, his dissenting opinions had been adopted on appeal as the majority view by the Supreme Court. When pressed during his own testimony at the confirmation hearings, Chief Justice Burger never qualified his expansive praise of Bork; and he was far from being alone in making such an assessment of the nominee. *Nomination of Robert H. Bork to be Associate Justice of the Supreme Court of the United States: Hearings Before the Senate Comm. On the Judiciary*, 100th Cong., 1st sess. 33 (1987), pp. 2096–2117. Hereinafter cited as *Hearings*. Burger insisted that Bork was a "very sound lawyer, and a very fair judge, on the whole record." Moreover, he said, "I surely do not understand the suggestion that he is not in the mainstream of American constitutional doctrine." Ibid., pp. 2101, 2104.

[4] Dissent in *Griswold v. Connecticut*, 381 U.S. 479 (1965), 522.

[5] Gerald Gunther, ed., *John Marshall's Defense of McCulloch v. Maryland* (Stanford, CA: Stanford University Press, 1969), pp. 167–169.

limited and enumerated powers. In his view, "the framers' intentions . . . are
the sole legitimate premise from which constitutional analysis may proceed."
Constitutionalism and the rule of law, if those ideas were to mean anything,
Bork believed, had to mean that "the moral content of law must be given
by the morality of the framer or the legislator, never by the morality of the
judge."[6] It could never be legitimate in a constitutional democracy for a
judge as a matter of interpretation to substitute his own moral judgment for
the considered moral judgments of the legislator or the Founder as expressed
in the written law. To his critics, this view meant that Judge Bork lacked
what they argued was proper "judicial temperament," and put him outside
what they insisted was "the mainstream" of legal opinion.[7]

In a sense, the critics were right. They feared – and probably correctly –
that his jurisprudential approach to constitutional law would almost certainly threaten the liberal tradition of expansive interpretation that had
begun in earnest when Earl Warren ascended to the center chair over thirty
years earlier. The Warren Court, after all, was praised by Bork's most committed critics for having taught more than one generation of lawyers and
judges, in the words of an early supporter of the Warren Court's activism,
that there need be "no theoretical gulf between law and morality," and that
the Supreme Court was the branch of the federal government best equipped
to speak "the language of idealism" for the nation. The result was nothing
less than a "revolutionary" jurisprudential stance in which the historic written Constitution is to be supplemented or supplanted by judicial recourse
to an allegedly unwritten constitution of a higher law that is in its essence
morally evolutionary.[8]

This notion of a "living" constitution denies that there is any settled
fundamental meaning to the Constitution whereby the politics of the nation
may be ordered and guided; rather, it embraces and celebrates quite the
opposite view, that judges should redefine the meaning of the Constitution
over time according to their own "fresh moral insight."[9] The goal of judicial
power after the Warren Court was no longer merely securing constitutional

---

[6] Robert H. Bork, *Tradition and Morality in Constitutional Law* (Washington, DC: American Enterprise Institute, 1984), pp. 10, 11.

[7] See Laurence H. Tribe, *God Save This Honorable Court: How the Choice of Supreme Court Justices Shapes Our History* (New York: Random House, 1985), pp. 106–124.

[8] J. Skelly Wright, "Professor Bickel, the Scholarly Tradition, and the Supreme Court," *Harvard Law Review* 84 (1970–71): 769, 804, 804. The intellectual relationship between Alexander M. Bickel and Robert Bork that grew during their time together on the faculty of the Yale Law School is given a masterful consideration by Johnathan O'Neill in "Shaping Modern Constitutional Theory: Bickel and Bork Confront the Warren Court," *Review of Politics* 65 (2003): 325–351.

[9] Ronald Dworkin, *Taking Rights Seriously* (Cambridge, MA: Harvard University Press, 1977), p. 137.

or legal rights – even judicially created ones. Rather, the goal had become the "moral evolution" of the nation to be led by the courts.[10]

At the most important level, the Bork defeat was about more than merely the partisan and ideological rejection of one highly qualified nominee to the Supreme Court. It was the very public affirmation by the Senate of this new ideological theory of moralistic judging that had been developing for quite some time – even before the advent of the Warren Court, in fact. And that new theory of judging was completely at odds with the great historical tradition of a jurisprudence of original intention of which Bork was so visible a part.[11] The defeat of Robert Bork was historic for what was clearly in danger of being lost when it came to a public understanding of the nature and extent of judicial power.

What was at stake was the original view of the Constitution, an understanding that took seriously the importance of its being a written document the terms of which are to be deemed permanent until and unless changed by the "solemn and authoritative act" of formal amendment.[12] This is the understanding that lies at the core of what may with propriety be called the Founders' Constitution. And it is this idea of a constitution at once fundamental and permanent that is most in danger of being eroded by the new idea of moral judging under an evolving constitution that so fully infuses contemporary constitutional law and theory.

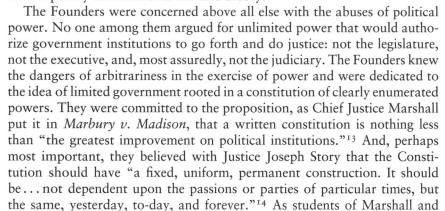

The Founders were concerned above all else with the abuses of political power. No one among them argued for unlimited power that would authorize government institutions to go forth and do justice: not the legislature, not the executive, and, most assuredly, not the judiciary. The Founders knew the dangers of arbitrariness in the exercise of power and were dedicated to the idea of limited government rooted in a constitution of clearly enumerated powers. They were committed to the proposition, as Chief Justice Marshall put it in *Marbury v. Madison*, that a written constitution is nothing less than "the greatest improvement on political institutions."[13] And, perhaps most important, they believed with Justice Joseph Story that the Constitution should have "a fixed, uniform, permanent construction. It should be...not dependent upon the passions or parties of particular times, but the same, yesterday, to-day, and forever."[14] As students of Marshall and Story, originalists such as Judge Bork argue for the recovery of the Founders'

---

[10] Michael Perry, *The Constitution, the Court, and Human Rights* (New Haven, CT: Yale University Press, 1980), p. 101.

[11] See Raoul Berger, "'Original Intention' in Historical Perspective," *George Washington Law Review* 54 (1985–86): 296–337.

[12] Jacob Cooke, ed., *The Federalist* (Middletown, CT: Wesleyan University Press, 1961), No. 78, p. 528. Hereinafter cited as *The Federalist*.

[13] 5 U.S. 137 (1803), 176.

[14] Joseph Story, *Commentaries on the Constitution of the United States*, 2 vols. (3rd ed.; Boston: Little, Brown and Co., 1858), I.426.303. Citation indicates volume, section, and page number.

Constitution and the idea that interpretation, in order to be legitimate, must be rooted in the text and the original intention behind that text.[15]

While this view may be more modest than the current dominant view, it is also safer, constitutionally and politically. For at bottom it accepts a basic truth of American constitutionalism. As James Wilson said at the Constitutional Convention, "laws may be unwise, may be dangerous, may be destructive ... and yet not be unconstitutional."[16] This older view of the Constitution – the Constitution understood as positive law – was premised on the belief that when it came to interpreting the Constitution there were limits to the influence of higher law, limits to judicial recourse to an allegedly unwritten constitution in interpreting the written text.

Where the Constitution's framers and ratifiers intended to protect rights, so argue the originalists, the document does so – clearly and simply. Where it is silent, it is silent. The due process clauses are not, nor were they intended to be, judicial wild cards whereby contemporary moral, political, or economic theories may be made to trump the Constitution's original meaning; the Ninth Amendment is not a statement of unenumerated rights so fundamental and sweeping as to render all the other rights explicitly mentioned in the text superfluous; most of all, Article III, which creates the federal judicial power, is not the primary means whereby rights are to find their protection. It would have struck the Founders not only as dangerous but as bizarre to have expected the security of their rights to depend upon a judiciary willing to plunge into a moral discourse unattached to the constitutional text and divorced from the intentions that lie behind the document itself.[17]

A jurisprudence of original intention appreciates the design and objects of the Constitution. It unflinchingly recognizes the limitations of popular government – such as the possibility of majority tyranny – and the need to secure individual rights. But it also denies that good government and the sound security of rights are ever to be expected from any body of judges even if (or perhaps especially if) dedicated to the judicial pursuit of an allegedly higher law contained within an unwritten constitution. The Constitution

---

[15] As Joseph Story put it, the "fundamental maxim ... in the interpretation of ... positive laws is that the intention ... is to be followed. This intention is to be gathered from the words, the context, the subject matter, the effects and consequences, and the spirit and reason are to be ascertained, not from vague conjecture, but from the motives and language apparent on the face of the law." Joseph Story, "Law, Legislation, Codes," in Francis Lieber, ed., *Encyclopedia Americana*, 13 vols. (Philadelphia: Lea & Blanchard, 1844), VII: 576–592, p. 576. This essay has been reprinted in James McClellan, *Joseph Story and the American Constitution* (Norman: University of Oklahoma Press, 1971), p. 365.

[16] Max Farrand, ed., *Records of the Federal Convention*, 4 vols. (New Haven, CT: Yale University Press, 1937), II: 73. Hereinafter cited as *Records of the Federal Convention*.

[17] On the facts of the relationship between framers' limited institutional provisions for the judiciary and their expectations of its role, see Gary L. McDowell, "Bork Was the Beginning: Constitutional Moralism and the Politics of Federal Judicial Selection," *University of Richmond Law Review* 39 (2005): 809, 813–817.

with its carefully contrived institutional balances and checks was devised precisely to supply, as James Madison said in *The Federalist*, "the defect of better motives."[18] Sturdy institutions replaced good intentions as the source of good government in the Founders' new science of politics. To allow the courts to enter the realm of substantive policy making denies the logic and the limits of the most basic idea of written constitutions. Distrusting the moral impulses of judges is not morally cynical; it is politically prudent.

The only way the inherently undemocratic power of judicial review can be reconciled with the demands of republican government is by keeping it tied to the written text of the fundamental law. Only by conforming to the "intention of the people"[19] as expressed in the document can the judges legitimate what they do; as they range further from the text and intention, their power becomes increasingly suspect. "The Court," as Justice Byron White once argued, "is most vulnerable and comes nearest to illegitimacy when it deals with judge-made constitutional law having little or no cognizable roots in the language or design of the Constitution."[20]

This is the essential dilemma posed by the new anti-originalist jurisprudence, the wide-ranging moralistic judging rooted in a so-called "living" constitution that has come to characterize the exercise of contemporary judicial power. Not only does such judicial activism violate the separation of powers and make the judges policy makers at a given moment, but over time it weakens the role of the Court by undermining its only claim to legitimacy – that when it speaks it is only enforcing the clear will of the sovereign people as already expressed in their Constitution.

As Madison said of the legislatures of his day, so might it be said about the courts of the present: the judiciary has "every where extended the sphere of its activity and draw[n] all power into its impetuous vortex."[21] Where the Founders could say with confidence that "[j]udges ... are not presumed to possess any peculiar knowledge of the mere policy of public measures,"[22] more recent generations have come to believe that judges are indeed quite well equipped to deal with the most sensitive and politically controversial areas of policy. And as the courts have become ever more immersed in the "mere policy of public measures," the choice of who shall wield those vast extra-constitutional powers has become ever more politically important, with the sad result – made clear in the Bork confirmation fight – that the federal courts are no longer to be left above the fray.

---

[18] *The Federalist*, No. 51, p. 349.
[19] *The Federalist*, No. 78, p. 525.
[20] *Bowers v. Hardwick*, 478 U.S. 186 (1982), 194.
[21] *The Federalist*, No. 48, p. 333.
[22] Nathaniel Ghorum in the Constitutional Convention, *Records of the Federal Convention*, II: 73.

How did this state of affairs come about? It is not enough to say that the present dilemma is the result of power-grabbing judges bent on wielding their powers in order to achieve the policy ends they prefer. There is some of that, of course; but the whole answer is more complicated. The story involves not just judicial usurpation but also Congress's abdication of its responsibility to shape the judicial process by rules and regulations and to make exceptions to the Supreme Court's jurisdiction. In many ways, Congress has been more than willing to leave the federal courts to their own devices.[23]

But neither does the whole answer lie simply in the institutional relationship between the judiciary and the legislature. It has also involved something far more subtle. Since the last third of the nineteenth century there has been a change in the ideas about judicial power. The new ideas have been largely created and encouraged not by the courts themselves but by the scholarly community. Legal scholars have become adept at creating new theories of interpretation, and new understandings of what constitutionalism generally and the United States Constitution in particular demand of the judges. Indeed, the new dominant anti-originalist, aconstitutional constitutionalism has its roots as much in the classroom as in the courtroom. As Edward S. Corwin once put it, "if judges make law, so do commentators."[24] At the head of the fight against Robert Bork's nomination was a phalanx of professors that was able to persuade the public and the Senate that Bork's originalism was outside the "mainstream" of legal opinion that the professors themselves had helped to divert from its long-established, traditional path.[25]

More important, in a sense, than what led to the current state of affairs is what might reasonably be done about it. What might help restore an appreciation for the Constitution's original institutional design and thus a firmer understanding of the true nature and proper extent of judicial interpretation? It is in this sense that the vote over Judge Bork's nomination to the Supreme Court is not just a matter of quaint historical interest but the first great battle in the contemporary war for the Constitution – a continuing war that must be won if true self-government as envisioned by the Founders is to prevail. Time has shown that originalism as a theory of constitutional interpretation remains very much alive; Bork was defeated, but his central idea was not. That theory of interpretation and its implicit belief in restrained judging continues to guide those who believe that the inherent arbitrariness of government by judiciary is not the same thing as the rule of law.

---

[23] See Gary L. McDowell, *Curbing the Courts: The Constitution and the Limits of Judicial Power* (Baton Rouge: Louisiana State University Press, 1988).

[24] Edward S. Corwin, "Review: *The Law of the American Constitution*, by Charles K. Burdick," *Michigan Law Review* 22 (1923): 84, p. 84.

[25] For a listing of those in the legal academy who opposed the Bork nomination, see *Hearings*, pp. 1335–1341, 1342–1345, 3351–3354, 3355–3412.

Changing the public mind is never quick or easy. To recover the Founders' Constitution it will be necessary to demonstrate that recourse to original intention – John Marshall's "most sacred rule of interpretation" – is the true mainstream flowing from the well-established legal and constitutional traditions of the nation. This book is an attempt at that recovery of the intellectual and philosophic foundations of that jurisprudence of original intention as the most sound approach to judicial interpretation under our constitution of enumerated and limited powers and liberties.

The Constitution and the Scholarly Tradition

Recovering the Founders' Constitution

The Constitution of the United States was born in controversy, and thus has it lived. From the time of the ratification struggle and the debates between the Federalists and the Anti-Federalists, to disputes between the Jeffersonians and the Hamiltonians, to the debate between Chief Justice John Marshall and President Andrew Jackson, to the crisis of the house divided and the impassioned rhetoric of Abraham Lincoln and Stephen A. Douglas, throughout American history the question of how to interpret the Constitution has animated and divided public opinion. The reason, of course, is that the Constitution is a document explicitly designed to order the nation's politics; politically, a great deal hangs on the peg of interpretation.

Since the last quarter of the nineteenth century there has been a growing public debate of a rather different sort over constitutional interpretation. It is, at one level, a debate that is part of the earlier American political tradition; but at another level it is unlike the other great constitutional debates up to that time. In those earlier debates, the line was typically drawn between those who understood themselves to be "strict" constructionists (such as Thomas Jefferson) and those who saw themselves as "fair" or "reasonable" constructionists (such as Alexander Hamilton and John Marshall). The question for both groups was how to read the Constitution. The common objective of the two interpretive camps was to reveal the proper or true meaning of the text as explained and supported by the original intentions of the framers behind that text. Now, the debate is between those who continue to argue that constitutional meaning is to be found in text and intention, and others who insist upon an evolutionary interpretive approach that openly encourages judges to import new meaning into the text; the question now is largely not how but whether to read the Constitution in light of its original meaning.

This shift from text and intention to the moral intuition of a judge as the foundation of constitutional meaning is not a matter of ideology. Both political liberals and political conservatives at one time or another have embraced it by creating such doctrines as the "liberty of contract" and the "right to privacy" – neither of which appears in the Constitution. But whether from the left or the right, the price that is paid for this shift is the same: it is the abandonment of the original Founders' Constitution in favor of an allegedly "unwritten constitution" of higher law to which judges are encouraged to turn in order to ground their constitutional decisions in contemporary and evolving moral sentiments.

In the name of interpreting the Constitution, the new constitutional moralists attack the very foundations of constitutionalism by undermining the binding force of language. Words, they insist, no longer mean what they originally were understood to mean by those who used them; meaning is to be found in the mind of the reader rather than in the intention of the writer. The result has been a constitutionalism that is largely bereft of the Constitution itself. The idea that there is an unwritten constitution to which the judges may turn frees theory from form; it liberates contemporary judicial opinion from the shackles of historical truth.[1] Such a view goes completely against the Founders' view of judging, a view gleaned from centuries of experience.[2]

The most distinctive aspect of the current debate over interpretation is that it has not been simply political or judicial; it has also been academic. From the outset, the movement to abandon the Founders' Constitution has been encouraged by the scholarly community. From their earliest issues, law reviews and journals of history and political science have been friendly to scholars seeking to create new constitutional theories and willing to praise those on the bench who might adopt them. In the scholarly imagination, the Founders' Constitution largely ceased to exist a long time ago.

---

[1] As Laurence Tribe has described it: "constitutional interpretation is a practice alive with choice but laden with content; and ... this practice has both boundaries and moral significance not wholly reducible to, although never independent of, the ends for which it is employed." Thus the contemporary concern is with *"doing* constitutional law ... constructing constitutional arguments and counter-arguments or exploring premises and prospects of alternative constitutional approaches in concrete settings.... [T]he core ... concern is the making of constitutional law itself – its tensions and tendencies ... its limits as a form of activity; in a word, its horizons." Laurence Tribe, *Constitutional Choices* (Cambridge, MA: Harvard University Press, 1985), pp. 4, ix-x.

[2] Robert Cover's view of this history is enlightening. "Judicial review," Cover observed, "is tolerable because judges themselves are limited. The very instrument that affords them their power is also their master. For the judge may not properly act of his own 'will'. His function is one of 'judgment' assessing the indicia of the various 'wills' of others." As a result, "a conscientious execution of the judge's job involves self-limitation to explicit constitutional and legal authority, i.e., to positive law." In the view of the founding generation, Cover concludes, "the judge ... inherited a tradition binding him to the explicit sources of law. Constitutions were the highest examples of such explicit law. In their written form they justified judicial review precisely because they were positive law. The notion that out beyond lay a higher law to which the judge *qua* judge was responsible was never a part of the mainstream of American jurisprudence." Robert Cover, *Justice Accused: Anti-Slavery and the Judicial Process* (New Haven, CT: Yale University Press, 1975), pp. 27, 28, 29.

While the new understanding of constitutional interpretation as moral theory first came to dominance in the Warren Court, its intellectual roots run far deeper. The contemporary academic supporters of this jurisprudential school are, in fact, but the descendants of older schools of thought, schools whose leaders paved the political path for the ascendance of modern judicial activism. In particular, the current jurisprudence of constitutional moralism has grown from seeds planted during the last decades of the nineteenth century and brought to fruition during the early years of the twentieth century.

Between 1870 and 1925 the foundations of modern constitutional law and theory were laid largely by three scholars, one in law and two in political science. Christopher Columbus Langdell, the first dean of the Harvard Law School, and Woodrow Wilson and Edward S. Corwin, in succession each the McCormick Professor of Jurisprudence in the Politics Department at Princeton, successfully supplanted the grounds of the Founders' Constitution and prepared the way for the rise of the ideology of a "living constitution."

Langdell transformed the way law was taught and understood through three innovations. The first and arguably most important was his introduction of the case method of instruction in 1870, replacing the treatise as the focus of legal education with the decided cases of the courts in an effort to make the study of law scientific and thus worthy of inclusion in the curriculum of a university. Ultimately, the case method would produce "a far-reaching change in the general conception of the nature and purpose of legal education." In 1873, Langdell further startled the legal profession and irritated the university community by hiring the first purely theoretical law professor, James Barr Ames. Since law was a science, it required "philosophical" professors, not practitioners, to teach it. The third development during Langdell's tenure was the creation of the *Harvard Law Review* in 1887. Such student-edited law reviews would soon proliferate, becoming the "literary meeting place and powerful organ"[3] of the newly intellectualized professoriate. And in a short time they would become the avenue by which the latest theorizing in the law schools would routinely make its way into the judges' chambers. Together these changes would greatly contribute to the shift in thinking about the law from principles to precedents.

Woodrow Wilson, both a lawyer by training and a political scientist by profession, would seek to displace the theoretical foundations of the Founders' Constitution with a new science of politics. Like Langdell, Wilson embraced the scientific enthusiasms of the day and sought to replace what he described as the Founders' Newtonian conception of constitutional law and politics with a Darwinian notion; the result would be an argument

---

[3] Josef Redlich, *The Common Law and the Case Method in American University Law Schools* (New York: Carnegie Endowment, 1914), pp. 25, 49. Hereinafter cited as *Common Law and the Case Method*.

in behalf of a constitution of evolving meaning, a fundamental law that was evolutionary, not static. In works such as *Congressional Government* (1885) and *Constitutional Government in the United States* (1908), Wilson undertook to effect nothing less than a refounding of the constitutional order. And later, as president of the United States, Wilson could start to practice what he had preached by appointing to the Supreme Court of the United States in 1916 Louis Brandeis, long an open advocate of judges and justices undertaking to create a truly "living law."[4]

Over the better part of half a century, Edward S. Corwin would build upon Langdell's methodological focus on judge-made law and Wilson's idea of Darwinian constitutional development, enveloping both of those within his own appeal to a new notion of natural law. By 1925 he had developed his theory that the "higher law background" of the American constitutional order was to be found not in the Constitution, but in constitutional law. As he would put it, "the judicial version of the Constitution *is* the Constitution,"[5] an idea that for some would properly be seen as providing "the enduring canon of scholarship"[6] for the remainder of the twentieth century.

While during this same period there were many other scholars influencing the academic study and doctrinal development of the law – perhaps not least Roscoe Pound, Oliver Wendell Holmes, Jr., and Thomas Cooley – the views of Langdell, Wilson, and Corwin are fundamental in understanding precisely how and when the Founders' Constitution began to disappear.

I. CHRISTOPHER COLUMBUS LANGDELL'S REVOLUTION IN LAW

On September 27, 1870, the three members of the faculty of the Harvard Law School – Emory Washburn, Nathaniel Holmes, and Christopher Columbus Langdell – gathered in the office of the president of the university, Charles W. Eliot. Their purpose, following new regulations that had

---

[4] See, for example, Louis D. Brandeis, "The Living Law," *Illinois Law Review* 10 (1915–16): 461–471, p. 467. Brandeis had been a student of Langdell at the Harvard Law School and an early supporter of the *Harvard Law Review*. He understood the power of transforming the law by the proper collection of precedential cases and their analysis in the reviews as a means of making new law. See especially Samuel D. Warren and Louis D. Brandeis, "The Right to Privacy," *Harvard Law Review* 4 (1890): 193–220, an article that would, in time, serve as one of the foundational stones of the new constitutional moralism when the Supreme Court undertook to create the "right to privacy" in a constitutional sense in *Griswold v. Connecticut* (1965).

[5] Edward S. Corwin, "Judicial Review in Action," in Richard Loss, ed., *Corwin on the Constitution*, 3 vols. (Ithaca, NY: Cornell University Press, 1981–88), II: 203. Unless otherwise noted, all citations to Corwin's law review articles will be to this collection, hereinafter cited as *Corwin on the Constitution*.

[6] William M. Wiecek, *The Lost World of Classical Legal Thought: Law and Ideology in America, 1886–1937* (New York: Oxford University Press, 1998), p. 258.

been adopted that past April, was to choose the first dean of the Law School. The group quickly elected to the deanship Langdell, who had been named Dane Professor of Law only in January of that year and who up to that appointment had been an "obscure New York lawyer."[7] He was about to assume a new and largely undefined administrative office whose duties were expected to be merely "formal and trifling."[8] Yet as is often the case in such positions, the deanship would prove to be open to all that Langdell might make of it. And President Eliot, who had known and admired Langdell since his own undergraduate days at Harvard College (he thought him nothing less than "a man of genius"),[9] would see to it that the new dean was able to transform the Law School – and in the process to revolutionize the study and teaching of law.

Founded in 1817, the Law School had reached its peak under the leadership of Justice Joseph Story from 1829 to 1845. As the first Dane Professor of Law, Story, by his distinguished reputation as a justice of the United States Supreme Court and by his seemingly boundless energy, had made the school into one of national prominence and had invigorated the university study of law, not least by the production of his own learned treatises on various aspects of the common law and the law of the United States Constitution.[10] But since Story's day, the school had declined and faded. By 1870, when Langdell assumed the deanship, it was clear he had his work cut out for him.[11] By the time he retired as dean in 1895, Langdell could look back at great success.[12]

Yet the administrative and institutional changes he imposed on the Law School in order to heighten its professionalism and make it the great institution of legal learning that it would eventually become would prove to be the least of Langdell's accomplishments. By far the "most startling and fruitful" change he introduced was in the way the law was studied and taught.[13] In his first year of teaching, Langdell initiated an approach to teaching law

[7] *Common Law and the Case Method*, p. 15.

[8] Arthur E. Sutherland, *The Law at Harvard: A History of Ideas and Men, 1817–1967* (Cambridge, MA: Harvard University Press, 1967), p. 167.

[9] Ibid., p. 159.

[10] Ibid., p. 106.

[11] "He found at Cambridge a school without examination for admission or for the degree, a faculty of three professors giving but ten lectures a week to one hundred and fifteen students of whom fifty-three percent had no college degree, a curriculum without any rational sequence of subjects, and an inadequate and decaying library." James Barr Ames, "Christopher Columbus Langdell," in *Lectures in Legal History and Miscellaneous Legal Essays* (Cambridge, MA: Harvard University Press, 1913), p. 477.

[12] "He lived to see a faculty of ten professors, eight of them his former pupils, giving more than fifty lectures a week to over seven hundred and fifty students, all but nine being college graduates, and conferring the degree after three years' residence and the passing of three annual examinations." Ibid.

[13] Ibid., p. 478.

that he had been thinking about since his own student days at Harvard Law School.[14] His approach was to insist that law was a science and that students would be best prepared for the practice of law if they turned to its "original sources," the adjudged cases that made up the common law tradition. By focusing on the judicial decisions directly, by making the students teach themselves to deal with the difficulties of finding fundamental legal principles in those cases, Langdell's so-called case method eventually turned legal education upside down. Cases were no longer deemed merely illustrative of preexisting principles, but were seen as revealing fundamental principles in the first instance.[15] As a result, the traditional reliance on treatises and lectures in order to teach the students about antecedent principles was lessened in favor of making them actually grapple with the black-letter law that had emerged from the judicial resolution of concrete cases and controversies. Langdell's pedagogic goal was to teach students to think like lawyers, not merely to train them to remember like historians. And his method "created an extraordinarily radical change . . . at a single stroke."[16] So pervasive has been his influence that only by recalling the older mode of legal education can the radicalism of the dean's new scheme be truly appreciated.

No small part of Eliot's and Langdell's design was to make legal education in universities not only respectable but expected. By and large, most lawyers were still trained as apprentices reading law in the offices of established practitioners who would take them on for a fee. Their education was hit-and-miss, at best, depending not least on the extensiveness of their mentor's personal library. School-based legal education had begun in earnest with the establishment in 1784 of the famous and well-regarded private law school of Judge Tapping Reeve in Litchfield, Connecticut.[17] There had also been several appointments to chairs of law at colleges, such as the appointment in 1779 of George Wythe at the College of William and Mary

---

[14] See the recollection of Judge Charles E. Phelps, a classmate of Langdell's, that it was over dinner conversations that "Langdell got the germ of the idea that he later developed into the case system of instruction which has made his name famous both here and abroad." Phelps to Charles Warren, as quoted in Charles Warren, *History of the Harvard Law School*, 3 vols. (New York: Lewis Publishing Co., 1908), II: 181–182.

[15] William Wiecek has described this methodological upheaval most succinctly: "As originally expounded by Blackstone, early legal science presumed the existence of universal principles, resting on theological or moral foundations. From these principles, judges deduced and applied norms of human conduct. In contrast, modern legal science was inductive in its approach, viewing cases as sources of law, from which judges derived principles inductively. The legal scientist's responsibility was to arrange those principles into a system." *The Lost World of Classical Legal Thought*, p. 89.

[16] *Common Law and the Case Method*, p. 12.

[17] See Sutherland, *The Law at Harvard*, p. 28.

to a professorship of law and police created in part by Wythe's former student, Thomas Jefferson, who was at the time governor of Virginia.[18] James Wilson, a signer of both the Declaration of Independence and the Constitution, assumed a professorship of law at the College of Philadelphia (later the University of Pennsylvania) in 1789 during his tenure as an associate justice on the Supreme Court of the United States. And Alexander Hamilton in 1794 worked to see the appointment of James Kent at King's College, later Columbia University.[19]

The earliest efforts to establish law schools were not without their political purposes.[20] There was a general agreement that republics such as the young United States depended upon a citizenry trained in the principles of republicanism. Not least would such a training require a familiarity with law and legal processes. After all, republics, above all other forms of government, boasted of being governments of laws, not simply governments of men. There was no suggestion that legal education should be politically neutral. As a result, there were certain shared assumptions when it came to what students in the law should read and by which their thinking should be guided. One sees this republican commitment clearly in the inaugural lectures of such teachers of the law as James Wilson, James Kent, and Joseph Story.[21] And it was spelled out without ambiguity in the work of yet another early republican professor of the law at the University of Maryland, David Hoffman, in his celebrated text, *A Course of Legal Study*, first published in 1817, with a second edition appearing in 1836.[22]

---

[18] For details on another of Wythe's students, see Charles T. Cullen, "New Light on John Marshall's Legal Education and Admission to the Bar," *American Journal of Legal History* 16 (1972): 345–351.

[19] For an account of the early efforts to establish law schools, see Alfred Zantzinger Reed, *Training for the Public Profession of the Law* (New York: Charles Scribner's Sons, 1921), pp. 107–159.

[20] See generally Anton-Hermann Chroust, *The Rise of the Legal Profession in America*, 2 vols. (Norman: University of Oklahoma Press, 1965), II: 173–223. See also Paul D. Carrington, "The Revolutionary Idea of University Legal Education," *William and Mary Law Review* 31 (1990): 527–574.

[21] James Wilson, "Of the Study of Law in the United States," in Robert G. McCloskey, ed., *The Works of James Wilson*, 2 vols. (Cambridge, MA: Harvard University Press, 1967), I: 69–96; James Kent, "An Introductory Lecture to a Course of Law Lectures," November 17, 1794, reprinted as "Kent's Introductory Lecture," *Columbia Law Review* 3 (1903): 330–343; Joseph Story, "The Value and Importance of Legal Studies," August 25, 1829, in William W. Story, ed., *The Miscellaneous Writings of Joseph Story* (Boston: C. C. Little and J. Brown, 1852), pp. 503–548.

[22] See Thomas L. Shaffer, "David Hoffman's Law School Lectures, 1822–1833," *Journal of Legal Education* 32 (1982): 127–138; Maxwell Bloomfield, "David Hoffman and the Shaping of the Republican Legal Culture," *Maryland Law Review* 38 (1979): 673–688; Carrington, "Revolutionary Idea of University Legal Education," pp. 566–568; and Reed, *Training for the Public Profession of the Law*, pp. 123–126.

Wilson's inaugural lecture in Philadelphia on December 15, 1789, was a great public event, and the newly appointed professor delivered his discourse in the presence of a most distinguished audience, including President and Mrs. Washington, the president's Cabinet, and members of Congress.[23] His series of lectures was broadly learned and deeply republican. As was typical, he began with a discussion of the nature of law generally and then proceeded to a discourse on the law of nature before eventually turning to the range and complexities of law in the new United States. The lectures covered the philosophical foundations of law, the nature of the common law, the particulars of the criminal law, and the institutional details of the law of the recently launched Constitution of the United States. No small part of Wilson's intention was to put the widely celebrated Blackstone in his proper place. Blackstone was, Wilson concluded, no "zealous friend of republicanism," and as a result, while the great English commentator was worthy of study, and for his contributions deserved to be "much admired," it would be a mistake should he be "implicitly followed."[24] In this Wilson the Federalist was at one with Jefferson the Republican, who also looked askance at the Vinerian Professor and his *Commentaries on the Laws of England.*[25]

Kent, like Wilson before him, made clear that his course of lectures was not to be on the law simply but "on the government and laws of our country." Indeed, he said, "the people of this country are under singular obligations, from the nature of their government, to place the study of law at least on a level with the pursuits of classical learning." Properly designed, a course of legal study would inculcate "a correct acquaintance with genuine republican maxims." There was, he insisted, a great "utility" to "academical learning" in establishing "the science of the law as a practical profession." Legal education should combine "the sciences of logic and mathematics," essential as they were to the "art of close reasoning," with "moral philosophy," the doctrines of which "form the foundation of human laws and must be deemed an essential part of juridical education."[26]

All this was necessary, Kent believed, because of the unique character of the American constitutional order in which the courts of justice were "authorized to bring the validity of a law to the test of the Constitution." Unlike the political arrangements of the Old World, America's constitutional

[23] Chroust, *Rise of the Legal Profession*, II: 179, n.2.
[24] Wilson, "On the Study of Law in America," *Works of James Wilson*, I: 79, 80.
[25] For an account of Jefferson's views on legal education, see Morris L. Cohen, "Thomas Jefferson Recommends a Course of Law Study," *University of Pennsylvania Law Review* 119 (1970–71): 823–844; and Morris L. Cohen, Edwin Wolf, and William Jeffrey, Jr., "Historical Development of the American Lawyer's Library," *Law Library Journal* 61 (1968): 440–462. See also W. Hamilton Bryson, "The History of Legal Education in Virginia," *University of Richmond Law Review* 14 (1979–80): 155–210.
[26] Kent, "Introductory Lecture," pp. 330, 331, 334, 341, 339.

design rested on the belief that there had to be "constitutional limits to the exercise of the legislative power." Such limitations are necessary because of the unfortunate truth that public opinion can never be safely assumed to be "correct and competent." Thus was legal education in America needed for constitutional law in this new sense as well as for the common law in its traditional sense. At its best, a legal education steeped in republican principles would eventuate in "a steady, firm, and impartial interpretation of the law," including that "law of the highest nature," the written Constitution.[27]

When Nathan Dane made his bequest for a professorship of law to Harvard University, he did so with the understanding that the chair would be offered in the first instance to Joseph Story. Like the earlier professors of the law, Story too understood that explaining the relationship of the common law to the fundamentals of the constitutional order was a primary part of his job. As he put it in his inaugural lecture, "a knowledge of the law and a devotion to its principles are vital to a republic, and lie at the very foundation of its strength." The reason was that republics are susceptible to dangers less likely to emerge in other forms of government. Governments, Story taught, are not always "overthrown by direct and open assaults," not always "battered down by the arms of conquerors or the successful daring of usurpers." In republics especially there may well be a "concealed... dry rot which eats into the vitals when all is fair and stately on the outside." Legal education is peculiarly essential in a republic, he argued, because in that form of government "every citizen is himself in some measure intrusted with the public safety, and acts an important part for its weal or woe." For Story, law was, and had to be understood to be, more than "a little round of manoeuver and contrivances" by skilled advocates to win their case. It was a collection of fundamental principles that had been revealed over time. In learning and respecting that tradition, those principles that had been "built up and perfected by artificial doctrines, adapted and moulded to the artificial structure of society," the students of the law would become the foundation of the public happiness and safety.[28]

In Story's view, "the common law, as a science, must be forever in progress; and no limits can be assigned to its principles or improvements." It is a body of law that is "flexible" and that is "constantly expanding with the exigencies of society." The essence of the common law is the experience of mankind in its social relations. Thus would Story issue a stern warning. "Great vigilance and great jealousy," he proclaimed, "are... necessary in republics to guard against the captivations of theory."[29] For it is that kind of intellectual carelessness that will cause the "dry rot" of republican institutions from within.

[27] Ibid., pp. 334, 334, 336, 336, 338.
[28] Story, "Value and Importance of Legal Studies," pp. 512, 513, 513, 518, 524.
[29] Ibid., pp. 526, 526, 513.

In 1817, the same year the Harvard Law School was founded and twelve years before he would ascend to the Dane professorship, Justice Story published a review in the *North American Review* of David Hoffman's *Course of Legal Study*. He was unstinting in his praise. It was, he said, "by far the most perfect system for the study of the law which has ever been offered to the public." Story was all too aware of how the study of law in the old days had been such a drudgery, what with the "whole of law ... locked up in barbarous Latin, and still more barbarous Norman French." As vexing to the learning of the law was the fact that the "great body of the law was to be principally extracted from the Year Books" and a series of "immethodical abridgments." What was not to be found in those books was to be learned only "by the dry practice of a black-letter office, and a constant and fatiguing attention upon courts of justice."[30] Yet as improved as the situation was, learning the law was still not simple or easy. The intellectual demands remained strenuous.[31]

At a minimum, Story believed, Hoffman's *Course of Legal Study* should be recommended to "all lawyers, as a model for the direction of the students who may be committed to their care." But in truth Hoffman's elaborate and comprehensive outline of study would demonstrate "the necessity" of law school education. Even the most cursory perusal would "dissipate the common delusion, that the law may be thoroughly acquired in the immethodical, interrupted, and desultory studies of the office of a practising counsellor." In Story's view, a law school education would prepare the student for his apprenticeship and subsequent plunge into the actual practice of the law by laying a sturdy "foundation in elementary principles, under the guidance of a learned and discreet lecturer." Such formal education was necessary to keep the young lawyer from becoming little more than "a patient drudge, versed in the forms of conveyancing and pleading, but incapable of ascending to the principles which guide and govern them."[32]

The model offered by Hoffman's *Course of Legal Study* would indeed be taken up in earnest at the law school in Cambridge, especially after the arrival of Story himself as Dane Professor. What Story found so appealing about the Hoffman approach was that it was both broad and deep, including sections for study beginning with Moral and Political Philosophy, moving on to The Feudal Law, The Law of Equity, The Lex Mercatoria, The Law of Crime and Punishments, The Maritime and Admiralty Law, federal and state constitutional law, and concluding with a section on Political Economy. Under each syllabus, Hoffman listed in detail the texts and treatises to be read, and accompanied those lists with his own detailed notes on most if

[30] *North American Review* 6 (1817): 45; reprinted as "Course of Legal Study," in Story, ed., *Miscellaneous Writings of Joseph Story*, pp. 66–92, pp. 91, 72, 72, 72.
[31] Ibid., pp. 72–73.
[32] Ibid., pp. 91, 91–92, 92, 92.

not all of the books suggested. If there was a defect in Hoffman's design, it was that the course as prescribed would probably take six or seven years to complete in its entirety. But as a guide to the emerging ideas informing university legal education, one could do no better.[33]

Story's influence at the Law School, and upon legal education more generally, is perhaps seen most clearly in his fulfillment of the clear terms of Nathan Dane's endowment.[34] Not only was the Dane Professor of Law to lecture, but he was to publish learned treatises on as many parts of the common law as possible. Story took the command seriously, but instead of merely preparing his lectures for publication, he undertook to write original treatises that were in turn the basis of his lectures in the Law School.[35] In January 1832 the first of Story's treatises appeared, *Commentaries on the Law of Bailments*, followed the next year by his *Commentaries on the Constitution of the United States*. The rest followed in a regular stream, and this from a man serving not only as a law professor but also as a sitting justice of the United States Supreme Court, a job that also included riding circuit: *Commentaries on the Conflict of Laws* (1834), *Commentaries on Equity Jurisprudence* (1835), *Commentaries on Equity Pleadings* (1838), *Commentaries on the Law of Agency* (1839), *Commentaries on the Law of Partnership* (1841), *Commentaries on the Law of Bills of Exchange* (1843), and *Commentaries on Promissory Notes* (1845). There were still other treatises planned when Story died just after the appearance of his work on promissory notes.

Story's approach to legal study remained the model at the Law School until Langdell arrived twenty-five years later. The procedure was for the professors to lecture from textbooks or treatises, more often than not merely reading from the texts while the students scrambled to copy down their every utterance.[36] It was not uncommon for the students to have twenty-five or thirty such books in each course.[37] There was attention to cases, of course, but only in a derivative way, presented to the students as the treatise writers had understood and digested them. The cases served simply to reveal a more fundamental principle deemed to have been antecedent to the case itself.[38] As Story had put it in his inaugural lecture, "judicial decisions are

---

[33] See generally David Hoffman, *A Course of Legal Study, Addressed to Students and the Profession Generally* (2nd ed.; Baltimore: Joseph Neal, 1836).

[34] See Sutherland, *The Law at Harvard*, p. 106.

[35] Ibid., p. 107.

[36] See Anthony Chase, "The Birth of the Modern Law School," *American Journal of Legal History* 23 (1979): 329–348, pp. 336–337.

[37] Samuel F. Batchelder, "Christopher C. Langdell," *The Green Bag* 18 (1906): 437–443, p. 437.

[38] Theodore Plucknett described the traditional treatise as an effort "to present the law in a strictly deductive framework." T. F. T. Plucknett, *Early English Legal Literature* (Cambridge: Cambridge University Press, 1958), p. 19.

deemed but the formal promulgation of rules antecedently existing, and obtain all their value from their supposed conformity to those rules."[39] The understanding was that the judge did not make law, but merely discovered it; the treatises then undertook to explicate and explain the principle that had been exposed by the controversy at hand. It was this approach that Langdell found stultifying and unscientific. The students were not being taught to think in ways that would be expected of them when they actually went into the courtroom; they were merely learning by rote what others had said without actually ever delving into the primary materials of the law, the decided cases.[40] Langdell, with the support of President Eliot, meant to put a stop to that.

Langdell and Eliot shared a commitment to science that was, in a way, their intellectual bond. Having been trained as a chemist, Eliot was naturally inclined to see law as a science in the way in which Langdell saw it, and to understand that cases were the original sources of the law, not the treatises and textbooks so long in fashion. Yet the talk of law as a science was not entirely new, nor was it the invention of Langdell.[41] At least since Blackstone had published his *Commentaries* a century before, many common lawyers were willing to think of the law as a science and not simply as a collection of isolated decisions over time. Even at Harvard, the view of law as a science had been around for some time. In a lecture at the beginning of the 1838 academic year, Professor Simon Greenleaf, who would succeed Story as Dane Professor in 1846, offered remarks with which Langdell would undoubtedly have agreed: "Adjudged cases are, to the philosophical student of law, what facts are to the student of natural science. They are the elements from which, by process of induction, his mind ascends to the higher regions of the science, scans its boldest outlines and familiarises itself with its great and leading principles."[42] But what had been a flicker of a scientific approach to law through the study of cases would be fanned to a full, roaring intellectual conflagration when Langdell arrived in Cambridge.

---

[39] Story, "Value and Importance of Legal Studies," p. 506. This was a view of long-standing respectability. Lord Mansfield had declared that "law does not consist of particular cases, but of general principles which are illustrated and explained by those cases." *Lex v. Benbridge*, 3. Dougl. 332, as quoted in W. L. Penfield, "Text-Books vs. Leading Cases," *American Law Review* 25 (1891): 234–248, p. 245.

[40] One of Langdell's most successful students, William Keener, insisted that the "mind of a student who studies under the text-book system has been compared to a sponge." William A. Keener, "The Inductive Method in Legal Education," *American Law Review* 28 (1894): 709–725, p. 714.

[41] See M. H. Hoeflich, "Law & Geometry: Legal Science from Leibniz to Langdell," *American Journal of Legal History* 30 (1986): 95–121, pp. 120, 121.

[42] As quoted in William P. LaPiana, *Logic and Experience: The Origin of Modern Legal Education* (Oxford: Oxford University Press, 1994), p. 31.

All told, a rather shocking development from a man deemed by those closest to him to be "by nature a conservative."[43]

During the 1870–71 academic year, Langdell startled his students by launching rather unexpectedly into his new approach to the study of law in his class on contracts:

The class gathered in the old amphitheatre of Dane Hall – the one lecture room of the School – and opened their strange new pamphlets, reports bereft of their only useful part, the head-notes. The lecturer opened his.

"Mr. Fox, will you please state the facts of the case of *Payne v. Cave?*"

Mr. Fox did his best with the facts of the case.

"Mr. Rawle, will you give the plaintiff's argument?"

Mr. Rawle gave what he could of the plaintiff's argument.

"Mr. Adams, do you agree with that?"

And the case system of law teaching had begun.[44]

The scheme was not celebrated. Indeed, his new methods were looked upon as the "novelties" that they were, and deeply "distrusted." They were generally "condemned"[45] – and not least by the students who turned from the new dean in droves. Yet those who stuck with him were among the best and the brightest, and knew that what he was doing was nothing less than an "act of great bravery."[46]

One of the more peculiar aspects of Langdell's pedagogic revolution was his reticence about it. As James Barr Ames would later recall, "after explaining his theory of legal education in the preface of his 'Cases on Contracts', Langdell never wrote a word in its behalf."[47] Perhaps there was no need; the system was not, after all, very complicated. Langdell introduced the new mode this way in his new form of legal publication, the casebook.

Law considered as a science, consists of certain principles or doctrines. To have such a mastery of these as to be able to apply them with constant facility and certainty to the ever-tangled skein of human affairs, is what constitutes a true lawyer; and hence to acquire that mastery should be the business of every earnest student of the law. Each of these doctrines has arrived at its present state by slow degrees; in other words, it is a growth, extending in many cases through centuries. This growth is to

---

43 Ames, "Christopher Columbus Langdell," p. 481. President Eliot would recall Langdell as having been "a curious mixture of the conservative and the radical, having the merits of both." Charles W. Eliot, "Langdell and the Law School," *Harvard Law Review* 33 (1919–20): 518–525, p. 524.

44 Batchelder, "Christopher C. Langdell," p. 440.

45 Franklin G. Fessenden, "The Rebirth of the Harvard Law School," *Harvard Law Review* 33 (1919–20): 493–517, pp. 500, 498.

46 Eugene Wambaugh, "Professor Langdell – A View of His Career," *Harvard Law Review* 20 (1906–07): 1–4, p. 1.

47 Ames, "Christopher Columbus Langdell," p. 479.

be traced in the main through a series of cases; and much the shortest and best, if not the only way of mastering the doctrine effectually is by studying the cases in which it is embodied. But the cases which are useful and necessary for this purpose at the present day bear an exceedingly small proportion to all that have been reported. The vast majority are useless and worse than useless for any purpose of systematic study. Moreover, the number of fundamental legal doctrines is much less than is commonly supposed; the many different guises in which the same doctrine is constantly making its appearance, and the great extent to which legal treatises are a repetition of each other, being the cause of much apprehension. If these doctrines could be so classified and arranged that each should be found in its proper place, and nowhere else, they would cease to be formidable from their number.[48]

Langdell, as far as one can tell, elaborated on his system on only one other occasion, in brief remarks after a dinner of the Harvard Law School Association celebrating the 250th anniversary of Harvard University. His original purpose, he confessed, had been to attempt to place the law school, "so far as differences of circumstances would permit, in the position occupied by the law faculties in the universities of continental Europe." The essence of his approach came to this: "law is a science, and . . . all the available materials for that science are contained in printed books." It was essential that law not be deemed a mere "species of handicraft" that could be picked up at a practitioner's side during an "apprenticeship."[49] Because "law is a science," it was clear to Langdell and his followers that "a well-equipped university is the true place for teaching and learning that science." And because the law is to be learned from its "ultimate sources," the adjudged cases, the law library is the place where the legal scientist learns. As Langdell put it, "the library is the proper workshop of professors and students alike; . . . it is to us all that the laboratories of the university are to the chemists and physicists, the museum of natural history to the zoologists, the botanical garden to the botanists."[50] And as will be discussed later, this view of the law as a science required a certain kind of teacher, a scientific theoretician of the law rather than merely a practitioner: "What qualifies a person . . . to teach law, is not experience in the work of a lawyer's office, not experience in dealing with men, not experience in the trial or argument of causes, not experience, in short, in using law, but experience in learning law."[51]

In some ways, Langdell's theory of legal education was better explained by others, not least by his most distinguished students. William Keener, first

---

[48] As quoted in Louis D. Brandeis, "The Harvard Law School," *The Green Bag* 1 (1889): 10–25, pp. 19–20.

[49] Ibid.

[50] Reprinted as Christopher Columbus Langdell, "Teaching Law as a Science," *American Law Review* 21 (1887): 123–125, pp. 123, 123, 123, 124, 124. This address, and one on the same evening by Justice Holmes, was also reprinted in the *Law Quarterly Review* 3 (1887): 118–125.

[51] Ibid., p. 124.

of Harvard and later of Columbia, where he would become dean, argued in his teacher's behalf that the study of law by cases was nothing more radical than was done in virtually every other department of the universities, the application of the scientific method to the raw materials of the field of inquiry. In his view, opposition to the scientific study of the law was merely a matter of "ignorance." The entire enterprise launched by Langdell was simply a matter of common sense. "If the authority of treatises and textbooks," Keener observed, "is derived from the cases, then the treatises and text-books must be derivative, while the cases are the original sources; and he who consults the text-book as a substitute for the cases, gets his information at second hand." But there is more to it than that. The object of the case method is not merely to develop in the student "a great memory for cases and their facts," but to spawn an "apprehension of the principles governing the decisions." Once the case method has developed in the student this necessary "habit of legal thought,"[52] there is no reason why a properly trained student cannot also benefit from the best writings on the legal subject at hand.[53]

The fear that any reliance at all on treatises and textbooks was being jettisoned in favor of cases and cases alone, was the most pervasive theme of the critics of Langdell's controversial method of instruction. The suggestion by that "rising Cambridge clique" that casebooks could adequately replace the treatises was, the critics said, simply wrong. The fact was, they insisted, that "such text-books as those of Coke, Blackstone, and Kent . . . have done more for the real development of our law in England and the United States than any of the opinions pronounced in any one case by any one English or American judge who can be pointed out."[54] But since cases had been a part of legal study from time immemorial, it was impossible simply to demand that cases be excluded in favor of the treatises. The more moderate critics of Langdell were willing to concede as much. "Treatises alone will not do," wrote one, "since the lawyer must learn to deduce the law on the facts; cases alone will not do, since he must have a broad general view of the subject, must know the general principles underlying it, and the reasons sustaining or modifying them, in order to deal intelligently with the facts."[55]

By the early twentieth century it was generally conceded that "a combination of the case-book and lecture system . . . is now made in every law school professing to follow the case method."[56] The fact was, to those who still

---

52 Keener, "The Inductive Method in Legal Education," pp. 709, 709, 712, 718, 724.
53 "The distinct feature of the case system is . . . to enable students to compare their own generalizations with those of the authors of standard works." Ibid., p. 722.
54 James Schouler, "Cases without Treatises," *American Law Review* 23 (1889): 1–10, pp. 2, 4.
55 Penfield, "Text-Books vs. Leading Cases," p. 242.
56 Simeon E. Baldwin, "Education for the Bar in the United States," *American Political Science Review* 9 (1915): 437–448, p. 442.

harbored misgivings about the case method, that "law is both science and art – a philosophy and a trade." And it remained firmly rooted in the thinking of those critical of that "rising Cambridge clique" that "[p]rinciples, not cases, are the building stones of law, here and everywhere, now and always." Properly understood, adjudged cases should be regarded "less as sources of law than as channels of law." It was essential that the use of cases in legal instruction be within a context of the more elevated and enduring principles of the law. From this viewpoint, "to teach the law by cases only, or by cases mainly, without first grounding the learner in the elements of the subject is, so far as scientific methods of instruction are concerned, to begin at the wrong end. It is to explain the foundation of a building by examining the roof, or rather by scrutinizing a few of the shingles."[57] Simply put, "no science can be learned purely from particulars. The universals must be studied to discover what the particulars mean and whence they sprang."[58] And a reported case, as such, is nothing more than "a statement of how a particular court decided a particular cause by applying particular rules to particular facts."[59]

But there was also a nagging awareness that however prevalent treatises and textbooks might have seemed, they were now clearly in the second tier of materials being used to teach the law. By the time of Langdell's death in 1906, his revolution in law was all but complete, with the scholarly "shift of attention from principle to precedent" having become nearly universal.[60] And both his advocates and his critics understood that there is a necessarily "close relation between the forms of legal literature and lawyers' ideas of what they are doing, and of the appropriate way for jurists to behave."[61] At a minimum, the shift in focus to judicial decisions as the fount of law would in time help to legitimate the idea of judicial lawmaking and contribute to the idea of a living or evolutionary Constitution.[62]

From Langdell's own first casebook, it was clear that implicit in the idea of the case method was a belief that each of the binding doctrines of the law had "arrived at its present state by slow degrees," and that the study of the law generally reveals in such doctrines "a growth extending in many cases through centuries." Thus the main point of the method he devised: "This growth is to be traced in the main through a series of cases; and much the shortest and best, if not the only way of mastering the doctrine effectually

[57] Simeon E. Baldwin, "The Study of Elementary Law, the Proper Beginning of a Legal Education," *Yale Law Journal* 13 (1903): 1–15, pp. 2, 15, 3, 13.
[58] Simeon E. Baldwin, "Teaching Law by Cases," *Harvard Law Review* 14 (1900–01): 258–261, p. 259.
[59] Baldwin, "The Study of Elementary Law," p. 9.
[60] Reed, *Training for the Public Profession of the Law*, p. 376.
[61] A. W. B. Simpson, "The Rise and Fall of the Legal Treatise: Legal Principles and the Forms of Legal Literature," *University of Chicago Law Review* 48 (1981): 632–679, p. 633.
[62] Paul D. Carrington, "Hail! Langdell!", *Law & Social Inquiry* 20 (1995): 691–760, p. 752.

is by studying the cases in which it is embodied."[63] Ultimately, the case method is concerned not merely with what the law is, but with what the law "ought to be."[64]

One of Langdell's most preeminent students, Joseph Beale, was unambiguous about this implicitly evolutionary notion of the case law. The "common law changes," he acknowledged, in a progressive way. "The law of today must of course be better than that of seven centuries ago, more in accordance with the general principles of justice, more in accordance with the needs of the present age, more humane, more flexible, and more complex."[65] Thus the legal principles that are revealed by the scholarly scrutiny of cases are not principles transcendently antecedent to the case or controversy in which the judicial opinion is rendered; they are rather derived from the time in which the decision is reached. "The spirit of the time molds and shapes its law, as it makes and shapes its manner of thought and the whole current of its life," Beale explained. "For law is the effort of a people to express its idea of right; and while right itself cannot change, man's conception of right changes from age to age as his knowledge grows."[66]

John Chipman Grey, another of Langdell's supporters at Harvard, insisted that his colleague's approach to the study of the law through cases had the salutary effect of disabusing the students of the erroneous notion that the law was "merely . . . a series of propositions having, like a succession of problems in geometry, only a logical interdependence." Rather, it instilled in them an appreciation for the fact that the law is "a living thing, with a continuous history, sloughing off the old, taking on the new."[67] And the new that was to be taken on was that spirit of the age to which judges seemingly had easy access. The source of this spirit of the age that was to give substance to the law was the "popular sense of right" that both legislators and judges have "forced upon them" by the "social forces which are at play in every organized society." Thus was it wrong to suggest that the law is made by the judges; it is not. It is only "promulgated by them."[68] Law evolves because society evolves. Abstract notions of justice are no match for the "popular sense of right" of the here and now.

At the heart of Langdell's notion of law as a growing, evolving body of doctrines was the nineteenth-century belief in the evolutionary science

---

[63] As quoted in Brandeis, "The Harvard Law School," p. 20.

[64] S. Stanwood Menken, "Methods of Instruction at American Law Schools," *Columbia Legal Times* 6 (1892–93): 168–170, p. 169.

[65] Joseph H. Beale, Jr., *Treatise on Conflict of Laws* (Cambridge, MA: Harvard University Press, 1916), p. 149.

[66] Joseph H. Beale, Jr., "The Development of Jurisprudence during the Past Century," *Harvard Law Review* 18 (1904–05): 271–283, p. 272.

[67] John Chipman Grey, "Methods of Legal Instruction," *Yale Law Journal* 1 (1891–92): 159–160, p. 159.

[68] Christopher G. Tiedeman, "Methods of Legal Instruction," *Yale Law Journal* 1 (1891–92): 150–158, p. 154.

of Charles Darwin.[69] Where the older legal science – that of Blackstone, Kent, and Story – understood fundamental legal principles as resting on a moral, ethical, or even a theological foundation, Langdell and his followers abandoned that idea in favor of an unflagging belief in modern science and the modern scientific method, not unlike what one would find in the work of biologists. Thus it was not empty rhetoric when Langdell likened the library's role for lawyers as akin to that of the laboratory for the natural scientists. "Law and its fundamental doctrines displayed one salient characteristic, growth."[70]

As Langdell's new methodology was taking root and spreading, there was a parallel development occurring that would contribute to the shift already under way from principle to precedent in the way the law was understood. That development was the establishment of a series of national reporters that would publish all the cases decided in all the appellate courts around the United States, both state and federal. John West of St. Paul, Minnesota, a former traveling book salesman, hit upon a scheme to provide for the profession – lawyers and judges alike, and soon professors too – a system of reliable national reports and digests of the decisions being handed down that would be both comprehensive and affordable.

West's goal was "to collect, arrange in an orderly manner, and put into convenient and inexpensive form in the shortest possible time" for those in need of such information, "everything which the courts have said on any given subject up to the last decision just rendered." No small part of his broader purpose was to facilitate the uniformity of the law by "enabling the courts to harmonize conflicting decisions."[71] Indeed, such uniformity would prove to be West's greatest contribution,[72] despite the flood of opinions he unleashed.[73]

In the view of some, the "rapid accumulation of reports" was clearly a "growing evil." Not only was the number overwhelming, but there was no quality control in the publish-everything approach that West adopted.

---

[69] As Thomas Grey has explained, "the classical legal scientists... accepted the nineteenth-century evolutionary idea that law, even in its fundamentals, was not unchanging, but progressively evolving; as Sir Henry Maine had argued, the legal order grew from the primitive to the advanced, from a regime based on status to one based on contract." Thomas C. Grey, "Langdell's Orthodoxy," *University of Pittsburgh Law Review* 45 (1983–84): 1–53, pp. 28–29.

[70] Wiecek, *The Lost World of Classical Legal Thought*, p. 92.

[71] John B. West, contribution to "A Symposium of Law Publishers," *American Law Review* 23 (1889): 400–407, pp. 406, 403, 406.

[72] Thomas A. Woxland, "'Forever Associated with the Practice of Law': The Early Years of the West Publishing Company," *Legal Reference Services Quarterly* 5 (1985): 115–124, p. 123.

[73] "In 1810 there were only eighteen published volumes of American reports; in 1848, about eight hundred; by 1885, about 3,798; by 1910, over 8,000." Lawrence M. Friedman, *A History of American Law* (New York: Simon and Schuster, 1973), p. 539.

There was no doubt that "the volumes that are constantly falling from the press teem with cases of no interest to the profession or to the public, and important only to the parties litigant." There was no reason a case should be reported unless it carried within itself "enunciation of some legal principle." In the long run, it was feared, such an indiscriminate spread of decided cases would serve only to weaken the foundations of the legal system "by the substitution of precedents for principles in the practical administration of justice." With the pressure to win the case at hand, what competent lawyer, it was wondered, could long be able to resist the "constant temptation to forget the underlying principle in the search for a precedent exactly on point."[74] It would be suggested by some that the "legal science pioneered at the Harvard Law School"[75] would greatly aid those seeking to isolate the development of principles from mere judicial blather.

The other abiding problem with Langdell's methodology was that it could only be highly subjective. Again, from the very beginning, as stated in the preface to his first casebook on contracts, he made that much clear. In the flood of cases that were then being pumped out of the courts, a scholar could not simply take all that was coming and make sense of them. As Langdell had unblushingly pointed out, the "vast majority" of cases coming from the courts were "useless and worse than useless for any purpose of systematic study." In order for the proper and true doctrines to be found in the case law, sorted out, arranged, and classified, it would take a truly critical ability on the scholar's part. To the academically trained eye, the number of cases that were actually worth studying constituted "an exceedingly small proportion to all that have been reported." Moreover, "the number of fundamental legal doctrines" themselves were in fact "much less than is commonly supposed."[76] In fact, they did not come to be known by the powerful understanding of the judges who actually employed them in their decisions; indeed, the judges in question might not have ever even appreciated the importance of their own opinion in revealing the true doctrinal foundation. That would depend not upon judicial understanding, but only upon professorial insight. And it was for that reason that Langdell drew a clear distinction between those who studied the law and those who merely practiced it.

The case method was not Langdell's only "startling" reform in legal education, and in some ways was not the most shocking to the bench and bar. Stemming from his dedication to the idea of developing law as a science to be gleaned from adjudged cases was Langdell's further radical belief that law thus understood could be properly taught only by legal scientists,

74 J. L. Hugh, "What Shall Be Done with the Reports?", *American Law Review* 16 (1882): 429–445, pp. 429, 429, 443, 439, 439.
75 Wiecek, *The Lost World of Classical Legal Thought*, p. 89.
76 As quoted in Brandeis, "The Harvard Law School," p. 20.

professors who were purely theoretical in their approach to the law. There were, in his view, two professions of the law, and he firmly believed that "a successful practitioner would not necessarily be a successful teacher, any more than a successful teacher must prove to be a successful practitioner."[77] Thus did Langdell's theory of teaching lead directly to what President Eliot would recall as the dean's "bold adventure," the appointment in 1873 of James Barr Ames as an assistant professor of law, a young man just out of the Law School himself with no experience whatsoever at either the bench or the bar.[78] This was pouring pedagogic salt into the not yet healed wounds Langdell had inflicted with the imposition of the case method itself.

Until Ames was appointed, all the members of the law faculty at Harvard, as elsewhere, had either been or were judges or distinguished practitioners. Joseph Story was undoubtedly the most prominent example of that model, serving as he did the whole time he was a professor as a justice on the nation's highest court. The fundamental reason for the professional staffing of the professoriate was the belief that law was an inherently practical profession and that the students would benefit most from instruction by those who had actually practiced. It was somewhat derivative of the idea of the apprenticeship way of legal education outside the law schools. To great criticism and long-lingering doubts, Langdell was seen as "breeding" a whole new class of legal intellectuals whose theoretical approach to the law would only exacerbate the mischief of the case method.

When Langdell moved to hire another of his former students, William A. Keener, the dean of the faculty of Harvard College, Ephraim W. Gurney expressed to President Eliot his grave misgivings about Langdell's personnel march from practice to theory. In his view, Langdell, whom he thought "as *intransigeant* as a French Socialist" at the best of times, was risking wrecking the Law School with his effort "to breed professors of law, not practitioners." In Gurney's view, the appointment of Keener suggested that the Law School was committing itself "to the theory of breeding within itself its corps of instructors" and thereby severing the school from "the great current of legal life which flows through the courts and the bar." Such a commitment, Gurney insisted, would constitute "the gravest error of policy which it could adopt."[79]

That was not all; there was another and perhaps equally dangerous professional problem with these lofty theoreticians of the law. Gurney was deeply concerned about "the contemptuous way which both Langdell and Ames have of speaking of Courts and Judges." And this was not simply about the ordinary judges of the time, but the expression of an intellectual contempt for "the men of the past to whom the profession looks up to as

---

[77] Fessenden, "Rebirth of the Harvard Law School," p. 512.
[78] Eliot, "Langdell and the Law School," p. 521.
[79] Sutherland, *The Law at Harvard*, p. 188.

its great ornaments." And this too was the result of Langdell's scientific shenanigans, in Gurney's opinion. "The trouble in their mind with those judges is that they did not treat this or that question as a philosophical professor, building up a coherent system would have done, but as the judges before whom the young men are going to practice will do." As Gurney saw it, this "attitude of mind" flowed directly from "a too academic treatment of a great practical profession."[80]

It seems Gurney's criticisms of Langdell likely fell on the deaf ears of President Eliot. Although Gurney was the president's "general right-hand man,"[81] Eliot never seemed to falter in his faith in the Law School dean's efforts to transform legal education. Speaking in praise of Langdell at a meeting of the Harvard Law School Association in 1895, Eliot recalled the "courageous adventure" undertaken by Langdell when he sought to appoint Ames to the assistant professorship. It was "an absolutely new departure in our country in the teaching of law." Eliot appreciated what the long-term effect of Langdell's vision was likely to be. "In due course, and that in no long term of years, there will be produced in this country a body of men learned in the law, who will never have been on the bench or at the bar, but who nevertheless hold positions of great weight and influence as teachers of the law, as expounders, systematizers, and historians."[82] One suspects this vision would have been Gurney's ultimate nightmare.

The implications of this shift from practitioners to theorists and historians were clear to most everyone, not least to James Barr Ames himself. At a minimum, he believed, the work of a law professor "demands an undivided allegiance"; it is, and must be seen to be, "a vocation and not an avocation." And this was fundamentally important because the activities of the law professor were "not limited to his relations with students, either in or out of the classroom." The new breed of law professor was to be not simply a teacher, but a scholar in as far-reaching a sense as possible. By his full-time position within the university, Ames suggested, the law professor has "an exceptional opportunity to exert a wholesome influence upon the development of the law by his writings."[83]

The fact was then, as now, that serious legal scholarship demands "an amount of time and thought that a judge or a lawyer in private practice can almost never give."[84] The new scholarly approach, exemplified not least by Ames himself, was characterized by "the existence of a permanent body of teachers devoting themselves year after year to the mastery of their respective

[80] Ibid.
[81] Ibid., p. 186.
[82] As quoted in ibid., p. 184.
[83] James Barr Ames, "The Vocation of the Law Professor," *American Law Register* 48 (1900): 129–146, pp. 137, 138, 140–141, 141.
[84] Ibid., p. 142.

subjects" and who, as a result, "are destined to exercise a great influence on the further development of [the] law."[85] Such an opportunity was no small part of "the inherent attractiveness of the professor's chair."[86] These new legal scholars were not to be scribbling quietly in their studies; their work was likely to have – indeed, was intended to have – a practical influence.

As Langdell had put it in his remarks to the Harvard Law School Association, his original scheme was to import into legal education in the United States many of the same advantages known by the law faculties in universities in continental Europe. So, too, was that the intention behind the new intellectualized professoriate. "If we turn to countries in which the vocation of law professors has long been recognized," Ames wrote, "we find a large body of legal literature, of a high quality, the best and the greatest part of which is the work of professors." That example demonstrated clearly that the influence of professors' "opinions in the courts is as great or even greater than that of judicial precedents." The time was "most propitious" in the United States for this new professoriate to achieve great things through its "legal authorship."[87]

Reflecting no small bit of the intellectual arrogance Dean Gurney had detected in him, Ames confessed that "the chief value of this new order of legal literature will be found in its power to correct . . . the principal defect in the generally admirable work of the judges."[88]

It is the function of the law to work out in terms of legal principle the rules, which will give the utmost possible effect to the legitimate needs and purposes of men in their various activities. Too often the just expectations of men are thwarted by the actions of the courts, a result largely due to taking a partial view of the subject, or to a failure to grasp the original development and true significance of the rule which is made the basis of the decision. . . . From the nature of the case the judge cannot be expected to engage in original historical investigations, nor can he approach the case before him from the point of view of one who has made a minute and comprehensive examination of the branch of the law of which the question to be decided forms a part.[89]

Thus the helpful role of the professor:

The judge is not and ought not to be a specialist. But it is his right, of which he has been too long deprived, to have the benefit of the conclusions of specialists or professors, whose writings represent years of study and reflection, and are illuminated by the light of history, analysis and the comparison of the laws of different countries.[90]

---

[85] Ibid., p. 144. See also James Barr Ames, "Law and Morals," *Harvard Law Review* 22 (1908–09): 97–113, p. 113.

[86] Ames, "Vocation of the Law Professor," p. 146.

[87] Ibid., pp. 141, 141, 141.

[88] Ibid., p. 142.

[89] Ibid., pp. 142–143.

[90] Ibid., p. 143.

Ames's view was perhaps best summed up by Arthur Goodhart, in explaining the primary difference between the law professors in his native land of America and those professors in his adopted home of England. "[T]he English teacher," Goodhart insisted, "emphasizes what the judge has said: the American professor explains what the judge should have said."[91]

An obvious question was exactly what type of legal literature might best accommodate the new professoriate in its desire to lend its expertise to the shaping of the law, allowing the judges their "right" to scholarly guidance. After all, although still used, the textbooks and treatises as standard sources had been nudged aside by the case method. And the legal periodicals of the day were not so much collections of substantive articles as they were places where the news of the profession could be announced and new cases summarized for the benefit of the practicing bar.[92] In the view of Louis Brandeis, himself a product of the school of Langdell and Ames, the new approach to law engendered by the case method was characterized by "intellectual self-reliance" and a "spirit of investigation" such that it led more or less inevitably to the founding of the *Harvard Law Review*, the first successful student-edited journal.[93] A new kind of periodical was needed, in part, to share with the world "some idea of what is done under the Harvard system of instruction."[94] It was perhaps most fitting that the new idea was given the support of James Barr Ames and that when the review appeared it was led by one of Ames's articles. In time this new kind of legal periodical would help the new theoretical professoriate to spread its influence widely.

The seeming inevitability of the rise of the law review in its modern form was primarily the result of Langdell's view of a legal profession divided between those with "experience in learning law" and those with "experience ... in using law."[95] To the degree to which his case method succeeded "so far as differences of circumstances would permit" in adapting to the American scheme of things the way of legal study in continental Europe, it began to contribute to the rise of what was described in the European case as "university-made law," a system of law in which "[i]ts spirit was academic ... its oracles ... law teachers." While America never went that entire distance, it did develop a legal world in which law became "the work of courts guided and inspired by jurists who were teachers in universities."[96]

It is often mistakenly assumed that the *Harvard Law Review* was the first to be established, but it was not. Prior to its establishment in 1887 no fewer

---

[91] As quoted in Robert Stevens, *Law School: Legal Education in America from the 1850s to the 1980s* (Chapel Hill: University of North Carolina Press, 1983), p. 133.

[92] See "American Law Periodicals," *Albany Law Journal* 2 (1870–71): 445.

[93] Brandeis, "The Harvard Law School," p. 23.

[94] Notes, *Harvard Law Review* 1 (1887–88): 35–37, p. 35.

[95] Langdell, "Teaching Law as a Science," p. 124.

[96] Roscoe Pound, "Types of Legal Periodicals," *Iowa Law Review* 14 (1928–29): 257–265, pp. 258, 263–264.

than 158 different legal periodicals had been published in the United States. While most had been more professional than scholarly in tone, there were exceptions. Such journals as the *American Law Register* (which would in time become the *University of Pennsylvania Law Review*) and the *American Law Review* had indeed been repositories of articles of a more theoretical and scholarly nature. And the law review at Harvard had two explicitly academic forerunners, as well. The students at the Albany Law School in 1875 published the *Albany Law School Journal*, and those at Columbia Law School in 1885 came out with the *Columbia Jurist*.[97] Neither journal was to be long-lived, but the *Columbia Jurist* seems to have been the spark that motivated the young men of Harvard Law School to launch their review, an effort that would transform the legal periodical both in format and in influence.

Looking back at the origins of the *Harvard Law Review* on the occasion of its fiftieth anniversary, John Jay McKelvey, who had served as the founding editor-in-chief of that review in 1887, noted that "the law review . . . [had become] the vehicle of thought between legal scholars and the practitioners and judges who can absorb and apply, but have not the time for personal research."[98] The law reviews that proliferated after the creation of the one at Harvard "had an almost immediate impact on the development of the law in the courts and in the legislatures."[99] It was seen by practitioners, scholars, and judges alike to be "an apparatus for instructive and constructive commentary on the living law which is the major product of the schools."[100] And no less a figure than Benjamin Cardozo was willing to applaud the fact that judges had finally "awakened . . . to the treasures buried in law reviews."[101] And in Cardozo's opinion, the reason for that was simple. "Judges and Advocates may not relish the admission," he wrote, "but the sobering truth is that leadership in the march of legal thought has been passing in our day from the benches of the courts to the chairs of universities." And there was no doubt in his mind that "academic scholarship is charting the line of development and progress in the untrodden regions of the law."[102]

---

[97] Michael I. Swygert and Jon W. Bruce, "The Historical Origins, Founding, and Early Development of Student-Edited Law Reviews," *Hastings Law Journal* 36 (1984–85): 739–791, pp. 742, 755–758, 763–769. A professional journal, the *Central Law Journal*, found the *Albany Law School Journal* to be "quite creditable . . . [but] not a man's law journal," as quoted at p. 764.

[98] John Jay McKelvey, "The Law School Review, 1887–1937," *Harvard Law Review* 50 (1936–37): 868–886, p. 877.

[99] Swygert and Bruce, "Historical Origins," p. 787.

[100] G. H. Robinson, *Cases and Authorities on Public Utilities* (Chicago: Callaghan & Co., 1926), p. iv.

[101] Benjamin N. Cardozo, *Growth of the Law* (New Haven, CT: Yale University Press, 1924), p. 14.

[102] Benjamin N. Cardozo, "Introduction" to *Selected Readings in the Law of Contracts from American and English Periodicals*, ed. Committee of the Association of American Law Schools (New York: Macmillan, 1931), pp. vii, ix.

The first citation to a law review article in the United States Supreme Court occurred in 1897 when Justice Edward White noted an article from the *Harvard Law Review*[103] in a dissenting opinion in *United States v. Trans-Missouri Freight Association.*[104] The first citation in a majority opinion came two years later in *Chicago, Milwaukee, and St. Paul Railway Co. v. Clark*[105] when Chief Justice Melville Fuller cited another *Harvard Law Review* article, James Barr Ames's "Two Theories of Consideration."[106] The reliance on law reviews, both in the Supreme Court and in the lower courts, continued apace until by the 1920s it was a common occurrence, with one writer noting that "law review material . . . aids [the judge] in 'finding the law' in ascertaining the state of informed opinion in disputed questions of law and social policy, and in giving written reasons for his decision."[107]

There was from the beginning among those manning the law reviews an implicit assumption that their most important role would be to contribute to "the progress of the law outside the school" and not to focus merely on what was taking place in the classrooms. By facilitating thinking about the formation of legal concepts, they would, it was hoped, be able to "influence human progress." In a sense, carrying forward Langdell's scientific metaphors, the law reviews understood themselves to be akin to "a testing laboratory for the immaterial and intangible principles in which so much of human justice has its origin." Filtered as their intellectual influence would be through both practitioners and judges, they had every reason to expect that their notes and articles could aid in "the prevention of injustice and the promotion of justice, in the interpretation and application of the principles of law to the complicated processes of modern civilization." This "broader usefulness" of the law review was nothing less than the pursuit of "the broad principles of truth and justice, as they may be applied to the building of a better civilization."[108]

The moral benefit to judges and thus to the law they would be providing would be incalculable. The true student of the law who possessed a "questioning or inquiring mind" should never be satisfied with the settled law, the firm precedent or the textbook doctrines derived from "a preponderance of decisions." Rather, being dedicated to "the progress of mankind," he knows that it is always "the minority which pioneers towards a truth, finally establishes it and creates a new majority for the truth established,

---

[103] The article was Amasa M. Eaton, "On Contracts in Restraint of Trade," *Harvard Law Review* 4 (1890): 128–137.

[104] 166 U.S. 290 (1897), p. 350, n.1.

[105] 178 U.S. 353 (1899), p. 65.

[106] *Harvard Law Review* 12 (1899): 515–531.

[107] Douglas B. Maggs, "Concerning the Extent to which the Law Review Contributes to the Development of the Law," *Southern California Law Review* 3 (1929–30): 181–204, p. 186. See also Chester A. Newland, "Legal Periodicals and the United States Supreme Court," *Midwest Journal of Political Science* 3 (1959): 58–74.

[108] McKelvey, "The Law School Review," pp. 880, 873, 873, 873, 877.

whereupon pursuit is again carried onward by a new minority and thus the sum of human knowledge and achievement is constantly being increased." To such an inquiring legal mind bent on progress in the law and in society, there is but one unchanging truth: "*stare decisis* means nothing."[109] And one of the most important vehicles of the change that is sought in the law would prove to be the law review, where the best thinking of Dean Gurney's "philosophical professor" could be brought to bear on the manipulation of legal doctrines in the hands of mere lawyers and judges.[110] It did not take long for the university law review to prove itself "an apt vehicle for speculative writing in the law," one especially well suited for "shorter works by the new class of teaching scholars."[111] With the spread of the case method,

---

[109] Ibid., pp. 877, 876–877, 877, 877.

[110] A stunning example of an article that would suggest new avenues for American jurisprudence was included in the first number of the *Harvard Law Review* by the future president of Harvard, A. Lawrence Lowell. In his essay on "The Responsibilities of American Lawyers," Lowell sought to address what he considered to be the "weighty duty" put on the bar by the American constitutional scheme of government. The essence of the responsibilities of American lawyers was nothing less than "watching over and guarding" the "fundamental principles" and "legal morals" posited by the Founders in the Constitution itself. It is that duty that gives to the courts the power of declaring invalid duly passed legislation. But that is not to say that the lawyers of the late nineteenth century ought to engage in the "fetish worship" of the Constitution as displayed in the early part of the century. Given the realities of the day, one can no longer expect the "blind veneration" of the Constitution that had distinguished those earlier decades, Lowell concluded. What is now needed, he insisted, is constitutional theory in a "higher" sense. "We need that ripe scholarship which regards theory as truth stated in an abstract form, to be constantly measured by practice as a test of its correctness; for theory and practice are in reality correlatives, each of which requires the aid of the other for its own development." And that theory was needed in particular to address the errors and mistakes of the state judges. The point of Lowell's argument was simply that "the fourteenth amendment to the Constitution of the United States has furnished an opportunity for a review of the decisions of the State courts upon a most important branch of the law," that being the meaning of the due process clause of that relatively recent amendment. The answer to Lowell's call for high theory would come shortly with a vengeance with the arrival three years later of the era of substantive due process, a doctrine already struggling within the courts to be born as Lowell was writing. A. Lawrence Lowell, "The Responsibilities of American Lawyers," *Harvard Law Review* 1 (1887–88): 232–240, pp. 232, 235, 237, 239.

[111] Friedman, *A History of American Law*, p. 547. The law reviews would never be without their critics, however. Fred Rodell famously dismissed the law reviews – albeit in a law review article – as nothing more than "citadels of pseudo-scholarship" in which the usual authors seemed "peculiarly able to say nothing with an air of great importance." Fred Rodell, "Goodbye to Law Reviews – Revisited," *Virginia Law Review* 48 (1962): 279–290, pp. 286, 280. This article reprints with a postscript Rodell's famous original essay, "Goodbye to Law Reviews," which first appeared in the *Virginia Law Review* 23 (1936–37): 38–45. Others have bewailed "the monster that our predecessors created." James Lindgren, "Reforming the American Law Review," *Stanford Law Review* 47 (1994–95): 1123–1130, p. 1123. Still others have been willing to condemn the modern law review as "a most unfortunate mass of ill-assorted, heterogeneous articles connected only by the fact that they appear in the same review." Alan W. Mewett,

the rise of the "philosophical" professoriate, and the proliferation of law reviews, Langdell's revolution in law and legal thinking was complete.

Yet, whatever Langdell's pretensions, his legal methodology was never able to achieve the completely objective "science" he had intended. No small part of the reason was that, in the end, his methodology was not the inductive process he assumed, but was very much a deductive exercise. The essence of Langdell's "science of the law" was his belief that the case law of the courts was somehow analogous to the physical specimens of the natural scientists. But it was not. Students of the particular cases of the common law do not stand in the same relation to them as the true scientist does to the phenomena of nature. "The latter are the result of forces of nature that are to be investigated," while the opinions of judges "are special acts of the will, which have been reached by a process of logical interpretation from a more general declaration of the will contained in each positive legal principle." The judge-made law of the common law is still the result of the human will and thus is a kind of positive law, albeit declared by courts rather than enacted by legislatures. The idea that legal science is truly comparable to the physical sciences ultimately proved to be "an erroneous and merely superficial analogy." In the end, the intellectual effort of a judge is "essentially deductive."[112]

The essence of Langdell's science was, in the end, a Social Darwinist view of the law and legal doctrine, case law that was the result of the survival of the fittest. The judge-made norms that were viewed as principles had no real permanence beyond the willingness of later judges to accept and perpetuate them. And while this might be acceptable in the realm of the common law, because that law "is case law and nothing else but case law,"[113] when it came to be applied to the cases and controversies under a written constitution, the result would be far more pernicious. It would encourage a common law approach to constitutional law and lead to the mistaken notion that the Constitution is nothing more than what judges have to say about it.

This tendency would be exacerbated by the general relegation to second-class status of the treatises that had so dominated legal education prior to Langdell's reforms; that abandonment carried with it not simply a change in

---

"Reviewing the Law Reviews," *Journal of Legal Education* 8 (1955–56): 188–191, p. 188. A common indictment has been the poverty of the writing to be found in the student-edited reviews. The prose, said one commentator, is "predominantly bleak and turgid." Kenneth W. Lasson, "Scholarship Amok: Excesses in the Pursuit of Truth and Tenure," *Harvard Law Review* 103 (1989–90): 926–950, p. 942. But no one has been able to outdo Rodell's original pithy dismissal: "There are two things wrong with almost all legal writing. One is its style. The other is its substance." Rodell, "Goodbye to Law Reviews," p. 38.

[112] *Common Law and the Case Method*, pp. 55, n.1; 56–57.

[113] Ibid., p. 35.

literary format, but a substantive jurisprudential loss, as well.[114] The greatest of legal commentators, such Hugo Grotius, Samuel Pufendorf, Emerich Vattel, Thomas Rutherforth, and Sir William Blackstone, in whose works earlier generations of law students had been steeped, had all rooted their discussions on interpretation in the idea that the fundamental task of the interpreter was to discern the intention of the law giver.[115] So, too, had the great works of the American treatise writers such as William Rawle, James Kent, and Joseph Story built upon that principled foundation of finding the meaning of the law.[116] And it was this common view of intention as the bedrock of interpretation that lay behind John Marshall's willingness to call it nothing less than "the most sacred rule of interpretation."

At the beginning, the study of constitutional law was only intermittently taught in the Law School, at least at Harvard during Langdell's reign. The

---

[114] See Elizabeth Kelley Bauer, *Commentaries on the Constitution, 1790–1860* (New York: Columbia University Press, 1952), p. 9.

[115] "The true end and design of interpretation is, to gather the intent of the man from most probable signs." Samuel Pufendorf, *The Law of Nature and Nations*, trans. Basil Kennet (3rd ed.; London: R. Sare, et al., 1717), V.XII.II, p. 301. Citation indicates book, chapter, section, and page number. "[T]he sole object of lawful interpretation ... ought to be the discovery of the thoughts of the author or authors.... This is the general rule for all interpretations." Emerich Vattel, *The Law of Nations* (4th ed.; London: W. Clarke and Sons, 1811), II.XVII, p. 247. Citation indicates book, chapter, and page number. "The end which interpretation aims at, is to find out what was the intention of the writer; to clear up the meaning of his words, if they are obscure; to ascertain the sense of them, if they are ambiguous; to determine what his design was, where his words express it imperfectly." Thomas Rutherforth, *Institutes of Natural Law* (2nd American ed.; Baltimore: William and Joseph Neal, 1832), p. 405. "The fairest and most rational method to interpret the will of the legislator, is by exploring his intentions at the time when the law was made, by *signs* the most natural and probable. And these signs are either the words, the context, the subject matter, the effects and consequence, or the spirit and reason of the law." William Blackstone, *Commentaries on the Laws of England*, 4 vols. (8th ed.; Oxford: Clarendon Press, 1778), I: 59. See Chapter 4 of this volume for an expanded discussion of these theories of interpretation and their influence on the early Americans.

[116] "By construction we can only mean the ascertaining the true meaning of an instrument, or other form of words, and by this rule alone ought we to be governed in respect to this constitution. The true rule therefore seems to be ... to deduce the meaning from its known intention and its entire text, and to give effect, if possible, to every part of it, consistently with the unity and harmony of the whole." William Rawle, *A View of the Constitution of the United States of America* (Philadelphia: H. C. Carey and I. Lea, 1825), p. 28. "It is an established rule ... that the intention of the lawgiver is to be deduced from a view of the whole, and of every part of a statute, taken and compared together.... The real intention, when accurately ascertained, will always prevail over the literal sense of the terms." James Kent, *Commentaries on American Law*, 4 vols. (4th ed.; New York: For the Author, 1840), I: 461–462. "The first and fundamental rule in the interpretation of all instruments is, to construe them according to the sense of the terms, and the intention of the parties." Joseph Story, *Commentaries on the Constitution of the United States*, 2 vols. (3rd ed.; Boston: Little, Brown and Co., 1858), I.400.283. Citation indicates volume, section, and page number.

common law was supreme. The subject of constitutional law had peaked under Story with his incomparable *Commentaries on the Constitution of the United States*, but by the time Oliver Wendell Holmes came to teach constitutional law at Harvard just prior to his brief appointment in the Law School, it was in Harvard College.[117] In the meantime, the study of constitutional law flourished more in departments of history and political science than in the law schools. And that was particularly true of Princeton University's Department of Politics. Not only was there a growing interest there in constitutional law, but it was a faculty congenial to the new Langdellian approach to the study of the law. But where Langdell's science of law had been only implicitly Darwinian, there were others willing to make the case for an evolutionary understanding of the law in far more explicit terms, especially when it came to the study of the Constitution and the judicial interpretations of it. One of the most important of these advocates was Woodrow Wilson, whose influence would be felt not only in his own publications but especially in the career of one of those he recruited to Princeton.

II. WOODROW WILSON'S NEW SCIENCE OF POLITICS

As students of the Enlightenment, Woodrow Wilson observed, the makers of the Constitution "constructed a government as they would have constructed an orrery – to display the laws of nature." They understood politics as "a variety of mechanics"; their constitution "was founded on the law of gravitation" and was intended by them "to exist and move by virtue of the efficacy of 'checks and balances'"[118] But what struck the founding generation as sensible would in time strike a later generation as an encumbrance; a written constitution of enumerated and balanced powers gets in the way of the ordinary impulses of politics.

If the Founders are to be given credit for having created and bequeathed to their posterity this mechanical or Newtonian conception of the constitutional order – "a machine that would go of itself"[119] – Wilson must be

---

[117] It was primarily after the appointment of James Bradley Thayer as Royall Professor of Law in 1873 that the return to the serious study of constitutional law was foreshadowed, if not immediately achieved, at the Harvard Law School. In 1893 he published in the *Harvard Law Review* a seminal article that would help make the serious study of the Constitution, or at least the study of the law under it, an acceptable subject in the law schools. See James Bradley Thayer, "The Origin and Scope of the American Doctrine of Constitutional Law," *Harvard Law Review* 7 (1893): 129–156. See also James Barr Ames, "James Bradley Thayer," in Ames, *Lectures on Legal History*, pp. 464–466.

[118] Woodrow Wilson, *The New Freedom* (New York: Doubleday, Page & Co., 1913), pp. 46–47.

[119] James Russell Lowell, "The Place of the Independent in Politics," in *Political Essays* (Boston: Houghton Mifflin & Co., 1888), p. 312.

credited for first challenging that conception in the popular mind with an organic or Darwinian alternative.[120] It was not enough, Wilson thought, to see the Constitution as a perpetual motion machine; it was more accurate to see it as an adaptable "living thing" capable not only of growth but of evolution. As such, Wilson believed, constitutional government "falls not under the theory of the universe, but under the theory of organic life. It is accountable to Darwin, not to Newton."[121] All "[l]iving political constitutions must be Darwinian in structure and in practice."[122]

In Wilson's view, the government, to achieve the noble ends for which it was intended, had to be a dynamic human enterprise. To allow that, the Constitution itself, the source of that government, had to be understood as dynamic, not static. In Wilson's progressive view of the world, a static Constitution was at odds with the most basic principles of democratic governance. Had the government of the United States "been a machine governed by mechanically automatic balances," Wilson once observed, "it would have had no history; but it was not, and its history has been rich with the influences and personalities of the men who have conducted it and made it a living reality."[123] Even though he insisted that he harbored "an inveterate reverence for the text and meaning of the Constitution," Wilson was not one who thought "an undiscriminating and almost blind worship" of the Constitution was either necessary or appropriate.[124] Indeed, he took pride in the fact that he was part of that generation that found itself "in the first season of free outspoken, unrestrained constitutional criticism."[125] But unlike others of his generation, Wilson was far more inclined to celebrate than

---

[120] For insightful discussions of Wilson's understanding of constitutionalism, see Michael Kammen, *A Machine that Would Go of Itself: The Constitution in American Culture* (New York: Knopf, 1987), pp 166–170; and Christopher Wolfe, *The Rise of Modern Judicial Review: From Constitutional Interpretation to Judge-Made Law* (New York: Basic Books, 1986), pp. 203–222. For an astute assessment of Wilson's science of politics more generally, see Ronald J. Pestritto, *Woodrow Wilson and the Roots of Modern Liberalism* (Lanham, MD: Rowman & Littlefield, 2005). For an account of Wilson's transition from the academic to the political world, see W. Barksdale Maynard, *Woodrow Wilson: Princeton to the Presidency* (New Haven, CT: Yale University Press, 2008).

[121] Woodrow Wilson, *Constitutional Government in the United States* (New York: Columbia University Press, 1908), p. 56. Hereinafter cited as *Constitutional Government*. There are doubts as to the true influence of Newtonian thinking on the Founders' constitutionalism. See James A. Robinson, "Newtonianism and the Constitution," *Midwest Journal of Political Science* 1 (1957): 252–266.

[122] *Constitutional Government*, p. 57.

[123] Ibid.

[124] Woodrow Wilson, "Address to the Short Ballot Organization," January 21, 1910, in Arthur Link, ed., *The Papers of Woodrow Wilson*, 69 vols. (Princeton, NJ: Princeton University Press, 1966–94), XX: 37; Woodrow Wilson, *Congressional Government: A Study in American Politics* (Boston: Houghton, Mifflin, and Co., 1885), p. 4. Hereinafter cited as *Congressional Government*.

[125] *Congressional Government*, p. 5.

to criticize the Constitution. The reason was that to his way of thinking the Constitution was nothing more than what each successive generation could make of it. As Wilson bluntly put it: "The Constitution contains no theories."[126]

This view that there is an absence of theory in the Constitution was essential to Wilson's Darwinian understanding of the Constitution as against the Founders' Newtonian conception. The virtue of this atheoretical text, Wilson believed, was that it not only allowed, but demanded that each successive generation bring to the fundamental law the current, evolved meaning. The key was a confidence in the possibility of constitutional "evolution," the need "to interpret the Constitution according to the Darwinian principle."[127] "As the life of the nation changes," Wilson wrote in 1908, "so must the interpretation of the document which contains it change, by a nice adjustment, determined, not by the original intention of those who drew the paper, but by the exigencies and the new aspects of life itself." This was not a radical proposition to Wilson; indeed, it was inherently conservative; it was "a process not of revolution but of modification." Such a view of the Constitution as a living, evolving organism was, he believed, in the best sense "conservative, not of prejudices, but of principles, of established purposes and conceptions, the only things which in government or in any other field of action can abide."[128]

But given that the Constitution itself "contains no theories," those necessary "established purposes and conceptions" had to be brought to the Constitution from sources external to it. They were to be found, as Wilson said, not in the "original intention" but in "the new aspects of life." To do otherwise, he concluded, would be to regard the Constitution as "a mere legal document" rather than what it was truly meant to be: "a vehicle of life."[129]

This importation of meaning to fill the Constitution's void was to be achieved especially, though not exclusively, by a Supreme Court understood to be – and which understood itself to be – "a constitutional convention in continuous session."[130] The very structure of the Constitution demanded it. "The process of formal amendment of the Constitution was made so difficult by the provisions of the Constitution itself that it has seldom been feasible to use it; and the difficulty of formal amendment has undoubtedly made the courts more liberal ... in their interpretations than they otherwise would have been." For Wilson, it was good that the "chief instrumentality by which the Constitution has been extended to cover the facts of national development [had] ... been judicial interpretation" This was as it should be;

---

[126] *Constitutional Government*, p. 60.
[127] *The New Freedom*, pp. 46–48.
[128] *Constitutional Government*, pp. 192, 194, 194.
[129] Ibid., p. 190.
[130] As quoted in Kammen, *A Machine that Would Go of Itself*, p. 265.

it ensured flexibility. Properly, Wilson thought, the Constitution "does not remain fixed in any unchanging form, but grows with the growth and is altered with the change of the nation's needs and purposes." When it came to constitutional government, he said, "its atmosphere is opinion."[131]

Thus did Wilson the progressive see constitutional legitimacy springing from political expediency; the political end justified the constitutional means. And the constitutional means were to be shaped, in large measure, by a politically sensitive judiciary. The fact that the Supreme Court had on occasion adapted the Constitution with "boldness and audacity" did not bother Wilson.[132] He took too much comfort from his belief that principles were to be gleaned less from what ought to be in some abstract sense than from what is in a concrete sense.

Wilson was not, of course, a voice in the wilderness; but of a chorus that included such luminaries as Oliver Wendell Holmes, Jr., and Theodore Roosevelt, his was voice was still loud, clear, and resonant. His progressive political concerns went beyond constitutional law, as such, then just beginning to appear as a field of political science. Wilson brought his views to bear on everything from Congress to the bureaucracy to political parties. His influence in the academy and in the political world was nearly unequaled. One place that his enormous influence did come to bear on the study of constitutional law, albeit somewhat indirectly, was in the young man Wilson recruited to Princeton in 1905, Edward S. Corwin.[133]

III. EDWARD S. CORWIN'S CORROSIVE CONSTITUTIONALISM

By the professional standards of today's academic world, Edward Samuel Corwin was an anomaly. Born in 1878, he earned his doctorate in history at the University of Pennsylvania. Handpicked by Wilson, he became a professor of politics at Princeton University, eventually succeeding Wilson as McCormick Professor of Jurisprudence. Acclaimed by his adopted profession, Corwin the historian later served as president of the American Political Science Association. And at the time of his death in 1963, the professor was one of the ten authorities on the Constitution and constitutional law most frequently cited in the opinions of the Supreme Court of the United States. Few scholars have ever crossed over into so many academic disciplines with such obvious success.

---

[131] *Constitutional Government*, pp. 193, 193. "The underlying understandings of a constitutional system are modified from age to age by changes of life and circumstances, and corresponding alterations of opinion." Ibid., p. 22.

[132] *Constitutional Government*, p. 193.

[133] For an overview of Corwin's life and work, see the introductory essays to Alpheus T. Mason and Gerald Garvey, eds., *American Constitutional History: Essays by Edward S. Corwin* (New York: Harper & Row, l964), pp. ix-xxiii; and Richard Loss, ed., *Presidential Power and the Constitution: Essays by Edward S. Corwin* (Ithaca, NY: Cornell University Press, 1976), pp. ix-xx. Hereinafter cited as *Presidential Power and the Constitution*.

But Edward Corwin was not simply a scholar silently scribbling in his study; he was a public man as well. As his last graduate student at Princeton, Clinton Rossiter, once put it, Corwin "changed the minds of men in seats of power in Washington as in the seats of learning around the country." Indeed, it is not too much to say, as Rossiter said, that "American constitutional law – not just the law taught by professors, but the law debated by senators and proclaimed by judges – has never been quite the same since he first took his incisive pen in hand."[134] In terms of legal theory, Corwin is the father of the age in which we still live.[135]

When Corwin began his academic career, the study of the law and the Constitution was largely devoid of the philosophical pretensions of our day. Those who sought to explicate constitutional meaning were largely those, like Corwin himself, who had been trained as historians; political science as a discipline separate from history was only then emerging. Teachers of law seem to have been more concerned with deciphering the black-letter law of court opinions than with anything else. Thus was it left to Corwin to cultivate the then-fallow field of constitutional law understood in light of political theory.[136]

Throughout his long career Corwin wrestled with two seemingly contradictory theories of law. On the one hand, he was attracted to the legal realism of his mentor Wilson and those realists writing in law such as Oliver Wendell Holmes and Benjamin Cardozo; he was tugged downward by the gravitational pull of the here and now, of politics in the ordinary sense of the word. But on the other hand, he was drawn to the notion of a higher-law tradition, the natural law as that had been understood from Aristotle down to John Locke with all its twists and turns of principle; Corwin was tugged upward toward notions of justice in the highest sense. Corwin's essays are often a muddled amalgam of these conflicting views of the legal universe.[137] In the end, he appeared to achieve a workable reconciliation of these contradictory premises of law; but the inherent tensions remained.

Following in the progressive tradition of Wilson, Corwin launched the idea that there is a meaningful distinction between what he saw as the Constitution properly understood and what he dismissed as simply the "documentary constitution." He was blunt: "As a *document*, the Constitution came from the framers ... but as *law*, the Constitution comes from and derives all its force from the people of the United States of this day and hour." For

---

[134] Clinton Rossiter, "Introduction and Biographical Sketch," in Edward S. Corwin, *The "Higher Law" Background of American Constitutional Law* (Ithaca, NY: Cornell University Press, 1955), pp. xii, xi. This book originally appeared as two articles in the *Harvard Law Review* 42 (1928–29): 149–185, 365–409. All citations to this work are to the book version, hereinafter cited as *Higher Law Background*.

[135] See Wiecek, *The Lost World of Classical Legal Thought*, p. 258.

[136] There were exceptions such as Thomas Cooley and Christopher Tiedeman.

[137] See, for example, his essay on "Natural Law and Constitutional Law," *Presidential Power and the Constitution*, pp.1–22.

him, proper interpretation of the Constitution eschews any "concerns for theories as to what was intended by a generation long since dissolved into its native dust." The bottom line for Corwin was what has since come to be called the "living" Constitution; the document is to be regarded as "a living statute, palpitating with the purpose of the hour, reenacted with every waking breath of the American people."[138] Put a bit differently, for Corwin, the Constitution "must mean different things at different times if it is to mean what is sensible, applicable, feasible."[139]

For Corwin, as for contemporary advocates of such an evolutionary Constitution, the dilemma was how to make sure a written document did indeed palpitate with "the purpose of the hour." And for Corwin, as for his ideological descendants, the answer was the same: "The Court's opinion of the Constitution . . . becomes the very body and blood of the Constitution."[140] His point was simple: "the judicial version of the Constitution *is* the Constitution."[141] In his view, "the constitutional document . . . has been absorbed into constitutional law." Believing that "the judges alone really *know* the law," Corwin was willing to allow the "documentary" Constitution to be reduced to nothing more than "the social philosophies, outlooks, and predilections of members of the Bench."[142]

Yet Corwin was no simple positivist. In his view, "the *legality* of the Constitution, its *supremacy*, and its claim to be worshipped, alike find common standing ground on the belief in a law superior to the will of human governors." As he put it, "[t]here is . . . discoverable in the permanent elements of human nature itself a durable justice which transcends expediency, and the positive law must embody this if it is to claim the allegiance of the human conscience."[143] But in Corwin's analysis of this "higher" law, he refused or failed to draw distinctions that must be drawn. He was unwilling or unable

---

[138] Corwin, "Constitution v. Constitutional Theory," *Corwin on the Constitution*, II: 191, 191, 192. This is in stark contrast to the Founders' view of the Constitution. See, for example, James Madison to Henry Lee, June 25, 1824, where he argued that not interpreting the Constitution as it had been "accepted and ratified by the nation" would cause a "metamorphosis" in the law. *Letters and Other Writings of James Madison*, 4 vols. (New York: Lippincott, 1865), III: 441.

[139] Corwin, "Moratorium over Minnesota," *Corwin on the Constitution*, II: 334.

[140] "[I]n relation to constitutional law . . . the constitutional document has become hardly more than a formal point of reference. For most of the Court's excursions in the constitutional sphere, the constitutional document is little more than a taking-off ground; the journey out and back occurs in a far different medium, of selected precedents, speculative views regarding the nature of the Constitution and the purposes designed to be served by it, and unstated judicial preferences. All of which signifies that in the constitutional field, the Court is a *legislature*; and to the extent that the doctrine of the finality of its interpretations of the Constitution actually prevails, it is a *super-legislature*." Corwin, "Standpoint in Constitutional Law," *Corwin on the Constitution*, II: 294.

[141] Corwin, "Judicial Review in Action," *Corwin on the Constitution*, II: 203.

[142] Corwin, "Standpoint in Constitutional Law," *Corwin on the Constitution*, II: 281, 282.

[143] *Higher Law Background*, pp. 5, 11.

to grasp the philosophical differences in the various ideas of natural law and "higher" law (not necessarily the same thing) that had obtained throughout history.[144] As a result, his "higher" law becomes a mixture of ancients and moderns, lawyers and philosophers, case law and treatises. But the essence of Corwin's confusion is the blending of the natural law with the common law.

The problem, as he saw it, was "not how the common law became *law* but how it became *higher*, without at the same time ceasing to be enforceable through the ordinary courts even within the field of its more exalted jurisdiction." Indeed, as Corwin explained it, before the common law "was higher law, it was positive law in the strictest sense of the term, a law regularly administered in the ordinary courts in the settlement of controversies between private individuals." There had to be a decisive moment, it seems, when the positive law became the higher law: that moment, for Corwin, began with "the establishment by Henry II in the third quarter of the twelfth century of a system of circuit courts with a central appeal court."[145]

At the outset, the common law was nothing more elevated than custom, custom rendered "national, that is to say common, through the judicial system" created by Henry II. But custom is never self-selecting, so, strictly speaking, the common law could not be merely custom alone. And therein lies the climactic moment: "For in their selection of what customs to recognize in order to give them national sway, and what to suppress, the judges employed the test of 'reasonableness,' a test derived in the first instance from Roman and continental ideas." It was precisely this "notion that the common law embodied right reason" that furnished the common law's "chief claim to be regarded as higher law." And that notion of "right reason which lies at the basis of the common law . . . was from the beginning *judicial* right reason."[146]

With this belief, Corwin argues, came a deference toward the judges' decisions as "the act of experts," a willingness to accept judicial opinion as "an act of knowledge or discovery." This tendency was compounded with the advent of "that series of judicial commentators on the common law which begins with Bracton" and by whose pens is secured the common law's "elevation to the position of a higher law binding upon supreme authority." With the contribution of Sir John Fortescue's *De Laudibus*, law comes to be seen – and celebrated – as "a professional mystery, as the peculiar science of bench and bar."[147] By the time of Sir Edward Coke's

---

[144] "Natural law is a 'higher law' but not every higher law is natural." Leo Strauss, "On Natural Law," in *Studies in Platonic Political Philosophy* (Chicago: University of Chicago Press, 1983), p. 137.

[145] *Higher Law Background*, pp. 24, 24, 26.

[146] Ibid., pp. 26, 26.

[147] Ibid., pp. 26, 26–27, 37.

opinion in *Bonham's Case*,[148] in Corwin's account, this "artificial reason" of the law, this "'common right and reason' is . . . something fundamental, something permanent; it is higher law."[149]

It is his blurring of the philosophic and legal borders of the various schools of thought of Coke's time that led to Corwin's fundamental error. "The receptive and candid attitude . . . evinced toward natural law ideas . . . enabled Coke to build upon Fortescue, and it enabled Locke to build upon Coke. It made allies of sixteenth century legalism and seventeenth century rationalism."[150] In short, for Corwin, there was not so great a difference between Coke's conception of higher law and Locke's; each ultimately drew his conclusions from the materials of ages past. However new the ideas of Locke and others might appear at first glance, the fact was, in Corwin's view, they were "far from novel."[151] Indeed, by Corwin's reckoning, "Locke's indebtedness" to those who took up "the thread of later medieval thought" and thereby "revived the postulates of popular sovereignty which underlay Roman law and institutions" was "immense."[152] Even Locke's natural rights teaching had its roots in ancient ground.[153]

[148] The only oft-repeated passage of Coke's opinion in *Bonham's Case* became the foundation of Corwin's understanding of the so-called higher law background of American constitutional law. As Coke had put it: "And it appears in our books, that in many cases, the common law will controul acts of parliament, and sometimes adjudge them to be utterly void: for when an act of parliament is against common right and reason, or repugnant, or impossible to be performed, the common law will controul it and adjudge such act to be void." *Bonham's Case*, 8 Co. Rep. 118a.

[149] *Higher Law Background*, p. 47. But this is to view the past through the lens of the present. "[T]o some extent at least, later doctrines of natural law have been reflected backward upon Coke's statement, giving it a content it did not in fact have." Samuel E. Thorne, "Dr. Bonham's Case," *Law Quarterly Review* 54 (1938):543–552, p. 545.

[150] *Higher Law Background*, p. 46. It is this passage that Thorne uses as his example of the false view of contemporary scholarship that Coke thought himself engaged in divining new rules from natural law. Thorne, "Dr. Bonham's Case," pp. 548–549.

[151] *Higher Law Background*, p. 60.

[152] Ibid., p. 63. In many ways, Corwin's logic parallels, and was no doubt influenced by, the older view of Frederick Pollock, who argued that "the history of the law of nature" had "no real break in it." Frederick Pollock, "The History of the Law of Nature," *Columbia Law Review* 1 (1905): 11–32, pp. 32, 31.

Pollock's view of Hobbes is especially at odds with the evidence. Hobbes himself surely thought otherwise: "Natural philosophy is . . . but young; but civil philosophy yet much younger, as being no older . . . than my own book *De Cive*." Thomas Hobbes, *De Corpore*, in William Molesworth, ed., *The English Works of Thomas Hobbes*, 11 vols. (London: John Bohn, 1839–45), I: ix. It is also fair to say that generations – including Hobbes's own – would agree with him as against Pollock. See generally William S. Holdsworth, *History of English Law*, 17 vols. (London: Metheun & Co., 1922–72), V: 480–485; VI: 294–301.

[153] *Higher Law Background*, p. 16. For precisely how Locke differed from the tradition, see Leo Strauss, *Natural Right and History* (Chicago: University of Chicago Press, 1953); Thomas L. Pangle, *The Spirit of Modern Republicanism: The Moral Vision of the American Founders and the Philosophy of Locke* (Chicago: University of Chicago Press, 1988); Ruth

In his own way, Corwin seemed to believe that a judicial reliance on a "higher law" would serve to keep judicial review from "obliterat[ing] the frontier between constitutional law and policy."[154] Yet by his own logic he simultaneously reduced natural law or higher law to mere judicial discretion. "As the matrix of American constitutional law," Corwin wrote, "the documentary Constitution is...natural law under the skin." But by his definition of the Constitution as merely what the judges say it is, Corwin was reduced to a dependence on judicial will in order to make the written Constitution – the "documentary" Constitution – comport with the higher demands of natural law. This will be achieved, Corwin argued, "by judicial massage – sometimes a rather rugged massage" of the Constitution's text. As he viewed it, to suggest that "judicial review is confined to the four corners of the written Constitution" is to deny the necessary place of "natural law ideas" in judicial review.[155]

Corwin's fundamental error was threefold. First, he did not grasp the degree to which Coke's reverence for the common law was inextricably linked to his appreciation for the forms of the common law; it was his regard for the maxims and forms of the law, its technicalities and medieval procedures and pleadings, that led him to praise it (as against, for example, Francis Bacon's view of equity) as the perfection of reason.[156] Indeed, it is not too much to say that Coke's view in *Bonham's Case* derived more from the concrete political circumstances of his time; in this sense, it is more accurate to speak of Coke's philosophy of politics than of any political philosophy broadly and properly understood. Coke's concern was never with "law"; he focused all his attention rather on the "laws of England." To the degree to which one can speak of Coke's jurisprudence – and it is not at all clear that one should so speak – his juridical science was particular and concrete, never abstract and universal.[157]

W. Grant, *John Locke's Liberalism* (Chicago: University of Chicago Press, 1987); and the editors' introduction to John Locke, *Questions Concerning the Law of Nature*, ed. R. Horwitz et al. (Ithaca, NY: Cornell University Press, 1990). The Godlessness of Locke's natural law was a profound movement away from all that had preceded him and Hobbes. For a sense of this, see Locke's "Second Reply to the Bishop of Worcester," in *The Works of John Locke*, 3 vols. (3rd ed.; London: Bettesworth, 1727), I: 432–575.

[154] Corwin, "The Dissolving Structure of Our Constitutional Law," *Presidential Power and the Constitution*, p. 154.

[155] Corwin, "The Debt of American Constitutional Law to Natural Law Concepts," *Corwin on the Constitution*, I: 195, 203, 203.

[156] As Stephen A. Siegel has pointed out: "Coke's de-emphasis of right reason and equity as sources of English law is supported conceptually by his view that the common law is the wisdom of ages." "The Aristotelian Basis of English Law, 1450–1800," *New York University Law Review* 56 (1981): 18–59, p. 30.

[157] "There are wide differences between the philosophy of law, as actually administered in any country, and the abstract doctrine, which may, in matters of government, constitute in many minds the law of philosophy." Joseph Story, *Commentaries on Equity Jurisprudence*, 2 vols. (12th ed.; Boston: Little, Brown, and Co., 1877), I: 25–26, n.1. Coke's view of the

One of the most stunning errors Corwin made in creating his history of the common law's elevation is what is meant by "reason" in the sense in which Coke seems to be using it. For Coke, reason was not untethered natural reason in any philosophic sense, that is, individual judgments of right and wrong. When he spoke of reason, he meant *legal* reason – what he called the "artificial reason" of the law that was comprised of those maxims and decisions that had been passed down through the ages.[158] As Coke himself had argued to the king, the "causes which concern the life, or inheritance, or goods, or fortunes of his subjects, are not to be decided by natural reason, but by the artificial reason and judgment of the law."[159] By "artificial reason" Coke meant reasoning from precedents, maxims, and other authorities. Artificial reason was inextricably linked in Coke's mind to "judgment of the law." It is this idea of the internal structure of the common law, the "artificial reason" that lies at the heart of precedential law and custom, that Coke was speaking of in *Bonham's Case* when he invoked "common right and reason."[160]

Coke's judges were bound to the lessons of experience of many generations as they had been handed down by courts and polished and fashioned by commentators. Reason, in the sense in which Coke used it, was in fact more a matter of legal custom than of abstract natural equity. This idea of reason in Coke derived its legitimacy in his mind not from his independent calculation of right and wrong in light of some transcendent higher natural law, but from the authorities of the common law, writers such as Henrici de Bracton, Ranulf Glanvill, Sir John Fortescue, and Christopher St. Germain.[161] While such sources as St. Germain's *Dialogues Between a*

---

law was in marked contrast to Hobbes's later view: "My designe is not to shew what is law here and there; but what is law." Thomas Hobbes, *Leviathan* (Oxford: Clarendon Press, 1909), p. 203.

[158] "Coke did not maintain that natural law supplied judges with roving commissions. Coke's natural law was a rather tame creature, satisfied with the inalienable rights to indictment and jury trial." Frank H. Easterbrook, "Substance and Due Process," *The Supreme Court Review: 1982* (Chicago: University of Chicago Press, 1983), pp. 85–125, 97–98.

[159] *Prohibitions del Roy* (1607), 12 Co. Rep. 65.

[160] Thomas Jefferson, long an admirer of Coke over Blackstone, captured the essence of Coke's view well: "The common law is a *written law*, the text of which is preserved from the beginning of the 13th century downwards, but what has preceded that is lost; its substance, however, has been retained in the memory of the people & committed to writing from time to time in the decisions of the judges and treatises of the jurists, insomuch that it is still considered as a *lex scripta*, the letter of which is sufficiently known to guide the decisions of the courts. In this department, the courts restrain themselves to the letter of the law." Thomas Jefferson to Philip Mazzei, November 1785, in Paul L. Ford, ed., *The Works of Thomas Jefferson*, 12 vols. (New York: G. P. Putnam's Sons, 1904–05), IV: 473.

[161] Coke did not embrace "the theory that 'an Act of Parliament may be void from its first creation' because of a conflict between its provisions and fundamental, natural, or 'higher' law." Samuel E. Thorne, ed., *A Discourse upon the Exposicion & Understandinge of Statutes* (San Marino, CA: Huntington Library, 1942), "Introduction," p. 89.

Doctor of Divinity and a Student of the Laws of England and Fortescue's *De Laudibus* were conduits of the Aristotelian natural law tradition of the scholastics, they were not deemed as setting judges free to follow their own discretion in fashioning new rules of natural justice or equity.[162]

While Coke shared St. Germain's and Fortescue's basic Aristotelian presuppositions, he was unwilling to find the sources of English law in conscience or synderesis. To Coke's way of thinking, "the natural reason of an individual or of an entire generation is inferior to the common law's accumulated wisdom."[163] For Coke, "right reason" was the collective reason of the many from time immemorial: "what speaks through the judge is the distilled knowledge of many generations of men, each decision based on the experience of those before and tested by the experience of those after, and it is wiser than any individual... can possibly be."[164]

At a minimum, Coke's great political battles during his judicial tenure – in behalf of the rules and rigidities of the common law against the looseness of equity – stand in stark contrast to Corwin's conclusion that Coke was the father of a freewheeling judicial discretion hemmed in only by the judge's sense of justice and natural law. The effort of Coke in behalf of the common law against what he saw as the pretensions of the ecclesiastical courts and the canon law, on the one hand, and those of kingly prerogative in the Chancery on the other is further evidence of this more restrictive view of his understanding of "common right and reason."[165]

Corwin's second fundamental error was no less egregious than his first. He failed to understand just how decisive was the break with tradition effected by Thomas Hobbes and John Locke over the idea of natural law; as a result, he diminished the difference between the old idea of a higher law and the new, between what he misunderstood as the essence of Coke and what he superficially attributed to Locke. Whereas to the degree to which Coke embraced the traditional understanding of the natural law, it was one

---

[162] See Paul Vinogradoff, "Reason and Conscience in Sixteenth Century Jurisprudence," *Law Quarterly Review* 24 (1908): 373–384.

[163] Siegel, "The Aristotelian Basis of English Law," p. 30.

[164] J. G. A. Pocock, *The Ancient Constitution and the Feudal Law*, rev. ed. (Cambridge: Cambridge University Press, 1987), p. 35. See also Pocock, *The Machiavellian Moment* (Princeton, NJ: Princeton University Press, 1975), pp. 3–30.

[165] See, for example, *Fuller's Case* (1607), 12 Co. Rep. 41, and *The Case of Proclamations* (1611), 12 Co. Rep. 74. "Under the leadership of Coke, the common lawyers were seeking to test the legality of political action by the standards and procedural techniques of the medieval common law." John P. Dawson, "Coke and Ellesmere Disinterred: The Attack on Chancery in 1616," *Illinois Law Review* 36 (1941): 127–152, p. 130. Coke himself summed it up unambiguously: "[F]or any fundamental point of the ancient common laws and customs of the realm, it is a maxim of policy, and a trial by experience, that the alteration of any of them is most dangerous; for that which hath been refined and perfected by all the wisest men in former succession of ages, and proved and approved by continual experience to be good and profitable for the commonwealth, cannot without great hazard and danger be altered or changed." 4 Co. Rep. Pref. v, vi.

that saw that law of natural reason and natural equity written in the hearts of men by the hand of God, the modern view of natural law articulated by Locke was drastically different. To Locke, as to Hobbes, natural law was "nowhere to be found but in the minds of men"[166] as the result of nothing but human reason.

Finally, having thus confused the philosophical issues, Corwin's third error was to see Locke as doing little more than rescuing "Coke's version of the English Constitution from a localized *patois* [and] restating it in the universal tongue of the age."[167] The Lockean idea of modern natural rights is thus made as compatible with the common law tradition as the ancient and medieval tradition had been for Coke. Locke's radicalism is denied, while Coke's is exaggerated.

Ultimately, by narrowing the philosophical distance between them, Corwin was able to collapse Locke into Coke, thereby reducing modern natural right into the common law; natural right thus becomes indistinguishable from, because it is identical to, judicial discretion. Locke's standard that the "people shall judge" becomes in Corwin's formulation a standard that the judges shall judge. He reduces the written Constitution to nothing more than a part of the common law to be molded by judicial reflection upon the cases and commentaries antecedent to it. But such reflection is not bound by any rules external to the reflection itself; Coke's standard of "right reason" becomes for Corwin merely judicial opinion "palpitating with the purpose of the hour."[168] The result is that Corwin establishes the common law as the higher law background of American *constitutional law* at the expense of understanding the modern political philosophy of natural rights as the higher-law background of the American *Constitution*. The Constitution, thus misunderstood, becomes indistinguishable from constitutional law.[169]

---

[166] As Coke argued in *Calvin's Case*: "The law of nature is that which God at the time of creation on the nature of man infused into his heart, for his preservation and direction; and this is *Lex aeterna*, the moral law, called also the law of nature. And by this law, written with the finger of God in the heart of man, were the people of God a long time governed before the law was written by Moses, who was the first reporter or writer of law in the world." 7 Co. Rep. 1, 12b. See Peter Laslett, ed., *Locke's Two Treatises of Government* (2nd. ed; Cambridge: Cambridge University Press, 1970), *Second Treatise*, 376: 136 (citation is to the page followed by the section).

[167] *Higher Law Background*, p. 72. To be fair, Corwin does go further and notes that when it comes to Coke's version of the English constitution that Locke "also supplements it in important respects." But in the end, they have more in common than not. See ibid., pp. 87–89.

[168] Corwin, "Constitution v. Constitutional Theory," *Corwin on the Constitution*, II: 192.

[169] Allowing courts to judge according to the principles of "natural law and justice," noted Story, would be to establish "the most formidable instrument of arbitrary power that could well be devised." And, he warned: "It would literally place the whole rights and property of the community under the arbitrary will of the judge... according to his own notions and conscience; but still acting with a despotic and sovereign authority." *Commentaries on Equity Jurisprudence*, I.19.15.

But it is precisely the written Constitution as the higher law – binding upon and limiting courts as well as legislatures, as Chief Justice John Marshall said in *Marbury v. Madison* – that makes the American constitutional order original in the history of the world. It was one point on which Jefferson and Marshall could agree: to Marshall, the written constitution was the "greatest improvement on political institutions;" to Jefferson, it was nothing less than "our peculiar security."[170] Its supremacy derives not from the common law tradition of Coke but from the philosophic tradition of Hobbes and Locke and their new notions of popular sovereignty and the consent of the governed. For it is in that modern rejection of the tradition of which Coke was a part that the roots of the modern doctrine of constitutionalism and its new "higher law" were planted.

In the end, Corwin's common law constitutionalism is severed from the common law itself, from that body of maxims and rules deemed permanent and binding. The common law, properly understood, consisted of principles not deemed dependent upon the circumstances of the moment. Such a view is fundamentally inconsistent with Corwin's insistence, born of the legal realism of his time, that the meaning of the Constitution can only be found by judicial recourse to "the purpose of the hour." Constitutional theory, as such, ideas about what the Constitution was intended to mean – including, apparently, the antecedent common law provisions that actually were incorporated into the Constitution – is to be avoided. "Such ideas," Corwin insisted, "whatever their historical basis . . . have no application to the main business of constitutional interpretation, which is to keep the Constitution adjusted to the advancing needs of time."[171]

When higher law and legal realism collided in Corwin's thinking, legal realism prevailed. All that remained of the higher-law tradition was the methodology of the common law judge. But bereft of the common law itself, Corwin's judge is left only recourse to a far more amorphous conception of higher law; natural law in that most abstract sense does indeed become a "brooding omnipresence in the sky" to be summoned down arbitrarily as the judge sees fit.[172] In Corwin's constitutional calculus, the "juristic connotations" of the concept of the natural law "under the skin" of the Constitution turned out to be simple and sweeping: "[N]atural law is entitled by its intrinsic excellence to prevail over any law which rests solely on human authority . . . [and] may be appealed to by human beings against injustices sanctioned by human authority."[173]

---

[170] 5 U.S. 137 (1803), 178; Thomas Jefferson to Wilson C. Nicholas, September 7, 1803, in Andrew Lipscomb and Andrew Bergh, eds., *The Writings of Thomas Jefferson*, 20 vols. (Washington, DC: Thomas Jefferson Memorial Foundation, 1905), X: 419.

[171] "Constitution v. Constitutional Theory," *Corwin on the Constitution*, II: 108.

[172] Justice Holmes in *Southern Pacific Co. v. Jensen*, 244 U.S. 205 (1917), 222.

[173] "Natural Law and Constitutional Law," *Presidential Power and the Constitution*, p. 2.

What this means for Corwin's theory of judicial review is that once the mediating structure of the common law is removed, there is nothing between the judge and the judge's personal view of natural justice. Since the Constitution itself is a law that ultimately rests on human authority, it too can have appeals made against it to natural law. Such appeals intended to square the Constitution with the demands of natural law will be made through the courts. The result will be for judges to create judicial doctrines derived from what they perceive to be the dictates of natural law by Corwin's "rugged massage" of the Constitution's text. To believe, Corwin said, that "judicial review is confined to the four corners of the written Constitution" does no justice to the influence of "natural law ideas" on judicial review.[174]

Whereas for a jurist like Sir Edward Coke judges were understood to decide cases "not by natural reason, but by the artificial reason and judgment of the law," Corwin's judges were not so encumbered.[175] Indeed, constitutional law understood as derived from natural law not only allows but demands that a judge exercise his "natural reason" in his quest to do what is right and just; a Constitution understood as a theoretical vacuum meant to be kept up with the times simply cannot survive without it. If the Constitution is to be kept attuned to the "intrinsic excellence" of the natural law, it is up to the judges to do the tuning.

Toward the end of his career, one begins to see in Corwin flickers of doubt about the potential dangers of such a jurisprudential view. In an article appropriately entitled "The Dissolving Structure of Our Constitutional Law," he argued that "[t]he fundamental elements of American constitutional law reduce . . . to a single element, judicial review, and this has gradually emancipated itself from all documentary and doctrinal restraints, and even from the restraint which was originally implicit in common law jurisdictions in the judicial function as such – the principle of stare decisis." The "result of this self-achieved emancipation" has been to reduce "judicial review" to a mere "instrument of policy."[176]

But oddly enough, Corwin's main concern with the dissolution of constitutional law was not with the enhancement but with what he saw as the diminution of judicial review as such. With the advent of the New Deal, Corwin saw constitutional law being transformed to allow "the concentration of governmental power in the United States, first in the hands of the national government; and, secondly, in the hands of the national executive." In his view, such principles as federalism, separation of powers, and judicial

---

[174] Ibid., p. 11. See also "Judicial Review in Action" and "The Basic Doctrine of American Constitutional Law," *Corwin on the Constitution*, II: 198; III: 30.

[175] *Prohibitions del Roy*, 7 Co. Rep. 63–65 (1609).

[176] "The Dissolving Structure of Our Constitutional Law," *Presidential Power and the Constitution*, pp. 154–155.

review had come to be eroded by "an altered expectation" on the part of the American people as to "what government can do if it only tries hard enough." At the root of these changed political expectations was a new public ideology, the "theory of the equality of man." Rather than the older libertarian conception of constitutional liberty against government that had held sway from the beginning, the New Deal heralded the inauguration, in Corwin's view, of a new egalitarian conception of constitutional equality through government. Such non-political factors as "social superiority and economic power" were to be corrected by a national government increasingly bent on a policy of "social levelling."[177]

While Corwin could look at the passing of the old constitutional world with a sense of melancholy, and at the coming of the new with at least a twinge of apprehension and uncertainty, he seemed never to grasp how at home was his theory of constitutional law with the transformation. But this was precisely his notion of the Constitution as "a living statute palpitating with the purpose of the hour" writ large. For if there is no substantive theoretical core to the Constitution, if it is bereft of any discernible political theory, and if its meaning is to come only from judicial interpretation, then one must accept what comes. With the elevation of constitutional law to higher-law status and the diminution of the Constitution itself to a mere derivative of constitutional law, there is no objective standard by which to judge and control the judges. There will be a tendency for judges to cease seeing themselves as merely lawyers and begin to think of themselves more as moral philosophers; their concern will no longer be the Constitution in a legal sense but justice in the most abstract sense. They will come to see themselves empowered "to give voice to the conscience of the country."[178] Or, in another more recent formulation, they will believe they are "invested with the authority to . . . speak before all others for [the people's] constitutional ideals."[179]

The tension inherent in Corwin's understanding of the Constitution and the role of the Court under it – his muddled amalgam of higher law and legal realism – came into clearest focus with the Warren Court's revolution in law and its effort to effect "a fusion of constitutional law and moral theory."[180] The result was a new and troubling "political jurisprudence"; Warren's own belief that his appointment was a "mission to do justice" subsequently inspired a growing number of other judges that they too possessed

---

[177] Ibid., pp. 149, 156, 155.

[178] Edward S. Corwin, *Constitutional Revolution, Ltd.* (Claremont, CA: Pomona College, Scripps College, Claremont Colleges, 1941), p. 111.

[179] Justice Anthony Kennedy in *Planned Parenthood of Southeastern Pennsylvania v. Casey*, 505 U.S. 833 (1992), 868.

[180] Ronald Dworkin, *Taking Rights Seriously* (Cambridge, MA: Harvard University Press, 1977), p. 149.

"roving commissions to do good."[181] Constitutional rights and powers in the traditional sense were no longer simply the point: "the task of the judge is to give meaning to constitutional values . . . by working within the constitutional text, history, and social ideals. He searches for what is true, right, and just."[182]

There is something of an irony in the fact that Corwin was born into an America just edging into the juridically mystical world of substantive due process and died in an America a decade into the Warren Court. The era of conservative judicial activism of 1875 to 1937 was not much different from the current world of liberal activism. Corwin's career parallels the time during which the notion of substantive due process and the so-called rule of reason as the measure of constitutionality were being woven ever more tightly into the fabric of American constitutional law. But his career ultimately did more than merely parallel a doctrinal development; Corwin encouraged and guided that development, often seemingly unaware of how his scholarship was contributing to it. In the end, his efforts to supplant the intentions of the framers with what has been rightly called his own "primitive nihilism" cloaked as higher law has proved to be a corrosive constitutionalism at odds with the Constitution itself and destructive of the very idea of the rule of law.[183]

IV. RECOVERING THE FOUNDERS' CONSTITUTION

Corwin's influence has proved to be both deep and lasting. "All who work in the field of constitutional history today," one scholar has confessed, "tread in the tracks that Corwin blazed."[184] Ultimately, the difference between Corwin's constitutional jurisprudence and that of today's constitutional moralists is one of degree, not of kind. While Corwin might object to the extremes to which modern theorists are willing to go in infusing the Constitution with moral theories, they are in truth only following the path he helped clear between law and politics. They are simply fulfilling Corwin's prophecy that the constitutional revolution of the New Deal would, in time, prove to have extricated the Court from "suspicion of political or partisan entanglement" over questions of policy and left it free "to support the humane values of free thought, free utterance, and fair play."[185]

---

[181] Martin Shapiro, "Judge as Statesman, Judge as Pol," *New York Times*, November 21, 1981, Book Review Section, p. 42; G. Edward White, *Earl Warren: A Public Life* (New York: Oxford University Press, 1982), pp. 350–369; Alexander M. Bickel, *The Supreme Court and the Idea of Progress* (New York: Harper & Row, 1970), p. 134.

[182] Owen Fiss, "The Forms of Justice," *Harvard Law Review* 93 (1979): 1–58, p. 9.

[183] Loss, "Introduction," in *Corwin on the Constitution*, II: 15.

[184] Wiecek, *The Lost World of Classical Legal Thought*, p. 258.

[185] "Statesmanship on the Supreme Court," in Mason and Garvey, eds., *American Constitutional History: Essays by Edward S. Corwin*, p. 144.

To an extraordinary degree, Corwin's work from the early decades of the twentieth century continues to inform and shape much of contemporary constitutional scholarship. The basic premises of the contemporary scholars who embrace so-called noninterpretivist judicial review, or who suggest that there is historical justification for judges to appeal to an unwritten constitution, or who argue that to ignore the original intention is to fulfill that intention, are all the same as Corwin's.[186] They are united in the belief that the Constitution leaves in the hands of the judges "the considerable power to define and enforce fundamental rights without substantial guidance from constitutional text and history."[187]

The need is to recover the Founders' Constitution and the philosophic base on which it originally stood. For the Founders' understanding of the relationship between the "higher law" and their constitution was far removed from the view that has come to dominate the scholarly tradition.[188] To them, the creation of the Constitution signaled acceptance of the belief that it was possible for men to create their governments from "reflection and choice" and not be doomed to what fate may bring as a result of mere "accident and force." The tyrannies of "arbitrary kings and cruel priests," the result in large measure of that "wicked confederacy" of the canon and the feudal law of the Middle Ages, were consigned to the past.[189] At the heart of the idea that constitutions can be created from "reflection and

---

[186] The literature of this sort is truly voluminous, dominating in every sense of the word most scholarly publications from the peer-reviewed journals of political science and history to the student-edited law reviews. Among the most influential articles are Thomas C. Grey, "Do We Have an Unwritten Constitution?", *Stanford Law Review* 27 (1975): 703–718, and "Origins of the Unwritten Constitution: Fundamental Law in American Revolutionary Thought," *Stanford Law Review* 30 (1978): 843–893; H. Jefferson Powell, "The Original Understanding of Original Intent," *Harvard Law Review* 98 (1985): 885–948; and Suzanna Sherry, "The Founders' Unwritten Constitution," *University of Chicago Law Review* 54 (1987): 1127–1177. Three worthy correctives of this point of view are to be found in Walter Berns, "Judicial Review and the Rights and Laws of Nature," *Supreme Court Review: 1982* (Chicago: University of Chicago Press, 1982), pp. 49–84; Raoul Berger, "'Original Intention' in Historical Perspective," *George Washington Law Review* 54 (1985–86): 296–337; and Helen K. Michael, "The Role of Natural Law in Early American Constitutionalism: Did the Founders Contemplate Judicial Enforcement of Unwritten Individual Rights?", *North Carolina Law Review* 69 (1990): 421–490.

[187] Grey, "Do We Have an Unwritten Constitution?", p. 714.

[188] One of the most succinct statements of the Founders' understanding of the relationship of higher law to the Constitution and constitutional law was made by Justice John McLean. "It is for the people," Justice McLean argued, "in making constitutions and in the enactment of laws, to consider the laws of nature. . . . This is a field which judges cannot explore. . . . They look to the law, and to the law only." *Miller v. McQuerry*, 17 F. Cas. (No. 9583) 332, 339 (CCD Ohio, 1853).

[189] Jacob Cooke, ed., *The Federalist* (Middletown, CT: Wesleyan University Press, 1961), No. 1, p. 3; John Adams, "Dissertation on the Canon and the Feudal Law," in Charles Francis Adams, ed., *The Life and Works of John Adams*, 10 vols. (Boston: Little, Brown, and Co., 1856), III: 447–464.

choice" lies the confidence that language, as Locke said, is indeed "the great instrument and common tye of society." The American founders held that their written and ratified constitution of limited and enumerated powers was understood to be the "fundamental law," the embodiment of "the intention of the people."[190]

The recovery of that original foundation of the Founders' Constitution begins with the premises not of the medieval natural law theorists or common law judges to whom Corwin and his intellectual descendants look, but of those who stood at the beginning of modernity, especially Thomas Hobbes and John Locke. For it is in their political philosophies of natural rights that one sees most clearly the moral grounds of originalism as the standard of interpretation; it is rooted in the belief that men are all created equal and may not legitimately be ruled arbitrarily by another – and that to avoid such tyranny all legitimate government must rest upon the consent of the sovereign people from whom all power flows.

[190] John Locke, *An Essay Concerning Human Understanding*, ed. P. Nidditch (Oxford: Oxford University Press, 1975), III.I.1, p. 402; *The Federalist*, No. 78, p. 525.

2

Nature and the Language of Law

Thomas Hobbes and the Foundations of Modern Constitutionalism

Thomas Hobbes was born in 1588 – prematurely, legend has it, due to his mother's anxiety over the Armada.[1] A century later, England was shaken to its roots and exulted in the political implications of the Glorious Revolution. Between those two seemingly disparate events the idea of natural-rights constitutionalism was born. It was Hobbes – "the monster of Malmesbury" – who had helped to plant the seeds of that juridical revolution, an upheaval of tradition that eventually would far exceed the tumultuous political events of his own seventeenth-century England.[2]

Hobbes has been called "the greatest, and certainly the most original and stimulating philosopher that England... ever produced."[3] Yet he was doomed to be reviled in his own time in his own land – and for centuries to come.[4] Indeed, Hobbes was never without his critics. From the beginning, he was assailed by all those whose power he called into question – the

---

[1] Leslie Stephen, *Hobbes* (Ann Arbor: University of Michigan Press, 1961), p. 3.

[2] See generally Paul A. Rahe, *Republics Ancient and Modern: Classical Republicanism and the American Revolution* (Chapel Hill: University of North Carolina Press, 1994); Vickie B. Sullivan, *Machiavelli, Hobbes and the Foundation of a Liberal Republicanism in England* (Cambridge: Cambridge University Press, 2004); Lee Ward, *The Politics of Liberty in England and Revolutionary America* (Cambridge: Cambridge University Press, 2004); and Paul A. Rahe, *Against Throne and Altar: Machiavelli and Political Theory under the English Republic* (Cambridge: Cambridge University Press, 2008).

[3] William S. Holdsworth, *History of English Law*, 17 vols. (London: Methuen & Co., 1922–72), VI: 294. Hobbes, Holdsworth would suggest, "approached English constitutional law and the political theories which underlay it from a new and critical standpoint." Ibid., V: 480.

[4] See John Bowle, *Hobbes and His Critics: A Study in Seventeenth-Century Constitutionalism* (London: Frank Cass & Co., 1951; rev. ed., 1969); Samuel I. Mintz, *The Hunting of Leviathan: Seventeenth-Century Reactions to the Materialism and Moral Philosophy of Thomas Hobbes* (Cambridge: Cambridge University Press, 1970); G. A. J. Rogers, ed., *Leviathan: Contemporary Responses to the Political Theory of Thomas Hobbes* (Bristol: Thoemmes Press, 1995); Noel Malcolm, *Aspects of Hobbes* (Oxford: Oxford University

priests, professors, and lawyers whose views he dismissed with such glittering contempt.[5]

But for all his critics, Hobbes was no intellectual outcast whose thought was doomed to die a wretched death of dismissal and derision. He had disciples in his own lifetime, and his works had a substantial following among many of Europe's leading intellectuals.[6] His influence was not simply overt, either; there were those who dared not speak his name who still took his philosophy seriously.[7] One sees, for example, far more than mere traces of Hobbes's philosophic project in John Locke's *Two Treatises of Government* and his *Essay Concerning Human Understanding*, despite the fact that Locke was forced by the intellectual politics of his day to proclaim the name of Hobbes as "justly decry'd."[8]

Others who came later – including Samuel Pufendorf, Jean Jacques Burlamaqui, Emerich Vattel, Thomas Rutherforth, Sir William Blackstone, and John Trenchard and Thomas Gordon – revealed in their works an abiding debt to Hobbes and presented to yet newer generations his teachings about sovereignty by institution, the centrality of language to politics, and the necessity of law to liberty.[9] And a century after his death his influence

Press, 2002); and Jon Parkin, *Taming the Leviathan: The Reception of the Political and Religious Ideas of Thomas Hobbes in England, 1640–1700* (Cambridge: Cambridge University Press, 2007).

5 "Hobbes...failed to influence his contemporaries because his theories were detested by statesmen like Clarendon, by lawyers like Hale, and of course by all theologians, for the very sufficient reason that his political philosophy attacked the practice and theories of all." William S. Holdsworth, *Some Lessons from Our Legal History* (New York: Macmillan, 1928), p. 127

6 See Noel Malcolm, "Hobbes and the European Republic of Letters," in *Aspects of Hobbes*, pp. 457–545; Quentin Skinner, "Thomas Hobbes and His Disciples in France and England," *Comparative Studies in Society and History* 8 (1966): 153–167; and Mark Goldie, "The Reception of Hobbes," in J. H. Burns and Mark Goldie, eds., *The Cambridge History of Political Thought, 1450–1700* (Cambridge: Cambridge University Press, 1991), pp. 589–615. See also Quentin Skinner, "The Ideological Context of Hobbes's Political Thought," *The Historical Journal* 9 (1966): 286–317.

7 See G. A. J. Rogers, "Hobbes's Hidden Influence," in G. A. J. Rogers and Alan Ryan, eds., *Perspectives on Thomas Hobbes* (Oxford: Clarendon Press, 1988), pp. 189–205.

8 John Locke, "Second Reply to the Bishop of Worcester," in *The Works of John Locke*, 3 vols. (3rd ed.; London: Bettesworth, 1727), I: 566. See Chapter 3 of this volume, for a detailed account of how Locke took his bearings from Hobbes.

9 "The introduction of superiority, as a necessary part of the definition of law, is traced from Sir William Blackstone to Puffendorf. This definition of Puffendorf is substantially the same as Hobbes." James Wilson, "Of the General Principles of Law and Obligation," in Robert G. McCloskey, ed., *The Works of James Wilson*, 2 vols. (Cambridge, MA: Harvard University Press, 1967), I: 105.

   While Hobbes's name was, as Locke said, "decry'd"; while he was pilloried as "the monster of Malmesbury"; and even while in 1683 the "thinkeing men of Oxford" held a public book burning in order to dispose of, among other works, "Thomas Hob's *Leviathan* and *De Cive*," his influence was spreading. His influence is seen not only in Locke, but also would be felt across the sea, where his "thinking... had penetrated the minds of Americans more pervasively than Americans knew or would have found it politic to admit."[10]

One of the most troubling aspects of Hobbes's thought for those seeking the sources of liberal constitutionalism is his famous assertion that the sovereign is not bound by the civil laws.[11] Most often this is taken as proof that Hobbes's true purpose is a defense of an absolute monarch. But given his repeated insistence that the sovereign need not be a monarchy – it may even be "a Democracy, or Aristocracy" – there is another way of understanding what he means when he says that the sovereign is above the law. His argument is in fact the first sustained effort to fashion a conception of fundamental law that is distinct from and superior to ordinary civil law yet does not depend upon the medieval belief in a higher natural or divine law. In the end, Hobbes's sovereign, his "mortal god,"[12] has more in common with a constitution based upon popular sovereignty than with any notion of institutional absolutism. It is for this reason that Hobbes is properly deemed the father of what would become modern, liberal constitutionalism.[13]

To a far greater degree than his philosophic successor Locke, Hobbes was explicitly concerned with the nature and extent of law. In all of his great

---

in other sources the Americans drew upon while crafting their new constitutional order. In the natural law treatises of Pufendorf, Burlamaqui, Vattel, and Rutherforth one sees clearly "a natural law teaching that is Hobbesian in every essential respect." Walter Berns, "Judicial Review and the Rights and Laws of Nature," *Supreme Court Review: 1982* (Chicago: University of Chicago Press, 1983): 49–83, p. 67.

Pufendorf was willing to argue that Hobbes's civil philosophy as presented in his *De Cive* was "for the most part extremely acute and sound." Vattel openly acknowledged his own debt to Hobbes, whose work, he said, "in spite of its paradoxes and detestable principles, shows us the hand of the master." And Trenchard and Gordon would repeatedly praise him simply as a "great philosopher." See Chapter 4 of this volume.

[10] Forrest McDonald, *The American Presidency: An Intellectual History* (Lawrence: University Press of Kansas, 1994), p. 44. See also Frank M. Coleman, *Hobbes and America: Exploring the Constitutional Foundations* (Toronto: University of Toronto Press, 1977).

[11] "The Soveraign of a Common-wealth, be it an Assembly or one Man, is not subject to the civill lawes. For having power to make, and repeale Lawes, he may, when he pleaseth, free himselfe from that subjection by repealing those lawes that trouble him, and making of new; and consequently he was free before." Thomas Hobbes, *Leviathan* (Oxford: Clarendon Press, 1909), p. 204. Hereinafter cited as *Leviathan*.

[12] Ibid., p. 132.

[13] For a powerful argument that Hobbes is properly called "the founder of liberalism," see Pierre Manent, *An Intellectual History of Liberalism* (Princeton, NJ: Princeton University Press, 1994), pp. 20–38. See also Harvey C. Mansfield, Jr., "Hobbes and the Science of Indirect Government," *American Political Science Review* 65 (1971): 97–110, p. 107. For a set of views on the liberalism-versus-republicanism debate and Hobbes's place in it, see Quentin Skinner, *Hobbes and Republican Liberty* (Cambridge: Cambridge University Press, 2008); Rahe, *Against Throne and Altar*; Sullivan, *Machiavelli, Hobbes and the Foundation of a Liberal Republicanism in England*; Ward, *The Politics of Liberty in England and Revolutionary America*; and Rahe, *Republics Ancient and Modern*.

works Hobbes's political attention was drawn to the role to be played by law in any healthy regime. From his first scholarly publication, his translation of Thucydides' *History of the Peloponnesian War* (1629) to the *Elements of Law* (1640) to *Leviathan* (1651) to *Behemoth* (1668) to *A Dialogue Between a Philosopher and a Student of the Common Laws of England* (1681), he sought to explore and explain how law served as the common border between politics and philosophy.

Hobbes was familiar with, or at least had access to, some of the major legal writers of his time as a member of the earl of Devonshire's household. On the shelves of the family's libraries at Chatsworth and Hardwick Hall were to be found copies of such civil and common law works as Justinian's *Corpus Juris Civilis*, Bracton's *De Legibus et Consuetudinibus Angliae*, St. Germain's *Doctor and Student*, Littleton's *Tenures*, Coke's *Institutes*, Grotius's *De Jure Belli ac Pacis*, Selden's *De Jure Naturali et Gentium*, and Zouch's *Cases and Questions Resolved in the Civil Law*. These treatises were supplemented by copies of reports of the common law courts prepared by Sir Henry Hobart, Sir Edward Coke, and Sir James Dyer. There seems also to have been a copy of John Rastell's law dictionary, *Termes of the Law*. Some of the works available to Hobbes at Chatsworth and Hardwick Hall eventually made their way into his own writings.[14]

But Hobbes was not a legal theorist as such. His interest in law was more philosophical than practical, more a matter of political sovereignty than judicial doctrine. "My designe," he confessed, "is not to shew what is law here and there; but what is law."[15] Hobbes's concern with the law was as part of his broader project of refashioning the foundation of political legitimacy in light of the lessons of English history. And it was this focus that drew him to confront the common law of England in particular and the medieval legal mind more generally. Indeed, it is that context that helps to explain Hobbes's own ideas pertaining to law. Hobbes, after all, never wrote simply abstractly; he always had his enemies, he always had his targets.[16]

---

[14] For lists of the books and references to the citations in Hobbes's writings, see James Jay Hamilton, "Hobbes's Study and the Hardwick Library," *Journal of the History of Philosophy* 16 (1978): 445–453; Robinson A. Grover, "The Legal Origins of Thomas Hobbes's Doctrine of Contract," *Journal of the History of Philosophy* 18 (1980): 177–194; and Samuel I. Mintz, "Hobbes's Knowledge of the Law," *Journal of the History of Ideas* 31 (1970): 614–615. This article by Mintz is a reply in an exchange over Hobbes's views on the law of heresy. See Samuel I. Mintz, "Hobbes on the Law of Heresy: A New Manuscript," *Journal of the History of Ideas* 29 (1968): 409–414; and Robert Willman, "Hobbes on the Law of Heresy," *Journal of the History of Ideas* 31 (1970): 607–613.

[15] *Leviathan*, p. 203.

[16] As Quentin Skinner has put it, "even the most abstract works of political theory are never above the battle; they are always part of the battle itself." Skinner, *Hobbes and Republican Liberty*, p. xvi.

I. THE MEDIEVAL LEGAL MIND

To understand the radicalism of Hobbes's project – and to appreciate just how much offense he gave to so many – it is important to keep in mind that there was nothing less than a "jungle"[17] of medieval theories of law – an intellectually sprawling and ideologically diverse jungle that Hobbes took it upon himself personally to clear from the ground of politics. Yet for all the diversity of theories there was a common ground, and that was the powerful and pervasive influence of Christianity that was to be found in every aspect of medieval intellectual life. Indeed, "all departments of thought were conceived as subordinate to theology, in such a way that the methods of theology fettered and strangled the development in science or art or literature."[18] Law was no exception.

There were four primary influences that shaped the contours of the medieval legal mind, as they shaped the medieval mind more generally. First was the rise of universities, especially those at Paris, Oxford, and Bologna, and the formal establishment of the scholastic method of teaching and learning.[19] Second was the rediscovery of the *Corpus Juris Civilis* of Justinian, which made a science of the law seem possible.[20] Third, the publication of Gratian's *Concordia Discordantium Canonum* around 1140 established the canon law as a major body of legal knowledge.[21] And finally, there was the discovery of the works of Aristotle and the subsequent rise of Aristotelianism. Together these influences, over a great stretch of time, prepared the way for the transition from the medieval to the modern conception of law and constitutionalism. These elements that made up the medieval "juridical culture . . . formed a kind of seed bed from which grew the whole tangled forest of early modern constitutional thought."[22]

The single most important influence, however, was the scholastic method of dialectical reasoning. Through early translations of Aristotle's rediscovered works on logic, the medieval way of thinking was firmly established;

[17] Hermann Kantorowicz, *Studies in the Glossators of the Roman Law* (Cambridge: Cambridge University Press, 1938), p. 50. Charles Homer Haskins noted that "[n]othing would have astonished medieval philosophers more than to be told they all thought alike." *The Renaissance of the Twelfth Century* (Cambridge, MA: Harvard University Press, 1927), p. 362. And C. R. S. Harris has argued that "the twelfth and thirteenth centuries contain a diversity which quite belies the notion of any orthodoxy vigorously imposed from without." *Duns Scotus*, 2 vols. (Oxford: Clarendon Press, 1926), I: 40.

[18] John Neville Figgis, *The Divine Right of Kings* (2nd ed.; Cambridge: Cambridge University Press, 1914), p. 257.

[19] See generally Hastings Rashdall, *The Universities of Europe in the Middle Ages*, ed. F. M. Powicke and A. B. Emden, 3 vols. (Oxford: Clarendon Press, 1936).

[20] See Kantorowicz, *Studies in the Glossators of the Roman Law.*

[21] See Stephan Kuttner, *Gratian and the Schools of Law, 1140–1234* (London: Variorum Reprints, 1983).

[22] Brian Tierney, *Religion, Law, and the Growth of Constitutional Thought, 1150–1650* (Cambridge: Cambridge University Press, 1982), p. 1.

throughout the Middle Ages it dominated every area of thought. As Charles Homer Haskins once put it, those "later centuries turned with avidity to Aristotle's dialectic and stretched themselves on the frame of his thought."[23] But the approach was especially suited to the study of law.[24] There was, in fact, more to the scholastic method than merely logical reasoning. "Its criteria were moral as well as intellectual; it was a way of testing justice and not only the truth."[25]

In the process of subjecting authoritative texts such as those of Aristotle and Justinian to dialectical scrutiny, the schoolmen produced glosses on the texts that in many cases supplanted the texts themselves as authority. By this process the priests and professors and lawyers endeavored to demonstrate that by their own scholastic cleverness the works of the great authors "could be interpreted so as to make them say what they ought to have said."[26]

The significance of the scholastic method thus lay in the fact that not all was as it appeared. Not infrequently new doctrines were introduced into the gloss but disguised and presented as merely straightforward interpretations of the text in question. It thus was not unusual to find new philosophical problems introduced by the glossator that might have only a "very tenuous" connection with the problems originally raised in the passage under consideration. In time these substantive glosses and commentaries took on a life of their own. Rarely would anyone attempt to read the original text without the scholarly guides.[27]

The scholastic method reached its most important stage in the middle of the thirteenth century when Aristotle's ethical and political works were rediscovered and given dependable Latin translations. With the naturalistic philosophy of such works as the *Politics* and the *Nicomachean Ethics* joined to Aristotle's merely logical treatises, the schoolmen faced the daunting task of attempting to reconcile that pagan Greek philosophy with the teachings of the Christian church.

There arguably has never been an impact in the history of ideas comparable to that of the recovery of Aristotle on the medieval mind. But in truth an "unadulterated Aristotle was not what made the impact." In their ceaseless striving to reconcile the most glaring philosophical contradictions, the schoolmen were committed to making Aristotle "fit to live with."[28] As

---

[23] Haskins, *The Renaissance of the Twelfth Century*, p. 343.

[24] None of the achievements of the civilians or the canonists "would have been possible without the so-called scholastic or dialectical method." Walter Ullmann, *Law and Politics in the Middle Ages* (Ithaca, NY: Cornell University Press, 1975), p. 87.

[25] Harold J. Berman, *Law and Revolution: The Formation of the Western Legal Tradition* (Cambridge, MA: Harvard University Press, 1983), p. 142.

[26] Norman Kretzmann, Anthony Kenny, and Jan Pinborg, eds., *The Cambridge History of Later Medieval Philosophy* (Cambridge: Cambridge University Press, 1982), p. 101.

[27] Ibid., pp. 29, 102.

[28] Walter Ullmann, *Principles of Government and Politics in the Middle Ages* (London: Metheun, 1961), pp. 231, 232.

a result, it was Aristotelianism rather than Aristotle himself that exerted such an influence on medieval thinking. The various rivulets of Aristotelianism – that is, Aristotle's teaching as interpreted, modified, and adapted by Christianity, Augustinian philosophy, Platonic and Neoplatonic ideas, and Thomistic doctrines – all "converged into one broad stream." The banks of that stream may have been carved by Aristotle, but the current itself was above all the "Christian element."[29] Thus in time scholasticism became "not only a method but a jurisprudence and a theology."[30]

Scholasticism and the Perversion of Language

By the sixteenth century, the metaphysical subtleties of the scholastic method had begun to strike many as absurd and pointless; the logical and grammatical refinements of the schoolmen, by becoming ends in themselves, wreaked havoc on common sense and, thereby, on philosophy properly understood.[31] Their descriptions took precedence over what had originally been the object to be described.[32] The law – more important, the *idea* of law – had suffered accordingly. "[T]here is scarce any thing so clearly written," Hobbes would note, "that when the cause thereof is forgotten, may not be wrested by an ignorant Grammarian, or a Cavilling Logician, to the injury, oppression, and perhaps destruction of an Honest man."[33]

To Hobbes, the schools and their pointless doctrines revealed at once "the presumption and the impotence of over intellectualism." The scholastic methods of the art and science of language served only to increase "the ambiguity of common speech by deliberately separating words from clear mental thoughts."[34] The dialectical or disputative methods of the schools had elevated language for its own sake over the proper regard for the true

---

[29] Walter Ullmann, *The Medieval Idea of Law* (London: Metheun, 1941), p. 3.

[30] Berman, *Law and Revolution*, p. 143.

[31] While at Oxford, Hobbes had found many subjects "above his understanding; but it did not apparently occur to him till a later period that they were unintelligible because nonsensical." By 1610, Hobbes had "discovered that the scholastic doctrine... was everywhere treated with contempt by the intelligent and was passing out of fashion." To say the least, Hobbes dedicated himself to hastening its demise. Stephen, *Hobbes*, pp. 5, 8.

The "founders of modernity – Bacon, Machiavelli, Descartes, Galileo, Hobbes, Spinoza, and Locke... in the sixteenth and seventeenth centuries sought to overthrow the Aristotelian-Scholastic tradition in the universities and to redefine philosophy or science." Thus there was an explosion of thinking about thinking. See Robert P. Kraynak, *History and Modernity in the Thought of Thomas Hobbes* (Ithaca, NY: Cornell University Press, 1992), pp. 97, n.2; 103.

[32] As Descartes would say, he had never "noticed that the arguments carried on in the schools have ever brought to light a truth which was previously unknown." Rene Descartes, *Discourse on Method, and Meditations* (New York: Liberal Arts Press, 1960), pt. 6, p. 44.

[33] Thomas Hobbes, *A Dialogue Between a Philosopher and a Student of the Common Laws of England*, ed. Joseph Cropsey (Chicago: University of Chicago Press, 1971), pp. 97–98. Hereinafter cited as *Dialogue*.

[34] Kraynak, *History and Modernity in the Thought of Thomas Hobbes*, pp. 61, 79.

purpose of language. To Hobbes, the result was a repulsive rhetoric that meant nothing: scholasticism was debate and wrangling for the sake of debate and wrangling. From their elevated station, the learned doctors had come to control opinion; true knowledge had been supplanted by obscure doctrines. Truth had been "strangled with the snares of words."[35]

To no small extent the perversity of the schoolmen grew from the unhealthy blending of faith and philosophy, of reason and religion; to Hobbes, neither had fared very well by the union. The scholars, who, "striving to make good many points of faith incomprehensible, and calling in the philosophy of Aristotle to their assistance, wrote books of school-divinity, which no man else, nor they themselves, are able to understand." The scholastic method of disputation and dialectics led to "unintelligible distinctions" with which these servants of the Pope's doctrines sought "to blind men's eyes." Such obscure language served "to make it seem... want of learning in the reader." From the earliest scholastics, such as Lombard and Duns Scotus, the method was fixed.[36] As Hobbes saw it:

[F]rom these the schoolmen that succeeded learnt the trick of imposing what they list upon their readers, and declining the force of true reason by verbal forks; I mean, distinctions that signify nothing, but serve only to astonish the multitude of ignorant men. As for the understanding readers, they were so few, that these new sublime doctors cared not for what they thought.

And more:

These schoolmen were to make good all the articles of faith which the Popes from time to time should command to be believed: amongst which there were very many inconsistent with the rights of kings, and other civil sovereigns, asserting to the Pope all authority whatsoever they should declare to be necessary... in order to [aid] religion.

From the Universities also it was, that all preachers proceeded, and were poured out into city and country, to terrify the people into absolute obedience to the Pope's canons and commands, which, for fear of weakening kings and princes too much, they durst not yet call laws.

From the Universities it was, that the philosophy of Aristotle was made an ingredient in religion, as serving for a salve to a great many absurd articles, concerning the nature of Christ's body, and the estate of angels and saints in heaven; which articles they thought fit to have believed, because they brought some of them profit, and others reverence to the clergy, even to the meanest of them.[37]

---

35 Thomas Hobbes, *De Corpore*, in William Molesworth, ed., *The English Works of Thomas Hobbes*, 11 vols. (London: John Bohn, 1839–45), vol. I, ep. ded., p. viii. Hereinafter cited as *De Corpore*.

36 Thomas Hobbes, *Behemoth*, ed. Ferdinand Tönnies (2nd ed.; New York: Barnes and Noble, 1969), pp. 17, 40, 43. Hobbes was especially contemptuous of Lombard and Scotus, whom he described as "two of the most egregious blockheads in the world, so obscure and senseless are their writings." Ibid., pp. 40–41. Hereinafter cited as *Behemoth*.

37 *Behemoth*, p. 41.

The result of this tradition of scholastic arrogance and popular igno-rance – its calculated design, in Hobbes's view – was simple: to bolster "the Pope's doctrine, and . . . his authority over kings and their subjects by school-divines."[38] This they achieved by appropriating language, by infusing it with contrived and "barbarous terms,"[39] whereby to render words arbi-trary and in need of final and authoritative definition. The use of Aristotle was essential to this: "[N]one of the ancient philosophers' writings are comparable to those of Aristotle, for their aptness to puzzle and entan-gle men with words, and to breed disputation, which must at last be ended in the determination of the church in Rome."[40] By the schoolmen's dupli-citous arts, speech became "a spider's web" wherein "by the contexture of words tender and delicate wits are ensnared and stopped."[41] By these methods the "crafty ambitious" schoolmen were able to "abuse the simple people."[42]

The schoolmen had produced a "vain philosophy"[43] by their "learned madness,"[44] their impenetrable and meaningless "jargon."[45] To see the absurdity of scholasticism, Hobbes insisted, one need only "take a Schoole-man into his hands, and see if he can translate any one chapter concerning any difficult point; as the Trinity; the Deity; the Nature of Christ; Transub-stantiation; Free-will, etc., into any of the moderne tongues, so as to make the same intelligible; or into any tolerable Latine, such as they were acquainted withall, that lived when the Latine tongue was Vulgar." To emphasize his point, Hobbes took "into his hands" Francisco Suarez. "What is the mean-ing of these words," Hobbes asked: "*The first cause does not necessarily inflow any thing into the second, by force of the Essentiall subordination of the second causes, by Which it may help it to worke?*" To Hobbes, such "questions of abstruse philosophy" were simply and profoundly "incom-prehensible." Hobbes was sure of that: "When men write whole volumes of such stuffe, are they not Mad, or intend to make others so?"[46]

---

[38] Ibid., p. 17.
[39] *De Corpore*, I.3.4, p. 34.
[40] *Behemoth*, pp. 41–42.
[41] *De Corpore*, I.3.8, p. 36.
  As Bacon had written, the schoolmen "did out of no great quantity of matter, and infinite agitation of wit, spin unto us those laborious webs of learning . . . admirable for the fineness of thread and work, but of no substance or profit." Francis Bacon, *The Advancement of Learning*, in Basil Montagu, ed., *The Works of Francis Bacon*, 3 vols. (Philadelphia: A. Hart, 1852), I: 171–172.
[42] *Leviathan*, p. 18.
[43] See especially *Leviathan*, Ch. 46.
[44] Thomas Hobbes, *Elements of Law: Natural and Politic*, ed. Ferdinand Tönnies (2nd ed.; New York: Barnes and Noble, 1969), I.10.9, p. 52. Hereinafter cited as *Elements of Law*. Citation indicates part, chapter, section, and page number.
[45] *Leviathan*, p. 524.
[46] Ibid., p. 63.

The schools, in Hobbes's view, were morally as well as intellectually corrupt. The "philosophy" that poured from the universities "was rather a dream than science." Put forward in "senselesse and insignificant language," the moral philosophy of the schoolmen was not philosophy properly so called, but merely "a description of their own passions"; they fashioned their own categories by their own brand of "logique," which was nothing more than "captions of words." Thus, he argued, they were able to "make the rules of *Good* and *Bad*" by nothing more substantial than "their own *Liking* and *Disliking*." In the name of Aristotelian metaphysics, the schoolmen denied the possibility of philosophy and, thereby, the possibility of a stable political order; their doctrines were "pernicious to the publique state." The teaching of "Aristotle and the other Heathen philosophers" was not only unintelligible; it was, said Hobbes, "repugnant to natural reason."[47] The inherent absurdities of Aristotle's works were such as to allow the Aristotelians (who ultimately "made more use of his obscurity than his doctrine")[48] to "resolve their conclusions before they knew their premises." Politically, with such lessons learned mindlessly by rote, the scholastics were able "not onely to hide the truth, but also to make men think they have it, and desist from further search."[49]

Sir Edward Coke's common law was a case in point. In its form and purpose, Coke's *First Institute*, his commentary upon Littleton's *Tenures*, revealed the problem perfectly. This work of inestimable importance to the history of English law was a text in which Coke "glossed" Littleton's medieval treatise on land law. He was ever trying thereby, Hobbes said, "to insinuate his own opinions among the people for the law of England." This he did, among other tricks, "by inserting *Latin* Sentences, both in his Text and in the Margin, as if they were Principles of the law of Reason, without any authority of Antient Lawyers, or any certainty of the Law of

---

47 Ibid., pp. 522, 531, 524. Aristotelianism, Hobbes noted, "reasoned only from the names of things, according to the scale of the *Categories*." In his view, such "reasoning" consisted only in the exchange of "words whereby we conceive nothing but the sound." Such words, he concluded, "are those we call *Absurd, Insignificant*, and *Non-sense*." *Dialogue*, p. 124; *Leviathan*, p. 34.

48 *Behemoth*, p. 41. Leo Strauss observed that there is a puzzling ambiguity in Hobbes's view – or at least in his use – of Aristotle. On the one hand, Hobbes's view of man and the nature of politics is shockingly at odds with Aristotle's; on the other hand, there are traces of strong similarity to Aristotle's *Rhetoric* in Hobbes's works. See *The Political Philosophy of Hobbes: Its Basis and Its Genesis* (Oxford: Clarendon Press, 1936), p. 42.

49 *Leviathan*, pp. 531, 535. As Roscoe Pound pointed out: "While they made the gloss into law in place of the text, and made many things over, as they had to be made over if they were to fit a wholly different social order, the method of dialectical development of absolute and unquestioned premises made it appear that nothing had been done but to develop the logical implications of an authoritative text." *An Introduction to the Philosophy of Law* (New Haven, CT: Yale University Press, 1954), p. 13.

England."[50] In Coke's hands it had been made clear that the common law was not immune to the perversions of scholasticism.

Sir Edward Coke and the Common Law

When Hobbes focused on the legal tradition of the common law, with all its customs and confusions, there was no question that he would bear down vigorously on the person he thought more than any other personified that tradition. Sir Edward Coke was the exemplar of the common lawyer. His understanding of law and politics was "essentially medieval" and was largely drawn from the scholastic teachings of the universities.[51] He was convinced that a student of the common law (be he a lawyer or a judge) could only benefit by coming to the law after his exposure to "the liberall arts, and especially logick" in the universities.[52] Coke was unblushing in his praise for the schools and their methods of study, and this alone would have been enough for Hobbes to hold him in contempt. There was hardly anyone who more disliked the intellectual confusions wrought by the scholastic method in the universities than Hobbes. And here was Coke willing to sing the praises of all that Hobbes despised. "In school divinity," wrote Coke, "and amongst the glossographers and interpreters of the civil and canon laws, in logick, and in other liberal sciences, you shall meet with a whole army of words, which cannot defend themselves *in bello grammaticali*, in the grammatical war, and yet are more significant, compendious, and effectual to express the true sense of the matter, than if they were expressed in pure Latin."[53]

Where Coke saw brilliance, Hobbes saw only "learned madness";[54] where Coke saw clarity of thought and depth of understanding, Hobbes saw only "vain and erroneous philosophy";[55] where Coke saw a firm foundation for society and a proper understanding of man's place in the world, Hobbes saw false doctrines that were "pernicious to the publique state."[56]

---

[50] *Dialogue*, p. 96. As Holdsworth has noted: "Since Coke in his readiness to explain and justify the many anomalies which disfigured the law, displayed the besetting sins of the historical lawyer in an exaggerated form, it was natural that Hobbes should select his writings as the type of that obsolete medievalism in law and politics which he had made it his life's work to combat." William S. Holdsworth, *Sources and Literature of English Law* (Oxford: Clarendon Press, 1925), p. 145.

[51] Holdsworth, *History of English Law*, V: 480. For the works with which Coke was familiar and which he apparently took seriously, see W. O. Hassall, ed., *A Catalogue of the Library of Sir Edward Coke* (New Haven, CT: Yale University Press, 1950).

[52] Sir Edward Coke, *The First Part of the Institutes of the Laws of England*, ed. F. Hargrave and C. Butler, 3 vols. (15th ed.; London: E and R. Brooke, 1794), II: 235b.

[53] Ibid., I: Pref. p. xxxix.

[54] *Elements of Law*, I.10.9, p. 52.

[55] *Leviathan*, p. 473.

[56] Ibid., p. 531.

In Hobbes's view, Coke's "obsolete medievalism"[57] was what his own new theory of sovereignty had to supplant.

The essential difference between Hobbes and Coke came to this: for Hobbes, the foundation of the law is the command of the sovereign; for Coke, the foundation is the reasonableness of the law.[58] The reasonableness of the common law was to be judged, in part, by its antiquity; rules that had endured through the ages could only be the result of the fact that they were reasonable to "grave and learned men" over a long period of time. Coke made clear his view throughout his *Institutes* and *Reports*, all variations on the same theme:

For reason is the life of the Law, nay the Common Law it selfe is nothing else but reason, which is to be understood of an artificiall perfection of reason gotten by long studie, observation and experience and not every man's naturall reason, for *nemo nascitur artifax* [no one is born skillful]. This legall reason *est summa ratio* [is the highest reason]. And therefore if all the reason that is dispersed into so many severally heads were united into one, yet could he not make such a Law as the Law of England is, because by many succession of ages it hath beene fined and refined by an infinite number of grave and learned men, and by long experience grown to such a perfection for the government of this Realme, as the old rule may be justly verified of it *Neminem oportet esse sapientiorem legibus:* No man (out of his owne private reason) ought to be wiser than the Law, which is the perfection of reason.[59]

But even though Coke did not root the law in the individual "naturall reason" of particular men, the role of articulating the reasonableness of the law still fell to the common law judges. And this was, by Hobbes's calculation, a power that could only undermine the idea of true sovereignty.[60]

This was not speculation on Hobbes's part. Coke had said as much. In the case of *Prohibitions del Roy* (1607) Coke recounted a confrontation between the king and his judges in which the question of the power to decide cases came up. The issue was whether because the "Judges are but the delegates of the King . . . the King may take what causes he shall please to determine, from the determination of the Judges, and may determine them himself." To this assertion, Coke "in the presence, and with the clear consent of all

---

57 Holdsworth, *History of English Law*, V: 480.
58 A fine assessment of the differences between Coke and Hobbes on the nature of law can be found in D. E. C. Yale, "Hobbes and Hale on Law, Legislation, and the Sovereign," *Cambridge Law Journal* 31 (1972): 121–156. See also James R. Stoner, *Common Law and Liberal Theory: Coke, Hobbes, and the Origins of American Constitutionalism* (Lawrence: University Press of Kansas, 1992).
59 Coke, I. Inst., 97b. This is quoted with parenthetical translations from Stoner, *Common Law and Liberal Theory*, p. 23.
60 In Coke's case, Hobbes found his definitions of law "so far from Reason" as to be easily dismissed as "Ridiculous." Thus the danger of leaving law to the artificial reason of the lawyers such as Coke. Said Hobbes: If Coke's "[d]efinitions must be the rule of law; what is there that he may not make Felony, or not Felony, at his pleasure." *Dialogue*, p. 119.

the Judges of England, and Barons of the Exchequer" replied that "the King in his own person cannot adjudge any case"; the cases must be "determined and adjudged in some court of justice according to the law and custom of England." After citing the appropriate authorities, the king was apparently not convinced, and said to Coke and the assembled jurists that "he thought the law was founded upon reason, and that he and others had reason, as well as the Judges." To this, Coke recorded that he responded as follows:

[T]rue it was, that God had endowed his Majesty with excellent science, and great endowments of nature; but His Majesty was not learned in the laws of his realm of England, and causes... are not to be decided by natural reason but by the artificial reason and judgment of law, which law is an act which requires long study and experience before that a man can attain to the cognizance of it.

The King, still unpersuaded – indeed, by this time "greatly offended" – responded that in such a case he would then "be under the law, which was treason to affirm." To this, Coke allegedly replied "that Bracton saith, *quod Rex non debet esse sub homine, sed sub Deo et lege* [the king ought to be under no man, but under God and the law]."[61]

Although Hobbes had first taken on Coke and his common law in *Leviathan*,[62] his sustained critique came in his most clearly legal work, *A Dialogue Between a Philosopher and a Student of the Common Laws of England*. In one sense, Hobbes takes up in the *Dialogue* where Francis Bacon had left off in his political struggles with Coke half a century before. But Hobbes, who had at one point served as an amanuensis to Bacon, took the debate to a higher level. Undistracted by the politics of the moment, Hobbes was able, as Bacon was not, to offer a probing inquiry into what they both viewed as the pretensions of the common lawyers. But this required going beyond the common law simply; to Hobbes, that law had been corrupted, as had all other political thinking, by the scholastic tradition and its attendant confusions of Aristotelian logic and school divinity.[63]

It was thus no accident that Hobbes titled his *Dialogue* as he did.[64] It was an obvious reference to one of the most basic of common law texts, Christopher St. Germain's *Dialogues Between a Doctor of Divinity and a Student of the Laws of England*; but it was a reference with a glaring

---

[61] *Prohibitions del Roy*, 12 Co. Rep. 63–65.

[62] *Leviathan*, p. 207.

[63] See Stephen A. Siegel, "The Aristotelian Basis of English Law, 1450–1800," *New York University Law Review* 56 (1981): 18–59.

[64] While it seems likely that the title by which Hobbes's dialogue on the common law has come to be known is one that Hobbes himself "might easily have chosen," there is doubt that he actually did so choose. See Alan Cromartie's superb introduction to the new edition of Thomas Hobbes, *A Dialogue between a Philosopher and a Student, of the Common Laws of England*, ed. A. Cromartie (Oxford: Clarendon Press, 2005), p. xxii.

difference.[65] St. Germain's "Doctor of Divinity," one of the schoolmen whom Hobbes detested, had been replaced by a "Philosopher." And it was not hard to discern that this philosopher was of a decidedly different cast than most of the philosophers of Hobbes's day; this was no Aristotelian. Thus, although nominally addressed to Coke, Hobbes's *Dialogue* stretches past the chief justice to grapple with the broader philosophic tradition of which the medieval common law was a part.

By broadening the rhetorical context of his philosophical critique of the common law, Hobbes was able to attack the more clearly Aristotelian logic that is to be found in such writers as St. Germain and Sir John Fortescue. To Hobbes, Coke's common law reasoning was ultimately as confused and confusing as anything the schoolmen had come up with, and not least because Coke was willing to rely on such theorists as Fortescue and St. Germain.[66] And, in a very real sense, it was far more threatening to the commonwealth. After all, scholastic disputation and logical "wrangles" were truly academic questions. Their corruption of the public mind, while serious, was not simply direct. The common law, on the other hand, directly affected the welfare of the community. To the degree the common law undermined the sovereignty that was necessary to good political order, it was more to be feared than what Hobbes regarded as the scholastic shenanigans in Oxford and Cambridge.

Hobbes's contrary view was simple: "It is not wisdom, but authority that makes a law." And what that meant was equally clear: "A law is a command of him, or them, that have the sovereign power, given to those that be his or their subjects, declaring publickly and plainly what every of them may do, and what they must forbear to do." To the extent that reason had a role, it was this: "the law of reason commands that every one observe the law which he hath assented to, and obey the person to whom he hath promised obedience and fidelity."[67]

The command of the properly recognized authority as the basis of law did not depend for its legitimacy on whether the law was reasonable or not. The command of the sovereign might be deemed unreasonable, unwise, or unfair and it would still be the law to which the people were obliged to conform. This is what Hobbes meant when he argued that outside civil society words such as "justice" and "injustice" have no meaning. Most assuredly such words could not legitimately take their meaning from the moral musings of judges, such as Coke, who presumed more authority than they in fact

---

[65] Christopher St. Germain, *Dialogues Between a Doctor of Philosophy and a Student of the Laws of England*, ed. William Muchall (Cincinnati: Robert Clarke & Co., 1874). It has been noted that St. Germain was himself, as was Hobbes, a nominalist and a fierce critic of clerical power. Franklin Le Van Baumer, "Christopher St. German: The Political Philosophy of a Tudor Lawyer," *American Historical Review* 42 (1937): 631–651.

[66] See, for example, Coke's explicit and enthusiastic reliance on St. Germain in *Calvin's Case* (1610), 7 Co. Rep. 1, 12a-12b.

[67] *Dialogue*, pp. 55, 71, 158.

had.[68] The common law was, in Hobbes's opinion, more akin to scholastic philosophy "and other disputable arts" than it was to law in any true and meaningful sense.[69]

The common law with its belief in and reliance on the so-called artificial reason of the judges was a direct threat to the political order. It undermined sovereignty by its interpretive pretensions; its firm belief that no one but a judge – not even the king himself – could exercise the power of judgment in the King's own courts was, to Hobbes, simply preposterous. There was, Hobbes insisted, no such thing as "artificial reason" in the sense in which Coke understood it, or in any other sense. In the same way he deemed the philosophers' notion of "right reason" to be "not existent," so did he regard Coke's common law idea of "artificial reason." In both cases such ideas were likely to be invoked to settle a controversy by those whose standards of "right reason" or "artificial reason" looked unsurprisingly like their own opinions.[70]

By discrediting Coke and the scholastics, Hobbes sought to return men to the search for truth, arm them with true philosophy, and thereby to refound the science of politics and law on a more realistic, that is to say natural, foundation.[71] The entire project depended to no small degree upon recovering language as a natural element in politics as well as philosophy. For it is out of language that men's opinions of right and wrong, justice and injustice, are formed and shared; and, Hobbes argued, "the Actions of men proceed from their Opinions; and in the wel governing of Opinions consisteth the well governing of men's Actions, in order to their Peace, and Concord."[72] Ultimately, the very possibility of civil society, in Hobbes's political philosophy, rests upon the power of language to reconcile the undeniable fact of man's individuality with his absolute need for community through the social contract.

II. HOBBES'S NEW CIVIL PHILOSOPHY

Hobbes's most fundamental criticism of the scholastic tradition he so reviled and against which he so strenuously revolted, was that it was against nature. Nature had been buried by artifice and convention, and human reason

---

[68] Hobbes could not resist pointing out that "Sir Edw. Coke himself, who whether he had more or less use of reason, was not thereby a judge, but because the king made him so." *Dialogue*, p. 62.

[69] Ibid., p. 69.

[70] *Elements of Law*, II.10.8, p. 188.

[71] Scholasticism was simply inherently "fatal to any real knowledge of the facts of the physical world, to any historical understanding of the ancient world, and to any real originality of thought." Holdsworth, *History of English Law*, II: 131.

[72] *Leviathan*, pp. 136–137.

was left to suffocate beneath layers of intellectual fashion.[73] Truth – clear-headed, keen-eyed, scientific truth – had been supplanted by the affectations of learned opinion. The various schools of such opinion – school divinity, Aristotelian metaphysics, and the English common law – had served only to generate conflict and controversy.[74] In the confusions of opinion, in Hobbes's view, lay the roots of public disorder; in the certainty of opinion lay mankind's political salvation. The reason was compelling: "[O]ur wills follow our opinions, as our actions follow our wills. In which sense they say truly and properly that say the world is governed by opinion."[75] To Hobbes, the solution was simple: "those things that lie in confusion must be set asunder, distinguished, and every one stamped with its own name [and] set in order."[76] The problem of politics is the problem of opinion.

What Hobbes found especially vexing to good order was the myth that authoritative opinions such as those pronounced by the priests, professors, and lawyers derived not from the simple reflections of ordinary men but from some allegedly higher and unimpeachable authority – God, nature, or custom, respectively. This was the great and pernicious lie Hobbes set out to expose. As he saw it, those who spoke authoritatively of such concepts as justice, duty, and honor were in fact merely appropriating words to serve their own selfish purposes.[77] Such doctrines were nothing more elevated than the ordinary private opinions of those who decreed them. They each sought "to determine every question according to their own fancies."[78] The power of the doctrines imposed by the priests, professors, and lawyers derived not from any intrinsic truth of the ideas, but only from their "claims of authoritative wisdom and expert knowledge."[79]

What the various experts shared, in Hobbes's view, was reasoning not from truth, from nature, but merely from words, from scholarly contrivance. In their discourses, these men "speak such words, as put together, have in them no signification at all; but are fallen upon by some, through misunderstanding of the words they have received and repeat by rote; by others, from intention to deceive by obscurity." The result was "non-sense."[80] By relying

---

[73] As Hobbes viewed the history of the schools, he saw that authoritative opinion came to have a life of its own. The vague and confused texts in the first instance had required commentaries; then the "commentaries will need explications; and in the process of time, these explications expositions; those new expositions new commentaries, without any end." Thomas Hobbes, *De Cive*, volume II, in Molesworth, ed., *English Works*, XVII.18, p. 275.

[74] Kraynak, *History and Modernity in the Thought of Thomas Hobbes*, p. 81.

[75] *Elements of Law*, I.12.6, p. 63.

[76] *De Corpore*, "Author's Epistle to the Reader," p. 1.

[77] "For these words of Good, Evill, and Contemptible, are ever used with relation to the person that useth them: there being nothing simply and absolutely so; nor any common Rule of Good and Evil to be taken from the nature of the objects themselves." *Leviathan*, p. 41.

[78] *De Corpore*, p. x.

[79] Kraynak, *History and Modernity in the Thought of Thomas Hobbes*, p. 73.

[80] *Leviathan*, pp. 62, 34.

on "vain and erroneous philosophy," "uncertain traditions," and "uncertain history," the authorities had blocked the light of natural reason and had plunged mankind into a veritable "kingdome of darknesse," a "kingdome" ruled by a *"confederacy of deceivers,* that to obtain dominion over men in this present world, endeavor[ed] by dark and erroneous doctrines, to extinguish in them the light, both of nature and the gospel."[81]

Good government depended upon the destruction of this false "aristocracy of orators."[82] By proving there was no authority higher than man, no transcendent divine or natural law that spoke clearly and unequivocally of right and wrong, justice and injustice, to a favored few, Hobbes would be able to free mankind from the tyrannical shackles of false doctrine and superstition; such a lifting of the chains of ignorance was necessary to render men truly free.

Hobbes's philosophic project was enlightenment in the most literal sense: "I intend now, by putting into a clear method the true foundations of natural philosophy, to fright and drive away this metaphysical *Empusa*; not by skirmish, but by letting in the light upon her." By correcting "the ugly absurdity of false opinions"[83] that had derived from men's delusion that there was superhuman support for justice in the world, Hobbes believed that he could thereby sever men's dependence on the tradition.[84] This was the presupposition of Hobbes's radically new doctrine of sovereignty.

Hobbes's theory of sovereignty was not simply an ahistorical construct of his single, albeit vivid, imagination; it was, rather, related to a struggle that had been going on English legal history since at least the fourteenth century. It was at that moment that the idea of statutes, the idea of laws as more than the mere declaration of custom, began to emerge. This new understanding of law as command lay at the heart of his new concept of sovereignty by institution.[85]

Sovereignty by Institution

Hobbes's idea of "sovereignty by institution" was the central element of his science of politics, which was in turn derived from his science of man. His new and original "civil philosophy" was part of the modern understanding

---

[81] *Leviathan*, pp. 62, 34, 473, 472. Reasoning from such "senselesse and ambiguous words," Hobbes argued, was merely "wandering amongst innumerable absurdities; and their end, contention, and sedition, and contempt." Ibid., p. 38.

[82] *Elements of Law*, II.2.5, p. 120.

[83] *De Corpore*, p. xi; I.3.8, p. 36.

[84] See Kraynak, *History and Modernity in the Thought of Thomas Hobbes*, p. 159.

[85] See Theodore F. T. Plucknett, *Statutes and Their Interpretation in the First Half of the Fourteenth Century* (Cambridge: Cambridge University Press, 1922); and Samuel E. Thorne, ed., *A Discourse upon the Exposicion & Understanding of Statutes* (San Marino, CA: Huntington Library, 1942).

of natural philosophy in which all the world was reduced to its component parts and their motion.[86] Thus did he begin his political teaching with the characteristics most basic to man's nature: sense and speech. His reason for beginning as he did was that what he repeatedly called "meer nature" [87] was devoid of any institutions and was a place of arbitrariness, war, and horror. Life in the state of nature, as he so famously put it, was "solitary poore, nasty, brutish, and short."[88]

This state of nature was to be escaped not merely on the grounds of man's "bare preservation," but as well for "all the other contentments of life, which every man by lawful industry, without danger or hurt to the commonwealth, shall acquire to himself."[89] What was missing in "the condition of meer nature" were all the elements in which civilization consists. Because of the uncertainty of existence in the state of nature, there was no sense of future but of present only; each man could live only for the moment.[90] But at a minimum, civilization or civil society depends upon a sense among men that there can be, and will be, a future. And that sense of tomorrow depends upon a power today that is above each man and capable of keeping them all in awe and maintaining the peace.

The most basic dilemma man faces in the state of nature and the cause of his distress is his own nature. The fact is, "the passions of men are commonly more potent than their reason." There is no order to things, for "in the state of nature, to have all, and do all, is lawful for all." There is no common measure that governs "all things that might fall into controversy" such as "what is to be called right and good, what virtue, what much, what little, what *meum* and *tuum*; what a pound, what a quart, etc." Because there is no agreed-upon common or public measure, all is a matter of "private judgments [that] may differ and beget controversy."[91]

Existence outside civil society is fraught with danger and uncertainty not because men do not opine about justice, but precisely because they do. It is in the diversity of opinions as to what constitutes justice that men find their greatest "combat of wits,"[92] their most enduring disagreements that ultimately give rise to "quarrels and breach of peace." Because "our

---

[86] *De Corpore*, p. ix.
[87] Some of Hobbes's various uses of "meer nature" are to be found in *Leviathan*, pp. 98, 105, 205, 274; and *Elements of Law*, I.14.2, p. 70.
[88] *Leviathan*, p. 97.
[89] Ibid., p. 238.
[90] "In such a condition," Hobbes said, "there is no place for industry; because the fruit thereof is uncertain: and consequently no culture of the earth; no navigation, nor use of commodities that may be imported by sea; no commodious building; no instruments of moving, and removing such things as require much force; no knowledge of the face of the earth; no account of time; no arts; no letters; no society; and which is worst of all, continual fear, and danger of violent death." *Leviathan*, pp. 96–97.
[91] *Leviathan*, p. 144; *De Cive*, I.10, p. 11; *Elements of Law*, II.10.8, p. 188.
[92] *De Cive*, I.5, p. 7.

wills follow our opinions, as our actions follow our wills," if "every man were allowed this liberty of following his conscience, in such differences of consciences, they would not live together in peace an hour."[93]

Absent a common authority in man's original situation, "the right of protecting [themselves] according to [their] own wills, proceeded from [their] danger, and [their] danger from [their] equality." Most troubling, this war of every man against every man will be "perpetual" precisely because all who strive are by nature equal, and thus their conflict "cannot be ended by victory."[94] Man's absolute equality means he is possessed of an "absolute liberty" that can only result in "anarchy, and the condition of warre." Because nature makes no provision for governance, peace will come only as a result of an agreement, the creation of a sovereign power by "covenant of everyone to everyone." Only by the creation of a sovereign with the power to make civil laws can "the natural liberty of man . . . be abridged and restrained" and the possibility of peace be found.[95]

Man is capable of finding his way out of this bleak condition of "meer nature" not by the "right reason" of the philosophers, which does not exist, but by man's own "purely *analytical*" rationality. What begins with sense perception, Hobbes argued, ends with "the invention of principles."[96] This is the result of man's ability to imagine things that do not by nature actually exist. Man can take account of his situation and on the basis of his concrete experience create institutions that will obviate the inconveniences of nature. Although man cannot, strictly speaking, have in his mind a "conception of the future," he can have "conceptions of the past" drawn from what he has come to know. He is capable of seeing "like antecedents . . . followed by like consequents" sufficiently to be able to "conjecture" about things to come.[97]

Since the world is "governed by opinion,"[98] any agreement as to the creation of a sovereign power depends upon individuals being able to share with one another their opinions on the most fundamental matters. And this can occur only through the medium of speech. Thus it is by speech that what begins with sense perception ends with the invention of principles and sovereignty by institution. In Hobbes's view, it was clear that "there is no conception in a man's mind, which hath not at first, totally, or by parts, been begotten upon the organs of sense." By his observations of the natural world man accumulates "evidence"; this evidence, in turn, forms the basis for his formulation of "definitions"; and these definitions come to form the conceptions about the good and the bad, the just and the unjust, the virtuous

---

93 *Elements of Law*, II.10.8, p. 188; I.12.6, p. 63; II.5.2, p. 139.
94 *De Cive*, I.14, p. 13; I.13, p. 12.
95 *Leviathan*, pp. 224, 167, 206.
96 *De Corpore*, I.6.4, p. 69; I.6.7, p. 75.
97 *Elements of Law*, I.4.7, p. 15.
98 Ibid., I.12.6, p. 63.

and the vicious about which men can then reach agreement as to how best to constitute their fundamental law. Speech allows this agreement to be reached by allowing each man to "signifie to another what he thinks expedient for the common benefit." It is language that makes the social contract possible and "sovereignty by institution" a reality.[99]

It is because "private consciences are but private opinions" that men undertake to create a common power to keep them all in awe and to remove "the terror of . . . private revenge" that had made the state of nature so inhospitable and incommodious a place. The purpose of sovereignty by institution is to supplant private judgments of individuals with a collective public judgment as to what constitutes the just and the unjust, the right and the wrong. By the terms of the social contract and the fundamental law establishing the "essential rights of sovereignty" the civil law becomes the "publique conscience" and justice is reduced from metaphysical abstraction to simple law-abidingness.[100]

The act of agreeing to the social contract, this covenant of every man with every man, establishes the "fundamental law in any commonwealth," that law "which being taken away the commonwealth faileth, and is utterly dissolved; as a building whose foundation is destroyed." It is this law, this basic arrangement, "by which subjects are bound to uphold whatsoever power is given to the sovereign." That is to say, the sovereign is not simply absolute and arbitrary but absolute only within the fixed context of the powers given to him by the institutional design to which the people have freely consented. The office of the sovereign "consisteth in the end for which he was trusted with sovereign power, namely the procuration of the safety of the people." It is in this sense that for Hobbes "the good of the sovereign and people cannot be separated."[101]

The essence of the sovereign's power is the obligation of "the making of good laws." Hobbes was clear as to what constitutes a good law: it is that "which is *needful*, for the *good of the people*, and withall *perspicuous*."[102] It was important to Hobbes that it be understood that laws are means to the only end that justifies the creation of the mighty Leviathan in the first place. The use of laws, he argued. "is not to bind people from all voluntary actions; but to direct and keep them in such a motion, as not to hurt themselves by

---

99 *Leviathan*, pp. 11, 130. "[T]he most noble and profitable invention of all other, was that of speech, consisting of names or appellations, and their connexion; whereby men register their thoughts; recall them when they are past; and also declare them one to another for mutuall utility and conversation; without which, there had been amongst men, neither common-wealth, nor society, nor contract, nor peace, no more than amongst lyons, bears, and wolves." Ibid., p. 24.
100 *Leviathan*, p. 249, 230, 258, 249.
101 *Leviathan*, pp. 222, 222, 258, 268.
102 Ibid., p. 268.

their own impetuous desires, rashnesse, or indiscretion; as hedges are set not to stop travellers, but to keep them in the way."[103]

Put slightly differently, in cases "where the sovereign has prescribed no rule, then the subject hath the liberty to do, or to forbeare, according to his own discretion." A law that is not necessary for the good of the people, but is only for the benefit of the sovereign, is not a good law. To think such a law to be a good law is to misunderstand both the nature of law and the nature of sovereignty.[104]

The law establishing the office of the sovereign is fundamental; the civil laws imposed by the sovereign are not. The commonwealth does not stand or fall by these laws; the sovereign can change them as he sees fit to serve the interests of the people. These civil laws are those that seek to govern and settle "controversies between subject and subject,"[105] in part by creating "a common measure for all things that might fall into controversy."[106] Whereas the people should seek to make the constitution of the sovereign power "everlasting," there is no need to seek to make the ordinary civil laws permanent. It is the rightful power delegated by the people to the sovereign to "make or repeale laws" as may be most likely in his judgment to conduce to their safety and happiness.[107]

Hobbes's theory of "sovereignty by institution" and the inherently legal nature of the commonwealth leads inevitably to the necessity of written law. This is true for the fundamental law, "the constitutions . . . of the sovereign power by which the liberty of nature is abridged." It is essential that these "are written, because there is no other way to take notice of them."[108] So, too, does it follow that the civil laws, those that are not fundamental in the same sense as the social contract, be committed to writing, as well.

---

[103] Ibid. This was one of the many Hobbesian insights that Locke would take to heart. "Law, in its true notion, is not so much the limitation as *the direction of a free and intelligent agent* to his proper interest, and prescribes no further than is for the general good of those under that law. Could they be happier without it, the *law*, as a useless thing would of itself vanish; and that ill deserves the name of confinement which hedges us in only from bogs and precipices. So that, however it may be mistaken, *the end of law* is not to abolish or restrain, but *to preserve and enlarge freedom*: For in all the states of created beings capable of laws, *where there is no law, there is no freedom*. For *liberty* is to be free from restraint and violence from others which cannot be, where there is no law: but freedom is not, as we are told, *a liberty for every man to do what he lists*: (For who could be free, when every other man's humour might domineer over him?) But a *liberty* to dispose, and order, as he lists, his person, actions, possessions, and his whole property within the allowance of those laws under which he is; and therein not to be subject to the arbitrary will of another, but freely follow his own." Peter Laslett, ed., *Locke's Two Treatises of Government* (2nd ed.; Cambridge: Cambridge University Press, 1970), *Second Treatise*, 323–324: 57.
[104] *Leviathan*, pp. 168, 268.
[105] Ibid., p. 222.
[106] *Elements of Law*, II.10.8, p. 188.
[107] *Leviathan*, pp. 260, 204.
[108] *Elements of Law*, II.10.10, p. 190.

Hobbes was unambiguous on this point. "The law of nature excepted, it belongeth to the essence of all other lawes, to be made known, to every man that shall be obliged to obey them, either by word, or writing, or some other act, known to proceed from the sovereign authority." Although he speaks of the possibility of "some other act," the fact is the only means of promulgation of the laws that he explicitly defends is that "the law be written and published."[109]

Language, "Intendment," and the "Authentique"
Interpretation of the Law

The presumed knowledge of the law, or the allegedly special wisdom of the judges, are not what make law, law. Judges cannot be lawmakers for the simple reason that the act of judging, of interpreting, is subordinate to the act that creates that which is to be interpreted. Judges are merely the creatures of the sovereign; their power derives only from the power of the sovereign will. "Sir *Edw. Coke* himself, who whether he had more or less use of reason, was not thereby a judge, but because the king made him so."[110] The body of custom from which the common law derives its power, and thereby the lawyers their authority, was, in Hobbes's view, utterly lacking in legitimacy: "For if custom were sufficient to introduce a law, then it would be in the power of everyone that is deputed to hear a cause, to make his errors law."[111] Such custom as is the common law cannot be truly law because even the unwritten law that may necessarily continue alongside the written law after the social contract is entered into, can only take its "authority and force from the will of the common-wealth, that is to say, from the will of the representative." Thus an appeal by a judge to custom or to allegedly unwritten laws of nature, absent the mark of the sovereign making them binding, is an appeal neither to custom nor to higher law but only to the judge's personal opinion. Judges therefore are "to take notice of the law, from nothing but the statutes and constitutions of the Sovereign."[112]

To assure the certainty in rules that distinguishes civil society from the state of nature, it is necessary above all else that the laws promulgated by the sovereign avoid as much as possible the confusion and ambiguity that inevitably attend any and all written law. This is to be achieved by making clear in each law "the causes, and the motives, for which it was made." As a result of this need, it "belongeth therefore to the Office of the Legislator . . . to make the reason perspicuous, why the law was made; and the body of the lawe it selfe, as short, but in as proper, and significant termes, as may be."[113]

---

[109] *Leviathan*, pp. 209; 210.
[110] *Dialogue*, p. 62.
[111] *Elements of Law*, II.10.10, p. 190.
[112] *Leviathan*, pp. 206, 208, 216.
[113] Ibid., pp. 268, 269.

But the problem is that "all words are subject to ambiguity"; as a result, "all laws...have need of interpretation." The dilemma for Hobbes's commonwealth is precisely the dilemma that led him to seek to supplant the tradition: what is the proper basis of true or "authentique" interpretation of the laws? One "weak and false principle" that Hobbes banishes is the notion "that men shall judge what is lawfull or unlawfull not by the law itself, but by their own consciences; that is to say, by their own private judgments."[114]

That law can never be against Reason, our lawyers are agreed; and that not the letter (that is every construction of it) but that which is according to the intention of the legislator is the law. And it is true: but the doubt is, of whose reason it is, that shall be received for law. It is not meant of any private reason; for then there would be as much contradiction in the lawes, as there is in the Schooles; nor yet (as Sr. Ed. Coke makes it) an *Artificial Perfection of Reason, gotten by long study and observation and experience* (as his was.) For it is possible long study may encrease and confirm erroneous Sentences: and where men build on false grounds, the more they build, the greater is the ruine: and of those that study and observe with equall time, and diligence, the reasons and resolutions are, and must remain discordant: and therefore it is not that *Juris Prudentia*, or wisdome of subordinate judges; but the Reason of this our Artificiall Man the Common-Wealth, and his Command that maketh Law.[115]

As against the pretensions of the common lawyers, Hobbes's view was clear: "The abilities required in a good interpreter of the law, that is to say, in a good judge, are not the same with those of being an advocate; namely the study of the lawes."[116] Nor is a good judge likely to be found among those who have written commentaries on the written law; such glosses serve only to confuse and to obscure true meaning.[117] Still less should one seek moral philosophers for judges; unless explicitly adopted by the sovereign, such theories have no legal weight.[118] Hobbes saw a much more limited, a much more legitimate function for the judges.

Whatever misgivings about judges Hobbes may have harbored, he understood very well that the power of "judicature" was essential to any commonwealth men might choose to constitute. It was precisely the absence of an impartial judge to hear and decide disputes between free and equal men in the state of nature that rendered life there so precarious. Without such a power "of hearing and deciding all controversies, which may arise

[114] Ibid., pp. 268, 212, 264.
[115] Ibid., p. 207.
[116] Ibid., p. 216.
[117] "In like manner, when question is of the meaning of written lawes, he is not the interpreter of them, that writeth a commentary upon them. For commentaries are commonly more subject to cavill, than the text; and therefore need other commentaries; and so there will be no end of such interpretation." Ibid., p. 215.
[118] "The interpretation of the Lawes of Nature, in a common-wealth, dependeth not on the books of morall philosophy. The authority of writers, without the authority of the common-wealth, maketh not their opinions Law, be they never so true." Ibid., p. 212.

concerning law," Hobbes insisted, there would be "no protection of one subject, against the injuries of another; the lawes concerning *meum* and *tuum* are in vaine; and to every man remaineth, from the naturall and necessary appetite of his own conservation, the right of protecting himselfe by his private strength, which is the condition of warre; and contrary to the end for which every common-wealth is instituted."[119] The problem lay in devising an understanding of judicature that would produce the right sort of judge.

The key to a properly constructed judiciary was to make clear that there was no doubt that the judges were subordinate to the sovereign. As Hobbes put it, "judges in courts of justice" no less than the "magistrates of towns" and "commanders of armies" were "but ministers of him that is the magistrate of the whole common-wealth." It was a question of jurisdiction, "the power of hearing and determining causes," and the lines of authority were clear: "[T]he civil sovereign in every common-wealth is the *head*, the *source*, the *root*, and the *sun* from which all jurisdiction is derived." The judges are not to be lawmakers; their only task is to take the laws that are promulgated by the sovereign and "to make them obligatory"[120] by giving effect to the original intention of the lawmaker properly understood:

For it is not the letter, but the intendment, or meaning; that is to say, the authentique interpretation of the law (which is the sense of the legislator) in which the nature of the law consisteth; And therefore the interpretation of all Laws dependeth on the Authority Sovereign; and the interpreters can be none but those, which the Sovereign (to whom only the subject oweth obedience) shall appoint. For else, by the craft of an interpreter, the law may be made to beare a sense, contrary to that of the sovereign; by which means the interpreter becomes the legislator.[121]

This resort to the intention of the writer was not limited to the law. As Hobbes argued, "it is not by the bare words, but by the scope of the writer that giveth the true light, by which *any* writing is to be interpreted." Along with Scripture, the words of the law were of greatest moment to the peace and security of the commonwealth, and it was of paramount importance that the meaning of the law be accurately determined. In the best of all situations, the connection between the word used and the meaning intended to be conveyed would be both close and clear; this "literall sense is that which the legislator intended [and which] by the letter of the law be signified." That is to say, "the letter, and the sentence or intention of the law, is all one."

[119] Ibid., p. 138.
[120] Ibid., pp. 422, 446, 211.
[121] Ibid., pp. 211–212. Hobbes's use of "craft" in the case of the judges is suggestive of his view of them generally. Earlier he had defined "craft" as "crooked wisdom." Ibid., p. 56.

There is a need to assume, in the first instance, that the sovereign said what he meant, and meant what he said.[122]

Although "a judge may erre in the interpretation of even written lawes," there is no way that such an "errour of a subordinate judge can change the law." The only true or "authentique" interpretation is that which exposes and gives effect to the meaning "the legislator intended." That even holds for those occasions on which judges may find that an "incommodity... follows the bare words of a written law" and therefore seek to give an interpretation that would ease the incommodity according to the original intention of the lawgiver. But never can such an incommodity "warrant a Sentence against the law." Should a judge disregard "the reason which moved his sovereign to make such a law" in order to do what the judge may, according to his conscience, think right, he thereby supplants the public judgment of the sovereign with his own private judgment; and that, warns Hobbes, would be "unjust." As Hobbes insisted, "there is only one sense of the law," and neither judicial ignorance nor honest error nor wilful deceit can legitimately "change the law which is the general sentence of the sovereign."[123]

By keeping the language of the law precise and well defined, such problems are avoided. "When a man upon the hearing of any speech, hath those thoughts which the words of that speech, and their connexion, were ordained and constituted to signifie," as Hobbes put it, "then he is said to understand it: *understanding* being nothing else, but conception caused by speech."[124] Properly constructed, the signs or words used in the law to convey the intention of the sovereign will be sufficient to cause the same notion in the mind of the judges.

This is essential to Hobbes's notion of a properly constituted commonwealth. For by the laws of nature, individually free men, by mutual and voluntary agreement, issuing from their natural reason, create by formal covenant their commonwealth – their sovereign – in order to make certain that they are governed not by the private opinions of other men but only by the public opinion of their own legitimate authority. This "sovereignty by institution... by covenant of every one to every one" is the only way to establish a political order in which concepts of just and unjust, right and wrong, can have any meaning.[125] Insofar as all men are born free and equal,

---

[122] Ibid., pp. 471 (emphasis supplied), 215. This is why Hobbes insisted, as noted earlier, that a judge must "take notice of the law from nothing but the statutes and constitutions of the sovereign." Ibid., p. 216.

[123] Ibid., pp. 215, 216, 208, 215.

[124] Ibid., p. 31. "The first use of language, is the expression of our conceptions, that is, the begetting in another the same conceptions that we have in ourselves." *Elements of Law*, I.13.2, p. 64.

[125] *Leviathan*, p. 167. As Berns has observed: "Where government is built entirely out of materials supplied by the will – or a union of wills – that will must be expressed. In a world where all opinions of justice and injustice are understood to be merely private opinions, no

they may be governed legitimately only by their own opinion, by their own view of justice. But that independence of mind and motive renders men's ability to define justice prone to injustice, to the chaos and confusions of the state of nature. This is why each man willingly, *rationally* cedes the power to make the laws under which he will live, not to another man, but only to that "artificial person" that is the commonwealth. Thus man is able to govern himself – albeit indirectly. For the sovereign is, in a sense, every man; the laws of the sovereign are the judgments by which each man chooses to govern himself. By obeying the sovereign, each man, in effect, obeys himself. In this way sense is made of Hobbes's strange assertion that "the law of nature and the civil law contain each other and are of equal extent."[126]

The virtue of the subject is comprehended wholly in obedience to the laws of the commonwealth. To obey the laws, is justice and equity, which is the law of nature, and, consequently, is civil law in all nations of the world; and nothing is injustice or iniquity, otherwise, than it is against the law.[127]

Language, Hobbes taught, is the essence of law. The confidence that law can bind and direct human behavior ultimately rests only upon the belief that the words of the law mean something. It is in the definition and clarity of the language that the power of law is to be found. It is by this device and this device alone that the momentary fluctuations of politics can ever be made to yield to the permanence of principle. This truth lies at the heart of the idea of constitutionalism generally; it is the essence of the modern faith in written constitutions in particular.

III. THE RISE OF MODERN CONSTITUTIONALISM

To say that Hobbes is the father of modern constitutionalism is not to say that those who came after him, who took his thinking seriously and passed it along, were merely middlemen in the commerce of ideas. Rather, they took those ideas, thought them through, and made them their own in the process, drawing out implications here, correcting problems there. It was, of course, Locke who made Hobbes more acceptable by adjusting his notion of sovereignty and drawing a necessary line between the sovereign and the government. For Locke, it was essential that the people be understood never to cede their natural sovereignty in the process of entering into the social contract. They would always retain their power to alter or abolish any government that failed to secure their safety and happiness and to establish a new government in their sovereign capacity. That removed the appearance

man can rationally agree to an arrangement where another man is authorized to convert his opinion into fundamental law." "Judicial Review and the Rights and Laws of Nature," p. 74.
[126] *Leviathan*, p. 205.
[127] *Behemoth*, p. 44.

of an unalterable absolutism that had drawn such opprobrium on Hobbes's original formulation.

Yet for all their adjustments, all their embellishments, all their polishing, the essentials of modern constitutionalism are still seen in their fundamentals in Hobbes's political philosophy of natural rights. It was his belief that the tradition had to be supplanted and that in that act traditional notions of a higher law would be replaced. No longer would it come from on high, but would well up from below, not from God's word but from the independent wills of free and equal men. Natural law properly understood required nothing less than the legal positivism that is the essence of modern constitutionalism. Thus would it fall to Locke and those who followed him to devise the structures of modern constitutionalism that would come to rest upon the sturdy foundation Hobbes had laid.

3

Language, Law, and Liberty

John Locke and the Structures of Modern Constitutionalism

In May 1652, only a year after Thomas Hobbes had shaken the intellectual world to its scholastic roots with his infamous *Leviathan*, John Locke was elected to Christ Church, Oxford. For the rest of his life, Locke would labor in the mighty shadow Hobbes cast, drawing out the implications of Hobbes's thought all the while denying any influence.[1]

To say that the philosophic specter of Hobbes haunted the "thinkeing men of Oxford" in Locke's day is to understate the case.[2] In 1683, at the very time Locke was immersed in the intellectual excursions that would eventuate in the *Essay Concerning Human Understanding* (1689) and the *Two Treatises of Government* (1689), in the last book burning held at Oxford, "Hob's *De Cive* and *Leviathan*" were deemed good fuel for the flames of scholarly intolerance. For Locke, the lesson was hardly ambiguous; the art of writing was far from being free of persecution. If the ages were not still dark, they were surely dim; enlightenment and toleration were for another day.[3]

The Oxford that Locke entered was little changed from the one that Hobbes had left decades before. The arid scholasticism Hobbes had encountered and detested at Magdalen was still in control of Christ Church. Locke was no more impressed with the forms and substance of the tradition than Hobbes had been. To Locke, the tedious and pointless exercises in formal

---

[1] See generally the introductions to Peter Laslett, ed., *Locke's Two Treatises of Government*, (2nd. ed.; Cambridge: Cambridge University Press, 1970), pp. 67–91; Philip Abrams, ed., *John Locke: Two Tracts on Government* (Cambridge: Cambridge University Press, 1967), pp. 63–83; and Leo Strauss, *Natural Right and History* (Chicago: University of Chicago Press, 1953).

[2] James Tyrrell to John Locke, 30 June 1690, *The Correspondence of John Locke*, ed. E.S. de Beer, 8 vols. (Oxford: Clarendon Press, 1976–89), IV: 101.

[3] As Locke noted: "I would be quiet and I would be safe, but if I cannot enjoy them together, the last must certainly be had at any rate." As quoted in the introduction to Abrams, ed., *Two Tracts on Government*, p. 8.

logic and rhetoric were mere "hogshearing."[4] The future philosopher seems to have preferred romance novels.

The problem, in Locke's estimation, was that the schools misunderstood both nature and man's place in it; the lessons of the tradition had been precisely backward. Whatever rules nature offered for the guidance of men in their earthly affairs had to be discerned by that same cool and clear observation of nature that Hobbes himself had advocated. There were no lessons written on the hearts of men by the finger of God; there were no innate principles of right and wrong, of justice and injustice. Such standards derived not from without but from within; they were matters of the understanding – of *human* understanding. The task was to reduce politics to a science, to do for politics what the great Isaac Newton had done for physics: to show "how far Mathematicks, applied to some Parts of Nature, may, upon Principles that Matter of Fact justifie, carry us in the knowledge of some, as I may also call them, particular Provinces of the Incomprehensible Universe."[5]

I. THE HOBBESIAN FOUNDATIONS OF LOCKEAN LIBERALISM

It is not too much to say that a common revulsion over the pointlessness of scholasticism was in part the shared ground from which the theories of Hobbes and Locke sprang. For Locke, as for Hobbes, the strangling grip of the schools had to be broken if doctrinal politics was to be tamed and freedom made to flourish. At a minimum, that entailed the recovery of nature from beneath the academic rubble that over the past several centuries had come to bury it.

The intermingling in the schools of Aristotelian philosophy with Holy Scripture had been to the detriment of both, but especially to Scripture. The doctrines produced by the school divines had served only to confuse and abuse the ordinary people. As Hobbes had so memorably put it, "the universities have been to this nation, as the wooden horse was to the Trojans."[6] The scholastic attempt to render God an Aristotelian and Aristotle a Christian not only had resulted in "foolish and false"[7] doctrines, but by their practice of ever finer distinctions on points of faith had also rendered those

---

[4] As quoted by Laslett, *Locke's Two Treatises of Government*, p. 23. See W. N. Hargreaves-Mawdsley, *Oxford in the Age of John Locke* (Norman: University of Oklahoma Press, 1973); and J. R. Milton, "Locke at Oxford," in G. A. J. Rogers, ed., *Locke's Philosophy: Content and Context* (Oxford: Clarendon Press, 1994), pp. 29–47.

[5] John Locke, *Some Thoughts Concerning Education*, in James L. Axtell, ed., *The Educational Writings of John Locke* (Cambridge: Cambridge University Press, 1968), p. 306.

[6] Thomas Hobbes, *Behemoth*, ed. Ferdinand Tönnies (2nd. ed.; New York: Barnes and Noble, 1969), p. 40. Hereinafter cited as *Behemoth*.

[7] Thomas Hobbes, *De Corpore*, in William Molesworth, ed., *The English Works of Thomas Hobbes*, 11 vols. (London: John Bohn, 1839–45), vol. I, ep. ded., p. x. Hereinafter cited as *De Corpore*.

points of faith simply "incomprehensible."[8] In Locke's view, the result was "learned gibberish" that had only served to bury the true tenets of Christianity as revealed in the Bible.[9]

Locke agreed with Hobbes's view that such nonsense tended to "abuse the simple people."[10] The reason was clear: "The greatest part cannot know, and therefore they must believe."[11] Given the necessity of belief over knowledge for most men, the pernicious priests, reared on school divinity, had come "to fill their heads with false notions of the deity, and their worship with foolish rites, as they pleased: And what dread or craft once began, devotion soon made sacred, and religion immutable." It was much safer if "the instruction of the people were but still to be left to the precepts and principles of the Gospel" to be gleaned by the normal faculties of ordinary men.[12]

The essence of the problem Locke confronted, as had Hobbes, was the scholastic notion that there were incorporeal substances that lay behind the objects detected in the sensible world. Not only was there such a realm of incorporeal being, but man, properly trained in the philosophic arts, could have access to it. The result of this belief was the generation of that "learned gibberish" of which Locke complained, that "learned madness" that had so irritated Hobbes.[13]

To Locke's way of thinking, such a view was simply absurd. He believed, as Hobbes had said, that "essence without existence is a fiction of our mind,"[14] and that "there is nothing universal but names."[15] In Locke's view, the "essences . . . are nothing else but . . . abstract ideas" that are only "the workmanship of the understanding." Simply put, for Locke as for Hobbes, "knowledge goes not beyond particulars."[16] This was not a view that either

---

[8] *Behemoth*, p. 17.

[9] John Locke, *An Essay Concerning Human Understanding*, ed. P. H. Nidditch (Oxford: Oxford University Press, 1979), III.X.9, p. 495. Hereinafter cited as *Essay*. Citations indicate book, chapter, section, and page number.

[10] Thomas Hobbes, *Leviathan* (Oxford: Clarendon Press, 1909), p. 18. Hereinafter cited as *Leviathan*.

[11] John Locke, *The Reasonableness of Christianity*, in *The Works of John Locke*, 3 vols. (3rd. ed.; London: Bettesworth, 1727), II: 471–541, p. 535. Hereinafter cited as *Reasonableness*. This is the result of the very "nature of mankind." The fact is, "most men cannot live, without employing their time in the daily labours of their callings; nor be at quiet in their minds, without some foundation or principles to rest their thoughts on. . . . [R]everenced propositions . . . are to him the principles on which he bottoms his reasonings, and by which he judgeth of truth and falshood, right and wrong." *Essay*, I.III.24, p. 82.

[12] *Reasonableness*, p. 530.

[13] Locke, *Essay*, III.X.9, p. 495. Thomas Hobbes, *The Elements of Law: Natural and Politic*, ed. F. Tönnies (2nd. ed.; New York: Barnes & Noble, 1969), I.10.9, p. 52. Hereinafter cited as *Elements of Law*.

[14] As quoted in Noel Malcolm, "Thomas Hobbes and Voluntarist Theology" (Ph.D. dissertation, Gonville and Caius College, Cambridge University, 1983), p. 44.

[15] *Elements of Law*, I.5.6, p. 20.

[16] *Essay*, III.III.12, pp. 414, 415; IV.VI.16, p. 591.

Hobbes or Locke had crafted out of whole cloth, but rather was part of the older theological movement of voluntarism, especially as voluntarism had been expressed by William of Ockham.[17] The essence of voluntarist theology is that it is beyond man's meagere faculties to know God's will. Mankind is left to accept, as Hobbes said, that "[t]hat which he does is made just by his doing."[18] Despite man's pretensions to the contrary, some things are simply "above reason."[19] For a voluntarist, "existence can be described, but such descriptions will not lead up to definitions of the natures of things or interpretations of their meanings or purposes."[20] The gulf between faith and philosophy is ultimately unbridgeable because, as Hobbes starkly put it, "the nature of God is incomprehensible."[21]

The essential point of the understanding for Locke is that there are limits to what it can truly know. The medieval tradition against which he and Hobbes rebelled was a dangerous mixture of theology and philosophy. For Hobbes and Locke, the fact is that the human mind cannot know for certain that there is a God; it can only assemble facts from which the inference of God can be drawn. God exists in the realm of human faith, not in the understanding. Once freed from the delusions of medieval theological speculations, philosophy properly understood can focus on what the human mind can know in reality. While man might think the wonders of nature can only be the handiwork of an all-knowing God, he cannot prove it; it is a matter of faith, not philosophy, for philosophy, as Locke said, "is nothing but the true knowledge of things."[22]

To Locke, nothing was more worthwhile than "to search out the *Bounds* between opinion and knowledge." This was no small task; it required an uncommon sense of modesty on the part of a person to accept that certain things exceed human comprehension, "and to sit down in a quiet ignorance of those things, which, upon examination, are found to be beyond the reach

---

[17] See especially Malcolm, "Thomas Hobbes and Voluntarist Theology"; Michael Allen Gillespie, *The Theological Origins of Modernity* (Chicago: University of Chicago Press, 2008); Francis Oakley, "Medieval Theories of Natural Law: William of Ockham and the Significance of the Voluntarist Tradition," *Natural Law Forum* 6 (1961): 65–83; David W. Clark, "Voluntarism and Rationalism in the Ethics of Ockham," *Franciscan Studies* 31 (1971): 72–87; and Heiko Oberman, "Some Notes on the Theology of Nominalism," *Harvard Theological Review* 53 (1960): 47–76.

[18] Thomas Hobbes, *The Questions Concerning Liberty, Necessity, and Chance*, in Molesworth, ed., *English Works of Thomas Hobbes*, V: 114–115. As Locke put it: "God's infinite duration being accompanied with infinite knowledge, and infinite power, he sees all things past and to come... And there is nothing, which he cannot make exist each moment he pleases. For the existence of all things, depending upon his good pleasure; all things exist every moment, that he thinks fit to have them exist." *Essay*, II.XV.12, p. 204.

[19] *Leviathan*, p. 260.

[20] Malcolm, "Thomas Hobbes and Voluntarist Theology," p. 82.

[21] *Leviathan*, p. 304.

[22] *Essay*, "Epistle to the Reader," p. 10. See also *Essay*, II.XI.15, p. 162.

of our capacities." The tendency of man is much in the other direction, "to let loose [his] thoughts into the vast ocean of *Being*, as if all that boundless extent, were the natural, and undoubted possession of our understandings, wherein there was nothing exempt from its decisions, or that escaped its comprehension."[23]

It was this latter tendency that had brought humanity to the sad state in which it found itself: "Men, extending their enquiries beyond their capacities, and letting their thoughts wander into those depths, where they can find no sure footing; 'tis no wonder, that they raise questions, and multiply disputes, which never coming to any clear resolution, are proper only to continue and increase their doubts, and to confirm them at last in perfect scepticism." Human nature demanded a certain modesty. "Our business here," Locke argued, "is not to know all things, but those which concern our conduct." Thus, the first task of political philosophy is to find that "horizon... which sets the bounds between the enlightened and dark parts of things; between what is, and what is not comprehensible by us."[24]

The world in which Locke undertook to define the boundary within the human understanding between the regions of light and the regions of darkness was a world of infinite and unknowable proportions. Sense can be made of the world in which man finds himself only by the imposition of human categories such as place and time in order to bridge "those infinite abysses of space and duration."[25] So vast is the ocean of being that even the "sensible parts of the universe" prove taxing to the human mind: "Reason... comes far short of the real extent of even corporeal being."[26] The undeniable fact is that humanity is "far from being admitted to the secrets of nature"; it is roped off from "that mass of knowledge, which lies yet concealed in the secret recesses of nature."[27] So bleak is our condition that we cannot even begin to imagine what we do not know: "For how much the being and operation of particular substances in this our globe, depend on causes utterly beyond our view, is impossible for us to determine."[28] The fact is

---

[23] Ibid., I.I.3, p. 44; I.I.4, p. 45; I.I.7, p. 47. By nature the only "Dominion of man" is the "little world of his own understanding," in an otherwise "vast, stupendous universe." *Essay*, II.II.3, p. 120.

[24] Ibid., I.I.7, p. 47; I.I.6, p. 46; I.I.7, p. 47.

[25] Ibid., II.XV.6, p. 199. See also II.XV.5, pp. 198–199.

[26] Ibid., IV.X.7, p. 622; IV.XVII.9, p. 681. "'Tis a hard matter to say where sensible and rational begin, and where insensible and irrational end: and who is there quick-sighted enough to determine precisely, which is the lowest species of living things, and which the first of those which have no life?" *Essay*, IV.XVI.12, p. 666.

[27] Ibid., IV.VI.11, p. 585; IV.XVII.6, p. 679.

[28] Ibid., IV.VI.11, p. 587. As Locke explained by means of analogy: "'Tis of great use to the sailor to know the length of his line, though he cannot with it fathom all the depths of the ocean." Later, he returned to the same example to make the point even more forcefully: "All that we thus amass together in our thoughts, is positive, and the assemblage of a great

that man's understanding is prisoner to the senses; for Locke "the simple ideas we receive from sensation and reflection, are the boundaries of our thoughts; beyond which, the mind, whatever efforts it would make, is not able to advance one jot." In attempting to look beyond those ideas borne of sensation, the only discovery that the mind can hope to make is its "own short-sightedness."[29]

With such difficulties facing man in sorting out the details of the corporeal world, the situation he confronts in attempting to know God is even more desperate. Being so "destitute of faculties" to go beyond sense and reflection, man cannot hope to know "the infinite incomprehensible GOD." God is simply "beyond the reach of our narrow capacities"; "His power, wisdom, and goodness and other attributes... are properly inexhaustible and incomprehensible."[30] While we may, by God's grace, come to have a "perfect, clear, and adequate knowledge" of His creation, we are blocked by "our own blindness and ignorance" from knowing Him in the strictest sense. The finite cannot know the infinite.[31] We possess faculties sufficient only "to discover enough in the creatures, to lead us to knowledge of the Creator."[32]

It is the ultimate incomprehensibility of both the universe and God that demands that people fashion their knowledge of the world about themselves from the ideas that come to them from the senses and reflection; these are ideas about particulars, not about universals. While, for the sake of convenience, man might sort things according to their nominal essences, this in no way means that there is anything beyond the sum of the parts. Given that man is dependent for his knowledge on what he knows about the various parts of the comprehensible universe, he looks to bolster his

number of positive ideas of space or duration. But what still remains beyond this, we have no more a positive distinct notion of, than a mariner has of the depth of the sea, where having let down a large portion of his sounding-line, he reaches no bottom: whereby he knows the depth to so many fathoms, and more; but how much that more is, he hath no distinct notion at all: And could he always supply a new line, and find the plummet always sink, without ever stopping, he would be something in the posture of the mind reaching after a compleat and positive idea of infinity." *Essay*, I.I.6, p. 46; II.XVII.15, pp. 217–218.

[29] *Ibid.*, II.XXIII.29, p. 312; II.XXIII.28, p. 312.

[30] *Ibid.*, II.XXIII.32, p. 313; II.XIII.18, p. 174; II.XVII.1, p. 210.

[31] "If you do not understand the operations of your own finite mind, that thinking thing within you, do not deem it strange, that you cannot comprehend the operations of that external infinite mind, who made and governs all things, and whom the Heaven of Heavens cannot contain." *Essay*, IV.X.19, p. 630. As Locke further noted, "what lies beyond our positive idea towards infinity, lies in obscurity." The fact is, infinity is simply "an object too large and mighty, to be surveyed and managed" by the minds of men. Further, "nothing finite bears any proportion to infinite; and therefore our ideas, which are all infinite, cannot bear any." *Essay*, II.XVII.15, p. 218; II.XVII.21, p. 223; II.XXIX.16, p. 371.

[32] *Ibid.*, II.XXIII.12, p. 302.

knowledge by "the mechanical drudgery of experiment and enquiry."[33] The knowledge of God's "harmonious and beautiful" world must be brought home "piecemeal" to the minds of men where some sense can be made of it.[34] Only by the methods of empirical science can nature come to be sufficiently known to man to prepare him to handle his "business" on earth.[35]

Locke's effort to find the boundary between the knowable and the unknowable would reach its fullest expression in the *Essay Concerning Human Understanding*, which finally appeared in 1689. But the philosophical trek to that point stretched back nearly thirty years, to Locke's earliest writings on government and the status of natural law as a guide to human affairs. And it is in those earliest writings that Locke's essentially Hobbesian roots are first seen, and from which his later thought develops.

Two Tracts on Government and Questions on the Law of Nature

Locke's first effort in political philosophy appears in two tracts written in 1660, eight years into his studentship at Christ Church. The tracts were written – one in English, a second in Latin – to refute a pamphlet recently published by Edward Bagshaw, *The Great Question Concerning Things Indifferent in Religious Worship* (1660).[36] Bagshaw's argument was that "none can Impose, what our Saviour in his Infinite Wisedome did not think necessary, and therefore left free."[37] Immersed as Locke then was in the traditional scholastic training, the issue of indifferency would have been one of great significance.[38] The relationship between the powers of the civil magistrate and the freedom of sects to fashion the modes of their worship as they saw fit in areas that were deemed indifferent was of crucial political importance; it was, said Locke, "a hotly disputed subject."[39] The peace

---

[33] *Conduct of the Understanding*, in *Works of John Locke*, III: 389–428, sec. 42, p. 424. As Locke pointed out elsewhere: "That wealth which has been hidden in the darkness must be excavated with great labor. It does not offer itself up to the idle and indolent, nor indeed to all who seek it, since some we see toil to no avail." John Locke, *Questions Concerning the Law of Nature*, ed. and trans. R. Horwitz, J. S. Clay, and D. Clay (Ithaca, NY: Cornell University Press, 1990), II: 135. Hereinafter cited as *Questions*. The citation indicates the number of Locke's question followed by the page number.

[34] *Conduct of the Understanding*, sec. 37, p. 420.

[35] See ibid., sec. 38, p. 420.

[36] The history of this debate, and an excellent account of the arguments, are to be found in the extensive introduction to Abrams, ed., *Two Tracts on Government*.

[37] As quoted in John Locke, *Essays on the Law of Nature*, ed. W. von Leyden (Oxford: Clarendon Press, 1954), pp. 24–25. Hereinafter cited as *Essays on the Law of Nature*.

[38] "By indifferent things both Bagshaw and Locke mean the time and place of meeting for religious worship, bowing at the name of Jesus and towards the altar, the making of the sign of the cross in baptism, the wearing of the surplice in preaching, kneeling at the Lord's Supper, set forms of prayer, etc." *Essays on the Law of Nature*, p. 25, n.3.

[39] *Second Tract*, p. 221. (All citations hereinafter to either the *First Tract* or the *Second Tract* are to the Abrams edition.)

had been too frequently disrupted by what Locke saw as the "tyranny of a religious rage."[40] History made it clear that all too often "a predatory lust under the guise of Christian liberty and religion" had brought a great many "calamities" to the nation.[41] In particular, the "great question" of the moral status of indifferent things had itself been "attended by a train of as many violent acts as there are points of view."[42] At its deepest level, the political debate over the status of indifferent things was a debate over the relationship between private conscience and public order. In their premises and in their conclusions, Locke's *Two Tracts on Government* are essentially Hobbesian.[43]

Locke lived in an age during which sectarian strife was a constant concern. It seemed that people were far too "ready to conclude God dishonoured upon every small deviation from that way of worship which either education or interest hath made sacred to them." These were not mere academic disputes; they were public concerns of the first order. As Locke put it, men are too willing "to vindicate the cause of God with swords in their hands . . . and so in the actions of greatest cruelty applaud themselves as good Christians."[44] By Locke's calculation, religious differences "are more likely to be signs of men striving for power and empire than signs of the Church of Christ."[45] With the claim of virtuous "reformation," moved in truth more by "ambition and revenge" than by faith, men had picked up "religion as a shield" and roused the people to evil heights: "the overheated zeal of those who know how to arm the rash folly of the ignorant and passionate multitude with the authority of conscience often kindles a blaze among the populace capable of consuming every thing."[46] Thus was it imprudent for the civil magistrate to remain indifferent to the political status of indifferent things. Indeed, "civil indifferencies" mattered as much as those in religion. It was a question of legitimate power and political obligation.[47]

The question was where and how to draw the line between oppression, on the one hand, and disorder on the other: "'Tis not without reason that tyranny and anarchy are judged the smartest scourges can fall upon mankind, the plea of authority usually backing the one, and of liberty inducing the other: and between these two it is, that human affairs are perpetually kept tumbling." Between these extremes Locke sought to find the means to provide "security to each and peace to all." The most vexing question was to

[40] *First Tract*, p. 120.
[41] *Second Tract*, p. 211.
[42] *Ibid.*, p. 210.
[43] See the introduction to Abrams, ed., *Two Tracts on Government*, p. 24.
[44] *First Tract*, pp. 161, 161–162. See also pp. 160–161.
[45] John Locke, *A Letter on Toleration*, ed. Raymond Klibansky (Oxford: Clarendon Press, 1968), p. 59.
[46] *First Tract*, pp. 161, 160; *Second Tract*, p. 211.
[47] *Second Tract*, p. 240.

determine "the very foundations of authority." Ultimately Locke concluded that the means to civil peace and the quelling of religious strife was to create a "supreme magistrate" with an "absolute and arbitrary power over all the indifferent actions of his people." But this sovereign magistrate would not be simply untethered; he would be bound to "provide for the common good and the general welfare."[48]

The foundation of the magistrate's authority ultimately rests in the consent of the governed. Men, by nature, are possessed of an "equal liberty"; until and unless they choose to divest themselves voluntarily of that natural liberty, they cannot unite into a commonwealth.

Moreover, there is no residual power on the part of the people once the contract is entered into. For the magistrate "concentrates in his person the authority and natural right of every individual by a general contract; and all indifferent things, sacred no less than profane, are entirely subjected to his legislative power and government."[49]

The essence of this sovereignty is the supreme legislative power against which individual conscience will have no right; states where private conscience could "nullify the edicts of the magistrate" would be as insecure as in a state where no government existed at all. Sovereignty is absolute, there being "no superior on earth to which it is bound to give an account of its actions." The governed are obliged to obey even "those laws which it may be sinful for the magistrate to enact." To allow any exception to this supremacy of the magistrate's pronouncements would be to endanger the civil peace, for once the consciences of the people against the magistrate are loosed, "their hands will not be long idle or innocent." Failure to create and maintain a properly supreme magistrate will lead to "no peace, no security, no enjoyments, enmity with all men and safe possession of nothing, and those stinging swarms of miseries that attend anarchy and rebellion."[50]

How government is constituted was to Locke a matter of political indifference; as long as sovereignty was complete and absolute, the form of the civil authority did not matter. "By magistrate I understand the supreme legislative power of any society not considering the form of government or the number of persons wherein it is placed." Indeed, there was not even any need for the civil magistrate to be a single man, for an assembly, "which acts like one person," is as capable of exercising a complete and arbitrary power

---

[48] *First Tract*, p. 119; *Second Tract*, p. 210; *Second Tract*, p. 229; *First Tract*, p. 123; *Second Tract*, p. 219.

[49] *Second Tract*, p. 231.

[50] *Second Tract*, pp. 226–227; 231; *First Tract*, pp. 152, 154, 156. It is not too much to say that this unpublished account of life without a properly sovereign magistrate is a fair description of what Locke's state of nature in the *Second Treatise* inevitably degenerates into, a state comparable to that sketched by Hobbes where the life of man is "solitary, poore, nasty, brutish, and short." *Leviathan*, pp. 96–97.

as a monarch. The choice of form is a matter of indifference to Locke for the simple reason that "nature gives no superiority of dominion." As a matter of fact, "God doth nowhere by distinct and particular prescriptions set down rules of governments and bounds to the magistrate's authority, since one form of government was not like to fit all people, and mankind was by the light of nature and their own inconveniencies sufficiently instructed in the necessity of laws and government, and a magistrate with power over them."[51] All that is required is that private conscience yield to public law.

The most basic assumption of Locke's attempt to address the problem of indifferent things was this: "A general freedom is but a general bondage."[52] Yet the solution is a voluntary one, man being "so much the master of his own liberty that he may by compact convey it over to another and invest him with a power over his actions, there being no law of God forbidding a man to dispose of his liberty and obey another."[53] The process is to transform the naturally diverse opinions about indifferent things into a general public consensus; private judgments are supplanted by public law. The one necessity of government in order "to settle a peace and society amongst men [is] that they should mutually agree to give up the exercise of their native liberty to the disposure and prudence of some select person or number of men who should make laws for them which should be the rule of their actions one towards another and the measure of their enjoyments."[54]

In plumbing the depths of the problems posed by the moral status of indifferent things, Locke was pushed to confront the nagging problem of divine and natural law. For if some things are indifferent, others are not; and how to know, truly know, those that are indifferent from those that are not is a problem not of theology but of epistemology. Confronted with the questions he had exposed in the two early tracts on government, Locke moved next to consider the status of the law of nature; the fundamental questions concerning indifferencies, both civil and religious, demanded it.

Although Locke's first efforts to grapple with the law of nature have come to be known as his *Essays on the Law of Nature*, they are not truly essays as such. Rather, they are in the form of scholastic questions, *quaestiones disputatae*. They were left untitled by Locke in manuscript form, apparently not intended for publication, although his friend James Tyrrell seems to have seen them. He repeatedly urged Locke to publish his "Treatise or

---

[51] *First Tract*, pp. 125, 125, 126, 172.
[52] Ibid., p. 120. This is a subject to which Locke returns in the *Second Treatise*, 327: 63. Citation to the *Treatises* will indicate the page number followed by the section number in the Laslett edition.
[53] *First Tract*, pp. 124–125.
[54] Ibid., pp. 137–138. But even under the law of the sovereign magistrate, the people still retain their right to exercise once again their natural liberty should the law of the sovereign be "abolished" or rendered "in anyway inoperative." *Second Tract*, p. 226.

Lectures upon the Law of nature," a plea Locke ultimately ignored.[55] These preliminary thoughts on the law of nature were probably written sometime between 1661 and 1663. Their importance to understanding the development of Locke's political thought is that they serve as the bridge between the *Two Tracts on Government* and the first draft of the *Essay Concerning Human Understanding* of 1671.[56]

The significance of the *Questions Concerning the Law of Nature* lies in how they depart from the traditional, Christian natural law tradition of Locke's time. This was a tradition Locke was disinclined to follow, being always a doubter about the safety of simply conforming to tradition and custom; he was never one to blindly follow the "beaten path."[57] In these earliest forays into this deepest of questions, Locke began to develop an understanding of the law of nature that was hardly consistent with the received tradition.

The tradition from which Locke began to fall away was one that held the law of nature to be the result of God having inscribed it in the hearts of men; it was part of conscience or synderesis. As was explained by one early writer, "synteresie [is] the inward conscience: or a naturall qualitie ingrafted in the soule, which inwardly formeth a man, whether he do well or ill."[58] Richard Carpenter, in *The Conscionable Christian*, explained how the conscience worked: "Now the whole or entire work of conscience...consists, as I conceive it, in a practicall syllogisme: the major proposition whereof ariseth from the *synteresis* or treasury of morall principles, and of sacred rules wherewith the practicall understanding is furnished, for the saving direction of us in all actions." This conscience, Carpenter said, is "written by the finger of God, in such plaine characters, and so legible, that though thou knowest not a letter in any other book, yet thou maiest read this."[59] It was from this inscription that men found the law of nature: "The law of nature, is that rule of pietie, and honestie, that the Lord hath written in the hearts

---

[55] The best history of these manuscripts is to be found in Diskin Clay, "Translator's Introduction," in *Questions*, pp. 76–79. This edition is intended to supplant the original publication of these manuscripts, von Leyden, ed., *Essays on the Law of Nature*. Unless otherwise indicated, all references to Locke's manuscripts will be to the Horwitz edition. The reasons are to be found in Horwitz's introduction, pp. 45–62.

[56] See *Essays on the Law of Nature*, pp. 29, 62; and R. I. Aaron and Jocelyn Gibb, eds., *An Early Draft of Locke's "Essay," together with Excerpts from His Journals* (Oxford: Clarendon Press, 1936).

[57] In the *Essay*, Locke would denigrate those who "servilely confine themselves to the rules and dictates of others." Such men, Locke wryly noted, were merely "cattel" who could safely follow only "beaten tracts." IV.XVII.7, p. 680.

[58] John Bullokar, *An English Expositor* (London, 1616), as quoted in John W. Yolton, *John Locke and the Way of Ideas* (Oxford: Clarendon Press, 1956), p. 31.

[59] (London, 1623). As quoted in Yolton, *John Locke and the Way of Ideas*, p. 31.

of all men: whereby they know confusedly, and in generally, what is good; what is evill; what is to be done; what is to be forborn."[60]

It was into the midst of this tradition that Hobbes had dropped his *Leviathan*, causing such shock and revulsion.[61] In 1655, John Bramhall, in *A Defence of True Liberty*, reaffirmed the traditional Christian view of natural law, that "the will of God, and the Eternall Law which is in God himself, is properly the rule and measure of Justice" and that therefore "all lawes are but participations of the eternall law, from whence they derive their power."[62] Nathanael Culverwel would make a similar argument a few years later in *An Elegant and Learned Discourse of the Light of Nature*. "As Aquinas does very well tell us," he wrote, "the Law of Nature is nothing but the copying out of the eternal law, and the imprinting it upon the breast of a rational being, that eternal law was in a manner incarnated in the law of *Nature*."[63] This in turn reflected the sentiments of Richard Hooker in his *Laws of Ecclesiastical Polity*.[64] Locke's excursion into the politics of natural law theology was a trip fraught with potential dangers, for the fundamental questions he posed called the received tradition radically into question.

Locke posited eleven questions pertaining to the law of nature, three of which he did not answer beyond a simple denial.[65] Through his responses to those questions he saw fit to answer, Locke sought to carve out a new understanding of natural law, one that went far afield from the notions of such theologically inspired writers as Carpenter, Culverwel, and Hooker. The core of Locke's theory is that natural law is a matter of human reason, not drawn from consensus among men, tradition, their natural inclinations, or their private interests. It begins with the senses, finds its expression through reason, and thus can only be binding on human beings. Beasts, bound as

---

[60] William Sclater, *A Key to the Key of Scripture* (London, 1611), as quoted in ibid., p. 33.

[61] See Jon Parkin, *Taming the Leviathan: The Reception of the Political and Religious Ideas of Thomas Hobbes in England, 1640–1700* (Cambridge: Cambridge University Press, 2007); and Samuel I. Mintz, *The Hunting of Leviathan: Seventeenth-Century Reactions to the Materialism and Moral Philosophy of Thomas Hobbes* (Cambridge: Cambridge University Press, 1962).

[62] As quoted in Horwitz, "Introduction," *Questions*, p. 6, n.11. Bramhall went on to castigate Hobbes directly: "See then how grossely T[homas] H[obbes] doth understand that old and true principle, that *the Will of God is the rule of Justice*, as if by *willing things in themselves unjust, he did render them just, by reason of his absolute dominion and irresistible power.... This were to make the eternall Law a Lesbian* rule." Ibid.

[63] Nathanael Culverwel, *An Elegant and Learned Discourse of the Light of Nature*, ed. Robert A. Greene and Hugh MacCullum (Toronto: University of Toronto Press, 1971), p. 34.

[64] See Richard Hooker, *Of the Laws of Ecclesiastical Polity*, in *The Works of Richard Hooker*, ed. John Keble, 3 vols. (Oxford: Clarendon Press, 1888), I: 278.

[65] The three questions are: "III. Does the Law of Nature become known to us by tradition? It does not." "VI. Can the Law of Nature be known from the natural inclination of mankind? It cannot." "IX. Is the Law of Nature binding on brutes? It is not." *Questions*, p. 93.

they might be by laws of natural instinct, cannot be said to be bound by natural law in the sense in which Locke develops it.

Locke begins his quest for the proper understanding of the law of nature with the commonsense observation that men differ greatly over what the law of nature commands. "When it comes to this law [of nature]," he notes, "men depart from one another in so many different directions; in one place one thing, in another something else, is declared to be a dictate of nature and of right reason; and what is held to be virtuous among some is vicious among others." The fact that "most mortals have no knowledge of this law" means that in its place most people rely on custom and tradition. The idea of *"right reason"* becomes nothing but a cover; it is what everyone "claims for himself" and that over which "the various sects of men contest so fiercely among themselves and the guise in which everyone presents his own opinion."[66]

Among men these various notions of what constitutes right reason grow up as received tradition. As Locke saw it, "the greater part of mankind . . . pattern their own conduct on the example and opinion of those men among whom they happen to be born and educated, and have no other rule for right and virtue than the customs of the state and the common opinion of the men among whom they dwell." This is not the case simply with those of mean capacities; it is an affliction that affects especially the "more civilized peoples, who have been refined by education and regulations for their conduct." Among these people "there exist certain definite and unquestioned opinions concerning morals which . . . they recognize as the law of nature and believe to be inscribed in their hearts by nature."[67] As a result of these taught traditions, men are convulsed and divided by what constitutes the law of nature or right reason; everywhere one looks "traditions are everywhere so varied, men's opinions . . . manifestly contradictory and in conflict with one another."[68] And what tradition sows, nature finds it hard to uproot.[69] The result of tradition's power is thus of enormous consequence for political life, for there is, as it were, a natural propensity for men to divide among themselves and to clash.

Such variations and conflicts reveal what was to Locke the fundamental fact of the law of nature: "there exists no such law of nature inscribed in our hearts."[70]

---

[66] *Questions*, IV: 141; III: 133; I: 98–99. See also I: 111.

[67] Ibid., IV: 147.

[68] Ibid., II: 127; IV: 147; II: 127.

[69] "[W]e embrace with all our might those opinions of our earliest youth which have been instilled in us by others, set a high value on them, stubbornly believe in them; nor do we suffer anyone to call them into question, and, since we call these 'principles', we do not permit ourselves to question them, or others to challenge them, for we believe they are 'principles'." Ibid., IV: 149

[70] Ibid., IV: 139.

If this law of nature were inscribed in men's minds, how does it come about that the very young, the uneducated, and the barbarian nations, without institutions, without laws, without any learning or culture, do not know this law better than any and are not most expert in it? . . . If the law of nature were inscribed in the hearts of men, one would be obliged to believe that it would be discovered among these people without a blot or a flaw. . . . Were this law of nature in our hearts, why do fools and madmen have no knowledge of this law?[71]

Because there are no innate ideas, no law of nature inscribed on the hearts, minds, or souls of men,[72] there simply "does not exist among men a universal and common consensus concerning moral matters," with the unhappy result that "there exists among men no common consensus concerning right conduct."[73]

Yet Locke, with a nod toward tradition, insists that there is a law of nature and that it is "the command of the divine will, knowable by the light of nature, indicating what is and what is not consonant with a rational nature, and by that very fact commanding or prohibiting."[74] And it is at this level that Locke must move away from that tradition in which he seems to be working, for the notion of the law of nature as an expression of the divine will traditionally meant innate ideas, notions of right and wrong written on the human heart by the finger of God. By the "light of nature" Locke means human reason. But to make his case that it is in fact the divine will that human reason, as the "light of nature," comes to know, he must gently change what he means by "reason."

At the outset, Locke insists that "reason does not so much lay down and decree this law of nature as it discovers and investigates a law which is ordained by a higher power and has been implanted in our hearts." More emphatically, he insists that reason is not "the maker of this law, but its interpreter." But as his disputations proceed, Locke arrives at a rather different view of reason. "[W]hen we say something is known by the light of nature, we would signify nothing but the kind of truth whose knowledge man can, by the right use of their faculties with which he is provided by nature, attain by himself and without the help of another." What this means exactly becomes clear: "[T]here remains nothing that can be called the light of nature except reason and sense." Thus does natural law seem to be less than divine will in any traditional sense; rather, "all of our knowledge of it is derived from those things we can perceive by our senses."[75]

---

[71] Ibid., IV: 145, 151.

[72] Locke keeps changing what it is that there is nothing inscribed upon, often using the terms synonymously.

[73] *Questions*, VII: 181.

[74] Ibid., I: 101.

[75] Ibid., I: 101; II: 119; V: 153; and II: 133. See also *Essay*, II.I.24, p. 118.

The implications of this view for the received tradition of natural law were significant.[76] The senses, by Locke's measure, "furnish the entire and primary matter for discourse and introduce it into the hidden recesses of the mind." There is no other way to know anything: "every conception of the mind . . . always comes from some pre-existent matter." As a result, "without the help of the senses and their service, reason can produce nothing more than can a workman in the dark behind closed shutters." Thus can Locke conclude, in contradiction to his initial argument that reason makes nothing, that the law of nature is indeed "a fixed and eternal rule of conduct, *dictated by reason itself*, and for this reason something fixed and inherent in human nature."[77]

But there is no possibility of any law without a known legislator. Thus must reason create "some god," for "god and the immortality of the soul . . . must . . . be necessarily assumed for the existence of the law of nature, for there can exist no law without a legislator and law will have no force if there is no punishment." It is from the "legitimate method for establishing axioms" that this creation comes about, that is, "by induction and the observation of particulars." In observing the sensible world, man can only be struck by the order of it all, it being "so perfect everywhere and wrought with such skill." By such observation man makes the necessary "inference that there must exist some powerful and wise creator of all . . . things." With "sense to show the way," man's reason eventually leads him to "a knowledge of a legislator, or some superior power, to whom we are necessarily subject, which was the first requirement for the knowledge of any law."[78]

As a result of this power of reason, man sees that by the will of the superior creator he is "impelled to form and preserve a union of his life with other men, not only by the needs and necessities of life, but he is driven by a certain natural propensity to enter society and is fitted to preserve it by the gift of speech and the commerce of language."[79] Man's most natural state is civil society, defined by "the fixed form of a commonwealth and constitution of a regime." Such a situation prevents "that part of the commonwealth which has the greatest power to harm . . . [from doing] anything at its own pleasure."[80] As Locke asked: "Where . . . would human affairs stand, what would the privileges of a society be, if mortals gathered together in a state

---

[76] See *Questions*, II: 133.

[77] Ibid., V: 157; V: 155; and X: 227 (emphasis supplied).

[78] Ibid., II: 133; VII: 193; V: 161, and V: 161, 163.

[79] Ibid., V: 169. As will be seen later, language is the bridge between Locke's epistemology and his political philosophy. See especially *Essay*, III.I.I, p. 402; and *Second Treatise*, 336–337: 77. On the context of Locke's work on language, see Hannah Dawson, *Locke, Language and Early-Modern Philosophy* (Cambridge: Cambridge University Press, 2007); and Walter Ott, *Locke's Philosophy of Language* (Cambridge: Cambridge University Press, 2004).

[80] *Questions*, I: 115.

only to become more readily prey to the power of others?"[81] Such is civil society that "the saner part of mankind" eschew any desire to shake off "the yoke of all authority" and plunge into a state of "natural liberty" where "all right and justice should be determined not by another's law, but by the interest of each individual."[82] It is the law of nature, properly understood, that divides civil liberty from licentiousness. But in the end, that law of nature for Locke is reasonably modest; it consists of nothing more than a dictate"which bids obedience to superiors, and keeping the public peace."[83] And it is at this level that one can understand how "the laws of the civil magistrate derive all their force from the binding power of this law."[84] For governments are instituted among men to secure the rights that nature gives but leaves insecure; it is the only rational thing to do.

II. THE LAW OF NATURE AND THE NATURE OF LAW

The *Essay Concerning Human Understanding* and the *Two Treatises of Government*

The influence of the works of Thomas Hobbes on John Locke is one of the enduring questions in the history of ideas as well as in political philosophy. It is of no small moment to understanding Locke's contributions to constitutionalism in particular and to the science of politics in general. While it is not uncommon to dismiss Hobbes's views as a mere "irrelevance" to Locke's political philosophy, or even to argue that Locke wrote his political treatises in order to refute Hobbes, such views ignore abundant evidence to the contrary. At the deepest level, Locke's debt to Hobbes was immense.

Locke's relationship to Hobbes is most clearly revealed in the relationship between the younger man's two great works, the *Essay Concerning Human Understanding* and the *Two Treatises of Government*. Taken separately, they have struck some as works whose "literary continuity . . . was about as slight as could be."[85] In this view, each work "was written for an entirely different purpose and in an entirely different state of mind." This interpretation begs credulity, especially when one considers that by all evidence the two works "were in gestation at the same time."[86] A more convincing account

---

[81] Ibid. See also *Second Treatise*, 346: 93.

[82] *Questions*, XI: 237.

[83] Ibid., I: 115. This is a clear echo of Hobbes's sketch of the laws of nature. See *Leviathan*, pp. 100, 110.

[84] *Questions*, VIII: 213. See *Leviathan*, p. 205.

[85] Laslett, ed., *Locke's Two Treatises of Government* p. 82. Laslett insists that Locke did not "consciously recollect" the sources of his Hobbesian sentiments: "He seems to have been in the curious position of having absorbed Hobbesian sentiments, Hobbesian phraseology in such a way that he did not know where they came from." Ibid., p. 72.

[86] Ibid., pp. 83, 35.

is the one that sees the *Essay* as containing "the defense of the method of the *Two Treatises* in its defense of the possibility of demonstrative moral science."[87] This view seems bolstered by circumstantial evidence concerning the appearance of the two great works.

First is the simple fact that two works of such power and depth appeared within a few weeks of each other in 1689; the *Two Treatises* in mid-November and the *Essay* in December. That neither work contains any clear notice of the other is not terribly puzzling insofar as Locke saw fit to hide his authorship of the *Two Treatises* yet signed his name clearly, if somewhat timidly, to the "Epistle Dedicatory" in the *Essay*. The view that this tactic was used because Locke "was quite aware that it was no easy simple matter to reconcile their doctrines" ignores how easily their doctrines are in fact reconciled. Indeed, it seems far more likely that Locke claimed the authorship of one but not the other precisely because had the two works been taken together Locke's broader philosophical scheme would have been all too clear.

The second suggestive fact is presented by Locke himself in the preface to the *Two Treatises*. Locke begins that work in a strikingly odd way: "Thou hast here the Beginning and the End of a Discourse concerning Government; what Fate has otherwise disposed of the Papers that should have filled up the middle, and were more than all the rest 'tis not worthwhile to tell here." Beyond the obvious fact that a scholar as careful and fastidious as Locke would hardly seem likely to "lose" the central portion of a work lies the odd fact of his seeing fit to mention it at all. If the missing portion of the work were of such a quality as "*should* have filled up the middle," it seems implausible that Locke would have made no effort to reconstruct the missing section.[88] On the other hand, if the vanished portion were of no significance to the work in hand, it seems even odder that a writer as judicious as Locke would see fit to point it out. To begin with such a tease raises more questions than the author answers; at least, that is, in a forthright way.

There is no doubt that Locke understood the prudence of esoteric writing; persecution of those whose ideas challenged the reigning orthodoxies was yet a very real political problem.[89] Indeed, 1683, the same year that Oxford held its last book burning, also saw Algernon Sidney's beheading for his republican sentiments. Such events sent a strong message to those who would

---

[87] Ruth W. Grant, *John Locke's Liberalism* (Chicago: University of Chicago Press, 1987), p. 23. See also Thomas L. Pangle, *The Spirit of Modern Republicanism: The Moral Vision of the American Founders and the Philosophy of Locke* (Chicago: University of Chicago Press, 1988).

[88] Locke, "Preface," *Two Treatises of Government*, p. 155 (emphasis supplied).

[89] See Pangle, *The Spirit of Modern Republicanism*, pp. 137–138. For a very interesting argument about the "missing middle" of the *Two Treatises*, see Steven N. Zwicker, *Lines of Authority: Politics and English Literary Culture, 1649–1689* (Ithaca, NY: Cornell University Press, 1994), pp. 130–172.

dig too deeply beneath the foundations of existing arrangements, and thereby become liable to censure for "pulling up the old foundations of knowledge and authority."⁹⁰ Thus it is not unlikely that Locke's teasing preface in the *Two Treatises* is a veiled hint that when his authorship of the *Two Treatises* was found out, his readers might look elsewhere to bring together the "Beginning and End" of his discourses on government. That elsewhere would be to the *Essay*; for it is the logical bridge between the *First Treatise* and the *Second Treatise*.

By separating the *Essay* from the *Two Treatises* Locke was able to disguise his true principles. In the first pages of the *First Treatise*, in fact, he noted in Sir Robert Filmer's *Patriarcha* the same caution. Filmer's basic theory was not simply in *Patriarcha* but rather "lies scatter'd in the several Parts of his writings." Should Filmer have "given up the whole Draught together in that Gigantic Form, he had painted it in his own Phancy," Locke suggested, his theory would likely have made "a very odd and frightful Figure." Therefore, noted Locke, "like a wary Physician, when he would have his patient swallow some harsh or *Corrosive Liquor*, he mingles it with a large quantity of that, which may dilute it; that the scatter'd Parts may go down with less feeling, and cause less Aversion."⁹¹

The great and abiding fear of Locke's philosophic (and political) life was that he would be thought a "Hobbist." There was no more damning indictment that one could suffer in his time; he avoided it at all costs, all of his life. But looking back over his works and papers, it seems his distance from Hobbes was too great to be real. In his massive notebooks, where he kept references and citations to the important books "referenced and arranged with monumental carefulness," one finds not a single passage from Hobbes's works.⁹² Surely a mind as inquisitive as Locke's would have been led to include extracts from the most important books published in his lifetime on the very subjects in which he was immersing himself. And surely he could have covered himself well by attacking Hobbes in some direct way.

---

⁹⁰ *Essay*, I.IV.23, p. 100. Earlier in the *Essay* Locke had confessed that: "'Tis possible, men may sometimes own rules of morality, which, in their private thoughts, they do not believe to be true, only to keep themselves in reputation, and esteem amongst those, who are persuaded of their obligation." I.III.11, pp. 72–73.

⁹¹ *First Treatise*, 164: 7. Citations indicate page number followed by the section number in the Laslett edition of the *Two Treatises of Government*.

⁹² Laslett has identified one citation to Hobbes "on a fly-leaf of a volume in his library published in 1668." It does not seem to strike Laslett as significant that the passage in question, not identified by Locke as being taken from Hobbes, is one concerning the abuses of speech from *Leviathan*: "In wrong or noe definitions, lyes and first abuse of speech, from wch. proceeds all false and useless tenets; wch. make those men who take their instruction from the authority of books, not from their owne meditation to be as much below the condition of ignorant men, as men indued with true science are above it. For between true science and erroneous doctrines Ignorance is in the middle." "Introduction," *Locke's Two Treatises of Government*, pp. 73–74.

Yet he never did – not even when urged to do so directly by his good friend Tyrrell, who had himself endeavored to refute Hobbes's principles.[93] The reason Locke refused to engage Hobbes was arguably the same as that which prompted him to keep separate his epistemology and his politics: he was in agreement with Hobbes's fundamental principles.

This is not to say that Locke was a mere transcriber of Hobbes.[94] By Locke's own standard, such would have been pointless. The "stock of knowledge," he would write, "is not increased by being able to repeat what others have said, or produce the arguments we have found in them."[95] Blind reverence for authority was anathema to Locke: "Reading furnishes the mind only with materials of knowledge, 'tis thinking makes them ours."[96] And by his thinking through the deepest implications of Hobbes's political philosophy, Locke very much made them his own; and it was by that process of absorption that Hobbes's theories would reach a far broader audience than was willing to take seriously Hobbes's work presented in his own name.

The *First Treatise of Government*

Locke's vicious rejection of Sir Robert Filmer's *Patriarcha* in the *First Treatise* is, in one sense, akin to "a wolf making lint out of a teddy bear";[97] by Locke's own estimate, Filmer's works were "so much glib nonsense," no longer taken seriously by anyone. Yet what made Filmer a significant target for Locke was the fact that his writings had come to be "publickly owned" by the pulpit, his doctrine made into "the Currant Divinity of the Times." Filmer had been embraced by those who took themselves "to be Teachers" but who had by Filmer's dim lights served only to "dangerously mislead others." To those who have "done the Truth and the Publick wrong," Locke urged this reflection: "That, there cannot be a greater mischief to Prince and People, than the propagating wrong Notions concerning Government, that so at last all times might not have reason to complain of the DRUM ECCLESIASTICK." By means of the *First Treatise* Locke intended to overthrow those pernicious principles that had so infected those who had come to preach "them up as Gospel."[98]

---

93 In Tyrrell's view, Hobbes's principles were the very essence of "falsehood and absurdity," principles of the most profound "wickedness." James Tyrrell, *A Brief Disquisition of the Law of Nature* (2nd. ed.; London: W. Rogers, 1701), pp. 252, 379.

94 This view has been taken by some. See Frank Coleman, *Hobbes and America: Exploring the Constitutional Foundation* (Toronto: University of Toronto Press, 1977).

95 *Conduct of the Understanding*, sec. 19, p. 406.

96 Ibid., sec. 19, p. 405. Anyone who fails to question what he reads, Locke suggested, "makes his understanding only the warehouse of other men's lumber." Ibid., sec. 41, p. 424.

97 Pangle, *The Spirit of Modern Republicanism*, p. 134.

98 Locke, "Preface," *Two Treatises of Government*, pp. 155–156.

In this, Locke was echoing Hobbes's criticism of the "Gown-men," those "sublime doctors" of school divinity who had undertaken "to mingle the sentences of heathen philosophers" with "the decrees of Holy Scripture" in order to produce their pernicious doctrines of faith and philosophy.[99] It was from the universities "that all preachers proceeded . . . were poured out into city and country to terrify the people into an absolute obedience."[100] By this "vain philosophy," the schools were able to nourish superstition whereby "crafty ambitious persons" were able to "abuse the simple people."[101] By Locke's measure, Filmer's patriarchal politics and his doctrine of the divine right of kings were a classic example of those sophistical teachings Hobbes had attacked.[102] As Filmer himself put it, Aristotle's *Politics* "agrees exactly with the Scripture."[103]

Given that Filmer's theory of politics, strictly speaking, had been largely annihilated by the time Locke got to him, it is necessary to look for another purpose in his having seen fit to write the *First Treatise*.[104] Surely his open contempt for Filmer in the preface is something of a nudge away from the substantive argument contained in *Patriarcha*. The real purpose of the opening essay is to expose what is truly the issue for Locke: the utter dishonesty of Filmer's interpretation of so-called authoritative sources and the disingenuousness of his argument. By laying bare Filmer's "peculiar way of writing" Locke will be able to demonstrate how easily falsehood can be made to pass for truth and how by the "use of words, one may say anything."[105] In all of *Patriarcha*, Locke argues, there is "not any thing that looks like an argument." According to Filmer's method, once "having named the text, [he] concludes without any more ado, that the meaning is as he would have it." Filmer zealously builds on allegedly authoritative expressions "of whose signification interpreters are not agreed." The result is that he necessarily builds his theory upon a foundation at once "false and frail." Indeed, at

---

99 Thomas Hobbes, *A Dialogue between a Philosopher and a Student of the Common Laws of England*, ed. Joseph Cropsey (Chicago: University of Chicago Press, 1971), p. 157 (hereinafter cited as *Dialogue*); *Behemoth*, p. 41; *De Corpore*, p. x.

100 *Behemoth*, p. 49

101 *Leviathan*, p. 18.

102 As Peter Laslett has argued, "the whole concept of naturalistic politics is part of the Aristotelian tradition, as Filmer himself fully realized." Indeed: "It is possible . . . to trace the patriarchal family in all . . . respects in the conventional theology, the political thinking and the legal opinion of the age." Peter Laslett, ed., *Patriarcha and Other Political Works of Sir Robert Filmer* (Oxford: Basil Blackwell, 1949), pp. 27, 28. Hereinafter cited as *Patriarcha*.

103 *Patriarcha*, p. 79.

104 By both "Sydney's outraged blusterings" and "Tyrrell's laborious pedantry," Laslett has suggested, Filmer, "a profoundly unoriginal writer," had been severely mauled. *Patriarcha*, pp. 39, 31.

105 *First Treatise*, 190: 44; 205: 63.

his worst, Filmer baldly undertakes to persuade his readers "against the express words of the Scripture."[106] Filmer's "ingenuity and the goodness of his Cause," said Locke, "required in its Defender Zeal to a degree of warmth able to warp the Sacred Rule of the Word of God, to make it comply with his present occasion."[107] As Locke snidely noted, "God must not be believed, though he speaks it himself, when he says he does anything, which will not consist with Sir Robert's Hypothesis."[108]

Robert Filmer was, Locke suggested, a man of great "skill in distinctions," nothing less than a "great...master of style." Yet even "a little attention" to Filmer's text would reveal myriad contradictions. Ultimately, Filmer's political teaching was all form and no substance; from the very core of his theory of patriarchal politics this was the case. Such was Filmer's tack: "Incoherencies in Matter and Suppositions without proofs put handsomely together in good words and a plausible style, are apt to pass for strong Reason and good Sense." That is, Locke sharply noted, "till they come to be look'd into with Attention." And when they are "look'd into with Attention," concluded Locke, one sees at once that Filmer is guilty of "garbling," and that his theory is simply "absurd."[109]

Throughout his assault on Filmer's house of cards, Locke endeavors to restate Filmer's "arguments" in "plain *English*" in order better to expose the author's duplicity and the "argument's" doubtfulness.[110] By giving his words a "good construction" Locke could at once demolish what was left of Filmer's substantive argument and expose the dishonesty of the method whereby opinion would be shackled by the authority allegedly derived from Scripture. It was not God but merely Filmer who created the logic of *Patriarcha*.[111]

The deepest flaw of Filmer's thesis is its denial of human reason as the guide to human affairs. The "law of nature, which is the law of reason," Locke responded, is that by which the world is governed; and human beings have been made by God to be directed by "Senses and Reason" in the same way inferior creatures were made to be directed by "their Sense, and Instinct." The one thing that God has not done is to indicate by "marks" anyone who is by nature or by divine right to rule over others. Thus one cannot know who is the proper heir to Adam; one cannot even guess in whose hand such a divinely conveyed scepter ought to rest. But at a minimum, even by Filmer's odd logic, "a man can never be oblig'd in Conscience to submit to any power, unless he be satisfied who is the person, who has a Right to

---

[106] Ibid., 190: 44; 205: 63; 167: 11; 193: 49; 208: 67; and 181: 32.
[107] Ibid., 202: 60. See also *Conduct of the Understanding*, pp. 409–412.
[108] *First Treatise*, 182: 32.
[109] Ibid., 172: 18; 239.110; 214: 74; 173: 20; 202: 61; 257: 134.
[110] Ibid., 219: 79; 240: 112.
[111] Said Locke: "I never, I confess, met with any man of parts so dexterous as Sir *Robert* at this way of arguing." Ibid., 259–60: 137.

exercise that power over him." Further, Locke pointed out: "To settle therefore men's consciences under an obligation to obedience, 'tis necessary that
they know not only that there is a power somewhere in the world, but that
the person who by Right is vested with this power over them."[112]

Filmer's inability to show who has this divine right to rule will "serve
only to give a greater edge to man's natural ambition, which of itself is
but too keen." Filmer's theory of "Omnipotent Fatherhood...can serve
for nothing but to unsettle and destroy all the Lawful governments in the
world and to establish in their room, Disorder, Tyranny, and Usurpation."
Rather than conduce to "that Peace and Tranquility, which is the business of
Government, and the end of Humane Society," Filmer's ambiguous right to
sovereignty will only "lay a sure and lasting foundation of endless contention
and disorder." History teaches this harsh truth clearly: "The great question
which in all ages has disturbed mankind, and brought on them the greatest
part of those mischiefs which have ruined Cities, depopulated Countries, and
disordered the peace of the world, has been, not whether there be power in
the world, nor whence it came, but who should have it."[113]

Filmer's doctrine "cuts up all Government by the roots" insofar as it
provides no guide for answering the basic political question: who shall
govern? The idea of a divine right to rule breaks down at precisely the point
where one must ask to whom that right is to be conveyed from one generation
to the next. For there is no "plain Natural or Divine Rule concerning it."
The answer to this most fundamental of questions Filmer "leaves like the
Philosopher's Stone in Politicks, out of reach of any one to discover from
his writings." Having failed to establish the grounds for the descent of
divine dominion from Adam onward, Filmer has failed to refute those who
have argued – his primary targets – that the natural liberty and equality of
mankind is "a Truth Unquestioned." With this foundational failure, Filmer's
entire "fabric falls with it, and Governments must be left again to the old
way of being made by contrivance, and the consent of men...making use
of their reason to unite together into Society."[114]

While neither God nor nature marks clearly who is by right to rule, both
God and nature indicate the focus of man's natural reason: his preservation.
Since "the preservation of every man's right and property" is the only true
end of government, it is only by conducing to that end that the rulers have
any claim on the consciences of men to obey the laws. Thus understood,
the only legitimate foundation for the claim to rule is by the consent of those
to be so governed. The very dilemmas of upheaval and contention, of war
and argument, spawned by Filmer's divine right of kings theory are "safely
provided against" by "positive laws and Compact." Thus does Locke's plan

[112] Ibid., 233: 101; 223: 86; 220: 81; 221: 81; 221: 81.
[113] Ibid., 237: 106; 212: 72; 237: 1061; 236–237: 106.
[114] Ibid., 251: 126; 239: 109; 208: 67; and 162: 6.

seem clear: to supplant "the Ordinance of God" as the foundation of political power with the "*Ordinances* of man." Since there is no divine right, there is only the human right to rule "depending upon the Will of man." And thus "men may put government into what hands, and under what form they please."[115]

The rejection of Filmer and patriarchal politics left a void to be filled; the state of nature and social contract teaching of the *Second Treatise* fill that void. But the state of nature and social contract construct Locke presents seems to come out of thin air. It is only when the epistemological assumptions of the *Essay Concerning Human Understanding* are interjected that one has a bridge between the first and the second treatises. With the view of human understanding presented in the *Essay* there is a firm grounding for the political teaching of the social contract presented in the *Second Treatise*.

The origins of the *Essay*, Locke hints in his "Epistle to the Reader," began in another discussion entirely; he only backed into an account of the understanding, it seems. Although Locke mentions that this project began when "five or six" of his friends met in his chambers to discuss "a Subject very remote from this," he does not see fit to reveal what that fruitful topic happened to be.[116] Yet his friend James Tyrrell, who was present at the session, noted in his copy of the *Essay* that the original discussion dealt with "the Principles of morality, and reveal'd Religion."[117]

The *Essay* is not, on its surface, directly concerned with the problem of revealed religion. Yet when placed in the context of Locke's attack on Filmer (a concern common to Tyrrell, it will be recalled), a central concern of the *Essay* becomes more intelligible precisely as a response to the political problem posed by revealed religion. The third book of the *Essay* dealing with language is, in effect, the continuation of Locke's most fundamental critique of Filmer: the abuse of words and the subsequent distortion of the truth. As Locke makes clear, it is the abuses to which language is subject that render revealed religion an overwhelming – indeed, insurmountable – political problem.

Locke sees the political problem posed by revealed religion in precisely the same light as had Hobbes; and, indeed, he sees the same solution. Man must not depend on expert opinion about religion or law or morality; human reason must be freed from the impositions of the priests, lawyers, and philosophers. In place of that tradition Locke sought to bolster Hobbes's solution of natural reason and the social contract. Thus was politics to be grounded in human nature in the strict sense and not on allegedly higher sources of

---

[115] Ibid., 223: 86; 227–228: 92; 251: 126; 261: 140.
[116] *Essay*, p. 7
[117] "Foreword," *Essay*, p. xix.

authority. Man, for Locke as for Hobbes, had to be seen as the measure of all things.

Unlike Locke, Hobbes had explicitly grounded his political theory in *Leviathan* on his reflections on man and his nature. That notorious book begins, not insignificantly, with Hobbes's consideration of man, not with any concern for politics or ethics. By seeing the *Essay* as the missing section between the *Two Treatises*, one finds in Locke the same progression that characterized Hobbes's account of the "Matter, Forme, and Power of a Common-Wealth." In Locke as in Hobbes, the state of nature and the idea of the consent of the governed make sense only when based on the radical individuality of men. But that radical individuality stems from their natural equality; that natural equality is born of the natural moral and political equality of the human understanding.

By nature no man has the right to rule another – the reason, for Locke as for Hobbes, was that by nature all opinions of justice are in the first instance equal. Because of that natural equality of ideas it is necessary that men voluntarily enter into a mutual covenant whereby they create a body politic with the power to fashion rules of justice, binding notions of public right. The implicit attack on the traditional notion of natural law in this view is severe; revelation, while still nodded to, is in fact and effect supplanted by human reason undirected by any divine power. Natural law is no longer seen as written in the hearts of men by the finger of God; rather, it is "nowhere to be found but in the minds of men."[118] Taken together, Locke's two greatest works do not contradict but rather form a unified whole.

An Essay Concerning Human Understanding

The teaching for which Locke is most often remembered is his theory of the state of nature and man's escape from it by entering into a social contract that he presents in the *Second Treatise*. But on the basis of the *Second Treatise* alone, or even taken in light of his argument in the *First Treatise*, there is no foundation for the idea of how a social contract based upon consent can work; to understand how it works, there must be presupposed an understanding of the understanding. Without such an understanding, there can be no real sense of legitimacy for the contractual foundation of civil society, any more than there was for Filmer's notion of the divine right of kings. It is this fact that makes the *Essay Concerning Human Understanding* the most deeply political of all Locke's works.

By the understanding, man is able to make sense of the otherwise incomprehensible world. The important teaching of the *Essay* is how, precisely, man does that; how does he come to draw that essential line between

[118] *Second Treatise*, 376: 136.

the knowable and the unknowable; how does his grasp of the distinction between knowledge and opinion come to bear on his conduct? Those were the pressing questions to which Locke had to provide answers if the misguided reliance on the belief in innate ideas was to be supplanted.

A. The Way of Ideas

When Locke viewed the world around him, he saw absolutely no evidence that there were innate ideas; indeed, there was no doubt that ideas are not innate, but rather are "acquired." No theory could have struck more directly at the heart of the traditional natural law teaching than that. It called into question in a most radical way the belief, the faith, that God Himself had imprinted certain moral dictates in the human heart. If He had, why is it that men seem so disinclined to follow those dictates? "I cannot," Locke concluded, "see how any men, should ever transgress those moral rules, with confidence, and serenity, were they innate, and stamped on their minds." The ugliness of human affairs suggested a far bleaker state of morality.

"View but an army at the sacking of a town," Locke urged his readers, "and see what observation, or sense of moral principles, or what touch of conscience, for all the outrages they do. Robberies, murders, rapes, are the sports of men set at liberty from punishment and censure." The truth of the matter was plain to Locke: "[T]he supposition of such innate principles, is but an opinion taken up at pleasure."[119] What most men think innate are really nothing deeper than doctrines and principles that have become customary.[120] The proof that such sentiments are not innate is clearly seen in the fundamental disagreements men have over such notions.

The world is characterized by a "great variety of opinions, concerning moral rules." Such variety would not be the case "if practical principles were innate, and imprinted in our minds immediately by the hand of God." But "there is scarce that principle of morality to be named, or rule of virtue to be thought on... which is not, somewhere or other, slighted and condemned by the general fashion of whole societies of men, governed by practical opinions, and rules of living quite opposite to others." Common sense suggested that "it will scarce seem possible, that God would engrave principles in men's minds, in words of uncertain signification, such as virtues and sins, which amongst different men, stand for different things." The historically demonstrable fact is that "there are no practical principles wherein all men agree; and therefore none innate."[121]

---

[119] *Essay*, I.II.15, p. 55; I.III.9, p. 70. I.III.14, p. 76.
[120] See *Essay*, I.III.21, p. 81. This was precisely a problem Locke pointed to in the *First Treatise*: "And when fashion hath once established, what folly or craft began, custom makes it sacred, and 'twill be thought impudence or madness, to contradict or question it." 201: 58.
[121] *Essay*, I.III.6, pp. 68–69; I.III.10, p. 72; I.III.19, p. 79; I.III.27, p. 84.

Locke understood that it was necessary to set about "pulling up the old foundations of knowledge and certainty." At a minimum this required supplanting the traditional notion of natural law with a new understanding, one that took seriously human reason. Only by challenging the way men viewed natural law could Locke hope to survey and mark the proper boundary between the knowable and the unknowable. "There is a great deal of difference between an innate law, and a law of nature," Locke argued, "between something imprinted on our minds in their very original, and something that we being ignorant of may attain to the knowledge of, by the use and due application of our natural faculties."[122]

For Locke, the *law* of nature in the traditional, Christian sense must be replaced by the *laws* of nature in a modern, scientific sense; metaphysics is replaced by physics, Aristotle and Aquinas by Hobbes and Newton. Traditional natural law teaching was rooted in the realm of the unknowable, in the realm of faith rather than the realm of philosophy. The stunning thing about the idea of innate principles, noted Locke, is that "those who talk so confidently of them are so sparing to tell us . . . which they are."[123] This was the same characteristic of the received tradition of the law of nature. As he would later put it, when it came to that notion of natural law, no one had been able "to give it us all entire, as a law; no more, nor no less, than what was contained in, and had the obligation of that law."[124] In the hands of the priests, the law of nature had proved itself to be "the law of convenience, too."[125] Natural law was the most basic problem the new philosophers like Hobbes and Locke had to confront. On the one hand, the "most unshaken rule of morality and foundation of all social virtue, *That one should do as he would be done unto*," was generally "more commended than practised."[126] Yet, on the other hand, it was a rule deemed above question as the foundation of the traditional understanding of the law of nature. Locke argued that such was human reason that it would not be absurd to "ask a reason why?" If even that most basic of truths was up for questioning in Locke's project, there was likely to be little left of the doctrine of innate ideas when he finished. Indeed, there was nothing left.

The belief in innate ideas was only part of the problem Locke sought to address; the other was the perverse teachings of the schools when it came to Aristotelian metaphysics and logic. This nagging Aristotelianism was the more vexing part of the situation. For while the doctrine of innate ideas was a matter of belief, the teachings of the schools were understood to be the result of reason of the highest order; to combat the schoolmen was to engage

---

[122] Ibid., I.IV.23, p. 100; I.III.13, p. 75.
[123] Ibid., I.III.14, p. 76.
[124] *Reasonableness*, p. 533.
[125] Ibid., pp. 530, 535.
[126] *Essay*, I.III.4, p. 68; I.III.7, p. 70.

the enemy on the field of philosophy rather than on the bogs of faith. It was to call into question the single most powerful intellectual influence of the past five hundred years, Aristotle. Although for Locke the real problem, as it had been for Hobbes, was less Aristotle than the Aristotelians.

Locke's contempt for the schoolmen knew no bounds; nearly all the passion that is to be found in the soberly rational *Essay* is reserved for them, although his indictment is delivered at a very general level, with no individuals being named (unlike that of Hobbes, who could not resist the occasional swipe at such figues as Aquinas and Suarez.) Still, it is in Locke's assault on the schoolmen and their dangerous teachings that one finds the core of his modern teaching on the nature of law and the importance of language to human understanding and the foundations of civil society.[127]

Locke introduced his *Essay* modestly, insisting that it was nothing more elaborate than an effort to remove "some of the rubbish that lies in the way to knowledge."[128] That rubbish was the intellecual litter of the schools. The greatest pile of clutter that had accumulated came from the perverse practice of the scholarly disputation, moved as it was by the medieval academic arts of rhetoric – "that powerful instrument of error and deceit," Locke called it – and logic. This academic practice had not only served "to perplex the knowledge and truth of things"; it had also reduced the entire enterprise of philosophy to nothing more than "eminent trifling," simply "huffing opinions" spewed forth by those "mistaken pretenders to knowledge." By "taking words for things" the scholars had reduced true learning to nothing more than "jargon" and "gibberish" by which they sought to "palliate men's ignorance and cover their errors."[129] These "profound Doctors" knew what power and influence were to be had in keeping people "lost in the great wood of words."[130]

The price had been high. The schoolmen had been able to teach "doubtful systems for complete sciences" and to pass off "unintelligible notions for scientific demonstrations." The means they had employed was the syllogism, a way of arguing that had been put forth in the schools as "the only proper

---

[127] "Vague and insignificant forms of speech, and abuse of language, have so long passed for mysteries of science; and hard or misapply'd words, with little or no meaning, have, by prescription, such a right to be mistaken for deep learning, and height of speculation, that it will not be easie to persuade, either those who speak, or those who hear them, that they are but the covers of ignorance, and hindrance of true knowledge. To break in upon the Sanctuary of Vanity and Ignorance, will be, I suppose, some service to human understanding." *Essay*, "Epistle to the Reader," p. 10.

[128] Ibid.

[129] *Essay*, III.X.34, p. 508; III.X.6, p. 493; III.IV.8, p. 422; III.V.16, p. 438; III.IX.2, p. 475; II.XIII.18, p. 174; III.IV.9, p. 423; III.X.14, p. 497.

[130] Ibid., IV.III.30, p. 561. The schoolmen were savvy; they knew well that "there is no such way to gain admittance, or give defence to strange and absurd doctrines, as to guard them round about with legions of obscure, doubtful, and undefined words." Thus did they cloak their theories in "a curious and unexplicable web of perplexed words." Ibid., III.X.9, p. 495; III.X.8, p. 494.

instrument of reason and means of knowledge." This was the essence of the Aristotelian domination of the schools. So powerful was the hold of the syllogism that an innocent observer could be forgiven for concluding that "before Aristotle there was not one man that did or could know anything by reason." Locke was scornful of such a view: "But God has not been so sparing to men to make them barely two-legged creatures, and left it to Aristotle to make them rational." The result of the reliance on the syllogism and Aristotelian logic had been to render frivolous what was deeply serious. The "scholastique forms" had been "adopted to catch and entangle the mind, [rather] than to instruct and inform the understanding."[131]

Scholasticism had rendered philosophy a verbal game in which the "artificial and cumbersome fetters" that were the syllogistic method of reasoning served only to "clog and hinder the mind." This "art of reasoning" not only offered no new knowledge; it also actively confused what knowledge there might be at hand. Since the greatest end was nothing more than victory for the learned doctor who could prevail in this bout of "fencing," men were "allowed without shame to deny the agreement of ideas that do manifestly agree." The deepest problem, however, was not that the schools had undertaken to teach "a very useless skill" in syllogistic reasoning and scholarly disputations; it was that this so-called skill was undermining political life.[132] The "logical niceties" and "empty speculations" of the schools had "invaded the great concernments of human life and society; obscured and perplexed the material truths of law and divinity; brought confusion, disorder, and uncertainty into the affairs of mankind" and had largely "rendered useless those two great rules, religion and justice."[133] By the careless "scholastick proceedings," the schools had reduced language to so much "insignificant noise." This was the focus of Locke's attack: "Language, which was given us for the improvement of knowledge, and bond of society, should not be employ'd to darken truth, and unsettle peoples rights; to raise mists, and render unintelligible both morality and religion."[134]

It was in the schools where the line between the knowable and the unknowable had been encrusted and obscured by forms of reasoning inherently unnatural. At the deepest level, the schoolmen had assumed themselves able to explain all being, never assuming for a moment that there were secrets of nature to which they had no access. In their zeal to explain everything, they wound up explaining nothing. This was seen most clearly in their efforts to teach such doctrines as those of substantial forms and incorporeal being. Locke saw his task as showing that "real essences or substantial forms . . . come not within the reach of our knowledge."[135]

---

[131] Ibid., IV.XII.12, p. 647; IV.XVII.4, p. 671; IV.XVII.4, p. 677.
[132] Ibid., IV.XVII.4, p. 672; IV.XVII.6, p. 679; IV.XVII.4, p. 675; III.X.8, p. 494.
[133] Ibid., III.X.12, p. 496.
[134] Ibid., IV.XVII.6, p. 679; III.X.13, p. 497. See also III.XI.5, p. 510.
[135] Ibid., III.VI.33, p. 461.

The battle line that separated Locke from the schoolmen was that which had separated theologians since the time of William of Ockham, with the realists on the one side and the nominalists on the other. The nominalists rejected the realists' claim that true being lay beyond the sensible physical world, that there was a metaphysical realm in which the real or universal essences of particular things were to be found. In that realm, the true or substantial forms of things – such as man, rose, dog – were said to have real existence of which the visible, physical world was but a pale and inadequate reflection. To the nominalists or voluntarists, such an understanding of the world was mistaken mysticism. As Ockham had bluntly put it, "no universal is existent in any way whatsoever outside the mind of the knower."[136] As Locke would say, there was nothing accessible to man but the "little world of his own understanding."[137] Anything else was, strictly speaking, incomprehensible.

To Locke's way of thinking, the word "substance" was a "doubtful... term" that had come to suffer a most "promiscuous" use in the schools. It was used to try to explain everything from "the infinite incomprehensible God, to finite spirit, to body." This promiscuity was what Locke meant when he repeatedly charged the schools with generating "jargon" and "insignificant noise" by "taking words for things." At his most generous, Locke was willing to concede when it came to "substance" only that "we have no idea what it is, but only a confused, obscure one of what it does." At his more honest, he argued simply that "whatever exists anywhere at any time excludes all the same kind and is there itself alone"; as a result of that fact, "the real constitution of things... begin and perish with them." "There is nothing like our ideas, existing in the bodies themselves," Locke argued.[138]

It was not hard to understand why so dubious a concept had gained acceptance among the learned; such was the unfortunate human impulse to explain all, and to refuse, as Locke put it, to sit down quietly in ignorance about things we simply cannot know. There is something inherently unsatisfying in seeing the world as nothing more than simple ideas spawned by the senses. As Locke pointed out, "not imagining how these simple ideas can subsist by themselves, we accustom ourselves to suppose some substratum wherein they do subsist, and from which they do result which therefore we call substance." The lust to explain the "cause of their union" when we observe the simple ideas in the sensible world about us, led men to believe that "ideas of particular sorts of substances... flow from the particular

---

[136] As quoted in David Knowles, *The Evolution of Medieval Thought*, ed. D. E. Luscombe and C. N. L. Brooke (2nd. ed.; London: Longman, 1988), p. 293. The parallel to Locke's description of natural law is striking; see *Second Treatise*, 376: 136.

[137] *Essay*, II.II.2, p. 120.

[138] Ibid., II.XIII.18, p. 74; II.XIII.19, p. 175; II.XXVII.1, p. 328; III.III.19, p. 419; II.VIII.15, p. 137.

internal constitution, or unknown essence of that substance." Given that we can "have no knowledge...of the internal constitution, and nature of things, being destitute of faculties to attain it," the result of the efforts to know substances and universal essences caused men to stop short of true knowledge. This was the greatest and least forgiveable sin of the schoolmen. For when it comes to the real essences or hidden constitutions of things, Locke was guided by a simple, demonstrable truth: "men are ignorant and know them not."[139]

In place of the idea of real essences defining the world, Locke argued that "substances are determined into sorts or species...by the nominal essence." This nominal essence is nothing more than the collection of "sensible ideas" that man creates in his mind by the observation of the world around him and to which he affixes a name. The world in which man finds himself is a world of particular things: "*General* and *Universal* belong not to the real existence of things; but are the inventions and creatures of the understanding, made by it for its own use, and concerns only signs, whether words or ideas." The reason is simply that man can come to know the existence of things only by experience, and "it is beyond the power of human capacity to frame and retain distinct ideas of all the particular things we meet with." The creation of such general terms is thus "the effect...of reason and necessity."[140]

The fact is, nature does not provide the order of the universe man perceives; such order as is to be found is the result of human "contrivance." That is not to say that nature is nothing but the creation of man's imagination; the nominal essences man creates to explain and order the world must be derived from those things actually in the world and not arbitrarily put together by the understanding. Yet, "if we suppose...that things existing are distinguished by nature into species, by real essences, according as we distinguish them into species by names, we shall be liable to great mistakes." To do so would be to "confound truth and introduce uncertainty into all general propositions, that can be made about them."[141] One can do no better than to remember that "the abstract idea for which the name stands, and the essence of the species, is one and the same."[142] Put a bit more strongly, "the essences...of things are nothing else but abstract ideas."[143]

Locke's understanding that substance and universality are merely names is the foundation on which he builds his theory of knowledge and ultimately his notion of consent as the foundation of political society. The primary

[139] Ibid., II.XXIII.1, p. 295; II.XXIII.6, p. 298; II.XXIII.3, p. 296; II.XXIII.32, p. 313; II.XXXI.6, p. 378. See also III.VI.9, p. 444. See also *Leviathan*, pp. 81–84.

[140] Ibid., III.VI.7, p. 443; III.VI.9, p. 444; III.III.11, p. 414; IV.III.31, p. 562; III.III.2, p. 409; III.III.1, p. 409. See also III.III.6, pp. 410–11; and II.XI.9, p. 159.

[141] Ibid., IV.IV.14, p. 570; III.VI.28, p. 455; III.VI.13, p. 448; IV.VI.4, p. 581.

[142] Ibid., III.III.12, p. 415. "[H]e that thinks general names and notions are anything else...will, I fear, be at a loss where to find them." Ibid., III.III.9, p. 412.

[143] Ibid., III.III.12, p. 414.

fact of human existence is that "in particulars our knowledge begins, and so spreads itself, by degrees, to generals." And it is in that movement from the sensible world of particular things to the world of abstract generalisations drawn from those particulars that man comes to have certain knowledge of the world about him, for such certainty is to be found only in the realm of ideas. Yet, Locke repeatedly insists, it must ever be remembered that "our knowledge goes not beyond particulars."[144] It is in the definition of those ideas and the language used to make those ideas known to those around him that man finds the foundation of civil society. It is a world made not from on high, but from below, built not by divine guidance but by human reason. In the end, it is a world in which man, by his nature, is the necessary measure of all things.[145]

For Locke, knowing begins with sensation, sensation that is "produced in us, only by different degrees and modes of motion in our animal spirits, variously agitated by external objects." Human understanding thus depends upon two things, sensation and reflection: "External material things, as the objects of sensation; and the operations of our own minds within, as the objects of reflection, are... the only originals from whence all our ideas take their beginning." These powers of sense and reflection alone "are the windows by which light is let into this dark room." In Locke's mechanistic view, thinking was to the soul what motion was to the body, "not its essence, but one of its operations." The implications, especially the moral implications, of what men can know were striking. "All those sublime thoughts, which tower above the clouds, and reach as high as Heaven itself," Locke argued, "take their rise and footing there: In all that great extent wherein the mind wanders, in those remote speculations, it may seem to be elevated with, it stirs not one jot beyond those ideas, which sense and reflection have offered for its consideration."[146]

Knowing begins with the simple act of perceiving, "the first operation of all our intellectual faculties, and the inlet of all knowledge into our minds." Next to the initial act of perception, the memory is the most essential step in building the understanding, for it is "the storehouse of our ideas." From this storehouse, man is able to call up perceptions he has had before, with the added perception that he, indeed, has had those perceptions before. Without the memory, knowledge would not be possible.[147]

From his perception of the world about him, man sorts, names, and stores his perceptions. As we have seen, because all reality is a collection of particulars, and since man lacks the faculties to name and record each and every particular thing he encounters, he depends on his power of abstraction

---

[144] Ibid., IV.VII.11, p. 603; IV.VII.16, p. 591.
[145] Ibid., IV.III.29, p. 560.
[146] Ibid., II.VIII.4, p. 133; II.I.4, p. 105; II.XI.17, pp. 162–163; II.I.10, p. 108; II.I.25, p. 118.
[147] Ibid., II.XI.15, p. 149; II.X.2, p. 150; II.X.8, p. 153.

to give order to the world by creating general ideas to which he affixes general names. This power alone "is that which puts perfect distinction betwixt man and the brutes." By sense and reflection and memory, man is made capable of society: "Those who cannot distinguish, compare, and abstract, would hardly be able to understand, and make use of language, or judge, or reason to any tolerable degree."[148]

Simple ideas are the most basic building blocks of knowledge; these the mind gets directly from sensation.[149] The mind itself cannot produce within it any simple idea it has not received from sensation; nor can divine revelation itself impart such ideas. All simple ideas come from without, but all complex ones come from within. By its own powers, the mind can "put together those ideas it has, and make new complex ones, which it never received so united." In this constructive ability, "the mind has great power in varying and multiplying the objects of its thoughts, infinitely beyond what sensation or reflection furnished it with."[150] Yet the foundation remains securely those basic inlets of sense and reflection.[151]

All great and abstract thoughts – from time to space to infinity to God to natural law – are the products of the inward motions of the mind based on information received from the senses about the world in which man moves. The mind itself is nothing more than "white paper, void of all characters, without any ideas."[152] Beyond the simple ideas lie the paths to more elevated notions to be held by the mind, these being the various complex ideas of modes, substances, and relations. Of these, the most significant is that of mixed modes, the realm in which the foundations of moral ideas are to be found. Whereas mens's ideas of substances, even though lacking any notion of substantial form, are still rooted in things that actually exist in nature, mixed modes are not so encumbered; rather, they are "scattered and independent ideas" that the mind puts together in creative ways. The essence of mixed modes is an inherent arbitrariness. The combination of ideas man assembles in his mind simply "does not always exist together in nature." Every man has complete liberty in forming these notions, so much

[148] Ibid., II.XI.10, p. 159; II.XI.12, p. 160.

[149] "Simple ideas... are only to be got by those impressions objects themselves make on our minds, by the proper inlets appointed to each sort." III.IV.11, p. 424.

[150] Ibid., II.XII.3, p. 164; II.XII.2, p. 164.

[151] "[W]e shall find, if we warily observe the originals of our notions, that even the most abstruse ideas, how remote soever they may seem from sense, or from any operation of our own minds, are yet only such, as the understanding frames to itself, by repeating and joining together ideas, that it had either from objects of sense, or from its own operations about them: so that those even large and abstract ideas are derived from sensation or reflection, being no other than what the mind, by the ordinary use of its own faculties, employed about ideas received from the objects of sense, or from the operations it observes in itself about them, may and does attain unto." Ibid., II.XII.8, p. 166.

[152] Ibid., II.I.2, p. 104.

so that one man's idea of justice is often quite different from another's.[153] These complex ideas of mixed modes and moral ideas have "no other reality but what they have in the minds of men."[154] Locke put it starkly: "The names . . . of mixed modes stand for ideas perfectly arbitrary."[155]

The mind sets about to put together into mixed modes such ideas as it finds "convenient." All that keeps these various and disparate ideas together, in the case of mixed modes as well as substances, is the name given to the collection; it is "the knot that ties them fast together." Because these collections of ideas to which various names are given exist only in name and not in nature, there is a far greater tendency for their significations to be doubtful. While in the case of substances, nature stands as a means for men to "rectify and adjust" the significations given them, this is not so in the case of mixed modes. Not even such words as "murder" and "sacrilege," Locke insists, can be known from the things themselves; it is all a matter of human definition. As a result, moral words are "little more than bare sounds" in the mouths of most men, and hence beset by "obscure and confused signification."[156]

In spite of all this confusion, however, Locke insists that "morality is capable of demonstration as well as mathematicks" insofar as, being made by the mind of man, "the precise and real essence of things moral words stand for may be perfectly known."[157] Being man-made, and meaning nothing more than what men would arbitrarily have them mean, moral words admit of such definition that "their meaning may be known certainly, and without leaving any room for contest about it."[158] Because our moral ideas are original in and of themselves, they are archetypes, and hence, once defined, cannot be wrong or false. Definitions, carefully drawn, bridge the gap of obscurity and confusion between the word and the idea for which it stands. "Moral truth . . . is speaking things according to the persuasion of our own minds, though the proposition we speak agree not to the reality of things."[159]

Man's fate when it comes to having true knowledge of things is a precarious one. Not only does he totter dangerously close to an "abyss of darkness" and ignorance, he constantly confronts the fact that he can know nothing about the existence of any thing except as his senses inform him. The fewer

---

[153] Ibid., II.XXII.1, p. 288; II.XXII.4, p. 289; II.XXX.3, p. 373.

[154] Ibid., II.XXX.4, p. 373. This is the basis of Locke's assertion in the *Second Treatise* that natural law "exists only in the minds of men."

[155] *Essay.*, III.IV.17, p. 428.

[156] Ibid., III.V.10, p. 434; III.IX.7, p. 478; III.IX.7, p. 478; III.IX.9, p. 480.

[157] Ibid., III.XI.16, p. 516.

[158] Ibid., III.XI.17, p. 517. "Because an artificial thing being a production of man, which the artificer design'd, and therefore well knows the idea of, the name of it is supposed to stand for no other idea, nor to import any other essence, than what is certainly to be known, and easy enough to be apprehended." III.VI.40, p. 464.

[159] Ibid., IV.VI.11, p. 578.

the senses, the weaker the faculties a man might have; the farther removed he will ultimately be from his more far-sighted and quick-witted fellows; the less distinct and more confused will be his ideas. Men are not equal in all respects. Moreover, each man's faculties in the pursuit of truth are ever beset by "vices, passions, and domineering interest." True and certain knowledge is difficult to obtain. Yet, Locke insists, morality is the "proper science and business of mankind," and it is that which allows "enquiries of rational men after real improvements."[160] Given the facts of nature, however, the best man can hope for is to fashion his affairs and his conduct based on "probable truth."[161] The faculty "which God has given man to supply the want of clear and certain knowledge, in cases where that cannot be had is judgment."[162]

The basic premise of Locke's theory of the understanding is that "our knowledge cannot exceed our ideas"; knowledge consists in "nothing but the perception of the connexion and agreement, or disagreement and repugnancy of any of our ideas." Such agreement is to be found by proofs, intervening ideas that connect two otherwise separate ideas or propositions. Indeed, for Locke, "truth properly belongs only to propositions." The steps by which these proofs are fashioned and whereby they connect the propositions are carried out by man's reasoning faculty. Since the truth of most propositions cannot be known with absolute certainty, it is left to the judgment to presume the certain agreement or disagreement of such ideas thus put together.[163]

This power of reason is the only "light in the understanding": "To talk of any other light . . . is to put ourselves in the dark, or in the power of the prince of darkness, and by our own consent, to give ourselves up to delusion to believe a lie." So fundamental is the power of reason to reach judgments about probable truths by which men can govern their lives and conduct that for Locke error is a mistake of the judgment, not of our knowledge, by "giving assent to that, which is not true." Truth, for Locke, can come only from "proofs and argument." Judgment is thus nothing more than "determining on which sides the odds lie." Ultimately, "moral principles require reasoning and discourse and some exercise of the mind to discover the certainty of their truth."[164]

---

[160] Ibid., IV.III.22, p. 553; IV.III.24, p. 535; IV.XI.13, p. 638; IV.III.18, p. 549; IV.XII.11, p. 646; IV.XII.12, p. 647.

[161] Ibid., IV.XVI.2, p. 658. "He that in ordinary affairs of life would admit of nothing but direct plain demonstration, would be sure of nothing, in this world, but of perishing quickly." IV.XI.10, p. 636.

[162] Ibid., IV.XIV.3, p. 653.

[163] Ibid., IV.XII.14, p. 648; and IV.III.1, p. 538; IV.I.2, p. 525; IV.V.2, p. 574; IV.XIV.3, p. 653; IV.XIV.4, p. 653; IV.XV.2, p. 655. See also IV.VIII.3, p. 611; and IV.VII.11, p. 598.

[164] Ibid., IV.XIX.13, p. 703; IV.XX.1, p. 706; IV.XVII.22, p. 687; II.XXI.67, p. 278; I.III.1, p. 66.

Man is possessed of two faculties, reason and will, and ultimately, it is reason that controls and directs the will. It does this by discovering the probable truths by which men must order their conduct.[165] It is nothing less than man's "duty as a rational creature . . . to search and follow the clearer evidence and greater probablity." The fact is, "the greatest part of knowledge depends upon deductions and intermediate ideas"; but "the greatest part of our ideas are such that we cannot discern their agreement or disagreement, by an intermediate comparing them," and thus "we have need of reasoning, and must by discourse and inference, make our discoveries." It is for this reason that Locke deemed reason to be of necessity "our last judge and guide in everything."[166]

The power of reason is that "it finds out, and . . . so orders the intermediate *ideas*, as to discover what connection there is in each link of the chain, whereby the extremes are held together."[167] It is by this process, and this process alone, that man can come to know that "portion of truth" that lies within the reach of his natural faculties. But simply relying on the powers of reasoning cannot assure truth; there are many times when reason may fail us.[168] "Reason is far from clearing the difficulties which the building upon false foundations brings a man into, that if he will pursue it, it entangles him the more and engages him deeper in perplexities."[169] This extends even to divine revelation and matters of faith.

"*Faith*," Locke argues, as distinguished from reason, "is the assent to any proposition, not thus made out by the deduction of reason; but upon the credit of the proposer, as coming from GOD, in some extraordinary way of communication. This way of discovering truths to men we call revelation." Yet there is an obligation to be sure that what we perceive to be a divine revelation is indeed so, and that "we understand it right." As Locke's argument about faith proceeds, it becomes increasingly clear that his notion of divine revelation is a far cry from the traditional one; by the end of his effort, faith is dependent upon reason. "Faith can never convince us of any thing that contradicts our knowledge." It has no authority "against the plain and clear dictates of reason."[170] To say, as Locke insists, that of an assumed divine revelation "reason must judge" is to reduce the possibility of divine

---

[165] See the *First Treatise*: "The imagination is always restless and suggests variety of thoughts, and the will, reason being laid aside, is ready for every extravagant project." 200: 58.

[166] Ibid., IV.XVII.24, p. 688; IV.XVII.2, p. 669; IV.XVII.5, pp. 683–684; IV.XIX.14, p. 704. As Locke had put it in his *Questions Concerning the Law of Nature*, human reason is but the "faculty for making arguments." V: 157. See also *Essay* IV.XVIII.2, p. 689; IV.XVII.2, pp. 668–669; and IV.XVII. 3, p. 669.

[167] Ibid., IV.XVII.2, pp. 668–669. See also IV.XVII.4, p. 673; and IV.XVII.3, p. 669.

[168] Ibid., IV.XIX.4, p. 698; IV.XVII.9, p. 687.

[169] Ibid., IV.XVII.12, pp. 682–683.

[170] Ibid., IV.XVIII.2, p. 689; IV.XVI.14, p. 667; IV.XVIII.5, p. 692; IV.XVIII.6, p. 694. See also IV.XVII.8, pp. 694–695.

revelation to the level of sensation and reflection, the only way man can come to have simple ideas, and hence complex and elevated ideas. Such a firm rationalist view, Locke argues, is nothing less than the ultimate praise of God, for to assume revelation more certain than knowledge would be to

overturn all the principles and foundations of knowledge he has given us; render all our faculties useless; wholly destroy the most excellent part of his workmanship, our understanding; and put a man in a condition, wherein he will have less light, less conduct than the beast that perisheth. For if the mind of man can never have a clearer (and, perhaps, not so clear) evidence of any thing to be a divine revelation, as it has of the principles of its own reason, it can never have a ground to quit the clear evidence of its reason, to give place to a proposition, whose revelation has not a greater evidence, than those principles have.[171]

This applies with equal force to alleged examples of truths being revealed to others that come to be conveyed down to them by "the tradition of writings, or word of mouth."[172] As he says elsewhere, the reason is that "everyone's philosophy regulates everyone's interpretation of the word of God."[173]

Locke's purpose in subjecting faith to the scrutiny of reason is to establish more clearly than traditionally had been the case the boundaries between faith and reason. The failure properly to observe that line had been "the cause, if not of great disorders, yet at least of great disputes, and perhaps mistakes in the world." As a result, "religion which should most distinguish us from the beasts, and ought most peculiarly to elevate us, as rational creatures, above the brutes, is that wherein men often appear most irrational, and more senseless than beasts themselves." The reason for this perversion of faith is that some men are inclined to assume that their opinions are "under the peculiar guidance of Heaven" and to flatter themselves that they enjoy "an immediate intercourse with the Deity, and frequent communications from the divine spirit."[174] It is only by subjecting allegedly divine revelations to reason that one can separate the true from the false. When it comes to proving whether the inspiration one might feel is indeed a "light or motion from Heaven," there is "nothing can do that but the written word of GOD without us, or that standard of reason which is common to us with all men."[175] And in the end, it is reason more than anything else that will lead men to truth.

[171] Ibid., IV.XVIII.5, pp. 692–693.
[172] Ibid., IV.XVIII.6, p. 693.
[173] John Locke, *An Essay for the Understanding of St. Paul's Epistles, by Consulting St. Paul Himself*, in *Works of John Locke*, III: 100–112, p. 111 (hereinafter cited as *Essay on St. Paul*). See also *Essay*, III.IX.23, pp. 489–490.
[174] *Essay*, IV.XVIII.1, p. 688; IV.XVIII.11, p. 696; IV.XIX.5, p. 699. See also IV.XIX.14, p. 704.
[175] Ibid., IV.XIX.16, p. 706.

B. *The Foundations of Liberty*

While there is no room for innate ideas in Locke's political philosophy, he was willing to grant that there were certain impulses or tendencies in man by nature. It was a very Hobbesian vision of man that saw both "a desire of happiness" as well as "an aversion to misery" as nothing less than "innate practical principles" that "constantly . . . operate and influence all our actions without ceasing." While man's faculty of reasoning is bereft of any innate guidance, his only other faculty, the will, is not. These "natural tendencies imprinted on the minds of men . . . never cease to be the constant springs and motives of all our actions, to which, we perpetually feel them strongly impelling us."[176]

The innate practical principles that so constantly impel men to actions of one sort or another, are all moved in the first instance by the most basic of impulses, man's "strong desire of self-preservation."[177] It is toward this end, and this end alone, that God gave men both sense and reason and thus elevated him over all the lower beasts. This native instinct is ultimately rooted in man's sense of self and personal identity, in his vigorous appreciation of his individuality.[178] The ultimate motive force of all human endeavor is this most basic desire for preservation. "The great business of the senses being to make us take notice of what hurts or advantages the body." Self-interest is the ultimate foundation of morality.[179]

It is by reflection on this natural impulse to preserve himself that man comes to fashion his notions of good and evil. These notions are not those towering, abstruse, and abstract notions of antiquity reflecting some transcendent realm of natural right; rather, they are the more earthly reflections of man's sense of pleasure and pain, those indicators that point him toward his preservation and away from annihilation. "Things are good or evil," Locke argues, "only in reference to pleasure or pain"; these "are the hinges on which our passions turn." Locke represents this calculus of pleasure and pain by the idea of "uneasiness." Uneasiness results from "the very first instances of sense and perception [that] there are some things, that are grateful, and some things unwelcome to them." The power of these perceptions in man is without equal: "The motive to change is always some uneasiness: nothing setting us upon the change of state, or upon any new action but some uneasiness."[180]

---

[176] Ibid., I.III.3, p. 67.

[177] *First Treatise*, 223: 86.

[178] "This very intelligent being, sensible of happiness and misery, must grant, that there is something that is himself, that he is concerned for, and would have happy; that this self has existed in a continued duration more than one instant, and therefore 'tis possible may exist, as it has done, months and years to come, without any certain bounds to be set to its duration; and may be the same self, by the same consciousness, continued on for the future." *Essay*, II.XXVII.25, p. 345.

[179] Ibid., II.X.3, p. 150. See also II.XXVII.17, p. 341; and II.XXVII.18, pp. 341–342.

[180] Ibid., II.XX.2–3, p. 229; I.III.3, p. 67; II.XXI.29, p. 249.

This "spur to industry," this sense of uneasiness or dissatisfaction, "alone operates on the will, and determines its choice." It is the engine that drives men in their "pursuit of... happiness" and by which men are "conducted... to different ends." While the notion of some "absent good" is capable of moving man toward its realization, this attractive sense of pleasure is nothing when compared to the repellent sense of pain in man's calculations. Says Locke, "every little trouble moves us, and sets us at work to get rid of it."[181] By comparison, "absent good does not at any time make a necessary part of our present happiness, nor the absence of it make a part of our misery."[182] The sad fact is that "[p]leasure operates not so strongly on us as pain." When it comes to man's judgment, "that which... determines the choice of our will to the next action will always be the removing of pain... as the first and necessary step toward happiness," because "every less degree of pain... has the nature of a good."[183]

From sense and reflection come the standards of good and evil that man will embrace: "[W]hat has an aptness to produce pleasure in us, is what we call good, and what is apt to produce pain in us, we call evil... wherein consists our happiness and misery." Reason gives man the "opportunity to examine, view and judge of the good or evil of what we are going to do." What distinguishes human "senses and reason" from the "sense and instinct" of the lower animals is man's ability to hold back, to suspend the action of the will until he has had an opportunity for "a fair examination" of the choices confronting him; such deliberation and determination is the "very end of our freedom."[184] To the degree that man departs from such an exercise of his free will he moves ever closer to a state of "misery and slavery."[185] Yet there is a deeper obligation on man by nature, and that is to resist the inducements of momentary gratifications of the appetite in favor of "true happiness": "[T]he highest perfection of intellectual nature, lies in a careful and constant pursuit of true and solid happiness; so the care of ourselves, that we mistake not imaginary for real happiness, is the necessary foundation of our liberty."[186] It is by pleasure and pain, and the choices

---

[181] Ibid., II.XXI.36, p. 254; II.XX.6, p. 230; II.XXI.36, p. 254; II.XXI.47, p. 264; II.XXI.33, p. 252; II.XXI.42, p. 259; II.XXI.44, p. 260.

[182] Ibid., II.XXI.44, p. 260. "Objects, near our view, are apt to be thought greater, than those of a larger size that are more remote: And so it is with pleasures and pains, the present is apt to carry it, and those at a distance have the disadvantage of the comparison." II.XXI.63, p. 275.

[183] Ibid., II.XX.14, p. 232; II.XXI.36, p. 254; II.XXI.44, p. 259.

[184] Ibid., II.XXI.42, p. 259; II.XXI.47, p. 263; II.XXI.47, p. 264; II.XXI.48, p. 264. "[E]very man is put under a necessity by his constitution, as an intelligent being, to be determined in willing by his own thought and judgment, what is best for him to do: else he would be under the determination of some other than himself, which is the want of liberty." Ibid., II.XXI.48, p. 264.

[185] Ibid., II.XXI.48, p. 264.

[186] Ibid., II.XXI.51, p. 266. See also II.XXI.52, p. 267.

freely made by men in pursuit of their true happiness, that man can chart the
knowable part of the otherwise incomprehensible universe. By the existence
of human reason, rooted as it is in sense and reflection, God has given
mankind "faculties sufficient to direct him in the way he should take" to
fulfill the ends of his nature.[187]

Locke's great concern to come to grips with the mechanics of the human
understanding was an inherently political one. His objective was to fashion
an understanding of liberty, where it originates and how best to secure
it. "Without liberty," Locke wrote, "the understanding would be of no
purpose: And without understanding, liberty (if it could be) would signify
nothing." For it is by the understanding that men exercise their wills, and
hence act. "So far as a man has the power to think, or not to think, to move
or not to move, according to his preference or direction of his own mind, so
far is a man free." In the absence of such liberty, man confronts necessity, for
"wherever thought is wholly wanting, or power to act or forbear according
to the direction of thought, there necessity takes place." The essence of
liberty, for Locke, was freedom of the mind: "liberty cannot be where there
is no thought, no volition, no will; but there may be thoughts, there may
be will, there may be volition, where there is no liberty." That is to say,
the will is always free, although man may not always be: "[T]he question is
not proper whether the will be free, but whether a man be free." Ultimately
liberty, properly understood, consists "in a power to act, or to forbear from
acting, and in that only."[188]

The true importance of liberty is to allow man to avoid "blind precipi-
tancy": "The principal exercise of freedom is to stand still, open the eyes,
look about, and take a view of the consequences of what we are going to
do." Since the purpose of the will is to pursue pleasure and avoid pain, and
thereby to seek the good and avoid the evil, its very existence presupposes
"knowledge to guide the choice." This knowledge, over time and through
experience, eventuates in man determining what Locke calls moral relations, guides to man's judgment based on past experience as to what is more
likely to conduce to his freedom and happiness, and what to a condition
of slavery and misery. These judgments come to be posited as rules against
which behavior is to be judged as good or evil, that is, as leading to pleasure
or pain. These are the result of the mind by its free choice pulling otherwise disparate ideas together into various complex, moral ideas. Man's true

---

[187] Ibid., IV.XX.3, p. 707. See also IV.XI.8, pp. 634–635.
[188] Ibid., II.XXI.67, p. 278; II.XXI.8, p. 237; II.XXI.13, p. 240; II.XXI.8, p. 238; II.XXI.21,
p. 244; II.XXI.24, p. 246. As Locke explained: "[A] man that sits still, is said to be at
liberty, because he can walk if he wills it. A man that walks is at liberty also, not because
he walks or moves; but because he can stand still if he wills it. But if a man sitting still
has not a power to remove himself, he is not at liberty; so likewise a man falling down
a precipice, though in motion, is not at liberty, because he cannot stop that motion, if he
would." II.XXI.24, p. 246.

freedom is this power to "make any complex ideas of mixed modes, by no other pattern, but by his own thoughts"; this is the same liberty that Adam had in the beginning, and "the same have all men ever since had."[189] There is no restriction on any man to form such complex moral rules, name them, and act by them. And therein lies the dilemma.

Based as such rules are on man's judgment of happiness, there will likely be a great diversity of such rules, because "the same thing is not good to everyman alike."[190] That which is common to all men, the desire for happiness, paradoxically leads to different ends. And there is no inherent moral problem with this; it is simply a matter of fact, for although men may choose different things, yet they all choose right insofar as they guide their individual wills toward that which is their true happiness.[191] There is, by nature, no *summum bonum*: "We have our understandings no less different than our palates."[192] Politically, this is a most significant fact for Locke, for politics is more siginficant than palates: "[T]here is nothing more common than contrariety of opinions; nothing more obvious, than that one man wholly disbelieves what another only doubts of; and a third steadfastly believes, and firmly adheres to."[193] Locke knew, as Hobbes had taught, that unless there is something that transcends each individual's natural right to calculate his happiness as he sees fit, and to act upon that calculation, there will not be peace for a moment. Life will be a war of all against all, each forming his own conception of right and justice, and seeking to make all others conform to it. Thus must there be rules of man's own making that give political order to what would otherwise be moral chaos. This is what Locke meant when he wrote in the *First Tract on Government* that complete liberty is complete bondage.[194]

Men are moved to fashion rules to which each will be obligated; it will be by such rules, and such rules alone, that men can come to enjoy a consensual measure of right and wrong, justice and injustice. The price for such rules is a structuring of individual liberty, not to diminish it but to secure it: "[N]o government allows absolute liberty: the idea of government being the establishment of society upon certain rules or laws, which require conformity to them; and the idea of absolute liberty being for anyone to do whatever he pleases." Locke was, he insisted, "as certain of the truth of this proposition,

---

[189] Ibid., II.XXI.67, p. 279; II.XXI.52, p. 267; III.VI.51, p. 470. See also *Second Treatise*, 323: 57.

[190] Essay, II.XXI.54, p. 268. "Happiness consists in having those things which produce the greatest pleasure; and in the absence of those which cause any disturbance, any pain. Now these to different men are very different things." II.XXI.55, p. 269.

[191] Ibid., II.XXI.55, p. 270.

[192] Ibid., "Epistle to the Reader," p. 8.

[193] Ibid., IV.XX.1, p. 706.

[194] *First Tract*, p. 120.

as of any in mathematicks."[195] The foundation of such rules or laws becomes the critical measure of good political order because all calculations of what is morally "good and evil" can only be "conformity or disagreement of our voluntary actions to some law, whereby good and evil is drawn on us, from the will and power of the law-maker."[196] It is only in civil society, a society of law, that one can reasonably speak of justice and injustice; for only in civil society have men tempered their complete liberty in order to secure their true liberty and thus their true and solid happiness.

The mechanics of consent begin with the defects of human understanding. Man finds himself in a position where "his thoughts are but of yesterday, and he knows not what tomorrow will bring." Thus in attempting to fashion rules for the future he is limited merely to calculations of probabilities. "Probability," Locke argued, "then being to supply the defect of our knowledge, and to guide us where that fails, is always conversant about propositions, whereof we have no certainty, but only some inducements to receive them as true." This "necessity of believing without knowledge," as Locke termed it, is the essence of political life; all is calculation, every judgment an effort to hedge one's bets against uncertainty. The foundation for coming to grasp such probable truths is twofold, according to Locke. The first is "the conformity of anything with our own knowledge, observation, and experience"; the second is "the testimony of others, vouching their observation and experience."[197] Social order rests, and can only rest, upon probability.[198]

It is in this uncertainty that Locke roots his argument for toleration of opinions with which one might disagree. The various opinions of right and wrong, good and evil, that men come to hold, shaped as the are by each man's calculation of his greatest happiness and how to attain it, are, at the most fundamental level, irreconcilable; they can be drawn together only as a matter of agreement to allow disagreement. Where is the man, Locke asked, "that has uncontestable evidence of the truth of all that he holds, or of the falshood of all he condemns; or can say, that he has examined, to the

---

[195] *Essay*, IV.III.18, p. 550. This was a theme that saturated Locke's works. In the *Second Tract on Government* he argued that "a commonwealth without human laws never has existed and never could." pp. 230–231. He returned to the theme in the *Second Treatise*: "[A] government without laws is, I suppose, a mystery in politicks, unconceivable to humane capacity, and inconsistent with humane society." 429: 219. He made a more expansive argument, reaching beyond civil society simply, in the *Letter on Toleration*: "[N]o society can hold together, however free it may be, or for however slight a purpose it may be formed, whether it be a society of men of letters for philosophy, or merchants for commerce, or men of leisure for mutual conversation and intercourse, but it will at once dissolve and perish, if it is entirely without laws." p. 73.

[196] *Essay*, II.XXVIII.5, p. 351.

[197] Ibid., II.XV.12, p. 204; IV.XV.4, pp. 655–666; IV.XVI.4, p. 660; IV.XV.4, p. 656.

[198] As Locke put it: "The grounds of probablity . . . are the foundations on which our assent is built." Ibid., IV.XVI.1, p. 657.

bottom, all his own or other men's opinions?"¹⁹⁹ In light of this fact, Locke sought to construct a common ground of mutual toleration in which men could "maintain peace" amid a great "diversity of opinions." Rather than "imposing on others," Locke urged a more politically salutary tack in which men are well advised "to commiserate [their] mutual ignorance" and give to each other's beliefs the benefit of the doubt.²⁰⁰

This is not to say that all ideas men may hold are simply equal. Some ideas will be intrinsically better than others in that they come closer to certain knowledge by the power of reasoning of one person that is stronger than that of others. This is a fact that "no body, who has ever had any conversation with his neighbors, will question."²⁰¹ The disparity of ideas reflects the very differences one sees in men themselves; and those differences can be great indeed.²⁰² The difficulty arises because, while equality does not mean all ideas are of equal value when objectively considered, it does mean that they are all politically equal. Men, by nature equal, have complete liberty to fashion their complex ideas of moral things as they like and as they are able; to be denied that freedom, Locke argued, would reduce a man so denied to the status of a slave. The question is how men might, in "gentle and fair ways," reach a consensus as to what ideas of right and wrong merit each man's assent. In Locke's science of politics, these simple facts of human nature point to the necessity of deliberative government.

It is by rational argument, by laying out the proofs that connect various ideas in a chain of reasoning, that men can come to some agreement about the most important ideas. Such agreement demands "diligence, attention, and exactness . . . to form a right judgment, and to proportion the assent to the different evidence and probability of the thing."²⁰³ This foundation of consent is what Locke called the "*Argumentum ad Judicium*," the effort to persuade others of one's views by "proofs drawn from any of the foundations of knowledge or probability." Of the four methods of reasoning with others, this method "alone . . . brings true instruction with it and advances us in our way to knowledge."²⁰⁴ The key to such rational argument and reasoned consent is language, "the great bond that holds society together, and the

---

¹⁹⁹ Ibid., IV.XVI.4, p. 660.

²⁰⁰ Ibid., IV.XVI.4, pp. 459–60; IV.XVI.4, p. 661; IV.XVI.4, p. 660.

²⁰¹ Ibid., IV.XX.5, p. 707.

²⁰² "[T]here is a difference of degrees in men's understandings, apprehensions, and reasonings, to so great a latitude that one may, without doing any injury to mankind, affirm that there is a greater distance between some men and others, in this respect, than between some men and some beasts." Ibid., IV.XX.5, p. 709.

²⁰³ Ibid., IV.XVI.9, p. 663.

²⁰⁴ Ibid., IV.XVII.22, p. 686. The other three methods of reasoning Locke calls *Argumentum ad Verecundiam*, *Argumentum ad Ignorantiam*, and *Argumentum ad Homienem*. IV.XVII.19–22, pp. 685–687.

common conduit whereby the improvements of knowledge are conveyed from one man, and from one generation to another."[205]

C. Language and Law

Locke thought his treatment of language in the third book of the *Essay Concerning Human Understanding* was "new, and a little out of the way"; and, although perhaps a bit lengthy, it was, he believed, essential to address the great harm to society that comes from the abuse of words.[206] This, of course, was the essence of his indictment of the schoolmen; in their hands "all sorts of knowledge, discourse, and conversation" had come to be "pester'd and disordered by the careless and confused use and application of words." The language of the schools, and some pulpits, had been filled "with an abundance of empty unintelligible noise and jargon, especially in moral matters."[207] By encouraging a careful consideration of the importance of language, Locke believed his treatment "shall . . . have done some service to truth, peace, and learning."[208] For the proper use of language was essential to the "comfort and advantage of society."[209] This was the case because without language and the means of communication it afforded, man would be doomed to a radically isolated existence; language alone makes society possible.[210]

Language, as Locke presents it, is completely conventional. There is "no natural connexion . . . between particular articulate sounds and certain ideas"; as a result, there is no "one language amongst all men." It is only by a "voluntary" and "perfectly arbitrary imposition" that a word comes to stand for a particular idea.[211] As a general matter, each man is presumed to possess the liberty of fashioning names as he sees fit for the complex ideas he so arbitrarily puts together. The reality, however, is that men usually come to names already in use, names to which, if they are to be understood, their notions must conform. In most cases, the meanings of words in use are of

---

[205] *Ibid.*, III.XI.1, p. 509.

[206] *Ibid.*, III.V.16, pp. 437–438.

[207] Ibid., III.V.16, p. 438; III.IX.4, p. 492. Locke repeatedly condemned those "philosophers . . . who had learning and subtlety enough . . . to destroy the instruments and means of discourse, conversation, instruction, and society." III.1X.10, p. 495.

[208] Ibid., III.V.16, pp. 437–438. "Would it not be well," Locke asked, "that the use of words were made plain and direct?" III.10.13, p. 497.

[209] Ibid., III.II.1, p. 405.

[210] It is, he argued, the "common tye of society." III.I.1, p. 402.

[211] Ibid., III.II.1, p. 405; III.II.8, p. 408. As Locke further argued: There is a "great store of words in one language, which have not any that answer them in another. Which plainly shews, that those of one country, by their customs and manner of life, have found several occasions to make several complex ideas, and give names to them, which others never collected into specifick ideas. This could not have happened, if these species were the steady workmanship of nature; and not collections made and abstracted by the mind, in order to naming, and for the convenience of communication." III.V.8, pp. 432–433.

primitive origin, more the result of common sense and necessity than of speculative philosophy and scholarly disputations: "[T]he general names, that are in use amongst the several nations of men . . . have for the most part, in all languages, received their birth and signification from ignorant and illiterate people, who sorted and denominated things, by those sensible qualities they found in them, merely to signify them, when absent, to others, whether they had an occasion to mention a sort or a particular thing." This commonsense approach to making sense of the world was, for Locke, greatly superior to the "vain ostentation of sounds" that was blaring from the schools, that "artificial ignorance and learned gibberish." It was, he pointed out, "to the unscholastick statesman, that governments of the world owed their peace, defence, and liberties; and from the illiterate and contemned mechanick (a name of disgrace) that they received the improvements of useful arts." The fact is, "vulgar notions suit vulgar discourses: and both . . . yet serve pretty well the market, and the wake. Merchants and lovers, cooks and tailors, have words wherewithal to dispatch their ordinary affairs." Locke was ever the admirer of "native rustick reason."[212]

From the earliest formation of languages, "common use, by a tacit consent, appropriates certain sounds to certain ideas."[213] This is not an inconvenience, giving as it does a certain stability to civil conversations: "[T]here comes by constant use to be such a connexion between certain sounds, and the ideas they stand for that the names heard almost as readily excite certain ideas, as if the objects themselves, which are apt to produce them, did actually affect the senses."[214] Once "men in society have . . . established a language amongst them, the signification of words are very warily and sparingly to be alter'd." The reason is that once framed, languages are no longer any man's "private possession" but become the "common measure of commerce and communication."[215] That is not to say that the meaning of common words cannot change; but only to insist that it rarely be done and be clearly stated when it does occur.[216]

The great purpose of language, in Locke's view, was simple: "[T]he ends of language in our discourse with others being chiefly these three: first, to make known one man's thoughts or ideas to another; secondly, to do it with as much ease and quickness, as is possible; and thirdly, thereby to convey the knowledge of things. Language is either abused, or deficient, when it fails in any of these three." Words, in Locke's theory, are "the instruments

---

[212] Ibid., III.XI.7, p. 512; III.X.9, p. 495; III.X.9, p. 495; III.XI.10, p. 514; IV.XVII.6, p. 679.

[213] Ibid., III.VI.25, pp. 452–453; III.II.8, p. 408. See also III.VI.28, p. 456.

[214] III.II.6, p. 407. Locke saw that such convenience was subject to abuse, as well. See III.X.22, p. 503.

[215] Ibid., III.VI.51, pp. 470–471; III.XI.11, p. 514. See also III.VI.51, p. 471.

[216] "[C]ommon use, being a very uncertain rule, which reduces itself at last to the ideas of particular men, proves often a very variable standard." III.XI.25, p. 522.

whereby men communicate their conceptions and express to one another these thoughts and imaginations they have within their breasts." Words are sounds that "stand as marks for the ideas within [a man's] own mind, whereby they might be made known to others, and the thoughts of men's minds be conveyed from one to another."[217]

Properly used, words will elicit in the mind of the hearer the same idea that is in the mind of the speaker: "When a man speaks to another, it is that he may be understood; and the end of speech is, that those sounds, as marks, may make known his ideas to the hearer." Thus is it critical that there be a common understanding in the speaker and the hearer that "the same sign stands for the same idea."[218] If there is not, communication will not take place and the words used will be "unintelligible noise." This is no small feat, given that "the very nature of words, makes it almost unavoidable, for many of them to be doubtful and uncertain in their significations." Thus must an effort be made to define the words used in civil discourse as strictly and as clearly as possible; there is an obligation "to ask the meaning of any word, we understand not, from him that uses it." For it is the intention of the user that gives words their power and purpose. On this point, Locke was firm: "Words in their primary or immediate signification, stand for nothing, but the ideas in the mind of him that uses them."[219]

To facilitate communication, "men learn names and use them in talk with others, only that they may be understood: which is then only done, when by use or consent, the sound I make by the organs of speech, excites in another man's mind, who hears it, the idea I apply it to in mine, when I speak it." The arbitrariness of the signification of words demands that due attention be paid to definitions. "Words having naturally no signification," Locke pointed out, "the idea which each stands for must be learned and retained by those who would exchange thoughts, and hold intelligible discourse with others, in any language." Because all words in every language are subject to "obscurity, doubtfulness, or equivocation," those who would seek the truth of things, especially of moral notions, are "obliged to study" how to obviate the inconveniences to which all languages are prone. Ultimately, "a definition is the only way whereby the precise meaning of moral words can be known."[220]

The essence of language, for Locke, is the meaning or intention behind the words used. The power to make articulate sounds or words is "not enough to produce language; for parrots and several other birds, will be taught to make articulate sounds distinct enough, which yet, by no means

[217] Ibid., III.X.23, p. 504; III.II.6, p. 407; III.I.2, p. 402
[218] Ibid., III.II.2, p. 405; III.VI.45, p. 467. See also *Essay*, "Epistle to the Reader," p. 13.
[219] Ibid., IV.VIII.7, p. 614; II.IX.1, p. 476; II.VI.45, pp. 467–468; III.II.2, p. 405.
[220] Ibid., III.III.3, p. 409; III.IX.5, p. 477; III.XI.3, p. 509; III.XI.17, p. 517.

are capable of language."[221] Yet the connection between the sound and the idea is without any standard but that of man's own making; the sounds or words are imitations of nothing real; they are merely what men make them. This looseness becomes especially troubling when it comes to the complex ideas men put together and infuse with moral significance. Such moral ideas "are the creatures of the understanding, rather than the works of nature." This fact is at once the cause of likely confusion and the possibility of complete precision in definition. Although such complex ideas will likely vary from man to man, they admit of common defintion to such a degree as to remove such differences. As it happens, it is in those "matters of the highest concernment," in man's "discourses of relgion, law, and morality" where there is the greatest difficulty and the greatest need.[222]

Having uprooted the traditional conception of innate ideas in which it was believed that moral principles were inscribed on the hearts of men by the hand of God, and having reduced man's understanding to the motions of the physical world on his senses, and having further reduced morality to mere abstract ideas derived from sense and reflection, Locke had obliterated any notion of natural justice. Like all other complex ideas, *justice* was nothing more than a name man chooses to give to a particular set of ideas. The "idea in our minds, which we express by the word *justice*," Locke could write, "may, perhaps, be that, which ought to have another name."[223] The idea of justice, like any other moral word, is purely arbitrary, and likely to differ from place to place and over time.[224] The only standard by which true and false ideas of *justice* can be judged is a strikingly conventional one: "When a man is thought to have a false idea of *justice or gratitude or glory* it is for no other reason, but that his agrees not with the ideas which each of those names are the signs of for other men."[225] It is reasonably easy "for men to frame in their minds an idea which shall be the standard to which they will give the name *justice*." For all "they need but know is the combination of ideas that are put together in their own minds"; they need not bother themselves with attempting to inquire into the "abstruse hidden constitution, and various qualities of a thing existing without them."[226] Thus is justice a matter of definition.[227]

---

[221] Ibid., III.I.1, p. 402. See also IV.VIII.7, p. 614. The example of the parrot was also one taken as apt by Hobbes: "[I]f words alone were sufficient, a parrot might be thought as well to know a truth as to speak it." *Elements of Law*, 1.6.3, p. 25.

[222] *Essay*, III.V.12, p. 435; III.IX.22, p. 489.

[223] Ibid., II.XXXII.10, p. 387. "When we say this is . . . *justice*, that cruelty . . . what do we else but rank things under different specifick names, as agreeing to those abstract ideas of which we have made these names the signs." III.III.13, p. 415.

[224] Ibid., III.IX.6, p. 478.

[225] Ibid., II.XXXII.11, p. 387. See also III.V.12, p. 436.

[226] Ibid., III.XI.17, p. 517.

[227] See Ibid., III.XI.18, p. 518

Put most simply, justice is what men choose to make it. The difficulty is that most moral words "are, in most men's mouths, little more than bare sounds." Men generally come to learn the word first and only later grasp the ideas for which such a moral word stands. It is for this reason that such words are only vaguely understood.[228]

Justice is a word in every man's mouth, but most commonly with a very undetermined loose signification: which will always be so, unless a man has in his mind a distinct comprehension of the component parts, that complex idea consists of; and if it be decompounded, must be able to resolve it still on, till he at last comes to the simple ideas that make it up: And unless this be done, a man makes an ill use of the word, let it be *justice*, for example, or any other.[229]

The most likely source of definition for the word *justice* will be laws, rules posited by society to give definition to good and evil and to which men are obligated to conform their actions.[230]

There being no conception of justice prior to men arbitrarily assembling various ideas into a complex notion to which they attribute that name, the only standard of "moral rectitude" is conformity or nonconformity to the rules men fashion as the definitions of moral good and evil.[231] Such conformity to received rules becomes the very essence of justice "whether the rule be true or false."[232] When attached with a sanction for not conforming to such a rule, that rule, as the expression of the will of a recognized lawmaker, becomes a law. Law is distinguished from other moral rules: "[W]e must, whenever we suppose a law, suppose also some reward or punishment annexed to that law."[233] This notion of a sanction to back up moral rules, said Locke, "is the nature of all law, properly so-called."[234] And it is the ability in man to be able "to understand general signs, and to deduce consequences about general ideas," as in the case of knowing the rewards and punishments for conformity or deviation from the law, that makes man, man. Being subject to law by the exercise of reason is what truly distinguishes man from the beasts.[235]

---

[228] Ibid., III.IX.9, p. 480.

[229] Ibid., III.XI.9, p. 513.

[230] Ibid., IV.III.18, p. 550. "He that ... shall lay it down as a principle, that right and wrong, honest and dishonest, are defined only by laws, and not by nature, will have other measures of moral rectitude and pravity than those who take it for granted, that we are under obligations antecedent to all humane constitutions." IV.XII.4, p. 642.

[231] Ibid., II.XXVIII.14, p. 358.

[232] Ibid., II.XXVIII.20, p. 362. In the *Letter on Toleration*, Locke confessed that "laws are not concerned with the truth of opinions, but with the security and safety of the commonwealth and of each man's goods." p. 121.

[233] *Essay*, II.XXVIII.5, p. 351.

[234] Ibid.

[235] "For were there a monkey, or any other creature to be found, that had the use of reason ... he would be a man, how much soever he differ'd in shape from others of that name." III.XI.16, p. 517

It is in his discussion of language and law in the *Essay* that Locke comes closest to showing the Hobbesian roots he first revealed in the *Two Tracts on Government*. Yet, as ever, he is less than simply forthright. In two places in the *Essay* Locke sketches three sorts of law: divine, civil, and philosophical. There are various parallels he follows among them, from their introduction in the first book during the discussion that there are no innate practical principles through their reappearance in the second book during the argument about moral relations. He begins the discussion with a decidedly Hobbesian concept, that it is a matter of morality that men keep their compacts:

That men should keep their compacts, is certainly a great and undeniable rule in morality: but yet, if a Christian, who has the view of happiness and misery in another life, be asked why a man must keep his word, he will give this as a reason: Because God, who has the power of eternal life and death, requires it of us. But if an Hobbist be asked why; he will answer: because the publick requires it, and the *Leviathan* will punish you, if you do not. And if one of the old Heathen philosophers had been asked, he would have answer'd: Because it was dishonest, below the dignity of man, and opposite to virtue, the highest perfection of humane nature, to do otherwise.[236]

When Locke returns to the topic of law in the second book, he there announces the three sorts of law; the scheme follows that about the obligation of compacts, but with a slight variation. "The laws that men generally refer their actions to, to judge of their rectitude, or obliquity, seem to me to be these three. 1. The divine law. 2. The civil law. 3. The law of opinion or reputation, if I may so call it."[237] The divine law is that which comes to man from God, either "by the light of nature or the voice of revelation." It is the law – "the only true touchstone of moral rectitude," Locke calls it – that posits what duties and sins are "likely to procure them happiness or misery, from the hand of the ALMIGHTY." God has the power to enforce this divine law "by rewards and punishments of infinite weight and duration, in another life."[238] And therein lies the problem with divine law: it lacks immediacy. At its best, divine retribution is an absent pain or pleasure. "The penalties that attend the breach of God's laws, some, nay, perhaps, most men seldom seriously reflect on: and amongst those that do, many, whilst they break the law, entertain thoughts of future reconciliation, and making their peace for such breaches."[239] The possibility of forgiveness mitigates the severity of the sanction, and thereby diminishes the fear of that sanction that must lie behind any law.

The law of political societies is another matter; it is the "law no body over-looks." The reason is that its "rewards and punishments" are both real

---

[236] Ibid., I.III.5, p. 68.
[237] Ibid., II.XXVIII.7, p. 352.
[238] Ibid., II.XXVIII.8, p. 352.
[239] Ibid., II.XXVIII.12, p. 357. There is also the problem of how likely it is for ordinary men to be able to grasp the full implications of the infinity of God and his law. See II.XXIX.15, p. 369; II.XXIX.16, p. 371.

and immediate in the "power to take away life, liberty, or goods, from him, who disobeys."[240] But even with this law, men "frequently flatter themselves with the hopes of impunity."[241]

The law most men find it nearly impossible to disobey, because the sanction is so severe, is that of reputation. This law, first denominated as the philosophical law of virtue, has been transformed in the second book into first the "law of opinion or reputation" and then finally into "the law of fashion."[242] The greatest part of mankind, Locke suggests, "govern themselves chiefly, if not solely, by this law of fashion; and so they do that, which keeps them in reputation with their company, little regard the laws of God, or the magistrate."[243] Whereas man is likely to calculate that the probability is good that he can escape the wrath of God, or even the sanction of the Leviathan, he will tread most cautiously when it comes to judging whether he will be able to escape the "punishment or censure . . . of the company he keeps, and would recommend himself to."[244]

When Locke turns to his discussion of language in the third book of the *Essay*, he picks up the tripartite distinction once again, noting that the imperfections and abuses of language cause the greatest difficulty in "discourses of religion, law, and morality."[245] While divine law has remained as religion, and the civil law of political society has remained as law, the notion of the law of fashion or opinion has become "morality." Locke returns to this list once again later in the third book where he argues that only good could come from men using language in a way that would be "plain and direct." It is in this passage that Locke argues that "[l]anguage, which was given us for the improvement of knowledge, and bond of society, should not be employ'd to darken truth, and unsettle peoples rights; to raise mists, and render unintelligible both morality and religion."[246] The significance is that "law" has been dropped, leaving only religion and morality, that is to say, the law of God on the one hand, and that of fashion or opinion on the other. When viewed in the context of his earlier pronouncements on civil law as the most certain in its principles and its punishments, the least likely to be overlooked, one is left to draw the conclusion that ultimately

---

[240] Ibid., II.XXVIII.9, pp. 352–353.

[241] Ibid., II.XXVIII.12, p. 357.

[242] Ibid., II.XXVIII.7, p. 352; II.XXVIII.13, p. 357. See also II.XXVIII.10, p. 353.

[243] Ibid., II.XXVIII.12, p. 357.

[244] Ibid., II.XXVIII.12, p. 357. "He must be of a strange, and unusual constitution, who can content himself, to live in constant disgrace and disrepute with his own particular society. Solitude many men have sought, and been reconciled to: but no body, that has the least thought, or sense of a man about him, can live in society, under the constant dislike, and ill opinion of his familiars, and those he converses with. This is a burthen too heavy for humane sufferance: And he must be made up of irreconcilable contradictions, who can take pleasure in company, and yet be insensible of contempt and disgrace from his companions." Ibid.

[245] Ibid., III.IX.22, p. 489.

[246] Ibid., III.X.13, p. 497.

the greatest security (albeit not perfect) for men's rights lies in the civil law of political societies. For however powerful is the hold of the law of fashion or opinion, it is, at bottom, nothing more than the measure of the majority's self-interest, to which men in all times and in all countries will be "constantly true."[247] As Locke described it, "the desire of esteem, riches, and power, makes man espouse the well endowed opinions in fashion, and then seek arguments either to make good their beauty, or varnish over and cover their deformity."[248] It is a matter of "a secret and tacit consent" that differs from place to place; and, born as it is of everyone's self-interest, it inevitably serves only to elevate the concern for the private over concern for the public interest. It lacks the legitimacy of civil law in that it is the result of passion, not reason, and is in truth prejudice, not knowledge.[249]

Like Hobbes, Locke understood that the security of men's rights depended upon the civil law, promulgated by the commonwealth, and enforced by the common power to which each man had ceded his rightful power of enforcement. This, and this alone, was the way to make law transcend men's mere opinions about justice. Known and standing laws based on consent are a kind of public definition; they give meaning to moral ideas.[250] This comes from the expression of the will of the lawmaker.[251] "Lawmakers," Locke argues, "have often made laws about species of actions, which were only the creatures of their own understanding; beings that had no other existence, but in their own minds."[252] Thus is the intention of the lawmaker the essence of the law. As a result, there is a danger in allowing the law of the commonwealth to be subjected to constant interpretation and commentary.[253]

---

[247] Ibid., II.XXVIII.11, p. 356.

[248] Ibid., IV.III.20, p. 552.

[249] *Conduct of the Understanding*, sec. 10, p. 400. "[T]his great and dangerous imposter prejudice, who dresses up falsehood in the likeness of truth, and so dextrously hoodwinks men's minds, as to keep them in the dark, with a belief that they are more in the light than any that do not see with their eyes." Ibid.

Locke was unstinting in his condemnation of such passions: "Matters that are recommended to our thoughts by any of our passions, take possession of our minds with a kind of authority, and will not be kept out or dislodged, but as if the passion that rules, were, for the time, the sheriff of the place, and came with the posse, the understanding is seized and taken with the object it introduces, as if it, had a real legal right to be alone considered there." *Conduct of the Understanding*, sec. 44, p. 425.

[250] *Essay*, IV.IV.10, pp. 567–568.

[251] "[T]he right of making its laws can belong to none but the society itself; or at least, which comes to the same thing, to those whom the society has authorized by consent." *Letter on Toleration*, p. 73.

[252] *Essay*, III.V.5, p. 430.

[253] See what seem to be Locke's own views as expressed in Article LXXX of the Constitutions of Carolina: "Since multiplicity of comments, as well as of laws, have great inconveniences, and serve only to obscure and perplex; all manner of comments and expositions on any part of these FUNDAMENTAL CONSTITUTIONS, or any part of the common or statute law of Carolina, are absolutely prohibited." As reprinted in John Locke, *Political Writings*, ed. David Wootton (London: Penguin Books, 1993), p. 226.

[I]n the interpretation of laws, whether divine or humane, there is no end; comments beget comments, and explications make new matter for explications: And of limiting, distinguishing, varying the signification of these moral words, there is no end. These ideas of men's making are, by men still having the same power, multiplied *in infinitum*. Many a man, who was pretty well satisfied of the meaning of a text of scripture, or clause in the code, at first reading, has by consulting commentators, quite lost the sense of it, and, by those elucidations, given rise or increase to his doubts, and drawn obscurity upon the place.[254]

By this process of scholastic commentary, glosses on the text and then glosses on the glosses, the shrewd expositor can make the words of the law "signifie either nothing at all, or what he pleases."[255] Such interpretations render obscure and confused what should be clear and certain, the original intention of the law. They undermine law as law. That which applies to the laws of God in Scripture applies with equal force to the laws of man. When reading them there is an obligation on the part of the reader to grasp the meaning intended by the writer. Whoever the author, whatever the law, the reader must endeavor to "understand his terms in the sense he uses them, and not as they are appropriated by each man's particular philosophy to conceptions that never enter'd the mind of the [author]."

We shall...in vain go about to interpret their words by the notions of our philosophy, and the doctrines of men delivered in our schools. This is to explain the Apostles' meaning by what they never thought of whilst they were writing, which is not the way to find their sense in what they delivered, but from our own, and to take up from their writings not what they left there for us, but what we bring along with us in ourselves.[256]

Thus is great "attention, study, sagacity, and reasoning...required to find out the sense of ancient authors."[257] To do otherwise is to abuse the language of the law and, as Locke said, "to darken the understanding, and unsettle peoples rights."

D. The Problem of Custom

The most vexatious political problem in Locke's view was custom, which he held to be "a greater power than nature." Most men most of the time are prisoners of the time and place in which they find themselves. And to the ordinary man it is "reveranvced propositions which are to him the principles on which he bottoms his reasonings, and by which he judgeth of truth and falshood, right and wrong." The power of custom is such that inevitably

---

[254] *Essay*, III.IX.9, p. 480. "What have the greatest part of the comments and dispute, upon the laws of God and man served for, but to make the meaning more doubtful and perplex the sense?"

[255] Ibid., III.X.12, p. 496

[256] *Essay on St. Paul*, p. 111.

[257] *Essay*, III.IX.10, p. 481.

"men worship the idols that have been set up in their minds." The danger is that such "idols" may have been "derived from no better an original that the superstition of a nurse, or the authority of an old woman [and] may, by length of time, and consent of neighbors, grow up to the dignity of principles in religion or morality." Such doctrines, bolstered as they are by the familiar sources of authority, will come "to have the reputation of unquestionable, self-evident, and innate truths." The political danger is that men are usually not content to have their differences of opinion in silence; rather, they "contend... fight, and die in defense of their opinions." The problem is that "contrary tenets, which are firmly believed, [and] confidently asserted" inevitably come to be supported by "great numbers... ready at any time to seal with their blood."[258]

This propensity to confuse for innate what is merely familiar allows the people to be kept in check by "fear of the magistrate's sword, or the neighbor's censure."[259] They cease to question; they cease to wonder; they become prisoners of the "Empire of Habit."[260] And this benefits those who aspire to control or, as Hobbes said, abuse the people:

[I]t was of no small advantage to those who affected to be masters and teachers, to make this the principle of principles, that principles must not be questioned: For having once established this tenet, that there are innate principles, it put their followers upon a necessity of receiving some doctrines as such; which was to take them off from the use of their own reason and judgment, and put them upon believing and taking them upon trust, without farther examination: In which posture of blind credulity, they might be more easily governed by, and made useful to some sort of men, who had the skill and office to principle and guide them. Nor is it a small power it gives one man over another, to have the authority to be the dictator of principles, and teacher of unquestionable truths; and to make a man swallow that for an innate principle, which may serve to his purpose, who teacheth them.[261]

The underlying problem for Locke is that such opinions, however passionately held, are only rarely true and are almost always wrong. "Fashion and the common opinion having settled wrong notions, and education and custom ill habits, the just values of things are misplaced and the palates of men corrupted." So powerful is this tendency that neither God nor the magistrate is equal to its power. In time, these opinions come to be assumed nothing less than natural, so familiar and common are they: "Custom settles habits of thinking in the understanding, as well as determining in the will, and of motions in the body; all which seems to be but trains of motion in the animal spirits, which once set a going continue on in the same steps they

---

[258] Ibid., I.III.25, p. 82; I.III.24, p. 82; I.III.26, p. 83; I.III.22, p. 81; I.III.22, p. 82; I.III.26, p. 83; I.III.27, p. 84.

[259] Ibid., I.IV.8, p. 88.

[260] *Conduct of the Understanding*, sec.40, p. 422.

[261] *Essay*, I.IV.24, pp. 101–102.

have been used to, which by often treading are worn into a smooth path, and the motion in it becomes easy and as it were natural."[262]

Men are blinded to the truths to be found in the world around them by virtue of having sacrificed their native power of reasoning on the altar of authoritative belief bolstered by custom.[263] This leads naturally to a "universal... perverseness." The power to delude ordinary minds by the force of custom and authority is the focus of Locke's assault in the *Essay* for the same reason it was his focus in the *First Treatise*:[264] The deepest problem for Locke is that this is not simply a matter of men occasionally being duped; it is the result of human nature. The dilemma posed by custom to Locke's theory of the understanding, and hence to his theory of civil society, is that most men, most of the time, in most places are not much skilled in the ways of "proofs and arguments" upon which truths, even only probable truths, depend. For most, believing is easier than knowing:

[T]he greatest part of mankind... are given up to labour, and enslaved to the necessity of their mean condition; whose lives are worn out, only in the provisions for living. These men's opportunity of knowledge and enquiry are commonly as narrow as their fortunes; and their understandings are but little instructed, when all their whole time and pains is laid out, to still the croaking of their own bellies, or the cries of their children.

The monotonous drudgery of being is the inescapable lot of most men:

'Tis not to be expected, that a man who drudges on, all his life, in a laborious trade, should be more knowing in the variety of things done in the world, than a pack-horse who is driven constantly forwards and backwards, in a narrow lane, and dirty road, only to market, should be skilled in the geography of the country.

And the political price for such a reality is high:

[A] great part of mankind are, by the natural and unalterable state of things in this world, and the constitution of humane affairs, unavoidably given over to invincible ignorance of those proofs, on which others build, and which are necessary to establish

---

[262] Ibid., II.XXI.69, p. 281; II.XXVIII.12, p. 357; II.XXXIII.6, p. 396.

[263] "That which thus captivates their reasons," Locke noted, "and leads men of sincerity blindfold from common sence, will, when examin'd, be found to be what we are speaking of: some independent ideas, of no alliance to one another, are by education, custom, and the constant din of their party, so coupled in their minds, that they always appear there together, and they can no more separate them in their thoughts, than if they were but one idea, and they operate as if they were so." Ibid., II.XXXIII.18, pp. 400–401.

[264] "This gives sense to jargon, demonstration to absurdities, and consistency to nonsense, and is the foundation of the greatest, I had almost said, of all the errors in the world; or if it does not reach so far, it is at least the most dangerous one, since so far as it obtains, it hinders men from seeing and examining." Ibid., II.XXXIII.18, p. 401. See *First Treatise*, 200–201: 58.

those opinions: the greatest part of men, having much to do to get the means of living, are not in a condition to look after those of learned and laborious enquiries.[265]

Such men – most men – must depend upon others for the proofs and arguments of the truths by which their conduct must be guided; they are forced to assent to "the common received opinions, either of our friends or party; neighborhood, or country." This assent is given "without examination"; the standard of agreement is merely "what they find convenient and in fashion."[266] The problem is that in taking on trust what they should accept only on evidence, most men find themselves in the grip of those who make the arguments, those "strict guards . . . whose interest it is to keep them ignorant, lest, knowing more, they should believe the less in them." Such men "are confined to the narrowness of thought, and enslaved in that which should be the freest part of man, their understandings."

This is generally the case of all those, who live in places where care is taken to propagate truth, without knowledge; where men are forced, at a venture, to be of the religion of the country; and must therefore swallow down opinions, as silly people do empiricks pills, without knowing what they are made of, or how they will work, and have nothing to do, but believe that they will do the cure.[267]

This is political power at its rawest and crudest:

Whilst the parties of men, cram their tenets down all men's throats, whom they can get into their power, without permitting them to examine this truth or falsehood; and will not let truth have fair play in the world, nor men the liberty to search after it; what improvements can be expected of this kind? What greater light can be hoped for in the moral sciences?[268]

The point, of course, is neither enlightenment nor liberty; the point is loyalty and obedience:

[Such men] are resolved to stick to a party, that education or interest has engaged them in; and there, like the common soldiers of an army, shew their courage and warmth, as their leaders direct, without ever examining, or so much as knowing the cause they contend for.... 'Tis enough for him to obey his leaders, to have his hand and his tongue ready for the support of the common cause, and thereby approve himself to those, who can give him credit, preferment, or protection in that society.[269]

To those who by their wiles or wits come to be the "dictator of principles, and teacher of unquestionable truths," there comes this added advantage

---

[265] *Essay*, IV.XX.2, p. 707.
[266] Ibid., IV.XX.17, p. 718; IV.XX.6, p. 710.
[267] Ibid., IV.XX.4, pp. 708–709.
[268] Ibid., IV.III.20, p. 552.
[269] Ibid., IV.XX.18, p. 719.

among their loyal but ignorant followers: "Those being generally the most fierce and firm in their tenets, [are those] who have least examined them."[270]

Over time, such received opinions become "rivetted . . . by long custom and education [and] beyond all possibility of being pull'd out again."[271] The reason is that by such a process men come to have settled opinions and beliefs about the world; they find, even in the errors with which they surround themselves, a security and certainty they cannot live without. Opinion is more comforting than knowledge, and it is unlikely that men can be freed of their opinions and put upon the course for true knowledge. Such an expectation is simply against human nature.[272]

Life is such that most men will prefer to hunker down in their huts, however intellectually shabby and morally primitive, if they offer the sense of security men naturally crave; truth is no match for such passion. "Earthly minds, like mud walls, resist the strongest of batteries: and though, perhaps, sometimes the force of a clear argument may make an impression, yet they nevertheless stand firm, keep out the every truth, that would captivate or disturb them."[273]

The longer opinions hold sway, the more secure they become. Even propositions "evidently false or doubtful" come to be "thought to grow venerable by age, and are urged as undeniable."[274] Woe be to those who would seek to question such received and venerable truths, much less deny them. The censure of one's neighbors can be severe for those who would stand against intellectual fashion and the law of opinion and reputation.[275] Such a passionate embrace of things thought true seals a society off from those who do not share its belief in those fundamental, received truths. Ultimately, such basic, shared tenets of neighborhood, party, or country are what draw otherwise radically isolated individuals together in society; they are what transforms human beings into citizens. In time such shared tenets will come to be seen as necessary rules of behavior and will likely be, eventually, transcribed into laws of the commonwealth. And it is this relationship between the law of opinion or reputation and the law of civil or political societies that is the ultimate paradox of Locke's political teaching.

The inherent tension in Locke's thought lies in the relationship between custom or the law of reputation, and liberty. On the one hand, custom is suffocating, keeping new ideas out as it bolsters and perpetuates the received

---

[270] Ibid., IV.XVI.3, p. 659.
[271] Ibid., IV.XX.9, p. 712.
[272] Ibid., IV.XX.11, p. 714. See also IV.XVI.4, p. 660.
[273] Ibid., IV.XX.12, p. 715.
[274] Ibid., IV.XVI.10, p. 664. It was along these lines that Hobbes quipped of precedents in the common law that "prove only what was done, and not what was well done." *Dialogue*, p. 129.
[275] *Essay*, I.III.25, p. 83.

tradition and dominant opinions. On the other hand, if men are freed from custom, and rely only on their individual understandings to explain the world around them, the diversity of their opinions will issue in social and political chaos. It would be a situation in which each, by virtue of his claims to liberty and freedom of the will, would presume to articulate moral rules of behavior and make those around him conform to them. If his reason were not persuasive, he would likely resort to force to impose his vision of justice on the rest. As Locke asked: "What strange notions will there be of *justice* and *temperance*? What confusion of virtues and vices, if every one may make what ideas of these he pleases."[276]

Thus there is a need for custom, for that law of opinion and reputation most will not try to escape. In such custom lies the roots of a needed consensus of right and wrong, just and unjust. Social order is ultimately to be found in both "punishment and censure"; the civil law is bolstered by the law of opinion that knits a society together beneath the institutional arrangements the people may come to erect. This foundation of the political order is what a later generation of Americans would term the "genius of the people." Locke's fundamental teaching, then, is that good government will depend upon there being a solid foundation for both the civil law and the law of opinion; they are better rooted in reason than in the myths of tradition.

Locke was not blind to the advantages of "that veneration which time bestows on everything."[277] There was a salutary political effect to come from being supported in the hearts as well as the minds of the people. The difficulty was simple: how to encourage that veneration for those notions that were right and true as opposed to those that were simply old and familiar. Locke's solution to the problem of received opinion would ultimately be the same as his solution to the problem of divine revelation; nothing was worthy of regard that was against reason. Thus myths and traditions, both sacred and secular, however salutary they might be, had to pass the same rigorous test; they had to measure up well against the proofs and arguments reason and judgment could fashion. They had to be seen as moral ideas that were, by the measure of how well their internal notions agreed, true. As with any other proposition, by meeting these standards of reason, the law of opinion is quite capable of being properly seen as an eternal truth.[278] In the end, civil peace must depend both upon the "fear of the magistrate's sword [and] the neighbor's censure"; they are mutually reinforcing.[279]

Related to this law of opinion or censure is man's need of God, for it is ultimately by those "two great rules, religion and justice" that man governs

---

[276] Ibid., IV.IV.9, p. 566.
[277] *The Federalist*, ed. Jacob Cooke (Middletown, CT: Wesleyan University Press, 1961), No. 49, p. 340.
[278] See *Essay*, IV.XII.14, pp. 638–639.
[279] Ibid., I.IV.8, p. 88.

his conduct.[280] Opinion founded on God's word, properly and accurately understood, will serve as a support for the law of the commonwealth. For all his efforts to reduce the traditional notion of God to intellectual rubble, Locke then had to reconstruct the idea of "a god" in order to take account of the great majority of men, those who cannot know but can only believe. Having denied, on the one hand, that there is any innate idea of God, and proclaiming, on the other, that the knowledge of "God is infinitely beyond the reach of our narrow capacities," Locke had to refound the idea of God on a ground that was within man's reach.

Locke's argument is that by sense and reflection man comes to observe the physical world in which he finds himself, and by that observation man is led to conclude that such order must be the result of a maker, an "eternal wise being who had no beginning."[281] The ultimate proof of God is to be found within each man's consciousness of himself: "since we have sense, perception, and reason, [we] cannot want a clear proof of him as long as we carry ourselves about us."[282] That is, each man knows one thing above all others: "that he is something that actually exists." From this fact it follows that "non-entity cannot produce any real being"; further, man deduces that "from eternity there has been something; since what was not from eternity, had a beginning; and what had a beginning, must be produced by something else." It is clear, then, Locke insists, that such an "eternal source of all being must also be the source and original of all power; and so this eternal being must be also the most powerful." Given that man is a knowing creature, that which created him must also be a knowing, intelligent being from eternity.[283] "Thus from the consideration of our senses, and what we infallibly find in our own constitutions, our reason leads us to the knowledge of this certain and evident truth, that there is an eternal, most powerful, and most knowing being; which whether anyone will please to call God, it matters not."[284] Yet this "demonstration" is nothing short of shocking. Not only is it a matter of indifference to Locke whether such a powerful creator be called God, he sidesteps the most pressing of questions, especially in a work about the understanding. "How far the idea of a most perfect being, which a man may frame in his mind, does, or does not prove the existence of a God," he asserts, "I will not here examine." The only thing Locke is willing to concede as demonstrably true, by the terms of the argument of the *Essay*, is that ultimately "all religion and genuine morality depend" upon such a proof of the existence of "a God."[285]

[280] Ibid., III.X.12, p. 496.
[281] Ibid., II.XVII.17, pp. 219–220.
[282] Ibid., IV.X.1, p. 619.
[283] Ibid., IV.X.2, p. 620; IV.X.3, p. 620; IV.X.4, p. 620; IV.X.5, p. 620.
[284] Ibid., IV.X.6, p. 621.
[285] Ibid., IV.X.7, p. 621; IV.X.7, p. 622.

Not being innate, the idea of God is merely one more complex assemblage made by man from the evidence of his sense and reflection. Looking at the various facts of existence, men cobble them together in order to "make our complex idea of god." Ultimately, says Locke, "it is infinity, which joined to our ideas of existence, power, knowledge, etc., makes that complex idea whereby we represent to ourselves the best we can, the supreme being." Our complex idea of God originates in our sense of self: "[E]ven the most advanced notion we have of God, is but attributing the same simple ideas we have got from reflection on what we find in ourselves, and ... attributing ... those simple ideas to him in an unlimited degree." Locke's demonstration of God is complete: "[W]e need go no farther than ourselves, and that undoubted knowledge we have of our own existence."[286] Put a bit more plainly, we are not made in God's image, but He in ours.[287]

Locke's "proof" of the existence of "a God" follows his method of proving probable truths in complex ideas generally. One idea is connected to another by intervening proofs or logical steps. In the case of God, no less than in all other cases, these ideas are only the creation of the understanding. They have no foundation in nature, any more than any other complex moral idea man sees fit to assemble. By Locke's own method, God is merely a logical construct – hence his repeated references to "a God" as opposed to simply "God." One presumes that, as with other complex moral ideas that are put together arbitrarily by men, the ideas of God men come to have will, in fact, be notions of gods, created as different men in different times and places may find "convenient." Man universally engages in this activity because it gives him a way of explaining the otherwise incomprehensible universe in which he finds himself. It is by the idea of an all powerful, omniscient, eternal being that man bridges the gulf between what he can know by his sense and reflection and what remains the "hidden constitution" of things. Reason must be bolstered by faith. While man cannot prove beyond doubt that there is a God, neither can he prove that there is not. Despite Locke's claim that the existence of God is a matter of knowing, by his own standards, it is not. His logical construct of God renders it still a matter of belief, at best based on probability; there is no proof, no certain knowledge. Without such a belief in God, ordinary men would be adrift on the incomprehensible "ocean of being" with no surer guide than their often faulty and always limited reason.

It was for this reason that Locke sought to defend the "reasonableness" of Christianity, especially the written word of God as given in the sacred

---

[286] Ibid., II.XXIII.33, p. 314; II.XXIII.35, p. 315; III.VI.11, p. 445; IV.X.1, p. 619.

[287] Locke is less than enthusiastic in his defense: "[T]he having the idea of anything in our minds, no more proves the existence of that thing than ... the visions of a dream make thereby a true history." *Essay*, IV.XI.1, p. 630. In the end, "we must content ourselves with the evidence of faith." Ibid., IV.XI.12, p. 637.

Scriptures. This was a necessary effort given that for the great "bulk of mankind" it is "too hard a task for unassisted reason, to establish morality in all its parts upon its true foundation, with a clear and convincing light." It is not hard to understand why: "[T]he reason . . . [is] to be found in men's necessities, passions, vices, and mistaken interests, which turn their thoughts another way; and the designing leaders, as well as following herd, find it not to their purpose to employ much of their meditations this way." For all the talk about the law of nature being the law of reason, it is clear that "human reason unassisted failed men in its great and proper business of morality. It never, from unquestionable principles, by clear deductions, made out an entire body of the law of nature." The fact was that the "rules of morality were in different countries and sects, different. And natural reason no where had, nor was like to cure the defects and errors in them."[288]

Until the time of Christ there had been no "sure standard" of morality, the reason being that the "just measures of right and wrong, which necessity had any where introduced, the civil laws prescribed, or philosophy recommended, stood not on their true foundations." That missing foundation was the notion of a lawmaker. The advent of the Savior provided that foundation and offered a law that could be the "sure guide of those who had a desire to go right." For once a man is "persuaded that Jesus Christ was sent by God to be a king, and saviour of those who believe in him, all his commands become principles; and there needs be no other proof for the truth of what he says, but that he said it." By reference to His word, in the "inspired books," man will find moral instruction: "All the duties of morality lie there clear, and plain, and easy to be understood."[289] To Locke the basic question had been answered: "And I ask, whether one coming from Heaven in the power of God, in full and clear evidence and demonstration of miracles, giving plain and direct rules of morality and obedience, be not likelier to enlighten the bulk of mankind, and set them right in their duties, and bring them to do them, than by reasoning with them from general notions and principles of human reason?"[290] For most men, "the precepts and principles of the Gospel" provide quite enough guidance for the "business" of life.[291]

No small part of the power of the Gospel to bring men around is the promise of "endless, unspeakable joys of another life" if only they will believe and obey.[292] To those who labor in the endless drudgery of existence here, who strive to survive against often daunting odds, nothing could be more powerful: "The view of Heaven and Hell will cast a slight upon the short pleasures and pains of this present state, and give attractions and

[288] *Reasonableness*, pp. 535, 532, 532, 532–533, 534.
[289] Ibid., pp. 534, 534, 535, 535.
[290] Ibid., p. 535.
[291] Ibid.
[292] Ibid., p. 537.

encouragements to virtue, which reason and interest, and the care of ourselves, cannot but allow and prefer. Upon this foundation, and upon this only, morality stands firm, and may defy all competition."[293] Such is the promise of Christ's teaching that men can find quiet comfort there, and in that comfort, hope: "To a man under the difficulties of his nature, beset with temptations, and hedged in with prevailing custom; 'tis no small encouragement to set himself seriously on the courses of virtue, and the practice of religion, that he is from a sure hand, and an almighty arm, promised assistance to support and carry him through."

By Locke's measure, however, the simple truths of the Savior's teachings had been obscured by the priests, "those wary guardians of their own creeds and profitable inventions." They had, by their perverse interpretations, tainted as they were by the prevailing philosophy of the day, turned religion from a source of hope to a source of terror; they had, as Locke described it, filled the heads of the people with "false notions of the deity" and imposed on their worship "foolish rites." The result was that "what dread or craft once began, devotion soon made sacred, and religion immutable."[294] So powerful are such ecclesiastical teachings that "men will disbelieve their own eyes, renounce the evidence of their senses, and give their own experience the lye, rather than admit of anything disagreeing with these sacred tenets."[295]

When it came to the written word of God, the core problem was that layer after layer of interpretation and commentary had all but covered the original meaning. The opinions of the priests had come to encrust the clear word of the Savior as reported by the apostles. "There are fewer that bring their opinions to the sacred scripture to be tried by that infallible rule, than bring the sacred scripture to their opinions, to bend it to them, to make it as they can a cover and guard of them."[296] This denied the natural basis of religion Locke sought to establish, and substituted learned criticism for God's word. Thus was the proper role of religion as a support to civil society an important one to establish. The basic need was to return God to the people directly, and remove the interfering influence of the authoritative interpreters. The way to achieve that was to remove religion from the public sphere and make it a matter of private conscience. By such a movement, all the private virtues of faith might be retained, while its public vices would be lessened. The need was to introduce toleration as a general matter; the separation of church and state would be to the advantage of both.

In preparation at the same time, and appearing in 1689, just before the publication of *An Essay Concerning Human Understanding* and the

[293] Ibid.
[294] Ibid., p. 530.
[295] *Essay*, IV.XX.10, p. 713.
[296] *Essay on St. Paul*, p. 105.

Two Treatises of Government, was Locke's other great work, *A Letter on Toleration.* Locke's ultimate goal in pushing the idea of toleration in both the *Essay* and the *Letter* was not so much to free religion from governmental intrusions as it was to free government from religious interference. There was a danger, as history had amply shown, of men of the cloth "meddling in politics." Indeed, history was in great part a catalogue that showed "how easily religions and the salvation of souls became a pretext for rapine and ambition." There was a great deal of danger to be apprehended when "zeal for the church...combined with the desire of dominion." Sectarian strife was usually the result of "trivial matters"; but even though trivial, they were sufficient to "breed implacable enmities among Christian brethren." History was replete with examples of how "for the sake of religion subjects are often maltreated and live wretchedly." Such disruptive bouts of "religious rage" as men had suffered could be prevented only by keeping the church and all its doctrinal squabbles separate from the powers of the state.[297]

The way this was to be achieved in practice was to keep religion a strictly private matter: "churches have no jurisdiction in earthly matters, nor are sword and fire proper instruments for refuting errors or instructing and converting men's minds."[298] To argue, Locke said, that

the orthodox church...has power over the erroneous or heretical...is to use great and specious words to say nothing at all. For every church is orthodox to itself and erroneous or heretical to others. For whatever any church believes, it believes to be true, and the contrary it condemns as error. Thus the controversy between...churches about the truth of their doctrines and the purity of their worship is equal on both sides; nor is there any judge...upon earth, by whose sentence it can be determined.[299]

Civil peace is only to be had when the passions of faith are finally pushed from the public councils, for "no security or peace, much less friendship, can ever be established or preserved amongst men, if the opinion prevails that dominion is founded in grace and that religion is to be propagated by force of arms."[300]

What this means in practice is that religion affords men no immunity from the demands and dictates of the civil law. "Things which in themselves are harmful to the commonwealth, and which are forbidden in ordinary life by laws enacted for the common good, cannot be allowed for sacred use in church, nor can they deserve impunity." When it comes to obeying the law of the commonwealth, individual conscience is not enough to merit exemption. In Locke's view, "the private judgment of any person concerning a law enacted in political matters, and for the public good, does not take

---

[297] *Letter on Toleration,* pp. 149, 115, 114, 93, 139.
[298] Ibid., p. 83.
[299] Ibid.
[300] Ibid., p. 85.

away the obligation of that law, nor does it deserve toleration." When it comes to political safety and religious toleration, it is essential that the boundaries between church and civil authority be "fixed and immovable." The concern of the former is the "salvation of souls," that of the latter the "safety of the commonwealth."[301]

The two concerns find common foundation in a properly constructed commonwealth, one that understands itself "to be a society of men constituted only for preserving and advancing their civil goods." Through "impartially enacted equal laws" the magistrate will seek to secure the safety and happiness of the people, including their right to exercise their wills freely when it comes to matters of conscience. The reason is simple: "Neither the care of the commonwealth, nor the right of enacting laws, reveals the way that leads to heaven more certainly to the magistrate than a private man's study reveals it to himself." As a result, "it is not the magistrate's business to censure with laws or check with his sword everything he believes to be a sin against God." When it comes to the private judgment of any person, including the magistrate, that judgment is not a part of the public power; he has no right to impose laws governing matters of conscience, as he sees it, on the people.[302] "No man," as Locke wrote elsewhere, "has power to prescribe to another what he should believe or do in order to the saving his own soul, because it is only his own private interest and concerns not another man. God has nowhere given such power to any man or society, nor can man possibly be supposed to give it to another over him absolutely."[303] When it comes to the realm of private morality and conscience, the "care of every man's soul belongs to himself, and is to be left to him." Such care simply "does not belong to the magistrate." The prerogatives in making laws that the magistrate enjoys are shaped and limited by their rightful ends: "[T]he public good in earthly or worldly matters... is the sole reason for entering society and the sole object of the commonwealth once it is formed."[304]

The separation of church from state does not diminish but actually enhances the salutary influence of religion in political life. Such a reduction of concerns of conscience and the quest to save souls to a matter of purely private concern will save the commonwealth from the "fiery zeal" of those who would seek to impose the dictates of their religion on others, and who would perhaps hope to enlist the "magistrate's rods and axes" in aid of their powers of persuasion. By denying that there is any one faith to which all must subscribe, by allowing all manner of diversity in religious

---

[301] Ibid., pp. 111, 127, 85, 65.

[302] Ibid., pp. 65, 93, 115, 129.

[303] John Locke, *Toleration*, as quoted in J. W. Gough, "Introduction," *Letter on Toleration*, p. 27.

[304] *Letter on Toleration*, pp. 91, 127.

conviction, the well-ordered commonwealth will find peace more readily. On this, Locke believed, history was clear: "It is . . . the refusal of toleration to people of diverse opinions, which could have been granted, that had produced most of the disputes and wars that have arisen in the Christian world on account of religion." Freedom of religion and conscience will come from a multiplicity of sects in which none will be more politically important than the rest. The result of such an encouragement of religion, within the legal boundaries of the public interest, will be that the commonwealth will enjoy a citizenry that will be subject to the restraint of two moral masters, the law of the magistrate, on the one hand, and the law of private conscience on the other.[305]

With all the defects of the human understanding, with all the dangers posed to judgment by self-interest, received opinion, and religious faith, Locke still believed that reason was the only law of nature, and that for any government to be legitimate it had to be based on that reason. And it was to the foundation of legitimate government that he turned his attention in the *Second Treatise of Government*, having finally cleared away the "rubbish" that had been so long strewn in the path to true knowledge.

The *Second Treatise of Government*

Nearly three decades before John Locke's *Two Treatises of Government* appeared, he neatly captured the enduring dilemma of politics that fascinated him all his life and that informed all his works, especially his *Second Treatise*. "'Tis not without reason," he wrote in his *First Tract on Government* in 1660, "that tyranny and anarchy are judged the smartest scourges can fall upon mankind, the plea of authority usually backing the one, and of liberty inducing the other: and between the two it is, that human affairs are perpetually kept tumbling."[306] How to keep human affairs on an even keel, to keep politics from the wild fluctuations between tyranny and anarchy, was the essential demand of political philosophy, Locke thought. To bring peace and stability to political life would be the greatest good one could imagine.

From his days at Oxford, when he first broached the subject, through the appearance of his great works in November and December 1689 and beyond, the political world in which Locke lived was one of tumult and uncertainty; his abiding interest in seeking to fashion a surer ground for politics was not simply a matter of bookish speculation.[307] He knew well how high were the stakes in that public world that vibrated between tyranny

---

305 Ibid., pp. 89, 145, 123.
306 *First Tract*, p. 119.
307 For an account of Locke and his political times, see generally Maurice Cranston, *John Locke: A Biography* (London: Longmans, Green and Co., 1953); see also Roger Woolhouse, *Locke: A Biography* (Cambridge: Cambridge University Press, 2007).

and anarchy. In January 1649 Locke had been a schoolboy in Westminster School "within earshot of the awe stricken crowd" when Charles I was executed in the name of liberty; and 1683, the year he left Oxford forever, saw Sidney beheaded as an exercise of sovereign authority, proving that one might indeed publish and perish.[308] Locke's own increasingly precarious position as one of Shaftesbury's inner circle had also impressed upon him the dangers of political life; spies watched his every move in Oxford.[309] The *Second Treatise* was his attempt to reconcile the competing claims of authority and liberty that he knew so well. The result was nothing less than the transformation of how men in generations to come would understand the grounds of legitimate government. Locke knew it was radical enough to demand anonymity; only in death did he confess to being the author, and then only with typical caution.[310]

Locke addressed himself in the *Second Treatise* to correcting "the great mistakes of late about government."[311] His nominal target, as he had made clear in the *First Treatise*, was Sir Robert Filmer and his followers. But Locke's objective was not merely the refutation of Filmer; rather, it was something far more important. He sought nothing less, as he said in the title of the work, than to establish "the true original, extent, and end of civil government." The purpose was to prove false the belief "that all government in the world is the product only of Force and Violence, and that men live together by no other rules but that of beasts, where the strongest carries it." The misguided notions put forward by the likes of Filmer and his followers, Locke argued, were such as to have laid "a Foundation for perpetual disorder and mischief, tumult, sedition and rebellion."[312] To Locke's way of thinking, mankind was capable of more. He believed that through reason man could fashion a new foundation for legitimate authority, one that would draw unto itself the voluntary obedience of the people.[313]

Locke began his account, like Hobbes before him, by arguing that man must be understood in his most pristine, natural state, free of such encrustations of society as customs, traditions, and institutions. The reason this was necessary for Locke, as for Hobbes, was his belief that the essence of politics was human understanding; how men made sense of the natural world in which they found themselves determined how they would go about creating the political world in which they would choose to live. While man by nature is "quickly driven" into society, the society in which he resides is purely a

---

[308] Laslett, "Introduction," *Locke's Two Treatises of Government*, p. 17.

[309] See Cranston, *John Locke*, pp. 201–203.

[310] Laslett, "Introduction," *Locke's Two Treatises of Government*, p. 4.

[311] *Second Treatise*, 398: 169.

[312] Ibid., 285–286: 1.

[313] Mankind was able, as he said in the *First Treatise*, to "lay a sure and lasting foundation of . . . peace and tranquility, which is the business of government, and the end of humane society." 237: 106.

matter of his creation. Given that the true origin, extent, and end of government is the result of reason, it is essential to see how men rationally decide to enter into society. As Locke had made clear in the *Essay Concerning Human Understanding*, the mechanics of human reason are rooted in man's nature, and, as a result, it is essential to understand that nature and how it moves men to join together in civil society, from their first simple ideas to moral language to social contract and civil laws and constitutiions.

A. *The State of Nature and Its Law*

The state of nature portrayed by Hobbes in his much reviled *Leviathan* was a bleak and forbidding place where life was "poore, solitary, nasty, brutish and short," and all existence reduced to the chaos of an endless "warre of every man against every man." But that was not all. Prior to the establishment of a commonwealth by institution, Hobbes argued, "this also is consequent: that nothing can be unjust. The notions of right and wrong, justice and injustice, have there no place. Where there is no common power, there is no law: where no law, no injustice." More chillingly, in the state of nature, Hobbes insisted, "the lawes of nature . . . are not properly lawes" insofar as they are not enforced; they are little more than moral "qualities" that may, or may not, suggest themselves to men in that natural state.[314] No small part of the public outrage leveled at Hobbes was generated by the picture he painted of the dark and apparently godless world of the state of nature.

Locke seems to present an entirely different picture of man in his natural state; if not simply idyllic, it certainly appears more commodious and hospitable than Hobbes's jungle. The state of nature for Locke is not only a "state of perfect freedom," but a "state also of equality" with "men living together according to reason" under a law of nature accessible to every one. But such appearances are deceiving. Locke's state of nature differs very little from that of Hobbes; it is merely a matter of presentation. The more one pulls together the various elements of Locke's state of nature that he scattered throughout the *Second Treatise*, the dimmer and more dangerous does his "one community of nature" grow, until in the end men do not simply opt for civil society, but rather are driven to it by many of the same horrors that characterized Hobbes's vision.[315] The reason was much the same: the terrors of life in the state of nature for Locke, as for Hobbes, are the result of a very imperfect human nature.

It is precisely the natural equality and freedom of men in the state of nature that is the problem. "The natural liberty of man is to be free from any superiour power on earth, and not to be under the will or legislative authority of man, but to have only the law of nature for his rule." The fact that men are "promiscuously born to all the same advantages of nature and

[314] *Leviathan*, pp. 97, 205.
[315] *Second Treatise*, 287: 4; 298: 19; 289: 6.

the use of the same faculties" means that by nature all are equal; the "Lord and master of them all" made no distinctions among men granting to some but not to others "an undoubted right to dominion and sovereignty." Since nature has made no choice as to who shall rule and who shall be ruled, the law of nature under which all men find themselves in the state of nature is left for its enforcement to each man. "The execution of the law of nature is in that state put into everyman's hands, whereby everyone has a right to punish the transgressions of that law to such a degree as may hinder its violation." Since the law of nature is in fact reason, and since it is accessible to "all mankind, who will but consult it," it would seem that Locke's state of nature would suffer none of the difficulties of Hobbes's. But, as Locke had demonstrated in the *Essay Concerning Human Understanding*, human reason is fallible, and men's passions strong; it is precisely for those reasons that the law of nature is the essential problem of the state of nature. With each man by right the judge and executioner of the law of nature, that law in practice and effect is reduced to nothing more than the opinions of individual men. The power of each man "to punish offences against the law of nature" will inevitably be exercised "in prosecution of his own private judgment" in pursuit of "his own private separate advantage."[316]

Admittedly, Locke argues that there are limits to each man's power to enforce the law of nature. It is not an "absolute and arbitrary power," he insists; no man may rightfully seek to enforce the law of nature "according to passionate heats, or [the] boundless extravagancy of his own will." Any punishment meted out is to be fashioned in proportion to the transgression of the law of nature. By "calm reason" and the dictates of "conscience," each man in enforcing the law of nature should be guided by the standards of "reparation and restraint," the ends for which he is given the power to enforce the law of nature in the first place. "Each transgression may be punished to that degree, and with so much severity as will suffice to make it an ill bargain to the offender, give him cause to repent, and terrifie others from doing the like." But such cool reason is unlikely to prevail. It turns out that knowing the law of nature is not as easy a proposition as Locke originally seemed to suggest; and, even if one knows it, there is no guarantee it will be followed, much less enforced according to the reasonable standards of reparation and restraint Locke posits. The fact is, there is a "baseness of human nature" that renders such a reasonable world nearly impossible.[317]

Human nature is such that most men, most of the time, will be more self-regarding than Locke's original appraisal of that nature might suggest.

---

[316] Ibid., 301: 22; 287: 4; 289: 7; 343: 88; 416–417: 199. Locke had first addressed this in his *Questions Concerning the Law of Nature*, where he argued that in a state of "natural liberty . . . all right and justice should be determined not by another's law, but by the interest of each individual." XI: 237.

[317] *Second Treatise*, 290: 8; 293: 12; 345: 92.

Although the law of nature is "plain and intelligible to all rational creatures," he later points out, "men being biassed by their interest, as well as ignorant for want of study of it, are not apt to allow of it as a law binding to them in the application of it to their particular cases." But ignorance is not the real problem: "men being partial to themselves, passion and revenge is very apt to carry them too far and with too much heat in their own cases; as well as negligence and unconcernedness, to make them too remiss, in other men's." Upon reflection, however, it becomes clear that not even self-interest is the most nagging problem. The deepest concern, and that which ultimately renders the state of nature no more agreeable for Locke than for Hobbes, is that most men, most of the time, are "no strict observers of equity and justice." It is, in fact, the "corruption and vitiousness of degenerate men" that renders the state of nature a place to be escaped.³¹⁸ With every man being a judge in his own cause, there is no standard of right and wrong save that of each man's impulse; what is missing in the state of nature is an impartial judge to whom all might appeal for remedy if mistreated at the hands of their fellows.³¹⁹

With each man being the measure of all things in the enforcement of the law of nature, with no superior power over him, each will find himself "subject to the unconstant, uncertain, unknown, arbitrary will of another man." Such is the demand of natural equality: "if anyone in the state of nature may punish another, for any evil he has done, everyone may do so." Thus is the natural liberty men are supposed to enjoy in the state of nature the primary casualty in the state of nature. It cannot endure. Although in that state each man has the right to be "the absolute lord of his own person and possessions, equal to the greatest and subject to no body," the enjoyment of that right "is very uncertain, and constantly exposed to the invasion of others." Rather than a peaceful, secure, and idyllic condition, Locke's state of nature proves to be "full of fears and continual dangers," a place that is "very unsafe, very unsecure."³²⁰

The ultimate paradox of Locke's account of the state of nature and the law of nature that governs it, is that "the fundamental law of nature" is nothing other than "the preservation of mankind." It is a law that is not only fundamental, but also "sacred and unalterable." But although fundamental, sacred, and unalterable, it is obviously not inalienable. Even though reason teaches that, by virtue of all men being both free and equal, "no one ought to harm another in his life, health, liberty or possessions," it is a rule more likely to be ignored than upheld.³²¹ In the state of nature, moral claims of

---

³¹⁸ Ibid., 369: 124; 369: 125; 368: 123; 370: 128.
³¹⁹ Ibid., 376–377: 136.
³²⁰ Ibid., 302: 22; 289–290: 7; 368: 123.
³²¹ Ibid., 376: 175 and passim; 385: 149; 289: 6.

right based on the law of nature are too easily trumped by the sheer force of man's unruly nature.

What reason does allow men in their natural state is the calculation necessary to see the state of nature for what it is, a place to be shunned in order to seek the conditions where the law of nature, that right of self-preservation, can be secured. "Thus mankind, notwithstanding all the privileges of the state of nature, being but an ill condition, while they remain in it, are quickly driven into society." And for Locke, the reason is clear: "The inconveniences, that they are therein exposed to, by the irregular and uncertain exercise of the power every man has of punishing the transgressions of others, make them take sanctuary under the established laws of government, and therein seek the preservation of their property." It is in civil society that man will find the three things most glaringly absent in the state of nature: clearly promulgated laws; impartial judges to whom appeal can be made, and legitimate political power authorized to enforce those laws. These three defects were what made the state of nature so intolerable, "so unsafe and uneasie" – that sense of "uneasiness," as Locke explained it in the *Essay*, being the ultimate spark in men to improve their condition.[322]

Ultimately, for Locke, men being judges in their own causes meant that the natural liberty due them was but a hollow promise. In truth, in the state of nature, each man had nothing more than " a liberty to shift for himself." What men had in the state of nature thus was not liberty at all, but "pure anarchy." The state of nature is simply inconsistent with true liberty, for there is in that state no protection from the "restraint and violence from others." True liberty is possible only through law. As Locke insisted, "where there is no law, there is no freedom."[323] The absence of law in the state of nature rendered it for Locke, as for Hobbes, a potential war of all against all. Indeed, by Locke's own definition, the state of nature would inevitably degenerate into a state of war.

The state of war was a condition described by Locke as being characterized by the use of "force without authority." And "authority . . . is founded only in the constitution and laws of the government." Thus in the state of nature, where there is no government and hence no positive law, the use of force would be, by definition, without authority. To ignore the command of reason in the state of nature is, in effect, to ignore the law of nature, and thereby to ignore its demand to preserve mankind. As Locke explained: "Whoever uses force without right, as every one does in society, who does it without law, puts himself into a state of war with those against whom he so uses it, and in that state all former ties are cancelled, all other rights cease, and every one has a right to defend himself, and to resist the aggressor." Locke's description is graphic: "For quitting reason, which is the rule

[322] Ibid., 370: 127; 371: 131; *Essay*, II.XXI.29, p. 249.
[323] *Second Treatise*, 424–425: 211; 433: 225; 324: 57.

between man and man, and using force the way of beasts, he becomes liable to be destroyed by him he uses force against, as any savage, ravenous beast, that is dangerous to his being." It is to flee this sad and savage condition of war and potential war that men rationally give up their tawdry "Empire" that is the state of nature for the security promised by civil society.[324]

It is only in civil society that the law of nature will be rendered secure. "The obligations of the law of nature," Locke suggests, "cease not in society, but only in many cases are drawn closer, and have by human laws known penalties annexed to them, to enforce their observation."[325] For Locke, as for Hobbes, the law of nature outside civil society is nothing more than moral "qualities," worthy perhaps in themselves, but unlikely to be observed. Without the support of the civil law, backed by clear and severe sanctions, the law of nature is next to nothing. Civil or political society is defined by law, conventional standards of right and wrong that transcend the individual judgment of each man in the state of nature.[326] In the end it is man's capacity for reason that proves to be the "common bond whereby humane kind is united into one fellowship and societie." For ultimately people enter into society "to be preserved, one intire, free, independent society, to be governed by its own laws." For justice is to be had only where such laws are "received and allowed by common consent to be the standard of right and wrong."[327]

B. Consent, Contract, and Civil Society

The foundation of civil society for Locke is ultimately grounded in God's silence. God "governs the universe," he argues, by a purely "arbitrary power." His will is unknowable to man, except where and when God condescends to speak to him. When it comes to governance, to how men ought to

---

[324] Ibid., 434: 277; 433: 226; 437: 232; 407: 181; 368: 123. "[W]here there is an authority, a power on earth, from which relief can be had by appeal, there the continuance of the state of war is excluded, and the controversie is decided by that power." Ibid., 300: 21. See also *Second Treatise*, 430: 222. The primary defect of the law of nature in the state of nature, it is worth recalling, was precisely the failure "to determine the rights and fence the properties of those that live under it." Ibid., 376–377: 136. Locke explains in the *Essay* and elsewhere how no one has ever made clear precisely what is demanded and prohibited by the law of nature. See *Questions*, IV: 141; *Essay*, I.III.14, p. 76; and *Reasonableness*, pp. 532–533.

[325] *Second Treatise*, 375–376: 135.

[326] *Second Treatise*, 342: 87.

[327] Ibid., 401: 172; 428: 217; 369: 124. As Locke said in the *Essay*: "Morally good and evil, then, is only conformity or disagreement of our voluntary actions to some law, whereby good and evil is drawn on us, from the will and power of the lawmaker; which good and evil, pleasure or pain, attending our observation or breach of the law, by the decree of the lawmaker, is what we call reward and punishment." II.XXVIII.5, p. 351.

This was a view held by Hobbes, as well: "Civil law is to every subject, those rules, which the commonwealth hath commanded him, by word, writing, or other sufficient sign of the will, to make use of, for the distinction of right and wrong; that is to say, of what is contrary, and what is not contrary to the rule." *Leviathan*, p. 203.

fashion the institutions of the world they inhabit, God is strikingly reticent. He has not, by any "manifest declaration of his will," set one man above another; he has placed no scepter in any hand thus conferring "an evident and clear appointment of undoubted right" to govern.[328] The essence of the natural freedom man enjoys or, more often, suffers in the state of nature is a complete equality; and this holds true until and unless God chooses to elevate anyone above the rest.[329]

The most man has to go on is the one example of "the voice of God in him" which is but reason, which moves him naturally to seek to give effect to that "strong desire for self-preservation" God has implanted in him.[330] Following this native impulse of the will to avoid pain and seek pleasure will prompt him toward figuring out how to secure "the peace and preservation of all mankind"; this exercise of reason, for Locke, constitutes "the right rule of reason."[331] But this "rule of reason," it is worth noting, is not the rule of "right reason" that had so characterized medieval notions of the law of nature. This is not reason understood as rules inscribed in the human heart by the finger of God. Rather, this is reason as logical calculation, man figuring out which of several actions will have the greatest probability of securing his safety and preservation.[332] This natural reason, this voice of God, "tells us, that men, being once born, have a right to their preservation."[333] This divine voice is nothing more than a direction to man "by his senses and reason" to preserve himself, and, as far as possible, his fellow men.[334] Beyond this starkest of messages, God's advice does not extend; He simply moves men, as He does "all other animals," to seek to preserve themselves.[335] The means to that end, God leaves to man's reason and voluntary agreement or consent.

The idea of consent as explained in the *Second Treatise* is the direct result of the epistemological system Locke puts forward in the *Essay Concerning Human Understanding*. If all men are equal, and if there are no innate ideas, then the idea of justice will vary from man to man. The differences among men's understandings demand agreement if peace is to obtain; this agreement focuses on what constitutes good government, and is, as such, not a natural agreement but a conventional one. The process of consent –

---

[328] *Second Treatise*, 396: 166; 287: 4.

[329] *First Treatise*, 208: 67.

[330] *First Treatise*, 223: 86.

[331] *Second Treatise*, 289: 7; 291: 10.

[332] In the *Essay*, Locke explained man's predicament this way: "The principal exercise of freedom is to stand still, open the eyes, look about, and take a view of the consequences of what we are going to do." The essence of reason for man thus understood is simply a "faculty for making arguments." *Essay*, II.XXI.67, p. 279; *Questions*, V: 157.

[333] *Second Treatise*, 303: 25.

[334] *First Treatise*, 223: 86; *Second Treatise*, 374: 134.

[335] *First Treatise*, 223: 86.

what Hobbes called "sovereignty by institution" – is open as to the actual form the government will take.

The state of nature apparatus Locke embraces to such powerful effect in the *Second Treatise* is not meant to be understood as an actual, historical state in which men find themselves. Locke's own references to primitive peoples and their development give the lie to such an actual state of nature. Looking at the histories of such peoples one sees their rise from rudeness to progress; that rise confirms the epistemological status of the state of nature. As primitive men experience the world around them, they learn from those experiences, share the lessons they have learned, and begin to fashion the structures of civilization. In many ways, Sir William Blackstone's phrase, the "state of uncivilized nature," better captures Locke's point.[336]

The essence of Locke's teaching about man's move from the state of nature into civil society is that it is only the result of experience over time. Insofar as there are no innate ideas, all ideas men come to have depend only upon experience. As events occur, experience is gained, and ideas are formed. Locke explains at the outset of the *Essay* that his method is "historical." Man's understanding comes in bits and pieces, as the result of "time and observation." Man's grasp of the world around him grows "by degrees."[337] Locke strove to make the point absolutely clear. "Let us suppose the mind to be, as we say, white paper, void of all characters, without any ideas," he urged, "how comes it to be furnished? . . . To this I answer, in one word, from *Experience*: In that all our knowledge is founded; and from that it ultimately derives itself."[338]

The essential feature of Locke's state of nature is that it is man's pristine state, not politically but psychologically. The free and uncluttered mind begins to apprehend the things about it; matters of fact are noted, sorted, named, and remembered; those ideas are subsequently shared among men. The key to Locke's theory of consent and the social contract, indeed of the very idea of civil society itself, is language. It is only by language that one radically isolated, free and independent man can make known his ideas to his equally isolated, free and independent fellows. And it is through the exchange of such ideas by means of language that men come to know what is in each other's minds; it is by this method that men come to reach agreements over certain things.[339] It is only by this foundation of consent, of shared opinions as to what constitutes the best course for the safety of each

---

[336] Sir William Blackstone, *Commentaries on the Laws of England*, 4 vols. (8th ed.; Oxford: Clarendon Press, 1778), IV: 181–182.

[337] *Essay*, I.I.2, p. 44; I.I.16, p. 56; I.II.20, p. 58; II.II.23, p. 60.

[338] Ibid., II.I.1, p. 104.

[339] "God's having made man such a creature, that, in his own judgment, it is not good for him to be alone, put him under strong obligations of necessity, convenience, and inclination, to drive him into society, as well as fitted him with understanding and language to continue and enjoy it." *Second Treatise*, 336–367: 77.

and the preservation of all, that man is able to overcome the limitations of natural liberty imposed by his natural equality. Consent is the reciprocal of the claim to equal liberty that each man has by nature.[340]

What renders life in the state of nature so intolerable is the inherent arbitrariness of daily existence; there is nothing beyond mere force by which a man might shield himself from the invasions of his peers. What drives men from the state of nature into civil society is the fear they come to know in that primitive state where each is subject to the arbitrary will of the stronger. There is there no certainty, so security, no peace. The power of each and all to enforce the law of nature as they might see fit, however distorted their interpretation might be by their viewing that fundamental and sacred law through the prism of their self-interest, means that the law of nature is of no value to man in the state of nature. Each is prisoner of the circumstances created by others; there is no calm, all is chaos. "This freedom from absolute, arbitrary power," Locke argued, "is so necessary to, and closely joyn'd with a man's preservation, that he cannot part with it, but by what forfeits his preservation and life together."[341]

It is only by the "declared laws" that characterize civil society that man is ultimately able to escape the terrors of the state of nature and thus, by slipping on the "bonds" of civil society, come to know true freedom. What man leaves behind as he enters into the social contract is the unrestrained lawlessness of man outside civil society, where each is moved by his own impulse toward despotic control of all those around him. For ultimately, it is despotic power, that "absolute, arbitrary power one man has over another, to take away his life, whenever he pleases," that will nearly always be the manifestation of each man's right in the state of nature to enforce the law of nature. In civil society, man finds the possibility of peace and security precisely because the "laws of society confine the liberty he had by the law of nature."[342] Thus does Locke in the *Second Treatise* seek to give institutional expression to the truth he expressed in the *Essay* as being a proposition as "certain . . . as any in mathematicks," namely, that "no government allows absolute liberty."[343]

The idea of consent Locke presents in the *Second Treatise* consists of two distinct steps. The first is when men in the state of nature enter into

---

[340] "Men being . . . by nature, all free, equal, and independent, no one can be put out of this estate, and subjected to the political power of another, without his own consent. The only way whereby one divests himself of his natural liberty, and puts on the bonds of civil society, is by agreeing with other men to joyn and unite into a community, for their comfortable, safe, and peaceable living one amongst another, in a secure enjoyment of their properties, and a greater security against any that are not of it." *Second Treatise*, 348–349: 95.

[341] Ibid., 301: 23.

[342] Ibid., 377: 136; 400: 172; 370: 129.

[343] *Essay*, IV.III.18, p. 550.

agreement to form a civil society; the second is when men thus constituted as a civil society decide upon a form of commonwealth or government. As Locke argued, "the beginning of politick society depends upon the consent of the individuals to joyn into and make one society; who, when they are thus incorporated, might set up what form of government they thought fit." In the first instance, men separate from the "great and natural community, and by positive agreements combine into smaller and divided associations." This is the result of each giving up his natural power to enforce the law of nature and turning it over to the community; from this original act arises "the original right . . . of both the legislative and executive power, as well as of the governments and societies themselves." It is this second form of consent, as to governing structures, which is, in fact, the most significant, for as Locke says, "government is hardly to be avoided amongst men that live together."[344] The actual form of that government is a matter of indifference to Locke; what is not a matter of indifference, however, is that whatever the form, it must rest upon the consent of the governed.

It is by the "justice" of consent that both civil society broadly considered, and particular governments as well, are kept limited.[345] Both society and any resulting consensual government are directed toward the one unfaltering demand in political life, the preservation of each person and of the society of which he is a part. It is that preservation, that ultimate fulfillment of the law of nature, that constitutes the common or public good. Both civil society and government are means to a higher end, "the public good of society."[346]

The mechanics of civil society of necessity rest upon majority rule. Once in the bonds of society, it is a matter of common sense that "the majority have a right to act and conclude the rest." The majority is deemed "by the law of nature and reason" to have the right to exercise "the power of the whole."[347] To this rule by the majority, each member of the society is obligated.[348]

The majority must be understood to be able to act for the whole or the entire notion of a civil society dissolves, for each would have the power to trump the whole, one man's will, in effect, governing the rest; thus a man

---

[344] *Second Treatise*, 355: 106; 370: 128; 370: 127; 355: 105.

[345] As Locke argued, in civil society each man "is to part . . . with as much of his natural liberty in providing for himself, as the good, prosperity, and safety of the society shall require: which is not only necessary, but just; since the other members of the society do the like." *Second Treatise*, 371: 130.

[346] Ibid., 375: 135.

[347] Ibid., 349: 95; 350: 96.

[348] "And thus every man, by consenting with others to make one body politick under one government, puts himself under an obligation to every one of that society, to submit to the determination of the majority, and to be concluded by it; or else this original compact, whereby he with others incorporates into one society, would signifie nothing, and be no compact, if he be left free, and under no other ties than he was before in the state of nature." Ibid., 350: 97.

cannot be allowed to pick and choose which he will accept among the acts of the society. It is all or nothing.[349]

In this, Locke was in firm agreement with Hobbes, and in defending this proposition makes his only direct allusion to Hobbes to be found in the *Second Treatise*.

Such a Constitution as this would make the mighty *Leviathan* of a shorter duration, than the feeblest creatures; and not let it outlast the day it was born in: which cannot be suppos'd, till we can think, that rational creatures should desire and constitute societies only to be dissolved. For where the majority cannot conclude the rest, there they cannot act as one body, and consequently will be immediately dissolved again.[350]

In Locke's estimation, this was simply an undeniable truth of political life. It is "the consent of any number of freemen capable of a majority... which did, or could give beginning to any lawful government in the world." There is simply no other foundation for legitimate authority: "Voluntary agreement gives... political power to governours for the benefit of their subjects, to secure them in the possession and use of their properties." For it is only through this process of consent and the mechanics of majority rule within civil society that each man comes to enjoy the "privilege of his nature to be free."[351] And the means to that civil liberty, in Locke's estimation, is law, the perfection of reason. It is the possibility of law that elevates man above the brutes, all the while it is the necessity of law that continues to emphasize the gulf between man and God.

C. Commonwealth by Constitution and the Rule of Law

For Locke, the essence of freedom is the power of man to live according to his own will.[352] That is the deepest meaning of natural equality; that is the ultimate goal of natural liberty; it is, said Locke, the "very end of our freedom."[353] And it is precisely that freedom which is threatened by the arbitrary power of others in the state of nature. To secure that basic freedom is the reason men enter civil society and create governments.

"Freedom of men under government, is, to have a standing rule to live by, common to everyone in that society, and made by the legislative power

---

[349] Said Locke: "No man in civil society can be exempt from the laws of it." To be able to pick and choose by one's private judgment "would be still as great a liberty, as he himself had before his compact, or any one else in the state of nature hath, who may submit himself and consent to any acts of it if he thinks fit." *Second Treatise*, 348: 94; 350: 97.

[350] *Second Treatise*, 351: 98.

[351] Ibid., 351: 99; 401: 173; 327: 63. See also 301: 22.

[352] As Locke put it in the *Essay*: "[E]very man is put under a necessity by his constitution, as an intelligent being, to be determined in willing by his own thought and judgment, what is best for him to do: else he would be under the determination of some other than himself, which is the want of liberty." II.XXI.48, p. 264.

[353] Ibid.

erected in it; a liberty to follow my own will in all things, where the rule prescribes not; and not to be subject to the unconstant, uncertain, unknown arbitrary will of another man." It is by law, and by law alone, that arbitrariness in human affairs is reduced to order. "Law," Locke argued, "in its true notion, is not so much the limitation as the direction of a free and intelligent agent to his proper interest, and prescribes no farther that is for the general good of those under that law." The fact is, said Locke, that the true end of law "is not to abolish or restrain, but to preserve and enlarge freedom." It is only by following the paths created by the fences erected by the "positive laws of an established government" that men can find their way to true freedom and the fulfillment of their nature. "The freedom... of man and liberty of acting according to his own will, is grounded on his having reason, which is able to instruct him in that law he is to govern himself by, and make him know how far he is left to the freedom of his own will."[354] Thus is the power to make laws the most fundamental power in a commonwealth and that to which the greatest attention must be given in establishing any form of government.

While Locke is generally hailed as the founder of modern democratic theory, he was hardly wedded to that form. His concern in establishing the true grounds for understanding the origin, extent, and end of civil government lay not in the everyday operations of governance, but in the foundation of political legitimacy. To his way of thinking, anything short of an absolute monarchy was a possible form of government.[355] His point was to make the case not for "a democracy," or for any particular form of government, but for the idea of "any independent community."[356] Locke's political science is characterized by his insistence that any legitimate government, whatever the form, will have certain well-defined attributes, and thus the success of such a "constituted commonwealth" depends to no small extent on the ideas that form the "original constitution."[357]

There is no ambiguity in Locke's theory as to what constitutes the most basic necessity in any fundamental constitution: "[W]hatever form the commonwealth is under, the ruling power ought to govern by declared and received laws, and not by extemporary dictates and undetermined resolutions."[358] To allow such "exorbitant and unlimited decrees"as may arise from the "sudden thoughts, or unrestrained and until that moment unknown wills" of the governors would be to import into the confines of

---

[354] *Second Treatise*, 302: 22; 323: 57; 324: 57; 325: 59; 327: 63.
[355] As Locke bluntly put it: "absolute monarchy... is indeed inconsistent with the civil society, and so can be no form of civil government at all." *Second Treatise*, 344: 90.
[356] *Second Treatise*, 373: 133. In Locke's view "the community may make compounded and mixed forms of government, as they think good." Ibid., 372: 132.
[357] Ibid., 388: 153–155; 389: 156.
[358] Ibid., 378: 137.

civil society all the dangers that characterized the state of nature. Thus was Locke clear on those features of any good government:

[W]hoever has the legislative or supreme power of any commonwealth is bound to govern by established standing laws, promulgated and known to the people, and not by extemporary decrees; by indifferent and upright judges, who are to decide controversies by those laws; and to employ the force of the community at home, only in the execution of such laws, or abroad to prevent or redress foreign injuries, and secure the community from inroads or invasion. And all this directed to no other end, but the peace, safety, and publick good of the people.[359]

The essence of any properly constituted commonwealth is a legislative power well ordered by "the original frame of government." Thus are the obligations great on "the first framers of the government."[360]

The only legitimate ground for the foundation of the commonwealth of whatever form is the consent of the people who will live under it: "The people alone can appoint the form of the commonwealth, which is by constituting the legislative, and appointing in whose hands that shall be." This "constitution of the legislative being the original and supream act of the society, antecedent to all positive laws in it, and depending wholly on the people, no inferiour power can alter it." This fundamental constitution of the commonwealth is "derived from the people by a positive, voluntary grant and institution" and can be only what the people by that original grant intended to convey. It is assumed to be perpetual until and unless the people in their collective and constitutive capacity determine that the duly constituted legislative has violated the trust the people have placed in it; at such a time, it remains the basic power of the people to alter or abolish such a government, and to establish a new one, laying its foundations upon such principles as to them shall seem most likely to conduce to their safety and happiness.[361]

The importance of a well-ordered legislative power is repeatedly emphasized by Locke. It is, he says, "the soul that gives form, life and unity to the commonwealth: from hence the several members have their mutual influence, sympathy and connexion." For the most basic fact of civil society and civil government is bringing men together in community, by which action their independent wills are to be knitted together into a public will by which each man subsequently agrees to be governed. But what is most important for Locke is that civil society not be looked upon as simply a holding pen wherein the unruly and irregular passions of independent men are kept in check; the creation of civil society and the subsequent constitution of a civil government is more fundamental a change than that. And it is "in their

---

[359] Ibid., 371: 131.
[360] Ibid., 392: 158; 389: 156.
[361] Ibid., 380: 141; 390–391: 157; 385: 149.

legislative that the members of a commonwealth are united, and combined together into one coherent living body."[362] It is by this act of fundamental consent that naturally independent human beings transform themselves into a community of citizens.

Thus, says Locke, it is important to understand that "it is not names that constitute governments, but the use and exercise of those powers that were intended to accompany them." When it comes to the idea of a properly constituted legislative, there are other considerations than mere representation or the power to create laws. What makes that body the "soul of the commonwealth," that place where all members are pulled together "into one coherent living body," is what must go on there. It is in that council where human reason is to express itself within the structures of civil order: "'tis not a certain number of men, no, nor their meeting, unless they have also freedom of debating, and leisure of protecting what is for the good of the society wherein the legislative consists."[363] It is deliberation, the exercise of reason, that constitutes the core of the legislative power and thereby the essence of civil society. And what renders those who participate in the legislative function part of one living coherent body is that they too are part of the whole that is governed by the part; there is no gulf between the rulers and the ruled.[364] That standard of the public good is the result of the law of nature that carries over into the civil society; that fundamental law, that all men are to be preserved, "is to govern even the legislature itself." It is that "fundamental law of nature and government," and that alone, that legitimates the consent of the people as the foundation of civil society and government.[365]

This legislative is not only the supream power of the commonwealth, but sacred and unalterable in the hands where the community have once placed it; nor can any edict of any body else, in what form soever conceived, or by what power soever backed, have the force and obligation of a law, which has not its sanction from that legislative which the publick has chosen and appointed. For without this the law could not have that, which is absolutely necessary to its being a law, the consent of society, over whom no body can have a power to make laws, but by their own consent, and by the authority received from them; and therefore all the obedience which by the most solemn ties anyone can be obliged to pay, ultimately terminates in this supream power, and is directed by those laws which it enacts.[366]

This standard imposed on all governments and all positive laws those governments create is the result of that law of nature which is antecedent

[362] Ibid., 425–426: 212; 425: 212.
[363] Ibid., 427: 215.
[364] Ibid., 382: 143.
[365] Ibid., 373–374: 134; 392–393: 159.
[366] Ibid., 374: 134.

to all human institutions and laws. Thus "the legislative...is not, nor can possibly be absolutely arbitrary over the lives and fortunes of the people," the reason being that "the law of nature stands as an eternal rule to all men, legislators as well as others."[367] This forms the very essence of Locke's understanding of constitutionalism:

For all the power government has, being only for the good of society, as it ought not to be arbitrary and at pleasure, so it ought to be exercised by established and promulgated laws: that both the people may know their duty, and be safe and secure within the limits of the law, and the rulers too kept within their bounds, and not be tempted, by the power they have in their hands, to employ it to such purposes, and by such measures, as they would not have known, and own not willingly.[368]

The legislative power, even though the fundamental power in the commonwealth, is but "a fiduciary power to act for certain ends."[369] And the meaning of a "constituted commonwealth" is precisely that those ends limit the powers to be wielded. It is that end, the fundamental right of preservation, that serves as a limit to the means of its attainment, civil government. It is for this reason that "there remains in the people a supream power to remove or alter the legislative, when they find the legislative act contrary to the trust reposed in them."[370]

The reason Locke is so insistent that the people retain the fundamental right to alter or abolish the forms of government they may have earlier created, whenever any form becomes destructive of the end for which it was established, is that the political power granted by voluntary consent to the legislative is enormous; it is the "right of making laws with penalties of death, and consequently all less penalties, for the regulating and preserving of property, and of employing the force of the community, in the execution of such laws, and in defence of the commonwealth from foreign injury, and all this only for the publick good."[371] Such power without the restraints imposed by the original constitution would render man's situation even more precarious in civil society than it had been in the state of nature. Such

---

[367] Ibid., 375–376: 135.
[368] Ibid., 378: 137.
[369] Ibid., 385: 149.
[370] "For all power given with trust for the attaining of an end, being limited to that end, whenever that end is manifestly neglected, or opposed, the trust must necessarily be forfeited, and the power devolve into the hands of those that gave it, who may place it anew where they shall think best for their safety and security. And thus the community perpetually retains a supream power of saving themselves from the attempts and designs of any body, even of their legislators, whenever they shall be so foolish, or so wicked, as to lay and carry on designs against the liberties and properties of the subject." Ibid., 385: 149.
[371] Ibid., 286: 3.

an arrangement would be against reason, that fundamental law of nature itself.[372]

The standard against which the legislative power of a government is to be measured is the authority granted that legislature in the first instance by the original grant of the people. That authority is "founded only in the constitution and laws of the government" and is the public will.[373] It is the permission granted by the people to those designated to hold power to do certain things. It is that public will, that authority, that gives legitimacy to the actions of the governors. Power must be exercised according to the rules laid down: "And whosoever in authority exceeds the power given him by the law, and makes use of the force he has under his command, to compass that upon the subject, which the law allows not, ceases in that to be a magistrate, and acting without authority, may be opposed as any other man, who by force invades the right of another."[374] This is a standard for anyone presuming to exercise power under the original grant of the people, kings no less than other officials. By Locke's measure, even the "king's authority [is] given him only by law." This is why, in Locke's view, an absolute monarchy can never be a legitimate civil government. "For exceeding the bounds of authority is no more a right in a great than in a petty officer; no more justifiable in a king than in a constable." Ultimately, "the people shall be judge" as to when and how the powers of the government have exceeded their rightful bounds of authority. Even in the case of the king, "whenever the authority ceases, the king ceases too, and becomes like other men who have no authority."[375]

Locke has a word for the exercise of power beyond the limits of proper authority. That word is "tyranny." The essence of tyranny, Locke argues, "is making use of the power anyone has in his hands; not for the good of those, who are under it, but for his own private, separate advantage."[376] The law of the commonwealth, as the expression of the legitimate public will, is the only source of authority. To this extent, Locke says, "the publick person vested with the power of the law, and so to be considered as the image, phantom, or representative of the commonwealth, acted by the will of the society, declared in its laws; and thus he has no will, no power, but

---

[372] "Whensoever . . . the legislative shall transgress this fundamental rule of society; and either by ambition, fear, folly, or corruption, endeavour to grasp themselves, or put into the hands of any other, an absolute power over the lives, liberties, and estates of the people; by this breach of trust they forfeit the power the people had put into their hands, for quite contrary ends, and it devolves to the people, who have a right to resume their original liberty, and, by the establishment of a new legislative (such as they shall think fit) provide for their own safety and security, which is they end for which they are in society." Ibid., 430–431: 222.

[373] Ibid., 433: 226.

[374] Ibid., 418–419: 202.

[375] Ibid., 421: 206; 419: 202; 442: 239. Locke was blunt: "against the law there can be no authority." Ibid., 421: 206.

[376] Ibid., 416–417: 199.

that of the law." It is for this reason that the "command of any magistrate, where he has no authority, [is] as void and insignificant, as that of any private man." Thus is it for Locke a certain truth that "[w]here-ever law ends, tyranny begins."[377]

Where anarchy was the greatest fear confronting men in the state of nature, so it is tyranny in civil society. What keeps man from "perpetually . . . tumbling" between those extremes is the rule of law. It is law that keeps both anarchy and tyranny at bay. What lies at the very foundation of the rule of law, by Locke's measure, is the legitimate exercise of power by those whom the people must entrust with its exercise. As a result, the fundamental constitutions of government must provide not simply for the power to make laws, but for the procedures whereby those who will govern will have the legitimate authority bestowed upon them. For it is in the procedures staked out in advance by the people, in their original constitution, that one finds the line between lawful and unlawful government, between the authorized and the arbitrary exercise of power.[378] The exercise of political power by anyone other than those appointed by the "settled methods" of conveying the proper authority on them, will be regarded as usurpation and hence unjust.[379]

Laws in Locke's view were "not . . . made for themselves, but to be by their execution the bonds of society, to keep every part of the body politick in its due place and function." The very possibility of human society depended upon man's capacity both to create and to abide by law: "Where the laws cannot be executed, it is all one as if there were no laws, and a government without laws, is, I suppose, a mystery in politicks, unconceivable to humane capacity and inconsistent with humane society."[380] What makes law the bond of society is the power granted to the legislative to attach penalties for its violation, including penalties of death. This necessity of severity in fashioning punishments for the transgression of the law is rooted in man's dependable impulse toward self-preservation. For Locke, no less than for Hobbes, the fear of death is the most basic and enduring of human passions, rooted ultimately in the fact that man's concept of himself is the basis of his understanding of all reality. It is that sense of self, that appreciation of existence, that makes man, man. It is in that sense of self that man's calculations of pleasure and pain are to be found. It is that power to calculate pleasure and pain, and thereby to fashion notions of good and bad, that moved man in the state of nature to act arbitrarily in exercising his natural power to enforce the law of nature. By choosing to enter civil society and relinquishing the power to enforce the law of nature to the community

---

[377] Ibid., 386: 151; 421: 206; 418: 202.
[378] Ibid., 415–416: 198.
[379] Ibid., 416: 198.
[380] Ibid., 429: 219.

itself, man sought to create an artificial man, the body politic, in whose hands the power of punishment could be legitimately placed by consent, there impartially to rest; each man would no longer be a judge in his own case, but rather that power, that right, would be channeled into authorized institutions.

For this to work, it is essential that law be both declared and received; it must be clearly promulgated. The mechanics of declaring and receiving law depends upon the signs men use to convey their thoughts from one to another. Thus is language the essence of law. By words clearly promulgated, the law will spawn in the mind of the citizen or subject the same idea that was in the mind of the lawmaker. It is through the understanding each man has of the lawmaker's will as expressed in certain rules, and the implications of the rewards and punishments attached thereto, that prompts each man in society to bend his private will to conform to the dictates of the public will as made clear in the law.

III. HOBBES, LOCKE, AND THE FOUNDATIONS OF MODERN CONSTITUTIONALISM

The relationship between Locke's earliest writings and his more mature published works can be seen on one level as being characterized by a weakening of his youthful enthusiasm for the principles of Thomas Hobbes, principles thought by many to be the very essence of "falsehood and absurdity" – indeed, the very essence of "wickedness."[381] Yet there remains in his most important works, especially the *Essay Concerning Human Understanding* and the *Two Treatises of Government*, a solid Hobbesian core. Rather than abandoning the clearly Hobbesian sentiments he had expressed in the *Two Tracts on Government* and the *Questions Concerning the Law of Nature*, Locke simply chose to present them more discreetly. Locke's refusal to bare his true beliefs as to the nature of man and his place in the world was the result of prudent calculation on the part of an inherently cautious man rather than a complete turning away from the philosophic place where he had begun.

This is not to suggest that Locke merely followed Hobbes in every particular. As discussed earlier, he sought to make Hobbes's principles his own by thinking them through to their deepest level and drawing out as fully as he could all the implications of the political theories that so captivated him. As Filmer had famously said of Hobbes that "[i]t may seem strange I should praise his building and yet mislike his foundation," so might Locke have said of him that while he admired the foundation Hobbes had laid, he thought his building needed a bit of remodeling. Locke had no intention of

[381] Tyrrell, *A Brief Disquisition of the Law of Nature*, pp. 252, 379.

using his understanding simply as a warehouse for Hobbes's philosophical lumber; he set about to build a sturdier structure out of it.

No one could suggest that a man possessed of so keen an intellect as Locke's would never change his mind; ideas on the most important things may well evolve, especially between a young man's student writings at the age of twenty-eight and the published works of a man in his late fifties. Yet there remains a close tie between those early works and his great publications. In the only two places in his major works where Locke speaks of Hobbes or his writings in a substantive way, he clearly embraces the principles that he finds in Hobbes. Indeed, the two Hobbesian principles Locke singles out serve as the very foundation of his own argument about civil society and man's place in it. These are worth recalling.

In the *Essay*, Locke speaks of Hobbes in his discussion of the power of the civil law to keep people in line. When considering the way men are made to keep their compacts, he notes that "if an Hobbist be asked why; he will answer: because the publick requires it, and the *Leviathan* will punish you."[382] The way such enforcement works, of course, is through the instrumentality of the civil law. And in fleshing out his understanding of the civil law, Locke is unblushingly Hobbesian: "The civil law ... [is the] law no body over-looks: the rewards and punishments, that enforce it, being ready at hand, and suitable to the power that makes it: which is the force of the commonwealth."[383] When compared to the divine law and especially the Christian "view of happiness and misery in another life," the civil law of the *Leviathan* is far more likely to curb men's wills in this world, its sanctions being far more immediate.[384] Eternal damnation is one thing, the executioner's block is quite another.

In the *Two Treatises*, Locke mentions Hobbes by name in the preface to the work and in the *First Treatise* only in passing, when he makes reference to Filmer's work, *Observations on Hobbs*.[385] But in the *Second Treatise*, he attributes, if only by allusion, one of his most important teachings to Hobbes. In the critical discussion of the right of the majority to govern the whole, Locke argues that to allow any man or small number of men to exempt themselves from the rules of the majority would lead to the government grinding to a halt and eventually lead to the dissolution of civil society. For Locke, while no institutions made by men can be deemed permanent, they must at least aspire to make them long-lasting. And it is in making this important point that Locke pulls Hobbes to his side, arguing that it "cannot be suppos'd" that "rational creatures" would opt for anything less than the

---

[382] *Essay*, I.III.5, p. 68.
[383] Ibid., II.XXVIII.9, pp. 352–353.
[384] Ibid., I.III.5, p. 68.
[385] "Preface" to the *Two Treatises of Government*, p. 157; *First Treatise*, 168: 14.

"mighty Leviathan."[386] Feebleness and uncertainty would generate the very "inconveniences" of the state of nature that men sought to avoid by entering civil society.

These two inherently Hobbesian principles – the intended perpetuation of the "mighty *Leviathan*" once established, and the power and the utility of the civil law in keeping the peace – lie at the very heart of Locke's most profound political teaching, his elaborate theory of commonwealth by constitution. They provide for Locke, as they had for Hobbes, the only rational alternative to the bleak and threatening state of nature in which man finds himself, a world in which man comes to see that he is his own worst enemy.[387]

The Hobbesian undercurrent that runs beneath the surface of all Locke's works can also be seen clearly in his valedictory address as moral censor in Christ Church in 1664. The question he posed for himself was "Can Anyone by Nature be Happy in this Life?" His answer was unambiguous: "No." The argument he sets out, while also serving to meet a more good-natured and celebratory requirement, sketches a view of nature and man's place in it from which Locke was never to depart in his later works.

Locke's valedictory discourse, like his *Questions Concerning the Law of Nature* of the same period, rejected the medieval natural law view that God has placed in man a moral light by which he can find his way to a preordained state of happiness on earth. This view, this understanding of a dependable conscience or power of synderesis, was, in Locke's view, sadly mistaken. Man's state on earth falls far short of divine intervention and guidance; he is doomed to a life not unlike a "prison," a place bereft of "tranquility and peace" where "no one is free from hardship or suffering."[388] In response to the ancient idea that by divine light man can find his way out of this jungle of despair, Locke was blunt: "And if perchance there is in us a small flame of divine origin, yet by that flickering and restless motion whereby it strives perpetually towards its original dwelling place, it gives us more trouble and anxiety than light, and it bestows on this clay of ours merely the awareness that it is ablaze and is both consumed and tormented with the silent torture of an imprisoned fire."[389]

Not even the great works of moral and political philosophy had succeeded in revealing a path out of man's awful situation: "in the midst of its noble utterances unhappy mankind feels itself powerless and pitiable." Such empty

---

[386] *Second Treatise*, 351: 98.
[387] As shown earlier, Locke had argued in his *Valedictory Address* in 1664 that "[i]f you seek the end of evils you must yourself cease to be." Reprinted in *Essays on the Law of Nature*, pp. 217–243, p. 229.
[388] *Valedictory Address*, p. 221.
[389] Ibid.

efforts had all been in vain: "Those pointed and shrewd discourses concerning the highest good do not heal human misfortunes any more than fist and sword cure wounds." Like nature itself, ancient philosophy was from its inception "disquieted and fretful."[390] The enthusiasm of those who "rattle off the praises of former times" is dangerously misplaced; the ancients hold out no cure for the distemper of being. This quest for happiness prompted by anxiety and uneasiness is man's true natural state. It is an endless cycle in which nature allows no man to be "content with himself, but sends him away, panting and ever empty, after remote and future goods."[391] Life, in Locke's view, as has been said, is but "the joyless quest for joy."[392] Perhaps the saddest aspect of the man's predicament is that he finds no immediate and natural comfort in the arms of his fellows; each, by nature, is alone and suspicious of the others, separated from the rest by his sense of self, his passions, and his interests.[393]

It is for all these reasons that man must eventually come to realize that "nature must be done away with," not in the metaphorical sense of Locke's valedictory address heralding his pedagogic "death" at the end of his tenure as censor, but truly in the sense that man escapes nature by entering civil society, moved by his uneasiness and desire both to pursue pleasure and happiness and to avoid pain. For in Locke's view, "nature mocks our prayers and grants us in this life no happiness at all except the desire for it."[394]

To escape nature, of course, is to attempt to escape the arbitrary laws by which God governs the universe, laws that upon reflection "are not so much the privileges of the happy as the fetters whereby the wretched are detained in this life."[395] It is by the enduring silence of an "incomprehensible God" that man is ultimately left to his own devices, not guided by a flickering inward moral light, but pushed by a robust and unyielding impulse to preserve himself. That command of self-preservation is the only voice of God that man routinely hears.[396] Thus does it ring hollow when Locke concludes in the *Second Treatise* that when civil governments betray their trust and civil society dissolves, men return to their native right to make their appeals to heaven.

---

[390] Ibid., pp. 221, 223, 225.

[391] Ibid., p. 227.

[392] Strauss, *Natural Right and History*, p. 251.

[393] "[T]here is no solace in distress for all alike to share, but the very people whom misfortune has joined in suffering a like fate are torn asunder and set in arms against one another by discord in their hearts. We hate rather than console our fellow sufferers, and we flatter ourselves with as much or as little right as we bear ill will against others." *Valedictory Address*, p. 229.

[394] Ibid., p. 221.

[395] See *Second Treatise*, 396: 166; *Valedictory Address*, p. 221.

[396] *First Treatise*, 223: 86.

It is man's seeking God's guidance and judgment by such appeals to heaven that plunges him again into the brutal state of nature, subject to the arbitrary wills of those around him. In the same way that each man in the state of nature is left as judge of the law of nature, so each will assume himself to be the true interpreter of the divine will. It was precisely Filmer's reliance on God, and his presumption that ordinary men can know the will of the extraordinary God, that was the reason Locke condemned his theory of politics, rooted as it was in divine guidance, as laying "a foundation for perpetual disorder and mischief, tumult, sedition and rebellion."[397] As Locke well knew, it is in the name of God that the most outrageous acts of human cruelty and depravity are often inflicted by men upon each other.[398] While Scripture may be a means of tempering men's private wills by its moral teachings, it can only wreak havoc if taken as the authoritative foundation of public judgment. For rather than God's clear guidance, man will be left under nothing more divine than the arbitrary opinion of ordinary men in power who presume to speak for God. As Locke argued, there was simply no doubt that experience had made clear the willingness to distort original meanings through interpretations that would seek "to bend" sacred Scripture to make it conform to the opinions of the interpreter.[399] Because of these facts, appeals to heaven by men of impure motives such as "ambition and revenge," through their "cunning and malice," will ultimately serve only "to pervert the doctrine of peace and charity into a perpetual foundation of war and contention."[400] The will of God thus presented by mere mortals can never be the legitimate foundation of authority.

Like Hobbes before him, Locke was moved by a desire to quell the civil unrest such appeals to heaven would inevitably cause. Thus from his earliest writings Locke sought to establish the "very foundations of authority" by which the obedience of men to "lawful government" could be assured, thus bringing to mankind safety for each and security for all. It is by that authority that words such as "justice" and "injustice" come to have accepted meanings, expressing as they do the will and power of the legitimate lawmaker, that most basic power to which the people have ceded their right to interpret the law of nature and punish those who transgress it.[401]

Locke's ultimate objective was to erect secure fences between liberty and anarchy on the one side, and between authority and tyranny on the other. This he sought to do by constructing a demonstrable moral science of ethics, an understanding of the understanding. His effort was not designed to make men virtuous but to leave them free; in that sense, Locke saw his task

---

[397] *Second Treatise*, 285–286: 1.
[398] *First Tract*, pp. 161–162.
[399] *Essay on St. Paul*, pp. 111, 105.
[400] *First Tract*, pp. 160–161.
[401] *Essay*, II.XXVIII.5, p. 351.

as a modest one.[402] To reach his objective, Locke undertook to "enquire into the original, certainty, and extent of humane knowledge" in order to establish "the true original, extent, and end of civil government."[403] This he did simultaneously but separately in the *Essay Concerning Human Understanding* and the *Two Treatises of Government*. And his conclusion as to the extent of human reason led him to argue that government was necessary to secure the rights nature gives but leaves insecure. In particular, man's natural liberty must be tamed, for absolute liberty is inconsistent with the safety and happiness of mankind. So sure was he of this "truth" that he insisted it was as certain as "any in mathematicks," the only idea about which Locke expressed such certainty.

The entire structure of Locke's constitutionalism is built with this one thought in mind, that true liberty is not natural liberty, but rather civil liberty derived from law. It is for that reason that Locke insists that "where law ends, tyranny begins," and that "where there is no law there is no freedom."[404] For it is only "under the positive laws of an Establish'd Government" that men finally come to enjoy the essence of constitutionalism, those "established laws of liberty" that make political life truly possible.[405]

Ultimately, for Locke, it is law alone that stands between man and the state of war, that condition in which force is exercised without authority.[406] For it is by law that man creates the legitimate foundations of political power, organizes its exercise, appoints those who are to administer it, and establishes limits to that power. That is to say, it is by properly constituted commonwealths that the people come to enjoy settled and established laws, impartial judges to whom appeal is to be made for protection and a redress of injuries, and the sanctions fashioned to make those settled and established laws achieve the ends for which they were created in the first place. For in the constituted commonwealth through the laws passed by the legislative power, man will enjoy that which distinguishes civil society from both tyranny and anarchy, that is, a judge on earth who renders unnecessary that most futile of appeals, the appeal to heaven.[407] The result is the creation of "one Body Politick" moved by "one will."[408] That is but another way of saying, as

---

[402] The most one can hope is "not to know all things," but to come to know only "those which concern our conduct." Ibid., I.I.6, p. 46.

[403] Ibid., I.I.2, p. 43; *Two Treatises of Government*, title page.

[404] *Second Treatise*, 418: 202; 324: 57.

[405] *Second Treatise*, 307: 59; 316: 42. It is by such laws, Locke repeatedly argued, that the ruler comes to practice well "the great art of government" whereby "to secure protection and incouragement to the honest industry of mankind against the oppression of power and the narrownesse of party." Ibid., 316: 42.

[406] *Second Treatise*, 434: 227.

[407] Such appeals to heaven, Locke agrees, are capable of causing "endless trouble" in the same way that "justice does, where she lies open to all that appeal to her." *Second Treatise*, 404: 176.

[408] *Second Treatise*, 350: 97; 425–426: 212.

Hobbes had said, that it is through consent and contract that men leave the state of nature and its incessant state of war for civil society and thereby establish, in the form of a constituted commonwealth, nothing less than a "*Mortal God.*"[409]

[409] *Leviathan*, p. 132.

4

The Limits of Natural Law

Modern Constitutionalism and the Science of Interpretation

Nearly from the moment when his two greatest works appeared, the contribution of John Locke to philosophy and politics proved to be enormous. Although his *Two Treatises of Government* was published anonymously, and was not officially attributed to him until after his death, he was widely known for his incomparable *Essay Concerning Human Understanding*, which had appeared under his own name. It instantly made him an internationally known philosopher whose influence spread far and wide; the *Essay* became the most influential book of the eighteenth century, with the sole exception of the Bible.[1] After his death, his importance only increased as new writers took their bearings from his writings, a group that would include, among many others, the English legal lexicographer Giles Jacob; the influential natural law theorists Jean Jacques Burlamaqui, Emerich Vattel, and Thomas Rutherforth; the widely read Whig polemicists John Trenchard and Thomas Gordon; and the great commentator on English law, Sir William Blackstone. In each of their works one sees how Locke's Hobbesian epistemology and the teachings of Hobbes and Locke about language informed the newer political and legal theories, especially on the importance of the definition of words and how best to interpret written instruments such as treaties, laws, and constitutions.

I. LAW DICTIONARIES AND THE LIBERAL TRADITION OF INTERPRETATION

Law dictionaries first appeared as part of the legal profession's contribution to the language of the modern liberal tradition and were meant for laymen as

[1] Kenneth MacLean, *John Locke and English Literature of the Eighteenth Century* (New Haven, CT: Yale University Press, 1936), p. v. See also William S. Howell, *Eighteenth-Century British Logic and Rhetoric* (Princeton, NJ: Princeton University Press, 1971).

well as lawyers.[2] The first law dictionary to be published, Rastell's *Exposiciones Terminorum Legum Anglorum* (1527), which came to be known simply as the *Termes de la Ley*, is a case in point.[3] Although Rastell's work had been preceded by something akin to dictionaries, the glossaries or vocabularies of Anglo-Saxon words, his law dictionary was distinguished by aspiring to be more.[4] It contained definitions of words and placed them in alphabetical order. But the most interesting thing about this early effort to define with some degree of precision the meaning of legal language is the extent to which Rastell anticipated the more theoretically sophisticated arguments that would eventually come from the founders of modern constitutional liberalism, Thomas Hobbes and John Locke. Rastell's purpose in creating his law dictionary was, at the deepest level, political.

While men are bound in their conduct by "the order & law of Nature," Rastell wrote, that law is not sufficient to the ultimate goal of civil peace. The fact is that "there is no multitude of people in no realm that can continue in unity and peace without they be thereto compelled by some good law & order." In Rastell's view, it is "a good reasonable common law" that ultimately will make "a good common peace." The emphasis on the commonality of law is essential, in Rastell's view, given the nature of mankind. As he points out, "as every man is variant from the other in visage, so they be variable in mind and condition, therefore one law & one governor for one realm and for one people is most necessary." The alternative, "diverse rulers & governors & diverse orders or laws one contrary to another," will lead only to conflict and division within society. One governor under one law will be able to "bringeth diverse & much people to one good unity."[5]

The essence of public order is law; it is both necessary "& a virtuous and good thing." It keeps people from committing wrongs "willingly" and guides them from doing so by negligence. In short, the law has an educating role to play. If the law is to fulfill its important social role, and to be both "virtuous & good," it is essential that "every man . . . have the knowledge of the law."[6] Rastell makes one of the earliest cases for the necessity of written law:

[I]t is necessary for every realm to have a law reasonable & sufficient to govern the great multitude of the people, ergo it is necessary that the great multitude of people have the knowledge of that same law, to which they be bound, ergo it followeth that

---

[2] On the American side, see Eldon Revare James, "A List of Legal Treatises Printed in the British Colonies and the American States Before 1801," in Roscoe Pound, ed., *Harvard Legal Essays* (Cambridge, MA: Harvard University Press, 1934), pp. 159–211.

[3] William S. Holdsworth, *History of English Law*, 17 vols. (London: Metheun, 1903–72), V: 401. Hereinafter cited as *History of English Law*.

[4] John D. Cowley, *A Bibliography of Abridgments, Digests, Dictionaries and Indexes of English Law to the Year 1800* (London: Selden Society, 1932) pp. lxxix-lxxxi.

[5] John Rastell, *Exposicions of the Termes of the Lawes of England* (London: R. Tottell, 1567), "Prologue," pp. Ai, Aii, Ai.

[6] Ibid., p. Aii.

the law in every realm should be so published, declared, & written, in such wise that the people so bound to the same, might soon and shortly come to the knowledge thereof or else such a law, so kept secretly in the knowledge of a few persons & from the knowledge of the great multitude, may rather be called a trap and a net to bring the people to vexation and trouble than a good order to bring them to peace & quietness.[7]

Rastell understood that if the law, having been "ordained and devised for the augmentation of justice," is indeed to be successful in its purpose, then it is essential that those who are to be bound and governed by it know what it says. One cannot be bound by the law, one cannot be restrained and guided by it, unless one knows what it commands and prohibits. Thus did he see his task in the dictionary as educating those who might otherwise be "ignorant of the law" by undertaking to "declare & to expound certain obscure and dark termes concerning the laws of this realm." For Rastell, it is only by knowledge of the law that "the true execution of the same law" is to be enjoyed, and thereby the preservation and increase of the fortunes of the commonwealth.[8]

These sentiments continued to inform legal lexicography, as can be seen in the relationship of law dictionaries to the broader tradition of the more modern constitutional and legal liberalism of the seventeenth century. This relationship is seen most clearly in the life and work of Giles Jacob. Although he is dismissed by some today as merely a writer of "undistinguished works,"[9] Jacob was in fact one of the most prolific and widely known compilers of legal texts in his day.[10] In addition to his *New Law Dictionary*, Jacob published no fewer than thirty-three legal texts, many of them running to several editions. His treatises, along with the dictionary, were to be found in many early American libraries, including those of John Adams and Thomas Jefferson.[11] In particular, Jacob's dictionary was in twice as many American

---

[7] Ibid., p. Aiii.

[8] Ibid., pp. Aiii, Aiv.

[9] A. W. B. Simpson, ed., *Biographical Dictionary of the Common Law* (London: Butterworths, 1984), p. 272.

[10] "Few men have left behind them more ample testimonies of their industry than Mr. Giles Jacob; his publications have been very numerous." His *New Law Dictionary* in particular was deemed a "very valuable work." Richard Whalley Bridgman, *A Short View of Legal Bibliography* (London: W. Reed, 1807), pp. 165, 169. Jacob's prodigious outpouring was undoubtedly as much a matter of sales as scholarship, and as a result many of his works do have the marks of haste. See *History of English Law*, XII: 340. For a glimpse of Jacob's successes, see the account book for one of his publishers, Bernard Lintot, in John Nichols, *Literary Anecdotes of the Eighteenth-Century*, 9 vols. (London: Nichols and Son, 1814), VIII: 296–297.

[11] See William Hamilton Bryson, *Census of Law Books in Colonial Virginia* (Charlottesville: University Press of Virginia, 1978); Nicholas Sellers, "The Smith Nicholas Law Library," *Law Library Journal* 83 (1991): 463–469; Herbert A. Johnson, *Imported Eighteenth-Century Law Treatises in American Libraries* (Knoxville: University of Tennessee Press,

law libraries as the second most popular legal lexicon, John Cowell's *Inter-preter*, and in colonial Virginia it was the fourth most popular of all law books available.[12] It was simply "the most widely used English law dictionary" in the early republic.[13]

Little is known of Giles Jacob beyond the few biographical strands he chose to weave into his various works.[14] From his nonlegal works it is clear that he aspired to a literary life, fancying himself both a poet and a playwright; he was thus outraged when he found himself the target of Alexander Pope's scorn in the *Dunciad* (1729) as nothing more than a "blunderbuss of law."[15] But it was the law and not literature that ultimately earned him his living and reputation. Indeed, he claimed he had been "bred to the law," and at the age of twenty-five embarked on his career as a legal scrivener.[16]

In 1720 Jacob began work on what would become an "entirely new departure in legal literature"; when his *New Law Dictionary* finally appeared in 1729, he had already published sixteen of his legal tracts and ten volumes of plays, poetry, and other nonlegal works.[17] But the originality of Jacob's own work and the political implications of his motives must be viewed in light of the evolution of law dictionaries down to his time. For over the course of the two hundred years that separated Jacob's dictionary from Rastell's *Exposiciones Terminorum Legum Anglorum*, the political and philosophical worlds had undergone tumultuous changes.[18] And it is within that context

1978); E. Millicent Sowerby, *Catalogue of the Library of Thomas Jefferson*, 5 vols. (Washington., DC: Library of Congress, 1952); and Lindsay Swift, ed., *Catalogue of the John Adams Library in the Public Library of the City of Boston* (Boston: The Trustees of the Boston Public Library, 1917).

12   Johnson, *Eighteenth-Century Law Treatises*, p. 61; Bryson, *Census of Law Books*, p. xvii.

13   Leonard W. Levy, "Origins of the Fifth Amendment and Its Critics," *Cardozo Law Review* 19 (1997): 821–860, p. 854.

14   He was born in 1686 in Romsey, one of eight children of Henry and his wife, Susanna, from the Thornburgh family of Wiltshire. His father was a maltster who died in 1734, leaving Jacob a modest inheritance. In 1733 Jacob married one Jane Dexter in the parish church of St. Andrew in Holborn.

15   Pope summed him up this way:

Jacob, the Scourge of Grammar, mark with awe,
Nor less revere him, Blunderbuss of Law.

See J. McLaverty, "Pope and Giles Jacob's *Lives of the Poets*: The *Dunciad* as Alternative Literary History," *Modern Philology* 83 (1985–86): 22–32.

16   Giles Jacob, *The Poetical Register*, 2 vols. (London: Bettesworth, 1723), I: 318; *The Modern Justice* (London: B. Lintot, 1720), p. iii. So, too, does he claim to have been the keeper of "very considerable estates for seven years together successively." *The Compleat Sportsman* (London: E. Nutt and R. Gosling, 1718), preface. See also *The Country Gentleman's Vade Mecum* (London: William Taylor, 1717).

17   Cowley, *Bibliography*, p. xc.

18   For a more complete discussion of the evolution of law dictionaries, see Gary L. McDowell, "The Politics of Meaning: Law Dictionaries and the Liberal Tradition of Interpretation,"

of Enlightenment liberalism and its concern with language that the rise of law dictionaries is best understood.

The epistemological revolution wrought in the science of politics by Hobbes and Locke, a revolution that would become the foundation of modern constitutionalism, as discussed earlier, took as its point of departure the belief that civil society rests only upon the voluntary consent of free and independent individuals. At the center of this understanding of consent lay an appreciation for the necessity of language as the means whereby society is formed and sustained.

Locke shared Hobbes's view of the importance of reaching a general agreement as to precise definitions of words. It is a matter of learning and retaining what meanings have been agreed upon.[19] This is especially critical when it comes to complex ideas and moral words, such as justice. A definition, Locke argued, "is the only way, whereby the precise meaning of moral words can be known; and yet a way, whereby their meaning may be known certainly, and without leaving any room for any contest about it."[20] It was precisely the fact that complex ideas and moral words are the contrivances of men that allowed Locke to suggest that morality is as capable of demonstration as pure mathematics.[21]

This idea is what led Locke to suggest in the *Essay Concerning Human Understanding* that human discourse and society would be greatly aided by the advent of a dictionary, an authoritative listing of definitions derived from the "sensible qualities" of observable things upon which men could depend. Although Locke thought that a truly philosophical dictionary of the sort he proposed, what he called a "natural history," would require "too many hands, as well as too much time, cost, pains, and sagacity, ever to be hoped for," he had no doubt there could be a compilation of a lesser sort, with definitions provided in "the sense men use them in."[22] Such a compilation would be the foundation of social and political intercourse, and would enhance both civil and philosophical exchanges among men. In time Locke's suggestion would come to fruition. The *Essay Concerning Human Understanding* eventually inspired Samuel Johnson to produce a dictionary

The American Journal of Legal History 44 (April 2000): 257–283, from which this section is drawn.

[19] "Words having naturally no signification, the idea which each stands for, must be learned and retained by those, who would exchange thoughts, and hold intelligible discourse with others in any language." John Locke, *An Essay Concerning Human Understanding*, ed. P. H. Nidditch (Oxford: Oxford University Press, 1979), III.IX.5, p. 477. Hereinafter cited as *Essay*. Citation indicates book, chapter, section, and page.

[20] *Essay*, III.IX.17, p. 517. As Hobbes had put it earlier, "the light of human minds is perspicuous words, but by exact definitions first snuffed, and purged, from ambiguity; reason is the pace; encrease of science the way; and the benefit of mankind the end." Thomas Hobbes, *Leviathan* (Oxford: Clarendon Press, 1909), p. 37.

[21] *Essay*, III.XI.16, p. 516.

[22] Ibid., III.XI.25, p. 522.

of the English language, the principles of which conformed to Locke's own theory of knowledge and language.[23]

By the time Johnson began work in 1746 on what would become his masterpiece, "Locke's ideas on language and the mind had become commonplaces."[24] But Johnson did not just share Locke's epistemological assumptions that "words are but the signs of ideas."[25] He also employed Locke in some 3,241 quotations in his *Dictionary*.[26] By incorporating works such as Locke's *Essay* along with numerous poems, histories, and other works by such esteemed authors as Addison, Donne, Dryden, and Shakespeare, Johnson contributed greatly to the "encyclopaedic tradition of lexicography." By adopting a version of a commonplace book of important quotations as the model for his dictionary, Johnson sought to go beyond mere linguistic analysis or etymology; rather, he created the *Dictionary* for educational and moral purposes. This he achieved by "presenting quotations that, besides illustrating the meanings of words, teach fundamental points of morality."[27] The encyclopedic approach of the *Dictionary of the English Language* would, from the time of its publication in 1755, dominate dictionary makers, including Noah Webster in the United States, upon whom Johnson's influence was indeed "considerable."[28]

But Johnson was not the first to follow Locke's lead. A quarter-century before Johnson published his monumental work, Jacob published his new kind of law dictionary, one that sought to provide for the legal profession the kind of "natural history" Locke had suggested such dictionaries should be.[29] Both Johnson and Jacob were part of a tradition of lexicography that stretched back at least to 1604 in the case of dictionaries of the English language, and to 1527 in the case of law dictionaries.[30] Such was the tradition

---

[23] See Allen Reddick, *The Making of Johnson's Dictionary, 1746–1773* (Cambridge: Cambridge University Press, 1990).

[24] Elizabeth Hedrick, "Locke's Theory of Language and Johnson's *Dictionary*," *Eighteenth Century Studies* 20 (1986–87): 422–444, p. 422.

[25] Samuel Johnson, *The Works of Samuel Johnson*, ed. Robert Lynam, 12 vols. (London: W. Baynes, 1825) V: 28.

[26] James McLaverty, "From Definition to Explanation: Locke's Influence on Johnson's Dictionary," *Journal of the History of Ideas* 47 (1986): 377–394, p. 384.

[27] Robert De Maria, Jr., *Johnson's Dictionary and the Language of Learning* (Oxford: Clarendon Press, 1986), pp. 7, 13, 19. But "just as he sought quotations from certain writers because of their political, moral, or religious beliefs, he rejected others, whatever the passage, because he feared that he would suggest approval of their ideas." Reddick, *The Making of Johnson's Dictionary*, p. 34.

[28] Ronald A. Wells, *Dictionaries and the Authoritarian Tradition* (The Hague: Mouton, 1973), p. 25. See also Olivia Smith, *The Politics of Language, 1791–1819* (Oxford: Clarendon Press, 1984).

[29] *Essay*, III.XI.25, p. 522.

[30] See De Witt T. Starnes and Gertrude E. Noyes, *The English Dictionary from Cawdrey to Johnson* (Chapel Hill: University of North Carolina Press, 1946). See also James A. H. Murray, *The Evolution of English Lexicography* (Oxford: Clarendon Press, 1900); Mary

that one might safely argue that "the whole history of English lexicography makes one slow to accept a claim of striking originality for any dictionary maker."[31] Yet Jacob, no less than Johnson, did indeed produce a work of striking originality. For his objective was nothing less than to produce "a kind of a library"[32] for a new, and largely Lockean, legal age.

Jacob's intellectual world was dominated by Locke, and Jacob's own career hovered around the edges of Locke's world. William Blathwayt, for whom Jacob worked, for example, served with Locke as a commissioner of trade and was a rival during Locke's control of the Board of Trade (1696–1700).[33] Upon his retirement Locke was succeeded by Matthew Prior, an acquaintance and occasional correspondent of Jacob. Jacob also dedicated one of his legal tracts to Peter King, Locke's nephew and close friend during his last years.[34] At a minimum, Jacob moved in a world where Locke's ideas were commonplace, and it is the influence of Locke on the ideas expressed in Jacob's various essays that provides the political context for the dictionary maker's legal thinking and his desire to render the law accessible through his new method of organization. The point was to enable the people to defend their rights and liberties.

The most clearly Lockean work Jacob produced is a small work entitled *Essays Relating to the Conduct of Life*.[35] In many ways, the *Essays* is an unremarkable work. But there are two reasons why it is of interest. First, the teachings Jacob seeks to instill through his essays very clearly take their bearings from the ideas one finds in Locke's *Essay Concerning Human Understanding* and his various tracts on education. The second reason Jacob's essays are of some interest is the light they shed on his possible motives in publishing his other works, especially his legal compilations and law dictionary.

Locke's purpose in constructing his *Essay Concerning Human Understanding*, it is worth recalling, was a reasonably modest one. "Our business here," Locke wrote, "is not to know all things, but those which concern

---

Segar, "Dictionary Making in the Early Eighteenth Century," *R.E.S.* 7 (1931): 210–213; and M. M. Mathews, *A Survey of English Dictionaries* (Oxford: Oxford University Press, 1933).

[31] James H. Sledd and Gwin J. Kolb, *Dr. Johnson's Dictionary: Essays in the Biography of a Book* (Chicago: University of Chicago Press, 1955), p. 4.

[32] Giles Jacob, *A New Law Dictionary* (London: E. & R. Nutt and R Gosling, 1729), p. ii.

[33] See Maurice Cranston, *John Locke: A Biography* (London: Blackwells, 1957), pp. 399–448; and G. A. Jacobsen, *William Blathwayt: A Late Seventeenth Century Administrator* (New Haven, CT: Yale University Press, 1932).

[34] Giles Jacob, *The Laws of Appeals and Murder* (London: B. Lintot, 1719).

[35] There are in the British Library three editions of this work. The first edition (1717) was published by Edmund Curll, the second (1726) by T. Cooke, and the third (1730) by J. Hooke. The case for attributing this work to Jacob is made in Gary L. McDowell, "Giles Jacob's *Conduct of Life*," *Notes and Queries* 242 (1997): 190–193, from which this section is taken.

our conduct. If we can find out those measures, whereby a rational creature put in that state, which man is in, in this world, may, and ought to govern his opinions, and actions depending thereon, we need not be troubled, that some other things escape our knowledge."[36] In his later works on education, it is precisely this objective that moves Locke. He seeks through education to make men fit for civil society, that is to say, to make them capable of being free. In a letter entitled "Instructions for the Conduct of a Young Gentleman," published in *The Remains of John Locke*, the author argues that it is by "knowing men and manners" that gentlemen can come to be guided by prudence, a quality he deems to be rightly "reckon'd among the cardinal virtues."[37] One can be expected to learn what one needs to know especially through the study of the history, institutions, and laws of one's own country. The lessons one gleans will be a safe guide to one's conduct.

These sentiments serve as Jacob's point of departure in the *Essays Relating to the Conduct of Life*. For Jacob, the "great art and accomplishment of mankind is that of prudence," and by his little book he sought to establish a method whereby "particular virtues are illustrated, and vices detected." The fact was that "the liberality of nature in the person, is frequently attended with a deficiency in the understanding." Thus was it necessary to "subdue passion," bringing it under the control of "true sense and right reason," for in human affairs "unruly passion is destructive to interest, and the greatest author of present and future misery." Jacob set out to impart moral

---

[36] *Essay*, I.I.6, p. 46.
[37] *The Remains of John Locke, Esq.* (London: E. Curll, 1714), p. 10. It is probably no coincidence that the first edition of *Essays Relating to the Conduct of Life* was published by the infamous publisher Edmund Curll just three years after he had published (also anonymously) *The Remains of John Locke, Esq.* Included in this collection of Locke's tracts, apparently given to Curll for publication by "R.K", described as "a near relative of Mr. Locke's," was a letter entitled "Instructions for the Conduct of a Young Gentleman, as to Religion and Government, etc." While it bears some similarity to Locke's other writings on education, especially that recently reprinted as "Some Thoughts Concerning Reading and Study for a Gentleman," it is not the same. The latter correspondence was acknowledged in a letter of 23 August 1703 from Samuel Bold thanking Locke on behalf of Roger Clavel, who had sought Locke's guidance in such matters. The letter included in Curll's *Remains of John Locke* was dated 25 August 1703 and apparently written to "R.K", the Reverend Richard King, a relation through Peter King. See James Axtell, ed., *The Educational Writings of John Locke* (Cambridge: Cambridge University Press, 1968), pp. 397–404; and Locke to [Richard King], 25 August 1703, letter no. 3328 in E. S. De Beer, ed., *The Correspondence of John Locke*, 8 vols. (Oxford: Clarendon Press, 1976–89), VIII: 56–59.

   Although there is no textual evidence to support it, it is at least possible that the anonymous editor of Curll's *Remains of John Locke* was indeed Jacob, who had written anonymously at least once before for the infamous publisher. The book was a "treatise" on hermaphrodites, oddly enough. *Tractatus de Hermaphroditis* (London: E. Curll, 1718). See Pat Rogers, *Grub Street: Studies in a Subculture* (London: Methuen, 1972), pp. 288–289. On Curll's reputation, see Ralph Straus, *The Unspeakable Curll* (London: Chapman & Hall, 1927).

instruction in order to provide for "a man's decent guidance through a difficult and capricious world." He was as modest in his expectations as Locke had been in the *Essay.* "To be perfectly just," he cautioned, "is beyond the attainment of human capacity; but to be so in some degree, is in every one's power, and to be so to the utmost of our power, is the greatest commendation of man."[38] Jacob's sketch of what such an education in worldliness for a gentleman should be closely followed Locke's prescriptions in *Some Thoughts Concerning Education.* The concerns were with history, geography, European languages, and "the laws, government, customs, and manners of other countries, as well as his own."[39]

Another glimpse of Locke's influence on Jacob is in the revision that occurs for the second edition of the *Essays,* in which Jacob undertakes to add "some essays on the government of society."[40] In those additions Jacob moves, as it were, from the Locke of the *Essay Concerning Human Understanding* and *Thoughts on Education* to the Locke of *Two Treatises of Government.* And in so doing, he follows Locke's clear teaching that there is an intimate connection between the conduct of the understanding and what may be called the moral foundations of legitimate government.

The focus of Jacob's excursion into political theory is tyranny and the role of law in preventing it. The line between tyranny and order, for Jacob no less than for Locke, was the idea that political power must be authorized. "Our king, altho' great," Jacob observes, "is bound by the laws, as well as his subjects; as we must not on the one hand transgress them, so he may not on the other incroach [sic] upon them."[41] The reason even the king must be deemed bound by the law is that the power he wields is held only by a grant from the people, a grant originally made to secure that political liberty that "makes the people of England more flourishing and formidable, than those of any other kingdom."[42]

For Jacob, as for Locke, no king or governor worthy of the name can act "without authority of the law of the land." To exceed the bounds of legality, to overleap the fences of the law, is for a ruler to roam at large in the trackless fields of his own will, sacrificing the public good to his private advantage. As

---

[38] Jacob, *Essays,* 2nd ed., p. 77; ibid., 1st ed., pp. v, 41, 69, 2; ibid., 2nd ed., pp. 108–109.

[39] Jacob, *Essays,* 1st ed., p. 18. For similarities to Locke, see especially *Some Thoughts Concerning Education,* pp. 187, 186, 295, and 324, in Axtell, ed., *The Educational Writings of John Locke.*

[40] Jacob, *Essays,* 2nd ed., title page.

[41] Ibid., 3rd ed., p. 111.

[42] Ibid., 2nd ed., p. 111. "To keep up order, rule and decorum, in the actions of men one towards another, and preserve them from violating each other, kings and governors were originally ordained. When they act as they ought, and make justice the pursuit of their power, they are the bulwarks of right and property; the promoters of virtue, piety, and humanity; and the fathers of their country: they deserve the highest reverence and obedience; and everything next to adoration is paid to them." Ibid.

Jacob put it, "a tyrannical prince...treats his subjects as a huntsman doth his game, and sets his ministers on the people, like unto other his hounds upon the prey, who are sure to worry them to death, or hunt them to dens and corners, whence they dare not stir abroad but for the sustentation of life, to give fresh pleasure to their cruel keeper." To so behave, in Jacob's estimation, is to descend from legitimate rule into tyranny, which of all the "publick violences and oppressions" one can imagine is the most destructive to society. "[I]f kings and princes abuse the authority repos'd in them: if instead of cherishing, they oppress their subjects, they are then no longer kings, but enemies to mankind."[43]

The intersection of Jacob's pedagogical and political concerns was at the point where it was understood that it is "by easy steps and loppings of liberty" that "tyranny is accomplished." Thus is it of critical importance to a true "country of liberty" to educate its people in their laws and institutions so that the first move against them, that first easy step or lopping of their liberty, will be the more easily detected and resisted.[44]

Jacob's contributions to law have tended to be ignored by virtue of their being primarily compilations of black-letter law put into alphabetical order. Yet in his various prefaces to those works Jacob touches repeatedly on the issues raised in *Essays Relating to the Conduct of Life*, the importance of educating the people in the laws of their country. As Jacob said elsewhere, "the subject of our law cannot be made too familiar," for it is by it that "rights and properties" of the people find protection.[45]

Jacob's understanding of politics began with the view that law is the only alternative to the barbarity of the state of nature. He knew, as Locke had taught, that "inclination has no law, and nature no restraint."[46] Outside of civil society and government by consent there is only the "primitive power" of self-defense, that "right of inflicting punishments" held by every man by virtue of his equality and independence.[47] Although there is most assuredly a law of nature that is, in and of itself, "just and good and binding in all places...being from God himself," without the "arbitrary laws"[48] of the commonwealth, there is no means of enforcement. While "all things proceeding from nature are not only respected in philosophy, but also in [the]

---

[43] Ibid., pp. 114–115, 114, 112, 111.

[44] Ibid., pp. 112, 114.

[45] *Every Man His Own Lawyer; or A Summary of the Laws of England in a New and Instructive Method* (London: J. Hazard, S. Birt, and C. Corbett, 1736), p. iii. This was one of Jacob's most popular titles, the seventh edition of which was published in New York in 1768 and reprinted in Philadelphia in 1769. See Levy, "Origins of the Fifth Amendment and Its Critics," p. 855, n.192.

[46] *Love in a Wood: or, The Country Squire, a Farce* (London: R. Burleigh, 1714), p. 35.

[47] *Lex Mercatoria: or, the Merchant's Companion* (London: B. Motte et al., 1729), pp. 2–3.

[48] *A Law Grammar: or, Rudiments of the Law* (London: Henry Lintot, 1744), p. 1

law,"[49] it is only by the force of the civil law – those "arbitrary laws" – that reason is brought to bear on an otherwise unruly world. It is the natural desire for self-preservation that moves men to create the institutions of government necessary for the maintenance of public order.[50] The only legitimate exercise of the legislative power is to give effect to those laws of nature that come to be known to human reason.

The civil law that each nation has "peculiarly established for itself" is essential to the protection of each man's "life, liberty, and property."[51] This law, this "well ordering of civil society," is a rule that goes beyond any private judgment of right or wrong.[52] All laws passed by the legislative power "are in their nature binding, and lay an obligation,"[53] an obligation of each member of that society to obey. "All lawful authority," Jacob argues, "is to be submitted to, and resisting it, is resisting the justice of the commonwealth."[54] In order for those necessary obligations to be met, it is essential that those governed by the laws be able to understand them.

While the common law of England was the very "perfection of reason,"[55] even there "statutes have been introduced on a deficiency of the common law."[56] In fact, as a general matter, the law was a mess. The common law Jacob found to be "lying confus'd in our books."[57] The abridgments were characterized by "great perplexity, confusion, and tautology."[58] Moreover, in many of the books of the law there was "a great deal of pedantick and affected stuff," with the result that the average reader was more likely to be confounded than instructed.[59] When confronting the tangle of the law, the average reader was "like a traveler in a wood without a guide, who, when once he is got in, is sure to be lost, and not find his way out."[60] Jacob's solution was his new method, which was a matter not of "laying

[49] *A Treatise of Laws* (London: T. Woodward and J. Peele, 1721), p. 102.

[50] *Law Grammar*, p. 1.

[51] Ibid., pp. 3, 5. "All countries require laws for their government, to prevent injuries and violence, and the invasions of men upon the rights and properties of each other." *The Student's Companion: or, the Reason of the Laws of England* (London: E. and R. Nutt and R. Gosling, 1725), p. 113.

[52] *Law Grammar*, p. 1. "[N]o person ought, out of his own private opinion, to be wiser than the law." Ibid., p. 54.

[53] *Lex Mercatoria*, p. 2.

[54] *The Student's Companion*, p. 128. Since not all men are honest and decent, it is necessary that civil law be built upon an abiding truth of human nature, that "evil men fear to offend, for fear of pain;" as a result, "'tis necessary that pains should be ordained for offences." Ibid., p. 206.

[55] *Treatise of Laws*, p. 115.

[56] *The Statute Law Common-Plac'd* (London: B. Lintot, 1719), p. 1.

[57] Ibid., p. 2.

[58] *The Compleat Chancery-Practiser*, 2 vols. (London: E. and R. Nutt and R. Gosling, 1730), p. viii.

[59] *City Liberties: or, the Rights and Privileges of Freemen* (London: W. Mears, 1732), p. viii.

[60] *The Student's Companion*, p. iv.

the ax to the root" but only of "skilful and judicious pruning, so as the law may remain an art and science, and justice at the same time be obtained on easy terms, not oppressive to the people."[61] His "good and easy method"[62] would allow him to clear "the plainest and easiest road"[63] whereby the people could come to know their law.

A proper public understanding of the law was essential to that great end of civil society, political liberty. Liberty was a "sacred thing... the sum of all our happiness here." Should it be lost, Jacob warned, "we should miserably find a Hell upon earth." In all forms of government, liberty is constantly threatened by the encroachment of tyranny – no less to be expected from rulers of free states than from kings – and there is "no other fence or security against it but... [the] laws." Liberty was not simply freedom in some limited sense; it was nothing less than the essence of "the welfare of mankind." By it men were spurred to action and gained their property; it was essential that both be secured by the law of the land. In particular, it was by the law of the land that the king's prerogative and the people's liberty were bound together, each with "certain limits beyond which they may not venture." When it came to the monarchy, "the king can do no wrong, for he has not the power to do it, he having no power but by law, and there being no law to do wrong."[64] Citing William Prynne as his authority, Jacob insisted that "the laws to which the king assents are more the people's than the king's... it is the... people only that make it a law to bind them. And... the chief legislative power is in the people and Houses of Parliament, not the king."[65] Confusion in the law, a disregard for its language and its meaning, would endanger the rights and liberties of the people.

The difficulty of all law, Jacob knew, was that it would inevitably require interpretation. What was essential, if law was to fulfill its important role in civil society, was that the words of the law be understood as they were intended, just as in ordinary speech. In every case, "the sense of the words is to be collected from the cause of the speech, and the subject of the matter." When it comes to law, that demand translates into the necessity that judges called upon to interpret the law never forget the essential distinction between "private knowledge and... judicial knowledge." Judges are not permitted to give effect to the law on the basis of their "own fancy, nor according to [their] own will," but only on the basis of the meaning of the law as created. Hardly original, Jacob was just following the great tradition that held that "judges have not the power to judge according to what they think

---

[61] Giles Jacob to G – e C – by, Esq., 30 October 1730, in Giles Jacob, *The Mirrour: or, Letters Satyrical, Panegyrical, Serious and Humorous on the Present Times* (London: J. Roberts, 1733), pp. 67–68.

[62] *The Law Military* (London: B. Lintot, 1719), p. 1.

[63] *The Compleat Chancery-Practiser*, p. vii.

[64] *The Laws of Liberty and Property* (London: E. and R. Nutt and R. Gosling, 1724), pp. i-ii, iii, i, iii, 53, 53.

[65] *Lex Constitutionis, or the Gentleman's Law* (London: In the Savoy, 1719), p. 122.

fit, but that which by the law they know to be right and consonant to the laws."[66]

It was by the rules of grammar that law was to be given its true meaning. The art of grammar and language is "the portal by which we enter into the knowledge of all acts and whereby we communicate ourselves and our studies to others."[67] When it came to the written law, judges, said Jacob, siding with Coke, "ought not make any interpretation against the express letter of the statute, for nothing can so well express the intent of the makers of the act as their direct words themselves."[68] By limiting themselves to the cause of the law and the subject of the matter, judges will be able to chain themselves to the law and not wander off into the wilderness of their own fancy. It is adherence to the law that constitutes judicial, as opposed to merely private, knowledge. That is to say, "statutes are to be interpreted reasonably, according to the meaning of the makers." This was true of the old as well as the new law, for "the strength of expression in ancient records should be preserved, which is often preferable to our modern refinements."[69]

The triumph of Jacob's effort to secure the liberties of the people by securing the language and meaning of the law, as well as his effort to bring the law into a "much narrower compass,"[70] was his "masterpiece,"[71] *A New Law Dictionary*. It was an attempt to give an account of the whole law, and this he did by combining three things into one law book – "a dictionary, an abridgment, and a vocabulary."[72] It was nothing less than a"legal encyclopedia," in which he "based upon the definition of each term a statement of the whole law on the subject."[73] It was not enough simply to define the words; he strove to put the meaning in context. Thus did he seek to include the forms and writs of the law in order to "contribute to the right understanding of the law." So, too, did he take to include "from the most ancient authors treating the British, Saxon, Danish, and Norman laws, such information as explain the history and antiquity of the law, with our manners, customs, and original form of government."[74] By his

---

[66] Ibid., p. 64. This was a common theme in Jacob's works: "A judge is to pronounce sentence according to the law, and what is alledjed [sic] and proved and not according to his own will and fancy. He hath no power to judge according to what he think fit, but that which by the law he knows to be right." *The Laws of Liberty and Property*, p. 57.

[67] *Law Grammar*, p. ii.

[68] *Treatise of Laws*, p. 15. As Coke had reported, "The judges said that they ought not to make any construction against the express letter of the statute; for nothing can so express the meaning of the makers of an act as their own direct words, for *index animi sermo*." *Edrich's Case*, 5 Co. Rep. 118a.

[69] *The Compleat Attorney's Practice*, 2 vols. (London: Dan Browne, 1737), I: i-ii.

[70] *Treatise of Laws*, p. iv.

[71] Cowley, *Bibliography*, p. xc.

[72] *History of English Law*, XII: 176.

[73] Cowley, *Bibliography*, pp. xci, xc.

[74] *A New Law Dictionary*, p. ii.

method would the "difficulty and disagreeableness" of the study of the law be overcome and the law be made manageable.

Jacob's belief that the true meaning of the law was to be found in the meaning of the words used by the makers of the law was the received tradition of his day, a juridical view with intellectual roots reaching back hundreds of years; it was also a view that would continue to flower and flourish.[75] It was a view that was embraced by those who created the American republic, and it continued to hold sway among the best minds of the next century. Those who turned their attention to the problem of interpretation, especially the interpretation of the written law and the Constitution, embraced the commonsense notion that the law means what it says and that it says what those who framed it intended. As Francis Lieber would put it a century later, "no... form of words can have more than one 'true sense,'" and it is this meaning that is "the very basis of all interpretation."[76]

II. NATURAL LAW AND THE SCIENCE OF INTERPRETATION

At the same time that Jacob was preparing the later editions of his revolutionary law dictionary, and when Johnson was simultaneously readying his *Dictionary of the English Language* for publication, there also was developing a new school of natural public law. These writers took their bearings primarily from Hugo Grotius, especially his *De Jure Belli ac Pacis* (1625), but they added to Grotius's theories of natural law and the law of nations their own reflections in light of the political philosophies of Hobbes and Locke.[77] Three of the most important works of these natural law theorists were Jean Jacques Burlamaqui's *The Principles of Law: Natural and Politic* (1747, 1751), Thomas Rutherforth's *Institutes of Natural Law* (1754), and Emerich Vattel's *Law of Nations* (1758). This new tradition of natural law theorizing had begun in earnest with the works of Samuel Pufendorf, not least with his widely celebrated *De Jure Naturae et Gentium* (1672), which, by building upon Grotius's work and attempting to reconcile that with Hobbes's new civil philosophy, would provide the intellectual framework for the later theorists, each of whom would "propound a natural law teaching that is Hobbesian in every essential respect."[78] None of these theories

---

75 See those dictionaries that followed in the path Jacob cleared: Timothy Cunningham, *A New and Complete Law Dictionary*, 2 vols. (London: S. Crowder and J. Coote, 1764–65); and, in the United States, John Bouvier, *A Law Dictionary Adapted to the Constitution and Laws of the United States of America*, 2 vols. (Philadelphia: T. & J. W. Johnson, 1839).

76 Francis Lieber, *Legal and Political Hermeneutics: or, Principles of Interpretation and Construction in Law and Politics* (Boston: Charles C. Little and James Brown, 1839), p. 86.

77 See generally Richard Tuck, *Natural Rights Theories: Their Origin and Development* (Cambridge: Cambridge University Press, 1979); and Michael P. Zuckert, *Natural Rights and the New Republicanism* (Princeton, NJ: Princeton University Press, 1994).

78 Walter Berns, "Judicial Review and the Rights and Laws of Nature," *The Supreme Court Review: 1982* (Chicago: University of Chicago Press, 1983), p. 67.

of natural law had anything to do with theology, and any notions of God were very "remote."[79]

Grotius and Pufendorf

Pufendorf is interesting in great part because, in a day when political prudence still dictated scholarly reticence, he was willing publicly not only to take Hobbes seriously but to praise him. In his *Elementorum Jurisprudentiae Universalis* (1660) he confessed "[n]o small debt" to Hobbes, "whose basic conception in his book, *De Cive*, although it savours somewhat of the profane, is never the less for the most part extremely acute and sound."[80] But he is also fascinating because he himself was highly praised, and his great work, *De Jure Naturae et Gentium*, was repeatedly recommended by no less a figure than Locke. In *Some Thoughts Concerning Education* (1693), Locke listed *De Jure Naturae et Gentium* as a text where a young reader could be properly "instructed in the natural rights of men, and the original and foundations of society, and the duties resulting from thence."[81] Indeed, he was rather unstinting in his praise: Pufendorf's treatise when compared with the great work of Grotius, Locke wrote, was "perhaps... the better of the two."[82] In *Some Thoughts Concerning Reading and Study for a Gentleman* (1703), Locke would again recommend *De Jure Naturae et Gentium* as a means of learning about "the original of societies and the rise and extent of political power" and proclaim it simply "the best book of that kind."[83] And this about an author who was clearly "the first and greatest herald of Hobbes's work" – about whom Locke himself had so little to say, at least explicitly.[84]

What is most important about this tradition of natural law theorists for the present consideration is that a common element of their works was a concern for how properly to interpret the positive laws, constitutions, and treaties that men might contrive for the ordering of their political affairs. There is a remarkable repetition, sometimes almost verbatim, of the principles first laid down by Grotius in his chapter "Of Interpretation" in *De Jure Belli ac Pacis*. There was a need, he said, for "some certain rule" to be agreed upon that would establish the "right interpretation" for the words

---

[79] A. P. D'Entreves, *Natural Law: An Introduction to Legal Philosophy* (New York: Hutchinson's University Library, 1951), p. 52.

[80] Samuel Pufendorf, *Elementorum Jurisprudentiae Universalis*, trans. W. Oldfather, 2 vols. (Oxford: Clarendon Press, 1931), II: xxx.

[81] Axtell, ed., *The Educational Writings of John Locke*, p. 294.

[82] Ibid. Four years later Locke would again recommend Pufendorf's works in response to a request from the countess of Peterborough for a list of readings for her son. See ibid., p. 395.

[83] Ibid., p. 400.

[84] Norberto Bobbio, *Thomas Hobbes and the Natural Law Tradition* (Chicago: University of Chicago Press, 1993), p. 106.

that might be used in such legal documents. Such rules were needed "because the inward acts and motions of the mind are not themselves discernible," and the words chosen to express the intention of the parties could not safely be left for a man "to put what construction he pleased upon them." In order to avoid such a chaotic state of affairs, Grotius made a simple proposal: "The best rule of interpretation is to guess at the will by the most probable signs, which signs are of two sorts, words and conjectures; which are sometimes considered separately, sometimes together." As a general matter, he argued, "the words are to be understood according to their propriety, not the grammatical one, which regards the entymon and original of them, but what is vulgar and most in use." Beyond such strict literal interpretation, conjectures might well be "necessary when words and sentences are . . . of several significations, which the rhetoricians call . . . doubtful and ambiguous."[85]

The essence of Grotius's rules of interpretation issued from his understanding of the importance of speech generally for the promises, oaths, covenants, and contracts men make use of in the conduct of their public lives. There was a binding power in words:

The duty of keeping faith arises from speech or anything that resembles speech. Speech is given to man alone amongst the animals for the better furtherance of their common interest in order to make known what is hidden in the mind; the fitness whereof consists in the correspondence of the sign with the thing signified, which is called "truth." But since truth considered in itself implies nothing further than the correspondence of the language with the mind at the actual moment when the language is used, and since man's will is from its nature changeable, means had to be found to fix that will for time to come, and, such means are called "promise."[86]

When he undertook to reconcile Grotius with Hobbes, Pufendorf also included a chapter "Of the Interpretation of Compacts and Laws" in *De Jure Naturae et Gentium*, to which he added another, following Hobbes, which he entitled "Of Speech, and the Obligation which Attends It."[87] At a minimum, Pufendorf knew that if man was to be protected from his own "wild and wandering impulse," law was essential.[88] And law had to be understood as "the instrument of sovereignty, by which the ruler makes his pleasure known to his subject, which being once discovered, an obligation to obedience is produced in them by virtue of his supreme authority."[89] If

[85] Hugo Grotius, *The Rights of War and Peace* (London: W. Innys et al., 1738), Book II, Chapter XVI, Section I, pp. 352, 352, 353, 353, 354.

[86] Hugo Grotius, *The Jurisprudence of Holland*, ed. and trans. R. W. Lee (Oxford: Clarendon Press, 1926), pp. 292–293.

[87] Samuel Pufendorf, *Of the Law of Nature and Nations*, trans. B. Kennet (3rd ed.; London: R. Sare, et al., 1717), "Of the Interpretation of Compacts and Laws," V.XII.I–XXII, pp. 300–318; "Of Speech, and the Obligation which Attends It," IV.I.I–XXI, pp. 94–117. Citation indicates book, chapter, section, page number.

[88] Ibid., II.III.I, p. 117.

[89] Ibid., I.VI.XIV, p. 73.

this obligation to obedience was to serve its true purpose as "a kind of *moral bridle . . .* upon our freedom of action,"[90] the meaning of the law had to be clear:

> *Civil laws* are conveyed to the subject's knowledge by a promulgation, publickly and perspicuously made. In which men use two conditions, which ought to be clear and certain; first that the laws proceed from him who hath the chief command in the state; and secondly, that the meaning of the law is such and no other. . . . As to the [second] point, that the sense of a law may be clearly apprehended, it is incumbent upon the promulgators, to use the greatest plainness that the thing is capable of. . . . If anything in the law seems obscure, the explication of it is to be sought, either from the legislator, or from those persons who are by him appointed to judge according to the laws. For it is their business, observing a right interpretation to apply the laws to particular cases, or upon the proposal of such and such a fact, to declare the sovereign's pleasure concerning it.[91]

Thus, echoing Grotius, Pufendorf makes clear the purpose of interpretation. "The true end and design of *interpretation* is to gather the intent of the man from most probable signs. These signs are of two sorts, *words* and *other conjectures* which may be considered separately or both together."[92] Pufendorf's was an understanding of interpretation that would continue to resonate.

Burlamaqui

Jean Jacques Burlamaqui (1694–1748) was a Swiss jurist and professor of civil and natural law at the University of Geneva. Near the end of his relatively short life he made arrangements to publish the definitive version of his lectures as *The Principles of Natural Law* (1747) and *The Principles of Politic Law* (1751). He did so largely to prevent from being published the corrupted versions of the lectures then being passed around in his former students' notes. An English translation in 1752 by Thomas Nugent (who would also render the French of Montesquieu's *The Spirit of Laws* available to his American readers) ensured a broad popularity for the treatise, especially in America.[93] Although deemed by some to be "not . . . a very original production,"[94] *The Principles of Law: Natural and Politic* would prove to

---

[90] Ibid., I.VI.V, p. 61.

[91] Ibid., I.VI.XIII, p. 69.

[92] Ibid., V.XII.II, p. 301.

[93] See Ray Forrest Harvey, *Jean Jacques Burlamaqui: A Liberal Tradition in American Constitutionalism* (Chapel Hill: University of North Carolina Press, 1937); and Morton White, *The Philosophy of the American Revolution* (New York: Oxford University Press, 1978).

[94] David Hoffman, *A Course of Legal Study*, 2 vols. (2nd. ed.; Baltimore: J. Neal, 1836), I: 112. Benjamin Fletcher Wright described it simply as "one of the least original books of the time." *American Interpretations of Natural Law: A Study in the History of Political Thought* (Cambridge, MA: Harvard University Press, 1931), p. 8.

be enormously influential, being translated into numerous languages and its various publications each running to several editions.[95] The popularity of the work stemmed in part from the fact that it was something of a clearly written primer on the works of Grotius, Pufendorf, and Locke, especially on the laws of nature and their relationship to the laws of man. But it was also seen not to be bereft of its own originality.[96] On more than a few occasions, Burlamaqui begs to differ with the views of Grotius and Pufendorf.

Like the other modern natural law theorists, Burlamaqui does not root his natural law in any innate principles etched in men's hearts by the hand of God, but rather derives them from "the nature and constitution of man" through man's own power of reason, reason understood as "nothing more than . . . calculation." What reason reveals to man is that the desire for self-preservation and happiness constitutes "the grand spring which sets [men] in motion." Given that "human conduct is susceptible of direction," the nature and constitution of man require "some rule" by which man can move from the insecurity of his natural condition to the more commodious confines of civil society. But that rule is not just any rule; it can only be law. As Burlamaqui developed Pufendorf's thought, he defined law as "a rule prescribed by the sovereign of a society to his subjects, either in order to lay an obligation upon them of doing or omitting certain things, under a commination of punishment; or to leave them at liberty to act, or not, in other things, just as they think proper; and to secure to them, in this respect, the full enjoyment of their rights." In an echo of Hobbes's thought, Burlamaqui argued that "the sovereign is willing to direct his people, better than they could themselves, and gives a check to their liberty, lest they should make a bad use of it, contrary to their own and the public good."[97] But in the end, this is possible only if the power of the sovereign is sufficiently absolute to keep the people "in awe."[98]

Like Pufendorf, and Hobbes before him, Burlamaqui agreed that the essence of sovereign power is that it "acknowledges no other superior power on earth." This "plentitude of . . . power" cannot be checked, nor is the sovereign "accountable to any person upon earth for his conduct." The "essence of sovereignty" is the legislative power, the power to make the laws

---

[95] For the bibliographic history of the work see Harvey, *Jean Jacques Burlamaqui*, pp. 188–192.

[96] Burlamaqui, for example, became a major authority for the likes of Blackstone in his *Commentaries on the Laws of England* and James Wilson in his law lectures in Philadelphia.

[97] See Hobbes, *Leviathan*, p. 268.

[98] Jean Jacques Burlamaqui, *The Principles of Natural and Politic Law* (Oxford and London: W. Green, 1817), I.I.V.II, p. 27; I.I.V.VI, p 29; I.I.V.V, p. 29; I.I.V.III, p. 28; I.I.VIII.III, p. 47; I.I.X.III, p. 60; II.I.IV.V, p. 199. The citations indicate volume, part, chapter, section and page. This edition is two volumes in one, with continuous pagination. Hereinafter cited as *Natural and Politic Law.*

that direct the people in their affairs and provide for their punishment should they fail to comply. Thus the very purpose of law is to express the intention or the will of the legislator as to what would contribute to the public good. For "the safety of the people [is] . . . the supreme law."[99] Thus, by making the people conform, obedience to the sovereign's will, the basic tenet of the original contract, was essential to the maintenance of civil society:

For . . . if each man was to follow his own private judgment in things relating to the public good, they would only embarrass one another, and the diversity of inclinations and judgments arising from the levity and inconstancy of man, would soon demolish all concord and mankind would thus relapse into the inconveniences of the state of nature.[100]

But there was more to Burlamaqui's theory. Like Pufendorf and Locke, but unlike Hobbes, Burlamaqui believed there were dangers in any notion of absolute sovereignty; indeed, "the experiences of ages" proved that much. The fact was, the sovereign was always going to be "a human creature . . . subject to the same prejudices and susceptible of the same passions" as everyone else. When people situated as sovereigns "discover they can do whatever they list," they just might do so, being as they are exposed to "temptations unknown to private people." Given this all-too-human nature of any sovereign, it was hardly far-fetched to think that sooner or later he will abuse the sovereign power granted him by the people. The solution, for Burlamaqui, was to remove as much of the temptation as possible by clearly defining exactly what the sovereign was permitted to do, and what not. Such regulations and restrictions would produce "a happy incapacity in kings not to be able to act contrary to the laws of their country."[101]

This arrangement was the result of what Burlamaqui denominated "the fundamental laws of the state." These laws were "the covenants betwixt the people and the person on whom they confer the sovereignty, which regulate the manner of governing, and by which the supreme authority is limited." These explicit arrangements are nothing less than the "foundation of the state, on which the structure of the government is raised."[102] This foreshadowing of the idea of a written constitution went further than had

---

[99] Ibid., II.I.VII.II, p. 211; II.I.VII.V, p. 212; II.II.VIII.XXIII, p. 267.

[100] Ibid., II.I.IV.V, p. 199. This is a rather direct echo of a point made by Hobbes: "if every man were allowed this liberty of following his conscience, in such difference of consciences, they would not live together in peace an hour." Thomas Hobbes, *The Elements of Law: Natural and Politic*, ed. F. Tönnies (2nd. ed.; New York: Barnes and Noble, 1969), II.5.2, p. 139.

[101] Burlamaqui, *Natural and Politic Law*, II.I.VII.XXVII, p. 216; II.I.VII.XXVIII, p. 217; II.I.VII.XXIX, p. 217; II.I.VII.XXXIV, p. 218.

[102] Ibid., II.I.VII.XXXV, p. 218; II.I.VII.XXXVI, p. 218; II. I. VII.XXXVII, p. 218.

either Pufendorf or Locke when they maintained that the people's natural sovereignty allowed them a right of resistance should any sovereign be deemed to be abusing his power.

Nor was Burlamaqui finished; he was willing to take yet a further step. So deeply rooted was his fear of an abuse of the sovereign power that he introduced a compelling argument for what he called "a kind of partition in the rights of sovereignty." This separation of powers between "the different bodies of the state" was no simplistic notion of a complete and nominal separation, but rather a more nuanced one arguing for a "mutual dependence" between the powers that were to be separated that would serve to restrain each of those who shared the sovereign authority. Each partial sovereign would help to patrol the boundaries of the others, and through this "balance of power" would come a healthy "equilibrium" that would serve to "hinder the one from subverting the other." By this means, Burlamaqui concluded, could the "public liberty" be best secured. Moreover, such internal contrivances could prevent those "fatal revolutions" that would inevitably occur when the people would rise up in resistance against any absolute power that had degenerated into a despotism.[103]

In order for this to work it was necessary that the laws – both fundamental and civil – be "fixed and determinate." The meaning of the people's intentions in the fundamental law and the sovereign's intention in the civil law had to remain the same – and to be understood as remaining the same – as when those intentions or wills were declared. Thus was it essential that both the fundamental law and the civil law be "duly promulgated"[104] so that those original meanings could be made known. Although *The Principles of Law* does not have sections devoted to "speech" or "interpretation," Burlamaqui's theory implicitly requires the same sorts of rules one sees in those who came before him, as well as in those who followed. One sees this especially in Emerich Vattel (1714–1767), a student of Burlamaqui, whose *Law of Nations* once again emphasized the importance of proper rules of interpretation.

Vattel

In Vattel's view, "the sole object of lawful interpretation . . . ought to be the discovery of the thoughts of the author or authors. . . . This is the general rule for all interpretation." It is this intention of the parties that must be the primary if not the only guide to those who undertake to interpret a document. "Let us figure to ourselves the intention or the will of the legislature or the contracting parties, as a fixed point. At that point precisely should we stop, if it be clearly known – if uncertain, we should at least endeavor to

---

[103] Ibid., II.I.VII.L, p. 221; II.I.VII.XXXIV, p. 217.
[104] Ibid., II.III.I.V, p. 274; II.III.I.XIX, p. 277.

approach it."[105] And this commitment to discerning the original intention is time-bound:

> The usage we here speak of, is that of the time when the treaty, or the deed, of whatever kind, was drawn up and concluded. Languages incessantly vary, and the signification and force of words changes with time. When, therefore, an ancient deed is to be interpreted, we should be acquainted with the common use of the terms at the time when it was written; and that knowledge is to be acquired from deeds of the same period, and from contemporary writers, by diligently comparing them with each other. This is the only source from which to derive any information that can be depended on.[106]

Indeed, for Vattel, the words alone, "without the intention by which they must be dictated" were worth "nothing."[107] About this, he was certain:

> Good-faith adheres to the intention: fraud insists on the terms, when it thinks that they can furnish a cloak for its prevarications. . . . To violate the spirit of the law while we pretend to respect the letter, is a fraud no less criminal than an open violation of it; it is equally repugnant to the intention of the law-maker, and only evinces a more artful and deliberate villainy in the person who is guilty of it.[108]

Ultimately, it is the original intention, the grand purposes for which laws are made, that must be the guide in their interpretation:

> The reason of the law . . . the motive which led to the making of it, and the object in contemplation at the time . . . is the most certain clue to lead us to the discovery of its true meaning; and great attention should be paid to this circumstance, whenever there is question either of explaining an obscure, ambiguous, indeterminate passage in a law . . . or of applying it to a particular case.[109]

These sentiments shared by Grotius, Pufendorf, Burlamaqui, and Vattel would receive their fullest and most complete articulation in Thomas Rutherforth's *Institutes of Natural Law* (1754). This work was especially important in that it would help transmit this tradition of interpretation understood as rooted in the intentions of the lawmaker in a very explicit way; it was adopted by Joseph Story as one of his primary guides to his own rules of interpretation in his highly influential *Commentaries on the Constitution of the United States.*

---

[105] *Law of Nations* (4th, ed.; London: W. Clarke and Sons, 1811), II.XVII, p. 247; II.XVII, p. 264. Citation indicates book, chapter, and page number.
[106] Ibid., II.XVII, pp. 248–249.
[107] Ibid., p. 249.
[108] Ibid., pp. 258–259.
[109] Ibid., p. 256.

Rutherforth

Thomas Rutherforth (1712–1771) was the Regius Professor of Divinity at Cambridge and archdeacon of Essex. His *Institutes of Natural Law*[110] formed the basis of a series of lectures on Hugo Grotius's *De Jure Belli ac Pacis* that he read in St. John's College, Cambridge. In Rutherforth's *Institutes* one sees very clearly how those who took natural rights seriously understood them in relation to a written constitution. Ultimately, Rutherforth's canons of construction are best understood within the broader context of his view of civil society and law more generally.

In Rutherforth's analysis of the grounds of civil society there is above all else a "constitutional compact" all societies must have. The essence of that compact is the creation and organization of the various powers of governance, not least the legislative power. The constitutional compact, for Rutherforth, is based upon the consent of those who have agreed to be bound by it; so, too, is the legislative power created by it tied to that original consent. As a result, it is necessary that the civil constitution be understood as "fixed and permanent," as lying beyond change by the ordinary legislative power. Such "fixed and permanent" constitutions, while they are changeable, are "not variable in their own nature." As Rutherforth puts it: "The constitution . . . may indeed be changed, but it is not variable in itself: such consent, as introduced it at first, may alter it afterwards."[111]

Any alteration dictated by anything less than that original consent would constitute a violation of the theory of natural rights that undergirds the constitutional compact. As the members of a civil society are obliged by the laws of nature, as a matter of their consent, to obey the civil laws, so, too, are those who wield power under the terms of the civil constitution obliged, by the laws of nature, to be bound by that original consent.[112] "[A]gents who are chosen and appointed by the people to exercise their constitutional share of the legislative power, act under the constitutional compact, and consequently are not authorized by such an appointment to change the terms of the compact."[113] The creature cannot legitimately recreate the creator. "The power of civil society . . . extends no farther than the purposes of the social compact, by which it was produced."[114] It is this

---

[110] 2 vols. (Cambridge: J. Bentham, 1754–56). All citations here will be to the second American edition: *Institutes of Natural Law* (2nd ed.; Baltimore: William and Joseph Neal, 1832). Hereinafter cited as *Institutes*.

[111] Ibid., pp. 293, 296.

[112] Ibid., pp. 357–358. "[T]he superiority of a civil legislator; that is, the right which a civil legislator has to prescribe laws to the members of a civil society, arises from their own consent. . . . [T]he obligation of civil laws, as well as the obligation of compacts, arises from the consent of those who are obliged by them." Ibid., p. 357.

[113] *Institutes*, p. 567.

[114] Ibid., p. 370. Thus the task of the constitution makers is great: "It is the business of the politician, in order to guard against such excess in the exercise of legislative power, to contrive some external checks upon the legislative body. . . . Such checks as these. . . . for

idea that the original purpose and intention of constitutional compacts bind the discretion of those who wield power under the terms of those compacts that lies at the heart of Rutherforth's canons of construction.

Rutherforth's fundamental premise is a simple one: "The end, which interpretation aims at, is to find out what was the intention of the writer; to clear up the meaning of his words, if they are obscure; to ascertain the sense of them, if they are ambiguous; to determine what his design was, where his words express it imperfectly."[115] This quest for intention is the foundation of all efforts at interpretation for a powerful reason: law obligates people to obey it; the essence of law is language; and thus "the obligations that are produced by the civil laws . . . arise from the intention of the legislator; not merely as this intention is an act of mind; but as it is declared or expressed by some outward sign or mark, which makes it known to us." The endeavor is not to ascertain what may have been the subjective intention of any one or even many lawmakers; the objective is to discern the purpose for which the law was enacted, what wrong it was intended to right, what problem it was intended to correct.[116] It is only if this purpose or intention can be known that the people are obliged to comply with the civil law.[117]

This interpretive effort is often easier said than done, however. Language is, in and of itself, problematic: "sometimes a man's words are obscure; sometimes they are ambiguous; and sometimes they express his meaning so imperfectly, as either to fall short of his intention and not express the whole of it, or else to exceed his intention and express more than he designed." On such occasions, Rutherforth suggests, "we must have recourse to some other means of interpretation, that is, we must make some use of other signs or marks, besides the words of the speaker or the writer, in order to collect his meaning." These other marks and signs, Rutherforth agrees with Grotius, are what are properly called "probable conjectures." But however difficult the task, the first duty of interpretation is to discern, to the degree possible, the meaning of the writer or the speaker according to "common use and custom."[118]

Rutherforth divides his approach to interpretation into three categories, "according to the different means that it makes use of, for obtaining its end." Those categories are: literal interpretation, mixed interpretation, and rational interpretation.[119] In Rutherforth's calculus of construction, these three methods form something of a continuum.

---

preventing any undue exercise of legislative power, are called constitutional checks. . . . This is the province of politics and not natural law." *Institutes*, pp. 371, 372.

[115] *Institutes*, p. 405.

[116] As Rutherforth says: "The meaning of a law is the design of the lawmaker in respect of what he commands or forbids. The reason of a law is his design in respect of the end or purpose for which he commands or forbids it." *Institutes*, p. 415.

[117] *Institutes*, p. 404.

[118] Ibid., pp. 405, 407.

[119] Ibid., pp. 407–408.

Literal interpretation is the most basic, text-bound approach: "when the words of a man express his meaning planely [sic], distinctly, and perfectly, we have no occasion to have recourse to any other means of interpretation." Yet even at this level, it is possible to take a word in either a "confined sense" or in a more "comprehensive sense." The key here is to try to discern the meaning of the words used from "the common consent of those who use them."[120] Thus to opt for taking the word in question in its more comprehensive sense is not to abandon the obligatory effort to get at the sense in which the word was actually used by the writer or the speaker. On this point Rutherforth is clear:

The principal rule to be observed in literal interpretation is to follow that sense, in respect both of the words and of the construction, which is agreeable to common use, without attending to etymological fancies or grammatical refinements. . . . By grammatical refinements . . . I mean such rules of construction, as are not justified by the common usage of the language before us, and have nothing else to support them, but some groundless conjecture or some supposed analogy between this language and others. . . . [S]uch rules of grammar, as, instead of being copied from common use, are intended to overrule its authority.[121]

But even when one conscientiously eschews such word games, and tries diligently to get at the writer's meaning through literal interpretation, there arise other problems. Not the least of the problems is the ambiguity of language. Sometimes the word used "will admit of two or more senses, and either of these . . . is equally agreeable to common usage." In such a case, when common usage will not settle the confusion, the interpreter "must have recourse to other conjectures to fix it." It is at this point that literal interpretation fades into mixed interpretation, a mode "partly literal and partly rational."[122] Yet these "other conjectures" are not simply untethered to the text. "In mixed interpretation . . . the topics from whence our conjectures are drawn, are either the subject matter of the writing, or the effect, that it will produce, according as we continue in this or in that sense, or lastly, some circumstances that are connected with it." This approach is bound down by certain rules of common sense:

When any words or expressions in a writing are of doubtful meaning, the first rule in mixed interpretation is to give them such a sense, as is agreeable to the subject matter, of which the writer is treating. For we are sure, on the one hand, that this subject matter was in his mind, and can, on the other hand, have no reason for thinking that he intended anything which is different from it, and much less, that he intended anything which is inconsistent with it. . . . The second rule, in mixed interpretation, is to give all doubtful words or expressions that sense which makes them produce some effect; this effect must in general be a reasonable one; and it must likewise be the

---

[120] Ibid., pp. 405, 420, 407.
[121] Ibid., pp. 408–409.
[122] Ibid., pp. 410, 408.

same, that a lawmaker or the testator or the contractor intended to produce.... [I]f we give [the lawmaker's] words such a meaning, as is agreeable to the reason of the law, or such a meaning as will make the law produce the effect, which he intended to produce by it, we give them such a meaning, as is agreeable to his intention.[123]

To go beyond these first efforts to resolve ambiguities and to seek guidance from circumstantial evidence surrounding the law, is still not an invitation to ignore or abandon the primary obligation to discern the intention of the writer. A basic circumstance from which meaning might be gleaned, is to examine what the same lawmaker has said or written on other occasions. Yet still, those other writings must have some connection with the language at hand: "nothing, which is wholly unconnected with such writing, can either be made use of to explore any ambiguous words in it, or with any propriety be called a circumstance of it." The presumption is that the writer will always have been of "the same mind" and thus is deemed likely to have been consistent in the meaning he presumed to convey by the language he used.[124]

Another means of arriving at "probable conjectures" about what the original meaning of a law might be is a reliance on what Rutherforth calls "contemporary practice." This approach embraces two standards: a reliance on common practices that may have prevailed at the time the law was passed, and an account of "what was done upon the law in the times immediately after the making of it." The first standard is "only a remote topic of inter- pretation" insofar as it can give only a sense of the probable reason the law was enacted in the first place. And the second standard is not to be confused with "contemporary construction," those interpretations given a law by the courts. Rather, for Rutherforth, contemporary practice means "the effect which the law produced in the behaviour of those, who were obliged by it, and who lived at the time of the making of it, [that] will help us to form a judgment about the meaning of the legislator, where his words have left it doubtful."[125]

This is not to say that contemporary judicial construction will not also assist in this problem of getting at the original intention of a particular law. While the adjudications of the courts of law are themselves "authentic interpretations," judges who confront the same law at a later date will no doubt find earlier judgments helpful.[126] Those first judicial determinations, those made by judges who were "contemporaries of the legislator," will

---

[123] Ibid., pp. 412, 413, 414.
[124] Ibid., pp. 416, 416.
[125] Ibid., pp. 417, 417, 418.
[126] Ibid. This is one of the many areas in which Rutherforth follows the lead of Hobbes. What makes such judicial determinations "authentic" for Rutherforth, as for Hobbes, is not the judge's private notion of what is right or just, but the power granted the judge by the sovereign to make such a determination. See Hobbes, *Leviathan*, pp. 212–213.

show later judges "in what sense the law was understood by those, who had the best opportunity of knowing the true sense, either by advising with the legislator himself, or at least by seeing the situation of things which led him to make the law."[127] This is, to Rutherforth's way of thinking, merely a matter of good sense:

Laws operate at a distance of time: those who live many years after the laws were made, are obliged to act upon them; and are, therefore, concerned to know their true meaning. But, in length of time the meaning of a law may become doubtful, though it was clear and precise when it was first made. And since, by looking back into the contemporary practice, that is, into the practice, which the law produced in the first instance, we may see in what sense it was then understood; a view of this practice will be a means of removing any doubts about the sense of it, which are owing only to our remoteness from its original establishment.[128]

At the farther end of the continuum of modes of interpretation, past literal and mixed interpretations, lies that mode that requires the greatest caution on the part of the interpreter: rational interpretation, that mode that does not seek to confine itself to the letter of the law. Indeed, the gulf that separates literal and mixed interpretations is not nearly so great as that which separates both from the mode of rational interpretation. Both literal and mixed keep close to the words being interpreted: "even mixed interpretation is so far literal, that it keeps strictly to the letter, without giving the words any sense, which common usage has not given them; it only ascertains the sense, in which the writer used the words, when common usage has given them more senses than one." Rational interpretation, which Rutherforth prefers to call "liberal or free" interpretation, is a method in which the interpreter may very well have to deviate from the letter and not confine himself to it.[129]

Yet this "liberal or free" mode of interpretation is not an approach that simply dismisses the intention of the writer in favor of the inclinations of the interpreter; it is still *interpretation* in the most meaningful sense. Even under this more liberal mode of considering a text, the interpreter is bound by the obligation to seek the intention of the legislator; that remains the only legitimate objective of the interpreter. "[T]he business of interpretation [is] to find out the meaning or design of the writer," and rational interpretation means nothing more than endeavoring "to collect . . . intention from something else besides his words." Relying solely on the "assistance of conjectures" beyond the literal import of the words used is still only a means to the higher end of determining intention.[130]

The essence of rational interpretation is not to supplant the original intention of the law but to flesh it out, to give it effect in those cases when a

[127] *Institutes*, p. 418.
[128] Ibid., p. 419.
[129] Ibid., pp. 421, 421, 420.
[130] Ibid., pp. 405, 405, 408.

strictly literal or even mixed mode would not be able to do it justice. The presumption in rational interpretation is, as it also is with literal or mixed interpretations, that the lawgiver intended to achieve something by the law in question. Whether it was to prohibit some action or to command another, the law, to make any sense at all, must be presumed to have had a purpose. Rational construction does not seek to alter or abolish that purpose, only to assist in having that purpose fulfilled.

There are two ways in which rational interpretation is to be employed: "sometimes the meaning of the writer is extended, so as to take in more, and sometimes it is restrained, so as to take in less, than his words import in their common acception."[131] In the one case, as Rutherforth says:

When we know what was the reason or final cause, which the writer had in view, what end he proposed, or what effect he designed to produce; and the meaning of the law...if we were to adhere closely to the words of it, would not come up to this reason, or would not produce this effect; we may then conclude that his words express his meaning imperfectly, and that his meaning is to be extended beyond his words, so as to come up to this reason, or so as to produce this effect. For it is much more probable that the writer should fail in expressing his meaning, than that his meaning should fall short of his purposes which he designed to obtain.[132]

So also does such common sense obtain in those cases where the language used must be restrained:

When we would restrain the meaning of a writer, and show, that it is less comprehensive than his words, or that some particular case, which is included in his words, is not within his meaning; we must argue, either for an original or for an accidental defect in his intention; either we must argue, that...the lawmaker...could not intend originally to include the case in question, however he may have so failed in his expression as to include it in his words; or else we must argue, that the case is an accidental one, which probably was not foreseen originally; and that, if the writer had foreseen it...he would have limited his expression and have particularly excepted the case in question.[133]

Neither extending the meaning nor restraining the meaning is understood by Rutherforth to empower the interpreter to abandon the serious business of ascertaining the original intention of the lawgiver. Rational interpretation, he argues, is still aimed at the end or the purpose that the lawgiver intended; "certainly we can never argue, that his meaning ought to be extended beyond his words, upon a reason which does not appear to have been in his mind." Similarly, "when we argue, that a particular case could not, originally, be included in the meaning of the law; either because some absurd consequence will follow from including it, or because some consequence will follow which

[131] Ibid., p. 421.
[132] Ibid.
[133] Ibid., pp. 422–423.

is inconsistent with the reason or end of the law; we plainly argue, in both instances, from the effect."[134] Rational interpretation, for Rutherforth, in the end is very similar to "equitable interpretation," especially as that was described by Joseph Story in his *Commentaries on Equity Jurisprudence*.[135] As Rutherforth put it: "By equity is here meant, a fair and honest correction, of a law . . . where it appears that the lawmaker . . . either would or ought to consent to such a correction, if they were to interpret their own act."[136]

Rutherforth's three types of interpretation – literal, mixed, and rational – are in the end united in their common purpose. Each is a means, and only a means, toward one overarching end: "to find out what was the intention of the writer; to clear up the meaning of his words, if they are obscure; to ascertain the sense of them, if they are ambiguous; to determine what his design was, where his words express it imperfectly."[137] Nowhere in his discussion of interpretation does Rutherforth argue that a judge's private notions of justice may legitimately supplant the intentions of the lawgiver. He most assuredly never suggests that there is some higher, unwritten law waiting to be summoned down by judges in order to make the polity conform to some abstract notion of justice; nor does he suggest that rational interpretation is a shorthand notation for a recourse to natural law.[138] His theory of interpretation is much more modest than that; it is much safer than that. For

---

[134] Ibid., pp. 421, 423.

[135] As Story succinctly put it: "[W]ords of a doubtful import may be used in a law, or words susceptible of a more enlarged or a more restricted meaning or of two meanings equally appropriate. The question, in all such cases, must be, in what sense the words were designed to be used; and it is the part of a judge to look to the objects of the legislature, and to give such a construction to the words that will best further those objects. This is an exercise of equitable interpretation." In no way, as Story pointed out, should one deem such equitable interpretation as embracing a jurisdiction "so wide and extensive, as that which arises from the principles of natural justice." Joseph Story, *Commentaries on Equity Jurisprudence*, 2 vols. (12th ed.; Boston: Little, Brown and Co., 1877), I.7.7, I.2.2. Citation indicates volume, section, and page number.

[136] *Institutes*, p. 427.

[137] Ibid., p. 405.

[138] Rutherforth's dim view of "abstract speculators" is worth remembering: "Some indeed, who are better pleased with amusing themselves in speculations, than with enquiring into facts, have endeavored to settle our notions of civil constitutions by abstract reasonings. . . . As this method favors the idleness of superficial politicians, it is no wonder that these abstracted philosophers should have many followers. . . . It would be a great expense of time and labour to read history, to collect and consider usages and customs, to search records, to examine and compare facts. But such abstract arguments are easily invented, as will serve to puzzle both the inventor and his disciples, though they should neither be convincing to himself, nor to anyone else. This seems to be the reason, why most of those who write or talk about the constitution in our own or in any other country, should deal more in metaphysical reasonings, than in arguments drawn from facts and observation, and should chuse to learn their political principles, rather from the subtleties of schoolmen, than from records and history." *Institutes*, p. 297.

Rutherforth, the line between natural law and constitutional interpretation is one that should not be crossed; moral theory and constitutional law are not the same thing.

III. TRENCHARD AND GORDON ON CATO'S CONSTITUTIONAL POLITICS

In the study of the American founding, the influence of John Trenchard and Thomas Gordon on political thinking in colonial Anglo-America is one of the few matters on which there is near-universal agreement.[139] *Cato's Letters* and *The Independent Whig* constituted two of the most basic texts of the colonial period, with the authority accorded *Cato's Letters* being especially "immense." Indeed, *Cato* has been described as "of the utmost importance in the creation of American republicanism." As a general matter, the "writings of Trenchard and Gordon ranked with the treatises of Locke as the most authoritative statement of the nature of political liberty and above Locke as an exposition of the social sources of the threats to it." Even those who doubt the pervasiveness of the classical republicanism usually attributed to *Cato's Letters* do not hesitate in describing them as "the most remarkable piece of English political writing since Locke's *Two Treatises*."[140] The popularity of Trenchard and Gordon stemmed in part from their role as "intellectual middlemen" during the Revolutionary period, for in their pages were to be found a host of writers who seemed to speak directly to the problems facing Americans.[141]

The resurrection of Trenchard and Gordon three decades ago demonstrated that the literature surrounding the creation of the American republic was far richer and more complicated than had theretofore been thought. Building on the work of Caroline Robbins, Bernard Bailyn's examination of the intellectual sources on which the pamphlets of the period drew placed such traditionally understood seventeenth-century sources as Locke's *Two Treatises* in the broader context of the works of the eighteenth-century

[139] The editions used in this chapter are John Trenchard and Thomas Gordon, *Cato's Letters*, ed. Ronald Hamowy, 2 vols. (Indianapolis: Liberty Fund, 1995); and John Trenchard and Thomas Gordon, *The Independent Whig, or A Defense of Primitive Christianity*, 2 vols. (7th ed.; London: J. Peele and J. Osborn, 1736).

[140] J. G. A. Pocock, *The Machiavellian Moment* (Princeton, NJ: Princeton University Press, 1975), p. 468; Ronald Hamowy, "Introduction" to *Cato's Letters*, I: xxxv; Robert E. Shalhope, "Toward a Republican Synthesis: The Emergence of an Understanding of Republicanism in American Historiography," *William and Mary Quarterly*, 3d ser., 29 (1972): 49–80, p. 58; Bernard Bailyn, *The Ideological Origins of the American Revolution* (Cambridge, MA: Harvard University Press, 1967), p. 36; and Michael Zuckert, *Natural Rights and the New Republicanism* (Princeton, NJ: Princeton University Press, 1994), p. 297.

[141] The phrase "intellectual middlemen" is Bailyn's; *Ideological Origins of the American Revolution*, p. 35.

English Whigs.[142] The natural rights political philosophy of Locke, important as it was, was but a part of a larger literary tradition. In due course
Bailyn's insight was expanded and, some say, distorted to the near exclu-
sion of any serious consideration of Locke and the natural rights thinkers
in favor of classical republicanism or civic humanism. Eventually, a great
many historians followed J. G. A Pocock's lead when he insisted that the
American Revolution was "less the first act of revolutionary enlightenment
than . . . the last great act of the Renaissance."[143]

This view of the origins of American politics has not been without its
critics, nor Locke without his defenders. The most penetrating critics have
shown that Trenchard and Gordon, far from being anti-Lockean, succeeded
admirably in bringing together "Whig political science and Lockean political
philosophy" as the foundation stones of a new conception of republicanism
upon which the Americans would eventually build.[144] Yet even those who
have sought to restore the natural rights tradition in explaining these matters
have missed one of the most important features of the political thought of
Trenchard and Gordon, namely, their teaching about the important role of
language in the establishment of civil society and the necessity of written
constitutions and laws to the security of political liberty. What is most striking about this aspect of their thought is not simply their reliance on Locke,
the *Essay Concerning Human Understanding* as well as *Two Treatises of
Government*, but their unblushing use of Thomas Hobbes.[145]

---

[142] Caroline Robbins, *The Eighteenth-Century Commonwealthman: Studies in the Transmis-
sion, Development and Circumstances of English Liberal Thought from the Restoration of
Charles II until the War with the Thirteen Colonies* (Cambridge, MA: Harvard University
Press, 1959), pp. 115–125; Bernard Bailyn, ed., *Pamphlets of the American Revolution,
1750–1776* (Cambridge, MA: Harvard University Press, 1965).

[143] J. G. A. Pocock, "Virtue and Commerce in the Eighteenth Century," *Journal of Interdisciplinary History* 3 (1972): 119–134, p. 127.

[144] Zuckert, *Natural Rights and the New Republicanism*, p. xix. See also Joyce Appleby,
Liberalism and Republicanism in the Historical Imagination (Cambridge, MA: Harvard
University Press, 1992); Steven M. Dworetz, *The Unvarnished Doctrine: Locke, Liberalism,
and the American Revolution* (Durham, NC: Duke University Press, 1990); Jerome Huyler,
Locke in America: The Moral Philosophy of the Founding Era (Lawrence: University Press
of Kansas, 1995); and Thomas L. Pangle, *The Spirit of Modern Republicanism: The Moral
Vision of the American Founders and the Philosophy of Locke* (Chicago: University of
Chicago Press, 1988).

[145] The relationship between Book III of Locke's *Essay Concerning Human Understanding*
and Hobbes's theory of language would have been obvious to those who knew those
works, especially given the fact that the *Essay* was perhaps even better known than the *Two
Treatises*. See John Dunn, "The Politics of Locke in England and America in the Eighteenth
Century," in John Dunn, *Political Obligation in Its Historical Context: Essays in Political
Theory* (Cambridge: Cambridge University Press, 1980), pp. 53–77; Martyn P. Thompson,
"The Reception of Locke's *Two Treatises of Government*, 1690–1705," *Political Studies*
24 (1976): 184–191; David Lundberg and Henry F. May, "The Enlightened Reader in
America," *American Quarterly* 28 (1976): 262–271; and Donald S. Lutz, "The Relative

The common ground shared by Hobbes, Locke, and Trenchard and Gordon in appreciating the importance of language to constitutionalism appears most clearly in their passionate rejection of Aristotelian scholasticism and what they saw as the confusions wrought by the schoolmen in political life. This was due in large measure, they charged, to the schoolmen's abuse of language (and thus of reason), which derived from their perverse intermingling of Aristotelian logic and Christian dogma.[146] The learned doctors had supplanted true knowledge with obscure doctrines; truth had been "strangled with the snares of words."[147] By ridding mankind of the philosophical obfuscation and theological confusions generated by the "Gown-men,"[148] both Hobbes and Locke believed a sturdier foundation would be prepared for politics; they sought to establish sound politics in part by emphasizing the importance of clear and solid language to political life.[149]

Similarly, Trenchard and Gordon repeatedly denounced "religious madmen and godly pedants," "fairy philosophers" and "dogmatic zealots," who, "by pretending to know the other world, cheated and confounded this one." The "fate of millions, and the being of states" had come to "stand or fall by the distinctions of monks, coined in colleges." Thus could Trenchard and Gordon conclude with Hobbes and Locke that "most of the mischiefs under which mankind suffers, and almost all their polemick disputes are owing to the abuse of words."[150] Those who authoritatively control the meaning of words, especially of Scripture and law, exercise immense power over those who are obliged to obey their interpretations, either by force or through ignorance.[151]

Trenchard and Gordon began their inquiry where Hobbes had begun his, with the nature of man. And, like Hobbes, they based their theory of politics on a fundamental premise: "Everything in the universe is in constant

Influence of European Writers in Late Eighteenth-Century American Political Thought," *American Political Science Review* 78 (1984): 189–197.

[146] See especially Hobbes, *Leviathan*, Chapter 46, pp. 524–537.

[147] Thomas Hobbes, *De Corpore*, in Thomas Molesworth, ed., *The English Works of Thomas Hobbes*, 11 vols. (London: John Bohn, 1839–45), ep. ded., I: viii. See also Thomas Hobbes, *A Dialogue between a Philosopher and a Student of the Common Laws of England*, ed. Joseph Cropsey (Chicago: University of Chicago Press, 1971), pp. 97–98. Hereinafter cited as *Dialogue*.

[148] Hobbes, *Dialogue*, p. 157.

[149] See Frederick G. Whelan, "Language and Its Abuses in Hobbes's Political Philosophy," *American Political Science Review* 75 (1981): 59–75, p. 60; John W. Danford, *Wittgenstein and Political Philosophy* (Chicago: University of Chicago Press, 1978), pp. 12, 13, 44; Eugene Miller, "Locke on the Meaning of Political Language," *Political Science Reviewer* 9 (1979): 163–194, pp. 165–166; and Cranston, *John Locke: A Biography*, pp. 38, 39, 270.

[150] *Cato's Letters*, No. 59, p. 410; No. 109, p. 769; *Independent Whig*, No. 30, p. 191; *Cato's Letters*, No. 59, p. 410; No. 12, p. 94; No. 117, p. 814.

[151] See especially *The Independent Whig*, Nos. 4, 5, 8, 20, 29, 30, 35, 48.

motion." The task of reason is to make sense of that motion, which it receives through the senses, its "subordinate instruments and spies." There are no innate ideas, Trenchard and Gordon insisted, noting that the absence of them had been "justly observed by Mr. Locke, and by Mr. Hobbes." All ideas are the impressions of objects in the physical world that are "let in upon the mind through the organs of sense." The implications of this view of human understanding are no less shocking in Trenchard and Gordon than in Hobbes and Locke: "[W]e can know nothing about . . . God's essence, or his attributes . . . or concerning his ways or motives for making or governing the universe." When it comes to the loftiest matters men are doomed "to know little or nothing about them," with the result that, in his natural state, each man is the sole measure of what he understands to be justice. That is why the state of nature is properly understood to be a "state of war" where life is characterized by "a continual state of uncertainty, and wretchedness, often an apprehension of violence, often the lingering dread of violent death."[152] As for Hobbes and Locke, so for Trenchard and Gordon: man is his own worst enemy.

Life in the state of nature is "precarious, always miserable, often intolerable" because of each man's natural love of himself, the "root" of all human passions. Man finds himself in an endless quest for happiness that drives him to seek "what is pleasant and profitable in his own eyes," no matter what the effect on his fellows; personal happiness is tangible, "misery upon multitudes" is a mere abstraction. The passions of men, "being boundless and insatiable, are always terrible when not controuled." But it is precisely man's selfish nature that offers the solution to his natural inclination to sacrifice the public interest to "private lust."[153]

Trenchard and Gordon learned well Hobbes's lesson that the most abiding passion in the human economy is fear, and that the fear necessary to influence men's behavior is brought to bear only by the sheer "terror of the laws" within the confines of civil society. This psychological approach to keeping the civil peace will work because the passions "direct and govern all the motions" of the mind in a "purely mechanical" way, and those who seek to control behavior need only "pull the proper ropes and turn the wheels which will put the machine in motion." Thus the science of politics is truly a science, one that understands the motions of the mind and how to affect man's actions by appealing to his passions, especially his most enduring passion of self-love.[154]

---

[152] *Independent Whig*, No. 53, p. 323; No. 35, p. 217; *Cato's Letters*, No. 116, p. 808; No. 111, pp. 781, 779; and No. 62, p. 430.
[153] *Cato's Letters*, No. 62, p. 430; No. 40, pp. 280–281; No. 75, p. 551; No. 33, p. 238; No. 40, pp. 278, 281; No. 33, pp. 238, 236; and No. 75, p. 551. See also No. 60, p. 417.
[154] *Cato's Letters*, No. 40, p. 281; No. 105, p. 742. As *Cato* put it: "The first elements, or knowledge of politicks, is the knowledge of the passions; and the art of governing is chiefly

Because all men are by nature equal, and because each has the fundamental natural right to preserve himself as he thinks fit, the social contract is the only legitimate foundation of civil society insofar as the contract is able to reconcile all the "various and contradictory . . . opinions and reasonings of men." Only by their voluntary consent can men legitimately be governed by the decrees of the magistrate, whose rightful power "arises only from the right of private men to defend themselves, to repel injuries, and to punish those who commit them." That natural right of self-preservation "being conveyed by the society to their publick representative, he can execute the same no farther than the benefit and security of that society requires he should."[155]

The problem facing those who seek to enter into a civil society by mutual consent is how to fashion the government so that the administration of power is kept in check, held within the original grant. Arbitrariness in the exercise of power had been more devastating to mankind than "all the beasts of prey and all the plagues and earthquakes ever were." Given the grim realities of human nature, no one can be trusted to wield power without restraint, for even "the best men grow mischievous when they are set above laws." Without laws to guide and restrain those who govern, the governed will inevitably be subjected to their "mere will and pleasure," thus incorporating within civil society the very problem that had forced men to flee from the state of nature. As *Cato* saw it, "those nations only who bridle their governors do not wear chains."[156]

What stands between tyranny and freedom, in the political science of Trenchard and Gordon, is a constitution of "fixed and stated rules" by which all good governments must proceed. In a properly constituted government, the magistrate will be obliged to "consult the voice and interest of the people." And it is this obligation to secure the safety and happiness of the people that truly distinguishes a free state from an enslaved one, where the magistrate is free to rule simply by his "private will, interest, and pleasure." The secret in framing a free government, *Cato* argued, following Hobbes, "is to make the interests of the governors and the governed the same, as far as human policy can contrive." Of this much, he was absolutely certain: "Liberty cannot be preserved any other way."[157]

The basic purpose of a constitution, for Trenchard and Gordon, was to make clear "the jurisdiction of governors, and its limits." It is by the terms of the constitution that the necessary "checks and restraints" are

the art of applying to the passions." No. 39, p. 276. See especially No. 44, p. 299; and No. 122, pp. 847–848.

[155] *Independent Whig*, No. 50, p. 303; *Cato's Letters*, No. 59, p. 407.

[156] *Cato's Letters*, No. 25, pp. 185, 180; No. 62, p. 433; and No. 115, p. 803.

[157] *Cato's Letters*, No. 25, p. 186; No. 38, p. 272; and No. 60, p. 417. See Hobbes, *Leviathan*, p. 268.

expressed. Thus was a fundamental law necessary to empower the magistrate to create the ordinary laws by which society is governed. At the same time, the fundamental law would leave "nothing, or as little as may be...to chance, or to the humours of men in authority." Only by the "stated rules" of that fundamental law are rulers chained down from mischief.[158] As with the constitution, so with the ordinary laws made pursuant thereto. In order to keep the people in line, they must be governed by "prudent and fixed laws," designed so that it is in their interest to be honest and decent. The aim of the laws is to define with precision the rights of the governed and to shelter these rights "under certain and express laws, irrevocable at any man's pleasure." Without clear promulgation, the law is not the law; it cannot work if it is not known and understood by those whose behavior it is meant to control.[159] Thus is language the essence of law no less for Trenchard and Gordon than for Hobbes and Locke.

The scholastic abuse of words through the "far-fetched interpretations" of those in power was an abiding problem in civil life. The methodology of the schools, so vigorously condemned before them by Hobbes and Locke, was not confined to the laws of God; it had also corrupted the laws of man. The "vain philosophy... and metaphysical gibberish" that comprised university education had produced "blockheads and accomplished dunces" aplenty. This "false learning" of the schools, a "hodge-podge of nonsense, jargon, and authority," posed the greatest threat to civil life and peace.[160] The civil law of the commonwealth was especially vulnerable:

[P]romulgation is of the essence of a law, which cannot be without plainness and perspicuity: It must not be expressed in doubtful and equivocal terms: It must not depend upon critical learning, or different readings; nor receive its explanation from the mysterious gibberish, and unintelligible jargon of the schools; but ought to be such, as a plain, open, simple-minded, sincere man may easily discover, amidst the numerous and contradictory schemes of the Ecclesiasticks.[161]

This idea of the law rested on a theory of language that derived directly from Hobbes and Locke; it is a theory based upon common sense. Put most simply, "words... are coined to convey finite conceptions." The use of language is inherently social in that words "are the signs of ideas... and are intended to convey the conceptions of men to one another." Words are not natural, but conventional, and all meaning attached to words is "wholly

---

[158] *Cato's Letters*, No. 60, p. 414; No. 59, p. 405; No. 25, p. 186; and No. 62, pp. 429, 433.
[159] *Cato's Letters*, No. 108, p. 766; No. 62, p. 433.
[160] *Independent Whig*, No. 36, p. 223; No. 1, p. 39; No. 8, p. 68; No. 22, p. 151; No. 18, p. 122 In their condemnation of the schools, Trenchard and Gordon followed Hobbes closely, going so far as to paraphrase the same argument from *Leviathan* that Locke had found of interest. *Independent Whig*, No. 30, pp. 189–190. This is taken from *Leviathan*, pp. 28–29.
[161] *Independent Whig*, No. 48, p. 292.

arbitrary." Thus is it essential that men define their words carefully and reach agreement as to the meaning. Moreover, unless they "annex the same conceptions to the same sounds, they cannot understand one another, or discourse together." If men fail to define words carefully and to stick to the definitions agreed upon, words will be "perfectly useless, will convey no ideas at all, can give us no rule, nor can communicate any knowledge." Without such agreed-upon definitions, all discourse will be like "discourse among jack-daws and parrots, meer sounds without sense or meaning."[162]

Given the great diversity in men's reasoning abilities, education, and beliefs, language is the necessary tie that can bind radically individual human beings into a civil society. Through language, consisting of words of agreed-upon meaning, men transform their "various and contradictory...opinions" into a basic agreement on the "common interests and conduct of the society."[163] Thus is there an obligation to find the meaning of language as it was understood by those who created the constitution or framed the laws. Meaning should not be derived from the prejudices or philosophic understanding of the interpreter; such infusion of new meaning would render subjective that meaning of the law that was intended to be objective once enacted by the legitimate authority. For Trenchard and Gordon, certainty in the language of the law maintained within civil society was the important distinction between arbitrary and free governments. And it was this distinction that was most important to their American readers.

By combining the theories concerning the language of law they found in Hobbes and Locke with other sources of political ideas, not least Algernon Sidney's *Discourses Concerning Government*, Trenchard and Gordon were able to fit natural rights theories of constitutionalism within a broader republican context. By transmitting the ideas concerning the nature of language and the problems posed to public order by the interpretive abuse of words first put forth by Hobbes and later refined and enlarged by Locke, Trenchard and Gordon assured that those theories became ever more embedded in the emerging logic of American constitutionalism, which would see a written constitution of enumerated and limited powers as essential to the maintenance of republican liberties.

IV. BLACKSTONE'S SCIENCE OF THE LAW

Of those who took seriously the teachings of Hobbes and Locke and transmitted them to later generations, perhaps none was ultimately more important than Sir William Blackstone (1723–1780), whose *Commentaries on the Laws of England* (1765–69) became one of the most widely used and

---

[162] *Cato's Letters*, No. 111, p. 780; No. 120, pp. 831–832, 835; and *Independent Whig*, "Letter to a Clergyman," p. 131.
[163] *Independent Whig*, No. 50, p. 303. See also No. 54, pp. 329–330.

influential books in the history of law.[164] The *Commentaries* were based on the lectures on English law that Blackstone began delivering in Oxford after he had been rejected for the Regius Professorship of Civil Law there in 1753. Before Blackstone began, the common law of England had never been taught in either of the universities, but had been left the preserve of the Inns of Court in London; it was deemed more the stuff of practitioners than of men of a more philosophical bent. But so popular were the lectures that in 1756 Blackstone was named the first Vinerian Professor in the University of Oxford, a post he retained until 1762. Although he also would serve as a member of Parliament (1761–70) and as a judge on both the Court of Common Pleas and King's Bench (1770–1780), it was on the basis of his four volumes of *Commentaries* that his undying fame would rest. As they were published between 1765 and 1769, they were an immediate success – and not just in England but in America, as well.[165]

Blackstone was himself a university man, having studied at Pembroke College, Oxford, and then having been appointed a fellow of All Souls. And the breadth of his education was on full display in the *Commentaries*, proving to many that he was both "a distinguished man of letters and a great lawyer."[166] Yet subsequent generations (inspired perhaps in the first instance by Jeremy Bentham's scathing dismissal of Blackstone and his work)[167] have been inclined not to take Blackstone seriously as a thinker of the first rank.[168] Some have suggested that he did not really understand the

---

[164] See *History of English Law*, XII: 702–737.

[165] For the biographical details of Blackstone's life, see David A. Lockmiller, *Sir William Blackstone* (Chapel Hill: University of North Carolina Press, 1938); and Wilfred Prest, *William Blackstone: Law and Letters in the Eighteenth Century* (Oxford: Oxford University Press, 2008). See also Daniel Boorstin, *The Mysterious Science of the Law* (Cambridge, MA: Harvard University Press, 1941); Albert W. Alschuler, "Rediscovering Blackstone," *University of Pennsylvania Law Review* 145 (1996–97): 1–55; and Dennis R Nolan, "Sir William Blackstone and the New American Republic: A Study of Intellectual Impact," *New York University Law Review* 51 (1976): 731–768.

[166] Holdsworth, *History of English Law*, XII: 706. Holdsworth reports that Blackstone had studied not only the classics but logic and mathematics, as well. The result was impressive: "Blackstone combined with an accurate knowledge of English law, which he had learned from books and by attendance in the courts, a knowledge of English history, political theory and Roman law, which he had learned at the University. It was this unique combination of the learning of the English lawyer and university learning which explains the distinctive excellence of the Commentaries." William S. Holdsworth, "Some Aspects of Blackstone and His Commentaries," *Cambridge Law Journal* 4 (1932): 261–285, pp. 263–264.

[167] See, for example, A. V. Dicey, who has suggested that Bentham's attack on Blackstone in his *Fragment on Government* had succeeded in proving the commentator to be "a lax thinker" and delivering a critical blow from which Blackstone's reputation as a profound jurist "[a]mong men of thought . . . never recovered." "Blackstone's Commentaries," *Cambridge Law Journal* 4 (1930–32): 286–307, p. 291. (This article was based on Dicey's inaugural lecture and is here reprinted from *The National Review* 54 [1909]: 653–675.)

[168] Daniel Boorstin argued, for example, that "Blackstone was not a rigorous thinker and his work does not rank with the great books which demonstrate the nicest intricacies of the mind of man." *Mysterious Science of the Law*, p. 189.

philosophical sources from which he drew most heavily – such as Pufendorf and Burlamaqui – but rather patched together theories from here and there in a way that ultimately undermined his presumed intention in writing the *Commentaries* in the first place.[169] But on the whole it seems true that "less than justice has been done to Blackstone's abilities as a political thinker."[170] Indeed, it seems clear that he was perfectly adept at handling his sources (he certainly understood what Pufendorf and Burlamaqui were up to) and that he set out with an intention that was not simply to capture the common law as it existed in his day. He was more intellectually ambitious than that. His true and avowed purpose was nothing less than developing a science of the law, a science, as he unambiguously put it in his inaugural lecture as Vinerian Professor, "which is to be the guardian of natural rights and the rule of ... civil conduct."[171] The essence of that science was the reconciliation of the common law and the new civil philosophy of natural rights.[172] The result was a theory of the law that would seem to many to be "remarkably Hobbesian."[173]

Natural Law and the Law of Human Nature

It has been suggested that Blackstone's highest purpose in the *Commentaries* was to address the relationship between natural law and positive law.[174] In a sense, that is true; nearly every writer in the common law tradition from Bracton onward had insisted that the law of nature was properly understood to be one of the grounds of the laws of England.[175] But in fact what Blackstone had to address was the relationship of the customary law to positive or municipal law, that is to say, law understood as the expression of the will of the sovereign. For no small part of what has been called the "contagious ambiguity"[176] of the natural law stemmed from its confusion with the law of custom. The tradition held that custom was "the life of the common law," that indeed, "the common law [was] nothing else but

---

[169] Michael Lobban, "Blackstone and the Science of Law," *The Historical Journal* 30 (1987): 311–335, p. 312.

[170] Holdsworth, "Some Aspects of Blackstone and His Commentaries," p. 283.

[171] Sir William Blackstone, *Commentaries on the Laws of England*, 4 vols. (8th ed.; Oxford: Clarendon Press, 1778), I: 4. Hereinafter cited as *Commentaries*.

[172] James R. Stoner, Jr., *Common Law and Liberal Theory: Coke, Hobbes, and the Origins of American Constitutionalism* (Lawrence: University Press of Kansas, 1992), p. 165.

[173] Ibid., p. 166. See also Lobban, "Blackstone and the Science of Law," p. 325, on Blackstone's "Hobbesian premises"; and Paul Lucas on Blackstone's "characteristic trait of devious cautiousness" in concealing his debt to Hobbes, in "Ex Parte Sir William Blackstone, Plagiarist: A Note on Blackstone and the Natural Law," *American Journal of Legal History* 7 (1963): 142–158, pp. 148, 149.

[174] Herbert J. Storing, "William Blackstone," in Leo Strauss and Joseph Cropsey, eds., *History of Political Philosophy* (2nd ed.; Chicago: Rand McNally, 1972), p. 595.

[175] See, for example, Christopher St. Germain, *Doctor and Student*.

[176] Boorstin, *Mysterious Science of the Law*, p. 65.

custom"; the dominant view in Blackstone's day was that "the first ground and chief cornerstone of the laws of England...is immemorial custom." But there was no guarantee that what was old was a matter of natural law rather than merely conventional law. It was clear to Blackstone that there was nothing more difficult than trying "to ascertain the precise beginning and first spring of an antient and long established custom." The problem, as he knew, was that men generally tend to "mistake for nature what [they] find established by long and inveterate custom." It was important to keep that distinction clearly in mind, especially since man-made statutes were to have priority over the customary common law.[177]

In keeping with the demands of the common law tradition, Blackstone was compelled to argue that "the sound maxims of the law of nature [were] the best and most authentic foundation of human laws." But that position was not without its problems. The "moral system" that had been framed by certain "ethical writers" and thus "denominated the natural law" was nothing more than what those writers were inclined to "imagine" that law to be. The fact was, the law of nature, properly so called, was not " a multitude of abstracted rules and precepts, referring...to the fitness or unfitness of things"[178] It was something lower, more accessible. When Blackstone spoke of the law of nature, he had in mind a far more modern view than that which had been embraced by the common lawyers up to his time. When it came to developing his science of the law, his objective was to do for "the English legal system what Newton had done for the physical world, and what Locke had done for the world of the mind."[179]

One sees this clearly in the movement of Blackstone's argument about the nature of laws in general. What begins as a discussion of the immutable and transcendent law of nature becomes a concern for "the immutable laws of human nature." However morally worthy one might think those "sound maxims" of the law of nature to be, they were not to be discovered "only upon the due exertion of right reason," not to be ascertained by "a chain of metaphysical disquisitions." Were that the case, then "the greater part of the world would have rested content in mental indolence, and ignorance its inseparable companion." God was more clever than that; He was not much given to metaphysical subtleties. He enabled ordinary human reason – reason understood as calculation – to be sufficient for men to discover "the eternal, immutable laws of good and evil...so far as they are necessary for the conduct of human actions." The Creator had seen fit "to contrive the constitution and frame of humanity, that [men] should want no other

177 *Commentaries*, II: 150; I: 472; I: 73; I: 67; II: 11. "Statutes are either declaratory of the common law, or remedial of some defects therein." Moreover, "[w]here the common law and a statute differ, the common law gives place to the statute." *Commentaries*, I: 86, 89.
178 *Commentaries*, I: 33, 42, 41.
179 Boorstin, *Mysterious Science of the Law*, p. 12.

prompter to inquire after and pursue the rule of right, but only [their] own self-love, that universal principle of action." Said Blackstone, God "has graciously reduced the rule of obedience to this one paternal precept, 'that man should pursue his own true and substantial happiness'." This was the law of nature that was "coeval with mankind" to such an extent that "no human laws are of any validity if contrary to this; and such of them as are valid derive all their force, and all their authority, mediately or immediately from this original."[180] But in the end, of course, such validity depended upon human judgment.

Thus was there yet a further problem. Human reason was inevitably "corrupt," and the human understanding "full of ignorance and error." Aware of their deficiencies, men would come to understand the need for civil society and for government. While the idea of a state of nature was "too wild to be seriously admitted," that did not diminish the reality that the "only true and natural foundations of society are the wants and fears of individuals." These wants and fears, spawned by men's own "sense of their weakness and imperfection," would show men the necessity of their union and thereby prove to be "the cement of civil society."[181]

For the principal aim of society is to protect individuals in the enjoyment of those absolute rights, which are vested in them by the immutable laws of nature; but which could not be preserved in peace without that mutual assistance and intercourse which is gained by the institution of friendly and social communities. Hence it follows that the first and primary end of human laws is to maintain and regulate these *absolute* rights of individuals.[182]

Such a union of otherwise free and independent individuals could occur only by what Blackstone accepted as the original contract, despite the absence of the efficacious fiction of a state of nature. This contract was the basis of his own view of sovereignty by institution.

Sovereignty by Institution

Even though he rejected the idea of a state of nature, Blackstone had no delusions that human history had been idyllic. The original contract was the means whereby his fellow men, or at least his fellow Englishmen, had escaped the "savage state of vagrant liberty" and "those rude and unlettered times," those "dark ages of monkish superstition." While there may not have been a time in which all the world was a war of all against all, the movement through the original contract to something better was motivated by the same concern that had moved Hobbes. "Peace," Blackstone insisted,

[180] *Commentaries*, I: 39–40, 40, 40, 40, 41, 41.
[181] Ibid., I: 41, 47, 47, 47.
[182] Ibid., I: 124.

is "the very end and foundation of civil society."[183] The mechanics of the original contract meant that it was by its terms that

the whole [of society] should protect all its parts, and that every part should pay obedience to the will of the whole; or, in other words, that the community should guard the rights of each individual member, and that (in return for this protection) each individual should submit to the laws of the community; without which submission of all it was impossible that protection could be certainly extended to any.[184]

The contract was absolute in its demands for obedience, rejecting any notion that individuals within society would be the arbiters of when to obey and when not. "[C]ivil liberty rightly understood," he argued, "consists in protecting the rights of individuals by the united force of society: society cannot be maintained, and of course can exert no protection, without obedience to some sovereign power: and obedience is an empty name if every individual has a right to decide how far he himself shall obey."[185] Men willingly enter into the original contract because it is rendered clear to them by their shrewdly calculating and self-loving reason that such a union of the natural many into the artificial one of the body politic will serve their true interests. "No man, that considers for a moment," Blackstone insisted, "would wish to retain the absolute and uncontrolled power of doing whatever he pleases; the consequence of which is, that every other man would also have the same power; and there then would be no security to individuals in any of the enjoyments of life."[186] It is this form of "legal obedience and conformity" that makes possible the idea of a "public good" that can be achieved only by the presence of a sovereign that will be the "supreme, irresistible, absolute, uncontrolled authority."[187] And such a sovereign, to be legitimate, can only be the result of consent.

---

[183] Ibid., II: 6, 228, 455; I: 349.

[184] Ibid., I: 48.

[185] Ibid., I: 251.

[186] Ibid., I: 125. Blackstone sketched the movement from natural liberty to civil liberty in some detail: "The absolute rights of man, considered as a free agent, endowed with discernment to know good from evil, and with power of choosing those measures which appear to him to be most desirable, are usually summed up in one general appellation, and discriminated the natural liberty of mankind. This natural liberty consists properly in a power of acting, as one thinks fit, without any restraint or control, unless by the law of nature; being a right inherent in us by birth, and one of the gifts of God to man at his creation, when he endued him with the faculty of the will. But every man, when he enters into society, gives up a part of his natural liberty, as the price of so valuable a purchase; and in consideration of receiving the advantages of mutual commerce, obliges himself to conform to those laws, which the community has thought proper to establish."

[187] Ibid., I: 125, 139, 49. As Blackstone elaborated: "Unless some superior be constituted, whose commands and decisions all the members are bound to obey, they would still remain as in a state of nature, without any judge upon earth to define their several rights, and redress their several wrongs." *Commentaries*, I: 48.

The great and abiding natural obstacle to the convention of civil society is man's free will. Given that the "state is a collective body, composed of a multitude of individuals ... intending to act together as one man," the mechanical difficulty is how to transform many wills into one. As Blackstone knew, such a transformation of many wills into one could not be achieved by "any *natural* union." The only means was a contract to be freely entered into by each individual. Such a union of wills into "one uniform will of the whole"[188]

can ... be no otherwise produced than by a *political* union; by the consent of all persons to submit their own private wills to the will of one man, or of one or more assemblies of men, to whom the supreme authority is entrusted: and this will of that one man, or assemblage of men, is in different states according to the [sic] their different constitutions, understood to be *law*.[189]

"By the sovereign power," Blackstone explained, "is meant the making of laws." Since it is "requisite to the very essence of a law that it be made by the supreme power," Blackstone concluded that "sovereignty and legislature are ... convertible terms; one cannot subsist without the other." And the essential feature of such law duly made and promulgated by the sovereign was the sanction it carried for noncompliance. As Blackstone put it, "the main strength and force of a law consists in the penalty annexed to it. Herein is to be found the principal obligation of human laws." Put a bit more bluntly: "nothing is compulsory but punishment." If the conscience "were the only, or most forcible obligation, the good only would regard the laws, and the bad would set them at defiance."[190]

The essential feature of the sovereignty duly "constituted" by free men was its absoluteness, in Blackstone's estimation. This absolute sovereignty manifested itself in both the king and Parliament. When it came to Parliament, it was "the place where that absolute despotic power, which must in all governments reside somewhere, is entrusted by the constitution of these kingdoms." There was simply no limit to the power of Parliament; it could do "everything that is not naturally impossible,"[191] and what it might choose to do, "no authority on earth can undo."[192] There could be no other way to preserve the union of civil society than by the agreement that "the power of Parliament is absolute and without control."[193]

---

[188] Ibid., I: 52, 52, 52.
[189] Ibid.
[190] Ibid., I: 49, 46, 57, 57, 57.
[191] Ibid., I: 160, 161.
[192] Ibid., I: 161. "An act of Parliament ... cannot be altered, amended, dispensed with, suspended or repealed, but in the same forms and by the same authority of Parliament: for it is a maxim in law, that it requires the same strength to dissolve as to create an obligation." *Commentaries*, I: 186.
[193] Ibid., I: 162.

To emphasize Parliament's freedom, Blackstone took as his example the old notion that it was inherently unjust for a man to be made a judge in his own cause. This was a maxim that to many was seen as having been derived from the natural law itself. Even so, should Parliament undertake by statute to allow for such a situation, there was nothing that could be done about it. Most assuredly, however unreasonable such a statute might be, no judge could declare it void.[194] The fact was, Blackstone insisted, "there is no court that has power to defeat the intent of the legislature, when couched in such evident and express words, as leave no doubt, whether it was the intent of the legislature, or no."[195]

The king was, by the nature of the original contract, subject to some limitation on his prerogatives. But within those powers "vested in the crown by the laws of England," his latitude was unrestricted. In order for the system to work it had to be understood that "in the execution of lawful prerogatives... there is no legal authority that can either delay or arrest him." In the exercise of his politically permissible powers, "the king is irresistible and absolute, according to the forms of the constitution." The foundation of this arrangement was a simple maxim: "The king can do no wrong." At least as long as he fulfilled his "principal duty," which was "to govern his people according to the law."[196]

The dilemma posed by Blackstone's theory of absolute sovereignty was the same as it had been for Hobbes's: what can be done should the power of government prove tyrannical and at odds with the obligation to secure the safety and happiness of the people? Locke, of course, had famously modified Hobbes's scheme by insisting that the people retained their natural sovereignty and were thus able to check abuses and perhaps even dissolve the government and form a new one more likely to secure their interests. But this solution Blackstone explicitly and forcefully rejected. However "just" such a solution might appear in theory, in practice it would be disastrous. To try to provide legally for such an eventuality was at best paradoxical and at worst contradictory. To provide for such a power to dissolve the legislature would undermine the original contract's intention to create absolute sovereignty. It would result in the people being thrown back into their state of natural equality – that "savage state of vagrant liberty" – where by "annihilating the sovereign power" such an action would also serve to repeal "all positive laws whatsoever before enacted."[197] While there may not have been an

---

[194] "[I]f the Parliament will positively enact a thing to be done which is unreasonable, I know of no power that can control it; and the examples usually alleged in support of this sense of the rule do none of them prove, that, where the main object of a statute is unreasonable the judges are at liberty to reject it; for that were to set the judicial power above the legislative, which would be subversive of all government." *Commentaries*, I: 91.

[195] Ibid.

[196] Ibid., I: 237, 233, 250, 251, 246, 233.

[197] Ibid., I: 162; II: 6; I: 162.

actual historical state of nature, the dissolution of the government and the repeal of all positive laws would come fairly close to creating one.

The reason this Lockean solution was unacceptable to Blackstone was that it was "the supposition of the law...that neither the king nor either house of Parliament (collectively taken) is capable of doing any wrong." Should "oppressions...spring from any branch of the sovereign power" they would, of necessity, be "out of the reach of any *stated rules* or *express legal* provision." Should the worst come to pass, it would fall to the people by "the prudence of the times" to fashion "new remedies upon new emergencies." Ultimately, Blackstone shared at least part of Locke's solution, agreeing that there were indeed "inherent (though latent) powers of society, which no climate, no time, no constitutions, no contract, can ever destroy or diminish."[198] Such inherent powers just could not be codified as part of the express legal structure.

Blackstone's commitment to absolute sovereignty was firm. The safety and happiness of the individual citizens depended upon it. Without a supreme sovereign with unrestrained compulsive power to enforce the law, the absolute rights of the people would enjoy no security. Even the potential of oppression was not enough to move him to shackle the sovereign, not even in principle. And in the end the reason was clear. For Blackstone, as for Hobbes, there was no doubt that "anarchy [is] a worse state than tyranny itself, as any government is better than none at all."[199]

The Nature of Law and the Limits of Judging

Blackstone's theory of sovereignty by institution led to his understanding of law generally and to his view of the positive or municipal law in particular. From these views about the law were derived his ideas about the nature and limits of the power of judging. The one point about which he was utterly unambiguous was the danger that would be posed to the civil society, and thereby to the security of the absolute rights of individuals, should the meaning of the law be left to the "arbitrary will of any judge."[200] Blackstone's understanding of sovereignty simply could not allow that.

The municipal law "is properly defined to be 'a rule of civil conduct prescribed by the supreme power in a state, commanding what is right and prohibiting what is wrong.'" This was not, in Blackstone's view, a matter of the sovereign merely transmitting notions of right and wrong that had been antecedently established by the law of nature. Rather, the essence of sovereignty meant that it was by the supreme power in the state that "the boundaries of right and wrong [would] be established and ascertained by

---

[198] Ibid., I: 244, 245, 245, 245.
[199] Ibid., I: 127.
[200] Ibid., I: 142.

the law." Those legal definitions of right and wrong depended not upon the law of nature or even the declared law of God, but only upon "the wisdom and will of the legislator"[201] in creating them.

The municipal law was not, strictly speaking, concerned with standards deemed to be "naturally and intrinsically right or wrong." Its focus was on those things that were "indifferent," things that were neither commanded nor prohibited by either the law of nature or God's law. These matters of indifference could by the municipal law be made "either right or wrong, just or unjust, duties or misdemeanors, according as the municipal legislator sees proper, for promoting the welfare of the society, and more effectually carrying out the purposes of civil life." It turns out that this realm of indifferent things open to legislative discretion is vast, and thus most of the laws that will govern the people are of this sort.[202] For Blackstone, "the bulk of human laws has no foundation in nature."[203] Thus any science of the law is primarily to be concerned with man-made laws.

It was in his discussion of the nature of the laws of England that Blackstone made clear that, whatever the natural law pretensions of earlier writers, the common law was part of the positive laws. Whatever its antiquity, "the *lex non scripta*, the unwritten or common law," was no less a part of the laws of man than was "the *lex scripta*, the written or statute law."[204] As such, both the common law and the statute law had to be understood as expressions of the sovereign will, either mediately or immediately.

The statute law, the *lex scripta*, is seen unambiguously to be the decree of the sovereign. Such a law was clearly a "command" to which obedience was owed not as a result of individual approbation but because it was "the maker's will."[205] These written laws are, in a sense, the hard edge of the sovereign power: they are resolved by his will, promulgated and made knowable by his words, and enforced with whatever sanction he thinks necessary to make the people conform to them. And, as discussed earlier, when that will is made clear by express words, there is no power on earth, no court of law, that can modify or thwart it.

The place of the *lex non scripta* or the customary common law as an expression of the sovereign will is more complicated. These customs or maxims of the law are to be made known by the judges in the courts of justice, who are acknowledged to be "the depositaries of the laws"; they are, Blackstone says, "the living oracles . . . who are bound by oath to decide [all cases before them] according to the law of the land."[206] What this means

---

[201] Ibid., I: 44, 53, 54.
[202] Ibid., I: 54, 55, 42.
[203] John Finnis, "Blackstone's Theoretical Intention," *Natural Law Forum* 12 (1967): 163–183, p. 181.
[204] *Commentaries*, I: 63.
[205] Ibid., I: 45, 44.
[206] Ibid., I: 69.

is that the common law is something more than the mere opinions of the judges.[207]

The idea that the judges are to rule according to the law of the land is the result of *stare decisis* or precedent. And it is in explaining the binding power of precedent – it is not merely a matter of judicial discretion – that Blackstone makes clear the limits of common law judging:

For it is an established rule to abide by former precedents, where the same points come again in litigation: as well as to keep the scale of justice even and steady, and not liable to waver with every new judge's opinion; as also because the law in that case being solemnly declared and determined, what before was uncertain, and perhaps indifferent, is now become a permanent rule, which it is not in the breast of any subsequent judge to alter or vary from, according to his private sentiments: he being sworn to determine not according to his own private judgment, but according to the known laws and customs of the land; not delegated to pronounce a new law, but to maintain and expound the old one.[208]

While it is essential to civil liberty that the judiciary be independent, it is also necessary that the judges not forget that they are magistrates subordinate to the king.[209] The "judges are the mirror by which the king's image is reflected." The long-standing tradition is that "all jurisdictions of courts are either mediately or immediately derived from the crown, their proceedings run generally in the king's name, they pass under his seal, and are executed by his officers."[210] What this means is that while the judiciary is institutionally independent, the judges are not personally so. They are, as was just pointed out, obliged by oath to follow the law of the land. A faithful adherence to precedent will keep the judges from roaming at will.

Given the priority Blackstone gives to the statute side of the municipal law, the interpretation of these laws is of fundamental importance to him. Since one cannot "interrogate the legislature" to determine the meaning of each law, it is essential that there be clear and sensible rules to guide judges as they seek to establish the will or intention of the sovereign in each case. Following Grotius and Pufendorf, Blackstone posits a rather straightforward list of rules for interpretation. Those rules all derive from his most basic view of the task. "The fairest and most rational method to interpret the will of the legislator, is by exploring his intentions at the time when the law was made, by signs the most natural and probable. And these signs are either the words, the context, the subject matter, the effects and consequences, or the spirit and reason of the law." When confronting the language of the

---

[207] "So...*the law*, and the *opinion of the judge*, are not always convertible terms, or one and the same thing; since it sometimes may happen that the judge may *mistake* the law." *Commentaries*, I: 71.

[208] *Commentaries*, I: 69.

[209] Ibid., I: 146.

[210] Ibid., I: 146, 270, 267.

law, the general rule is that the words are to be "understood in their most usual and known signification," not according to the rules of grammar but based upon "their general and popular use." Technical terms of art should be rendered according to "the learned in each art, trade, or science." Should words taken in their literal sense be found to bear "either none, or a very absurd signification," it could not be amiss for the interpreter to deviate a little from the received sense of them.[211]

As a general matter, it is often a great help in construing a law to take note of "the proeme or preamble" of it. At a minimum, this prefatory explanation of the law may offer sound guidance for discovering "the reason and spirit of it, or the cause which moved the legislator to enact it." This ascertaining of the reason or purpose of the law is, in Blackstone's view, simply "the most universal and effectual way of discovering the true meaning of the law."[212]

The danger of "interpreting laws by the reason of them" is that such an interpretive effort can allow or encourage a judge to stray from the confines of literal interpretation into a more equitable way of viewing the law in question. This could wrongly lead the judge to conclude that in order to be enforced, laws must simply be reasonable. Nothing could be more dangerous, in Blackstone's view. The idea that the unreasonableness of a statute would be sufficient grounds for a judge to reject it would be "to set the judicial power above that of the legislature, which would be subversive of all government." For Blackstone, the lesson was simple: "[T]he liberty of considering all cases in an equitable light must not be indulged too far, lest thereby we destroy all law, and leave the decision of every question entirely in the breast of the judge." The obvious reason for caution was that "law, without equity, though hard and disagreeable, is much more desirable for the public good, than equity without law: which would make every judge a legislator, and introduce a most infinite confusion; as there would be almost as many different rules of action laid down in our courts, as there are differences of capacity and sentiment in the human mind."[213] For Blackstone, the power of judges, whether in dealing with the common law or with the statute law, was limited. At a minimum, law was never to be defined by the arbitrary will of so subordinate a magistrate. The true meaning of the law can be nothing other than the expressed will of the sovereign lawmaking power in the society.

Blackstone's teachings about the nature and extent of law and, by implication, the nature and extent of the emerging notion of constitutionalism was not merely one book among many; it outranked the works of Locke himself and was second only to Montesquieu's celebrated *The Spirit of Laws*

---

[211] Ibid., I: 59, 59–60, 60, 61.
[212] Ibid., I: 60, 62, 62.
[213] Ibid., I: 91, 62, 62.

as to the frequency with which the founders explicitly relied upon it.[214] It seems to have been no exaggeration when James Madison in the Virginia ratifying convention described the *Commentaries on the Laws of England* as "a book which is in every man's hand."[215]

V. MONTESQUIEU AND THE ART OF JUDGING

One cannot speak of the influential writers who came in Locke's wake, those whose works would prove to be of fundamental significance in the creation of the American republic and the rise of American constitutionalism, without at least mentioning that widely read and justly acclaimed work by the aristocratic French jurist Charles Louis de Secondat, baron de la Brède et de Montesquieu, *The Spirit of Laws* (1748).[216] In the view of many his great treatise was simply the "single most important work of political analysis for Americans of the Revolutionary generation."[217] It was another of those books, like that of his disciple Blackstone, that seemed to be literally "in every man's hand."[218] Yet, as has often been noted, there is an intriguingly enigmatic quality to much of *The Spirit of Laws*, and this is certainly the case when it comes to his notion of judicial power and what one might call the art, if not the science, of judging.[219]

[214] See Donald S. Lutz, "Intellectual History and the American Founding," Chapter 5 of *A Preface to American Political Theory* (Lawrence: University Press of Kansas, 1992), pp. 113–140; the tables of relative influence are at pp. 136, 138, 139.

[215] Jonathan Elliot, ed., *The Debates in the Several State Conventions on the Adoption of the Federal Constitution*, 5 vols. (Philadelphia: J. B. Lippincott & Co., 1876), III: 501.

[216] For a brief sketch of the phenomenal publishing history of the work, see Paul A. Rahe, *Montesquieu and the Logic of Liberty* (New Haven, CT: Yale University Press, 2009), pp. xvii-xix. This great text is cited in different ways, either as *The Spirit of the Laws* or, as is the case here, as *The Spirit of Laws*. Earlier publishers used the latter title, and this will be used generally here, even though the practice of other authors who use the more recent style will not be changed.

[217] Jack P. Greene, *The Intellectual Heritage of the Constitutional Era: The Delegates' Library* (Philadelphia: Library Company of Philadelphia, 1986), p. 43.

[218] See Lutz, *A Preface to American Political Theory*, pp. 135, 136, and 138. See also Paul Merrill Spurlin, *Montesquieu in America, 1760–1801* (Baton Rouge: Louisiana State University Press, 1940), pp. 46–98.

[219] This is especially the case when it comes to anything approaching rules of interpretation. There is, for example, nothing in *The Spirit of Laws* comparable to the extensive discussions of language and the signification of words found in Locke and Hobbes or in those who followed them, from Jacob to Rutherforth to Blackstone. See the previous discussion; see also Chapters 2 and 3. For a guide to the often perplexing teachings of Montesquieu, see David W. Carrithers, Michael A. Mosher, and Paul A. Rahe, eds., *Montesquieu's Science of Politics: Essays on The Spirit of Laws* (Lanham, MD.: Rowman & Littlefield, 2001).

At first encounter Montesquieu seems to some to be somewhat removed from Hobbes and Locke and the tradition they had spawned.[220] His science of politics is not explicitly rooted in the idea of a horrifying state of nature from which rational men seek their preservation through escape into civil society.[221] Indeed, he argues that the state of war begins only *after* men enter into civil society.[222] He understands politics and government and law as springing less from such grand philosophical abstractions than from the concrete realities of man's true situation as revealed by a keen-eyed, social scientific, and comparative assessment.[223] Good laws depend not only on a sound *"politic law,"* a fundamental law "relative to the governors and the governed," but also upon such variable and rather mundane factors as climate, terrain, and soil quality as well as the "inclinations, riches, numbers, commerce, manners, and customs" of any particular people. In Montesquieu's view, "the government most conformable to nature, is that which best agrees with the humour and disposition of the people in whose favour it is established."[224]

Montesquieu does not risk leaving his differences from Hobbes and Locke to mere inference or conjecture. He proclaims at the outset of *The Spirit of Laws* that Hobbes's notorious account of man's nature being such that life is a war of all against all was "far from being well founded." Moreover, the Englishman had recklessly declared that "there is nothing just or unjust but what is commanded or forbidden by positive laws." To the contrary, Montesquieu judiciously insists that there are surely "relations of justice antecedent to the positive law by which they are established."[225] Thus from the start does he strive to appear to be in a completely different philosophical world from that of Hobbes and Locke. Yet a closer reading suggests that in fact his "political intentions" are essentially the same. It is simply that his prudence leads him to present his similar teaching in a way that is "radically different."[226]

---

[220] See especially Paul O. Carrese, *The Cloaking of Power: Montesquieu, Blackstone, and the Rise of Judicial Activism* (Chicago: University of Chicago Press, 2003).

[221] See Mark H. Waddicor, *Montesquieu and the Philosophy of Natural Law* (The Hague: Martinus Nijhoff, 1970), pp. 66–76.

[222] M. de Secondat, Baron de Montesquieu, *The Spirit of Laws*, trans. T. Nugent, 2 vols. (4th ed.; London: J. Nourse and P. Vaillant, 1766), I.II.6. The citation indicates book, chapter, and page number. Hereinafter cited as *Spirit of Laws*.

[223] On the comparative nature of his work, see Anne M. Cohler, *Montesquieu's Comparative Politics and the Spirit of American Constitutionalism* (Lawrence: University Press of Kansas, 1988); and Ran Hirschl, "Montesquieu and the Renaissance of Comparative Public Law," in Rebecca E. Kingston, ed., *Montesquieu and His Legacy* (Albany: State University of New York Press, 2009), pp. 199–219.

[224] *Spirit of Laws*, I.III.7; I.III.9; I.III.8.

[225] Ibid., I.II.6; I.I.3; I.I.3.

[226] Pierre Manent, *An Intellectual History of Liberalism* (Princeton, NJ: Princeton University Press, 1994), p. 53. See also Stoner, *Common Law and Legal Theory*, p. 159.

Ultimately, the distance between Montesquieu's political science and that of Hobbes and Locke is more apparent than real.[227] It becomes clear that he, like Locke before him, undertook in part to develop and to complete what Hobbes had left incomplete.[228] In the process, of course, he also famously developed and completed what Locke himself had left incomplete, namely, a theory of separated governing powers as the institutional key to a reasonably safe, if not simply a good government.[229] It is in the context of his theory of separation of powers that the necessity of an independent yet restrained judicial power emerges. And it is in his arguments about the nature and extent of the judicial power that Montesquieu reveals how relatively close is his theory of the art and science of judging to the views about language and interpretation that sprang from Hobbes and Locke in the first instance. Yet his views about judicial power in this regard are in no way simply straightforward and clear.

As with much of his treatise, no small part of the difficulty of coming to grips with Montesquieu's theory of judging is the structural complexity of *The Spirit of Laws*.[230] And one may reasonably suspect that the design of the work was intentionally rendered complex at least in part to shield the author from accusations that, despite his protests to the contrary, he was in fundamental agreement with the somewhat grimmer view of man's basic nature to be found in the works of his English forebears.[231] After all, it is, as he says in rather guardedly Hobbesian terms, the profound "wickedness of mankind" that demands government and laws in the first place; and, in somewhat Lockean terms, he insists that it is that same wicked nature that demands institutional arrangements within government to curb the inevitable impulse toward excess and abuse by those who will come to wield power. Such arrangements, he believes, are the means necessary to render a government "moderate" and thus safe to the liberty of the people.[232]

[227] Thomas L. Pangle, *Montesquieu's Philosophy of Liberalism: A Commentary on the Spirit of the Laws* (Chicago: University of Chicago Press, 1973), pp. 33–43; see also Michael Zuckert, "Natural Law, Natural Rights, and Classical Liberalism: On Montesquieu's Critique of Hobbes," in Ellen Frankel Paul, Fred D. Miller, Jr., and Jeffrey Paul, eds. *Natural Law and Modern Moral Philosophy* (Cambridge: Cambridge University Press, 2001), pp. 227–251.

[228] Pangle, *Montesquieu's Philosophy of Liberalism*, p. 35.

[229] See Robert Shackleton, *Montesquieu: A Critical Biography* (Oxford: Oxford University Press, 1961), pp. 284–288.

[230] On that complexity, see Ana J. Samuel, "The Design of Montesquieu's *The Spirit of the Laws*: The Triumph of Freedom over Determinism," *American Political Science Review* 103 (2009): 305–321.

[231] Pangle, *Montesquieu's Philosophy of Liberalism*, p. 33. For all his prudence and caution *The Spirit of Laws* was still condemned by the Catholic Church and placed on the Index of Prohibited Books in 1751. See Shackleton, *Montesquieu*, pp. 370–377.

[232] *Spirit of Laws*, VI.XVII.132; XI.IV.220; XI.IV.220.

The greatest danger to the governed is always going to be the tendency of rulers to subject them to "arbitrary decisions" as the result of a general "capriciousness" in the administration of power. As Locke had taught, there need to be known and settled laws the people can depend upon. The essence of despotic government, for Montesquieu no less than for Locke, was the fact that "all is uncertain, because all is arbitrary." In his view, the governed are "really free"when they are "subject only to the power of the law" and when that law is itself "express and determinate."[233] Despotic governments, by definition, are governed by nothing more certain than the whims of the governor, be the governor a single ruler or an assembly.

Montesquieu's greatest contribution to the new science of politics was his insight that law in and of itself is but a necessary condition for good government, not a sufficient one. Laws, without more, will always be subject to abuse by those officials who seek to "carry [their] authority as far as it will go." The solution was obvious, in Montesquieu's view: "To prevent this abuse, it is necessary, from the nature of things, power should be a check to power." The need within liberalism that he exposed was to make clear the nature and extent of the legislative, executive, and judicial powers and to position each in such a way as to enable them to maintain their independence from the others. This was essential to securing liberty against the abuses of power. "A government may be so constituted," Montesquieu argued, "as no man shall be compelled to do things which the law does not oblige him, nor forced to abstain from things which the law permits." The result of such internal contrivances would be liberty in the truest sense, that "tranquility of mind arising from the opinion each person has of his safety." Should the legislative and executive powers be united, he insisted, "there can be no liberty;" similarly, "there is no liberty if the judiciary power be not separated from the legislative and executive."[234] As Alexander Hamilton would later argue in *The Federalist*, the key for Montesquieu was to render the judicial power such that it would exercise "neither force nor will, but merely judgment."[235]

The judiciary in Montesquieu's science of politics is an institution of paradox. On the one hand, it wields a power potentially "terrible to mankind"; on the other, it is, "in some measure, next to nothing." Yet even though it may be "next to nothing," it is not to be presumed simply safe. As with any other institution, the judiciary might well abuse its powers, not least should judges presume to supplant the letter or even the spirit of the law with their own "private opinion." Such judicial arbitrariness is no more acceptable than any other variety. That is why Montesquieu insists that the judgments

[233] Ibid., XII.IV.270–271; XXVI.XVI.242; XI.VI.225; VI.III.109.
[234] Ibid., XI.IV.220, 220, 220; XI.VI.222, 222.
[235] Jacob E. Cooke, ed., *The Federalist* (Middletown, CT: Wesleyan University Press, 1961), No. 78, p. 523.

of the courts in monarchies as well as in republics must always be, as far as possible, "conformable to the letter of the law." In his view, judges are properly understood to be "mere passive beings" who serve as little more than "the mouth that pronounces the words of the law."[236] Thus the design of the laws is of the utmost importance in making sure that they serve the ends for which they have been adopted.

At the most basic level, the laws of a regime should be of a style that is "concise... plain and simple." The need to make clear the ends of the laws to those obliged to live under them requires that they be characterized by a "certain simplicity and candor." In short, the laws need to be a "direct expression" of the legislator's will and intention so that that will and intention, or even his "passions and... prejudices," may be "better understood." As Hobbes and Locke had taught, in order for the laws to do their job it is "essential" that "the words of the laws... excite in every body the same ideas." And once those same ideas are "fixt" they ought not to be weakened by the introduction of, or return to, any "vague expressions." The lawgiver must remember the audience for whom his handiwork is actually intended. "The laws," Montesquieu argues, as a result, "ought not to be subtle; they are designed for people of common understanding, not as an art of logic, but as the plain reason of a father of a family." It is by this means alone that the law can be made known to the governed while simultaneously providing "a fixed rule to the judge."[237]

Montesquieu's teaching about judging is rendered ambiguous in that he undertakes alternately to sketch the nature and extent of judicial power in both monarchies and republics. While both sorts of regimes require "courts of judicature," their requirements are very different. The task of judges in monarchies is rendered more arduous by the fact that they must consider not only "whatever belongs to life and property, but likewise to honor." And such a concern with honor introduces so many interests as to render adjudication anything but simple. The differences in "rank, birth, and condition" in monarchies tend to generate complexity and potential confusion in the laws to such a degree as is sufficient "to make of reason itself an art." As a result, in monarchies the judges pass judgment not as individual decrees but as a matter of arbitration among themselves. By this method "they deliberate together; they communicate their sentiments for the sake of unanimity; they moderate their opinions, in order to render them conformable to those of others; and the lesser number are obliged to give way to the majority." This approach, while necessary for monarchies, is simply "not agreeable to the nature of a republic."[238]

---

[236] *Spirit of Laws*, XI.VI.224, 228, 225, 225, 232.
[237] Ibid., XXIX.XVI.364, 369, 372, 364, 365, 366, 368.
[238] Ibid., VI.I.103, 104, 105, 103; VI.IV.110.

The reason such a deliberative function does not fit a republican judiciary is that such a body of decrees, built up over time, will more often than not prove to be uncertain or even contradictory and thus "contrary" to the spirit of moderate republican governments. Even though in monarchies the judges are expected to make "very scrupulous enquiries," the accumulated results can often be bewildering. This is not to say that in monarchies the judges are presumed to exercise a largely unbounded discretion. Quite to the contrary; where the laws are explicit, the judge in a monarchical system "conforms to them." But in such systems the judges are allowed, when the laws are not so explicit, to "investigate their spirit." In Montesquieu's view history had made it perfectly clear that such investigations – or what may be called interpretations or constructions – of the laws' spirit may in fact put the judges in a position of not really having "any laws to direct them," thus leaving their untethered wills to render purely "arbitrary judgments." This was, in Montesquieu's view, ultimately the greatest concern in both monarchies and republics.[239]

In monarchies and republics alike it is essential that the law as interpreted by the judges not fluctuate but have the same meaning "to-day as yesterday." That is the case so that "the lives and property of the citizens may be as certain and fixt as the very constitution of the state." As a result, it is necessary that the judgments of the courts of judicature not be corrupted by the political passions of the moment or tainted by the personal interests of the judge but rather exhibit a "certain coolness" and indeed an "indifference, in some measure, to all manner of affairs." It is by such known and settled laws being given a steady interpretation by disinterested and impartial judges that the people, by such a rule of law, come to be, as the author says, "really free." It is the sense of security that comes from confidence that the law truly governs that in great part assuages the people's nagging sense of uneasiness and gives them that "tranquility of mind" that is the very essence of liberty.[240]

All this is especially true the "nearer a government approaches toward a republic." Given the nature of that form of government it is simply requisite that "the manner of judging becomes settled and fixt." The demand on the judge is clear, to Montesquieu's way of thinking. "In republics," he insists, "the very nature of the constitution requires the judges to follow the letter of the law: otherwise the law might be explained to the prejudice of every citizen, in cases where their honours, property, or life are concerned."[241] It is by this "recourse to express and determinate laws" that the judges will be able to wield their potentially "terrible" power while at the same time remaining politically "next to nothing."

[239] Ibid., VI.I.105; VI.III.109, 109, 109.
[240] Ibid., VI.I.103; VI.VI.116; XI.VI.225, 222.
[241] Ibid., VI.III.109.

This is the result, in part, of the courts of judicature having relatively little to do with questions about the fundamental political or constitutional law that sets out the relationship between the governed and their governors. By and large, the courts are limited in their concerns to questions arising from the civil law (in which Montesquieu also includes the criminal law of the state); it is through them that the magistrate "punishes criminals, or determines the disputes that arise between individuals."[242] This is no small thing, in the Frenchman's view, insofar as the people will come to enjoy a state of liberty "only as they are governed by civil laws; and because they live under those civil laws, they are free."[243] But the judiciary in Montesquieu's scheme has no grand power akin to what will come to be known as judicial review, the power of courts to determine the constitutionality of ordinary legislation. And even when it comes to the separate powers keeping one another in their proper places, it is primarily the political give-and-take between the executive and the legislative, not the exercise of judicial power as a matter of constitutional law, that maintains that necessary system of balances and checks.

Where modern readers are inclined to think of judges as comprising the essence of judicial power, Montesquieu, in reflecting on the English constitution, saw primarily juries, groups of citizens who would be called upon to sit in judgment of their fellows and then to disperse. They would have the power to exert an influence on the spirit of the laws yet institutionally be all but "invisible."[244] Yet there is something more in Montesquieu's argument about an independent judiciary, something implicit in his account of both republican and monarchical judges, something that needs to be drawn out and fashioned into a recognizable idea of judicial power as such – something, in short, that has its roots in his notion of what the laws' spirit requires.[245] Indeed, he goes so far as to end the book in *The Spirit of Laws* most concerned with constitutional matters with a daring tease: "[W]e must not always exhaust a subject so as to leave no work at all for the reader. My business is not to make people read, but to make them think."[246] And there were those across the Atlantic – such as Alexander Hamilton and John Marshall – who would rise to the occasion by thinking through and drawing out the deeper implications of Montesquieu's somewhat meager

---

[242] Ibid., XI.VI.222. For a consideration of Montesquieu and the criminal law, see David W. Carrithers, "Montesquieu and the Liberal Philosophy of Jurisprudence," in Carrithers, Mosher, and Rahe, eds., *Montesquieu's Science of Politics*, pp. 291–334.

[243] Ibid., I.III.7; XXVI.XX.246.

[244] Ibid., XI.VI.224–225.

[245] See his highly suggestive, if somewhat cryptic, comment that "the master-piece of legislation [is] to know where to place properly the judiciary power." Further, he insists, it is the "true function of a prince ... to appoint judges, and not to sit as judge himself." Ibid., XI.XI.242.

[246] Ibid., XI.XX.267.

theory of judging and transforming it into an essential feature of American constitutionalism.[247]

VI. THE INTELLECTUAL FOUNDATIONS OF
AMERICAN CONSTITUTIONALISM

The intellectual foundations of American constitutionalism were rich and varied, with the various strands of thought – from philosophy to Whig politics to the common law – often "tangled and interdependent." This was the result of the Founders being actively engaged in a "continuing dialogue" with those writers whose works they took seriously, taking what worked for them from here and there and "adapting that heritage to their shifting purposes." They were not merely "passive recipients" of the ideas spawned by these various intellectual traditions.[248] Yet there were common concerns and objectives, not least among them a rather definite understanding of what constitutions and constitutionalism, properly understood, were all about.

Early in the revolutionary period a consensus began to emerge that "in all free states the Constitution is fixed" and that "vague and uncertain laws, and more especially constitutions, are the very instruments of slavery." Experience had taught the colonists the harsh lesson that any governor without restraint could make "mere humour and caprice" the most fundamental "rule and measure" of the administration of political power. Protection lay in maintaining the "essential distinction" between a "civil constitution," which was fundamental, and the form of government and the exercise of its powers, which was not.[249]

As the Americans moved closer to the call for independence, their thinking about constitutions hardened. A constitution to be deemed fundamental had to be able to "survive the rude storms of time" and to remain constant "however . . . circumstances may vary."[250] The most likely way to achieve

---

[247] See Chapters 5 and 7 of this volume.

[248] Greene, *The Intellectual Heritage of the Constitutional Era*, pp. 10, 11, 12.

[249] Samuel Adams, "The House of Representatives of Massachusetts to the Speakers of Other Houses of Representatives," 11 February 1768, in Harry Alonzo Cushing, ed., *The Writings of Samuel Adams*, 3 vols. (New York: Octagon Books, 1968), I: 185; "Candidus" [Adams], 3 February 1776, ibid., III: 262; Jonathan Mayhew, *A Discourse Concerning Unlimited Submission and Nonresistance to the Higher Powers* (Boston, 1750), in Bailyn, ed., *Pamphlets of the American Revolution*, pp. 241, 242; Daniel Shute, *An Election Sermon* (Boston, 1768), in Charles S. Hyneman and Donald S. Lutz, eds., *American Political Writing of the Founding Era, 1760–1805*, 2 vols. (Indianapolis: Liberty Press, 1983), I: 109–136, p. 117; *Berkshire's Grievances* (Pittsfield, 1778), ibid., I: 455–461, 457. See also *Four Letters on Interesting Subjects*, ibid., I: 368–389, 385; and Philodemus [Thomas Tudor Tucker], *Conciliatory Hints, Attempting, by a Fair State of Matters, to Remove Party Prejudice* (Charleston, 1784), ibid., I: 606–630, 627. Hereinafter cited as *American Political Writing*.

[250] [Theophilus Parsons], *The Essex Result* (Newburyport, 1778), *American Political Writing*, I: 480–522, 491. See also *Rudiments of Law and Government Deduced from the Law of*

such permanence was to make certain that the constitution was "contained in some written charter."[251] And for such charters to serve as a brake on government, it was further necessary that they be "plain and intelligible – such as common capacities are able to comprehend, and determine when and how far they are, at any time departed from."[252] The objective of those who would draft such constitutions was that "not a single point... be subject to the least ambiguity."[253] Such a "fixt" constitution was the only means whereby the people could safely make their way between "the arbitrary claims of rulers, on one hand," and their own "lawless license, on the other."[254]

A great part of the confidence of the Revolutionary generation in the constraining power of written law and constitutions was of course a matter of common sense and their own experience; by 1776 the idea of a written constitution was so widely accepted that it seemed nothing less than a self-evident truth.[255] From the beginning, Americans were familiar with documents – ranging from royal charters to the early state constitutions – that sought to reduce political and social agreements to writing.[256] This

Nature (Charleston, 1783), ibid., I: 565–605, 567. The anonymous author of *The People the Best Governors: Or a Plan of Government Founded on the Just Principles of Natural Freedom* (New Hampshire, 1776) gave a more Hobbesian version of the necessity of permanence for fundamental constitutions: "It is an old observation, the political bodies should be immortal – a government is not founded for a day or a year, and, for that very reason, should be erected upon some invariable principles." Ibid., I: 390–400, 395.

[251] *Four Letters on Interesting Subjects*, ibid., I: 382.

[252] Gad Hitchcock, *An Election Sermon* (Boston, 1774), ibid., I: 281–304, 294. This same point was stressed repeatedly. See *Rudiments of Law and Government Deduced from the Law of Nature*, ibid., I: 588–589; and John Tucker, *An Election Sermon* (Boston, 1771), ibid., I: 158–174, p. 164.

[253] Thomas Jefferson, "Albemarle County Instructions Concerning the Virginia Constitution," in Julian P. Boyd et al., eds., *The Papers of Thomas Jefferson*, 21 vols. to date (Princeton, NJ: Princeton University Press, 1950–), VI: 286.

[254] Tucker, *Election Sermon, American Political Writing*, I: 168, 169.

[255] Willi Paul Adams, *The First American Constitutions: Republican Ideology and the Making of the State Constitutions in the Revolutionary Era*, trans. Rita and Robert Kimber (Chapel Hill: University of North Carolina Press, 1980), p. 22.

[256] "Like all Englishmen the colonists were familiar with written documents as barriers to encroaching power.... Moreover, America's own past was filled with written charters to which the colonists had continually appealed in imperial disputes – charters and grants from the Crown which by the time of the Revolution had taken on an extraordinary significance in American life." Gordon S. Wood, *The Creation of the American Republic, 1776–1787* (Chapel Hill: University of North Carolina Press, 1969), p. 268. See also Clinton Rossiter, *Seedtime of the Republic: The Origin of the American Tradition of Political Liberty* (New York: Harcourt, Brace and Co., 1953), pp. 32–33; Benjamin F. Wright, "The Early History of Written Constitutions in America," in Carl Frederick Wittke, ed., *Essays in History and Political Theory in Honor of Charles Howard McIlwain* (Cambridge, MA: Harvard University Press, 1936), pp. 344–371; Charles H. McIlwain, "The Fundamental Law behind the Constitution of the United States," in Conyers Read, ed., *The Constitution Reconsidered* (New York: Columbia University Press, 1938), pp. 3–14; and Adams, *The First American Constitutions*, p. 27.

commonsense assessment was bolstered by the English philosophical and legal traditions on which the Americans drew for guidance in constitutional matters and for their notions of fundamental law.[257] These two sources pushed the Americans toward a new understanding of fundamental law in the form of "a written superior law set above the entire government against which all the law is to be measured."[258]

The creation and ratification of the American Constitution thus signaled a new beginning in the history of constitutionalism, bringing to fruition a conception of fundamental law that had been developing in America for over a quarter of a century. From that moment on, political science took seriously the claim that rights, to be secured, had to depend upon something more permanent than the uncertain passions of the moment or the arbitrary opinions of those who might at a given time wield power. That security depended upon a law deemed "paramount," "fundamental," and "permanent"; it depended upon a constitution that was created to "last for ages."[259] The founders sought to fashion a written document that would, in a sense, transcend history.[260]

For a collection of such early documents, charters, and covenants, see Donald S. Lutz, ed., *Colonial Origins of the American Constitution* (Indianapolis: Liberty Fund, 1998).

[257] See generally J. W. Gough, *Fundamental Law in English Constitutional History* (Oxford: Clarendon Press, 1955); H. Trevor Colbourn, *The Lamp of Experience: Whig History and the Intellectual Origins of the American Revolution* (Chapel Hill: University of North Carolina Press, 1965); Charles Howard McIlwain, *The High Court of Parliament and Its Supremacy* (New Haven, CT: Yale University Press, 1910); Charles F. Mullett, *Fundamental Law and the American Revolution* (New York: Columbia University Press, 1933); J. G. A. Pocock, *The Ancient Constitution and the Feudal Law* (Cambridge: Cambridge University Press, 1987); and Martyn F. Thompson, "The History of Fundamental Law in Political Thought from the French Wars of Religion to the American Revolution," *American Historical Review* 91 (1986): 1103–1128.

[258] Wood, *Creation of the American Republic*, p. 260.

[259] *The Federalist*, No. 53, p. 361; No. 78, p. 525; Max Farrand, ed., *Records of the Federal Convention*, 4 vols. (New Haven, CT: Yale University Press, 1938), I: 422.

[260] Joseph Priestley described the power of writing this way: "[B]y means of writing we become acquainted with the sentiments and transactions of men in all ages, and all nations of the world. It connects, as it were, the living, the dead, and the unborn: for, by writing, the present age can not only receive information from the greatest and wisest of mankind before them, but are themselves able to convey wisdom and instruction to the latest posterity." *A Course of Lectures on the Theory of Language and Universal Grammar* (Warrington: W. Eyres, 1762).

5

The Greatest Improvement on Political Institutions

Natural Rights, the Intentions of the People, and Written Constitutions

When the delegates gathered in Philadelphia in the summer of 1787 for the convention that had been called to address their common problems, they ostensibly did so in order to revise the ineffectual Articles of Confederation; their goal was to render that first national constitution capable of meeting the exigencies of the union. Rather than offer mere revisions, however, they soon found themselves embarked on the arduous task of writing a completely new fundamental law. Believing as they did that language is the essence of law and that law is the essence of liberty, they sought to craft their new constitution as carefully as possible, pulling its words and meaning from sources they believed clear and common.[1] At the most basic level, there would be neither place nor need in such a written constitution for "metaphysical or logical subtleties."[2] Freedom demanded that "there be no mysteries in the governing plan"; it had to be "plain and intelligible."[3] Their objective was "to form a fundamental constitution, to commit it to

---

[1] It had been "the intention and honest desire of the Convention to use those expressions that were most easy to be understood and least equivocal in their meaning," Rufus King, a delegate from Massachusetts, would later recall. Max Farrand, ed., *The Records of the Federal Convention*, 4 vols. (New Haven, CT: Yale University Press, 1937), III: 268. Hereinafter cited as *Records of the Federal Convention*.

[2] Joseph Story, *Commentaries on the Constitution of the United States*, 2 vols. (3rd. ed.; Boston: Little, Brown and Co., 1858), I.451.322. (Citation indicates volume, section, and page number.) This was not simply the view of Story, the ardent nationalist. Thomas Jefferson himself would instruct Justice William Johnson that constitutional meaning was never to be sought in "metaphysical subtleties" because to do so would be to "make anything mean everything or nothing, at pleasure." Thomas Jefferson to William Johnson, 12 June 1823, in Andrew Lipscomb and Albert Bergh, eds., *The Writings of Thomas Jefferson*, 20 vols. (Washington, DC: Thomas Jefferson Memorial Foundation, 1905), XV: 439–452, p. 450. Hereinafter cited as *Writings of Jefferson*.

[3] John Tucker, *An Election Sermon* (Boston, 1771), in Charles S. Hyneman and Donald S. Lutz, eds., *American Political Writing during the Founding Era, 1760–1805*, 2 vols. (Indianapolis: Liberty Fund, 1983), I: 158–174, p. 164. Hereinafter cited as *American Political Writing*.

writing, and place it among their archives where everyone would be free to appeal to its text."[4] They celebrated the written constitution as simply "the greatest improvement on political institutions."[5]

The founding generation took seriously the idea that "the fundamental and paramount law of the nation" had to be a written law. It was, after all, to serve as the foundation of all the power delegated by the sovereign people by which the powers and institutions of the government would in turn be "defined and limited." The constitution had to be written so "that those limits may not be mistaken, or forgotten."[6] Such was the logic of the founding generation that it could be presumed that anything the people intended to include in their Constitution "they would have declared . . . in plain and intelligible language."[7] The foundation of the Constitution was the natural rights of mankind; its substance, the political intention of the people. The Founders' Constitution thus exemplified the central and essential premise of the Declaration of Independence, "that to secure . . . rights governments are instituted among men deriving their just powers from the consent of the governed."[8]

judicial review? [handwritten margin note]

I. NATURAL RIGHTS, POPULAR SOVEREIGNTY, AND FUNDAMENTAL LAW

In his final letter, written on the eve of its fiftieth anniversary, Thomas Jefferson celebrated the Declaration of Independence as nothing less than "the signal arousing men to burst the chains under which monkish ignorance and superstition had persuaded them to bind themselves, and to assume the blessings and security of self-government." In the place of that "monkish ignorance and superstition" the founders of the American republic had

---

[4] Thomas Jefferson to John Cartwright, 5 June 1824, in *Writings of Jefferson*, XVI: 45–46.

[5] *Marbury v. Madison*, 5 U.S. 137 (1803), 178.

[6] Ibid., 176, 176.

[7] *Barron v. Baltimore*, 32 U.S. 243 (1833), 250.

[8] John Marshall encapsulated this original natural rights understanding succinctly: "That the people have an original right to establish, for their future government, such principles as, in their opinion, shall most conduce to their own happiness is the basis on which the whole American fabric had been erected. The exercise of this original right is a very great exertion; nor can it, nor ought it, to be frequently repeated. The principles, therefore, so established, are deemed fundamental. And as the authority from which they proceed is supreme, and can seldom act, they are designed to be permanent." The practical lessons were clear: "This original and supreme will organizes the government and assigns to different departments their respective powers. . . . The powers . . . are defined and limited; and that those limits may not be mistaken, or forgotten, the Constitution is written. To what purpose are powers limited, and to what purpose is that limitation committed to writing, if these limits may, at any time, be passed by those intended to be restrained? The distinction between a government with limited and unlimited powers is abolished, if these limits do not confine the persons on whom they are imposed, and if acts prohibited and acts allowed are of equal obligation." *Marbury v. Madison*, pp. 176–177.

established a form of government that had succeeded in restoring the "free right to the unbounded exercise of reason and freedom of opinion." The American revolutionaries had proved beyond doubt, Jefferson insisted, that "the mass of mankind had not been born with saddles on their backs, nor a favored few booted and spurred, ready to ride them legitimately by the grace of God." Indeed, by their achievement all eyes were "opened or opening to the rights of man."[9]

Yet there was something paradoxical about the handiwork of that "host of worthies"[10] who had labored so diligently five decades earlier to secure political liberty. For all the successes that had come from their Declaration, the fact was that the instrument never presumed to offer any "new principles, or new arguments" but merely to record the "harmonizing sentiments of the day." Rather than aspire to any "originality" the Declaration had been intended merely to offer to the "tribunal of the world" a clear "expression of the American mind." The relatively modest objective was "to place before mankind the common sense of the subject, in terms so plain and firm as to command their assent, and to justify ourselves in the independent stand we [were] compelled to take." So much were the Americans of "one opinion" on the important subject of independence that their formal declaration sought only to express the views that one could find in ordinary conversations, letters, essays, and the "elementary books of public right."[11]

Preeminent among the authors of those "elementary" treatises of public right was, of course, "the great and judicious Mr. Locke."[12] To Jefferson and his countrymen it was Locke's "immortal writings"[13] that had made clear the natural rights foundation upon which the Americans understood themselves

---

[9] Thomas Jefferson to Roger Weightman, 24 June 1826, *Writings of Jefferson*, XVI: 182. On the source of Jefferson's powerful metaphor, see Douglass Adair, "Rumbold's Dying Speech, 1685, and Jefferson's Last Words on Democracy, 1826," in Douglass Adair, *Fame and the Founding Fathers*, ed. Trevor Colbourn (New York: W. W. Norton, 1974), pp. 192–202.

[10] Jefferson to Weightman, 24 June 1826, *Writings of Jefferson*, XVI: 182.

[11] Thomas Jefferson to Henry Lee, 8 May 1825, *Writings of Jefferson*, XVI: 118, 118–119.

[12] Tucker, *An Election Sermon, American Political Writing* I: 164.

Jefferson's admiration for Locke was considerable. In ordering from John Trumbull copies of portraits of Locke along with Francis Bacon and Isaac Newton, Jefferson explained that he considered them "as the three greatest men that have ever lived, without any exception, and as having laid the foundation of those superstructures which have been raised in the Physical & Moral sciences." Thomas Jefferson to John Trumbull, 15 February 1789, in Merrill D. Peterson, ed., *Jefferson: Writings* (New York: Library of America, 1984), pp. 939–940. Hereinafter cited as *Jefferson: Writings*. So, too, did Jefferson see to it that Locke's treatises on government were included in the curriculum of the University of Virginia as one of the best books in which "the general principles of liberty and the rights of man, in nature and in society" were clearly elaborated. Ibid., p. 479.

[13] Samuel Cooper, *A Sermon on the Day of the Commencement of the Constitution* (Boston, 1780), in Ellis Sandoz, ed., *Political Sermons of the Founding Era, 1730–1805*, 2 vols. (2nd ed.; Indianapolis: Liberty Fund, 1998), I: 639. Hereinafter cited as *Political Sermons*.

to stand and from which they prepared to launch and to wage their battle to free themselves from what they saw as the illegitimate yoke of British rule. Among the widely shared sentiments of that age was the belief that "Locke by his discoveries in the intellectual world . . . [had] enlarged the boundaries of human knowledge and happiness." The American revolutionaries were convinced that their young country was the chosen land where the "political truths" Locke had "investigated with philosophic eye" were destined to take root and burst "spontaneous forth."[14]

Jefferson's genius in dealing with Locke in formulating an accurate "expression of the American mind" as it was in June and July 1776 went beyond merely reiterating the teachings to be found in *Two Treatises of Government*; it went beyond even the Virginian's artful substitution of the "pursuit of happiness" for "property" in the catalogue of the inalienable natural rights of mankind. Rather, Jefferson's true genius lay in his ability to distill Locke's political philosophy of natural rights and the consent of the governed to its essence – and then to use that distillate to establish a new standard for the true ground of legitimate government thereafter. What had begun as an appeal to Britain to recognize the Americans' rights as Englishmen became, within that Lockean context, a justification for revolution based on the rights of man.

The Declaration of Independence had two purposes, one political the other philosophic. Politically, the document was intended to demonstrate to potential allies that the Americans were not undertaking the dangerous business of revolution for mere "light and transient causes." It was only after long and deep consideration of what could be objectively seen as "a long train of abuses and usurpations" that the Americans had been moved to such radical action. Recent history had made clear that there was in Britain a conscious "design" to reduce the American colonists to a state of "absolute despotism." It was the Americans' "decent respect to the opinions of mankind" that prompted them, as Jefferson put it, to "declare the causes which impel[led] them to the separation." Indeed, the bulk of the Declaration was a catalogue of the particulars of Britain's tyrannical design.

The bill of particulars against Britain had to be seen as more than the usual grumbling of colonies against perceived slights by the colonizing power, however. Their complaints were deeper than that, the Americans insisted. As "the laws of nature and of nature's God" entitled them to a "separate and equal station" among "the powers of the earth," it was precisely the violation of those fundamental laws of nature and nature's God by Britain that legitimated the revolution. This was not merely a case of disgruntled

---

[14] Nathanael Emmons, *The Dignity of Man* (Providence, 1787), *Political Sermons*, I: 893; Bishop James Madison, *Manifestations of the Beneficence of Divine Providence Towards America* (Richmond, 1795), *Political Sermons*, II: 1311–1312.

Englishmen who thought their rights as subjects had been slighted by unwelcome taxes or other irritating regulations; this was a case of a concerted effort to violate the more fundamental natural rights of man that were, Jefferson would insist, inalienable. Thus was the American cause the cause of free men everywhere.

The Declaration may have lacked the originality in its principles that Jefferson claimed, but it did not lack any originality in the purposes to which those principles were put in practical terms. Never before had there been a revolution justified by recourse to a philosophy of politics. And Jefferson sought to leave no doubt as to the Americans' philosophic justification for their move for independence:

> We hold these truths to be self-evident: that all men are created equal; that they are endowed by their creator with certain inalienable rights; that among these are life, liberty, and the pursuit of happiness: that to secure these rights, governments are instituted among men, deriving their just powers from the consent of the governed; that whenever any form of government becomes destructive of these ends, it is the right of the people to alter or abolish it, and to institute new government, laying its foundation on such principle, and organizing its powers in such form, as to them shall seem most likely to effect their safety and happiness.

Because the existing British colonial order had indeed become destructive of the ends of securing the rights to life, liberty, and the pursuit of happiness of the Americans, the colonists had every legitimate reason to throw off that government and to establish a new one that to them would appear most likely to "effect their safety and happiness."

The philosophic truths upon which the Declaration rested its radical political cause were, as Jefferson said, deemed to be "self-evident," meaning that their truth did not depend upon their universal acceptance. They were true in and of themselves, whether everyone or anyone at any particular time recognized that truth or not; they were true in the same way that the laws of gravity and motion were true before Isaac Newton explained them in his celebrated *Principia*. The laws governing man's social relations, based upon his nature, are no less self-evidently true than the scientific laws governing the natural world. This is what Jefferson meant fifty years later when he told Roger Weightman that the principles of the Declaration would eventually be seen around the world – "to some parts sooner, to others later, but finally to all" – as freeing men to assume the blessings of self-government.[15]

The primal truth of the Declaration of Independence was the natural equality of all men. It was this truth that had banished as illegitimate the view that "the mass of mankind" had been born with saddles on their backs and a "favored few booted and spurred, ready to ride them legitimately, by

[15] Jefferson to Weightman, 24 June 1826, *Writings of Jefferson*, XVI: 182.

the grace of God."[16] Nature was silent on the important question as to who was to rule and who was to be ruled. Not only was each person born with certain rights that could not be taken away legitimately – life, liberty, and the pursuit of happiness – but implicit in that arrangement was the right of the people collectively to govern themselves as they might see fit. They would be free to choose whatever form they might think best, be it a democracy, an aristocracy, or a monarchy, and to arrange the internal institutions of that form as would seem to them most politically efficacious.[17]

Because all men are by nature created equal and because each is possessed of inalienable rights and because nature is silent as to who shall rule, it becomes clear that the only basis for a legitimate government will be the consent of those who are to be governed by it.[18] Consent is the reciprocal of man's natural equality.[19] The choice as to form and function is open, but the government to which consent is given should only be one that will by purpose and design secure the rights nature gives but leaves insecure. Given the insecurity man faces outside a civil society, and the continuing vulnerability of his rights to the actions of the stronger even within a civil society, there are certain minimal requirements.

It is worth recalling that Locke himself defined what any legitimate government must have as part of its structure. Those three requisites are, first, "an *establish'd*, settled, known *Law*, received and allowed by common consent to be the standard of right and wrong, and the common measure to

---

[16] Ibid.

[17] James Otis put it this way: "The form of government is by nature and by right so far left to the individuals of each society that they may alter it from a simple democracy or government of all over all, to any other form they please." James Otis, *The Rights of the British Colonies Asserted and Proved* (Boston 1764), in Bernard Bailyn, ed., *Pamphlets of the American Revolution, 1750–1776* (Cambridge, MA: Harvard University Press, 1965), pp. 408–482, p. 426. Hereinafter cited as *Pamphlets of the American Revolution*.

[18] "Men being...by nature, all free, equal and independent, no one can be put out of this estate, and subjected to the political power of another, without his own consent." Peter Laslett, ed., *Locke's Two Treatises of Government* (2nd ed.; Cambridge: Cambridge University Press, 1970), *Second Treatise*, 348: 95. Hereinafter cited as *Second Treatise*. Citation indicates page number followed by section number.

Long before Jefferson penned the Declaration of Independence, Jonathan Mayhew made the same point. When it came to the legitimate foundation of political power, Mayhew insisted, anything besides consent "is mere lawless force and usurpation, neither God nor nature having given any man a right of dominion over any society independently of that society's approbation and consent to be governed by him." Jonathan Mayhew, *A Discourse concerning Unlimited Submission and Nonresistance to the Higher Powers* (Boston 1750), *Pamphlets of the American Revolution*, pp. 203–247, p. 237 n.

[19] As Locke had put it, the "Lord and master" of all mankind had never by "any manifest declaration of his will" set anyone above the others or conferred on him "by an evident and clear appointment an undoubted right to dominion and sovereignty." *Second Treatise*, 287: 4.

decide all controversies"; second, there must be *"a known and indifferent judge*, with the authority to determine all differences according to established law"; and third, the government must have the *"Power* to back and support the sentence, when right, and to give it *Execution."*[20] All this must come from the bottom up, from the consent of the governed, and not from the top down, under some notion of sovereignty external to the people themselves such as the divine right of kings. In the view of Locke, as in the Declaration of Independence, the people alone are sovereign. To allow political power to be created and wielded by anything but institutions resting upon the consent of the governed would be inherently illegitimate and would subject the people to the same sort of arbitrary force that had rendered the state of nature so dangerous and inhospitable a place.

The Americans took the teachings of Locke and the Lockeans seriously when it came to their own thinking about the nature and extent of fundamental laws or constitutions and how such laws could be made to fit within the American political context. They were not seduced by the medieval moral claims that had been made in behalf of natural law;[21] nor were they blindly drawn to the British model of judge-made common law.[22] Rather, they were decidedly modern, seeing that the nature of "civil society or governments is a temporal worldly constitution, formed upon worldly motives, to answer valuable worldly purposes."[23] They knew, as Locke and his followers had taught them, that "the people... are the only source of civil authority on earth."[24] Thus were their expectations of what a fundamental constitution was all about properly limited. "A constitution," an anonymous writer noted, "when completed, resolves the two following questions: First, what shall the form of government be? And secondly, what shall be its powers?"[25]

---

[20] *Second Treatise*, 368–369: 124–126.

[21] "As [man] comes originally from the hands of his Creator, self-love or self-preservation, is the only spring that moves within him." Untitled article signed "U" (Boston, 1763), *American Political Writing* I: 33. James Winthrop would later put it this way: "No man when he enters into society does it from a view to promote the good of others, but he does it for his own good." [James Winthrop] "Agrippa Letters," in Paul L. Ford, ed., *Essays on the Constitution of the United States, Published During its Discussion by the People, 1787–1788* (Brooklyn: Historical Printing Club, 1892), p. 73.

[22] They were in general committed to the idea that law had to be "simple, clear, and intelligible to the meanest capacity": "Law from precedent should be altogether exploded.... What people in their senses would make the judges, who are fallible men, depositaries of the law; when the easy, reasonable method of printing, at once secures its perpetuity, and divulges it to those who ought in justice to be made acquainted with it." *Rudiments of Law and Government Deduced from the Law of Nature* (Charleston, 1783), *American Political Writing*, I: 589, 590.

[23] Abraham Williams, *Election Sermon* (Boston, 1762), *American Political Writing*, I: 7.

[24] Gad Hitchcock, *Election Sermon* (Boston, 1774), *American Political Writing*, I: 288.

[25] *Four Letters on Interesting Subjects* (Philadelphia, 1776), *American Political Writing*, I: 385.

Putting it a bit more fully, Thomas Tudor Tucker sketched the American reception of Locke's vision this way:

The constitution should be the avowed act of the people at large. It should be the first and fundamental law of the state, and should prescribe the limits of all delegated powers. It should be declared to be paramount to all acts of the legislature, and irrepealable and unalterable by any authority but the express consent of the majority of the citizens collected by such regular mode as may be therein provided.[26]

Of this much, the Americans were sure: "Where there is no system of laws, not liberty, but anarchy, takes place."[27] And they knew, as many of their own revolutionary essayists pointed out, that in order to prevent the "mischiefs of perverted law"[28] there had to be not just a system of laws but a fundamental law – a fundamental *constitution* – to which final appeal could be made. There was no doubt in the "American mind," as Jefferson called it, that the only thing that could make such a law or constitution truly fundamental was that it had its "moral foundation" in "the consent of the people."[29] The only remaining question was how that widely celebrated, frequently invoked, but still somewhat vague maxim of "the consent of the people" was to be transformed into a concrete political and constitutional reality.

II. A CONSTITUTION FROM REFLECTION AND CHOICE

When Richard Henry Lee of Virginia stood forth in the Continental Congress on June 7, 1776, to offer the resolution for independence, he argued that the "United Colonies" of America "are, and of right ought to be, free and independent states." But declaring independence was only the first step. Lee prudently included in his resolution a call that "a plan of confederation be prepared and transmitted to the respective colonies for their consideration and approbation." The Americans knew, as Locke had taught them, that men in a social state cannot really do without government.

The issue was more complicated than simply turning to the business of establishing a confederation national in its scope, however. There was also the need to fashion constitutions and governments for thirteen newly independent states. Between 1776 and 1780, the states thus turned their attention to just how such constitutions and governments ought to be created

---

[26] Philodemus [Thomas Tudor Tucker], *Conciliatory Hints, Attempting, by a Fair State of Matters, to Remove Party Prejudice* (Charleston, 1784), *American Political Writing*, I: 627.

[27] Nathaniel Niles, *Two Discourses on Liberty* (Newburyport, 1774), *American Political Writing*, I: 260.

[28] *A Letter to the People of Pennsylvania* (Philadelphia, 1760), *Pamphlets of the American Revolution*, p. 266.

[29] John Adams to James Sullivan, 26 May 1776, in Charles Francis Adams, ed., *The Works of John Adams*, 10 vols. (Boston: Little, Brown and Company, 1854), IX: 375.

and just what they should look like. All of the constitution making within the states took place on a political track parallel to the fashioning of the Articles of Confederation, a document that would not finally be unanimously ratified by the states until March 1, 1781 – having been before them for their consideration since November 15, 1777.

During that rather long stretch of time the Americans at both the state and federal levels had to grapple with reconciling high theory with their own practical governing experiences as they sought to make sense of the differences between democracies and republics; as they put their faith in a dominant legislative power and on occasion in unicameral legislatures; as they made every effort to come to grips with their profound fear of executive power; as they tried to translate their colonial experiences with the British common law tradition into a new understanding of the nature and extent of judicial power under written and more-or-less republican constitutions; as they struggled to determine the proper allocation of power between the states and the federal head; and as they undertook to weigh how, and to what extent, the reasonably abstract notions of "popular sovereignty" and the "common good" ought to hold sway over the routine conduct of public affairs. It was a period that produced lessons that eventually would be of great importance in the framing of the Constitution that would be ratified in 1788.[30]

At the state level, the tendency in nearly all of the new constitutions was toward greater democracy, clearly dominant and largely unchecked legislatures, and governors who were, by and large, politically impotent – executives who were "little more than cyphers," in James Madison's words.[31] At the national level, the Articles of Confederation not only failed to provide any independent executive or judicial powers but prided itself on being nothing more than "a firm league of friendship" among otherwise largely sovereign and independent states. Indeed, the sovereignty of the states was celebrated in the Articles themselves, which noted at the beginning that each state retained "its sovereignty, freedom, and independence, and every power, jurisdiction, and right which is not by this Confederation expressly delegated to the United States, in Congress assembled." This combination of nearly complete state sovereignty and federal weakness was increasingly seen to be a political disaster. As early as 1784 there were serious moves to amend the Articles of Confederation in order to render them competent to meet the exigencies of the union; so, too, would there be calls to curb what many saw as the dangerous tendency toward majority tyranny within the states.

---

[30] Willi Paul Adams, *The First American Constitutions: Republican Ideology and the Making of the State Constitutions in the Revolutionary Era*, trans. Rita and Robert Kimber (Chapel Hill: University of North Carolina Press, 1980), p. 4.

[31] *Records of the Federal Convention*, II: 35.

The governments of the several states had seen their largely omnipotent legislatures degenerate into legislative tyrannies where majorities ran roughshod over the rights of minorities. Elbridge Gerry's first remarks at the opening of the Constitutional Convention were to decry what he saw as the danger of the "levilling [sic] spirit" that had been loosed within the states by the "excess of democracy." And he was far from being alone in his fears about what Edmund Randolph called "the turbulence and follies of democracy." Both Gerry and Randolph along with a good many others believed that it was the inescapable turmoil of the democratic spirit that had rendered the states incapable of providing for "the security of private rights and the steady dispensation of justice."[32] Thus the task of the convention when it came to the states, as Madison famously put it, was to find a "republican remedy for the diseases most incident to republican government."[33]

The federal authority under the Articles of Confederation posed precisely the opposite problem. "The great fault of the existing confederacy," James Wilson noted, was "its inactivity." The complaint against Congress was never that it "governed overmuch" but that it "governed too little."[34] The result was that the confederation under the Articles had become a "lifeless mass."[35] The dilemma facing those committed to revising or reforming the Articles was the need to determine how to invigorate the national authority without simultaneously introducing into those councils the same pernicious elements that had come to mar the state governments. Crafting a truly "vigorous government"[36] carried with it formidable dangers.

One thing common to both the constitutions of the states and the Articles of Confederation was that their framers had not been concerned that the fundamental laws rest clearly upon the consent of the governed. Nearly all the state constitutions had been produced by the state legislatures and passed more or less like ordinary legislation.[37] So, too, had the Articles been the handiwork solely of the frequently distracted Continental Congress.[38] But things had changed. "Since the Articles of Confederation were established," Oliver Ellsworth pointed out, "a new sett [sic] of ideas seem to have crept in." In particular, the idea of "conventions of the people" or of conventions

---

[32] Ibid., I: 48, 51, 134. George Mason was also willing to admit that the state governments had been "too democratic," but was also afraid that the convention might "incautiously run into the opposite extreme." Ibid., I: 49.

[33] Jacob E. Cooke, ed., *The Federalist* (Middletown, CT: Wesleyan University Press, 1961), No. 10, p. 65. Hereinafter cited as *The Federalist*.

[34] *Records of the Federal Convention*, II: 10.

[35] *The Federalist*, No. 38, p. 247.

[36] Gouverneur Morris, *Records of the Federal Convention*, II: 479.

[37] See generally Adams, *First American Constitutions*.

[38] For the history of the confederation and its articles, see Jack N. Rakove, *The Beginnings of National Politics: An Interpretive History of the Continental Congress* (New York: Alfred A. Knopf, 1979).

"with power derived expressly from the people" had taken hold of the public mind.[39]

Although Ellsworth himself and some others did not warm to the new ideas about conventions of the people, it came to be generally agreed with regard to the new Constitution that it would prove to be "more stable and durable" if it were to rest upon – and be seen to rest upon – the "solid foundation of the people" rather than only upon "the pillars of the legislatures" of the several states.[40] This difference in foundations was of enormous consequence. It was the difference between "a mere compact resting on the good faith of the parties" and a true government possessed of "a complete and *compulsive* operation."[41] It was by the device of the convention – both to draft the constitution and to ratify it by conventions within the states – that America would be able to demonstrate that "societies of men" are indeed capable of "establishing good government from reflection and choice" and are not "forever destined to depend for their political constitutions on accident and force."[42] For the idea of "reflection and choice" was the very essence of the consent of the governed when it came to the people in their sovereign capacity creating the fundamental law.

In many ways the motivation underlying the founding generation's commitment to crafting a fundamental law from the reflection and choice of the sovereign people sprang from a republican truth that had been made painfully clear to them by the tumultuous politics they had endured in the years since independence. As they watched their public affairs veer toward a dangerous fluctuation between the "extremes of tyranny and anarchy," they came to appreciate how it was that in a republic "liberty may be endangered by the abuses of liberty, as well as by the abuses of power." The demagogues of the day, springing as they did from "a certain class of men in every state," had made clear that a "dangerous ambition more often lurks behind the specious mask of zeal for the rights of the people, rather than under the forbidding appearance of zeal for the firmness and efficiency of government." The result of all this was to see the states so corrupted by the "mischiefs of faction" that the governments were rendered "unstable" and the "public good" was nearly always "disregarded in the conflicts of rival parties," leading to many of the most important public measures being decided "not according to the rules of justice, and the rights of the minor party, but by the superior force of an interested and over-bearing majority." Justice demanded that the unruly opinions and passions and interests of the

[39] *Records of the Federal Convention*, II: 91. See Chapter 8, "Conventions of the People," in Gordon S. Wood, *The Creation of the American Republic, 1776–1787* (Chapel Hill: University of North Carolina Press, 1969), pp. 306–343.

[40] James Madison, *Records of the Federal Convention*, I: 50.

[41] Gouverneur Morris, ibid., I: 34.

[42] *The Federalist*, No. 1, p. 3.

people be made to yield by "the forms of the Constitution" to the "permanent and aggregate interests of the community." But given "the ordinary depravity of human nature" that would prove to be easier said than done.[43]

Depravity and Virtue

In many ways the early Americans' success in the Revolution encouraged a confidence that they as a people were, somehow, different – more virtuous, more public-spirited, more egalitarian than the rest of mankind. Thus did their early constitutions reflect a far greater sense of security from the excesses of democracy and the dangers of legislative dominance than history might otherwise have suggested was sound. The Americans of the Revolutionary generation were in for a rude awakening; their experiences during the confederal period would make clear to them that they had "no exemption from the imperfections, weaknesses and evils incident to society in every shape." Having been lulled into political complacency by their own "deceitful dream of a golden age," they were now awakened to the fact that as a political people they too were "yet remote from the happy empire of perfect wisdom and perfect virtue."[44]

When it came to assessing human nature there were few misty-eyed idealists among the delegates who gathered in Philadelphia in May 1787. Alexander Hamilton, always the realist, was convinced that the stakes were as high as they could be; the convention was in a position to "decide forever the fate of republican government," and if they failed to fashion their new constitution to give the government both "stability and wisdom," the republican form "would be disgraced & lost to mankind forever."[45] It was no time for "idle theories"[46] or any misplaced reliance on "pure patriotism." That had, after all, already proved to be "the source of many . . . errors"[47] in the recent past. Hamilton's charge to his fellow framers was blunt: "We must take man as we find him, and if we expect him to serve the public must interest his passions in doing so."[48] Left to his own self-interested devices, man would inevitably prove himself to be moved by a free will that was at once "ambitious, vindictive and rapacious." Of this there could be no doubt. Experience, that most trusted of teachers, demonstrated time and again that "momentary passions and immediate interests have a more active and imperious control over human conduct than general or remote considerations of policy, utility or justice."[49]

---

[43] *The Federalist.*, No. 9, p. 50; No. 63, p. 408; No. 1, p. 4; No. 1, p. 6; No. 10, pp. 58, 57, 60, 57; No. 78, pp. 529–530.
[44] *The Federalist*, No. 6, p. 35.
[45] *Records of the Federal Convention*, I: 424.
[46] *The Federalist*, No. 6, p. 35.
[47] *Records of the Federal Convention*, I: 376.
[48] Ibid.
[49] *The Federalist*, No. 6, pp. 28, 31.

The danger in popular forms of government would come whenever "the interests of the people are at variance with their inclinations" because man will nearly always seek to satisfy his inclinations, however detrimental that might be to his true interests.[50] "If the impulse and the opportunity be suffered to coincide," Madison would argue, "neither moral nor religious motives can be relied on as an adequate control." And when a number of citizens in a republic come together, "united and actuated by some common impulse of passion or of interest adverse to the rights of other citizens or to the permanent and aggregate interests of the community," they will likely prevail if they constitute a majority. Under the rules of how republics govern themselves that very form will enable such a factious majority "to sacrifice to its ruling passion, both the public good and the rights of other citizens." This sad fact was, Madison said, the great "opprobrium" under which the republican form had "so long labored."[51]

The deepest problem was that the causes of this republican predicament were "sown in the nature of man."[52] In the end it is not only depravity but also a most remarkable gift for self-deception and delusion within human beings that renders popular government so problematic.

As long as the reason of man continues fallible, and he is at liberty to exercise it, different opinions will be formed. As long as the connection subsists between his reason and his self-love, his opinions and his passions will have a reciprocal influence on each other; and the former will be objects to which the latter will attach themselves.[53]

The political consequences of man's nature flow ineluctably:

A zeal for different opinions concerning religion, concerning government and many other points, as well of speculation as of practice; an attachment to different leaders ambitiously contending for pre-eminence and power; or to persons of other descriptions whose fortunes have been interesting to the human passions, have in turn divided mankind into parties, inflamed them with mutual animosity, and rendered them much more disposed to vex and oppress each other, than to cooperate for their common good.[54]

The necessary solution is to so craft the fundamental law that these "various and interfering interests" will be refined and enlarged by being passed through a succession of institutional filtrations and will in the end, it is hoped, be rendered reasonably "consonant to the public good."[55]

There was no doubt in the minds of almost all of the founders that there was truly a "degree of depravity in mankind" that necessitated a "certain

---

[50] *The Federalist*, No. 71, p. 482.
[51] *The Federalist*, No. 10, pp. 61, 60–61, 61.
[52] Ibid., p. 58.
[53] Ibid.
[54] Ibid., pp. 58–59.
[55] Ibid., p. 62.

degree of circumspection and distrust." But so, too, did they believe that there were "other qualities in human nature" that in turn justified a "certain portion of esteem and confidence." It was the presence of these latter qualities that meant there was "sufficient virtue among men for self-government" and that something less than the "chains of despotism" could be relied upon to restrain men from "destroying and devouring one another."[56] Although these virtues, these "other qualities," are not catalogued, it seems safe to say that among them is man's ability to look unflinchingly at his own nature and then to fashion institutions that will take account of both his virtues and his vices.

This set of institutional devices would be the result of the improvements in the science of politics that had come to be made by the Enlightenment. Understanding how such arrangements could be used to supply man's "defect of better motives" revealed on the part of the founding generation both a firm grasp on the intricacies of human nature and an appreciation of the remedies necessary for its weaknesses. Such "auxiliary precautions" as bicameral legislatures, energetic executives, and independent judiciaries were undoubtedly a "reflection on human nature" in that they were necessary to "controul the abuses of government"; but that was not all.[57] Government itself, Madison said, was but "the greatest of all reflections on human nature":

If men were angels, no government would be necessary. If angels were to govern men, neither external nor internal controuls on government would be necessary. In framing a government to be administered by men over men, the great difficulty lies in this: you must first enable the government to controul the governed; and in the next place oblige it to controul itself.[58]

It was thus by the particulars of that new science of politics that the founders were to find that "republican remedy for the diseases most incident to republican government," the remedy that would rescue that form of government from its well-deserved opprobrium and allow it finally to be recommended to "the esteem and adoption of mankind."[59]

The New Science of Politics

The American founders understood well the Hobbesian lessons they had taken from Locke and his followers. What rendered civil society superior to man's complete freedom and equality in the state of nature, it will be recalled, was the order that derived from the people being governed by settled, known,

56 *The Federalist*, No. 55, p. 378.
57 *The Federalist*, No. 51, p. 349.
58 Ibid.
59 *The Federalist*, No. 10, p. 61.

and received laws. They never lost sight of the fact that governments were instituted at all because of the ugly truth that "the passions of men will not conform to the dictates of reason and justice without constraint."[60]

Government implies the power of making laws. It is essential to the idea of a law that it be attended by a sanction; or, in other words, a penalty or punishment for disobedience. If there be no penalty annexed to disobedience, the resolutions or commands will in fact amount to nothing more than advice or recommendation.[61] This point deserved emphasis. "A law," Hamilton would further explain, "by the very meaning of the term includes supremacy. It is a rule which those to whom it is prescribed are bound to observe. This results from every political association. If individuals enter into a state of society the laws of that society must be the supreme regulator of their conduct."[62] But this was only half of the problem. The rest of the dilemma was what to do to prevent the laws that were enforced and accompanied by a sanction from being unjust or unfair. The fundamental danger of the rule of law in a majoritarian scheme of government is that what Madison described as an "interested and over-bearing majority" may very well be able to "execute and mask its violence under the forms of the constitution." The distemper of all popular governments was the very real possibility that men "of factious tempers, of local prejudices, or of sinister designs" might gain office only "to betray the interests of the people."[63] While republics are safer than pure democracies in this regard, they are still not simply safe.

Acknowledging the "disorders that disfigure the annals of . . . republics," the American republicans took comfort in the fact that there had come to be devised "models of a more perfect structure," models that would render the republican form far from "indefensible." The science of politics, they insisted, had come nearer perfection in recent times and now provided the constitution makers with "powerful means by which the excellencies of republican government may be retained and its imperfections lessened or avoided."[64] Among the catalogue of improved principles and structures were the ideas of an extensive or large republic with a multiplicity of interests; representation; the separation of powers; bicameral legislatures; independent judiciaries; and energetic or "fortified" executives. And all of these devices would rest upon a foundation that fell between a pure confederal compact among sovereign states, on the one hand, and a simple consolidation of the states into one unitary government on the other. Where the Articles of Confederation and the constitutions of the several states had been crafted

---

[60] *The Federalist*, No. 15, p. 96.
[61] Ibid., p. 95.
[62] *The Federalist*, No. 33, p. 207.
[63] *The Federalist*, No. 10, pp. 60, 62.
[64] *The Federalist*, No. 9, p. 51.

during the "infancy of the science of constitutions & of confederacies,"[65] the new Constitution had the advantage of having been created at a time when the principles of republicanism had made their "principal progress towards perfection."[66]

A. Representation and Good Government

In confronting the evils of majority tyranny there was one thing that was clear to those who embraced the new science of politics. That truth was the fact that a "pure democracy...can admit of no cure for the mischiefs of faction." The reason was that it was erroneous to think that by "reducing mankind to a perfect equality in their political rights, they would, at the same time, be perfectly equalized and assimilated in their possessions, their opinions, and their passions." They would not. The diverse interests and passions around which factions could grow would be very much present and by and large uncontrollable. The solution lay in choosing a republic rather than a democracy, that form of government in which a "scheme of representation" takes place.[67]

The advantages brought to popular government by the republican form were primarily two. First, the government would be delegated to a select few, thus allowing all the raw opinions and passions and interests of the community to be filtered – refined and enlarged – by "passing them through the medium of a chosen body of citizens." It was to be hoped that this body of representatives would have sufficient "wisdom" to see what was the "true interest of their country" and would not be inclined to sacrifice that interest to "temporary or partial considerations." While there could be no guarantee, the proportional relationship of the representative to the represented was enough to make it likely that the people would choose as their representatives men of the "most attractive merit" who clearly possessed "the most diffusive and established characters."[68]

The second advantage that a republic had over a pure democracy was that it could extend over a "greater number of citizens and extent of territory."[69] This was essential to reaping the advantages not simply of a republic, but of an extended republic, one with a diverse and robust multiplicity of interests. This, especially, would help undermine the possibility of factious and tyrannical combinations.

B. The Extended Republic

Most of the details of the framers' new science of politics were borrowed from the various sources that comprised the most basic political library

---

[65] Edmund Randolph, *Records of the Federal Convention*, I: 18.
[66] *The Federalist*, No. 9, p. 51.
[67] *The Federalist*, No. 10, pp. 61, 61–62, 62.
[68] Ibid., pp. 62, 62, 63.
[69] Ibid., p. 62.

of the day. The teachings of such writers as Sidney, Locke, Montesquieu, and Trenchard and Gordon, as suggested earlier, found their way into the thinking of the founding generation and exerted a profound influence. But the framers were not themselves lacking in any real originality – not least when it came to understanding the relationship of geographic size to the very idea of sound republican government. Raised on the belief that republican liberties could be secure only in a small republic where there could be a great homogeneity of manners and morals among the people, Madison, in particular, turned that notion on its head. By his calculation, not only could such political and personal liberties be safe in a large or extended republic, they could in fact *only* be safe in such a configuration.

Madison had first broached the subject during the debates in Philadelphia in early June in a speech that would become the basis for his famous essay in the tenth number of *The Federalist*. Given that whenever "a majority are united by a common interest or passion, the rights of the minority are in danger," something had to be done to take account of that fact. The idea that smallness of the territory was a solution had been proved wrong by their own experience. Indeed, the smaller the territory, the greater the chance of majority tyranny. Experience thus "admonished" the Americans to "enlarge the sphere as far as the nature of the Govt. would admit." The fact was, enlarging the size of the territory was "the only defence agst. the inconveniences of democracy consistent with the democratic form of Govt."[70]

There was no doubt that this new theory would appear to many – perhaps even to most – as "novel" at best.[71] But it was central to the founders' new notion of a constitution of limited and enumerated powers that could at the same time produce a government sufficiently energetic both to secure private rights and to provide for the steady dispensation of justice. This new idea of the extended republic was, in fact, the very essence of that republican remedy that was necessary to cure the diseases most incident to republican government. In his more polished argument in *The Federalist*, Madison explained it this way:

The smaller the society, the fewer probably will be the distinct parties and interests composing it; the fewer the distinct parties and interests, the more frequently will a majority be found of the same party; and the smaller the number of individuals composing a majority, and the smaller the compass within which they are placed, the more easily will they concert and execute their plans of oppression. Extend the sphere, and you take in a greater variety of parties and interests; you make it less probable that a majority of the whole will have a common motive to invade the rights of other citizens; or if such a common motive exists, it will be more difficult for all who feel it to discover their own strength, and to act in unison with each other.[72]

[70] James Madison, *Records of the Federal Convention*, I: 135, 134, 135.
[71] *The Federalist*, No. 9, p. 52.
[72] *The Federalist*, No. 10, pp. 63–64.

Returning to the argument in the fifty-first number of the essays, Madison sought once again to reassure his readers. "In the extended republic of the United States, and among the great variety of interests, parties, and sects which it embraces," he insisted, "a coalition of a majority of the whole society could seldom take place on any other principles than those of justice and the general good."[73] It was in "the extent and proper structure of the Union"[74] that good republican government was to be secured. It was by this mechanical method that the "lifeless mass" of the Articles of Confederation could be transformed into a national government without simultaneously importing all the defects that had so disrupted the state governments. By a careful adjustment of the principle of federalism, the founders would be able to transform the confederacy into a nation of states.

C. *The Nation of States*

Before the convention in Philadelphia even sat, the idea that a simple consolidated republic was not only "unattainable" but would be "inexpedient" was a view with many advocates.[75] There were also those among the delegates who believed the convention had no power whatsoever to go any further than merely offering amendments to the Articles of Confederation that were truly of "a federal nature." Not only did the convention lack the authority to "go beyond the federal scheme," but the people as a whole were "not yet ripe for stripping the states of their powers." If the confederation was in fact "radically wrong," then the proper response of the delegates would be to adjourn, return to their home states, and then reconvene with the "larger powers" that would be necessary for more fundamental changes.[76]

There was no doubt in the minds of most that this debate between the advocates of a revised confederation based upon the states and those supporting a true national government based upon the people directly was the fundamental issue facing the convention. Hamilton, for example, was convinced that "no amendment of the confederation, leaving the states in possession of their sovereignty could possibly answer the purpose" of the convention. Other nationalists, like James Wilson, were willing to avow as to how he saw no "incompatibility between the national & state govts," but only as long as the states were "restrained to certain local purposes."[77]

The future and integral role of the states was secured by the compromise over the nature of representation. Rather than have in both houses of the

---

[73] *The Federalist*, No. 51, pp. 352–353.

[74] *The Federalist*, No. 10, p. 65.

[75] James Madison to George Washington, 16 April 1787, in Jack N. Rakove, ed., *Madison: Writings* (New York: Library of America, 1999), pp. 80–85, p. 80. Hereinafter cited as *Madison: Writings*.

[76] *Records of the Federal Convention*, I: 249 (John Lansing); I: 178 (William Paterson); I: 80 (Elbridge Gerry); I: 250 (William Paterson).

[77] Ibid., I: 283 (Alexander Hamilton); I: 137 (James Wilson).

legislature either a simple national representation based on population, or a confederal arrangement based upon the states, the bicameral legislature was put in service of making sure that the states as states were represented along with the people in their direct capacity. Thus the states would wield their power to select the members of the Senate by vote of the state legislatures, and those senators in turn would have a significant role in everything from the passing of laws to the approval of treaties to the confirmation of executive appointees from the cabinet to the courts. Further, their role of sitting as a court for the trial of impeachments was another meaningful concession to the lingering presence of the confederal view.

The ambiguity of a constitutional system that was "neither wholly federal, nor wholly national"[78] was not without its obvious dangers, as history would tragically demonstrate. There was something inherently irreconcilable about the tension between the nation and the states when it came to understanding where sovereignty finally lay. Elbridge Gerry, late in the meeting in Philadelphia, went so far as to voice his concern to the convention that the division was so fundamental and potentially so contentious that in due course "a civil war may be produced by the conflict."[79]

The final draft of the Constitution that was to be ratified by the conventions within the several states was, as Madison would famously put it in *The Federalist*, "in strictness neither a national nor a federal constitution, but a composition of both."[80] By this "judicious modification and mixture of the *federal principle*," the Constitution in practice would provide a "double security . . . to the rights of the people." The two different governments, states and nation, would be in a constitutional position to "controul each other" while each, by it own internal constitutional contrivances, "will be controuled by itself."[81]

D. Separated Powers and Bicameralism

The problem of majority tyranny within the states had manifested itself institutionally in the legislative branches. The fundamental tendency of legislatures is that they soon come to think themselves indistinguishable from the people and thereby assume a willingness to exercise powers not knowingly or willingly given to them.[82] "The legislative department," as Madison summed it up, "is every where extending the sphere of its activity

---

[78] *The Federalist*, No. 39, p. 257.
[79] Elbridge Gerry, *Records of the Federal Convention*, II: 387.
[80] *The Federalist*, No. 39, p. 257.
[81] Ibid., No. 51, p. 351.
[82] Hamilton summed it up this way: "The representatives of the people, in a popular assembly, seem sometimes to fancy that they are the people themselves; and betray strong symptoms of impatience and disgust at the least sign of opposition from any other quarter; as if the exercise of its rights by either the executive or judiciary, were a breach of their privilege and an outrage to their dignity." *The Federalist*, No. 71, pp. 483–484.

and drawing all power into its impetuous vortex."[83] The solution was twofold: first, divide the legislature itself into two houses, setting one against the other; second, hem in the bicameral legislature as a whole by positioning on one side of it an energetic executive power with a veto, and, on the other side, an independent judiciary with a power to declare invalid any laws that might be at odds with the text and intention of the Constitution.

The legislatures of the states had demonstrated the various evils that sprang from a "facility and excess of law-making." Not only had they enacted "improper acts of legislation" in the form of "unjust and partial laws," but they had also shown the dangers that come from such a multiplicity of laws that the statutes were so "voluminous" that they could not be read and so "incoherent" that they could not be understood. Moreover, the short terms and frequency of elections trusted by most states had issued in an overwhelming "mutability in the pubic councils" where a frequent "change of men" inevitably meant a frequent "change of opinions," which in turn had meant a frequent "change of measures." The legislatures had forfeited any sense of responsibility to the people and thereby squandered the necessary "attachment and reverence" for the government that republics depend upon being present in the "hearts of the people."[84] The objective of both bicameralism and separated powers was the same, to restore needed respectability to the constitutional processes of the government.

The problem was not simply the corrupt men who would likely "practice with success the vicious arts by which elections are too often carried," those representatives who would come to possess the people's "confidence more than they deserve it, and . . . those who seek to possess, rather that to deserve it." The real and most pressing problem arose from man's own fallible reasoning and the need to protect the people from their own "temporary errors and delusions." It was "a just observation," Hamilton noted, that "the people commonly intend the public good," but that they do not "always *reason right* about the means of *promoting* it." Thus was it essential that the institutions be in place in order to "suspend the blow meditated by the people against themselves, until reason, justice and truth can regain their authority over the public mind."[85]

Because the legislative power in a republican government "necessarily predominates," the most basic remedy is simply "to divide the legislature into different branches and to render them by different modes of election, and different principles of action, as little connected with each other, as the nature of their common functions, and their common dependence on

---

[83] *The Federalist*, No. 48, p. 333.
[84] *The Federalist*, No. 62, pp. 417, 417; No. 78, p. 528; No. 62, pp. 421, 419, 420; No. 62, p. 422.
[85] *The Federalist*, No. 10, p. 63; No. 71, p. 482; No. 63, p. 425; No. 71, p. 482; No. 63, p. 425.

the society, will admit." But that was not all. The creation of an upper house would do more than merely institutionalize an internal scheme of legislative checks and balances. It also gave the framers the opportunity to introduce into the government an institution that would be respectable for its contribution to the "order and stability" of the constitutional order. Because of its requirements of office and the staggered longer terms to be served (each term was three times the length of those in the House of Representatives), the Senate would be more likely than not a "temperate and respectable" body that would be able to supply the defects that are "common to a numerous assembly frequently elected by the people, and to the people themselves."[86]

When it came to separating the powers of the national government, it was essential that the design not rely on mere "parchment barriers," pronouncements simply decreeing that the powers are separated; for them to be truly separated would require an intricate and somewhat sophisticated scheme of what Madison would call *partial agency*," an arrangement in which each branch would exercise some direct control over the actions of the others. It was by this design that the branches would be "connected and blended"[87] so that there would be in practice as well as in theory a system of checks and balances, and the powers of the branches would be truly and effectively separated.

The danger posed by the legislature would require constant attention in that it would always find itself "inspired by a supposed influence over the people" and distinguished by "an intrepid confidence in its own strength." The assembly, by virtue of its being "sufficiently numerous to feel all the passions which activate a multitude, yet not so numerous as to be incapable of pursuing the objects of its passions," would inevitably display an "enterprising ambition." Thus would it be necessary to empower the executive and judicial branches sufficiently to maintain the intended "constitutional equilibrium"[88] between the branches of the government.

In the case of the executive branch, the power of the presidency would come not only from the powers accorded the office by the Constitution, but also from the fact that the office would be a unitary one, with all the powers granted to be wielded by one set of hands. This would create the energy necessary for good government and good administration. So, too, would a unitary executive contribute to the needed responsibility of the chief magistrate to the people. As the only nationally elected officer, the president would be the sole representative of the people as a whole. This would give the president the power necessary to resist the legislature's natural impulse "to exert an imperious control over the other departments."[89] This would

---

[86] *The Federalist*, No. 51, pp. 350, 350; No. 63, pp. 422, 425, 426.
[87] *The Federalist*, No. 48, p. 333; No. 47, p. 325; No. 48, p. 332.
[88] *The Federalist*, No. 48, p. 334; No. 49, p. 341.
[89] *The Federalist*, No. 71, p. 484.

only be enhanced by his unlimited re-eligibility to stand for election to the office.

Meeting the need to bolster the judiciary, the branch that would be "the weakest of the three departments of power," was seen as designing that branch so that it would be in a position to enjoy "complete independence." Its "natural feebleness" would be offset in the first instance by the judges' "permanency in office;" in the second place, there would be a "fixed provision for their support," with the legislature being denied the power to diminish judges' compensation during their time in office. Such institutional independence would allow the courts to serve as the "bulwarks of a limited constitution against legislative encroachments"[90] without the possibility of legislative retribution.

Taken together, these various provisions of the recently improved science of politics would allow the founders to create a government of limited and enumerated powers that would be designed to act wisely and responsibly. This would not be due to man's virtues, but in spite of his vices. Once drafted and ratified, that constitution would carry with it the supremacy that only a fundamental law that rested upon the consent of the governed could reasonably possess.

Supreme Law of the Land

Given the persistence of the attachment to the idea of a confederation, there could be little doubt that the new Constitution might well be beset by those in the several states who would be disposed "to curtail and evade" the legitimate authorities of the new government.[91] Mere parchment barriers would never be sufficient to thwart the self-interested machinations of determined "local demagogues"[92] to make every effort to "sap the foundations of the Union."[93] To proclaim the new Constitution and the laws and treaties made pursuant to it to be the supreme law of the land was but the necessary first step; binding all national and state officials to support it "by oath or affirmation" was essential. And no small part of securing the Constitution was to make clear that the state judges especially were to be bound by the new fundamental law "anything in the constitution or laws of any state to the contrary notwithstanding."

The necessary supremacy of the Constitution would stem in large part from the fact that it would be ratified and put into effect not by the state legislatures but by special conventions of the people called for that specific purpose. This would be the people acting in their sovereign capacity. The

---

90 *The Federalist*, No. 78, pp. 523, 524, 523; No. 79, p. 531; No. 78, p. 526.
91 *The Federalist*, No. 33, p. 205.
92 Edmund Randolph, *Records of the Federal Convention*, II: 89.
93 *The Federalist*, No. 33, pp. 205–206.

reasons it was deemed necessary to so bypass the state legislatures were both practical and theoretical. The practical problem was the inevitable conflict of interest that ratification by legislators would pose. They would be, after all, state officials whose positions would be "degraded"[94] in importance by the ratification of the new Constitution. James Madison agreed completely. To allow the state legislatures to ratify would be to introduce the "novel & dangerous doctrine" of allowing a state body to "change the constitution under which it held its existence."[95] The state legislators were simply too interested to be trusted.

The theoretical concern in behalf of ratification by the people in special conventions rested upon the basic belief in the ultimate sovereignty of the people. The state legislators, George Mason argued, were the "mere creatures of the state constitutions," which were, in turn, the mere creatures of the people. As such, they had "no power" to ratify the new arrangement. It was, after all, in the people themselves that "all power" resided. To circumvent the people and allow the legislatures to ratify the new Constitution would reduce its foundation from that of popular sovereignty to nothing more than the "weak and tottering foundation of an act of assembly." Logically, it would then follow that what one legislature had been empowered to approve could be altered or abolished by future legislatures independent of the people themselves. That would leave the fundamental law of the Constitution far from being the supreme law of the land. In order to avoid having the new document "exposed to the severest criticisms," it was essential that it rest upon, and be seen to rest upon, "the clear & undisputed authority of the people."[96]

The supremacy of the Constitution was secured by popular ratification because it was then understood to be the embodiment of the "intention of the people" and not the mere "intention of their agents." As such, its terms and meaning could not be changed by the ordinary institutions of the government it had created. "Until the people have by some solemn and authoritative act annulled or changed the established form," Hamilton argued, "it is binding upon themselves collectively, as well as individually, and no presumption, or even knowledge of their sentiments, can warrant their representatives in a departure from it prior to such an act."[97] And this meant all those selected by the people to represent them. Indeed, the written and ratified Constitution of fixed and known meaning was intended by its framers to be a "rule for the government of courts, as well as of the legislature."[98]

---

[94] Edmund Randolph, *Records of the Federal Convention*, II: 89.
[95] James Madison, in ibid., II: 92–93.
[96] George Mason, in ibid., II: 89, 88, 88, 89.
[97] *The Federalist*, No. 78, p. 528.
[98] *Marbury v. Madison*, 5 U.S. 137 (1803), 180.

III. THE PROPER AND PECULIAR PROVINCE OF THE COURTS

When Alexander Hamilton in *The Federalist* turned to defend the new federal judicial power as created by the third article of the Constitution, he thought there was no need to be expansive. He had only to point out the common sense of the subject. The situation, he thought, was simple and straightforward. The "want of a judiciary power," he argued, was one of the crowning "defects of the confederation." The reason was clear: "Laws are a dead letter without courts to expound and define their true meaning and operation."[99] Enough said; or so he thought.

Hamilton's somewhat uncharacteristic reticence was supported by the limited exchanges that had taken place in the Constitutional Convention itself. Few major issues received as little discussion as did the nature and extent of the judicial power under the proposed constitution. Among those who did speak, it was clear that they were largely in agreement. Elbridge Gerry resisted using the judiciary in league with the chief magistrate as part of a proposed council of revision because he thought the courts in their own, independent role would have the power to expound the laws as well as a "power of deciding on their constitutionality."[100] Such was to be expected, he noted, given that state judges had already exercised such a power.

In the debate over James Madison's ill-fated proposal that Congress should be given the power to negative state laws, Gouverneur Morris opposed the measure because it seemed clear to him that any such "law that ought to be negatived will be set aside by the judiciary department." Luther Martin concurred that the courts in their "official character" would possess such "a negative on the laws." Although Madison at one point wondered if such a power should not be limited to "cases of a judiciary nature," he too assumed that constitutional supremacy surely meant at a minimum that any "law violating a constitution established by the people themselves would be considered by the judges as null and void."[101]

There were others who were less sure that such a power could be safely given to the courts. Two leading Anti-Federalist critics of the Constitution somewhat unexpectedly pounced on the convention's provisions for an independent judiciary. To their way of thinking, such independence simply went too far. *Brutus* believed that the Constitution rendered the federal judges "independent in the fullest sense of the word," with no "power above them to controul any of their decisions." They were, he insisted, "independent of the people, of the legislature, and of every power under heaven." In truth, he warned, history had shown that men "placed in this situation will generally

---

[99] *The Federalist*, No. 22, p. 143.
[100] Elbridge Gerry, *Records of the Federal Convention*, I: 97.
[101] Ibid., II: 28 (Gouverneur Morris); II: 76 (Luther Martin); II: 430 (James Madison); II: 93 (James Madison).

soon feel themselves independent of heaven itself."[102] Left in such a position, could anyone really doubt that the judges would feel themselves empowered to "mould the government into most any shape they please"?[103]

The *Federal Farmer*, one of the most thoroughgoing of the Anti-Federalists, believed that the Constitution left the federal judges free to decide the cases that might come before them merely "as their conscience, their opinions, their caprice, or their politics might dictate." As a result, he warned, the people were "more in danger of sowing the seeds of arbitrary government in this department than in any other." The *Federal Farmer* was not speaking only for himself when he argued that such arbitrariness was simply "repugnant to the principles of free government."[104]

It was against such thinking, and to assuage such fears, that Hamilton was forced to return to his defense of the federal judiciary. It was perhaps a paradox that a limited constitution could be protected only by a judiciary that enjoyed nothing less than "complete independence." But that was the case. How could the "specified exceptions to the legislative authority" be enforced in practice, how could the courts "declare all acts contrary to the manifest tenor of the Constitution void" if they were in fact subject to legislative control? To give such a power to the courts is not to suggest their "superiority" to the legislative power but only to make it clear that "the power of the people is superior to both." In fact, the more accurate view is that "the courts were designed to be an intermediate body between the people and the legislature in order ... to keep the latter within the limits assigned to their authority."[105]

This design within the Constitution was derived from the basic fact that the "proper and peculiar province of the courts" is the interpretation of the laws. In this role, the judges are expected to regard the Constitution as the "fundamental law" against which all other laws must be measured. The essence of the judicial power of constitutional review derives from this basic principle. If there is any "irreconcilable variance" between the Constitution and "any particular act proceeding from the legislative body," then the "Constitution ought to be preferred to the statute, the intention of the people to the intention of their agents."[106] If they are to have the institutional strength "to regulate their decisions by the fundamental laws, rather than by those which are not fundamental," the courts simply have to be free from legislative interference or domination.

---

[102] Herbert J. Storing, ed., *The Complete Anti-Federalist*, 7 vols. (Chicago: University of Chicago Press, 1982), 2.9.189. (This system of citation indicates the quotation in question is to be found in paragraph 189, of item 9, in volume 2.)

[103] Ibid., 2.9.134–144.

[104] Ibid., 2.8.195; 2.8.185; 2.8.185.

[105] *The Federalist*, No. 78, pp. 524, 524, 525, 525.

[106] Ibid.

The essence of Hamilton's argument is the idea that the "intention of the people" that distinguishes the Constitution as a fundamental law is a knowable intention. Thus the judges are not free to import new meaning into old words, or to transform the Constitution by construction; rather, they are obligated by the very nature of their power to determine the contours of what Chief Justice Marshall would frequently refer to as the "mind of the convention."[107] Nor was such a view limited to Federalists like Marshall and Hamilton. Jefferson and Madison were in complete agreement.

As Jefferson saw it, "certainty in the law" had become so "highly valued" that the judges were expected to be bound in their judgments by the intention of the lawgivers, an "intention to be collected principally from the words of the law," and not to wander off into an equitable interpretation by which they might seek the "spirit and reason" of the law in question.[108] To Madison, such was a matter of common constitutional sense. "If the meaning of the text be sought in the changeable meaning of the words composing it, it is evident that the shape and attributes of the government must partake of the changes to which the words and phrases of all living languages are constantly subject." Such was unacceptable in a written and ratified constitution. To engage in such loose interpretation would result in nothing less than "a metamorphosis" in the fundamental law.[109]

Thus was there a general agreement among the founding generation that when it came to interpreting their new constitution there had to be rules that were, as Madison would put it, "analogous" to those rules that governed the interpretation of laws more generally.[110] These were, of course, the rules that that generation had learned from everyone from Grotius to Hobbes to Pufendorf to Locke to Rutherforth to Blackstone. The essence of that agreement was that by those rules it was the duty of the judge to find the original intention of the lawgiver or the constitutional framer. Yet such agreement on that fundamental point could not bridge the deep divide that separated the likes of Jefferson and Madison from Hamilton and Marshall.

---

[107] See below, Chapter 7, for an extended discussion of Marshall's views.

[108] Thomas Jefferson to Phillip Mazzei, November 1785, in Paul L. Ford, ed., *The Works of Jefferson*, 12 vols. (New York: G. P. Putnam's Sons, 1905); IV: 473–475, p. 474.

[109] James Madison to Henry Lee, 25 June 1824, *Madison: Writings*, p. 803.

[110] "As there are rules for interpreting laws, there must be analogous rules for interpreting constitutions; and among the obvious and just guides applicable to the Constitution of the United States may be mentioned –

1. The evils and defects for curing which the Constitution was called for and introduced;
2. The comments prevailing at the time it was adopted;
3. The early, deliberate, and continued practice under the Constitution, as preferable to constructions adopted on the spur of occasions, and subject to the vicissitudes of party or personal ascendencies."

James Madison to M. L. Hurlbert, May 1830, in *Letters and Other Writings of James Madison*, 4 vols. (Philadelphia: Lippincott & Co., 1865), IV: 75.

The former were convinced that the original design of the Constitution was that of a confederated republic with strictly enumerated powers that must be construed strictly; to the latter, the Constitution created a nation in every sense of the word, and thus its enumerated powers had to be construed reasonably. American constitutional history in many ways would prove to be a working out of those two alternatives of originalist interpretation.

6

Chains of the Constitution

Thomas Jefferson, James Madison, and the "Political Metaphysics" of Strict Construction

There is arguably no one among the founding generation more closely associated with a particular mode of constitutional interpretation than is Thomas Jefferson with the theory of "strict construction." Yet that association is not without its complexities. Jefferson's understanding of constitutionalism tended to be an "evolving" one,[1] often seemingly shaped as much by pressing political necessity as by antecedent philosophical commitment. During the time the Philadelphia Convention was meeting and during the ratification battle, for example, Jefferson's constitutional thought was largely devoid of deep and abiding concerns about the sanctity of state sovereignty and what might be the potential dangers posed to it by the reach of the new federal government. On the whole, he thought the handiwork of the Convention went far toward remedying the most serious defects of the existing confederation.[2] It was the period from 1788 until 1800 that became the crucible in which the ideological fires of Federalism would cause his Republican beliefs in states' rights and strict construction both to form and to harden.[3] But then, after the so-called revolution of 1800, there were occasions when President Jefferson seemed willing to embrace views at odds with the strict tenets of Republicanism he had expressed in the past, causing even some of his most devoted followers to wonder.[4]

---

[1] David N. Mayer, *The Constitutional Thought of Thomas Jefferson* (Charlottesville: University Press of Virginia, 1994), p. 88.

[2] "I approved, from the first moment, of the great mass of what is in the new Constitution." Thomas Jefferson to Francis Hopkinson, 13 March 1789, in Andrew Lipsomb and Albert Bergh, eds., *The Writings of Thomas Jefferson*, 20 vols. (Washington, DC: Thomas Jefferson Memorial Foundation, 1905), VII: 300. Hereinafter cited as *Writings of Jefferson*.

[3] See Stanley Elkins and Eric McKitrick, *The Age of Federalism: The Early American Republic, 1788–1800* (New York: Oxford University Press, 1993), hereinafter cited as *Age of Federalism*. See also Merrill D. Peterson, *Thomas Jefferson and the New Nation* (New York: Oxford University Press, 1970).

[4] "States' rights purists like John Taylor of Caroline and John Randolph were as much concerned about the consolidating policies of Jefferson and Madison, of the presidency and

Jefferson began as a moderate critic of the Articles of Confederation, arguing as early as 1785 that the failure of that first constitution to grant a federal power to Congress to regulate commerce among the several states was one of its more glaring imperfections. He confessed to James Monroe that he hoped the states might at some point agree to "a new compact" in order to correct such flaws and thereby create what he envisioned as a "more perfect" constitution.[5] When James Madison later informed him that a failed meeting of the states in Annapolis in September 1786 had led to an agreement for "a plenipotentiary Convention in Philada. in May next,"[6] Jefferson was hopeful that the gathering would lead to what he envisioned as an even "broader reformation"[7] of the fundamental law of the confederation.

In Jefferson's view, the "fundamental defect of the Confederation" went beyond such concerns as the regulation of commerce. The more basic problem was that the Congress under the Articles "was not authorized to act immediately on the people & by its own officers." Rather, the federal power was "requisitory" only, thus reducing the federal authority to a debilitating financial dependence on the legislatures of the several states. The only coercive power at hand was an appeal to "the moral principle of duty" – in Jefferson's opinion an appeal that almost never worked. The strictly confederal arrangement of the Articles, whatever it might have been in theory, in fact gave "a negative to every legislature on every question proposed by Congress." The result was a shackled federal authority incapable of meeting the exigencies of the union.[8]

When Madison's letters pertaining to the upcoming Philadelphia Convention began to reach Paris, Jefferson seemed heartened at the prospects of strengthening the "federal head" in order to enable it "to exercise the powers given it, to best advantage." This would be made possible in part by the separation of powers into the "legislative, executive and judicial," a feature missing in the Articles of Confederation.[9] Jefferson seems to have been in general agreement with those, like Madison, who insisted that a mere confederation of sovereign states with all the delegated powers vested

---

Congress, as they were about the nationalism of the Marshall Court." R. Kent Newmyer, "John Marshall and the Southern Constitutional Tradition," in Kermit L. Hall and James W. Ely, Jr., eds., *An Uncertain Tradition: Constitutionalism and the History of the South* (Athens: University of Georgia Press, 1989), p. 108.

[5] Thomas Jefferson to James Monroe, 17 June 1785, *Writings of Jefferson*, V: 12.

[6] James Madison to Thomas Jefferson, 4 December 1786, in James Morton Smith, ed, *The Republic of Letters: The Correspondence between Thomas Jefferson and James Madison, 1776–1826*, 3 vols. (New York: W. W. Norton & Co., 1995), I: 454. Hereinafter cited as *Republic of Letters* with sender and recipient indicated by surname only.

[7] Jefferson to Madison, 16 December 1786, *Republic of Letters*, I: 458.

[8] Thomas Jefferson, "Autobiography," in Merrill Peterson, ed., *Jefferson: Writings* (New York: Library of America, 1984), p. 71. Hereinafter cited as *Jefferson: Writings*.

[9] Jefferson to Madison, 16 December 1786, *Republic of Letters*, I: 458.

in a unicameral legislature could never in any meaningful sense be a true government.

Yet Jefferson was no mere nationalist. He had always harbored, and never lost his appreciation for, the idea of small republics and civic virtue and how the states as such could contribute to republican liberty.[10] "To make us one nation as to foreign concerns, and keep us distinct in domestic ones," he instructed Madison, "gives the outline of the proper division of powers between the general and the particular governments." Perhaps because he lived with the effects every day, Madison was more convinced than Jefferson that the "existing constitution" suffered "mortal diseases."[11] To Madison's way of thinking, the fundamental problem was the result of the state legislatures standing between the "federal head" and the people themselves. This was the most basic structural problem the Convention would have to confront.

On the eve of the Convention, Madison explained to George Washington that during his preparations for the coming debates in Philadelphia he had been led to seek "some middle ground" between the claims of the states as separate sovereignties and the needs of the nation. He concluded that "an individual independence of the states is utterly irreconcilable with their aggregate sovereignty, and that a consolidation of the whole into one simple republic would be as inexpedient as it is unattainable." Madison's "middle ground" was designed to "at once support a due supremacy of the national authority, and not exclude the local authorities where they can be subordinately useful."[12]

When the Convention was finally sitting, Madison had to write his old friend with news he suspected would not be well received by the ambassador to France. Sending Jefferson a list of the delegates who were to attend, Madison explained that the list "exhausted all the means which I can make use of for gratifying your curiosity." The reason, Madison went on, was that the Convention had thought it "expedient in order to secure unbiased discussion within, and to prevent misconceptions without, to establish some rules of caution which will for no short time restrain even a confidential communication of . . . [the] proceedings."[13]

Madison knew Jefferson well; he was not at all pleased at the veil of secrecy. "I am sorry," Jefferson groused to his fellow diplomat, John Adams, "they began their deliberations by so abominable a precedent as that of tying up the tongues of their members." In Jefferson's view, there was nothing else

---

[10] See especially his *Notes on the State of Virginia* in *Jefferson: Writings*, pp. 290–291.

[11] Jefferson to Madison, 16 December 1786; Madison to Jefferson, 19 March 1787, *Republic of Letters*, I: 458, 470.

[12] James Madison to George Washington, 16 April 1787, in Jack N. Rakove, ed., *Madison: Writings* (New York: Library of America, 1999), p. 80. Hereinafter cited as *Madison: Writings*.

[13] Madison to Jefferson, 6 June 1787, *Republic of Letters*, I: 478.

that could explain such a decision except "the innocence of their intentions, and ignorance of the value of public discussions." Still, in spite of so fundamental a miscalculation, Jefferson believed the Convention was nothing less than "an assembly of demigods" whose measures were likely to be "good and wise."[14] He shared Madison's belief that there could be no doubt that the result of the Convention's deliberations "will, in some way or other, have a powerful effect on our destiny."[15] Secrecy or not, Jefferson was willing to hope for the best.

In the middle of July, Madison once more sent his regrets to Jefferson that he was "still under the mortification of being restrained from disclosing any part of [the] proceedings," but assured him that there was "little doubt that the people will be as ready to receive, as we shall be able to propose, a government that will secure their liberties and happiness." But by early September Madison warned Jefferson that he "expected that certain characters will wage war against any reform whatever." By the end of the year, his fears were heightened. It seemed likely that in Virginia the formidable Patrick Henry would marshal forces in an effort to keep alive an "adherence to the principle of the existing confederacy." In Madison's estimation, Henry was "the great adversary" who was quite capable of rendering the entire ratification process "precarious." Madison feared for the worst: "If the present moment be lost, it is hard to say what may be our fate."[16]

Five weeks after the Convention adjourned, Madison sent Jefferson a detailed account of the proposed Constitution. He assured him that it had been "the sincere and unanimous wish of the Convention to cherish and preserve the Union of the states,"[17] but not without what Madison would later describe in *The Federalist* as a "judicious modification and mixture of the *federal principle*."[18] The Convention had concluded that "the objects of the union could not be secured by any system founded on the principle of a confederation of sovereign states." The new government, "instead of operating on the states, would operate without their intervention on the individuals composing them." Thus did the new Constitution rest upon a fundamental change in "the principle and proportion of representation."[19]

---

[14] Thomas Jefferson to John Adams, 30 August 1787, in Lester J. Cappon, ed., *The Adams–Jefferson Letters: The Complete Correspondence between Thomas Jefferson and Abigail and John Adams*, 2 vols. (Chapel Hill: University of North Carolina Press, 1959), I: 196. Hereinafter cited as *Adams–Jefferson Correspondence* with sender and recipient indicated by surname only.

[15] Madison to Jefferson, 6 June 1787, *Republic of Letters*, I: 478.

[16] Madison to Jefferson, 18 July 1787, *Republic of Letters*, I: 483, 484; 6 September 1787, *Republic of Letters*, I: 491; and 9 December 1787, *Republic of Letters*, I: 508–509.

[17] Madison to Jefferson, 24 October 1787, *Republic of Letters*, I: 496.

[18] Jacob Cooke, ed., *The Federalist* (Middletown, CT: Wesleyan University Press, 1961), No. 51, p. 353. Hereinafter cited as *The Federalist*.

[19] Madison to Jefferson, 24 October 1787, *Republic of Letters*, I: 496.

Jefferson wrote to Adams in London about the new Constitution to "confess there are things in it which stagger all my dispositions to subscribe to what such an assembly has proposed." Suddenly, the Articles of Confederation seemed to Jefferson to be nothing less than a "grand, old, venerable fabrick." He wondered why all the good parts of the Convention's handiwork could not have been "couched in three or four new articles" that would have been tacked onto the old scheme.[20]

Jefferson was slightly less candid with Madison. He allowed as how he very much liked "the general idea of framing a government which should go on of itself peaceably without needing continual recurrence to the state legislatures." So, too, did he approve of "the substitution of the method of voting by persons, instead of that of voting by states." He even liked the veto power of the president, although he "should have liked it better had the judiciary been associated for that purpose, or invested with a similar and separate power." He was not at all saddened that Madison's peculiar proposal to give the federal legislature a power to negative any laws passed by the states had not been accepted. From first hearing of it, he had thought that such a power was at best inappropriate and at worst dangerous.[21] Ultimately, the most deeply held reservation Jefferson had about the new Constitution was the absence of a bill of rights. But even that was not enough to push him into the camp of the Constitution's Anti-Federalist critics.

The discussion between Jefferson and Madison over the latter's proposed national legislative negative on state laws is especially instructive about the status of their states' rights constitutionalism at the time. When Madison first mentioned the idea to Jefferson, his response was blunt: "I do not like it." It seemed to him that the device was a remedy worse than the disease. In its place Jefferson suggested that "an appeal from the state judicatures to a federal court, in all cases where the act of confederation controuled the question [would] be as effectual a remedy and exactly commensurate to the defect." After the Convention repeatedly rejected the negative on state laws, Madison remained convinced that the "evils" of the "mutability" and "injustice" of state laws – evils that had driven the states to the Convention in the first place, in his view – would remain the greatest threat under the new government.[22]

Madison, the future advocate of states' rights both in the new Congress and in the public prints, was convinced that there was a need for at least "a controuling power . . . by which the general authority may be defended

[20] Jefferson to Adams, 13 November 1787, *Adams–Jefferson Correspondence*, I: 212.
[21] Jefferson to Madison, 20 December 1787; Jefferson to Madison, 20 June 1787, *Republic of Letters*, I: 512, 480
[22] Jefferson to Madison, 20 June 1787; Madison to Jefferson, 24 October 1787, *Republic of Letters*, I: 480, 481, 500. For a sound account of the politics surrounding this issue, see Charles F. Hobson, "The Negative on State Laws: James Madison, the Constitution, and the Crisis of Republican Government," *William and Mary Quarterly* 36 (1979): 215–235.

against encroachments of the subordinate authorities, and by which the latter may be restrained from encroachments on each other." He did not reject Jefferson's view that the judicial power might provide a solution out of a solicitude for the sovereignty of the states. Rather, he was simply convinced that a reliance on the courts would be ineffectual. Any state that would "violate the legislative rights of the union," Madison believed, would be very unlikely "to obey a judicial decree in support of them."[23]

What is most striking about Jefferson's reactions to the proposed Constitution is what is missing. There is no discussion of the importance of states' rights or fears that the new government would endanger them. Nor is there any mention of strict construction as the only method by which such a constitution of limited and enumerated powers should be interpreted. Those concerns – concerns that would ultimately lie at the very heart of the Jeffersonian Republicans' creed – would come later. For the moment, Jefferson was willing to acclaim as profound the political theory of *The Federalist*. The collection of essays was, he told Madison, simply "the best commentary on the principles of government which ever was written." He had read it, he said, "with care, pleasure, and improvement." The argument of the work, he assured Madison, "establishes firmly the plan of the government."[24]

Things were about to change – and quickly. Both Madison and Jefferson soon came to see great dangers looming in the efforts of the Federalist Party generally and in the concrete fiscal policies of Treasury Secretary Alexander Hamilton in particular. The clear design of Hamilton and his party was the pursuit of a large and truly national government, by and large at the expense of the states' powers. Both Madison and Jefferson firmly believed that the form of any government inevitably shapes the kinds of citizens that such a government produces. In their view, the Federalist vision had no room for cultivating a citizenry characterized by simple and sturdy republican virtue; the people likely to follow from the Federalists' successes would more likely than not be speculators, stock-jobbers, and other unsavory sorts. And it was this moral element of the extensive commercial republic that Jefferson and Madison feared most. They became increasingly convinced that the only place for the republican virtues to be safely nurtured would be within the sovereign states. In order to secure such an arrangement they would have to engage in what Chief Justice John Marshall would later deride as "political metaphysics,"[25] the advocacy of states' rights and the strict construction of the Constitution as the very essence of the Founders' original intentions properly understood.

[23] Madison to Jefferson, 24 October 1787, *Republic of Letters*, I: 498, 500.
[24] Jefferson to Madison, 18 November 1788, *Republic of Letters*, I: 567.
[25] John Marshall to Joseph Story, 31 July 1833, in Herbert A. Johnson and Charles F. Hobson, eds., *The Papers of John Marshall*, 12 vols. (Chapel Hill: University of North Carolina Press, 1974–2006), XII: 291. Hereinafter cited as *Papers of John Marshall*.

I. STATES' RIGHTS, STRICT CONSTRUCTION, AND REPUBLICAN CONSTITUTIONALISM

To many of the founding generation who served in the first administration or in the first Congress it might well have seemed easier to frame and ratify the Constitution than to put it into practice once ratified. The need to translate the sometimes general terms of the document into "concrete and functioning institutions" was no small task.[26] Nor was it made easier by the somewhat ambiguous notion that the new Constitution was in fact "in strictness neither a national nor a federal constitution but a composition of both." The new government soon came to realize that "the task of marking the proper line of partition between the authority of the general, and that of the state governments" was indeed, as Madison had put it in *The Federalist*, nothing less than "arduous."[27]

The arduousness of setting up the new government was exacerbated, in the view of Congressman Madison and Secretary of State Jefferson, by what they saw as the "monarchical" inclinations of Hamilton.[28] The secretary of the treasury was moved by a vision of republicanism on a grand national scale; no piddling agrarian republics loosely tied together by a compact for him. The phrase "states' rights" had no place in Hamilton's political or constitutional vocabulary. His goal, rather, was to secure the economic and financial foundations of the new constitutional order to such an extent that the nation would become a great and wealthy republican empire of commerce.[29] Jefferson and Madison had no doubt that he would be a most formidable adversary.[30]

Hamilton had come into government with three clear advantages. He enjoyed the confidence and admiration of President Washington, with whom he had served in the Revolution (Washington thought Hamilton's judgment to be "intuitively great")[31]; he possessed the keenest legal and financial mind of his generation (indeed, perhaps of any generation); and he had the courage and the willingness to do anything that was necessary to win in

---

[26] David P. Currie, *The Constitution in Congress: The Federalist Period, 1789–1801* (Chicago: University of Chicago Press, 1997), p. 3.

[27] *The Federalist*, No. 39, p. 257; No. 37, p. 234.

[28] Thomas Jefferson to George Washington, 23 May 1792, in *Jefferson: Writings*, pp. 985–990.

[29] For Hamilton's views of empire, see Gerald Stourzh, *Alexander Hamilton and the Idea of Republican Government* (Stanford, CA: Stanford University Press, 1970); and Karl-Friedrich Walling, *Republican Empire: Alexander Hamilton on War and Free Government* (Lawrence: University Press of Kansas, 1999).

[30] As William Maclay put it, "Mr. Hamilton is all powerful, and fails in nothing he attempts." As quoted in Dumas Malone, *Jefferson and the Rights of Man* (Boston: Little, Brown, 1951), p. 340.

[31] George Washington to John Adams, 25 September 1798, in John Rhodehamel, ed., *Washington: Writings* (New York: Library of America, 1997), p. 1013.

the often brutal political tugs-of-war that were going to be inevitable. Once ensconced at the Treasury Department, Hamilton moved quickly to dominate congressional efforts to create both policies and institutions necessary to put the new government into motion. He put forward his program in a series of reports, but it was especially in three major efforts that he sought to build as sturdy a foundation as possible for his great commercial republic. Taken together, his *Report on the Public Credit*,[32] *Report on a National Bank*,[33] and *Report on the Subject of Manufactures*[34] made clear his agenda. By 1792 the principled breach between Hamilton and Jefferson was wide, deep, and irreconcilable.

Jefferson's reaction to Hamilton's plans was "less as a political economist than as a republican constitutionalist."[35] The same was true of Madison. He saw very little of the Constitution he and Hamilton had so eloquently defended in *The Federalist* in the New Yorker's program for the new government. He shared Jefferson's view that Hamilton was determined to transform the new constitutional order into an entirely different kind of government through what Jefferson called simply "legislative constructions."[36] The Federalists, by their liberal interpretations of the Constitution, were transforming a republican constitution of limited and enumerated powers into a "blank paper."[37] If allowed to stand, the result would no longer be a constitution that was "partly federal, and partly national"[38] but one that would be not simply national but consolidated as well.

In the view of Jefferson and Madison, the "true theory" of the Constitution was dramatically at odds with Hamilton's political and economic vision. The states, as they saw it, were properly understood to be "independent as to everything within themselves, and united as to everything respecting foreign nations."[39] That the states remained a vital part of the new order had been made clear by the Tenth Amendment, which provided that "powers not delegated to the United States by the Constitution, nor prohibited by it to the states, are reserved to the states respectively, or to the people." But more than that, they even had Hamilton to this effect in his own words.

Madison, as might have been expected, defended his "middle ground" theory of federalism in *The Federalist* by arguing that the "jurisdiction" of

---

[32] 9 January 1790, in Harold E. Syrett, ed., *The Papers of Alexander Hamilton*, 26 vols. (New York: Columbia University Press, 1961–79). VI: 51–168. Hereinafter cited as *Papers of Alexander Hamilton*.

[33] 13 December 1790, ibid., VII: 236–342.

[34] 5 December 1791, ibid., X: 1–340.

[35] Peterson, *Thomas Jefferson and the New Nation*, p. 459.

[36] As quoted in ibid., p. 466.

[37] Thomas Jefferson to Wilson Cary Nicholas, 7 September 1803, *Writings of Jefferson*, X: 419.

[38] *The Federalist*, No. 39, p. 257.

[39] Thomas Jefferson to Gideon Granger, 13 August 1800, *Writings of Jefferson*, X: 168.

the general government was "limited to certain enumerated objects, which concern all the members of the public," while the states were to be understood as retaining their "due authority" over "all those other objects, which can be separately provided for." This "partly federal, and partly national" design of the Constitution, Madison insisted, would provide a "double security . . . to the rights of the people" in that the "different governments will controul each other; at the same time that each will be controuled by itself."[40]

At the time, Hamilton seemed to be in complete agreement. It was, he said, "an axiom in our political system, that the state governments will in all possible contingencies afford complete security against invasions of the public liberty by the national authority." The states would have the means to "discover danger at the distance" and be able to fashion among themselves "a regular plan of opposition." And that was not all. The state legislatures, Hamilton further argued in *The Federalist*, "who will always be not only vigilant but suspicious and jealous guardians of the rights of the citizens against incroachments from the Federal government, will constantly have their attention awake to the conduct of national rulers and will be ready enough, if anything improper appears, to sound the alarm to the people and not only to be the VOICE but if necessary the ARM of their discontent."[41]

In time, Jefferson and Madison would take such ideas seriously and weave that logic into their Kentucky and Virginia Resolutions. But before the partisan battle reached that pitch with the hated Alien and Sedition Acts, they first turned to making the case – a compelling and irrefutable case, in their estimation – that a written and ratified federal constitution of limited and enumerated powers had to be construed strictly. It was simply the common sense of the matter. Hamilton's plan for a national bank, based on nothing more substantial than powers alleged to be implied by the Constitution's enumerated powers, served to focus their attention and helped to sharpen their argument as to what they believed to be the proper limits of constitutional interpretation.

The National Bank, Implied Powers, and Strict Construction

When the second session of the First Congress adjourned on August 12, 1790, Jefferson and Madison left New York and headed home to Virginia. The first two sessions had made clear to them what they were up against with Hamilton and the Federalists. Moreover, they feared that their influence with their fellow Virginian, President Washington, was beginning to wane. By the time they traveled back to Philadelphia for the third session (December 6,

[40] *The Federalist*, No. 14, p. 86; No. 51, p. 351.
[41] Ibid., No. 28, pp. 179–180, 180; No. 26, p. 169.

1790 – March 3, 1791), their long round-trip journey had given them "ample opportunity . . . to talk things over and to consider plans."[42] And it was a good thing they did because on December 13 the secretary of the treasury submitted the final draft of his *Report on a National Bank*.[43] Madison took the lead against the bank legislation in the House of Representatives; Jefferson, echoing Madison's arguments within the cabinet, endeavored to persuade the president to veto the bill when it reached his desk. But the odds were stacked against them.[44]

Hamilton's report made a powerful case that a national bank was "a political machine of the greatest importance to the State."[45] Congress was easily convinced that the bank was a necessary institution of great administrative convenience, and one that was not prohibited in any sense by the Constitution. It seemed obvious to most members of Congress that the creation of such a national bank was clearly within the implied powers of Congress to give effect to such enumerated powers as taxing and providing for the general welfare and the common defense. The bank's supporters in the House outnumbered its opponents two to one; in the Senate, three to one.[46] With such numbers, Madison calculated that mere political or ideological arguments were likely to have little if any persuasive effect. Thus did he repair to the higher ground of the Constitution. He would have to demonstrate that the incorporation of a national bank was beyond the limited powers that had been delegated to Congress by the Constitution itself. The measure was not simply unwise and unnecessary but was unconstitutional.

With his opposition to the bank bill Madison became the first person of "eminence" to articulate the theory of strict construction.[47] From that moment it would come to occupy an increasingly central place in the political thought of those who would come to think of themselves as the party of Jeffersonian Republicans. It would be developed, polished, and propagated by Jefferson himself, and then taken up by such influential followers as Judge Spencer Roane and John Taylor of Caroline. But it would never be lost on others (not least on his opponents in Congress) that the interpretive doctrine had its roots in the political thinking of Madison himself. After all, here was a preeminent Philadelphia framer who had been one of the staunchest defenders of the Constitution as creating a strong national government that was empowered to give effect to the enumerated powers by "construction and implication."[48] That he would now rise to defend the idea of strict

---

[42] *Age of Federalism*, p. 223.
[43] *Papers of Alexander Hamilton*, VII: 305–342.
[44] "The bank legislation was well planned, organized, and managed from the outset." *Age of Federalism*, p. 228.
[45] *Papers of Alexander Hamilton*, VII: 329.
[46] *Age of Federalism*, p. 228.
[47] Ibid., p. 224.
[48] *The Federalist*, No. 44, p. 303.

construction against his former collaborator Hamilton demonstrated clearly just how deep was the division between the two camps.

But there was more to Madison's situation than simply now finding himself backing away from views he had clearly and strongly held in the Philadelphia Convention and expressed in the pages of *The Federalist*. He was also stepping back from positions he had held – and had vigorously argued – in earlier sessions of the First Congress. In the debate over the power of the president to remove executive branch officers whom he had appointed "by and with the advice and consent of the Senate," Madison had defended the power of removal by the president alone – a power nowhere mentioned in the Constitution itself. He reached his conclusion not by a strict construction of the text but by what he then called a "fair construction," one that sought to give effect to the true "spirit and intention" behind the text by recourse to the idea of implied powers. That was the only sensible interpretive method unless an alternative and unambiguous understanding had been, he said, "saddled upon us expressly by the letter of that work."[49]

Madison stood forth in Congress to oppose Hamilton's proposed national bank on February 2, 1791. As was usual, he had come prepared. He had made detailed notes both on banks in general and on the Bank of England in particular.[50] Thus armed, he began his speech with a few comments setting out the advantages and disadvantages of banks as such. This general survey was followed by his sharing a personal recollection "that a power to grant charters of incorporation had been proposed in the general convention and defeated," seeming to suggest that what had been the convention's intentions on such matters was reasonably clear. He then plunged to the essence of his opposition, and that was, he said, "the peculiar manner in which the federal government is limited." That inherent limitation stemmed from the fact that there was not in the Constitution "a general grant, out of which particular powers are excepted"; rather, there was "a grant of particular powers only, leaving the general mass in other hands." This, Madison insisted, was how the Constitution as ratified "had been understood by its friends and its foes, and so it was to be interpreted." To permit a more expansive or liberal interpretation not only would fly in the face of "[c]ontemporary and concurrent expositions," but also would threaten to destroy "the essential characteristic of the government" itself as a scheme of strictly "limited and enumerated powers."[51]

When it came to particular enumerated powers, such as those delegated to Congress to "collect taxes to pay the debts and to provide for the common

---

[49] 12 June 1789; 19 May 1789, *Madison: Writings*, pp. 465, 435.

[50] William T. Hutchinson et al., eds., *The Papers of James Madison* (vols 1–10, University of Chicago Press, 1962–77; vols. 11 –, University Press of Virginia, 1977 –), XIII: 364–369. Hereinafter cited as *Papers of James Madison*.

[51] *Papers of James Madison*, XIII: 374, 374, 374, 374, 376.

defense or provide for the general welfare," or "to borrow money on the credit of the United States," none was sufficient to suggest by implication and inference that Congress had the power to incorporate a bank. Nor was the power to "make all laws which shall be necessary and proper" a grant of "unlimited discretion to Congress" to do whatever it might think best. That clause was "merely declaratory" of what otherwise would have "resulted by unavoidable implication," that is to say, that Congress was empowered to pass whatever laws might be strictly necessary to give effect to the enumerated powers, but that each such implied power had to be drawn from "the nature" of the enumerated power in question. The point to Madison was obvious: "no power... not enumerated, could be inferred from the general nature of the government." No power, he insisted, could be exercised by implication "which is not evidently and necessarily involved in an express power."[52] Congressional discretion did not reach that far.

"The doctrine of implication," Madison warned the members of the House, "is always a tender one." It is all too easy for implications to be "linked together" in order to form "a chain" of interpretive reasoning "that will reach every object of legislation, every object within the whole compass of political economy." The fact was, Madison noted, that the "latitude of interpretation required by the bill is condemned by the rule furnished by the Constitution itself." The Constitution's rule of construction, in Madison's view, came to this: "if it was thought necessary to specify in the Constitution... minute powers, it would follow that more important powers would have been *explicitly* granted had they been contemplated."[53] It was that rule of construction that demanded that the Constitution be strictly construed.

Madison's understanding of strict construction was ultimately rooted in the idea of states' rights. As the Jeffersonians would make increasingly clear in the years ahead, in their view the Constitution was a compact among the states. As a result, the general government possessed only those powers that were specifically and unambiguously delegated to it by the states. This was no abstract theory but was clearly stated in the "explanatory" Tenth Amendment to the Constitution, which decreed that all powers not delegated to the general government were constitutionally "reserved to the states... or to the people." Those first amendments, after all, "had not only been proposed by Congress, but ratified by nearly three-fourths of the states." The Tenth Amendment unambiguously excluded "every source of power not within the Constitution." This amendment was meant to be a confirmation, Madison pointed out, of "the sense in which the Constitution was understood and adopted."[54]

[52] Ibid., pp. 375, 379, 379.
[53] Ibid., pp. 377, 378, 378, 386.
[54] Ibid., pp. 380–381, 381, 381.

To create an implied power to charter corporations on the basis of such enumerated provisions as the common defense or general welfare clauses "would give to Congress an unlimited power; would render nugatory the enumeration of particular powers; would supercede all the powers reserved to the state governments." If accepted as constitutionally legitimate, the power to create corporations could easily extend beyond banks to everything from "companies of manufacturers" to "companies for cutting canals" to the power to "establish religious teachers in every parish." The exercise of the power in question, Madison argued, "involves the guilt of usurpation, and establishes a precedent of interpretation, leveling all the barriers which limit the powers of the general government, and protect those of the state governments."[55] For Madison, the conclusion was obvious:

It appeared on the whole... that the power exercised by the bill was condemned by the silence of the Constitution; was condemned by the rule of interpretation arising out of the Constitution; was condemned by its tendency to destroy the main characteristic of the Constitution; was condemned by the expositions of friends of the Constitution, whilst depending before the public; was condemned by the apparent intention of the parties which ratified the Constitution; was condemned by the explanatory amendments proposed by Congress themselves to the Constitution; and he hoped it would receive its final condemnation, by the vote of this house.[56]

It would not be condemned by the House of Representatives due in large measure to the power of the arguments of those aligned against Madison. For the next several days leaders in the opposing camp such as Fisher Ames, Elbridge Gerry, Theodore Sedgwick, and Elias Boudinot hammered at Madison's so-called rules of interpretation until passage of the act was all but assured.

Evidence is abundant that the members of the First Congress were genuinely concerned to give effect to what Fisher Ames called simply "the true intent of the Constitution." But that did not mean, he responded sharply to Madison on February 3, that they were to consider themselves as chained to the mere "letter of the Constitution." Such a literal or strict construction would prove to be dangerously short-sighted, Ames insisted. "The Constitution," he argued, "contains principles which are to govern in making laws; but every law requires an application of the rule to the case in question." Such was always a matter of legislative "discretion." The danger posed by Madison's rules of strict construction came to this, Ames insisted: "Not exercising the powers we have may be as pernicious as usurping those we have not."[57]

[55] Ibid., pp. 375, 375, 381.
[56] Ibid., p. 381.
[57] *Annals of the Congress of the United States 1789–1824*, 42 vols. (Washington, DC), 1st Cong., 3rd. Sess., 3 February 1791, pp. 1954, 1955.

Ames was not insensitive to the potential dangers of construction. He acknowledged that "many worthy persons" did indeed view interpretation by implication to be a "bugbear." He understood that they "apprehended that Congress by putting constructions upon the Constitution will govern by its own arbitrary discretion" and thus that Congress should "be bound to exercise the powers expressly given, and those only." In his view, it was simply a matter of necessity that Congress had to be understood as empowered to "exercise... powers which are not expressly given in the Constitution, but may be deduced by a reasonable construction of that instrument." The reason was that it would be impossible "to declare in detail everything that government can do." Such an effort would in practice prove to be "endless, useless, and dangerous."[58]

Even though "some interpretations of the Constitution" would have to be "indulged," the practice was still to be governed by certain rules. But such rules were not to be found in the intellectually cramped confines of Madisonian literalism. "The construction may be maintained to be a safe one," Ames concluded, "which promotes the good of the society, and ends for which the government was adopted, without impairing the rights of any man, or the powers of any state." In his estimation, such an understanding clearly warranted the creation of a national bank, and not least because the new Congress had itself for the past two years accepted that it was "a safe rule of action to legislate beyond the letter of the Constitution."[59]

The next day Ames was supported by Sedgwick and Boudinot. Sedgwick, following Ames and anticipating both Hamilton and Marshall, argued that simply as a matter of common sense "probably no instrument for the delegation of power could be drawn with such precision and accuracy as to leave nothing to necessary implication." But abstract theory or common sense were not the whole of it. Sedgwick had been convinced of the necessity of "construction and implication" by the earlier and energetic reasoning of Madison himself. He had been present, after all, when the Virginian had skillfully "impressed on the minds of a majority of... [the] House a conviction that the power of removal from office... was, by construction and implication, vested by the Constitution in the President, for there could be no pretence that it [was] expressly granted to him."[60]

Elias Boudinot of Connecticut was equally adamant about construction by implication. "Whatever power is exercised by Congress," he argued, " must be drawn from the Constitution; either from express words or apparent meaning, or from a necessary implication arising from the obvious intent of the framers."[61] The justly celebrated "Publius" had made that clear in

[58] Ibid., pp. 1954, 1954, 1955.
[59] Ibid., pp. 1956, 1954.
[60] Ibid., 4 February 1791, p. 1960.
[61] Ibid., p. 1970.

the estimable pages of *The Federalist*. At this point Madison had to listen as Boudinot quoted against him chapter and verse of Madison's own earlier argument. "Had the convention attempted a positive enumeration of the powers necessary and proper for carrying their other powers in to effect," Madison as "Publius" had argued,

the attempt would have involved a complete digest of laws on every subject to which the Constitution relates; accommodated too not only to the existing state of things, but to all possible changes which futurity may produce: For in every new application of a general power, the *particular powers*, which are the means of attaining the *object* of the general power, must always necessarily vary with that object; and be often properly varied whilst the object remains the same.[62]

Madison had been insistent that had the necessary and proper clause not been included, "the whole Constitution would be a dead letter." Without recourse to the "doctrine of *construction* and *implication*" the government would have been forced to find itself "distressed with the alternative of betraying the public interest by doing nothing; or of violating the Constitution by exercising powers indispensably necessary and proper, but at the same time, not *expressly* granted." This view, Madison had concluded, rested on a fundamental truth: "No axiom is more clearly established in law, or in reason, than that wherever the end is required, the means are authorized; wherever a general power to do a thing is given, every particular power necessary for doing it, is included."[63]

Of those who stood in opposition to Madison none was more scathing in his rebuttal than Elbridge Gerry, whose argument against strict construction was rooted in Sir William Blackstone's *Commentaries on the Laws of England*. It is all the more interesting since Gerry, like Madison, was not a lawyer. The Massachusetts congressman began by arguing that Madison's so-called rules of interpretation seemed to have been conveniently "made for the occasion." His "rules" were merely "the result of his interpretation" alone and were not "his interpretation of the rules ... sanctioned by law exposition, or approved by experienced judges of the law." It appeared to Gerry that Madison was making it up as he went along. As against what he saw as Madison's pedantic presumptions, Gerry offered to meet him on the "fair ground" of rules of interpretation that had in fact been "laid down" by the "learned Judge Blackstone." Surely, Gerry asserted, Madison would not dare to "refuse to be tried by this standard."[64]

Gerry began by stating Blackstone's famous formulation on the necessity of finding the intentions of the lawgiver, a formulation that embodied the received tradition of the rules of interpretation from at least Grotius

---

[62] *The Federalist*, No. 44, p. 304.
[63] Ibid., pp. 303, 303–304, 304–305.
[64] *Annals of Congress*, 7 February 1791, p. 1998.

and Pufendorf onward.[65] Those rules, Gerry reminded his listeners, were straightforward:

The fairest and most rational method to interpret the will of the legislator, is by exploring his intentions at the time when the law was made, by signs the most natural and probable. And these signs are either the words, the context, the subject matter, the effects and consequences, or the spirit and reason of the law.[66]

He then proceeded to examine the proposed bill to establish a national bank in light of the Constitution as construed through the prism of Blackstone's categories – from words, to context, to subject matter, to effects and consequences, to the reason and spirit of the document. On all counts, Madison's restrictive interpretation failed – and not least when measured by the "reason and spirit" of the Constitution.

The causes which produced the Constitution were an imperfect union, want of public and private justice, internal commotions, a defenceless community, neglect of the public welfare, and danger to our liberties. If these weighty causes produced the Constitution, and it not only gives power for removing them [as indicated in the Preamble] but also authorized Congress to make all laws necessary and proper for carrying these powers into effect, shall we listen to assertions that these words have no meaning, and that this Constitution has not more energy than the old?[67]

Of course not, Gerry concluded. Rather, the obligation was "to promote the great and important objects thereof" by "a candid and liberal construction of the powers expressed in the Constitution." The fact was, Gerry argued, that the "interpretation of the Constitution, like the prerogatives of a sovereign may be abused," but from such potential for abuse "the disuse of either cannot be inferred." Madison may well be right that a "liberal construction" could be dangerous, but a restrictive one such as that advocated by Madison himself might be even more so.[68]

Madison did not go quietly. Returning to the floor on February 8, he insisted that the "constructions of the Constitution...which have been maintained on this occasion go to the subversion of every power whatever in the several states."[69] But in the end, Madison was more passionate than persuasive. The House of Representatives voted 39 to 20 to pass the bank bill. Yet his misgivings were still taken seriously by President Washington. Before he would decide whether to cast his first veto as president against the bank bill, Washington exercised his constitutional power to request the

[65] See Chapter 4 of this volume, for an extended analysis of Blackstone's theory of interpretation.

[66] Sir William Blackstone, *Commentaries on the Laws of England*, 4 vols. (8th ed.; Oxford: Clarendon Press, 1778), I: 59.

[67] *Annals of Congress*, 7 February 1791, p. 2002.

[68] Ibid., pp. 2002, 2003, 2003.

[69] *Papers of James Madison*, XIII: 386.

opinions in writing of his attorney general, secretary of state, and secretary of the treasury. So unsure was he of his final decision that he also asked Madison to draft a veto message, should that be his conclusion.[70]

Washington first invited Attorney General Edmund Randolph and Secretary of State Jefferson to offer their views on the constitutionality of the bill to create a national bank. Both Randolph and Jefferson followed Madison's lead in opposing the bill as unconstitutional. Jefferson's opinion, the more significant of the two, was relatively brief and to the point. "I consider the foundation of the Constitution," Jefferson began, "as laid on this ground: That 'all powers not delegated to the United States by the Constitution, nor prohibited by it to the States, are reserved to the States or to the people'." Given this strict definition of delegation as derived from the Tenth Amendment it would be a grave danger, Jefferson argued, to "take a single step beyond the boundaries thus specially drawn around the powers of Congress." To do so, he warned, would be "to take possession of a boundless field of power, no longer susceptible of any definition." The power to charter a national bank was simply outside the line and was "not among the powers specially enumerated."[71] That left unanswered, of course, the harder question of implication.

Jefferson's argument against an expansive notion of construction by implication focused on the general welfare clause and the necessary and proper clause. The liberal construction of the former came very close to establishing the proposition that Congress somehow possessed a "universal power" to do good. To interpret the general welfare clause as "giving a distinct and independent power to do any act they please, which might be for the good of the Union, would render all the preceding and subsequent enumerations of powers completely useless."[72]

It would reduce the whole instrument to a single phrase, that of instituting a Congress with power to do whatever would be for the good of the United States; and as . . . [the members of Congress] would be the sole judges of the good or evil, it would be also a power to do whatever evil they please.[73]

The use to which the necessary and proper clause was being put by such a loose construction was also troubling. On this point, Jefferson was equally adamant. The Constitution's provision of a standard of necessity and propriety "allows only the means which are *necessary*, not those which are merely convenient for effecting the enumerated powers." By using the word "necessary" the framers had intended to restrict Congress to "those means without which the grant of power would be nugatory." Moreover, he concluded, "a little *difference* in the degree of *convenience* cannot constitute

70 "Draft Veto of the Bank Bill," *Papers of James Madison*, XIII: 395–396.
71 Thomas Jefferson, "Opinion on the Constitutionality of a National Bank," in *Jefferson: Writings*, pp. 416, 417.
72 Ibid., p. 418.
73 Ibid.

the necessity which the Constitution makes the ground for assuming any non-enumerated power."[74]

Tough as his position was, Jefferson then pulled back. "It must be added," he assured Washington, "that unless the president's mind on a view of everything which is urged for and against this bill, is tolerably clear that it is unauthorized by the Constitution . . . a just respect for the wisdom of the legislature would naturally decide the balance in favor of their opinion." The presidential veto, Jefferson argued, was to be limited to those cases where the members of Congress had been "clearly misled by error, ambition, or interest."[75] Thus did Jefferson himself leave open the door for Hamilton's influence to sway Washington's final judgment.

Hamilton had the advantage of Washington's giving him the "opportunity of examining & answering the objections contained in the . . . papers" that had been submitted by Randolph and Jefferson. As Hamilton was the author and advocate of the bill in question, Washington wanted to give him every chance to establish clearly the "validity & propriety" of the act. With Hamilton's views alongside those of Randolph and Jefferson, the president would thus feel himself to be "fully possessed of the arguments *for* and *against* the measure" before he expressed his own opinion either in signing the bill into law or vetoing it.[76] Hamilton knew an opportunity when he saw one. He provided Washington not only with a convincing argument in support of the bill's constitutionality in the instant case, but also with a brief treatise on how properly to interpret the Constitution more generally.

The idea of a strict construction of the Constitution such as Jefferson and Randolph had put forward, he warned Washington, would be "fatal to the just and indispensable authority of the United States." The fact was, Hamilton argued, that while "the exercise of constructive powers is indispensable," that exercise is not without its dangers; yet the simplistic solution of a "restrictive interpretation" would be equally dangerous. "The moment the literal meaning is departed from, there is a chance of error and abuse," the treasury secretary conceded. "And yet an adherence to the letter of its powers would at once arrest the motions of the government." Against such a restrictive view as strict construction Hamilton insisted that it was clearly "the intent of the convention" that the necessary and proper clause was designed "to give a liberal latitude to the exercise of specified powers." That intention was not to be found in "extrinsic circumstances" such as "theories of individuals," but rather was "to be sought for in the instrument itself according to the usual and established rules of construction."[77] One thing

---

[74] Ibid., pp. 419, 420.

[75] Ibid., p. 421.

[76] George Washington to Alexander Hamilton, 16 February 1791, *Papers of Alexander Hamilton*, VIII: 50.

[77] "Opinion on the Constitutionality of an Act to Establish a Bank," *Papers of Alexander Hamilton*, VIII: 97, 106, 104, 106, 106, 102–103, 111, 132, 111.

Hamilton knew for sure was that the idea of strict construction was not to be found among those "usual and established" rules.

The essence of the constitutional question was the status of implied powers. In Hamilton's opinion there could be no doubt that implied powers "are as effectually delegated" as were the powers expressly enumerated. This stemmed from the very nature of a republican constitution, the idea of a fundamental law in which it is understood that "all government is a delegation of power."[78]

[E]very power vested in a government is in its nature *sovereign*, and includes by *force* of the *term*, a right to employ all the *means* requisite, and fairly applicable to the attainment of the *ends* of such power; and which are not precluded by restriction & exceptions specified in the Constitution; or not immoral; or not contrary to the ends of political society.[79]

The question was the exact nature and extent of the powers delegated, including those that were implied. The answer to that question was not to be found in an artificially contrived method of strict or narrow interpretation but was only to be "made out by fair reasoning & construction upon the particular provisions of the Constitution – taking as guides the general principles & general ends of government."[80] Foreshadowing Chief Justice Marshall's famous opinion in *McCulloch v. Maryland*, Hamilton summed it up this way: "If the end be clearly comprehended within any of the specified powers, & if the measure have an obvious relation to that end, and is not forbidden by any particular provision of the Constitution – it may safely be deemed to come within the compass of the national authority."[81]

Jefferson's error was in refusing to take the word "necessary" in its "obvious & popular sense" and thereby imposing upon it a uniquely "restrictive operation." The secretary of state seemed to read "necessary" as though "the word *absolutely* or *indispensably* had been prefixed to it." Neither word had been used to modify "necessary." This was not to say that the phrase "necessary and proper" was an empty one; after all, said Hamilton, "no government has a right to do merely what it pleases." In the end, Hamilton argued, the measure of a law's necessity can never be the proper test of the "*legal* right to adopt it." Such calculations of necessity "can only be a test of expediency," a matter of political discretion. The test of constitutionality is more rigorous than that: "The *relation* between the *measure* and the *end*, between the *nature* of the *mean* employed towards the execution of a power and the object of that power, must be the criterion of constitutionality, not the more or less of necessity or utility."[82] It was this test

[78] Ibid., p. 100.
[79] Ibid., p. 98.
[80] Ibid., p. 100.
[81] Ibid., p. 107.
[82] Ibid., pp. 103, 103, 103, 104, 104.

that the bank bill passed and by which it was to be deemed constitutional, Hamilton concluded. Washington agreed and signed the bill into law on February 25, 1791, two days after he received Hamilton's response. Neither Randolph nor Jefferson was given the opportunity to react to Hamilton's opinion.

To Jefferson, Madison, and their growing number of followers, an ominous die had been cast. By March 1792 the fires of partisanship were nothing less than a general conflagration, stoked not least by the Philadelphia party press. John Fenno's *Gazette of the United States* in service to the Hamiltonian cause was locked in a fierce battle with the *National Gazette* published by Philip Freneau, an ardent Jeffersonian.[83] The remainder of the decade would be consumed by constant conflict between the Federalists (both the high Federalists of Hamilton and, later, the more moderate Federalists of Adams) and the Republicans.

Through it all, Jefferson and Madison never faltered in their belief, as Jefferson put it to John Taylor, that the "body of our countrymen is substantially republican, through every part of the union." Writing on the eve of the passage of the Alien and Sedition Acts, Jefferson thought it clear that the tumultuousness of the past decade had been caused by "the irresistible influence & popularity of Genl. Washington, played off by the cunning of Hamilton." That combination had not only "turned the government over to anti-republican hands," but had also succeeded in turning "the republican members chosen by the people, into anti-republicans." Jefferson was not so much filled with despair as he was resigned to biding his time. "A little patience," he assured Taylor, "and we shall see the reign of witches pass over, their spells dissolve, and the people, recovering their true sight, restore the government to its true principles."[84] Jefferson's prophecy would be fulfilled by what he would call the "revolution of 1800," the general election in which his party swept the Federalists from power in both the legislative and executive branches. But that would come about only after the Republicans had been confronted by what they considered the most insidious part of the Federalists' legislative agenda.[85]

The Kentucky and Virginia Resolutions and States' Rights

The Alien and Sedition Acts comprised three out of four bills signed into law by President Adams beginning on June 18, 1798, with a naturalization act that made citizenship more difficult and ending on July 14, 1798, with the

---

[83] See *Age of Federalism*, pp. 282–292.

[84] Thomas Jefferson to John Taylor, 4 June 1798, in *Jefferson: Writings*, pp. 1049, 1049, 1050.

[85] The classic history of this episode is James Morton Smith, *Freedom's Fetters: The Alien and Sedition Laws and American Civil Liberties* (Ithaca, NY: Cornell University Press, 1956).

most controversial of the four, the Sedition Act.[86] Ostensibly, they were all designed to bolster the protections of the nation against foreign intrigue and treason during the unofficial war with France that was under way. To the Jeffersonians, however, there was no doubt that the legislation had more to do with electoral politics than with national security. They saw the laws as designed specifically to destroy their party. Moreover, the laws could only have been passed by doing great violence to the Constitution by the loosest of legislative constructions.

The *Alien Friends Act* empowered the president summarily to deport "such *aliens* as he shall judge dangerous to the peace and safety of the United States, or shall have reasonable grounds to suspect are concerned in any treasonable or secret machinations against the government."[87] In similar fashion, the *Alien Enemies Act* enabled the president to apprehend, restrain, secure, and remove "as alien enemies" any unnaturalized citizens from any enemy country who might be present in the United States. At a minimum, both alien laws undermined the Constitution's provisions for a scheme of separated powers by placing all power in the hands of the chief magistrate. Vice President Jefferson thought the detested laws were "worthy of the 8th or 9th century."[88]

But to the Jeffersonians the most egregious abuse of the Constitution was the *Sedition Act*. By the terms of that law it became a crime for "any persons" to "combine or conspire together, with intent to oppose any measure or measures of the government of the United States." Clearly designed to prohibit political criticism of the government, the most dangerous provisions – and the most obviously unconstitutional ones – were those aimed at shackling the free press and thereby silencing the party of opposition. The act was unambiguous in its design and seemingly unlimited in its reach. It would now be a criminal act

if any person shall write, print, utter or publish, or shall cause or procure to be written, printed, uttered or published, or shall knowingly and willingly assist or aid in writing, printing, uttering or publishing any false, scandalous and malicious writing or writings against the government of the United States, or either house of the Congress of the United States, or the President of the United States, with intent to defame the said government, or either house of the said Congress, or the said President, or to bring them, or either of them, into contempt or disrepute.

[86] *An Act to Establish a Uniform Rule of Naturalization*, Ch. 54, 1 Stat. 566; *An Act Concerning Aliens*, Ch. 58, 1 Stat. 570; *An Act Respecting Alien Enemies*, Ch. 66, 1 Stat. 577; and *An Act for the Punishment of Certain Crimes against the United States*, Ch. 74, 1 Stat. 596.

[87] Ch. 58, 1 Stat. 570, sec. 1, p. 571.

[88] Thomas Jefferson to Thomas Mann Randolph, 9 May 1798, as quoted in Smith, *Freedom's Fetters*, p. 53.

That was not all. It would also be a crime

to stir up sedition within the United States, or to excite any unlawful combinations therein, for opposing or resisting any law of the United States, or any act of the President of the United States, done in pursuance of any such law, or of the powers in him vested by the Constitution of the United States, or to resist, oppose, or defeat any such law or act, or to aid, encourage or abet any hostile designs of any foreign nation against the United States, their people or government.[89]

The question facing the Jeffersonians was, what could be done to thwart these unconstitutional efforts? More precisely, what institution could possibly curb the power of the general government when it exceeded its constitutional boundaries? In the view of Jefferson and his followers, that institution had to be outside the general government itself, and in some sense superior to it.[90] The answer that Jefferson and Madison, respectively, would offer in the Kentucky and Virginia Resolutions was that it fell to the states, as original parties to the compact creating and empowering the general government, to protect and defend the original design of the Constitution by standing between the general government and the people themselves. As with their arguments against the national bank, the foundation of their reasoning was the language and logic of the Tenth Amendment to the Constitution.

Jefferson planned to resist the political pretensions of the federal government that had now been made manifest in the form of the Alien and Sedition Acts was by rousing the states from their dangerous slumber and persuading them to stand together in defense of the rights and powers that were reserved to them by the Constitution itself. But the Alien and Sedition Acts were only the most recent examples of what Madison would describe as "a *deliberate, palpable* and *dangerous* breach of the Constitution by the exercise of *powers not granted by it.*" In the view of the Republicans, there had been, in fact – to borrow earlier language from Jefferson – "a long train of abuses and usurpations pursuing invariably the same object." And that line of abuses stretched back a least to the bank law of 1791 and the dangerous "latitude of construction" on which it was founded.[91]

To take the resistance in behalf of states' rights forward Jefferson persuaded Madison that each of them should draft a set of resolutions to be introduced in the legislatures of Virginia and Kentucky (although North Carolina had been the first choice.) The resolutions would be offered

---

[89] Ch. 74, 1 Stat. 596, sec. 2, pp. 596–597.

[90] Henry Adams would argue that "the essence of Virginia republicanism lay in a single maxim: *The government shall not be the final judge of its own powers.*" Henry Adams, *History of the United States during the Administration of Thomas Jefferson* (New York: Library of America, 1986), p. 174.

[91] James Madison, "Report on the Alien and Sedition Acts," in *Madison: Writings*, pp. 612, 615. Hereinafter cited as the "Virginia Report."

anonymously, betraying no link to the Republican leaders. John Taylor of Caroline would introduce Madison's resolutions in Virginia; John Breckinridge would propose Jefferson's draft in Kentucky. The legislature of the latter adopted Jefferson's resolutions on November 13, 1798; Virginia accepted Madison's on December 21.

The Virginia and Kentucky Resolutions were intended to be a protest that would merely "produce an opinion, by exciting reflection."[92] Madison would speak of the power of the states to "interpose" themselves against federal laws they deemed unconstitutional, and Jefferson, more radically, would insist in his draft of the resolutions that the "rightful remedy" for such infractions of the Constitution would be "nullification" (although that strong language would be removed from the version finally adopted by Kentucky.) But neither author suggested or even hinted at the most extreme reaction of secession. It would be a later generation that would turn their words to that purpose. But the Virginians did succeed in laying the principled foundation for the compact theory of the Constitution, a theory defined by the idea of states' rights and the concomitant necessity of a strict construction of the powers of the federal government under the Constitution.[93]

The Virginia and Kentucky Resolutions were essentially efforts to recover what Madison and Jefferson insisted was the true intention of the Constitution's makers to create nothing more than a "compact to which the states are parties."[94] Nearly from the beginning, that original and limited intention had been sacrificed to the "forced constructions"[95] made by the Federalists in order to liberate the powers of the general government from any meaningful constitutional restraints. Such expansive constructions of the powers of the general government had gone far toward "the very destruction of all limits prescribed . . . by the Constitution."[96] Madison and Jefferson saw their effort as an attempt to recover "the plain sense and intention of the instrument constituting that compact" in order to keep the general government tied to the powers explicitly delegated to it. Whenever the general government assumed "undelegated powers," its acts would be held to be "unauthoritative, void, and of no force."[97]

The foundation of this understanding was the idea that the states were the only original parties to the Constitution. As a result, its preservation depended upon any necessary constructions of it being made only "according

[92] Ibid., p. 659.

[93] See Adrienne Koch and Henry Ammon, "The Virginia and Kentucky Resolutions: An Episode in Jefferson's and Madison's Defense of Civil Liberties," *William and Mary Quarterly* 5 (1948): 145–176. See also Herman Belz, "The South and the American Constitutional Tradition at the Bicentennial," in Hall and Ely, eds., *An Uncertain Tradition*, pp. 17–59.

[94] Madison, "Virginia Resolutions," 21 December 1798, in *Madison: Writings*, p. 589.

[95] Ibid., pp. 589–90.

[96] Jefferson, "Draft of the Kentucky Resolutions," in *Jefferson: Writings*, p. 452.

[97] Ibid., p. 449.

to the plain intent and meaning in which it was understood and acceded to by the several parties" to it. And what those original parties had acceded to was the belief that they were constituting "a general government for special purposes" and thus choosing to delegate to that government only "certain definite powers," reserving the "residuary mass" to the states themselves for "their own self-government." As a result of this original compact, each state retained a "natural right" to protect itself from encroachments by the general government.[98]

The most basic "truths" about constitutional government, Madison would later explain – truths "which were at all times necessary to be kept in mind" – came to this: "the authority of constitutions over governments and the sovereignty of the people over constitutions." As a result of this logic, Jefferson would argue, "the government created by this compact was not made the exclusive or final judge of the extent of the powers delegated to it." This would have made no sense. To have done so would have made the government's "discretion and not the Constitution, the measure of its powers." Congress, after all, was "merely the creature of the compact." Because the states alone were parties to the compact, they were "solely authorized to judge in the last resort of the powers exercised under it." Not only were the states authorized to intervene when the general government might engage in a "deliberate, palpable, and dangerous exercise" of "powers not granted by the said compact," but they were in fact "duty bound" to do so in order to arrest the "progress of the evil" and thereby to protect all "the authorities, rights, and liberties" properly reserved to the states themselves.[99] This was the essence of the theory of states' rights and their residual sovereignty.

This understanding of the Constitution was essential if the original design of the government as "partly federal, and partly national" was to be maintained. But minimizing the "partly federal" aspect of the original Constitution was precisely the point of the Federalists' efforts at transformation through construction. Neither Jefferson nor Madison doubted for a moment that the objective was "to consolidate the states by degrees into one sovereignty."[100] Nor did they doubt that "to take from the states all powers of self-government and transfer them to a general and consolidated government, without regard to the special delegations and reservations solemnly agreed to in that compact, is not for the peace, happiness, or prosperity of these states."[101]

In the end, it all came down to the question of whether those who wielded the powers of the general government were to be trusted. The short answer

---

[98] Ibid., pp. 453, 449, 453.
[99] Madison, "Virginia Report," p. 614; Jefferson, "Kentucky Resolutions," pp. 449, 453, 453; Madison, "Virginia Resolutions," p. 589.
[100] Madison, "Virginia Resolutions," pp. 589–590.
[101] Jefferson, "Kentucky Resolutions," p. 453.

was that they were not. And in light of that it was important, Jefferson thought, to make clear the basic premises of republicanism. Free government, he argued, "is founded in jealousy and not in confidence; it is jealousy and not confidence which prescribes limited constitutions to bind down those whom we are obliged to trust with power." The conclusion was inescapable: "In questions of power, then, let no more be heard of confidence in man, but bind him down from mischief by the chains of the Constitution."[102]

Having made the case for the compact theory of the Constitution and the necessity of strict construction, the legislatures of Kentucky and Virginia appealed to the other states to join their efforts. None of them was willing to do so. Indeed, most were highly critical of the efforts, perhaps not least because of such vague and provocative ideas as "interposition." The legislature of Delaware found the proposals of the resolutions to be "a very unjustifiable interference with the general government." The Senate of New York expressed its "anxiety and regret" over the "inflammatory and pernicious sentiments and doctrines" in the documents. The General Assembly of Connecticut, its resolution said, "explicitly disavows the principles contained in the . . . resolutions." And Vermont's House of Representatives declared the Virginia and Kentucky Resolutions simply to be "unconstitutional in their nature and dangerous in their tendencies."[103]

Jefferson and Madison were not willing to allow "the principles . . . advanced by Virginia and Kentucky . . . to be yielded in silence." Yet neither were they in complete agreement as to just how robust the response should be to their unsupportive sister states. As usual, Madison was the more cautious of the two. While he agreed with Jefferson that the Constitution was the result of a compact among the states, he was beset from the beginning by nagging doubts that it followed from that premise that the states retained independent powers to declare federal laws they deemed unconstitutional to be "null, void, and of no effect." Nor was he willing to accept Jefferson's suggestion that they should declare that they were "determined . . . to sever ourselves from that union we so much value, rather than give up the rights of self government which we have reserved, and in which alone we see liberty, safety and happiness."[104]

Madison was able to calm Jefferson's passions. By November 1799 the latter was willing to acknowledge that the resolutions were in fact only "[p]rotestations against violations of the true principles of our Constitution, merely to save them, and prevent precedent and acquiescence from being

---

[102] Ibid., pp. 454, 455.

[103] *The Virginia Report of 1799–1800* (Richmond: J. W. Randolph, 1850), pp. 168, 174, 175, 177.

[104] Jefferson to Madison, 23 August 1799, in *Republic of Letters*, II: 1119; Koch and Ammon, "The Virginia and Kentucky Resolutions," p. 162; Jefferson to Madison, 23 August 1799, *Republic of Letters*, II: 1119.

pleaded against them." In restating and reaffirming the resolutions of 1798 in 1799, Jefferson agreed, there should be "nothing... said or done which shall look or lead to force."[105]

Madison was elected to the state legislature in time to serve as the chairman of the committee in the House of Delegates that turned to the defense of the Virginia Resolutions against the criticism of the other states. In January 1800 the legislature approved and issued what would come to be known simply as the "Virginia Report," a thoroughgoing and systematic defense of the principles of 1798.

In the "Virginia Report," Madison sought to achieve two things. First, he needed to assuage the fears among the other states that it was the intention of the resolutions to empower any state to "interpose" itself between the general government and the people, either routinely or for perceived infractions of "a light and transient nature." To the contrary, he insisted that "the interposition of the parties in their sovereign capacities" would occur only on those "occasions... deeply and essentially affecting the vital principles of their political system." Interposition would never be undertaken in any case that was "obscure and doubtful" but only when the erroneous construction of the Constitution was both "plain and palpable." It would be too dangerous to the system's necessary stability to exercise such a fundamental power as a result of any "partial consideration or hasty determination." Not only did violations of the Constitution have to be "plain and palpable," they also had to be clearly "*deliberate*."[106]

Madison's second objective was ultimately the more important. He had to make clear that the legislature of Virginia was going to stand its ground and hold firm to the principles that had been defended in the original resolutions as fundamental. These principles were, in a sense, few and clear. The "legitimate and solid foundation" of the authority of the Constitution was the fact that it had been "formed by the sanction of the states, given by each in its sovereign capacity." This original exercise in sovereignty came to this: "If the powers granted, be valid, it is solely because they are granted; and if the granted powers are valid, because granted, all other powers not granted, must not be valid."[107] The foundation of states' rights was clear:

The states then being the parties to the constitutional compact, and in their sovereign capacity, it follows of necessity, that there can be no tribunal above their authority, to decide in the last resort, whether the compact made by them be violated; and consequently, that as the parties to it, they must themselves decide in the last resort such questions as may be of sufficient magnitude to require their interposition.[108]

---

[105] Jefferson to Madison, 26 November 1799, in *Republic of Letters*, II: 1122.
[106] Madison, "Virginia Report," p. 612.
[107] Ibid., p. 611.
[108] Ibid.

What was undoubted was that the political system of the United States was "distinguishable from that of other countries by the caution with which powers are delegated and defined." As a result, it would be "incumbent in . . . every exercise of power by the federal government to prove from the Constitution that it grants the particular power exercised."[109]

Whenever . . . a question arises concerning the constitutionality of a particular power, the first question is, whether the power be expressed in the Constitution. If it be, the question is decided. If it be not expressed, the next inquiry must be, whether it is properly and incident to an express power, and necessary to its execution. If it be, it may be exercised by Congress. If it be not, Congress cannot exercise it.[110]

In such a constitution, "vague and violent" constructions by inference and implication have no place.[111]

The report went beyond the original resolutions and responded more fully to the arguments being made on the other side that the common law had been imported from Britain and was in effect under the Constitution as "a law for the American people as one community." It was, in fact, from this alleged federal common law that Congress sought to derive the authority by which it could justify its enactment of the Alien and Sedition Acts, exercising a power to create crimes such as seditious libel that was nowhere delegated in the Constitution. In Madison's view, it was clear that granting such a fundamental status to "the common law . . . would sap the foundation of the Constitution as a system of limited and specified powers."[112]

But that was not all. To so accept the common law would be to embrace a doctrine that was nothing less than "repugnant to the fundamental principle of the revolution." Should the common law be admitted as "of legal or of constitutional obligation," the result would be to "confer on the judicial department a discretion little short of a legislative power." There was not, Madison insisted, even a "vestige" of this "extraordinary doctrine" to be found in the records of the creation of the Constitution. Indeed, had "the common law been understood to be a law for the United States," surely it would have been "expressed in the enumeration" of powers in the Constitution.[113] It was not there listed and could not be put there by mere inference.

Madison's view of the common law and its place under the Constitution was one he had held for some time. In the Philadelphia Convention he had argued against James Wilson's view that such words as "felonies" were "sufficiently defined by common law" to necessitate no further definition in the Constitution itself. To Madison, that was dangerous. No foreign law, he

---

[109] Ibid., pp. 628, 621.
[110] Ibid., p. 642.
[111] Ibid., p. 650.
[112] Ibid., p. 641.
[113] Ibid., pp. 634, 639–640, 635, 638.

argued, "should be a standard farther than is expressly adopted."[114] Later, against George Mason's objection to the Constitution that it failed to secure "the enjoyment and benefit of the common law," Madison insisted that had it incorporated that body of law the Constitution would have succeeded only in having imported from Britain "a thousand heterogeneous & anti-republican doctrines."[115]

During the battle over the Alien and Sedition Acts Jefferson echoed Madison's sentiments from Philadelphia and anticipated his arguments in the "Virginia Report" five months before it appeared. "Of all the novel doctrines which have been broached by the federal government," he wrote to Edmund Randolph, "the novel one, of the common law being in force and cognizable as an existing law in their courts, is to me the most formidable." All the "other assumptions of ungiven powers," he insisted, were but "solitary, unconsequential, timid things in comparison with the audacious, barefaced, and sweeping pretention to a system of law in the U.S. without the adoption of their legislature." Should the incorporation of the common law be accepted, he later told Gideon Granger, the political system of the United States "would become the most corrupt government on the earth."[116]

In a very fundamental way, the Alien and Sedition Acts proved to be a classic instance of political overreaching. Nothing the Federalists had ever done had the effect of those laws in drawing together the Republican opposition. As the bills were making their way through Congress in the summer of 1798, Hamilton had warned his fellow Federalists that if they should take a "false step" and "push things to an extreme," the likely result would be to give Jefferson's "faction" both "body and solidarity."[117]

The Federalists would learn the harsh truth of Hamilton's warnings when the election of 1800 wrought a "revolution in the principles of... government." That revolution in principles was as real a revolution as had been that of 1776 as to the forms of government, Jefferson believed. But it was in a way even more impressive for the republic. It was a revolution that had been "not effected... by the sword... but by the rational and peaceable instrument of reform, the suffrage of the people." By its vote, the "nation declared its will by dismissing functionaries of one principle, and electing those of another, in the two branches, executive and legislative, submitted to their election."[118] Yet Jefferson was painfully aware that the Republican revolution was incomplete.

---

[114] Max Farrand, ed., *The Records of the Federal Convention*, 4 vols. (New Haven, CT: Yale University Press, 1936), II: 316.

[115] James Madison to George Washington, 18 October 1787, *Madison: Writings*, p. 141.

[116] Thomas Jefferson to Edmund Randolph, 18 August 1799; Jefferson to Granger, 13 August 1800, *Writings of Jefferson*, X: 125, 168.

[117] Alexander Hamilton to Oliver Wolcott, Jr., 29 June 1798, *Papers of Alexander Hamilton*, XXI: 522.

[118] Thomas Jefferson to Spencer Roane, 6 September 1819, *Writings of Jefferson*, XV: 212.

Jefferson's Federalist enemies had "retired into the judiciary as a strong-hold." And from that politically protected "battery," he warned, "all the works of republicanism are to be beaten down and erased." Not only had President Adams on his way out the door packed the judiciary generally with "useless judges to strengthen their phalanx," but he had installed as chief justice of the United States Jefferson's most enduring enemy, John Marshall. Not only would Marshall guide the Court through both of Jefferson's terms as president, but he would outlive Jefferson by a decade. In the quarter-century between his first inauguration and his death, Jefferson would watch with growing despair as the federal judiciary became a "subtle corps of sappers and miners, constantly working underground to undermine the foundation of . . . [the] confederated fabric." Until the end of his days, Jefferson would continue to fight against the judiciary on behalf of what he considered to be the "true principles of the revolution of 1800."[119] Those true principles, of course, were states' rights and the strict construction of the Constitution.

II. JEFFERSON AND THE JEFFERSONIANS

Jefferson's path to the presidency had not been an easy one. Not only had John Adams defeated him in 1796, leaving him to serve uncomfortably as a Republican vice president in a Federalist administration, but the complex methods of the electoral college in 1800 led to a tie between Jefferson and Aaron Burr. Burr's refusal to step aside threw the election to the House of Representatives for resolution. Still dominated by the Federalists, support in the lower house for Burr ran high. It took Alexander Hamilton openly giving his support to Jefferson – whom he hated only slightly less than he hated Burr – for Jefferson to be able to claim the presidency.[120] But that was only on the thirty-sixth ballot cast in the House over a stretch of seven seemingly endless days.[121]

The result was far less than what would have been hoped for a true revolution in principles. Still, Jefferson was in the chief magistracy, and his party controlled both houses of Congress. Yet he knew that after twelve years of Federalist rule and unremitting partisan strife, and after so vicious

---

[119] Thomas Jefferson to John Dickinson, 19 December 1801, X: 302; Thomas Jefferson to Thomas Ritchie, 25 December 1820, XV: 297; Jefferson to Roane, 6 September 1819, XV: 212, all in *Writings of Jefferson*. See Richard E. Ellis, *The Jeffersonian Crisis: Courts and Politics in the Young Republic* (New York: Oxford University Press, 1971).

[120] For Hamilton's views on Burr and Jefferson, see his letters to Gouverneur Morris, 26 December 1800; John Rutledge, 4 January 1801; and James A. Bayard, 16 January 1801, in *Papers of Alexander Hamilton*, XXV: 275, 293–295, 319–324.

[121] For an account of the election and the surrounding political chaos, see Edward J. Larson, *A Magnificent Catastrophe: The Tumultuous Election of 1800 and America's First Presidential Campaign* (New York: Free Press, 2007).

a campaign as that which had just taken place, the slightest overture toward reconciliation would not be misplaced. He began by asking Chief Justice Marshall to administer the oath of office; Marshall graciously reciprocated by immediately accepting the invitation "with much pleasure." Beneath Marshall's magnanimity, of course, lurked his belief that Jefferson was "unfit" for the presidency, and that he would undoubtedly "sap the fundamental principles of the government."[122]

On the morning of inauguration day, Marshall began a letter to Charles Cotesworth Pinckney expressing his nagging fear that under Jefferson the "public prosperity & happiness" would be diminished, if not lost altogether. He saw Jefferson's party as divided into "speculative theorists & absolute terrorists." He was willing to place the new president among the theorists rather than among the terrorists and simply hope for the best. After he had sworn Jefferson in at noon, Marshall returned to his interrupted letter to Pinckney. He was, he said, pleased to report that he had found Jefferson's inaugural address, on the whole, to be "well judgd [sic] & conciliatory," although it was undeniably "characteristic of the general cast of his political theory."[123]

In his address, President Jefferson insisted that it was incumbent upon both parties not to forget that "every difference of opinion is not a difference of principle." In fact, it had become the unfortunate political custom during the age of Federalism to call "by different names brethren of the same principle." But the truth came to this: "We are all Republicans, we are all Federalists." That said, he still thought it important that there should be no ambiguity in the public mind when it came to understanding what he deemed to be "the essential principles of our Government, and consequently those which ought to shape its administration." At the core of those "essential principles" he placed "the support of the state governments in all their rights, as the most competent administrations for our domestic concerns and the surest bulwarks against anti-republican tendencies."[124]

Speaking as he was in the shadow of the just-expired sedition law, the new president could not resist a jab at what he saw as the cowardly illiberality of the Adams administration. "If there be any among us," he implored, "who would wish to dissolve this Union or to change its republican form, let them stand undisturbed as monuments of the safety with which error of opinion may be tolerated when reason is left free to combat it."[125] There

---

[122] Thomas Jefferson to John Marshall, and John Marshall to Thomas Jefferson, 2 March 1801, VI: 86–87; John Marshall to Alexander Hamilton, 1 January 1801, VI: 46, all in *Papers of John Marshall*.

[123] John Marshall to Charles Cotesworth Pinckney, 4 March 1801, *Papers of John Marshall*, VI: 89, 89–90.

[124] Thomas Jefferson, "First Inaugural Address," in *Jefferson: Writings*, pp. 493, 493, 493, 494, 494.

[125] Ibid., p. 493.

would be no need for laws against seditious libel in the new Republican political world. But the private Jefferson was not quite so tolerant as he would have his enemies believe. When it came to the lingering presence of the Federalists, he assured Levi Lincoln, "I shall take no other revenge, than, by a steady pursuit of economy and peace, and by the establishment of republican principles in substance and in form, to sink federalism into an abyss from which there shall be no resurrection of it."[126]

No small part of the "substance and . . . form" of the Republican principles that Jefferson promised to establish in order to sink Federalism was the idea of strictly construing the Constitution in order to restore its original "chains" that had been intended by the framers to "bind down from mischief" those who would have to be entrusted with power. "The Constitution on which our union rests," Jefferson promised shortly after his inauguration, "shall be administered by me according to the safe and honest meaning contemplated by the plain understanding of the people of the United States at the time of its adoption." That meaning, he argued, "is to be found in the explanations of those who advocated, not those who opposed it." The quest for that original meaning was not all that difficult, Jefferson insisted: "These explanations are preserved in the publications of the time and are too recent in the memories of most men to admit of question."[127]

In Jefferson's view there were but "two canons" that were necessary to a safe interpretation of the Constitution. The first was to keep in mind always that "the capital and leading object of the Constitution was to leave with the states all authorities which respected their citizens only, and to transfer to the United States those which respected citizens of foreign or other states" – in short, "to make us several as to ourselves, but one as to all others."[128]

The second canon went beyond the residuary states' rights of the compact among the several states to interpretation as such. "On every question of construction," Jefferson explained to Justice William Johnson (his first appointee to the Supreme Court), we must "carry ourselves back to the time when the Constitution was adopted, recollect the spirit manifested in the debates, and instead of trying what meaning may be squeezed out of the text, or invented against it, conform to the probable one in which it passed." Together, these canons would guide the interpreters to the "true theory" of the Constitution, that to the states were reserved "the authority of preserving order, of enforcing moral duties and restraining vice, within their own territories."[129]

---

[126] Thomas Jefferson to Levi Lincoln, 25 October 1802, *Writings of Jefferson*, X: 339.

[127] Thomas Jefferson to Messrs. Eddy, Russel, Thurber, Wheaton, and Smith, 27 March 1801, *Writings of Jefferson*, X: 248.

[128] Thomas Jefferson to William Johnson, 12 June 1823, *Writings of Jefferson*, XV: 448, 449.

[129] Ibid., p. 449.

Against this sensible and simple Republican approach to interpretation had been the "irregular and censorable" practice of the Federalists of "forcing the meaning of words, hunting after possible constructions, and hanging inference on inference, from heaven to earth, like Jacob's ladder." The key was to take seriously the written nature of the Constitution and to assume that its words were neither mysterious nor malleable. "Laws are made for men of ordinary understanding, and should, therefore, be construed by the ordinary rules of common sense," Jefferson argued. "Their meaning is not to be sought for in metaphysical subtleties, which may make anything mean everything or nothing, at pleasure."[130]

That, after all, was the entire point of creating a "fundamental constitution" in the first place. The object was "to commit it to writing, and place it among... [the] archives, where everyone should be free to appeal to its text." Such a constitution was to be deemed to have a permanence of meaning until and unless changed by formal amendment by the people in their sovereign capacity; it was not to be subject to the distorting influence of judicially contrived "inferences, analogies, and sophisms" imposed upon it as though it were nothing more than "an ordinary law."[131]

Jefferson remained convinced that the Federalists' advocacy of a liberal or a loose construction of the Constitution in the Court no less than in Congress was aimed at consolidating the states into one "mass." John Marshall seemed to him the living proof of this effort. As Jefferson sought to distance himself from direct confrontation in the "polemical world" after he retired from the presidency, he looked to others to raise the defenses against any further movement toward consolidation of the several states into one simple republic – or worse, some sort of monarchy. There were two loyalists in particular to whom he looked to secure the grounds of Republicanism. He viewed the theoretical treatises of John Taylor of Caroline as the best efforts "ever yet... sent by heaven to our aid" and as texts that contained "the political faith to which every catholic republican should steadfastly hold." And beyond the bookish Colonel Taylor, Jefferson saw in Judge Spencer Roane the Republicans' "strongest bulwark" on the ground.[132] There was simply no one, Jefferson said, who possessed "the power and the courage" of Roane to stand up to Marshall, denying root and branch his understanding of both the nature and extent of judicial power and of the Constitution

---

[130] Ibid., pp. 447, 449–450, 450.

[131] Thomas Jefferson to John Cartwright, 5 June 1824, XVI: 45–46; Thomas Jefferson to Edward Livingston, 25 March 1825, XVI: 113, all in *Writings of Jefferson*.

[132] Thomas Jefferson to Archibald Thweat, 19 January 1821, XV: 307; Thomas Jefferson to Spencer Roane, 9 March 1821, XV: 325; Jefferson to Thweat, 19 January 1821, XV: 307; Thomas Jefferson to Spencer Roane, 27 June 1821, XV: 327–328; Jefferson to Thweat, 19 January 1821, XV: 307; Jefferson to Thweat, 19 January 1821, XV: 307, all in *Writings of Jefferson*.

itself. Armed with the "true principles of the revolution of 1800," Roane would go after the chief justice with a Republican vengeance.

Spencer Roane and the Politics of Federal Judicial Power

Spencer Roane was first elected to the General Court of Virginia in 1789 at the age of twenty-seven; six years later he was appointed to the state's supreme court, the Virginia Court of Appeals. He would sit on that court until his death in 1822. During his long professional career in the law, Roane was never a man to let his judicial duties interfere with his active interest in politics.[133] Taking his political bearings from the Virginia and Kentucky Resolutions, Roane became an indefatigable defender of states' rights and the compact theory of the Constitution. In time he would seem to many to be more doctrinaire a Jeffersonian than even Jefferson himself.

With the dawn of the new century and Jefferson's ascendance, Judge Roane (who was Patrick Henry's son-in-law) laid plans to transform Richmond, then "a stronghold of Federalism,"[134] into the bastion of Republicanism. In 1802 he formed the Richmond Junto, a secret society of the great and the good among Richmond's Republican ranks. In a very short time it would come to dominate Virginia politics. Two years later, Roane founded the *Richmond Enquirer* and placed in charge as editor his cousin Thomas Ritchie. The newspaper became the strong and clear national voice of Republican ideology.[135] All this in John Marshall's hometown. So successful was Roane at dominating the political landscape that the chief justice would ultimately despair that there was simply "no such thing as a free press in Virginia."[136]

For all his irascibility and what Marshall condemned as the "coarseness & malignity"[137] of his invective, Roane was no party hack. Classically educated, he was at home in the treatises of Grotius, Locke, and Montesquieu.[138] And when it came to the law, he had studied – as had so many of the leading Virginia lawyers such as Jefferson and Marshall – with the great George

---

[133] Rex Beach, "Spencer Roane and the Richmond Junto," *William and Mary Quarterly* 22 (1942): 1–17, p. 2.

[134] Ibid., p. 1.

[135] As Gerald Gunther has pointed out, the "*Enquirer* was not just another local newspaper. It was the organ of the Richmond Junto, one of the nation's most effective political leadership groups. Newspapers throughout the country frequently reprinted materials that the *Enquirer's* energetic editor, Thomas Ritchie, chose to put into its pages." Gerald Gunther, ed., *John Marshall's Defense of McCulloch v. Maryland* (Stanford, CA: Stanford University Press, 1969), "Introduction," p. 8. Hereinalter cited as *Marshall's Defense*.

[136] John Marshall to Joseph Story, 15 June 1821, *Papers of John Marshall*, IX: 167–168.

[137] Ibid., p. 167.

[138] William E. Dodd, "Chief Justice Marshall and Virginia, 1813–1821," *American Historical Review* 12 (1907): 776–787, p. 776.

Wythe at the College of William and Mary.[139] Steeped in Blackstone and Coke and Littleton, Roane was a lawyer's lawyer, and one especially drawn to the great and abiding questions of constitutional law.[140]

Roane was never a critic of judicial power. Indeed, as a member of the General Court in 1793, he had been one of the first judges in Virginia to argue on behalf of the power of judicial review in terms that clearly foreshadowed Marshall's landmark opinion a decade later in *Marbury v. Madison*. Roane believed that under a written constitution the judiciary was obligated to invalidate any law that was "plainly repugnant to the letter of the Constitution." His reasoning in *Kamper v. Hawkins*, like that of Marshall later, was that the people are "the only sovereign power" and that the legislature is "not sovereign but subordinate . . . to the great constitutional charter which the people have established as fundamental law."[141] Roane's problem was not with judicial power as such but with *federal* judicial power as against the powers of the state.

Judge Roane's first intellectual brawl with the Marshall Court came in the sprawling and seemingly endless property rights litigation that began in the early 1790s and that would culminate only in the Supreme Court's decision in *Martin v. Hunter's Lessee* (1816).[142] The litigation involved the disposition of the lands once held by Lord Fairfax. The question was whether the original landholder's descendants had a rightful claim to the lands left to them by Lord Fairfax or if the lands had been properly and legally confiscated by the commonwealth of Virginia, later to be sold in part to Daniel Hunter, a land speculator. Lord Fairfax's heir, Denny Martin, claimed the lands were rightly his to dispose of as he might see fit, insisting that the titles were protected from confiscation by the explicit terms of both the Anglo-American peace treaty of 1783 and the Jay Treaty of 1794. Hunter, on the other hand, argued that a Virginia statute was controlling and properly left the lands he had acquired in his hands.

The litigation's history was made all the more interesting by the early involvement of then-attorney John Marshall and his brother James. Both

[139] While at William and Mary, Roane, along with his classmates Marshall and the future justice Bushrod Washington, was one of the founding members of Phi Beta Kappa. "The Fifty Founders of Phi Beta Kappa," *William and Mary Quarterly* 16 (1936): 420–421.

[140] T. R. B. Wright, "Judge Spencer Roane," *Virginia Law Register* 2 (1896): 473–489, p. 478.

[141] 1 Va. Cas. 20 (Va. Gen. Ct., 1793), 20.

[142] The intricacies of the Fairfax litigation are admirably sorted out and explained in Charles F. Hobson, "Marshall and the Fairfax Litigation: From the Compromise of 1796 to *Martin v. Hunter's Lessee*," editorial note in *Papers of John Marshall*, VIII: 108–121. See also Maeva Marcus, ed., *Documentary History of the Supreme Court of the United States, 1789–1800* (New York: Columbia University Press, 2003), pp. 778–797. A splendid account of the litigation from a perspective that is not unsympathetic to the states' rights point of view is to be found in F. Thornton Miller, *Juries and Judges versus the Law: Virginia's Provincial Legal Perspective, 1783–1828* (Charlottesville: University Press of Virginia, 1994).

served as agents representing the interests of the Fairfax family in Virginia; they were also purchasers in their own names of some of the lands in question. Marshall had served as attorney to the Fairfax heirs and initiated one of the early case filings in the matter. For all these reasons he was forced to recuse himself once the cases made their way to the Supreme Court of the United States, although he seems to have been involved throughout to the degree to which the professional ethics of the day allowed.[143]

The litigation arrived at the Virginia Court of Appeals, where it was first argued on May 3, 1796. It was reargued on October 25, 1809, and on April 23, 1810, it was finally decided as *Hunter v. Fairfax's Devisee* by judges Roane and Fleming.[144] The Fairfax claims had been upheld in the Winchester District Court, and Hunter had appealed. The court determined that a compromise that had been struck between the claimants and the legislature of Virginia in 1796, and not the treaties invoked by Fairfax's devisee, was controlling. The lower court had erred in holding for Fairfax's heir, and that decision was thus overruled. The rights of the property went to Hunter. Fairfax appealed by writ of error to the Supreme Court of the United States as provided by the twenty-fifth section of the Judiciary Act of 1789. What had been merely a complicated and convoluted title dispute was about to become a major constitutional confrontation.

In *Fairfax's Devisee v. Hunter's Lessee*, handed down on March 15, 1813, Justice Story held for the Court that the Virginia Court of Appeals, and not the Winchester District Court, had in fact erred. The Jay Treaty alone protected the Fairfax interests in the land. In light of that, the Court reversed the decision of the Virginia Court of Appeals and affirmed the lower court's original judgment. In August 1813, the Supreme Court issued a mandate commanding the Virginia Court of Appeals to carry out its judgment. Judge Roane and his colleagues thought otherwise.

In the spring of 1814, Roane's court scheduled six days of arguments on the question of whether as a state court it was in any way obligated to follow the mandate of the highest federal court. Twenty months later, on December 16, 1815, the Virginia Court of Appeals unanimously announced that it was not so obligated. The four judges offered their opinions *seriatim*, as was the general practice, with the "most elaborate and provocative" being that of Judge Roane.[145] The judge began by dismissing the relevance of arguments drawn from *The Federalist* by those on the other side of the question. Those came, he said, from "a mere newspaper publication, written in the heat and hurry of the battle... before the Constitution was adopted"; and, of course, it was no secret that many of those essays had come from the pen of Hamilton, a "supposed favourer of a consolidated

---

[143] See Hobson, "Marshall and the Fairfax Litigation," pp. 120–121.
[144] 1 Munford Reports 218 (1810). Hereinafter cited as Munf.
[145] Hobson, "Marshall and the Fairfax Litigation," p. 117.

government."[146] Roane opted instead to base his defiance of what he saw as the pretensions of the Supreme Court on the Constitution as he read it through the states' rights prism of Madison's "Virginia Report" of 1799.

Roane began his assault on the Supreme Court's mandate with characteristic bluntness. There is, he argued, "a centripetal as well as a centrifugal principle [that] exists in the government," and as a result there could be "no calamity . . . more to be deplored by the American people, than a vortex in the general government which would engulf and sweep away, every vestige of the state constitutions." The federal Constitution, properly understood, made it clear that the government of the United States was not intended to be "a sole and consolidated government" but was in fact understood to be a "confederated" one. As a result, "the powers of the federal government result from the compact to which the states are parties" and are "no further valid than as they are authorized by the grants enumerated in the compact."[147] Upon the whole, Roane concluded,

I am of opinion, that the Constitution confers no power upon the Supreme Court of the United States to meddle with the judgment of this court, in the case before us; that this case does not come within the actual provisions of the twenty-fifth section of the judicial act; and that this court is both at liberty, and is bound, to follow its own convictions on the subject, any thing in the decisions, or supposed decisions of any other court, to the contrary notwithstanding.[148]

The four judges were in complete agreement as to what had to be the opinion of their court:

The court is unanimously of opinion, that the appellate power of the Supreme Court of the United States, does not extend to this court, under a sound construction of the Constitution of the United States; – that so much of the 25th section of the act of congress, to establish the judicial courts of the United States, as extends the appellate jurisdiction of the Supreme Court to this court, is not in pursuance of the Constitution of the United States; that the writ of error in this case was improvidently allowed under the authority of that act; that the proceedings thereon in the Supreme Court were *corum non judice* in relation to this court; and that obedience to its mandate be declined by this court.[149]

The opinion of the Virginia Court of Appeals was a direct challenge to the authority of his court that Chief Justice Marshall could not allow to stand. The application for a second writ of error was drafted by the chief justice himself and sent to Justice Bushrod Washington to make sure the case would get on the docket for the first possible hearing. The appeal was filed on February 5, 1816, and the decision in *Martin v. Hunter's Lessee*

[146] 4 Munf. 27.
[147] 4 Munf. 48, 55–56, 52.
[148] Ibid., p. 54.
[149] Ibid., pp. 58–59.

was handed down several weeks later, on March 20.[150] The decision by Justice Story would be considered by many in the years to come to be not only Story's finest constitutional opinion but perhaps the "ablest and most impressive" constitutional decision in the history of the Supreme Court.[151]

Story never doubted the "great importance and delicacy" of the issue before him. He began by going to the very heart of the dispute. "The Constitution of the United States," he decreed, "was ordained and established, not by the states in their sovereign capacities, but emphatically, as the preamble of the constitution declares, by 'the people of the United States'." The fundamental law was not "carved out of existing state sovereignties," and the sovereign powers of the state governments remained "unaltered and unimpaired except so far as they were granted to the government of the United States." This original understanding was confirmed, Story argued, by the language of the Tenth Amendment to the Constitution.[152]

That design, however, did not lead to an understanding that the document was to be subject to a strict construction. Rather, like every such charter, the Constitution was expected by its framers to be subject to a "reasonable construction." The most basic rule of construction, in Story's considered judgment, came to this: "The words are to be taken in their natural and obvious sense, and not in a sense unreasonably restricted or enlarged."[153] In anticipation of Marshall's opinion in *McCulloch v. Maryland*, Story made clear the nature and extent of the powers of the Constitution:

The Constitution unavoidably deals in general language. It did not suit the purposes of the people, in framing this great charter of liberties, to provide for minute specifications of its powers, or to declare the means by which those powers could be carried into execution. It was forseen that this would be a perilous and difficult, if not impracticable, task. The instrument was not intended to provide merely for the exigencies of a few years, but was to endure through a long lapse of ages, the events of which were locked up in the inscrutable purposes of Providence. It could not be foreseen what new changes and modifications of power might be indispensable to effectuate the general objects of the charter; and restrictions and specifications, which, at the present, might seem salutary, might, in the end, prove the overthrow of the system itself. Hence its powers are expressed in general terms, leaving to the legislature, from time to time, to adopt its own means to effectuate legitimate objects, and to mould and model the exercise of its powers, as its own wisdom and the public interests, should require.[154]

---

[150] Hobson, "Marshall and the Fairfax Litigation," p. 117.

[151] R. Kent Newmyer, *Supreme Court Justice Joseph Story: Statesman of the Old Republic* (Chapel Hill, NC: University of North Carolina Press, 1985), p. 111, quoting W. W. Crosskey, *Politics and the Constitution in the History of the United States*, 3 vols. (Chicago: University of Chicago Press, 1953), II: 811.

[152] *Martin v. Hunter's Lessee*, 14 U.S. 304 (1816), 324, 324, 325, 325.

[153] Ibid., p. 326.

[154] Ibid., pp. 326–327.

In light of this understanding of the Constitution, the legislature was properly empowered to pass the judiciary act in question giving to the Supreme Court of the United States appellate jurisdiction, by writ of error, over the decisions of the courts of the several states. Indeed, the "framers of the Constitution... contemplated that cases within the judicial cognizance of the United States not only might but would arise in the state courts, in the exercise of their ordinary jurisdiction." The fact was inescapable that "the appellate power of the United States must... extend to state tribunals."[155] That is the logical result of the Constitution's demand that the "judges in every state" shall be bound by the Constitution as "the supreme law of the law of the land." The conclusion was inevitable:

On the whole, the court are of opinion, that the appellate power of the United States does extend to cases pending in the state courts; and that the 25th section of the judiciary act, which authorizes the exercise of this jurisdiction in the specified cases, by a writ of error, is supported by the letter and spirit of the Constitution. We find no clause in that instrument which limits this power; and we dare not interpose a limitation where the people have not been disposed to create one.[156]

However emphatic and carefully reasoned was Story's opinion in *Martin v. Hunter's Lessee*, this was not to be the end of Judge Roane's battle against the Supreme Court, but only the beginning. He was not to be silenced. In many ways, his opinions in the Fairfax litigation would prove to be but rehearsals for what was to come in his responses to the Court's decisions in *McCulloch v. Maryland* and *Cohens v. Virginia*. But in these cases he would write not openly and officially as a sitting judge but as a party man, pseudonymously as "Hampden" and "Algernon Sidney," respectively – although there was no doubt in anyone's mind as to the author's true identity.

The Court's decision in *McCulloch v. Maryland* was handed down on March 6, 1819. The central holdings – that the creation of the second National Bank by Congress was a constitutional exercise of power and that the states could not legitimately tax and thereby threaten an institution of the federal government – aroused much less public reaction than might have been supposed. By and large, the public had become acclimated to such views; even Madison as president had agreed to the bank's creation in 1816.[157] But both Marshall and Roane knew that there were deeper issues at stake, not least the questions of implied powers and the interpretation of those powers.

When Marshall returned to Richmond, he quickly learned that the Republicans were stirring and looking for a fight. "Our opinion in the bank case,"

---

[155] Ibid., pp. 340, 342.
[156] Ibid., p. 351.
[157] See Gunther, "Introduction," in *Marshall's Defense*.

he wrote to Joseph Story, "has aroused the sleeping spirit of Virginia – if indeed it ever sleeps." He had picked up on the gossip that Ritchie's *Enquirer* was preparing to have the decision attacked "with some asperity." Three days later, he wrote to their colleague, Justice Bushrod Washington, with similar news. The "politicians of Virginia," he warned Washington, had found the reasoning of the unanimous court to be nothing less than "heretical" and "damnable." As with Story, the chief justice urged Washington to prepare himself to be "denounced bitterly in the papers" as part of "a pack of consolidating aristocrats." Given the stranglehold on the news held by Roane and Ritchie, Marshall knew there would be "not a word...said on the other side" leaving "the poor court" to suffer "all the obloquy."[158] On reflection, Marshall vowed not to let that happen.

The first ideological volley against *McCulloch* was fired by Judge William Brockenbrough, yet another cousin of Roane's and also a member of the Richmond Junto. Signed by "Amphictyon," Brockenbrough's two essays appeared in Ritchie's newspaper on March 30 and April 2. Marshall shot back under the pen name of "A Friend of the Union," with his two essays being printed in the Philadelphia *Union* on April 24 and 28. But that exchange was but a preface to what was to come.

Judge Roane's essays under the name of "Hampden" appeared in his cousin's pages on June 11, 15, 18, and 22. They were a formidable intellectual attack on Marshall's Federalist constitutional principles, which he had so clearly spelled out in *McCulloch*. In response, Marshall, this time writing as "A Friend of the Constitution" (although he toyed with changing his signature to "A Constitutionalist"), produced a total of nine essays in the *Alexandria Gazette* between June 30 and July 15, 1819. Marshall's responses to "Amphictyon" and "Hampden" would be the only time a sitting justice publicly defended his judicial decisions. Two years later, when Roane attacked *Cohens v. Virginia*, Marshall would silently endure the onslaught.

The Roane essays against the bank case had roused Marshall because he was convinced that "Hampden's" design was to "injure the Judges & impair the constitution." Orchestrating the publication of his essays discreetly through Justice Washington, Marshall insisted that the first of his "Friend of the Constitution" essays should not be published until he had "seen the last of Hampden."[159] He wanted to have the final word. He well knew that the essays were "designed for the country &...had considerable influence there."[160] Had Marshall known of Jefferson's letter to Roane applauding his "Hampden" essays as embodying "the true

---

[158] John Marshall to Joseph Story, 24 March 1819, VIII: 280, 280; John Marshall to Bushrod Washington, 27 March 1819, VIII: 281, all in *Papers of John Marshall.*
[159] John Marshall to Bushrod Washington, 17 June 1819, *Papers of John Marshall*, VIII: 317.
[160] John Marshall to Bushrod Washington, 28 June 1819, ibid.

principles of the revolution of 1800,"[161] he most assuredly would not have been surprised.

Marshall reported to Story that "the opinion in the Bank case" had inspired an effort by the "democracy in Virginia" (as he called the party of Jefferson) to attempt to "induce the legislature . . . to pass resolutions not very unlike those which were called forth by the alien & sedition laws in 1799." Marshall had been watching with amazement in Richmond as the argument in *McCulloch* had been "met by principles one would think too palpably absurd for intelligent men." But, then, he knew that prejudice was such as "will swallow anything." He had no doubt that were "the principles which have been advanced on this occasion to prevail," the "constitution would be converted into the old confederation."[162] That was, of course, precisely Roane's point and purpose.

Thomas Ritchie introduced Roane's "Hampden" essays by emphasizing that the bank case was "fraught with alarming consequences" that flowed from the Constitution being blatantly "misinterpreted," thereby leaving "the rights of the states and the people to be threatened with danger."[163] As Roane, writing as "Hampden," put it, the Court's opinion in *McCulloch* had to be seen by all true republicans (as well as all true Republicans) as the "*Alpha* and *Omega*, the beginning and the *end*, the first and the *last* – of federal usurpations." To make his case, Roane said, he would depend in part upon the "enlightened *advocates* of the Constitution, at the time of its adoption," such as the authors of *The Federalist*. After all, "Publius," as "Hampden" read him, had insisted that the Constitution created a general government of limited and enumerated powers only, leaving to the states residuary sovereignty over all other concerns. But beyond *The Federalist*, Roane would especially look to Madison's "Virginia Report" of 1799, which since that time had "never been surpassed" for "truth, perspicuity and moderation." Madison's great report was, he said, the Republicans' "*Magna Charta*."[164]

The most fundamental defect of the bank decision was the Court's abuse of the language of the Constitution. Rather than seeking to "construe the Constitution as it really is," the chief justice had intentionally strayed beyond the facts and the issue of the case in order to establish a "*general* and *abstract* doctrine," a doctrine that was simply "extrajudicial and without authority." Instead of focusing on the true meaning of the words "necessary and proper" in order to decide the case on the narrowest ground, the Court in effect had "expunged those words from the Constitution" and "granted . . . [a] general power of attorney to Congress." The dangers of loose construction

---

[161] Jefferson to Roane, 6 September 1819, *Writings of Thomas Jefferson*, XV: 212.
[162] John Marshall to Joseph Story, 27 May 1819, *Papers of John Marshall*, VIII: 314.
[163] *Marshall's Defense*, p. 106.
[164] Ibid., pp. 114, 113, 113, 113.

were made clear. In Roane's view, there was simply "no essential difference between expunging words from an instrument, by erasure, and reading them in a sense . . . which they do not naturally bear"[165] as Marshall had done in *McCulloch*. If a constitution was to serve as a fundamental law, its meaning had to be fixed.

However great might be the power of the Supreme Court, "it does not extend to everything; it is not great enough to *change* the Constitution." The fact is, courts are simply not "at liberty to change the meaning of . . . language." To allow them to do so would be to reduce the Constitution to the arbitrary opinion of the judge in question. The far-reaching implications of such an uncertain mode of construction were ominous: "The time will soon arrive, if it is not already at hand, when the Constitution may be expounded without ever looking into it." Those to whom it falls to interpret the fundamental law, Roane argued to the contrary, must understand themselves as "tied down to the terms used by the founders of the Constitution; terms . . . of limited, well defined, and established signification." What "the convention dared not to express" can never legitimately be judicially supplied by mere "implication."[166] The Constitution itself provided a means of change when necessary.

Time might well expose weaknesses in the original constitutional design; necessity might demand that new powers be added or old ones revised. But the correct way to make such changes is not by a textually untethered construction. If the powers of government are not "sufficiently ample" to meet the exigencies of the union, then they can be "extended by amendment." Until and unless such powers are thus extended or modified, the government can "only exercise such powers as are clear and undoubted."[167]

As with the original battle over the creation of a national bank in 1791, the substantive focus in *McCulloch* was the true meaning of the necessary and proper clause. Taking his lead from the earlier views of Madison and Jefferson, Roane reiterated their argument that "the words 'necessary and proper' . . . did not enlarge the powers previously given, but were inserted only through abundant caution." The inclusion of those now-vexing words was meant only to emphasize the obvious fact that a "general grant of a . . . power carries with it all the means, and those only, which are necessary to . . . the execution of the power." That meant, he emphasized, only such means could be adopted as were "essential to effectuate the power." The danger was obvious: "When you get beyond this criterion of necessity, you embark on a field without limits; and everything there depending on discretion, the rights of the weaker party will be swept away."[168] The weaker parties in question were the state governments.

[165] Ibid., pp. 129, 121, 110, 111.
[166] Ibid., pp. 111, 111, 109, 123, 153.
[167] Ibid., p. 118.
[168] Ibid., pp. 115, 117, 125, 125.

To play fast and loose with the language of the Constitution was to risk undermining the true nature of the Constitution. In the Jeffersonian view, the Constitution was "a *compact* between the people of each state, and those of all the states, and . . . nothing more than a compact." Noting Marshall's assertion in *McCulloch* that "we must never forget that it is a constitution we are expounding," Roane mockingly noted that the Court must also never forget that "it is also a compact, and a limited and defined compact." And that meant something, as Roane sought to remind his readers. To "construe the Constitution as it really is" meant to the Jeffersonians that a true interpretation would make clear that "the powers delegated to the general government are few and defined, and relate chiefly to external objects, while the states retain a residuary and inviolable sovereignty over all other subjects; over all those great subjects which immediately concern the prosperity of the people."[169]

Because the Constitution is a compact, and because the powers granted to the general government under it came from the several states "in their highest sovereign character," it could never be legitimate for the general government, "much less . . . one of its departments," to redefine the original distribution of powers between the federal government and the state governments. To do so would be to allow the general government "to tread under foot the principle which forbids a party to decide its own cause." The fact is that "the adjustment of . . . powers made by the Constitution, between the general and state governments . . . has been made by the *people* themselves, and they only are competent to change it." This understanding rested upon the most fundamental principle of modern constitutionalism, which Madison had made clear in his "Virginia Report": "The people only are supreme. The Constitution is subordinate to them, and the departments of the government are subordinate to that Constitution."[170] In light of these articles of the Republican faith, *McCulloch v. Maryland* was nothing less than a judicial transgression of the Constitution.

Roane had undertaken to write his attack on *McCulloch* in order to try and "concentrate public opinion and arrest . . . the progress of federal usurpation." But, he confessed, he was less than sanguine about the possibilities of success. "Such is the torpor of the public mind, and such the temper of the present times, that one can count on nothing with certainty." Still, it was worth the effort to at least remind each generation of the essence of the Jeffersonian view of the "true theory" of the Constitution – that it was a compact among equal sovereigns that could only be legitimately construed only strictly. What Marshall in *McCulloch v. Maryland* had undertaken to do was to "adjudicate . . . away"[171] the rights and powers reserved by the Constitution itself to the states. To Roane, that could not be allowed to

[169] Ibid., pp. 127, 128, 129.
[170] Ibid., pp. 140, 152, 152, 128–129, 130.
[171] Ibid., pp. 154, 154, 138.

go unanswered. And his responses to Marshall could not have been better received. Jefferson himself assured the judge when he read the essays of "Hampden" that he "subscribe[d] to every tittle of them" and could only hope that Roane would continue to defend "those principles on which . . . the future happiness of our country essentially depends."[172] Roane would not let him down, and when the Court handed down *Cohens v. Virginia*, he put aside the pen of "Hampden" and picked up that of "Algernon Sidney" to once again do battle for Jefferson's "true principles of the revolution of 1800."

In the same sense that *McCulloch v. Maryland* was a resurrection of the debate over the creation of a national bank in the 1790s, *Cohens v. Virginia* brought back to the fore the issues in *Martin v. Hunter's Lessee* regarding the role of the Supreme Court in assessing the competing claims of the governments within the federal system. At issue in *Cohens* was the substantive question of whether a federal law (this one creating a lottery in the District of Columbia) could trump a state law (in this case a Virginia law prohibiting lotteries); there was also the procedural question of whether the Supreme Court of the United States under section twenty-five of the Judiciary Act of 1789 had appellate jurisdiction over the decisions of the state courts. Its issues not dissimilar to those raised in *McCulloch*, *Cohens* moreover gave Chief Justice Marshall the opportunity to respond officially to the states' rights arguments Judge Roane had advanced in his "Hampden" essays two years earlier. In his response, Marshall did not flinch:

That the United States form, for many, and for most important purposes, a single nation, has not yet been denied. In war, we are one people. In making peace, we are one people. In all commercial regulations, we are one and the same people. In many other respects, the American people are one; and the government which is alone capable of controlling and managing their interests in all these respects, is the government of the Union. It is their government, and in that character, they have no other. America has chosen to be, in many respects, and to many purposes, a nation; and for all these purposes, her government is complete; to all these objects it is competent. The people have declared, that in the exercise of all powers given for these objects, it is supreme. It can, then, in effecting these objects, legitimately control all individuals or governments within the American territory. The constitution and the laws of a states, so far as they are repugnant to the constitution and laws of the United States, are absolutely void. These states are constituent parts of the United States; they are members of one great empire – for some purposes sovereign, for some purposes subordinate.[173]

Marshall made clear that the unanimous Court believed that Virginia's prohibition of the sale of lottery tickets within its borders was a purely state concern. In light of that, the Court upheld the conviction and the fines

---

[172] Jefferson to Roane, 6 September 1816, *Writings of Jefferson*, XV: 212, 216.
[173] 6 Wheaton 264 (1821), 413–414.

levied against the Cohen brothers for violating the Virginia law. But that was not enough to assuage the concerns of the Court's ever-vigilant critics. The main holding of the case was that the Supreme Court did indeed have the legitimate authority to review criminal cases on appeal from the state courts whenever any federal constitutional question was raised. It was this part of the opinion that outraged the states' rights advocates across the board.

Predictably, Roane, writing as "Algernon Sidney," found the "extravagant pretensions" of the Court to be fundamentally at odds with the true character of the United States as "a confederation of free states." He felt as morally obligated to respond to Marshall's "most awful decision" in *Cohens* as he had to the chief justice's constitutional confusions in *McCulloch*. The decision at hand, perhaps even more than *McCulloch*, Roane argued, "deeply and vitally endangered the liberties and constitution of our country." His main target was what he saw as "the despotic power... now claimed for the Supreme Court." The practical result of the judgment in *Cohens* ultimately was to deny "the idea that the American states have a real existence, or are to be considered, in any sense, as sovereign and independent states."[174]

Roane's essays against the lottery case appeared in the *Richmond Enquirer* on May 25 and 29 and June 1, 5, and 8, 1821. The danger he sought most to expose was that the "monstrous" *Cohens* decision had unleashed the "arbitrary discretion of the judges" to "amend the federal constitution at the mere will and pleasure of the supreme court." The result of amendment "by construction" was no less an amendment than if it had been carried out by the formal means provided in the Constitution itself. On the basis of the principle of *stare decisis*, the decision would become part of the fundamental law itself for all future purposes. The design of the Court's granting to the judges this "unlimited right... to alter the Constitution as they please" was clear to Roane. It was intended to elevate the federal judiciary above even the "power of the people" themselves so that the judges could destroy "the state governments altogether" and raise up on "their ruins, one great, national, and consolidated government." This, of course, struck at the very heart of the idea of the Constitution as a "compact by which the states are confederated together."[175]

The essence of the *Cohens* decision, as Roane saw it, was the Supreme Court claiming for itself the power to be the final arbiter of all constitutional questions, not least those between the general government and the states. But there was not any evidence, he was quick to point out, that so "immense and unreasonable" a power was actually given to the Court by the Constitution.

---

[174] Spencer Roane, "Algernon Sidney Essays on the Lottery Decision," in William E. Dodd, ed., *The John P. Branch Historical Papers of Randolph-Macon College*, 5 vols. (Richmond, VA: Taylor and Taylor, 1906), II, no. 2: 78–183, pp. 83, 97, 89, 78, 105, 80.

[175] Ibid., pp. 82, 84, 80, 80–81, 81, 85, 85, 83, 83–84.

Such a grant was nowhere to be found in the fundamental law. Indeed, "the extent of the judicial power is to be measured by the actual grant contained in the third article,"[176] and that article gives no such great and unlimited power to the Court.

The original design of the Constitution as a compact meant that there were two parties to the agreement, the general government and the governments of the several states. As a result, neither party alone was seen by the framers as "competent to settle conclusively the chartered rights of the other." By its "extravagant pretensions" to be the final arbiter between the nation and the states, the federal Supreme Court had, in effect, made itself a judge in its own cause – an idea that from time immemorial had been held to be "contrary to natural justice." The reason was obvious: "A compact between two parties is a nullity, as to one of them, if the other by itself, or its agents, has the power of expounding it as it pleases."[177]

Because the state governments are the "sovereign and independent members of which [the] confederacy is composed," their actions are not subject to the control of the general government unless that control is explicitly "authorized by the Constitution." There is no textual evidence of any such authorization in this case, Roane insisted. Thus the Court's assumption of power was illegitimate: "Unless a jurisdiction in this case has been 'delegated to the United States by the Constitution,' the court cannot assume it; and, on the contrary, an exemption from that jurisdiction is reserved to the states, or to the people, by not being 'delegated'."[178] Any reordering of the original assignment of powers between the federal head and the states required an amendment, not merely a judicial decree.

As in his decision in *McCulloch v. Maryland*, Marshall in *Cohens* had his own "ultra-federal" agenda, Roane insisted. He was determined to transform the constitutional order by construction from a confederation into a consolidated government. But to do so would be to abandon the original understanding of the Constitution completely. The sovereign people at the time of the creation of the Constitution had "wished only to enter into a federal government," and any idea of "one great national consolidated government was abhorrent to their minds." Guided only by his own "politics," the chief justice in *Cohens* had pushed his Federalist principles "to an extreme never until now anticipated."[179]

Roane's call to Republican arms against the Court rested on a simple premise: "The Constitution is not whatever the Court thinks it ought to be. . . . What the Constitution 'ought to be' is one thing, and what it actually *is*, is another. The last is the only question with which the Supreme Court has

---

[176] Ibid., pp. 106, 118.
[177] Ibid., pp. 97, 106–107, 137.
[178] Ibid., pp. 137, 143.
[179] Ibid., pp. 123, 130, 123.

any legitimate concern." The justices could have reached the decision they did in *Cohens* by following not the Constitution but only "their own prejudices and love of power."[180] Whatever that sort of judicial decision making might be, Roane believed, it most assuredly was not constitutionalism in any meaningful republican sense.

Marshall's battle with Roane would undoubtedly have continued; the chief justice, after all, would serve for another tumultuous fourteen years. But Roane died the next year, unexpectedly, at the age of sixty. Yet he had not been laboring alone. Where Roane the polemicist had left a collection of essays and judicial opinions, his more sober and studious contemporary, John Taylor of Caroline, would leave a shelf of treatises on states' rights and strict construction,[181] all designed to shore up the principles of Jeffersonian Republicanism. Taylor was a man, Jefferson had said, with whom he had "rarely, if ever, differed in any political principle of importance."[182]

John Taylor of Caroline and the Moral Foundations of States' Rights

John Taylor has been rightly described as a "stern Republican" and as a man who never ceased to see himself as "a Virginian first and an American second."[183] An ardent defender of the states and their sovereignty, he never faltered in his belief that a true republic "depended entirely upon the moral character of its people."[184] And that character, he believed, was to be nurtured not in a vast and morally indifferent commercial society, but by exposure to the virtues to be found in the agrarian way of life.[185] His republican writings over a public life of nearly three decades have been uniformly praised for their "consistency,"[186] their "remarkable coherence,"[187] and their "considerable contribution"[188] to American political thought. Though plagued by an "unfortunate literary style," Taylor's works were nevertheless

[180] Ibid., pp. 132–133, 159.

[181] For a bibliography of the works of Taylor, see Eugene Tenbroeck Mudge, *The Social Philosophy of John Taylor of Caroline* (New York: Columbia University Press, 1939), pp. 209–215.

[182] Jefferson to Ritchie, 25 December 1820, *Writings of Jefferson*, XV: 296.

[183] William E. Dodd, "John Taylor, Prophet of Secession," *Branch Historical Papers*, II, no. 3: 214–252, p. 237.

[184] Robert E. Shalhope, *John Taylor of Caroline: Pastoral Republican* (Columbia: University of South Carolina Press, 1980), p. 3.

[185] See John Taylor, *Arator: Being a Series of Agricultural Essays, Practical and Political* (Georgetown, DC: JM & JB Carter, 1813).

[186] Manning J. Dauer and Hans Hammond, "John Taylor: Democrat or Aristocrat?," *Journal of Politics* 6 (1944): 381–403, p. 395.

[187] Grant McConnell, "John Taylor and the Democratic Tradition," *Western Political Quarterly* 4 (1951): 17–31, p. 29.

[188] Benjamin F. Wright, Jr., "The Philosopher of Jeffersonian Democracy," *American Political Science Review* 22 (1928): 870–892, pp. 875–876.

"both read and used."[189] Jefferson himself did not hesitate to confess that he was deeply "indebted" to him for "many valuable ideas."[190] In many ways, John Taylor of Caroline was the chief theoretician of Jeffersonian Republicanism.[191]

Although more philosophically disposed in his writings than most public men, Taylor was not simply a closeted philosopher. He wrote in response to the pressing issues of the day. Thus his first book was a defense of President Jefferson's first term and an argument for his reelection.[192] He penned his *Inquiry into the Principles and Policy of the Government of the United States*[193] to refute the allegedly republican theories put forth by John Adams in *A Defence of the Constitutions of Government of the United States of America*[194] (a work Jefferson praised as having "completely pulverized"[195] Adams' arguments about the separation of powers.) When it came to the hated tariff, Taylor published *Tyranny Unmasked*.[196] And then, of course, there was the matter of John Marshall and the nationalistic Court he led. For a man like Taylor, who believed that the idea of "judicial independence" was nothing more than a means of "making Gods of men,"[197] it was perhaps inevitable that two of his most important works would take aim at his fellow Virginian. *Construction Construed and Constitutions Vindicated*[198] and *New Views of the Constitution*[199] in part sought to expose what Taylor saw as the philosophical corruption of Marshall's constitutional thought. Together the works were aimed at recovering and securing the firm republican foundation afforded by those "true principles of the revolution of 1800."

Construction Construed, which appeared in 1820, and *New Views of the Constitution*, published in 1823, of course appeared only after the Marshall Court had hit its full nationalism in such cases as *Martin v. Hunter's Lessee* (1816), *McCulloch v. Maryland* (1819), and *Cohens v. Virginia* (1821). But

---

[189] Ibid., p. 892.

[190] Jefferson to Ritchie, 25 December 1820, *Writings of Jefferson*, XV: 296.

[191] He was, as Vernon Parrington put it, "the intellectual leader of the Jeffersonian Republicans." *Main Currents in American Political Thought*, 3 vols. (New York: Harcourt Brace, 1927–30), II (1800–1860): 14.

[192] *A Defence of the Measures of the Administration of Thomas Jefferson, by Curtius* [pseud.] (Washington, DC: Samuel W. Smith, 1804).

[193] (Fredericksburg: Green and Cady, 1814).

[194] The first American edition was (Philadelphia: Hall and Sellers, 1787); this work was first published in London during Adams's time there as ambassador (London: C. Dilly, 1787).

[195] Thomas Jefferson to John Taylor, 28 May 1816, *Writings of Jefferson*, XV: 18–19.

[196] (Washington, DC: Davis and Force, 1822).

[197] Taylor, *Inquiry*, p. 202.

[198] (Richmond, VA: Shepherd and Pollard, 1820).

[199] (Washington, DC: Way and Gideon, 1823). As much as Jefferson admired Taylor, he feared that *New Views of the Constitution* was "the voice of one crying in the wilderness." Thomas Jefferson to Robert J. Garnett, 14 February 1824, *Writings of Jefferson*, XVI: 16.

Taylor did not need Marshall to show him the dangers of federal judicial power; he was more prescient than that. In fact, these later treatises were able to build upon the foundation of Taylor's initial critique of the judiciary that he had offered in his *Inquiry* of 1814. The object of his concern in the *Inquiry* was not the case law of the Supreme Court but rather the structure and design of the judicial branch in the Constitution itself. Given the complete "absence of responsibility"[200] imposed on the federal courts, the political jurisprudence of Chief Justice Marshall and his brethren was all too sadly predictable.

Such an absence of responsibility on the part of the Court within the context of the Constitution's institutional arrangements to check power (impeachment was the only real check, and not much of one at all in practical terms, he thought) was, in Taylor's view, "an evil moral principle," one from which "good moral effects" could never be expected to flow. Astonishingly, the original institutional scheme of the Constitution was the first example in history of a judicial power being created "completely independent of the sovereign power." Taylor's indictment was sharp: "a judicial sovereignty over the Constitution and law, without responsibility to the national sovereignty [of the people] is an unprincipled and novel anomaly, unknown to any political theory, and fitted to become an instrument of usurpation."[201]

The framers could have concocted such an arrangement only by ignoring all the clear and powerful lessons the past had to offer – lessons that were not at all hard to find. History, Taylor pointed out, "abounds with the political intrigues and oppressions of judicial power." To explicitly join the institutional independence of the judiciary to life tenure for the judges, as the Constitution had done, only compounded the mistake and served to create a judicial power from which "integrity and virtue can never be expected." The end result of the framers' judicial handiwork was "an insubordinate power" able to "knead and mould" the Constitution by mere construction.[202]

At its deepest level, the problem of construction generally is the problem of the limitations of the human understanding. The innate "frailties" of mankind are only exacerbated by the "defects" and "imperfections" of language itself. Thus when an interpreter confronts a written document, not least a written constitution that aspires to be fundamental law, he confronts a great "complexity of words and phrases," any one of which might be "tortured" to make it give up whatever meaning might most "appease [the] conscience" or "gratify [the] prejudice" of the interpreter.[203] This is most often accomplished by extracting a word or phrase from its rightful

---

[200] Taylor, *Inquiry*, p. 204.
[201] Ibid., pp. 207, 207, 204, 208.
[202] Ibid., pp. 199, 205, 207.
[203] Ibid., pp. 126, 96, 126, 126.

context and subjecting it to what Taylor condemned as the mere "science of verbality."[204] It is by this abuse of language that "mystical interpreters" are able to "extract from texts whatever doctrine is necessary for their purpose." And there is nothing more "fatal" to the science of politics that this "art of extracting erroneous conclusions from sound principles."[205]

Because of these facts of human nature, the constructive power bestowed upon the independent federal judiciary was, Taylor warned, "nearly equivalent to a power of legislating." The result of such largely untethered construction inevitably would be a Constitution and laws that were made to mean whatever the judges by their "passions and vices" should want them to mean. The true meaning of the Constitution and the laws would be obscured, covered by "the cobwebs of inference and construction."[206]

The essential problem of the most "pernicious species of construction," for Taylor, came down to the "machine called inference," a willingness on the part of an interpreter to abandon the true principles upon which a government has been established in favor of mere "prejudice or self-interest." In the instant case of the United States under the interpretations of the Marshall Court, the nation was in danger of "exchanging the pure principles of the revolution for the garbage of aristocracy, and compromises with venality." This was being achieved by the judiciary's "interpolation by construction" of the idea that the government was not one bound down by "specifications and restrictions on power," but was rather a complete sovereign power unto itself. What had been "wisely rejected" as unfit for the American system by the framers was now being surreptitiously slipped in by courts willing to "stretch" the language of the Constitution in order to satisfy "the temporal interest of the dominant sect."[207]

Sovereignty, Taylor argued, is a word that is at once "equivocal and illimitable," an idea that is one of "mystery" and "obscurity." In the most basic view, the idea of sovereignty is a threat to liberty because, by its very nature, it is "indefinite." In Taylor's estimation, a "sovereignty in governments of every form has universally claimed and exercised a despotick power over life, liberty, and property." The proper alternative, he argued, is to see "the term 'sovereignty' as an attribute of the right of self-government, and only applicable to the people." This republican truth was as simple as it was

---

[204] Ibid., p. 161. As Taylor explained it, "the art of verbalizing single words into a different system, may render the Constitution as unintelligible as a single word would be made by a syllabick dislocation, or a jumble of its letters; and turn it into a reservoir of meaning for which the expounder may have occasion." Ibid.

[205] Ibid., pp. 200, 259.

[206] Ibid., pp. 199, 206, 204. The problem with judges, in the end, is that they are all too human. "Names cannot change man's nature, and cure him of his passions and vices; if they could, this discovery would have superseded the necessity of all out inventions for curbing the passions and the vices of public officials, by calling them judges." Ibid., p. 206.

[207] Taylor, *Construction Construed*, pp. 22, 23, 21, 17, 26, 26, 26, 26.

compelling: "If the people are sovereign, their governments cannot also be sovereign." In practical constitutional terms, it all came down to the fact that neither the federal government nor the governments of the states could properly be deemed as sovereign. "Our maxim" Taylor argued, "is, that a government is not a sovereign, but a trustee of the sovereignty of the people, invested only with limited powers and composed of co-ordinate departments established to discharge specified duties."[208] The people, in *their* sovereign capacity, created both levels of government, state and federal, and the more fundamental of those levels is that of the governments of the several states. That fact was rooted in the Revolution itself:

By the revolution, each state became a perfect individual nation, possessed of all the natural rights of nations. As perfect nations, they have entered into two confederations.... By these confederations, they relinquished several national rights, and retained all not relinquished. As to their natural rights retained, they remain perfect nations; or in other words, their national individuality and independence of each other, respecting these rights, are unchanged.... [N]o specification of state rights reserved was necessary in establishing our union, because these rights were not conceded, as being national and antecedent to the compact. Being natural and national rights, and also never delegated, but reserved, they are held by the states in their original character as perfect national rights.[209]

The Constitution, the second confederation into which the states had entered, was not created to exclude "the idea of a compact between the states," but only to place that compact on a "better ground." The Constitution was not the result of the "consent of individuals" but of the consent of "bodies politick called states." Thus the illegitimacy of the new notion of a binding construction by the judiciary of a sovereign national government was clear: "If the states made the union...the same consent, necessary to create, is necessary to construe." And that power is truly supreme. By their "common consent" the states may not only construe the Constitution but might even "dissolve or modify" the union itself. This is the result of the states' "natural right of self-government, which they have never relinquished." As a result, when it comes to the union – its form or even its existence – the states "retain a complete supremacy." It is only by the "wantonness" or "licentiousness" of construction that the federal government could ever be made sovereign in such a way that there could come to be "a judicial supremacy without controul."[210]

Usurpations always begin, Taylor warned, under the seemingly innocent guise of confronting "little inconveniences and pretended necessities." When it came to the dangerously *novel doctrine* of federal judicial supremacy," the justification was that unless there be a supreme arbiter to construe the

[208] Ibid., pp. 25, 87, 67, 33, 143, 264.
[209] Ibid., pp. 171–172.
[210] Ibid., pp. 43, 44, 49, 127, 49, 126, 152.

Constitution in light of conflicting claims, the nation would be plagued by "clashing constructions." There was no doubt that this would be true, Taylor conceded. But the solution was not to transform by construction the rules laid down by the framers for "dividing, limiting, and checking power" but to encourage the people to exercise their constitutional power of amendment to remove the difficulty. To allow those who serve merely as the "trustees" of the people to have recourse to "expediency and convenience" as justification for stretching the fundamental law by construction would eventually leave the people with "no constitution at all."²¹¹

There was a further danger posed by construction than merely isolated cases of distorting the original meaning of the Constitution. There was the problem that came from the "omnipotence of precedents." Nothing could be more dangerous to a nation than "surrendering its constitution to precedents." To do so would be to strike at the very heart of republicanism. "Judicial precedents," Taylor pointed out, "are commonly the work of one man or a very few men. An opinion becomes an authority, and as it rolls along, it magnifies by others which adhere to it, not because it is right but because it is authority. . . . [I]t bears no resemblance to the species of consent by which we make constitutions."²¹² Such was simply not tolerable in a constitutional republic of limited, enumerated, and delegated powers.

Taylor believed that the only true check against the tyranny of judicially imposed "constructive innovations" was political recourse to what was the "plain intention of the Constitution," that is to say, to the original design of the framers and ratifiers. This original intention was to be ascertained by taking seriously the "words, spirit, and ratification" of the fundamental law; to be true to the document meant that there could be no "constructions unsustained by its letter." And the true construction would make clear that the original intention was that "a federal government was established and a national government rejected."²¹³

It was in the "creation of the federal government" that the states could be seen as having exercised the "highest act of sovereignty." It was only by their "moral co-equality" that the union could have been legitimately created. "By these political individual entities, called states," Taylor explained, "the Constitution was framed; by these individual entities it was ratified; and by these entities it can only be altered."²¹⁴ The states and their rights were the moral foundation of the American republic.

---

²¹¹ Ibid., pp. 116, 136, 144, 144, 163, 163.
²¹² Ibid., pp. 191, 197, 194. "What should we say to a husband," Taylor mused, "who would surrender the custody of his wife to a set of professed rakes? That which ought to be said of a nation, which intrusts its constitution to the care of precedents." Ibid., p. 196.
²¹³ Taylor, *New Views of the Constitution*, pp. 153, 134, 295, 268–269, 295.
²¹⁴ Ibid., pp. 37, 250, 173.

In confronting the evidence of what the Constitutional Convention intended, it seemed to Taylor "certain that the convention did not entertain the least suspicion that a constructive supremacy would be pretended to." Had there been such an intention, the framers would have made that clear. It is "doing the utmost violence to probability to imagine that the Constitution by inference without plain words ... have bestowed this enormous power exclusively on the federal court." Had they done so, the framers would have had to imagine that "a majority of one judge was equivalent to a majority of three-fourths of the states, to which the power of re-moulding the rights of the federal and state departments, is jealously confined." Had it been their intention to transfer this power to a "judicial aristocracy," they would have included among the other modes of changing the Constitution one of amendment "by a majority of the Supreme Court."[215] This they most obviously did not do.

The necessity for three-fourths of the states to concur in any change in the fundamental law reflected the framers' understanding of the states as "pre-existing political sovereignties" that retained their importance under the new scheme. At the time of the founding, each state "comprised a sovereign people and no people existed, invested with sovereignty over the thirteen states." Thus the union had been created, as it could only have been created, by the agreement and formal compact of the several states. The creation of the federal union demonstrated the framers' "solemn preference" for that form of government as the best means of securing "the liberty and happiness of the people." Ultimately, the framers' design and structure of the Constitution underscored their appreciation for the "compatibility between the union and the sovereignty of the several states."[216]

It was this understanding of the balance between the general government and the governments of the states that made Taylor "the father of the doctrine of states' rights."[217] His view of the relationship between the sovereign people and their two levels of government was a sophisticated one. He took no exception, as Patrick Henry had done in the Virginia ratifying convention, to the Preamble's beginning with "*We, the people,* instead of *We, the states.*"[218] Rather, Taylor held a view similar to that which Madison had expressed in response to Henry. "Who are the parties" to the Constitution, Madison asked. The answer, he thought was clear: "The people." But "not the people as composing one great body; but the people as composing

[215] Ibid., pp. 13, 22, 125, 125.
[216] Ibid., pp. 265, 8–9, 130, 263–264, 3.
[217] James McClellan, "Introduction" to John Taylor of Caroline, *New Views of the Constitution of the United States*, ed. James McClellan (Washington, DC: Regnery, 2000), p. xxiv.
[218] Jonathan Elliot, ed., *The Debates in the Several State Conventions on the Adoption of the Federal Constitution*, 5 vols. (Philadelphia: J. B. Lippincott & Co., 1876), III: 22.

thirteen sovereignties. Were it . . . a consolidated government, the assent of a majority of the people would be sufficient for its establishment; and as a majority have adopted it already, the remaining states would be bound by the act of the majority, even if they unanimously reprobated it." That was decidedly not the case, Madison insisted: "no state is bound to it, as it is, without its own consent."[219]

In the debates over the Virginia Resolutions in the Virginia House of Delegates in 1798, Taylor had summed up his view succinctly. "Although the framers of the Constitution chose to use the style, 'We, the people',", it was important to recall

> that in every step, from its commencement to its termination; the sense of the people respecting it, appeared through the medium of some representative State assembly, either legislative or constituent. That the Constitution itself, in many parts, recognizes that states as parties to the contract, particularly in the great articles of amendment, and that of admitting new states into the Union without a reference to the people; and that even the government of the Union was kept in motion as to one House of the legislature, by the act of the state sovereignties. That added to these incontestable arguments to show that the states are parties to the compact, the reservation of powers not given, was to the states as well as to the people, recognizing the states as a contracting party, to whom rights were expressly reserved. From all which it followed, though it be not denied that the people are to be considered as parties to the contract, that the states are parties also, and as parties, are justifiable in preserving their rights under the compact against violations; otherwise their existence was at an end; for, if their legislative proceedings could be regulated by Congressional sedition laws, their independency, and of course their existence, were gone.[220]

The essence of true republicanism, to Taylor, was the unfaltering belief that the "people are the only safe guardians of their own liberty." It fell to them in what Taylor called their "social jurisdiction" to police the government and to halt and correct any "unconstitutional political designs." If the Constitution itself could not be invoked by the people – its "creator" – to "prevent it from violation" by the departments of the federal government – the Constitution's mere "creatures" – then the fundamental law would be but a "dead letter," and the "rights of man" would be left unprotected and vulnerable to anything that government might choose to do. But it would not be a dead letter precisely because the people, through "the organs of the state legislatures," could and would enforce the fundamental law. This means of security was, Taylor insisted, "the happiest . . . which could have been devised."[221]

---

[219] Ibid., III: 94.
[220] Randolph, ed., *The Virginia Report*, p. 120.
[221] John Taylor, *An Enquiry into the Principles and Tendency of Certain Public Measures* (Philadelphia: Thomas Dobson, 1794), pp. 53, 53, 54, 54, 54, 55.

The state legislatures are the people themselves in a state of refinement, possessing superior information, and exhibiting the natural suffrage in the fairest and safest mode. They are annual conventions, subject to no undue influence . . . and actuated by the motive of the public good. Holding their power by an annual tenure, they are frequently accountable to the people, often changed, and incapable of forming combinations for their private emolument, at the public expense. Being more immediately within the view of their constituents, should they misinterpret the doings of the national government, or misrepresent the public mind, a detection, or a contradiction, would be almost instantaneous.

But that was not all; there was an existing institutional arrangement that clearly displayed the Founders' confidence in the state legislatures:

As electors of senators, they constitute a chief link connecting the general and state governments, through which the conduct of the former may be better understood, and the will of the people reacted; so as to fill up in some measure, the great space between Congress and the people. They may operate decisively upon the general government, by constituting the senate according to a republican standard. And finally, the state legislatures have at least as good a right to judge of every infraction of the Constitution as Congress itself.[222]

How, exactly, such construction by the states would work in practice was not made clear. Ultimately, Taylor's suggested solution to the problem of judicial tyranny was as intellectually vague and as institutionally undeveloped as was Madison's notion of "interposition" or Jefferson's more provocative idea of "nullification." In the end, they were all variations on the same theme, each a largely undefined ideological and political yearning for an older, more confederal form of government in which the states would somehow serve as a constitutional barrier between the people and an overreaching national government in order to protect the liberties of the people from those whom the people themselves had placed in power. That it has never truly worked in practice is not to say that the idea of states' rights has not been one that has echoed clearly and powerfully through American political and constitutional history.

John Taylor of Caroline died on August 21, 1824, "full of years and full of honor," as Thomas Ritchie's eulogy in the *Richmond Enquirer* put it. The "great lawyer," the "profound politician," and most of all "the friend of the Constitution in its original purity" was no more. "Let Virginia," wrote the editor, "weep over the ashes of the illustrious patriot."[223] Ritchie was not exaggerating. Not until Jefferson himself passed away nearly two years later would the Republican cause suffer as great a loss as the passing of Taylor, the "chief architect of states' rights doctrines."[224]

---

[222] Ibid., p. 55.
[223] As quoted in Elizabeth Kelley Bauer, *Commentaries on the Constitution, 1790–1860* (New York: Columbia University Press, 1952), p. 196.
[224] McClellan, "Introduction" to Taylor, *New Views*, p. xiii.

III. FROM BEYOND THE GRAVE

Few of the founding generation were as focused on their own mortality as was Thomas Jefferson. In his retirement years at Monticello his scientific curiosity would not allow him to ignore the evidence of his own physical and mental decline. He avoided any possibility of public embarrassment by simply refusing to participate directly in any of the great debates of the day. He knew that "the misfortune of a weakened mind is an insensibility of its weakness." By the age of eighty-two he would report to one correspondent that he found himself "with one foot in the grave and the other uplifted to follow it."[225] He would be gone within the year.

Jefferson was above all else, however, a man of politics. And, as such, he knew that there was a kind of immortality that was within reach of such public men and that it came from a well-tended reputation. For this, he turned to James Madison, his political partner of "half a century." In his last letter to Madison, he implored his friend simply: "Take care of me when dead." He took "great solace," he wrote, in knowing that Madison would indeed be "engaged in vindicating to posterity the course we have pursued for preserving to them, in all their purity, the blessings of self-government, which we had assisted too in acquiring for them." Such a devotion of a public lifetime would be above "reproach" if only "protected by truth."[226] Madison would not let him down.

But Jefferson's reputation depended as much upon what he had said as upon what he had done. Yet he had never reduced his political philosophy to a treatise, as had John Taylor; nor were there even extended essays making the arguments for republicanism, such as those of Spencer Roane. While Jefferson had spoken often and eloquently of the fundamental principles of his political faith, he had done so almost exclusively in the thousands of personal letters he had written over the course of his life. Fortunately, copies of a great many of those were preserved by Jefferson in his own files. As a result, many of his private thoughts on the great political events through which he lived and in which he participated would, soon after his death, become a very public record of his philosophy of politics generally and his republicanism in particular. The great man himself would thus be able to offer a final defense of states' rights and strict construction from beyond the grave.

Jefferson was ever mindful of history's claims. He feared that the opponents of his party were "far ahead ... in preparations for placing their cause favorably before posterity."[227] He never doubted, however, that "time will,

---

[225] Thomas Jefferson to Edward Livingston, 25 March 1825, XVI: 115; Thomas Jefferson to Frances Wright, 7 August 1825, XVI: 119, both in *Writings of Jefferson*.
[226] Thomas Jefferson to James Madison, 17 February 1826, *Writings of Jefferson*, XVI: 159.
[227] Thomas Jefferson to William Johnson, 12 June 1823, *Writings of Jefferson*, XV: 439.

in the end, produce the truth."[228] The "true history" of the tumultuous times of the American founding and the great "conflict of parties" that immediately descended upon the nation would only be told – indeed, could be told – only when "the letters of the day, now held in private hoards, shall be broken up and laid open to public view."[229] With his own "hoard" of letters at hand, Jefferson's acute "archival instinct"[230] allowed him to see his own "documentary legacy" as the best means by which he could influence, if not control, "how future historians would write the history of his life and times."[231] He knew those historians in whose hands his reputation would rest would know that his letters constituted the "only full and genuine journal of his life."[232]

Jefferson was not just concerned about his personal reputation – although that was certainly a primary focus. He was also committed to leaving behind the evidence to enable the historians to present an accurate history of the Republicans and their great battle with the Federalists during the "opening scenes"[233] of the present government. He hoped to contribute to any efforts that would take place after he was gone to see true republicanism triumph over those he always thought of as "monarchists." He knew that battle was not yet over.

Although it has been suggested that Jefferson's grip on his reputation and that of his party would have been firmer had he undertaken to publish his papers during his own lifetime, he thought he had done the next best thing by bequeathing his papers to his beloved grandson, Thomas Jefferson Randolph, in whom he had complete trust.[234] So trusted was his heir that Jefferson left no guide or instructions on how the papers ought to be treated; it was a matter of complete editorial discretion. The epistolary bequest was nothing less than a political and constitutional treasure trove – and a most controversial one, at that.

Scarred by the loss of his papers in the early years of his professional life when his home burned, Jefferson was determined to avoid such losses in the future "by such multiplication of copies as shall place them beyond the

---

[228] Thomas Jefferson to William Short, 8 January 1825, *Writings of Jefferson*, XVI: 95–96.

[229] Jefferson to Johnson, 12 June 1823, *Writings of Thomas Jefferson*, XV: 442. See also Jefferson to Short, 8 January 1825, *Writings of Thomas Jefferson*, XVI: 95.

[230] Lyman H. Butterfield, "The Papers of Thomas Jefferson: Progress and Procedures in the Enterprise at Princeton," *American Archivist* 12 (1949): 131–132, p. 131. See generally Francis D. Cogliano, *Thomas Jefferson: Reputation and Legacy* (Charlottesville: University Press of Virginia, 2006), Chapter 3, "Jefferson's Papers," pp. 74–105; and Merrill D. Peterson, *The Jefferson Image in the American Mind* (New York: Oxford University Press, 1960), pp. 29–36.

[231] Cogliano, *Thomas Jefferson: Reputation and Legacy*, p. 2.

[232] Thomas Jefferson to Robert Walsh, 5 April 1823, as quoted in Cogliano, *Thomas Jefferson: Reputation and Legacy*, p. 75.

[233] Jefferson to Johnson, 12 June 1823, *Writings of Jefferson*, XV: 442.

[234] Cogliano, *Thomas Jefferson: Reputation and Legacy*, p. 77.

reach of accident."[235] His preoccupation with the preservation of his papers happily coincided with his fascination with the latest machines and gadgets. Thus from roughly 1785 to 1804, he made copies of his papers by use of the copy press that had been invented by James Watt in 1780.[236] In 1804 he switched to using a polygraph, a double-quilled device that provided much better copies. But not only was Jefferson an inveterate copier, he was also fastidious in the organizing, cataloging, and filing of his various writings. While his grandson's editorial task was still formidable, it was made much easier by the attention Jefferson had paid to preparing his archive.

The first collection of Jefferson's works edited by Thomas Jefferson Randolph (with the assistance of various family members) was published in four volumes in 1829 as the *Memoir, Correspondence, and Miscellanies from the Papers of Thomas Jefferson.*[237] The first printing of six thousand copies sold out within the year. Later editions appeared in Boston, New York, London, and Paris.[238] To reviewers on both sides of the Atlantic, it was "one of the most important publications ever presented to the world."[239] And it was as politically explosive as one can only imagine Jefferson would have hoped it would be. "Have you seen Mr. Jefferson's *Works?*" Justice Joseph Story breathlessly queried a colleague. "If not," he went on, "sit down at once and read his fourth volume. It is the most precious melange of all sorts of scandals you ever read. It will elevate your opinion of his talents, but lower him in point of principle and morals not a little."[240] The fourth volume was in many ways the most politically titillating because the bulk of the volume contained Jefferson's many letters written in retirement.

It was there, for example, that Justice Story learned for the first time that Jefferson had condemned him as a "pseudo-republican" some twenty years earlier for sins he had committed against the party during Story's brief congressional career as a Massachusetts Republican.[241] So, too, could the justice learn from the master's own pen the theoretical underpinnings of the compact theory of the Constitution and the necessity of strict construction in important letters to Justice William Johnson (Story's colleague on the Supreme Court), Edward Livingston, and John Cartwright, as well as those to Judge Spencer Roane, John Taylor of Caroline, and Samuel Kerchival.[242]

---

[235] Thomas Jefferson to Mr. Hazard, 18 February 1791, *Writings of Jefferson*, VIII: 127.

[236] Silvio Bedeni, *Thomas Jefferson and His Copying Machines* (Charlottesville: University Press of Virginia, 1984), pp. 10, 204.

[237] (Charlottesville: F. Carr and Co., 1829). Hereinafter cited as *Memoir.*

[238] Peterson, *Jefferson Image in the American Mind*, pp. 30–31.

[239] As quoted in ibid., p. 29.

[240] Joseph Story to Judge Fay, 15 February 1830, in William W. Story, ed., *The Life and Letters of Joseph Story*, 2 vols. (Boston: C. C. Little and J. Brown, 1851), II: 33.

[241] Thomas Jefferson to General Dearborn, 16 July 1810, in Randolph, ed., *Memoir*, IV: 149

[242] Thomas Jefferson to William Johnson, 12 June 1823, IV: 368–375; Thomas Jefferson to Edward Livingston, 4 April 1824, IV: 391–393; Thomas Jefferson to John Cartwright,

As Jefferson had hoped, these and other letters like them would perpetuate the battle for the Constitution. And Justice Story rose to the challenge, using some of Jefferson's missives on matters constitutional as grist for the mill of his own three-volume *Commentaries on the Constitution of the United States.*[243]

Chief Justice Marshall had also read the Jefferson papers – with "astonishment and deep felt disgust," as he put it. Such a work was "never before given to the world." The "unwarranted aspersions" cast by Jefferson on Marshall himself were nearly enough to rouse the chief justice into "taking some notice of them and repelling them." But age, he said, had "blunted" his feelings, and he had grown too "indolent" to respond to Jefferson's "malignant censure."[244] Death had not softened Marshall's opinion of his ideologically estranged cousin.

Marshall had always found Jefferson to be among the "most ambitious & ... the most unforgiving of men," and the posthumous publication of his secret assaults did nothing to change that opinion. What never ceased to amaze Marshall was the vast influence Jefferson wielded and how so many people were inclined to "adopt his opinions however unsound they may be, & however contradictory to their own reason."[245] That was certainly the case when it came to Jefferson's insistence that the Constitution was a mere compact, and one that was to be construed strictly. In those fundamental principles, Marshall viewed Jefferson as he viewed Judge Roane, as a man who will be seen "to be the champion of state rights instead of being what he really is, the champion of dismemberment."[246]

Marshall knew that the *Memoir* would cause what he saw as the unsound principles of Jeffersonian Republicanism to continue to echo in American politics, corrupting the public mind and threatening to undermine the Constitution and the nation it was meant to create. At the time of Jefferson's death in 1826, Marshall had been engaged in a relentless battle with the Virginia Republicans for a quarter of a century over what he saw as the perversities of their ideology of states' rights and strict construction. Their claim that such a view constituted the true original intention of the Founders was, as the chief justice put it, a matter of "political metaphysics" against which all reasoning seemed doomed to be in vain. The idea of states' rights seemed to have taken on a dangerous charm made all the more threatening by Jefferson's personal power over the public imagination. It was for all

---

5 June 1824, IV: 393–399; Thomas Jefferson to Spencer Roane, 6 September 1819, IV: 316–318; Thomas Jefferson to John Taylor, 28 May 1816, IV: 274–277; Thomas Jefferson to Samuel Kerchival, 12 July 1816, IV: 285–292, all in Randolph, ed., *Memoir*.

[243] (Boston: Hilliard, Gray, and Co., 1833).

[244] John Marshall to Henry Lee, 25 October 1830, *Papers of John Marshall*, XI: 386, 386, 387.

[245] John Marshall to Joseph Story, 13 July 1821, *Papers of John Marshall*, IX: 179.

[246] John Marshall to Joseph Story, 15 June 1821, *Papers of John Marshall*, IX: 168.

these reasons that in his last years Marshall doubted the Constitution could even survive.

His melancholy could only have been the result of his view that the Court he led, and the federal judiciary generally, were institutionally restrained from responding to the attacks made on them by the likes of Jefferson, Roane, and Taylor. For over the course of his three and a half decades as chief justice the Supreme Court had amassed a body of constitutional law rooted in what Marshall and Story understood to be the true intentions of the Founders. And it would be this body of law that would serve as the basis of Justice Story's *Commentaries on the Constitution of the United States*, a work that in time would completely overshadow all other commentaries on the fundamental law with the exception of *The Federalist*. Marshall's legacy and his view of "the most sacred rule of interpretation" would be secure – at least for a while.

7

The Most Sacred Rule of Interpretation

John Marshall, Originalism, and the Limits of Judicial Power

John Marshall ascended to the chief justiceship of the United States in 1801 as a committed republican, an ardent nationalist, and a loyal member of the Federalist Party; but most important, he went to the Supreme Court as an unwavering constitutionalist.[1] In nearly one hundred constitutional cases over his thirty-four years on the highest court, Chief Justice Marshall endeavored to articulate the limitations on both the state and federal governments; he drew out the implications of the congressional power to regulate commerce among the states; and he made clear that under the new Constitution the obligation of contracts would be safe from governmental finagling. And, of course, in *Marbury v. Madison* he established under the Constitution what would come to be called judicial review, the power by which the federal courts declare legislative acts unconstitutional.[2] No judge

---

[1] "In heart and sentiment, as well as by birth and interest," Marshall wrote, "I am an American, attached to the genuine principles of the Constitution as sanctioned by the will of the people for their general liberty, prosperity, and happiness." That Constitution, he concluded, is "the rock of our political salvation which has preserved us from misery, division, and civil wars; – and which will yet preserve us if we value it rightly and support it firmly." John Marshall, "To a Freeholder," 20 September 1798, in Charles F. Hobson, et al., eds., *Papers of John Marshall*, 12 vols. (Chapel Hill: University of North Carolina Press, 1974–2006), III: 504. Hereinafter cited as *Papers of John Marshall*.

[2] *Marbury v. Madison*, 5 U.S. 137 (1803). Prior to Marshall's opinion in *Marbury* there had been arguments as well as cases that took seriously the power of courts to declare unconstitutional laws the judges found to be repugnant to the Constitution. See especially *Kamper v. Hawkins*, 1 Virginia Cases 20 (Va. Gen. Ct., 1793); *Commonwealth v. Caton*, 4 Call 5 (Va. Ct. Of App., 1782); and *Van Horne's Lessee v. Dorrance*, 2 Dallas 310 (U.S. Cir. Ct. Pa., 1795). See also Alexander Hamilton's seminal argument in *The Federalist*, No. 78, in Jacob Cooke, ed., *The Federalist* (Middletown, CT: Wesleyan University Press, 1961). For a discussion of the antecedents to *Marbury*, and its place within that tradition, see Robert Lowry Clinton, *Marbury v. Madison and Judicial Review* (Lawrence: University Press of Kansas, 1989); Sylvia Snowiss, *Judicial Review and the Law of the Constitution* (New Haven, CT: Yale University Press, 1990); and Charles F. Hobson, *The Great Chief Justice: John Marshall and the Rule of Law* (Lawrence: University Press of Kansas, 1996).

has ever had greater influence on the nation's political development. Yet for all that influence he was unfalteringly committed to the belief that judges, no less than other officials, were bound by the terms of the Constitution, and that for them to go beyond their strictly judicial powers and exercise something akin to political discretion would be to commit nothing less than "treason to the Constitution." Marshall took seriously the demands of a written constitution, and was dedicated to the proposition that its meaning was to be found in "the intentions of the framers" and not in the "sympathies" of the judge. "Courts," he insisted, "are the mere instruments of the law, and can will nothing."[3]

Marshall was stunningly consistent in his commitment to originalism over the three and a half decades he navigated the Supreme Court through often treacherous political waters, first churned up by the Jeffersonian Republicans and then later muddied by the Jacksonian Democrats.[4] While on occasion he appears to have flirted with finding his constitutional way by resting a decision on some notion of a higher or unwritten law antecedent to, and superior to, the Constitution itself, those flirtations are most striking simply by being so exceptional to his usual interpretive approach of a close and exacting textual analysis.[5] Marshall knew that the judicial search

---

The phrase "judicial review" seems to have been the twentieth-century creation of Edward S. Corwin. See Edward S. Corwin, "The Establishment of Judicial Review," *Michigan Law Review* 9 (1910): 102.

[3] *Cohens v. Virginia*, 19 U.S. 264 (1821), 404; *Sturges v. Crowninshield*, 17 U.S. 122 (1819), 199–200; *Cherokee Nation v. Georgia*, 30 U.S. 1 (1831), 15; *Osborn v. Bank of the United States*, 22 U.S. 738 (1824), 866.

[4] While "originalism" is something of an anachronism in speaking about Marshall, it nonetheless captures the essence of his commitment to the judicial obligation to discover the intention of the lawgiver.

[5] They are also striking in that such abstract principles are never used by Marshall as the ground of his decision. See, for example, Marshall's opinion in *Fletcher v. Peck*, 10 U.S. 87 (1810), 133, where he seemed to argue that his decision rested upon "certain great principles of justice, whose authority is universally acknowledged." But in fact he argued only that the actions of the Georgia legislature were "restrained by the general principles which are common to our free institutions, *or* by the particular provisions of the Constitution of the United States" (emphasis supplied). Rather than seeing Marshall, the ardent textualist, as arguing that "general principles ... common to our free institutions" might be invoked to judicially invalidate certain governmental actions, it is more likely that he was merely suggesting that such "general principles" were what had prompted those "particular provisions" of the Constitution that Marshall himself understood to be the grounds for his decision. Moreover, constantly striving to maintain a Court that spoke with one authoritative voice, Marshall's somewhat ambiguous phraseology in his opinion in *Fletcher* was most likely prompted by Justice William Johnson's concurring opinion, in which he famously suggested that the decision of the Court rested on "a general principle, on the reason and nature of things: a principle which will impose laws even on the deity." 10 U.S. 87, 143. Johnson was not a follower of Marshall's linguistic approach to constitutional exegesis. He did not put much stock, he once said, in "mere verbal criticism." *Gibbons v. Ogden*, 22 U.S. 1 (1824), 226–227.

for the original intention of the lawmaker was an approach that "from time immemorial" had "guided courts in their construction of instruments brought under their consideration."[6] When it came to the Constitution, the object, in Marshall's view, was to discern what he frequently called simply "the mind of the Convention."[7] John Marshall was never one to shy away from judicial confrontations with the more political branches of the federal government or with the governments of the several states. He was always willing to reach the judgments he thought the Constitution demanded and to let the political chips fall where they may, even when there were whispers of his possible impeachment. He understood that his originalism demanded from him not simply decisions but reasoned arguments that would explicate the meaning of the Constitution in ways that would make clear to the nation the principled basis of the Court's conclusions. There were, of course, many who disagreed with those conclusions,[8] and still others who thought his appeal to original intention was but a veil pulled more to deceive than to enlighten.[9] But through it all, Marshall stood his ground, knowing that if the Constitution did not have a meaning independent of what the judges would like it to mean, then there would be no security for that Constitution or for the republic that it created.

To understand fully the shape and the substance of the great chief justice's originalist jurisprudence it is necessary to consider the sturdy architecture of his constitutional thought more generally, from its foundation in the liberal,

---

See also Marshall's only dissent in a constitutional case, *Ogden v. Saunders*, 25 U.S. 213 (1827), 346, where he suggested that men do not derive their right to contract from government, but bring it with them when they enter civil society. But this line of argument also seems to have been necessary, in Marshall's view, not to offer a natural or higher-law ground for his views, as is often suggested, but to enable him to argue as powerfully as he could that so basic was the received tradition as to the sanctity of contract that there was only one possible reading that could be extracted from the letter and the spirit of the Constitution.

[6] *Cohens v. Virginia*, 19 U.S. 264, 398.

[7] *Sturges v. Crowninshield*, 17 U.S. 122, 202, 205. See also *Ogden v. Saunders*, 25 U.S. 213 (1827), 356; and *Dartmouth College v. Woodward*, 17 U.S. 518 (1819), 644. When it came to ordinary law, he insisted that the judge was similarly obligated to search for "the mind of the legislature," *Ex Parte Randolph* (United States Circuit Court of Appeals, 21 December 1833), *Papers of John Marshall*, XII: 316; the "sense of the legislature," *Postmaster v. Early*, 25 U.S. 136 (1827), 151; or "the intention of the legislature," *Craig v. Missouri*, 29 U.S. 410 (1830), 433.

[8] James Madison, for instance, thought Marshall's opinion in *McCulloch v. Maryland* was a stellar piece of "constructive ingenuity." James Madison to Robert S. Garnett, 11 February 1824, *Letters and Other Writings of James Madison*, 4 vols. (Philadelphia: J. P. Lippincott, 1865), III: 367–368.

[9] Thomas Jefferson, whose dislike of Marshall was both profound and well known, was convinced that the chief justice was determined to make the Constitution "a blank paper by construction." Thomas Jefferson to Wilson C. Nicholas, 7 September 1803, in A. Lipscomb and A. Bergh, eds., *The Writings of Thomas Jefferson*, 20 vols. (Washington, DC: Jefferson Memorial Foundation, 1905), X: 419. Hereinafter cited as *Writings of Jefferson*.

natural rights philosophy of the Enlightenment to its ultimate defense of the Constitution as written fundamental law deemed to be permanent until and unless changed by the sovereign voice of the people.

I. THE MORAL FOUNDATIONS OF REPUBLICAN GOVERNMENT

The moral foundation of John Marshall's republicanism was the same as that of his constitutionalism, the philosophy of natural rights; and together, his republicanism and his constitutionalism would give rise to his understanding of the limitations on judicial power. Like the other Founders, Marshall had thought long and hard about the great works of law and political philosophy that had comprised a common "course of reading" for his generation; they were all, as he put it, "intimately acquainted with the writings of those wise and learned men whose treatises on the laws of nature and nations" constituted the core of their political education.[10] They handled the works of such writers as Grotius, Hobbes, Pufendorf, Locke, Vattel, Burlamaqui, Rutherforth, Blackstone, and Montesquieu with an easy familiarity. These were, after all, treatises to be embraced not as mere artifacts of intellectual ostentation, but rather as practical guides to government and law to be used by practicing statesmen.[11]

At the most basic level, Marshall's political and jurisprudential views derived from an essentially Hobbesian understanding of human nature – albeit an understanding that had been filtered through the philosophic screens of Hobbes's "more refined and ingenious philosophic successors," not least Locke and Blackstone. The result was an understanding of natural rights, consent of the governed, sovereignty by institution, and fundamental positive law that would issue in Marshall's insistence that a written and ratified constitution of limited and enumerated powers was not merely the "greatest improvement on political institutions" but was, in fact, nothing less than "sacred."[12] And it was from this view of the Constitution as a "sacred" text that Marshall's understanding of the nature and extent of judicial power under that Constitution ultimately derived.

---

[10] *Ogden v. Saunders*, 25 U.S. 213 (1827), 353–354.
[11] See, for example, the notes from Marshall's argument before the circuit court in *Ware v. Hylton* in 1793, in which he invoked as authorities such writers as Vattel, Burlamaqui, and Blackstone. *Papers of John Marshall*, V: 300–329. For a general overview of the readings of the founders, see Jack P. Greene, *The Intellectual Heritage of the Constitutional Era: The Delegates' Library* (Philadelphia: Library Company of Philadelphia, 1986); Bernard Bailyn, *The Ideological Origins of the American Revolution* (Cambridge, MA: Harvard University Press, 1967); and Gordon S. Wood, *The Creation of the American Republic* (Chapel Hill: University of North Carolina Press, 1969).
[12] Robert K. Faulkner, *The Jurisprudence of John Marshall* (Princeton, NJ: Princeton University Press, 1968), p. 81; *Marbury v. Madison*, 5 U.S. 137 (1803), 178; *United States v. Maurice* (United States Court of Appeals, 22 May 1823), in *Papers of John Marshall*, IX: 306.

When Marshall considered man's existence in "the rudest state of nature," he viewed it through a finely polished Lockean lens. What defined life in the state of nature, he believed, was man's complete "free agency" that issued from his natural equality. In such a state, natural man could do as he pleased, unrestrained by the shackles of law. In that state, Marshall noted, man "governs himself and labours for his own purposes." He also enjoys there natural rights to "acquire property," to "barter" and thus to "dispose of that property according to his own judgment" through the mechanism of his fundamental "right to contract."[13] These rights, in Marshall's view, were derived from "laws whose authority is acknowledged by civilized men throughout the world."[14]

Following Locke's logic, Marshall insisted that in "the state of nature . . . individuals may contract, their contracts are obligatory, and force may rightfully be employed to coerce the party who has broken his engagement."[15] But as both Hobbes and Locke had taught, Marshall understood that it was precisely each man's right in the state of nature to enforce the law of nature that ultimately rendered the state of nature so dangerous and inhospitable a place. The reason was that, being naturally free and equal, men would have nothing to supply the defects of their nature. When there would come to be disagreements over the "intrinsic obligation"[16] of contracts, there would be no disinterested and impartial judge to resolve the dispute on the basis of what Locke had described simply as "an establish'd, settled, known law."[17] Force, not reason, was most likely to hold sway. That very "free agency" that is the essence of human liberty is also the cause of unceasing conflicts between men. The reason is that all too often man's "judgment is completely controlled by the passions," not least his self-interest.[18] When something as important and divisive as claims to property is involved, "men seldom allow much weight to the reasoning of an adversary."[19] On the whole, man is "an animal much less respectable" than one might hope.[20] Thus finding life in the state of nature so threatening, men in that primitive state had opted to surrender their right of coercion to the government, with the understanding

---

[13] *Ogden v. Saunders*, 25 U.S. 213 (1827), 345, 350, 345, 346, 345.

[14] *Gibbons v. Ogden*, 22 U.S. 1 (1824), 211. "Marshall viewed the Lockean political understanding as the true political perspective." Faulkner, *Jurisprudence of John Marshall*, p. 195. See also R. Kent Newmyer, *John Marshall and the Heroic Age of the Supreme Court* (Baton Rouge: Louisiana State University Press, 2002), pp. 210–266.

[15] *Postmaster v. Early*, 25 U.S. 136 (1827), 346.

[16] *Ogden v. Saunders*, 25 U.S. 213 (1827), 350.

[17] Peter Laslett, ed., *Locke's Two Treatises of Government* (2nd ed.; Cambridge: Cambridge University Press, 1970), *Second Treatise*, 369.124 (page number and section).

[18] John Marshall to Joseph Story, 13 July 1821, *Papers of John Marshall*, IX: 179.

[19] John Marshall, *The Life of George Washington*, 5 vols. (Fredericksburg, VA: Citizens' Guild of Washington's Boyhood Home, 1926), IV: 176. Hereinafter cited as *Life of Washington*.

[20] John Marshall to Charles Cotesworth Pinckney, 21 November 1802, *Papers of John Marshall*, VI: 125.

that the government would in turn offer the security to their lives, liberties, and property that would otherwise be lacking.[21]

The social contract by which men in the state of nature could make themselves into members of a civil society was, in Marshall's view, the means whereby men could come to know and enjoy true liberty. Marshall rejected those "erroneous opinions which confound liberty with an exemption from legal controul." He had learned well from his philosophic teachers "the indispensable necessity of clothing government with powers sufficiently ample for the protection of the rights of the peaceable and quiet, from the invasions of the licentious and turbulent part of the community."[22] He was in complete agreement with James Madison's view that "liberty may be endangered by the abuses of liberty, as well as by the abuses of power."[23]

What this meant in practice, by Marshall's reckoning, was that all those rights that man held in the state of nature "are surrendered... when he enters into a state of society in exchange for social rights and advantages." There was neither ambiguity nor equivocation in Marshall's view: "All natural rights... may be controuled by society and exercised by its permission." Even the most fundamental natural rights of "life and liberty... are at the disposition of society."[24]

As with life and liberty, so too with the rights of property, contract, and commerce. While it was surely true that these "rights are not given by society but are brought into it,"[25] the fact remained that "however absolute the right of an individual might be," it was still a fundamental part of "the nature of that right" that it might be regulated or restrained for the public good as "determined by the legislature."[26] Thus while the right to acquire property may be a natural one, property itself in any meaningful sense springs only from "the law of property [which] in its origin and operation, is the offspring of the social state; not the incident of a state of nature."[27] Even the "obligations created by contract," while they are understood to "exist anterior to and independent of society" and are "brought with man into society," may yet be "controuled... by human legislation."[28] Similarly, the right to engage in barter and commerce was a right that the Constitution did not create but merely found as "an existing right," but still Congress was given "the power to regulate it."[29]

---

[21] *Ogden v. Saunders*, 25 U.S. 213, 346–347.
[22] *Life of Washington*, IV: 221.
[23] *The Federalist*, No. 63, p. 428.
[24] John Marshall to James M. Garnett, 20 May 1829, *Papers of John Marshall*, XI: 247.
[25] *Ogden v. Saunders*, 25 U.S. 213, 346.
[26] *Providence Bank v. Billings*, 29 U.S. 514 (1830), 563.
[27] John Marshall, "Argument in the Supreme Court of the United States in *Ware v. Hylton*," *Papers of John Marshall*, III: 9.
[28] *Ogden v. Saunders*, 25 U.S. 213, 345.
[29] *Gibbons v. Ogden*, 22 U.S. 1, 211.

The solution to man's dire situation in the state of nature, for Marshall no less than for Hobbes and Locke, was the creation of political sovereignty, the establishment of fundamental law by the consent of the governed. The people have, by the laws of nature and of nature's God, "an original right to establish, for their future government, such principles as, in their opinion, shall most conduce to their own happiness." There was nothing preordained that had to be included in, or excluded from, the fundamental law. Its commands and prohibitions were entirely up to what the people, in their collective and sovereign capacity, might choose to decree. And no small part of the legitimacy of this creation of fundamental law depended upon the understanding that the "supreme and irresistible power to make or unmake, resides only in the whole body of the people; not within any subdivision of them."[30]

This complete freedom of the sovereign people to create the fundamental law of their constitution in whatever manner they thought most likely to conduce to their happiness did not demand a democracy or a republic any more than it rejected an aristocracy or a monarchy; their freedom to choose the form was plenary. Yet for Marshall's generation, there was no question what was right for America, what form of government best conformed to what the Founders always called the "genius" of the American people. True republican government was all that would do. It was the form most in line with the philosophic underpinnings of the very idea of the social contract, popular sovereignty. As such, it was the form most agreeable to man's nature. Thus, for Marshall, in America republicanism and constitutionalism properly understood were inextricably linked and formed the essence of the Constitution itself.

II. THE NATURE OF THE CONSTITUTION

The nature of the Constitution, in Marshall's view, was best grasped in the first instance by understanding the defects of the constitution that preceded it, the Articles of Confederation. By examining the mischiefs the framers of the Constitution meant to address, the problems they meant to correct, one could come to see their intentions and thus understand the proper meaning of the Constitution's terms and provisions. And for Marshall, the true original meaning or intention of the framers began with a fundamental truth: the Constitution created a government, not a league or a confederation of sovereign states. To understand this one fact, Marshall believed, was to understand everything.[31]

---

[30] *Marbury v. Madison*, 5 U.S. 137, 176; *Cohens v. Virginia*, 19 U.S. 264, 389.

[31] "[O]ur government is not a league. It is a government; and has all the constituent parts of a government. It has established legislative, executive, and judicial departments, all of which act directly on the people, not through the medium of the state governments." Gerald

For Marshall, the "mischief the Constitution intended to prevent"[32] was the result of both "the sacrifice which had been made of national interest on the altars of state jealousy" and "the complicated calamities which flowed from the inefficacy of the general government."[33] On the one hand, at the national level, the Confederation had "nominal powers, but no means to carry them into effect."[34] While on the other, "in the state governments generally, no principle had been introduced which could resist the wild projects of the moment, give the people an opportunity to reflect, and allow the good sense of the nation time for exertion."[35] Thus was the situation under the Articles of Confederation's aspiration to be nothing more than a "firm league of friendship" among the sovereign states, one of national incompetence and state chaos.[36] It was only a matter of time before the Confederation collapsed of its "mere debility."[37]

Horrified at the "wide spreading contagion of the times," such as state laws that abolished debts and interfered with the obligation of contracts, the more "enlightened friends of republican government," Marshall would later write, came to have "a deep conviction of the necessity of enlarging the powers of the general government."[38] The actions of those thirteen "jealous and independent sovereigns" had all but undermined the most basic "principles of moral justice, and... sound policy." The determination of "the wise and thinking part of the community" to incorporate "some principles into the political system, which might correct the obvious vices, without endangering the spirit of the existing institutions" would manifest itself in the Constitutional Convention of 1787, "an occasion... generally deemed momentous."[39]

Gunther, ed., *John Marshall's Defense of McCulloch v. Maryland* (Stanford, CA: Stanford University Press, 1969), p. 199. Hereinafter cited as *Marshall's Defense.*

[32] *Ogden v. Saunders*, 25 U.S. 213, 357.

[33] *Life of Washington*, IV: 180, 199.

[34] John Marshall, "Speech in the Virginia Ratifying Convention, 20 June 1788," *Papers of John Marshall*, I: 259.

[35] *Life of Washington*, IV: 195.

[36] Marshall saw the time of the "miserable confederation" as the "awful and instructive period" of the nation's history. During that time the "states were... truly sovereign and were bound together only by a league." The options facing the American people had been clear: "To change it into an effective government, or to fall to pieces from the weight of its constituent parts, & weakness of its cement, was the alternative presented to the people of the United States." Fortunately, Marshall said, the "wisdom and patriotism of our country chose the former." *Marshall's Defense*, pp. 155, 199, 200.

[37] *Life of Washington*, IV: 134.

[38] Ibid., IV: 233, 197, 233. As Marshall explained the situation in the Virginia Ratifying Convention: "That economy and industry are essential to our happiness will be denied by no man. But the present government will not add to our industry. It takes away incitements to industry, by rendering property insecure and unprotected. It is the paper on your table [the proposed Constitution] that will promote and encourage industry." "Speech in the Virginia Ratifying Convention, 10 June 1788," *Papers of John Marshall*, I: 266.

[39] *Life of Washington*, IV: 193, 197–198, 238.

In the broadest terms, the framers in Philadelphia deliberately undertook simultaneously to enhance the power of the new national government and to restrict the powers of the states. Marshall greatly admired these achievements of the Convention, especially the latter. "Whatever respect might have been felt for the state sovereignties," he would write,

> it is not to be disguised that the framers of the Constitution viewed, with some apprehension, the violent acts which might grow out of the feelings of the moment; and that the people of the United States, in adopting that instrument, have manifested a determination to shield themselves and their property from the effects of those sudden and strong passions to which men are exposed. The restrictions on the legislative power of the states are obviously founded in this sentiment; and the Constitution of the United States contains what may be deemed a bill of rights for the people of each state.

Beyond those restrictions, the United States itself was transformed by the Constitution from a mere league of quarreling, petty, self-interested states into a single nation in which "the American people are one, and the government which is alone capable of controlling and managing their interests . . . is the government of the Union." And the powers of that new government, Marshall insisted, were accordingly both "complete" and "competent."[40]

For Marshall, the nature of the Constitution was largely defined by four distinct but intimately related characteristics. First, its legitimacy derived from the natural sovereignty of the people, not from the artificial sovereignty of the states. Second, it was a written and ratified document whose true meaning, the original intention of the sovereign people, was to be found in the words of its text as adopted. Third, it was a "constitution . . . of enumeration and not definition" with only the "great outlines" marked, leaving the means necessary to its implementation to be "deduced." Fourth, the Constitution was to be understood as a rule for the government of courts no less than for the legislature, and the judges were to be "bound by that instrument."[41]

A Nation of States

On the eve of the Constitutional Convention, it will be recalled, James Madison had written to George Washington sharing his first thoughts on what he hoped would emerge from the coming deliberations in Philadelphia. "Conceiving that an individual independence of the states is utterly irreconcilable with their aggregate sovereignty," Madison wrote, "and that a consolidation of the whole into one simple republic would be as inexpedient as it is unattainable, I have sought for some middle ground, which may at once support a due supremacy of the national authority and not exclude

---

[40] *Fletcher v. Peck,* 10 U.S. 87 (1810), 137–138; *Cohens v. Virginia,* 19 U.S. 264, 413–414.

[41] *Gibbons v. Ogden,* 22 U.S. 1, 189; *McCulloch v. Maryland,* 17 U.S. 316 (1819), 407; *Marbury v. Madison,* 5 U.S. 137, 179–180.

the local authorities wherever they can be subordinately useful."[42] When the Convention concluded its business, the proposed constitution that was sent to the states for ratification was, as Madison would say, "in strictness neither a national nor a federal constitution; but a composition of both."[43] The political dilemma posed by this "incomplete national government," as Alexis de Tocqueville would describe it half a century later, was that Madison's "middle ground" would become a doctrinal battlefield over just where the constitutional line between nation and states was to be drawn. It was a question, Marshall said, that was "perpetually arising" and one which in such a nation of states would "probably continue to arise so long as our system shall exist."[44]

From the earliest beginnings there had developed what Marshall described as "the keen sighted jealousy with which any diminution of state sovereignty was watched."[45] The rise of Marshall's political enemy, Thomas Jefferson, only sharpened that states' rights squint. In the eyes of the Jeffersonian Republicans, Marshall argued, "every exercise of legitimate power is construed into a breach of the Constitution." The election of the Republicans in 1800 unleashed a concerted effort by the new party in power "to convert our government into a meer league of states," Marshall thought. This was no superficial policy dispute, but a "deep design" that was intended to transform "the Constitution . . . into the old confederation." At the heart of the Republican strategy was an effort to curb the courts by whatever means possible. "The whole attack," Marshall confidently wrote to Story, "if not originating with Mr. Jefferson, is obviously approved and guided by him." Eventually, all the pernicious efforts by Jefferson – that "great Lama of the mountains," Marshall sneeringly called him – would succeed in giving the "word 'state rights' . . . a charm against which all reasoning is vain."[46]

Marshall believed the most fundamental tenets of states' rights to be nothing more than "insane dogmas."[47] At the heart of the states' rights faith was the view that the Constitution was to be considered "not as emanating from the people, but as the act of sovereign and independent states. By their constitutional calculations, the "powers of the general government . . . are delegated by the states, who alone are truly sovereign; and must be exercised in subordination to the states, who alone possess supreme dominion."

[42] James Madison to George Washington, April 1787, in *Letters and Other Writings of James Madison*, I: 287.
[43] *The Federalist*, No. 39, p. 257.
[44] *McCulloch v. Maryland*, 17 U.S. 316, 405.
[45] *Life of Washington*, IV: 189.
[46] John Marshall to Joseph Story, 3 June 1833, *Papers of John Marshall*, XII: 281; 18 September 1821, *Papers of John Marshall*, IX: 184; 29 May 1819, *Papers of John Marshall*, VIII: 314; 18 September 1821, *Papers of John Marshall*, IX: 183; 31 July 1833, *Papers of John Marshall*, XII: 291.
[47] Marshall to Story, 25 December 1832, *Papers of John Marshall*, XII: 248.

Such an understanding, Marshall insisted, could not be sustained.[48] The underlying premises of the states' rights advocates were "principles totally repugnant to the words of the Constitution and to the recorded facts of its adoption."[49]

Marshall conceded, as Madison had conceded, that it had never been the intention of the Constitutional Convention to create a unitary or consolidated republic. "No political dreamer," the chief justice wrote, "was ever wild enough to think of breaking down the lines which separate the states and of compounding the American people into one common mass." But the mere fact that the people are organized within states does not mean that the "measures they adopt . . . cease to be the measures of the people themselves, or become the measures of the state governments." It was the approval of the people immediately, not that of the governments of the formerly sovereign states, that "ordained and established" the Constitution. The government thus created "proceeds directly from the people." This fact was, in Marshall's view, simply indisputable. "The government of the Union" he argued, " . . . is emphatically and truly a government of the people. In form, and in substance, it emanates from them. Its powers are granted by them, and are to be exercised directly on them and for their benefit."[50]

Because it is the "government of all," because its "powers are delegated by all," and because it "represents . . . and acts for all," the nation must be understood to be empowered to "bind its component parts."[51] There is no fundamental notion of "state rights" that can trump the national government; the parts cannot control the whole. The sovereignty and independence of the states had been radically and intentionally reduced by the people by the clear terms of their Constitution. There was now a truly national government in place, something more than the mere confederal sum of the state parts. Should the "postulates" of the party of states' rights succeed, then those premises would "explain away the Constitution . . . and leave it, a magnificent structure, indeed, to look at, but totally unfit for use."[52]

Even though the essence of the Constitution was its nationalism, in Marshall's eyes, there did remain a real realm for the exercise of state power. He believed that the Constitution was "not intended to furnish the corrective for every abuse of power which may be committed by the state governments."[53] Indeed, each state had its own constitution that "provided such limitations and restrictions on the powers of its particular government, as its judgment dictated."[54] And even where the national government

---

[48] *McCulloch v. Maryland*, 17 U.S. 316, 402, 402, 403.
[49] *Marshall's Defense*, p. 91.
[50] *McCulloch v. Maryland*, 17 U.S. 316, 403, 402, 403–404, 404–405.
[51] Ibid., pp. 405, 406.
[52] *Gibbons v. Ogden*, 22 U.S. 1, 222.
[53] *Providence Bank v. Billings*, 29 U.S. 514, 563.
[54] *Barron v. Baltimore*, 7 Peters 243 (1833), 247.

was granted a power by the Constitution, such as the power to regulate commerce among the several states, it did not mean that the states were pre-empted from exercising their own similar powers when they did not conflict with the powers of the national government.[55] The powers retained by the states "remained, after the adoption of the Constitution, what they were before, except so far as they may be abridged by that instrument."[56]

Given the theoretical and practical complexities of the Constitution – such as its new understanding of federalism and its structure of separated powers – it was essential that the fundamental law be written. It was not merely a matter of "human reason" to be left to courts, as was the unwritten common law, to apply "in a regular train of decisions, to human affairs, according to the circumstances of the nation, the necessity of the times, and the general state of things."[57] Rather, the Constitution was the result of what Hamilton had described as "reflection and choice."[58] It was a matter of conscious design, a design that could be understood only in light of the purposes and intentions of its designers. It had to be so understood because, as fundamental law that had been ratified and accepted by the people, it was ultimately the embodiment of the intentions of the people in their sovereign capacity. And it was in the written word that the people's sovereign intention was made known.

A Written Instrument Framed for Ages to Come

While it has become commonplace to dismiss or diminish Marshall's insistence on the significance of the Constitution being written, to him there was no doubting the power and importance of that seemingly simple fact. It was, as he famously said, "the greatest improvement" on the institutions of government.[59] In his eyes, the Constitution's provisions were not written because they were fundamental in some abstract and antecedent sense; rather, the Constitution's provisions were fundamental precisely because they were written. They were the concrete expression of the will of the sovereign people. "The people made the Constitution," he pointed out, "and the people can unmake it. It is the creature of their will, and lives only by their will."[60]

---

55 See, for example, *Willson v. Black-Bird Creek Marsh Co.*, 27 U.S. 245 (1829).

56 *Sturges v. Crowninshield*, 17 U.S. 122, 193. "That the framers of the Constitution did not intend to restrain the states in the regulation of their civil institutions, adopted for internal government, and that the instrument they have given us is not to be so construed, may be admitted." *Dartmouth College v. Woodward*, 17 U.S. 518, 628.

57 *Livingston v. Jefferson* (United States Court of Appeals, 5 December 1811), *Papers of John Marshall*, VII: 282.

58 *The Federalist*, No. 1, p. 3.

59 *Marbury v. Madison*, 5 U.S. 137, 176.

60 *Cohens v. Virginia*, 19 U.S. 264, 389. This was a view Marshall held from the earliest years. "It is the people that give power, and can take it back. What shall restrain them? They are

The people in their role as the sovereign creators of fundamental law, as has been pointed out, were completely free to create any institutional arrangements they might please; it was a matter left completely to their discretion, with no higher law or power binding them. That was, as Marshall argued, the very essence of their "original right" to create whatever form of government they might think most likely to "conduce to their own happiness." Because the "exercise of this original right is a very great exertion" and cannot be "frequently repeated," it logically follows that the "principles . . . so established, are deemed fundamental." Moreover, because "the authority from which they proceed is supreme, and can seldom act, they are designed to be permanent." And so that the details of their constitutional design, both the powers created and the limitations imposed, would not be "mistaken, or forgotten," Marshall said, "the Constitution is written."[61]

Given the difficulty of creating such a fundamental law, there needed to be in its favor the presumption of its permanence. As Marshall argued, "a constitution is framed for ages to come, and is designed to approach immortality as nearly as human institutions can approach it." That near-immortality is best effected, he thought, by understanding the words of the instrument to have a "true meaning" that can be known, a meaning that is to be presumed fixed and incapable of change either by legislative fiat or by judicial construction.[62] For Marshall, the meaning of the Constitution could be altered only by the "solemn and authoritative act" of formal amendment.

Marshall understood well, as Locke had taught, that words are the signs that represent or stand for the ideas in the minds of the men who use them. The "great object of language," Marshall argued, "is to communicate the intention of him who speaks," that is, to communicate the ideas from the mind of one person to the minds of others.[63] This is possible because the words used, especially in a law or a constitution, are understood as presenting "distinct ideas."[64] This was, by and large, simply a matter of common sense, in Marshall's view. One can only believe that "the mind impressed with a particular idea, readily employs those words which express it most appropriately."[65] It is always the desire of those framing "important instruments" such as laws and constitutions to use those words that most "directly and plainly express the cardinal intent." As Marshall argued, "it is rare indeed for a person of clear and direct perceptions,

---

the masters who give it, and of whom their servants hold it." John Marshall, "Speech in the Virginia Ratifying Convention, 10 June 1788," *Papers of John Marshall*, I: 267.

[61] *Marbury v. Madison*, 5 U.S. 137, 176.

[62] *Cohens v. Virginia*, 19 U.S. 264, 387, 399.

[63] *Marshall's Defense*, pp. 168–169.

[64] *Pennington v. Coxe*, 6 U.S. 33 (1804), 53.

[65] *The Brig Wilson v. United States* (United States Court of Appeals, 22 May 1820), *Papers of John Marshall*, IX: 34–35.

intending to convey one principal idea, so to express himself as to leave any doubt respecting that idea."[66]

To Marshall, these presumptions concerning language were especially valid when it came to the written Constitution. "As men . . . generally employ the words which most directly and aptly express the ideas they intend to convey," he wrote, "the enlightened patriots who framed our Constitution, and the people who adopted it, must be understood to have employed words in their natural sense and to have intended what they said." Thus when it comes to ascertaining the extent of powers or limitations under the Constitution, "it becomes necessary to settle the meaning of the words"[67] in order to discern the original intention. When it comes to interpretation properly understood, "the intention of the instrument must prevail; . . . this intention must be collected from its words; . . . its words are to be understood in the sense in which they are generally used by those for whom the instrument was intended; . . . its provisions are neither to be restricted into insignificance, nor extended to objects not comprehended in them, nor contemplated by its framers."[68] This original meaning or intention of the Constitution does not change with the fluctuations of time. The "peculiar circumstances of the moment," Marshall explained, "may render a measure more or less wise, but cannot render it more or less constitutional."[69]

These attributes of language, and especially of constitutional language, do not render the search for intention a simple matter. Such determinations of constitutional meaning "sometimes depend on a course of intricate and abstruse reasoning"[70] to move from text to intention, from the letter of the Constitution to its true spirit. The reason for the difficulty of interpretation is not the result of "some sinister design"[71] on the part of the penman, but rather the nagging "imperfection of human language,"[72] which means that the same words can mean different things depending upon the context of their usage. So, too, are there "nice shades and gradations" of meaning that can perplex the interpreter of an instrument.[73] Given these realities, when it comes to the search for the intention, everything that can be helpful is a matter of fair use: "The nature of the instrument, the words that are employed, the object to be effected, are all to be taken into consideration, and to have their due weight."[74]

---

[66] *Ogden v. Saunders*, 25 U.S. 213, 356.
[67] *Gibbons v. Ogden*, 22 U.S. 1, 188, 189.
[68] *Ogden v. Saunders*, 25 U.S. 213, 332.
[69] *Marshall's Defense*, pp. 190–191.
[70] Ibid., p. 156.
[71] Ibid., p. 85.
[72] *United States v. Burr* (United States Court of Appeals, 13 June 1807), *Papers of John Marshall*, VII: 40.
[73] *The Brig Wilson v. United States*, p. 34.
[74] *Marshall's Defense*, p. 169.

A Constitution We Are Expounding

The presumption of the permanence of constitutional language was the primary means whereby those who would be called upon to interpret the instrument would be kept chained to the original meaning. While the Constitution consisted of both letter and spirit, of both text and intention, the words had to hold sway as a curb to subjective excursions by those who would willingly supplant the framers' original meaning with one of their own. As Marshall explained it, "although the spirit of an instrument, especially of a constitution, is to be respected not less than its letter, yet the spirit is to be collected chiefly from its words."[75]

There was no doubting that on occasion some would try to invoke what they would insist to be "the spirit and true meaning of the Constitution" in order to reach the interpretive end they might seek; this would almost always be accomplished by ignoring the "plain" or "natural" meaning of the words actually used. In those cases, where the spirit or intention argued for is at odds with the literal language of the document, it would be necessary in order for the spirit or intention being invoked to prevail that it be "so apparent as to override words which its framers have employed." Otherwise, Marshall argued, the Court "would not feel itself authorized to disregard the plain meaning of words, in search of a conjectural intent to which we are not conducted by the language of any part of the Constitution." It would be all too easy to supplant the original meaning of the fundamental law by "some theory not to be found in the Constitution." That was why, in Marshall's opinion, the Court could never countenance "a construction of the Constitution not warranted by its words."[76]

It was precisely this sort of interpretive sleight-of-hand that characterized the approach of the states' rights advocates. They were all too willing to base their arguments against national power "not on the words of the Constitution, but on its spirit, a spirit extracted, not from the words of the instrument but from [their] view of the nature of the union and of the great fundamental principles on which the fabric stands." This was the essence of their argument on behalf of strict construction of the Constitution; it was demanded because, in their view, the Constitution did not in fact create a truly national government of full and complete powers, but instead had left largely in place the confederation in which the states, they argued, were still sovereign. At the core of the states' rights advocates' argument for strict construction was their belief that the Constitution had to be read literally, without any implied powers being attributed to it. If the Constitution did not, for example, explicitly extend to Congress the power to establish a

---

[75] *Sturges v. Crowninshield*, 17 U.S. 122, 202.
[76] *Cohens v. Virginia*, 19 U.S. 264, 379; *Craig v. Missouri*, 29 U.S. 410 (1830), 434; *Gibbons v. Ogden*, 22 U.S. 1, 188; *Dartmouth College v. Woodward*, 17 U.S. 518, 645.

national bank, then Congress did not have the power to create such an institution. It was against this view that Marshall sought to remind his brethren on the bench as well as the people of the country that it was imperative they "never forget that it is a constitution we are expounding."[77]

What distinguished a constitution from ordinary law, in Marshall's mind, was the absence of minute specificity. Had the framers undertaken to burden the fundamental law with "an accurate detail of all the subdivisions of which its great powers will admit, and of all the means by which they may be carried into execution," they would have succeeded in reducing the Constitution to a mere "legal code," the details of which "could scarcely be embraced by the human mind." The framers were too clever for that. Rather, they understood that the very nature of a constitution demanded that only "its great outlines should be marked, its important objects designated, and the minor ingredients which compose those objects, be deduced from the nature of the objects themselves." This was essential in that the framers understood that their Constitution was "intended to endure for ages to come, and consequently, to be adapted to the various crises of human affairs." Had the framers chosen instead to "have prescribed the means by which government should in all future time, execute its powers," they would have unwisely shackled the lawmakers by the chains of "immutable rules" and thus deprived the legislature "of the capacity to avail itself of experience, to exercise its reason, and to accommodate its legislation to circumstances."[78]

This is what Marshall meant when he described the Constitution as a fundamental law that was characterized by "enumeration . . . not . . . definition." While the government of the United States might be "emphatically . . . a government of laws, and not of men," there remained the necessity of leaving those men who would fill the offices sufficient discretion to choose the best means by which the Constitution's great objects could be achieved. The framers were prudent enough to include within the enumerated legislative powers that which granted to Congress the flexibility to pass all laws they might deem "necessary and proper" for carrying all the other powers into execution. "Let the end be legitimate," Marshall famously put it, "let it be within the scope of the Constitution, and all means which are appropriate, which are plainly adapted to that end, which are not prohibited, but consist with the letter and spirit of the Constitution, are constitutional."[79]

The "awful responsibility" of determining whether the legislative end sought was indeed legitimate and within the Constitution's scope, and whether the means chosen to effect that end were consistent with the text

---

[77] *Cohens v. Virginia*, 19 U.S. 264, 422; *McCulloch v. Maryland*, 17 U.S. 316, 407.
[78] Ibid., 407, 407, 415, 415.
[79] *Gibbons v. Ogden*, 22 U.S. 1, 189; *Marbury v. Madison*, 5 U.S. 137, 163; *McCulloch v. Maryland*, 17 U.S. 316, 423.

and intention of the Constitution, fell to the courts.[80] But the essence of the judicial duty "to say what the law is"[81] was not a power that extended to examining the substantive political motives of Congress in concluding that this law or that is truly necessary.[82] Such an inquiry as that, Marshall argued, "would be to pass the line which circumscribes the judicial department, and to tread on legislative ground."[83] The legislative motives behind the language did not matter.[84] The job of the judicial branch was to give the words of the Constitution, as well as those of the law in question, a "reasonable," "true," and "sound" construction.[85]

It was this understanding, so clearly and frequently expressed by Marshall, that so antagonized the defenders of states' rights; it antagonized them because it denied the compact theory of the Constitution, bereft of implied powers, that they tirelessly advocated. They sought not a "reasonable" but a "strict" construction. But they could do this, Marshall insisted, only by importing into the Constitution a theory that simply was not there. Not only was there not a word in the Constitution to suggest that the framers intended that "everything granted shall be expressly and minutely described,"[86] there was not even "one sentence" in the document that suggested that the framers intended that the enumerated powers "expressly granted by the people . . . ought to be construed strictly."[87] This was merely a case of the political wish being father to the constitutional thought. Had the framers intended such a restricted mode of interpretation or construction, they would undoubtedly have expressed that intention in clear and concise language. This they did not do, and thus were the courts free to give the Constitution a natural and fair construction, taking the words seriously and understanding that through those words the intention of the framers was to be found and followed. This was the limited sense of Marshall's proclamation that "[i]t is emphatically the province and duty of the judicial department to say what the law is."[88]

---

[80] *McCulloch v. Maryland*, 17 U.S. 316, 400.

[81] *Marbury v. Madison*, 5 U.S. 137, 177.

[82] As Marshall explained it: "Those political motives which induced the legislation . . . under particular circumstances, are not for judicial consideration." *Pennington v. Coxe*, 6 U.S. 33, 59.

[83] *McCulloch v. Maryland*, 17 U.S. 316, 423.

[84] When it came to weighing the substantive motives of the legislature, Marshall was clear: "On the policy of their motives . . . I am not to decide; such is their will and I am bound to obey it." *United States v. Burr, in Papers of John Marshall*, VII: 145.

[85] *Cohens v. Virginia*, 19 U.S. 264, 394–395.

[86] *McCulloch v. Maryland*, 17 U.S. 316, 406.

[87] *Gibbons v. Ogden*, 22 U.S. 1, 187. It was clear to Marshall that "the framers of the American Constitution omitted to use any restrictive term which might prevent its receiving a fair and just interpretation." *McCulloch v. Maryland*, 17 U.S. 316, 407.

[88] *Marbury v. Madison*, 5 U.S. 137, 177.

A Rule for the Government of Courts

Marshall's understanding of the nature and extent of the judicial power created by the Constitution was clear long before John Adams persuaded him to become the chief justice of the United States. In June of 1788, as a delegate to the Virginia Ratifying Convention in Richmond, Marshall defended a notion of judicial power under a written constitution that would later be the essence of his opinion in *Marbury v. Madison*. He understood, as Hamilton had argued in defense of the judiciary in *The Federalist*, that for a written constitution of fundamental and permanent principles to survive in practice there had to be an institution empowered to defend it. "To what quarter will you look for protection from an infringement on the Constitution," he asked the delegates, "if you will not give the power to the judiciary?"[89]

The courts were the only institution that could safely assume such a power, Marshall firmly believed. The reason, as he would later write, was that "judicial power, as contradistinguished from the power of the laws, has no existence."[90] In Hamiltonian terms, the courts "may truly be said to have neither force nor will but merely judgment."[91] And it would be by the exercise of their judgment that the judges would be able to protect the Constitution from legislative amendment. If the legislature, he told the convention, "were to make a law not warranted by any of the powers enumerated, it would be considered by the judges as an infringement of the Constitution which they are to guard," and, fittingly, "they would not consider such a law as coming under their jurisdiction" and would simply "declare it void."[92]

This fundamental judicial power "of preserving the Constitution as the permanent law of the land, even from legislative infractions," did not issue from the nature of judicial power abstractly considered, but from the nature of the particular constitution under which it was to be exercised. It derived from the fact that the Constitution was written. As Marshall would later explain at length in *Marbury*, "all those who have framed written constitutions contemplate them as forming the fundamental and paramount law of the nation." As a result, he went on, "the theory of every such government must be that an act of the legislature, repugnant to the Constitution, is void." The logic was clear: "This theory is essentially attached to a written constitution, and is consequently to be considered by this Court as one of the fundamental principles of our society." Indeed, this "great American principle, the judicial right to decide on the supremacy of the Constitution

[89] Marshall, "Speech in the Virginia Ratifying Convention, 20 June 1788," *Papers of John Marshall*, I: 277.

[90] *Osborn v. Bank of the United States*, 22 U.S. 738, 866.

[91] *The Federalist*, No. 78, p. 523.

[92] Marshall, "Speech in the Virginia Ratifying Convention, 20 June 1788," *Papers of John Marshall*, I: 277.

[is] a right which is inseparable from the idea of a permanent law, a written constitution." Such a power was "the very essence of judicial duty."[93]

Without the judicial power to enforce the supremacy of the Constitution against ordinary legislation, the "distinction between a government with limited and unlimited powers is abolished." It was thus the essential task of the judiciary to protect and perpetuate the Constitution as "a superior, paramount law, unchangeable by ordinary means." The failure to include such a power would have resulted in reducing such written constitutions to nothing more than "absurd attempts, on the part of the people, to limit a power, in its own nature, illimitable." But because in America the idea of written constitutions had been a matter of great political "reverence,"[94] the framers designed their written Constitution well. The courts were intended to be, as Hamilton had argued, "the bulwarks of a limited constitution against legislative encroachments."[95]

Even armed with so great a power, there was confidence that the judges would not "transcend the limits prescribed to the judicial department."[96] For one thing, the nature of the judicial power was such that the courts would not "unnecessarily and wantonly" assail the laws passed by the legislature.[97] Indeed, "the presumption is in favor of every legislative act and . . . the whole burden of proof lies on him who denies its constitutionality."[98] It would take more than "slight implication and vague conjecture" for the courts to assert that the legislature had "transcended its powers and its acts [were] to be considered void." The power to declare laws unconstitutional, Marshall insisted, should never be exercised in "a doubtful case," but only in those in which the "opposition between the Constitution and the law . . . be such that the judge feels a clear and strong conviction of their incompatibility with each other."[99]

The nature of the judicial power under the Constitution was largely defined by its extent. "Those who fill the judicial department," Marshall noted, "have no discretion in selecting the subjects to be brought before them." Nor do they have a "right to decline the exercise of jurisdiction, which is given . . . [any more] than to usurp that which is not given." Moreover, the courts are bound to say only "what the law is" and are never empowered, as the legislature is empowered, to "declare what the law shall be." It is the duty of the court "to discover the intention . . . and to respect

---

93 *Marshall's Defense*, p. 158.; *Marbury v. Madison*, 5 U.S. 137, 177, 178; *Marshall's Defense*, p. 209; *Marbury v. Madison*, 5 U.S. 137, 178.
94 *Marbury v. Madison*, pp. 176, 177, 177, 178.
95 *The Federalist*, No. 78, p. 526.
96 *United States v. Palmer*, 16 U.S. 610 (1818), 635.
97 *Ex Parte Randolph* (United States Court of Appeals, 21 December 1833), *Papers of John Marshall*, XII: 315.
98 *Brown v. Maryland*, 25 U.S. 419 (1827), 436.
99 *Fletcher v. Peck*, 10 U.S. 87, 128, 128.

that intention"; it is the intention of the lawgiver that ties down the judges. "Judicial power," Marshall argued, "is never exercised for the purpose of giving effect to the will of the judge" but "always for the purpose of giving effect to the will of the legislature, or, in other words, to the will of the law."[100]

The judges, Marshall insisted, must be ever mindful of the border between law and politics, recognizing that they must avoid issues that "are generally rather political than legal in their character."[101] There are simply some controversies that if resolved judicially would "savor too much the exercise of political power to be within the proper province of the judicial department."[102] The integrity of the judiciary depended upon the maintenance of this separation. "It is not for us to depart from the beaten path prescribed for us," Marshall admonished, "and to tread the devious and intricate path of politics."[103] And if the judges should be tempted to stray from the judicial fold, there would be the political fence provided by the Constitution itself. "Congress," Marshall pointed out in the Virginia Ratifying Convention, "is empowered to make exceptions to the appellate jurisdiction of the Supreme Court," and whatever exceptions Congress may make would "certainly go as far as the legislature may think proper, for the interest and liberty of the people."[104]

While the courts had a realm of discretion, it was discretion of a certain limited kind. The discretion of the courts, Marshall said, " is a mere legal discretion, a discretion to be exercised in discerning the course prescribed by law," and once that course is discerned, the courts are obligated "to follow it." What that means is that any "motion to the discretion of the court . . . is a motion not to its inclination, but to its judgment, and its judgment is to be guided by sound legal principles."[105]

The written Constitution was not to be altered by judicial construction any more than it was to be changed by ordinary legislative enactment. Judges no less than legislators and executives were understood to be bound by the framers' words and, thereby, by their intention. They were obligated to fulfill that intention, not to abandon or alter it. That was what Marshall meant when he concluded in *Marbury* that "the framers of the Constitution contemplated that instrument as a rule for the government of courts, as well

[100] *Worcester v. Georgia*, 31 U.S. 515 (1832), 541; *Cohens v. Virginia*, 19 U.S. 264, 404; *United States v. Palmer*, 16 U.S. 610, 634; *Pennington v. Coxe*, 6 U.S. 33, 59; *Osborn v. Bank of the United States*, 22 U.S. 738, 866.

[101] *United States v. Palmer*, 16 U.S. 610, 634.

[102] *Cherokee Nation v. Georgia*, 30 U.S. 1, 20.

[103] *The Nereide*, 13 U.S. 389 (1815), 422–423.

[104] Marshall, "Speech in the Virginia Ratifying Convention, 20 June 1788," *Papers of John Marshall*, I: 283.

[105] *Osborn v. Bank of the United States*, 22 U.S. 738, 866; *United States v. Burr*, in *Papers of John Marshall*, VII: 43.

as of the legislature." And that is why he understood the search for intention to be "the most sacred rule of interpretation."[106]

III. THE MOST SACRED RULE OF INTERPRETATION

As is clear from Marshall's writings on and off the bench, his approach to interpreting both the Constitution and the ordinary law was designed to discover the intention of the lawgiver. But in each case it was a quest for what he understood to be the objective intention; there was no place in his jurisprudence for subjective or private intention. A constitution especially, he believed, "ought to be construed *in its words*," and not in light of any of the framers' private opinions that "might have been expressed upon it." Marshall never varied in his stance that such "opinions... were not to regulate the construction of the Constitution, but its own words alone were to regulate the construction of it."[107] His standards of seeking to discern the "mind of the Convention," on the one hand, or the "mind of the legislature," on the other, did not mean discovering the personal views of the lawgivers. It meant only trying to understand the language they had actually used, and to discern the precise sense in which they had likely used it. The question was, what were they trying to achieve? Whatever the imperfections, the language of the law remained the most reliable guide to revealing the framers' true intention and original meaning.

Marshall brought to the interpretation of the Constitution the same methods that he used in the interpretation of statutes. These were rules of construction that had been "dictated by good sense, and sanctioned by immemorial usage;" indeed, they were rules that had been "consecrated by the wisdom of the ages." These rules of interpretation all derived from the simple truth that "[t]he words of an instrument, unless there be some sinister design which shuns the light, will always represent the intention of those who frame it." And these ancient rules all led logically from that premise to the conclusion that "the great duty of a judge who construes an instrument is to find the intention of its makers."[108]

The most basic underlying assumption of Marshall's rules of construction was that the words of every instrument mean something. The words used in laws and constitutions are not merely "empty sounds" and are "certainly not senseless." They are, rather, vehicles specifically chosen by the sovereign power to express its will, a will the sovereign wishes to be made known to those who must obey the particular law or constitutional provision. Given

[handwritten marginal note: Book on Orten Am.?]

---

[106] *Marbury v. Madison*, 5 U.S. 137, 179–180; *Marshall's Defense*, p. 167.
[107] John Marshall, "Speech in the Virginia Constitutional Convention, 13 January 1830," *Papers of John Marshall*, XI: 338.
[108] *The Mary Ann*, 21 U.S. 380 (1823), 387; *Sturges v. Crowninshield*, 17 U.S. 122, 206, *Marshall's Defense*, pp. 85, 168–169.

this purpose, it "cannot be presumed that any clause in the Constitution [or statute] is intended to be without effect."[109] And in some cases, the lawgiver actually succeeds in conveying his intention with clarity and precision.

"Where there is no ambiguity in the words," Marshall wrote, "there is no room for construction." When the language is plain, clear, and determinate, there need be nothing more than a straightforward literal construction of the words as used to discern their "plain and obvious meaning." That meaning will be found in the "common acceptation of language,"and the interpreter's task will be limited to an "inquiry into the meaning of words in common use." There will be those occasions when the words used are simply "incapable of being misunderstood."[110]

A literal construction of the plain and obvious meaning of the words is not to be taken lightly. When from the words used "the intent is plain, nothing is left for construction." But the temptation to depart from the plain meaning can be great. Given that it is a rule that "where great inconvenience will result from a particular construction, that construction is to be avoided," the inclination may well be to adjust the meaning accordingly in order to remove any perceived inconvenience, however slight. But for Marshall, that rule of avoiding an inconvenience was strictly limited; if "the meaning . . . be plain," it was to be obeyed whatever the inconvenience. The presumption should be that if the judge can see the inconvenience spawned by taking the plain language literally, so too must the lawgiver have seen it when the provision was contemplated in the first instance. Thus the judge in such circumstances must not by construction change terms that are "sufficiently intelligible" as to leave no doubt about the intention. Rather, it is to be presumed that the lawgiver concluded that, on reflection, the inconvenience caused by the provision "was probably overbalanced by the particular advantages it was calculated to produce."[111]

Marshall was firm on this limitation on the latitude of construction. "[I]f, in any case, the plain meaning of a provision, not contradicted by any other provision in the same instrument, is to be disregarded because we believe the framers of that instrument could not intend what they say, it must be one in which the absurdity and injustice of applying the provision to the case, would be so monstrous, that all mankind would, without hesitation, unite in rejecting the application." But for Marshall, not even the "abhorrent" and "unnatural" slave trade, which was clearly "contrary to the law of nature," was sufficient cause to "seduce" a court from its "path of duty" and justify

---

[109] *Craig v. Missouri*, 29 U.S. 410, 432; *Postmaster v. Early*, 25 U.S. 136, 148; *Marbury v. Madison*, 5 U.S. 137, 174.

[110] *United States v. Wiltberger*, 18 U.S. 76 (1820), 95–96; *Postmaster v. Early*, 25 U.S. 136, 148; *Cohens v. Virginia*, 19 U.S. 264, 408; *Sturges v. Crowninshield*, 17 U.S. 122, 197, 198.

[111] *United States v. Fisher*, 6 U.S. 358 (1805), 386, 386, 386, 390, 390.

it in ignoring the clear "mandate of the law" that rendered that odious trade legal. When intention was expressed with "irresistible clearness," a court was obliged to follow that intention even when the result might be that "rights are infringed," or "fundamental principles are overthrown," or "the general system of laws is departed from." It is only when the intention is not clear that a court might legitimately deny that the lawgiver could ever have intended "a design to effect such objects."[112]

The effort of the lawgiver to be clear and precise will not always succeed. Human language is simply too imperfect a medium. And from that "imperfection of human language," Marshall pointed out, "it frequently happens that sentences which ought to be the most explicit are of doubtful construction." Not only may meaning be lost in "a circuity of expression," but the very nature of words themselves admit of ambiguity in usage. "Such is the character of human language," Marshall noted, "that no word conveys to the mind, in all situations, one simple definite idea." Because "the same word has various meanings... the peculiar sense in which it is used in any sentence is to be determined by context."[113]

The consideration of the context of legal language as a means of determining the intended meaning was, in Marshall's estimation, one of "those plain rules laid down by common sense... which have been universally acknowledged."[114] It was a matter of taking the broad view of either the statute or the constitutional provision in its entirety and properly positioning the words in question. One of the clearest examples of Marshall's contextual search for constitutional meaning and intention is to be seen in his exegesis in *McCulloch v. Maryland* to determine the true meaning of "necessary" as used by the framers in the necessary and proper clause.

In the list of enumerated powers granted to Congress in the first article of the instrument, the framers of the Constitution saw fit to add one more, the power to "make all laws which shall be necessary and proper, for carrying into execution the foregoing powers, and all other powers vested by this Constitution, in the government of the United States, or in any department thereof." The state of Maryland, following the Jeffersonian script on this provision, insisted that this was the language of restriction, not of expansion, that the only plausible meaning was that Congress could pass only such laws as were absolutely or indispensably necessary to give effect to the other provisions. This was not a grant of broad discretion to the legislature, but the denial of it.

---

[112] *Sturges v. Crowninshield*, 17 U.S. 122, 202–203; *The Antelope*, 23 U.S. 66 (1825), 115–116, 120–121, 114; *United States v. Fisher*, 6 U.S. 358, 390, 390.

[113] *United States v. Burr*, in *Papers of John Marshall*, VII: 40; *United States v. Fisher*, 6 U.S. 358, 387; *McCulloch v. Maryland*, 17 U.S. 316, 414; *Cherokee Nation v. Georgia*, 30 U.S. 1, 19.

[114] *Pennington v. Coxe*, 6 U.S. 33, 52–53.

Marshall's refutation of this interpretation was dependent upon placing the phrase "necessary and proper" within its proper constitutional context. He did so in three steps. First, he undertook simply to point out the fact that there were several senses in which the word "necessary," taken alone, could be reasonably understood. Certainly it could mean an "absolute . . . necessity so strong that one thing to which another may be termed necessary, cannot exist without that other." But surely, Marshall noted, it is also often used in a less demanding sense, to mean "no more than that one thing is convenient, or useful, or essential to another." As the chief justice put it: "To employ the reasons necessary to an end, is generally understood as employing any means calculated to produce the end, and not as being confined to those simple means, without which the end would be entirely unattainable." The word "necessary," in and of itself, "has not a fixed character, peculiar to itself" but "admits of all degrees of comparison; and is often connected with other words, which increase or diminish the impression the mind receives of the urgency it imports." Thus he concluded, a "thing may be necessary, very necessary, absolutely or indispensably necessary."[115]

Second, the framers of the Constitution were quite capable of making explicitly clear those differences between the possible meanings of "necessary." For example, the framers restricted the states from laying imposts and exposts without the consent of Congress "except what may be absolutely necessary for executing its inspection laws." As Marshall shrewdly pointed out, surely in that instance "the Convention understood itself to change materially the meaning of the word 'necessary' by prefixing the word 'absolutely'."[116] Had they intended to suggest that the necessary and proper clause was similarly limited to those acts that were "absolutely necessary," they clearly were capable of saying so.

Finally, there was yet another contextual fact for determining the true meaning of the word "necessary" within the necessary and proper clause. Had the clause as a whole been intended by the Convention as a restriction on the powers of Congress, surely they would not have placed it "among the powers of Congress . . . [but] among the limitations on those powers." Had the intention been to make the clause restrictive, "it would unquestionably have been so in form as well as effect."[117] That the clause was placed in the eighth section of the first article enumerating the powers of Congress, and not in the ninth section listing the limitations on Congress's powers, was deeply significant for determining the framers' intended meaning.

Marshall was always guided by what he called the necessity of a "fair construction" of any instrument that was to be interpreted and applied. By "fair construction" he meant one "which gives to language the sense in

[115] *McCulloch v. Maryland*, 17 U.S. 316, 413, 413, 413–414, 414.
[116] Ibid., 415.
[117] Ibid., 419, 420.

which it is used." By that he meant that the states' rights advocates' demand for a strict construction was unacceptable, but so too was any demand for an expansive interpretation that would go beyond what the framers had in mind. The proper standard was that "medium between that restricted sense which confines the meaning of words to narrower limits than the common understanding the world affixes to them, and that extended sense which would stretch them beyond their obvious import." To confine the meaning or to expand the meaning would be to sacrifice the true meaning and original intention of the lawgivers to theories or policies other than those that had moved them. But there was no denying that there might be instances where a literal or an obvious contextual construction would not succeed in revealing the original meaning or intention. In those instances, a "fair construction" would require more of a judge if effect was to be given to the purpose of the instrument.[118]

The focus of the interpreter's attention – beyond the plain and common meaning of the words used, and beyond light that might be shed on their meaning by the context of the words – must be on the objects that the framers of an instrument sought to achieve. What were the purposes of the provision? No legal instrument, not least a constitution, is ever created purposelessly. There were mischiefs to be addressed, problems to be corrected. Attention to those ends can cast constructive illumination back on the words used and help to make clear the lawgivers' intentions. A case in point in Marshall's jurisprudence came in *Trustees of Dartmouth College v. Woodward.*

At issue in the college case was the clause of the Constitution prohibiting the states from passing "any . . . law impairing the obligation of contracts." While there was no doubt that the state laws interfering with the sanctity of contracts were one of the primary concerns that had led to the new Constitution, there was nothing in the text of the Constitution itself offering any definition as to what sort of contracts were to be included within the language of the clause. For Marshall, there was no doubt that the purpose of the contracts clause was reasonably clear: "these words were introduced to give stability to contracts." The question he confronted in the case itself was whether those words were to be construed to exclude protecting contracts such as the one at issue at the college, which was something rather different from the "ordinary contracts between man and man."[119]

Marshall's opinion in the Dartmouth College case was an example of how the objects sought could be brought to bear on the interpretation of constitutional language. Marshall began by stating the situation. "[A]lthough a particular and rare case may not, in itself, be of sufficient magnitude to induce a rule, yet it must be governed by the rule, when established, unless

[118] *Marshall's Defense*, pp. 92, 92, 167.
[119] *Dartmouth College v. Woodward*, 17 U.S. 518, 645, 647.

some plain and strong reason for excluding it can be given."[120] The question came down to just what was in "the mind of the Convention" when the delegates crafted the clause protecting the obligation of contracts. For Marshall, the way to answer this question was clear:

It is not enough to say, that this particular case was not in the mind of the Convention, when the article was framed, nor of the American people, when it was adopted. It is necessary to go farther, and to say that, had this particular case been suggested, the language would have been so varied as to exclude it, or it would have been made a special exception. The case being within the words of the rule, must be within its operation likewise, unless there be something in the literal construction so obviously absurd, or mischievous, or repugnant to the general spirit of the instrument, as to justify those who expound the Constitution in making it an exception.

And therein lay the complication. "On what safe and intelligible ground," Marshall asked, "can this exception stand?"

There is no expression in the Constitution, no sentiment delivered by its contemporaneous expounders, which would justify us in making it. In the absence of all authority of this kind, is there in the nature and reason of the case itself, that which would sustain a construction of the Constitution not warranted by its words? Are contracts of this description of a character to excite so little interest, that we must exclude them from the provisions of the Constitution, as being unworthy of the attention of those who framed the instrument? Or does public policy so imperiously demand their remaining exposed to legislative alterations, as to compel us, or rather permit us to say, that these words which were introduced to give stability to contracts, and which in their plain import comprehend this contract, must yet be so construed, as to exclude it?[121]

Marshall thought not. Such a conclusion could be reached only by ignoring the clear language of the Constitution and denying the objects the framers sought to achieve; it could be reached only by "a forced construction of that instrument."[122]

The tension between text and intention, between the words of the Constitution and its spirit, in one sense rested upon the premise that the framers meant what they said. The other side of that formulation also held true: the framers did not mean what they did not say. And to Marshall, it was part of the judicial duty to make certain that the spirit of the Constitution – even when that spirit was generally accurately discerned – is not allowed to control the language by adding to the meaning of the text an intention the framers clearly did not hold. This was demonstrated by Marshall in his last constitutional case, *Barron v. Baltimore.*

---

[120] Ibid., 644.
[121] Ibid., 644–645.
[122] Ibid., 645.

It would be hard to think of a set of facts more likely to touch Marshall's natural sympathies, or that would better comport with his general view of individual property rights under the Constitution, than those surrounding the fate of John Barron's wharf. Barron had seen the value of his wharf destroyed when the city of Baltimore altered the natural course of certain streams; the wharf was rendered useless. Barron had sued under the Fifth Amendment's clause prohibiting the taking of private property for public use without just compensation. Chief Justice Marshall denied his claim, and he did so based on the import of the language of the Bill of Rights. "These amendments," Marshall concluded, "contain no expression indicating an intention to apply them to the state governments." Absent such an expressed intention, he said, "[t]his Court cannot so apply them."[123]

The history of the amendments, and the objects they were intended to achieve, were the controlling factors in Marshall's refusal to extend their reach by implication. "The Constitution," he argued, "was ordained and established by the people of the United States for themselves, for their own government, and not for the government of the individual states." In creating the Constitution, the people conferred both powers to be exercised by, and limitations to be imposed on, their government. Where they also sought to restrict the power of the individual states in the body of the original Constitution, they did so with "words...which directly express that intent." This was not the case with the first ten amendments to the Constitution, which in fact had been demanded as "security against the apprehended encroachments of the general government – not against those of the local governments." There was no reason for "departing from...[the] safe and judicious course" of using language precisely. "Had the framers of these amendments intended them to be limitations on the powers of the state governments, they would have imitated the framers of the original Constitution and have expressed that intention...in plain and intelligible language."[124] The Court could not add an extended meaning to the original intention, even if they thought that might well serve the interests of justice and the security of property rights.

As significant as were the controversies in such cases as *McCulloch*, *Dartmouth*, and *Barron*, they were not issues, in Marshall's mind, that were plagued by ambiguities of language. But there would be cases, he knew, "in which the literal construction of an act is opposed to its spirit, and would defeat, in part, the object of the legislature." In the same way that intention should not control the words, neither should the words be allowed to thwart the intention. Such would be the case in a situation "in which words of some ambiguity are used, which, construed according to their common

---

[123] *Barron v. Baltimore*, 32 U.S. 243 (1833), 250.
[124] Ibid., 247, 249, 250, 250.

acceptation, would not reach a case within the mischief intended to be provided against." In those cases, the literal meaning of the words would have to be construed in light of reasonable conjectures about the true intention of the framers. When the legal or constitutional language was "sufficiently ambiguous to admit of different constructions among intelligent gentlemen of the [legal] profession,"[125] the duty of a judge would be to depart from the plain meaning in order to make the language comport with the true intention.

The rule in such cases, however, to Marshall's way of thinking, was clear; this was not to be done frivolously or routinely. "The case must be a strong one indeed," he insisted, "which would justify a court in departing from the plain meaning of the words . . . in search of an intention the words themselves did not suggest." But when such ambiguity exists, or when "words conflict with each other" or where "the different clauses of an instrument . . . would be inconsistent unless the natural and common import of the words be varied," then such a conjectural construction "becomes necessary, and a departure from the obvious meaning of words is justifiable." But in those cases, the "change of language . . . ought to be as small as possible, and [made] with a view to the sense of the legislature, as manifested by themselves." In no instance is such textual ambiguity a warrant for unbound judicial creativity. The task of the judge is merely to reconcile the text and intention in the same way the original lawgivers would have done had they been aware of the ambiguity in their language that would later surface. Only the words are to be adjusted to conform to the intention; never is the intention to be abandoned. Indeed, Marshall argued, "the cardinal rule of construction is, that where any doubt exists, the intent . . . if it can be plainly perceived, ought to be pursued."[126]

The importance of a focus on language as the point of access to the lawgivers' intention was as a barrier to those who would undertake by construction to smuggle into the Constitution theories foreign to it. As Hobbes and Locke had derided those of their day who would abuse words by interpretation, so Marshall saw the same dangers posed by those of a similar bent in his day. "Powerful and ingenious minds," he warned, "may by a course of well digested but refined and metaphysical reasoning . . . so entangle and perplex the understanding, as to obscure principles which were before thought quite plain, and induce doubts where, if the mind were to pursue its own course, none would be perceived."[127] Marshall saw as one such possibility

---

[125] *Coates's Executor v. Muses's Administrators* (United States Court of Appeals, 12 June 1822), *Papers of John Marshall*, IX: 213, 213, 212.
[126] *United States v. Wiltberger*, 18 U.S. 76, 96; *Sturges v. Crowninshield*, 17 U.S. 122, 202; *Huidekoper's Lessee v. Douglas*, 7 U.S. 1 (1805), 66; *Postmaster v. Early*, 25 U.S. 136, 152.
[127] *Gibbons v. Ogden*, 22 U.S. 1, 222.

the preposterous notion that "the Constitution meant to prohibit names and not things."[128] In the instant case, the issue was the Constitution's clear and unambiguous prohibition that "[n]o state shall... emit bills of credit." The state of Missouri had issued "certificates" that they carefully did not designate as "bills of credit." Marshall was not fooled. The language of the Constitution prohibiting states from "emitting bills of credit" was sufficient to "comprehend the emission of any paper medium, by the state government, for the purpose of common circulation." The distinction between Missouri's "certificates" and "bills of credit" was meaningless. "Had they been termed 'bills of credit' instead of 'certificates'," Marshall pointed out, "nothing would have been wanting to bring them within the prohibitory words of the Constitution." For Marshall, the conclusion was obvious: "We think the certificates emitted under the authority of this act [of Missouri] are as entirely bills of credit as if they had been so denominated in the act itself."[129]

When it came to construing the Constitution, the rule was plain. The idea that "the Constitution, in one of its most important provisions, may be openly evaded by giving a new name to an old thing" was simply absurd.[130] The words used by the Constitution were intended by the framers to stand for specific ideas; and those ideas were not to be ignored by insisting that it was the words alone, and not the ideas behind them, that were the objects of the framers' intentions. The Constitution was meant to prohibit not simply names but the things behind those names.

Marshall's rules of construction were ultimately derived from the common law tradition with which he was so intimately familiar. In particular, their roots were to be found in that common law treatise most influential with the American founding generation, Blackstone's *Commentaries on the Laws of England*. In Blackstone's view, as in Marshall's, the point of departure in interpreting legal instruments was the determination of the intention of the lawgiver. "The fairest and most rational method to interpret the will of the legislator," Blackstone argued, following the rules laid down by writers from Grotius to Pufendorf to Rutherforth, "is by exploring his intentions at the time when the law was made, by *signs* the most natural and probable." Like the other writers, Blackstone understood that "these signs are either the words, the context, the subject matter, the effects and consequences, or the spirit and reason of the law."[131]

Marshall had taken from Blackstone the idea that as a judge moved from the words, "understood in their usual and most known signification," to the more abstract reason and spirit of the law, "the causes which moved the

---

[128] *Craig v. Missouri*, 29 U.S. 410, 433.

[129] Ibid., 432, 433, 433.

[130] Ibid., 433.

[131] William Blackstone, *Commentaries on the Laws of England*, 4 vols. (8th ed.; Oxford: Clarendon Press, 1778), I: 59.

legislator to enact it," construction moved from the sign with the greatest certainty to that sign most likely to depend upon some degree of conjecture. Even though, for Blackstone, this recourse to the reason and spirit of the law was to be taken "when the words are dubious," it was also, in his view, "the most universal and effectual way of discovering the true meaning of the law" in that it was most clearly the true "intention" of the lawgiver, in its most obvious sense. So significant was this reason and spirit of the law that "where this reason ceases, the law itself ought likewise to cease with it."[132]

The purpose of binding judges to the intention of the lawgiver, for both Blackstone and Marshall, was to reduce the possibility that the judges' constructions or interpretations of the law would be based on nothing more substantial than the "arbitrary will" of the judges. By relying on the meaning of public words as the route to the intention of the lawgiver, judges would, it was hoped, be restrained from resting their judgments on their "private sentiments." If this were not the case, and if "the decision of every question" was to be found "in the breast of the judge," the effect, Blackstone said, would be to "make every judge a legislator." The effect of this would be "to set the judicial power above that of the legislature which would be subversive of all government."[133]

Marshall's great achievement was to adapt Blackstone's rules of construction meant for the municipal law of England to fit the needs of the new written American Constitution. This he did by building upon Blackstone's "Hobbesian premises"[134] as to both human nature and the nature of law. For as Hobbes had taught, the only "authentique interpretation" of the law is the one that gives effect to "the sense of the legislator." If the judges be not so restrained, then "by the craft of an interpreter, the law may be made to beare a sense contrary to that of the sovereign; by which means the interpreter becomes the legislator."[135] For Marshall no less than for Hobbes, such an outcome would be simply "unjust."[136]

IV. JOSEPH STORY AND THE LEGACY OF JOHN MARSHALL

For all his success on the Court, Marshall faced his last years with a nagging melancholy over the future of the republic. He was sure he had failed to preserve, protect, and defend the Constitution he had always held to be sacred. "I yield slowly and reluctantly to the conviction," he confided to

---

[132] Ibid., I: 59, 61, 61, 61.
[133] Ibid., I: 142, 69, 62, 91.
[134] Michael Lobban, "Blackstone and the Science of Law," *The Historical Journal* 30 (1987): 311–335, p. 325.
[135] Thomas Hobbes, *Leviathan* (Oxford: Clarendon Press, 1909), pp. 211–212, 56.
[136] Ibid., p. 208.

Joseph Story, "that our Constitution cannot last." He was convinced that North and South alike had come to be corrupted by "the political creed of Virginia." Marshall's hopes that north of the Potomack "national liberty" might be preserved had been dashed. "The union has been prolonged by miracles," he told Story. "I [fear] they cannot continue."[137]

Any hope for the future Marshall had was largely placed in the works of Story himself, not least in his *Commentaries on the Constitution of the United States.* When the treatise appeared in 1833, Marshall was thrilled with the work – as well he should have been. Story's masterpiece was nothing short of a monument to Marshall and his constitutional jurisprudence. "I am certain, in advance," Marshall wrote to Story, "that I shall read every sentence with entire approbation. [The Constitution] is a subject on which we concur exactly. Our opinions on it are... identical."[138]

Marshall wrote again to confirm his first impressions once he had read the *Commentaries.* Story's "great work," he told his friend, "is a comprehensive and an accurate commentary on our Constitution, formed in the spirit of the original text." He wished, he said, that "it could be read by every statesman and every would be statesman in the United States."[139]

Marshall was equally thrilled when Story's publisher produced an abridged version for use in the schools, although he feared that "South of the Potomack, where it is most wanted, it will be least used." In his beloved Virginia, he confessed, "we are so far gone in political metaphysics that... no demonstration can restore us to common sense." They were still "gathering the bitter [states' rights] fruits of the tree... planted by Mr. Jefferson." When it came to Virginia and the South generally, Marshall told Story, "[o]ur young men... grow up in the firm belief that liberty depends on construing our Constitution into a league instead of a government; that is has nothing to fear from breaking these United States into numerous petty republics." It at least gave Marshall some enjoyment to think how it "would give our orthodox nullifier a fever to read the heresies of your *Commentaries.*"[140]

One of the most important aspects of Story's *Commentaries on the Constitution of the United States* was its explication and elaboration of rules of interpretation for the fundamental law. In that important chapter, Story was able to perpetuate those rules Marshall had developed over so many years

---

[137] Marshall to Story, 22 September 1832, *Papers of John Marshall*, XII: 238; 25 December 1832, *Papers of John Marshall*, XII: 248; 22 September 1832, *Papers of John Marshall*, XII: 238, 238.

[138] Marshall to Story, 25 December 1832, *Papers of John Marshall*, XII: 247.

[139] Marshall to Story, 31 July 1833, *Papers of John Marshall*, XII: 291.

[140] Marshall to Story, 24 April 1833, *Papers of John Marshall*, XII: 273; 31 July 1833, *Papers of John Marshall*, XII: 291; 25 December 1832, *Papers of John Marshall*, XII: 249; 3 June 1833, *Papers of John Marshall*, XII: 281; 24 April 1833, *Papers of John Marshall*, XII: 273.

on the Supreme Court. Not least was he able to make clear that the plain meaning of the Constitution was not to fluctuate with the times, but was to have "a fixed, uniform, permanent construction," and was to be "the same, yesterday, to-day, and forever."[141] The Founders' Constitution, as Marshall had taught, was to be deemed both fundamental and permanent.

[141] Joseph Story, *Commentaries on the Constitution of the United States*, 2 vols. (3rd ed.; Boston: Little, Brown and Co., 1858), I. 426. 303. (Citation indicates volume, section, and page number.)

8

The Same Yesterday, Today, and Forever

Joseph Story and the Permanence of Constitutional Meaning

The death of Chief Justice John Marshall on July 6, 1835, left Joseph Story, his closest judicial colleague, in "wretched spirits." While there were rumors that Story might succeed Marshall to the chief justiceship (a hope Marshall clearly harbored), Story himself insisted that he "never for a moment imagined" such would be the case, thus leaving him "equally beyond hope or anxiety."[1] Story was too politically shrewd to delude himself into thinking that President Andrew Jackson would somehow bestow such an honor on him, whatever his own secret hopes truly might have been. Their constitutional views were too widely separated, and the president had made clear, as Story's son would later recall, that the "school of Story and Kent . . . could hope for but little favor at his hands."[2] It was no surprise when Jackson filled Marshall's seat with a true Jacksonian, his own former attorney general and secretary of the treasury, Roger Brooke Taney of Maryland. From that moment, Story would increasingly come to see himself as "the last of the old race of judges."[3]

Amid his own considerable personal grief, it fell to Story publicly to remember and to eulogize his great friend, stalwart colleague, and influential mentor; and he did so in a way that could only have confirmed Jackson's confidence in his own political instincts. Marshall, Story told the assembled members of the Suffolk bar on October 15, 1835, was not merely "the highest boast and ornament of the [legal] profession," but was as near "perfect" a man as Story had ever known, characterized as the late chief justice was by "a rare combination of virtues."[4]

---

[1] Joseph Story to Richard Peters, 24 July 1835, in William W. Story, ed., *Life and Letters of Joseph Story*, 2 vols. (Boston: C. C. Little and J. Brown, 1851), II: 201, 202, 203. Hereinafter cited as *Life and Letters*.

[2] *Life and Letters*, II: 208.

[3] Joseph Story to Harriet Martineau, 7 April 1837, *Life and Letters*, II: 277.

[4] Joseph Story, "Life, Character, and Services of Chief Justice Marshall," in William W. Story, ed., *The Miscellaneous Writings of Joseph Story* (Boston: C. C. Little and J. Brown, 1852), pp. 640, 677. Hereinafter cited as *Miscellaneous Writings*.

That combination of virtues included what Story described as the "inflexible integrity" that allowed Marshall through all the years on the Court to maintain "the same political principles with which he began." Those principles, Story insisted, had sprung from Marshall's "thorough mastery" of the intricacies of free government "between the close of the war of the Revolution, and the adoption of the present constitution of the United States," and they were the principles that would constitute "the basis of all the public actions of his subsequent life." That mastery included an intuitive sense of "the dangers incident to free institutions," an ability to see clearly where "the weaknesses of the republic lay," and a commitment to the Union so strong that he "nailed its colors to the mast of the Constitution,"[5]

Marshall's unrivaled greatness as "the Expounder" of the Constitution, Story insisted, grew from his view that "the republic is not destined to perish ... by the overwhelming power of the national government; but by the resisting and counteracting powers of the state sovereignties." Marshall's unfaltering dedication as a judge was to ensure the "perpetuity of the Constitution" which he believed was the "only solid foundation" of America's "national glory and independence." And there was, in Story's estimation, clear proof of the rightness of that view. When Marshall "first took his seat on the bench," Story reminded his distinguished audience, "scarcely more than two or three questions of constitutional law had ever engaged the attention of the Supreme Court." Three decades later, after Marshall's careful exposition of the Constitution "wrought out by general principles," the nation had "risen ... from a feeble republic to a wide-spreading empire." Such an accomplishment was enough for the people to remember Marshall not merely as "a great man," but as someone who "would have been deemed a great man in any age, and of all ages."[6]

Not only would Story's remembrance of Marshall likely have confirmed Jackson's view of him late in his judicial career, but so, too, would it have confirmed Thomas Jefferson's opinion of the then-young Massachusetts lawyer when his name first surfaced as a possible replacement for Justice William Cushing. When "old Cushing" died in September 1810, Jefferson rather heartlessly deemed it a most "fortunate" event, opening the real possibility that he could finally orchestrate "a Republican majority in the Supreme judiciary." But that would be no slight task. Jefferson never doubted how difficult it would be "to find a character of firmness enough to preserve his independence on the same bench with Marshall." When it came to Story, Jefferson thought him "too young" for the post; more important, he believed the thirty-two-year-old lawyer from Salem to be "unquestionably a Tory."[7]

5 Ibid., pp. 682–683, 651, 650, 684, 683.
6 Ibid., pp. 694, 684, 684, 695, 695, 661, 685.
7 Thomas Jefferson to Albert Gallatin, 27 September 1810 (III: 124); Thomas Jefferson to James Madison, 25 May 1810 (II: 416); Thomas Jefferson to James Madison, 15 October 1810 (III: 166), all in J. Looney, ed., *The Papers of Thomas Jefferson: Retirement Series*,

Even though Story was nominally a Republican, he had displayed too much of an independent spirit to be trusted, in Jefferson's opinion. During his brief time as a member of the United States House of Representatives, Story not only had opposed Jefferson's embargo against Britain, but had dared to speak out against it. Jefferson viewed the subsequent repeal of the embargo as the direct result of Story's perfidy and as "a wound on our interests that can never be cured." Story's disloyalty was simply unforgivable, and Jefferson never ceased to think of him as nothing more than a mere "pseudo-Republican."[8] Such an unreliable man hardly deserved a life-tenured appointment to the nation's highest court, and Jefferson was prepared to do anything to block it.[9] Fate was to thwart him.

Joseph Story became the youngest person ever to serve on the Supreme Court nearly by accident. President Madison, at least in partial deference to Jefferson, first offered the Cushing seat to Levi Lincoln, a Massachusetts lawyer who had served as Jefferson's attorney general. Lincoln was high on Jefferson's list as an undoubtedly sound and trustworthy nominee. The former president believed he would be a justice characterized by "integrity... & unimpeachable character" and not least by "political firmness" – that is to say, by "firm republicanism." Knowing Lincoln was likely to be "inflexible"[10] in declining the nomination for personal reasons, Madison implored him to accept this new job for the good of the country, insisting that Lincoln would take his "learning, principles, and weight to a Department which has so much influence on the course of our political system." In November, as expected, Lincoln declined the appointment due to his "encreasing years & difficulty of sight." He felt strongly that he had to confine his "future action to the narrow limits of private life."[11]

Vexed by the heated politicking surrounding the vacancy – generated both by Republicans pushing their favorite candidates and by Federalists making all they could of his apparent indecisiveness – the president sought to

---

4 vols. to date (Princeton, NJ: Princeton University Press, 2004–). Hereinafter cited as *Jefferson Retirement Papers.*

[8] Thomas Jefferson to General Dearborne, 16 July 1810, *Jefferson Retirement Papers*, II: 537–538, p. 537. Jefferson's public assessment of Story as a "pseudo-republican" came from beyond the grave, as it were. It appeared in the first collection of Jefferson's papers and correspondence published in 1829. (See Chapter 6 of this volume, above.) In his "Autobiography," Story was blunt in his response: "'Pseudo-republican' of course, I must be; as every one was in Mr. Jefferson's opinion, who dared to venture upon a doubt of his infallibility." Joseph Story, "Autobiography," *Miscellaneous Writings*, p. 33.

[9] For an account of Story's nomination, see Morgan D. Dowd, "Justice Joseph Story and the Politics of Appointment," *American Journal of Legal History* 9 (1965): 265–285.

[10] Jefferson to Gallatin, 27 October 1810 (III: 125); James Madison to Thomas Jefferson, 19 October 1810 (III: 178); Jefferson to Madison, 15 October 1810 (III: 165), all in *Jefferson Retirement Papers.*

[11] James Madison to Levi Lincoln, 20 October 1810 (II: 588); Levi Lincoln to James Madison, 27 November 1810 (III: 29), both in R. Rutland and J. Stagg, eds., *The Papers of James Madison: Presidential Series*, 4 vols. to date (Charlottesville: University Press of Virginia, 1984–).

persuade Lincoln to accept what would be an agreed interim appointment for the good of the party until Madison could see the bench happily filled with a more fitting regular appointment. He even went so far as to submit Lincoln's nomination to the Senate (without Lincoln's knowledge or approval), which immediately confirmed him on January 3, 1811. But Lincoln still refused to serve.

Madison then nominated Alexander Wolcott. The president's critics in the Federalist press pounced on what was an obviously political nomination, denouncing it as being "disgusting to the moral sense of the community."[12] The Senate quickly and overwhelmingly rejected Wolcott. In response, the president turned to John Quincy Adams, a former Federalist but most recently an independent who on occasion had politically supported Jefferson and Madison. Adams's nomination was formally submitted to the Senate in February and was unanimously confirmed. But Adams, like Lincoln, declined. Not only did he prefer to continue in his diplomatic post as minister in St. Petersburg, but his eye was on the presidency, not the judiciary. But it was not until June that Madison learned of Adams's disappointing refusal to accept the appointment. Things slowed but continued to grind on concerning the now nearly year-old vacancy. Finally, on November 15, 1811, President Madison sent Joseph Story's name to the Senate, where the nomination was quickly confirmed. Jefferson's worst fears were about to come true.

Story would serve on the Supreme Court for thirty-four years, twenty-five of those at Marshall's side. During his tenure, Story would write opinions in 286 cases: 269 of those were either the opinion of the Court or for the majority; three were concurrences; and fourteen were dissents.[13] Although they were not always in agreement, they were so close so often that Albert Beveridge concluded that "in the work of building the American nation, Marshall and Story may be considered one and the same person."[14] Together they laid an enduring foundation for much of American constitutional law in such landmark cases as *McCulloch v. Maryland, Dartmouth College v. Woodward, Cohens v. Virginia,* and *Gibbons v. Ogden.* And Story was there to concur when the chief justice offered his only dissent in a constitutional case, *Ogden v. Saunders,* as well as to write the opinion in the seminal case of *Martin v. Hunter's Lessee* [15] (from which Marshall recused himself), which anticipated both *McCulloch v. Maryland* and *Cohens v. Virginia.* And in

---

[12] As quoted in Charles Warren, *The Supreme Court in United States History,* 3 vols. (Boston: Little and Brown, 1922), I: 411.

[13] Elizabeth Kelley Bauer, *Commentaries on the Constitution, 1790–1860* (New York: Columbia University Press, 1952), p. 141.

[14] Albert Beveridge, *The Life of John Marshall,* 4 vols. (Boston: Houghton Mifflin, 1919), IV: 96.

[15] 17 U.S. 316 (1819); 17 U.S. 518 (1819); 19 U.S. 264 (1821); 22 U.S. 1 (1824); 25 U.S. 213 (1827); 14 U.S. 304 (1816).

the nine years he remained on the Court after Marshall's passing he would continue to do constitutional battle with the Taney Court in such cases as *Charles River Bridge v. Warren Bridge.*[16]

Jefferson's antipathy toward Story was not simply a matter of differences over various public policies. It was deeper than that. What concerned Jefferson most was the theory of judging and the understanding of the nature and extent of federal judicial power that were likely to be held by Story. From his earliest days, Jefferson had voiced his belief that in a republic a judge should be a "mere machine"[17] who would interpret constitutions and laws as they had been written, seeing himself strictly bound by the intentions of those who had framed them. The greatest danger posed to that view came from the common law in the hands of judges who would see that body of judge-made law as liberating them from the chains of legal or constitutional intention.

Ultimately, the focus of Jefferson's jurisprudential ire was the celebrated Sir William Blackstone, whose *Commentaries on the Laws of England* were said during the American founding to have been "a book which is in every man's hand."[18] Those four volumes had smuggled in a most pernicious political influence, Jefferson believed. "When ... the honied Mansfieldism of Blackstone became the student's hornbook," Jefferson later told Madison, "from that moment, that profession ... began to slide into toryism, and nearly all the young brood of lawyers now are of that hue."[19]

Jefferson's fear of the corrupting influence of the common law was not a matter of his imagination. The battle fought by the Republicans against the Federalists over the Alien and Sedition Acts in 1798 and 1799 had left him with deep scars. The idea that the common law was somehow "in force & cognizable" as an existing law in the federal courts was not merely a "formidable" notion but was nothing less than an "audacious, barefaced, and sweeping pretention."[20] To have on the Supreme Court a common lawyer who might share that "pretention" was no small risk to the

---

[16] 36 U.S. 420 (1837).

[17] Thomas Jefferson to Edmund Pendleton, 26 August 1776, in Merrill Peterson, ed., *Jefferson: Writings* (New York: Library of America, 1984), p. 757. Hereinafter cited as *Jefferson: Writings.*

[18] James Madison in the Virginia Ratifying Convention, in Jonathan Elliot, ed., *Debates in the Several State Conventions on the Adoption of the Federal Constitution,* 5 vols. (Philadelphia: J. B. Lippincott & Co., 1876), III: 501.

[19] Thomas Jefferson to James Madison, 17 February 1826, *Jefferson: Writings,* pp. 1513–1514.

[20] Thomas Jefferson to Edmund Randolph, 18 August 1799, *Jefferson: Writings,* p. 1066. For an expanded discussion of the tensions between the Constitution and the common law, see "The Constitution and the Common Law in the Early Republic," in Gary L. McDowell, *Equity and the Constitution: The Supreme Court, Equitable Relief, and Public Policy* (Chicago: University of Chicago Press, 1982), pp. 51–69.

constitutional republic of limited and enumerated powers as Jefferson and his party understood it.

There was no denying that Joseph Story was the common lawyer's common lawyer. He had published in 1805 his *Selection of Pleadings in Civil Actions*[21] and had offered new editions of common law treatises that he had updated for his American colleagues.[22] But his affection for the common law, was not rooted in a desire to liberate judicial power; rather, it was quite the opposite. The common law with its myriad procedural niceties and doctrinal complexities, was in fact a sound means of restraining judicial power. Story generally agreed with Chancellor James Kent's view that it was precisely those complexities of the common law that rendered it "a safe guide," one that would deny judges "a dangerous discretion... to roam at large in the trackless field of their own imaginations."[23] And that would be the fundamental lesson Story would draw from the common law tradition in shaping his understanding of the rules of interpretation concerning the written and ratified Constitution.[24]

I. STORY AND THE COMMON LAW

Like many a young lawyer of his day, Story's entry into his chosen profession was not without its rough patches. The scheme of legal education under which he trained, that of "reading" the law in a practitioner's office, was usually a solitary affair, one the success of which depended primarily upon the attention given the student by the mentor.[25] Story, in fact, fared better

---

[21] (Salem, MA: B. B. Macanulty, 1805).

[22] *A Practical Treatise on Bills of Exchange: New Edition from the Second Corrected and Enlarged London Edition with the Addition of Recent English and American Cases by Joseph Story*, by Joseph Chitty (Boston: Farrand, Mallory, 1809); *A Treatise of the Law Relative to Merchant Ships and Seamen: Second American from the Third English Edition with Annotations by Joseph Story*, by Charles Abbott (Newburyport, MA: Edward Little & Co., 1810); and *A Practical Treatise on Pleading, in Assumpsit, with the Addition of American Decisions by Joseph Story*, by Edward Lawes (Boston: James W. Burditt & Co., 1811).

So deep was his regard for the common law that in time he would secure in his most controversial opinion, *Swift v. Tyson* [41 U.S. 1 (1842)], the doctrine that there was indeed a federal common law of commerce in the United States. Story's position would stand until overruled nearly a century later in *Erie Railroad Co. v. Tompkins*, 304 U.S. 64 (1938).

[23] James Kent, *Commentaries on American Law*, 4 vols. (4th ed.; New York: Printed for the Author, 1840), I: 341.

[24] Story would insist that there were "limitations contained in the bosom of the common law" and that if the "rules of the common law [were] to furnish a proper guide to interpretation," then a court would be restrained from giving "any interpretation it may please, according to its own arbitrary will." *Commentaries on the Constitution of the United States*, 2 vols. (3rd ed.; Boston: Little, Brown and Co., 1858), I.158.105; p. 106, n.1. Citations to the *Commentaries* indicate volume, section, and page. Hereinafter *Commentaries on the Constitution*.

[25] Story believed firmly that it was a "common delusion, that the law may be thoroughly acquired in the immethodical, interrupted, and desultory studies of the office of a practicing counselor." Joseph Story, "Course of Legal Study," *Miscellaneous Writings*, pp. 91–92.

than most, studying first with Samuel Sewall in Marblehead and then with Samuel Putnam in Salem. It was under Sewall that Story came to appreciate "the law of England as a system of political and moral and economic rules."[26] But after he had encountered Blackstone's work – "that most elegant of all commentaries" – he found himself plunged into "the intricate, crabbed, and obsolete learning of Coke on Littleton." Story despaired when he thought the literature he loved most, "the profound writings of the great historians, metaphysicians, scholars, and divines, down to the lightest fiction," was likely to have to be sacrificed on the "dark and mysterious" altar that was the common law. Learning those "dry and technical principles," those "subtle refinements and intricacies of the middle ages," not to mention "the repulsive and almost unintelligible forms for processes and pleadings," struck young Story as a task nothing short of "Herculean." But he persisted and was converted, even though he had "wept bitterly" over old Coke.[27] He came to believe that the virtues offered by the common law were not just legal, but political as well.

The great and abiding danger in human affairs, Story thought, was the exercise of "arbitrary power," the imposition of the "arbitrary will and caprice of rulers." In his estimation, the institutional structures of a "government... ought to be arranged for permanence," and that meant especially that "in proportion as a government is free, it must be complicated." Story never ceased to believe that "the great mass of human calamities, in all ages, has been the result of bad government, or ill-adjusted governments; of a capricious exercise of power, a fluctuating public policy, a degrading tyranny, or a desolating ambition." The common law was well equipped to guard against such dangers. After all, it was "the law of liberty, and the watchful and inflexible guardian of private property and public rights."[28]

No small part of this fundamental problem of politics stemmed from what Story called "the silent but irresistible influence of public opinion."[29] All too often there was among people "a restless desire for novelty,"[30] an "inordinate love of innovation."[31] Without a scheme of institutional restraints, the result could easily be the political dominance of the "false

---

[26] Samuel Sewall to Joseph Story, 12 February, 1799, as quoted by R. Kent Newmyer, *Supreme Court Justice Joseph Story: Statesman of the Old Republic* (Chapel Hill: University of North Carolina Press, 1985), p. 43.

[27] *Life and Letters*, I: 73, 74, 74–75.

[28] Story, "Progress of Jurisprudence," p. 198; "The Science of Government," pp. 617, 617, 619, 618; "The Value and Importance of Legal Studies," p. 506, all in *Miscellaneous Writings*. See also "Characteristics of the Age," ibid., pp. 341–342.

[29] Joseph Story, "Law, Legislation, Codes," in Francis Lieber, ed., *Encyclopedia Americana*. 13 vols. (Philadelphia: Lea & Blanchard, 1844), VII: 576–592, p. 576. Story's unsigned articles in the *Encyclopedia Americana* have recently been reprinted in Joseph Story, *Joseph Story and the Encyclopedia Americana* (Clark, NJ: Lawbook Exchange, 2006).

[30] Story, "Characteristics of the Age," *Miscellaneous Writings*, p. 359.

[31] Story, "The Science of Government," ibid., p. 633.

and glossy theories of the day"[32] because governments, even those of laws and not just of men, are "subject to the control and influence of pubic opinion."[33] Human nature is such that the "servile adoption of received opinions and a timid acquiescence in whatever is established" is all too common.[34] One way to counteract that dangerous tendency was by the machinery of the common law. It was for this reason that Story believed that in a properly complicated system of government "the independence of the judges is the great bulwark of public liberty, and the great security of property."[35] Of this, he had no doubt: "Whatever of rational liberty and security to private rights and property is now enjoyed in England, and in the United States, may, in a great degree, be traced to the principles of the common law, as it has been moulded and fashioned from age to age by wise and learned judges."[36] There had to be enough "firmness in courts . . . to resist the fashionable opinions of the day,"[37] all the while keeping the judges themselves from acting arbitrarily.

The common law, as Story understood it, is "the unwritten law which cannot now be traced back to any positive text; but is composed of customs and usages and maxims, deriving their authority from immemorial practice, and the recognition of courts of justice."[38] Ultimately, the common law is concerned with particulars rather than with abstractions and thus appreciates "the paramount importance of facts over mere speculative philosophy."[39] Because of this, "the common law, above all others, employs a most severe and scrutinizing logic." As a result, it "follows out its principles with a closeness and simplicity of reasoning, which approach, as near as any artificial or moral deductions can, to the rigor of demonstration." The power and essence of the common law is "common sense," which has always "powerfully counteracted the tendency to undue speculation . . . and silently brought back its votaries to that, which is the end of all

[32] Story, "Progress of Jurisprudence," ibid., p. 231.
[33] Story, "Value and Importance of Legal Studies," ibid., p. 510. "Governments," Story believed, "are not always overthrown by direct and open assaults. They are not always battered down by the arms of conquerors, or the successful daring of usurpers. There is often concealed the dry rot, which eats into the vitals, when all is fair and stately on the outside." Ibid., p. 513.
[34] Story, "Characteristics of the Age," ibid., p. 350.
[35] Story, "Progress of Jurisprudence," ibid., p. 209.
[36] Story, "Course of Legal Study," ibid., p. 66.
[37] Story, "Progress of Jurisprudence," ibid., p. 229.
[38] Story, "Value and Importance of Legal Studies," ibid., p. 505.
[39] Story, "Developments of Science and Mechanic Art," ibid., p. 483. See also Story, "Law, Legislation, Codes," *Encyclopedia Americana*, p. 592: "[T]he part of true wisdom, is not so much to search out any abstract theory of universal jurisprudence, as to examine what, for each country in particular, may best promote its substantial interests, preserve it rights, protect its morals, and give permanence to its liberties."

true logic, the just application of principles to the actual concerns of human life."[40]

The commonsense judicial resolution of the various controversies and crises of ordinary life are collected over time into a body of binding precedents. And it is in that system of precedents that the political safety the common law provides is to be found. This common law rule of deferring to precedential authority "controls the arbitrary discretion of judges, and puts the case beyond the reach of temporary feelings and prejudices, as well as beyond the peculiar opinions and complexional reasoning of a particular judge; for he is hemmed round by authority on every side." The essence of this system is straightforward: "The sense of the law once fixed by judicial interpretation is forever deemed its true and only sense."[41]

The question thus arises: If the common law is but a collection of particular cases that have resolved human conflicts and controversies by the judicial creation of legal rules, what is the moral foundation of that body of law that gives it authority and renders it something more than arbitrary opinion? Story's answer was simple: the law of nature. This law, says Story, "is that system of principles, which human reason has discovered to regulate the conduct of man in all his various relations." Natural law thus "comprehends man's duties to God, to himself, to other men, and as a member of political society."[42] Its "obligatory force" derives from "its presumed coincidence with the will of the Creator."[43] It is, in fact, Christianity from which the common law "seeks the sanction of its rights, and by which it endeavors to regulate its doctrines." But that is not all. In Story's view, "Christianity becomes, not merely an auxiliary, but a guide to the law of nature; establishing its conclusions, removing its doubts, and elevating its precepts."[44] And this is not simply a matter of blind faith. "The truth is," Story argued, "that the farther our researches extend, the wider our philosophy explores, the deeper our discoveries penetrate, the more we are struck with the evidence of almighty contrivance, design, and power."[45]

God has given to man "the power of discerning between good and evil, and a liberty of choice in the use of these means which lead to happiness or misery." And it is this innate ability to know good from evil, and to choose happiness over misery, that leads men to form governments and create laws. "The science of government," Story insisted, "draws within its scope all the

---

[40] Story, "Value and Importance of Legal Studies," *Miscellaneous Writings*, pp. 508, 510, 508–509.

[41] Story, "Law, Legislation, Codes," *Encyclopedia Americana*, pp. 582, 583.

[42] Joseph Story, "Natural Law," *Encyclopedia Americana*, IX: 150.

[43] Ibid. "The whole duty of man therefore consists in two things: first, in making constant efforts to ascertain what is the will of God; and secondly, in obedience to that will when ascertained." Ibid., p. 151.

[44] Story, "Value and Importance of Legal Studies," *Miscellaneous Writings*, pp. 517, 535.

[45] Joseph Story, "The Influence of Scientific Studies," ibid., p. 564.

various concerns and relations of man, and must perpetually reason from the imperfect experience of the past, for the boundless contingencies of the future." It must seek "the great objects of all free governments," such as "the protection and preservation of the personal rights, the private property, and the public liberties of the whole people."[46]

Even though the common law has its foundation in natural law as revealed by natural reason, it is "at the same time built up and perfected by artificial doctrines, adapted and moulded to the artificial structure of society."[47] The common law and natural law were not, to Story, merely the same thing. Indeed, not even equity, that part of common law jurisprudence seen as closest to natural justice and characterized by its own "curious moral machinery,"[48] was that expansive. To assume that equity "embraced a jurisdiction so wide and extensive as... the principles of natural justice" would be, Story insisted, a "great mistake."[49] Were any court ever to possess such an "unbounded jurisdiction" as that of "enforcing all the rights, as well as all the charities arising from natural law and justice... it would be the most gigantic in its sway, and the most formidable instrument of arbitrary power, that could well be devised."[50] Its arbitrariness, in short, would be completely at odds with the very purposes and virtues of the common law. While the law of nature might constitute "the first step in the science of jurisprudence," it is far from being the final step.[51]

What the common law needed was to have all its "artificial doctrines" that had emerged since time immemorial – doctrines which lay scattered in court reports and treatises – reduced to an orderly system. When Nathan Dane began to think about endowing a professorship in law at Harvard University, it was precisely in order to encourage the legal scholarship that would allow the law to be taught "systematically" and to be seen, studied, and understood as a science. His vision went beyond mere classroom instruction and focused on the creation of written legal texts. It was perhaps altogether fitting that the author of the influential *General Abridgment and Digest of American Law* would choose to use his fortune for such a purpose.[52]

Dane seems from the beginning to have envisioned the professorship as a chair to be filled only by Story. Although the justice had earlier declined an appointment to the Royall professorship at the Law School, and was insistent that any professorial arrangement had to be "so arranged as not

46 Story, "Natural Law," *Encyclopedia Americana*, IX: 150–151; "The Science of Government," *Miscellaneous Writings*, pp. 615, 620.
47 Story, "Value and Importance of Legal Studies," ibid., p. 524.
48 Story, "Progress of Jurisprudence," ibid., p. 205.
49 Joseph Story, *Commentaries on Equity Jurisprudence*, 2 vols. (12th ed.; Boston: Little, Brown and Co., 1877), I.2.2. (Citation indicates volume, section, and page.)
50 Ibid., I.19.15.
51 Story, "Value and Importance of Legal Studies," *Miscellaneous Writings*, p. 583.
52 Nathan Dane, *A General Abridgment and Digest of American Law*, 9 vols. (Boston: Cummings, Hilliard, and Co., 1823–29). See *Life and Letters*, II: 2.

to interfere with [his] judicial duties," he was convinced that he and Dane shared a commitment to seeing law elevated "from a trade to a science."[53] They believed that such an approach to legal education would benefit not only the university and the legal profession but also the republic itself.

Dane had made sure Story was willing to accept the professorship before he formally arranged the bequest. Once he and Story had agreed, Dane made clear to the university his expectations for the Dane Professor of Law. "In the first place," the donor wrote in June 1829, "it shall be his duty to prepare and deliver, and to revise for publication, a course of lectures on the five following branches of Law and Equity, equally in force in all parts of our Federal Republic, namely: The Law of Nature, the Law of Nations, Commercial and Maritime Law, Federal Law, and Federal Equity."[54] So, too, was it made clear that it was Story or no one. Harvard quickly accepted Dane's gift on his terms, and two months later Story assumed his new duties.

On August 25, 1829, Story spoke of the "Value and Importance of Legal Studies" at his inauguration as Dane Professor of Law in Harvard University, a speech designed to celebrate and to explicate the "noble design of the founder." It would be his intention, Story assured his audience, to "expound the doctrines and diversities" of the branches of the common law to prepare not only those who might be "destined for the profession" but also any "scholars and gentlemen" who might "desire to learn its general principles."[55]

In outlining the "duties assigned to the Dane Professorship," Story's list of his planned lectures and treatises transformed Dane's "Federal Equity" into the more general "Equity Law," while changing "Federal Law" into "the Constitutional Law of the United States." The latter was a matter of "political law," and Story's lectures on it would endeavor to "explain its principles, as far as practicable, by the lights of those great minds, which fostered into being and nourished its infancy." His object was "to fix in the minds of American youth a more devout enthusiasm for the constitution of their country, a more sincere love of its principles, and a more firm determination to adhere to its actual provisions against the clamors of faction, and the restlessness of innovation."[56]

Story would handily fulfill his obligations both in the classroom and in his study. But instead of merely revising his lectures for publication, he set about to create "a series of systematic treatises" on the various aspects of the law he had outlined in his inaugural address. Between 1832 and

---

[53] Joseph Story to ?, May 19, 1829; Joseph Story to Asa Aldis, February 15, 1832, as quoted in Newmyer, *Supreme Court Justice Joseph Story*, pp. 241, 246.

[54] Nathan Dane to the President and Fellows of the Corporation of Harvard University, 2 June, 1829, *Life and Letters*, II: 4.

[55] Story, "Value and Important of Legal Studies," *Miscellaneous Writings*, pp. 503, 506.

[56] Ibid., pp. 533, 543, 544.

1845 he would publish nine substantial treatments of the law, including his celebrated *Commentaries on the Constitution of the United States*.[57] Of the treatises, the constitutional commentaries is the only one to include a chapter detailing the "Rules of Interpretation."

The reason was clear. When it came to "the interpretation of constitutional questions," recent history had shown there to be "an ample space of debatable ground, upon which the champions of all opinions may contend, with alternate victory and defeat." Too many had proved themselves "unwilling to admit anything to be settled," thus subjecting the constitutional text itself to the constant assault of interpretive "glosses of the most contradictory character."[58] But most dangerous, especially in republics, were those would-be interpreters inclined to import theories unsupported by the history and purpose of the text itself. "Great vigilance and great jealousy are therefore necessary in republics," Story admonished, "to guard against the captivations of theory, as well as the approaches of more insidious foes."[59]

As was clear, the focus of Story's concern about the "captivations of theory," the "clamor of factions," and the "restlessness of innovation" was the "states rights" republicanism that had been unleashed by Thomas Jefferson and subsequently nurtured by his fellow Republicans. By the 1820s the "metaphysics" of state sovereignty had degenerated into claims on behalf of the states to nullify national law or even of their right to withdraw from the union. Story had learned well from Marshall that those who embraced "the political creed of Virginia" seemed bent on transforming the Constitution back into the old confederation by imposing a theory that was unsupported by either the language or the intention of the Constitution itself.[60]

At the heart of the states' rights assault on the Constitution was Jefferson's theory of constitutional interpretation. Ironically, there was, Story insisted, an "utter looseness and incoherence" to Jefferson's canons of allegedly "strict construction." By insisting that interpreters should carry themselves

---

[57] *Life and Letters*, I: 69. *Commentaries on the Law of Bailments* (Cambridge: Hilliard and Brown, 1832); *Commentaries on the Constitution of the United States*, 3 vols. (Boston: Hilliard, Gray, and Co., 1833); *Commentaries on the Conflict of Laws* (Boston: Hilliard, Gray, and Co., 1834); *Commentaries on Equity Jurisprudence*, 2 vols. (Boston: Hilliard, Gray, and Co., 1836); *Commentaries on Equity Pleadings* (Boston: C. C. Little and J. Brown, 1838); *Commentaries on the Law of Agency* (Boston: C. C. Little and J. Brown, 1839); *Commentaries on the Law of Partnership* (Boston: C. C. Little and J. Brown, 1841); *Commentaries on the Law of Bills of Exchange* (Boston: C. C. Little and J. Brown, 1843); *Commentaries on the Law of Promissory Notes* (Boston: C. C. Little and J. Brown, 1845).

[58] Story, "The Science of Government," *Miscellaneous Writings*, p. 622.

[59] Story, "Value and Importance of Legal Studies," ibid., p. 513.

[60] For a general account of Story's intentions concerning the role of the *Commentaries on the Constitution* in combating the states' rights theories, see H. Jefferson Powell, "Joseph Story's Commentaries on the Constitution: A Belated Review," *Yale Law Journal* 94 (1985): 1285–1314.

"back to the time, when the constitution was adopted [and] recollect the spirit manifested in the debates," Jefferson had endeavored to supplant the true interpretation or construction of the Constitution's "own text" with a recourse to its *"probable meaning"* as might be gathered from "conjectures from scattered documents, from private papers, from the table-talk of some statesman, or the jealous exaggeration of others."[61] Story saw his task in the *Commentaries on the Constitution* in part as recovering long-standing interpretive methods that would reveal the "true meaning" of the text, the meaning that was intended by those who had framed and ratified the document. Thus was it essential to make clear what were the proper rules of interpretation for a written and ratified fundamental law that had been "ordained and established" by the "authority of the people in their sovereign capacity."[62]

II. THE *COMMENTARIES ON THE CONSTITUTION OF THE UNITED STATES*

The period between the adoption of the Constitution and the outbreak of the Civil War were years marked by an outpouring of treatises on the Constitution. The battles over fundamental questions as to the nature of sovereignty, national supremacy, and states' rights were fought not only in the halls of Congress and before the Supreme Court, but also in the court of public opinion. The model established by Blackstone's *Commentaries* inspired many an American to seek to make clear the nature and extent of the Constitution as fundamental law.

Such works as William Rawle's *View of the Constitution of the United States*,[63] Peter DuPonceau's *Dissertation on the Nature and Extent of the Jurisdiction of the Courts of the United States*,[64] James Kent's *Commentaries on American Law*,[65] William Alexander Duer's *Outlines of the Constitutional Jurisprudence of the United States*,[66] Timothy Walker's *Introduction to American Law*,[67] John Taylor of Caroline's *Views of the Constitution of the United States*,[68] and Abel Upshur's *Brief Enquiry into the True Nature and Character of Our Federal Government*[69] were all efforts to capture

---

[61] Story, *Commentaries on the Constitution*, vol. I, p. 289, n.1.

[62] Ibid., I.415.294. He had written his *Commentaries on the Constitution*, Story wrote to James Kent while the volumes were still in press, "with a sincere desire to commend, and to recommend the Constitution upon true, old, and elevated principles." Joseph Story to James Kent, 27 October 1832, *Life and Letters*, II: 109.

[63] (Philadelphia: H. C. Carey and I. Lea, 1825).

[64] (Philadelphia: A. Small, 1825).

[65] (New York: For the Author, 1826).

[66] (New York: Collins and Hannay, 1833).

[67] (Philadelphia: P. H. Nicklin and T. Johnson, 1837).

[68] (Washington City: For the Author by Way and Gideon, 1823).

[69] (Petersburg, VA: E. And J. C. Ruffin, 1840).

and define America's constitutional soul.[70] But of these, Story's *Commentaries on the Constitution* was both the most comprehensive and the most widely read.[71] Yet he has been accused of coming to his task "with his mind made up as to the relative positions of the states and the federal government in the American union."[72] His account is characterized, it is said, by a "pronounced bias" and should be considered as nothing more than a mere "partisan document."[73] Abel Upshur, in a treatise designed specifically to refute the nationalist account in the *Commentaries on the Constitution*, dismissed Story's three massive volumes as nothing more than a collection of "mere dogmas."[74] And John C. Calhoun, the chief theoretician of nullification, viewed the treatise as "essentially false and dangerous."[75] Yet even his harshest modern critics concede that his *Commentaries on the Constitution* will likely remain, along with Marshall's constitutional opinions and *The Federalist*, as one of the "classic interpretations of the Constitution and the Union as settled by the Civil War."[76] Story would have considered that high praise.

Justice Story prefaced his *Commentaries on the Constitution* with the confession that he had taken "the greatest part of . . . [the] most valuable materials" for his treatise from "two great sources," the "incomparable" commentary of *The Federalist* and "the extraordinary judgments of Mr. Chief Justice Marshall upon constitutional law." Because he relied on sources of such "profoundness and felicity" there was no need, Story said, for him to undertake to put forth "any novel views and novel constructions of the Constitution." His only objective was to offer the reader "the view of its powers, maintained by its founders and friends, and confirmed and illustrated by the actual practice of the government." In particular, he denied any "ambition to be the author of any new plan of interpreting the theory of the Constitution, or of enlarging or narrowing its powers, by ingenious subtleties and learned doubts." As he put it: "Upon subjects of government it has always appeared to me that metaphysical refinements are out of place. A constitution of government is addressed to the common sense of the people; and never was designed for trials of logical skills, or visionary speculation."[77]

---

[70] See generally Bauer, *Commentaries on the Constitution, 1790–1860.*

[71] Ibid., p. 309.

[72] Ibid., p. 311.

[73] Vernon Parrington, *Main Currents in American Political Thought* (New York: Harcourt Brace, 1930), II: 302, as quoted in Bauer, *Commentaries on the Constitution, 1790–1860,* p. 329.

[74] Upshur, *Brief Enquiry,* p. 53.

[75] John C. Calhoun to A. D. Wallace, 17 December 1840, in C. Wilson, ed., *The Papers of John C. Calhoun,* 28 vols. (Columbia: University of South Carolina Press, 1959–2003), XV: 389.

[76] Bauer, *Commentaries on the Constitution, 1790–1860,* p. 330.

[77] Story, *Commentaries on the Constitution,* I: vii, viii, viii, viii.

Story, as a historian of ideas, knew well the dilemmas posed to the common law in its earlier days by "the embarrassing subtleties of scholastic refinement." In that earlier period when "metaphysical inquiries" grew from the embrace of "speculative philosophy," mankind found itself beset by "endless... controversies" that served only to distract and confuse. The confusions of that epoch, Story argued, resulted from the fact that "the metaphysics of Aristotle, or rather the misuse of his metaphysics," had been used to hold "the human mind in bondage." It was not until "Lord Bacon... exposed the absurdity of the existing system of study, and of its unsatisfactory aims and results" that the dense fog of scholasticism was finally blown away. In its place arose the new thinking of men like "Locke and Newton," who, Story insisted, "still stand above in unapproached, in unapproachable majesty."[78]

Upon this new foundation were constructed the fundamental premises of modern constitutionalism, not least the belief in popular sovereignty, the idea that "the people themselves possess the supreme power to form, alter, amend, change and abolish at their pleasure the whole structure of their government and of course to reconstruct it in such manner, as from time to time may be most agreeable to themselves."[79] Henceforth constitutions of government would be the result, to borrow the language of Alexander Hamilton in *The Federalist*, of "reflection and choice," rather than mere "accident and force."[80] This meant that when it came to interpreting the textual result of such "reflection and choice" the judges would be bound by the original meaning.

In thinking through the necessity of securing "certainty and uniformity of interpretation" when it came to the Constitution, Story looked back, in part, to the methods of statutory construction that had emerged under the common law. There was, at a minimum, the need for antecedent "rules... for the construction of statutes," and among those rules the most "fundamental maxim of the common law" was that which stated that when it came to the "interpretation of... positive laws," the lawgiver's "intention... is to be followed." Story's interpretive standards for statutory construction under the common law were unambiguous. "The intention," he argued, following Blackstone, "is to be gathered from the words, the context, the subject matter, the effects and consequences, and the spirit or reason of the law. But the spirit and reason are to be ascertained, not from vague conjectures, but from

---

[78] Story, "Course of Legal Study," p. 72; "Developments of Science and Mechanic Art," pp. 478, 483, 478; "Characteristics of the Age," p. 351; "Developments of Science and Mechanic Art," pp. 478–479; "Characteristics of the Age," p. 342, all in *Miscellaneous Writings*.

[79] Joseph Story, "American Law," *American Journal of Comparative Law* 3 (1954): 9–26, p. 12.

[80] Alexander Hamilton, *The Federalist*, No. 1, p. 3, in Jacob Cooke, ed., *The Federalist* (Middletown, CT: Wesleyan University Press, 1961).

the motives and language apparent on the face of the law." By the "spirit and reason" of the law, he did not mean untethered speculations derived from the "private reasoning" of a judge "as to what a wise or beneficent legislature might or might not intend." Rather, it was what the actual legislature in question truly intended to achieve by the particular law in question. Thus would "the professed objects of the legislature in making the law often afford an excellent key to unlock its meaning."[81] As with the common law, so with the law of the Constitution.

In formulating his nineteen rules of interpretation in the *Commentaries on the Constitution*, Story did not simply turn to the common law tradition that included, among others, the treatises of William Blackstone, Richard Wooddeson, and Jean Louis De Lolme. He also looked to sources in the civil law, the law of nations, political philosophy, and even to his fellow American commentators on the Constitution. The lessons he drew from all those sources converged into what he called simply the "first and fundamental rule in the interpretation of all instruments," which is "to construe them according to the sense of the terms and the intention of the parties."[82] This was, as Story knew, the received tradition.

Jean Domat, for example, had argued that "human laws are positive and arbitrary laws, because men may enact them, change them, and abolish them." And when it comes to interpreting them, "it is by the spirit and intendment . . . that we are to understand and apply them." Writing serves to "fix the sense of the law" and bind the interpreter to "the intention of the legislature."[83]

As Blackstone had argued that the "most rational" method of interpreting the law was by "exploring [the lawmaker's] intentions at the time when the law was made, by *signs* the most natural and probable,"[84] so did his successor to the Vinerian chair at Oxford, Richard Wooddeson. Wooddeson believed simply that "the principal rule of interpretation is the reason of the law."[85] And De Lolme, in his consideration of the constitution of England, insisted that "all judicial power is an evil, though a necessary one [and] no care should be omitted to reduce as far as possible the danger of it." Not even in a court of equity is a judge permitted simply to "follow the dictates of his own private feelings." To allow judges to alter the law by their own private views would in effect allow them arbitrarily "to control the legislature."[86]

---

[81] Story, "Law, Legislation, Codes," *Encyclopedia Americana*, VII: 576–592, pp. 585, 583, 583, 584, 583.

[82] Story, *Commentaries on the Constitution*, I.400.283

[83] Jean Domat, *The Civil Law in Its Natural Order*, trans. W. Strahan, ed. L. Cushing, 2 vols. (Boston: Little and Brown, 1850), I: 72, 84, 108, 120.

[84] *Commentaries on the Laws of England*, 4 vols. (8th ed.; Oxford: Clarendon Press, 1778), I: 59.

[85] *Elements of Jurisprudence* (London: T. Payne and Son, 1783), p. 37.

[86] *The Constitution of England* (London: J. Cuthell, 1822), pp. 143, 117, 116.

William Paley was also painfully aware of the possible "abuses of judicial discretion." Such discretion was to be kept limited by guiding interpretation by the available "evidence of the intention of the legislature." To free interpreters from that restraint would be to "allow judges a liberty of applying the law which will fall very little short of the power of making it."[87]

Along the same lines, William Rawle argued that "the superior advantages" of a written constitution were "great and manifest." Such a written fundamental law was "most conducive" to the "safety and happiness" of the people under it. When it came to interpreting such a constitution, Rawle conceded, "construction... can only mean the ascertaining of the true meaning of an instrument... and by this rule alone ought [the people] to be governed in respect to this constitution." The "true rule" of interpretation was "to deduce the meaning from its known intention and its entire text, and to give effect... to every part of it, consistently with the unity, and the harmony of the whole."[88]

Of all his sources, however, the most important and influential was Thomas Rutherforth, whose *Institutes of Natural Law*[89] Story deemed to be a work that "deserves attentive perusal." In this commentary on Grotius, as discussed at length earlier, Rutherforth put forth a tripartite account of the styles of interpretation – "literal, rational, and mixed" – that Story believed sound. Indeed, he confessed that he had borrowed liberally from Rutherforth because he found his work to provide "a very lucid exposition of the general rules of interpretation."[90]

In approaching the Constitution, Story was insistent that there had to be drawn out of the text what he saw as the "rules of interpretation belonging to the instrument" itself. Such rules, of necessity, were to be followed in order to allow the document's "true meaning" to be expounded. It was all too easy to allow rules of interpretation to be "shifted" to meet the exigencies of the moment, allowing the "passions and prejudices of the day" or the "favor and odium of a particular measure" to determine the meaning of a provision. Such accommodations would inevitably lead to a "mode of argument" that would either leave the Constitution "crippled and inanimate" or "give it an extent and elasticity, subversive of all rational boundaries."[91] Rules of interpretation, properly laid down, would avoid such dangerous extremes.

To say that there were "rules of interpretation belonging to the instrument" was to say that in approaching the constitutional text one had to be

---

[87] William Paley, *The Principles of Moral and Political Philosophy*, 2 vols. (6th ed.; London: R. Faulder, 1788), II: 247, 259, 259.

[88] William Rawle, *View of the Constitution of the United States of America* (2nd ed.; Philadelphia: Philip H. Nicklin, 1829), pp. 15, 16, 31, 31–32.

[89] Thomas Rutherforth, *Institutes of Natural Law*, 2 vols. (Cambridge: J. Bentham, 1754–56).

[90] Story, *Commentaries on the Constitution*, vol. I, p. 285, n.1.

[91] Ibid., I.307.206; I.393.274; I.398.283.

mindful of the original intention, in its broadest sense, behind the fundamental law. At a minimum, it was clear that the "avowed intention" of the
framers had been "to supersede the old confederation, and substitute in its
place a new form of government." One could see this in the simple fact that
the new Constitution "not only transferred from the states some of the highest sovereign prerogatives, but laid prohibitions upon the exercise of other
powers." Moreover, the friends of the Constitution during the battle for
ratification had demonstrated "the utter imbecility of a mere confederation,
without powers acting directly upon individuals."[92]

When it came to the threat posed by the theoretical subversions of the
states' rights proponents, Story was quick to point out that "[t]here is
nowhere found upon the face of the constitution any clause intimating it
to be a compact, or in anywise providing for its interpretation as such."
There was simply no ambiguity on this point. The framers knew well "the
distinction between a constitution and a confederation," and they had made
themselves clear. The much-repeated claim of the states' rights advocates
that the states, not the people, were the true parties to the Constitution
was merely "a gratuitous assumption."[93] To argue that the Constitution is
a compact of sovereign states was to "draw inferences, not from what is,
but from what is not stated in the instrument." What is stated is that the
document was intended to be "a constitution of government framed for the
general good and designed for perpetuity." What this meant in practice was
that, unlike a true compact, "a constitution, though originating in consent,
becomes, when ratified, obligatory, as a fundamental ordinance or law."[94]

At the heart of the states' rights argument that the Constitution was in
fact a compact of sovereign states that created a confederation rather than
a nation was their hope to establish as a fact that there was no "common umpire" whose task it would be to construe the document. Each state
would be left to judge for itself. But this depended upon nothing more than
"artificial reasoning founded upon theory" that could only result in "false
constructions and glosses." True interpretation would result not from such
"artificial reasoning" but from "a careful survey of the language of the
Constitution itself," which would provide an accurate interpretation of the
intentions behind "its powers and its obligations."[95]

The danger posed by what both Marshall and Story thought of as the
"doctrine of Virginia" was the suggestion that a document intended as a
permanent frame of government for the nation as a whole would end up
being interpreted as though it were nothing more than "a petty charter
granted to a paltry corporation for the purpose of regulating a fishery or
collecting a toll." The battle against the states' rights forces had to be joined

---

[92] Ibid., I.355.237. I.287.194; I.294.198.

[93] Ibid., I.352.235; I.352.235; I.363.244. See also I.356.239.

[94] Ibid., I.368.250; I.369.250; I.352.235–236.

[95] Ibid. I.370.251; I.372.252; I.372.252–253; I.372.253.

[handwritten annotation: M© destrusto theory, not his rules of interpretation... are grounded in... not theory... a theory]

because, although their doctrines were clearly "insidious," they were also "often popular" and, worse, "not infrequently plausible."[96] The demagogic appeal of Jefferson and his followers, and the dangers that appeal posed to the Union, could not be overstated.

This was why for Story it was essential to establish rules that would in fact see the Constitution consistently construed as "a *frame of government*" and not as a mere compact.[97] At the least, it had to be made clear beyond doubt that the states in their individual capacities could never properly be the final interpreters of the Constitution. That ultimate authority was inherently a judicial power.[98] Under the methods of the common law, "the principles of the decisions are held as precedents and authority, to bind future cases of the same nature." Because of this, the law of the Constitution will be "justly deemed certain, and founded in permanent principles, and not dependent upon the caprice or will of particular judges." When it comes to construing "a fundamental law of a government," it is a "necessary postulate" that there be a "uniformity of construction." Failing in that would produce a "vague and uncertain jurisprudence" that would serve only to reduce those living under such a constitution to a "miserable servitude."[99] Story was dedicated to producing rules of interpretation that would not allow that to happen.

Story's approach to constitutional interpretation began with the words of the Constitution. The reason was a matter of common sense. "Nothing but the text itself," he insisted, "was adopted by the people." The objective of a "natural and just interpretation" is to get at the "obvious sense" of the words that were used. This means that just as the words are not to be taken automatically in "the most restricted sense," neither are they to be "stretched beyond their fair sense." Every interpretation is to be guided by a "constant reference" to the objects for which the Constitution was framed and ratified.[100]

The framers were not "philologists or critics" when it came to the use of language. Rather, they were "statesmen and practical reasoners." In undertaking to interpret their words, it is necessary to assume that they said what they meant and meant what they said. As a result, "every word employed in the Constitution is to be expounded in its plain, obvious, and common sense, unless the context furnishes some ground to control, qualify, or enlarge it."[101]

---

[96] Joseph Story to John Marshall, 27 June 1821, in Herbert Johnson and Charles F. Hobson, eds., *The Papers of John Marshall*, 12 vols. (Chapel Hill: University of North Carolina Press, 1974–2006), IX: 176. Hereinafter cited as *Papers of John Marshall*.

[97] Ibid., p. 176.

[98] Story, *Commentaries on the Constitution*, I.376.257.

[99] Ibid., I.377.258; I.377.258; I.383.264; I.384.264.

[100] Ibid., I.406.288; I.406.288; I.407.288; I.413.293; I.422.298; I.405.285

[101] Ibid., I.454.323; I.451.322.

For Story, this derived from the very essence of what a constitution created by the people in their sovereign capacity was all about. "Constitutions," he argued,

are not designed for metaphysical or logical subtleties, for niceties of expression, for critical propriety, for elaborate shades of meaning, or for the exercise of philosophical acuteness or judicial research. They are instruments of a practical nature, founded on the common business of human life, adapted to common wants, designed for common use, and fitted for common understandings. The people make them; the people adopt them, the people must be supposed to read them, with the help of common sense; and cannot be presumed to admit in them any recondite meaning, or any extraordinary gloss.[102]

This was not to suggest that the interpreter's task was an easy one. The "necessary imperfection of all human language" alone rendered constitutional interpretation a difficult and often vexing undertaking. To say the least, it was not simply a matter of "mere verbal criticism." That is why those "men of ingenious and subtle minds, who seek for symmetry and harmony in language" are not the best interpreters for a constitution of government.[103]

It is not only imperfections in language borne of men's faulty reasoning and defective expression that render interpretation difficult. There is also the fact that languages tend to be living things, growing and adapting over time. Thus do the "gradual deflections in the meaning of words from one age to another" also demand a scrupulous attentiveness on the part of the interpreter. So constant is this evolutionary process, Story argued, "that the daily language of life in one generation sometimes requires the aid of a glossary in another."[104] Because the "first and fundamental rule in ... interpretation" is to discern the "intention of the parties," an interpreter's most basic obligation is to understand the framers as they understood themselves.

Unlike the "daily language of life," the language of a constitution of fundamental law, as with all legal documents, must be understood to be fixed and stable. Its meaning does not depend upon the context of the times. The Constitution, Story insisted, "must be expounded as it stands; and not as that policy, or that interest may seem now to dictate." The obligation of a judge in interpreting the Constitution is "to construe, and not to frame the instrument." Because the Constitution was "adopted by the people in its obvious and general sense," any interpretive "departure from the import and sense" of its provisions would be, Story believed, "*pro tanto*, the establishment of a new constitution." Such an undertaking would be "doing for the people, what they have not chosen to do for themselves." Judges who would

---

[102] Ibid., I.451.322.
[103] Ibid., I.452.322; I.455.325; I.454.324.
[104] Ibid., I.452.322.

engage in such an effort would in fact be guilty of "usurping the functions of a legislator, and deserting those of an expounder of the law."[105]

Because the Constitution was "made by the people, made for the people, and is responsible to the people," it may by them – and by them alone, in their sovereign capacity – "be altered, and amended, and abolished" at their will.[106] Such sovereign permanence is the essence of constitutionalism.

Story was insistent that the perpetuation of the Constitution depended upon the perpetuation of its original meaning unless and until that original meaning might be changed by what *The Federalist* described as the "solemn and authoritative act" of formal amendment. As Story put it:

Temporary delusions, prejudices, excitements, and objects have an irresistible influence in mere questions of policy. And the policy of one age may ill suit the wishes or the policy of another. The Constitution is not to be subject to such fluctuations. It is to have a fixed, uniform, permanent construction. It should be, as far at least as human infirmity will allow, not dependent upon the passions or parties of particular times, but the same yesterday, to-day, and forever.[107]

Like Chief Justice Marshall's, Story's originalism was a textually based approach to interpreting the fundamental law. While there is surely a spirit to a constitution, it is not a disembodied subjective spirit imported from without. As Story argued, "although the spirit of an instrument, especially of a constitution, is to be respected not less than its letter, yet the spirit is to be collected chiefly from the letter." The meaning of the words, and hence the spirit of the document, is not to be found lurking in "the private interpretation of any particular man or body of men." Indeed, Story noted, it is "not to be presumed that, even in the convention which framed the Constitution ... the clauses were always understood in the same sense or had precisely the same extent of operation."[108] There was a word for such "private interpretation"; that word was opinion.

Because nothing but the "text itself" was adopted, the task of the judge is to begin with that text, with the words used, and extrapolate from them the true and intended purpose of the provision in question. What this meant in practical terms for Story was reasonably simple and straightforward. "In construing the Constitution of the United States," he wrote, "we are, in the first instance, to consider, what are its nature and objects, its scope and design, as apparent from the structure of the instrument, viewed as a whole, and also viewed in its component parts." The result is that it is highly unlikely that there can ever be found any one "uniform rule of interpretation" that will not demand "many modifications in its actual application to particular clauses." The "safest rule of interpretation," in Story's view, is to "look to

---

[105] Ibid., I.424.301; I.424.301; I.424.300–301; I426.302; I.426.302; I.426.302.
[106] Ibid., I.397.282.
[107] Ibid., I.426.303.
[108] Ibid., II.427.303; I.406.287;.406.288.

the nature and objects of the particular powers, duties, and rights, with all the lights and aids of contemporary history and to give to the words of each just such operation and force, consistent with their legitimate meaning, as may fairly secure and attain the ends proposed."[109] By gleaning the purposes of the framers, the judge will be able to come to understand, in Marshall's phrase, the "mind of the convention."

III. STORY'S RULES OF INTERPRETATION AND THE TRADITION

Story's effort to establish clear and compelling standards of interpretation for the law of the Constitution was not unique. He wrote at a time when treatises on interpretation, construction, and hermeneutics were becoming increasingly common. In England, for example, three years before the *Commentaries on the Constitution* appeared in the United States, Sir Fortunatus Dwarris published his highly regarded and influential *General Treatise on Statutes: Their Rules of Construction, and the Proper Boundaries of Legislation and of Judicial Interpretation*,[110] a work that would run to several editions, including in the United States. And two years after Marshall died, a momentous year for the change of the Supreme Court's direction under Chief Justice Taney, Story's friend and collaborator, the editor of *The Encyclopedia Americana*, Francis Lieber, produced a two-part essay on interpretation that was published in the *American Jurist* in October 1837 and January 1838.[111] The articles were later edited and enlarged and published in book form as *Legal and Political Hermeneutics, or Principles of Interpretation and Construction in Law and Politics*.[112] And following Lieber came a collection of treatises on interpretation that appeared regularly until near the end of the century, each of which was grounded in rules and maxims that would have been instantly recognizable to Story and others of his earlier generation. That tradition of treatises on interpretation, from Dwarris to Lieber to Joel Prentiss Bishop and Henry Campbell Black, at once provides the intellectual context of Story's effort and draws out implications of his rules of interpretation.

The Boundaries of Interpretation

Sir Fortunatus Dwarris (1786–1860) was a Jamaican–born, Oxford-educated barrister who had been called to the bar at the Middle Temple

---

[109] Ibid., I.406.288; I.405.285; I.405.286–287; I.405.287.
[110] Fortunatus Dwarris, *General Treatise on Statutes: Their Rules of Construction, and the Proper Boundaries of Legislation and of Judicial Interpretation*, 2 vols. (London: Saunders and Benning, 1830–31).
[111] *American Jurist* 18 (1837–38): 37–101, 281–294.
[112] (Boston: C. Little and James Brown, 1839).

in 1811. A fellow of both the Royal Society and the Society of Antiquaries, Dwarris had written essays on various legal subjects, but it was his *General Treatise on Statutes* that proved to be his "one solid contribution to legal learning." A work at once "comprehensive and learned," it not only enjoyed "considerable success" when it appeared, but also proved itself to be of "permanent importance and value" to the profession.[113]

As a practitioner, Dwarris had found himself frustrated by the fact that there had never been a "solid and systematic" treatment given to the subject of the interpretation and construction of statutes.[114] Such a treatise had "long been a *desideratum* with the profession," and it was this yawning gap in the legal literature that Dwarris intended his *General Treatise* to fill.

Dwarris's professional frustration stemmed not simply from the absence of any serious account of the rules of interpretation, but more deeply from the carelessness with which judges and legislators alike had come to disregard what Dwarris believed to be "the proper boundaries of legislation and judicial interpretation." Those boundaries had come to be "so vaguely defined, and so imperfectly understood that the judges were constantly either mistaking the principles, or erring in the application of them." So dire had the situation become, in Dwarris's view, that the "jurisdiction and methods of proceeding" in all the superior courts in the country had come to be "founded on usurpation and sustained by fiction."[115]

Dwarris was not naive. "Laws," he insisted, "must be accommodated – or laws will accommodate themselves – to the growing necessities of mankind, and the varying state and condition of human society." The question was not whether there would be the need for change but only whether such change would come directly from the parliament by legislation or indirectly from the courts by interpretation. In Dwarris's view, there was only one correct answer. Such legal change should be left to the superior "competency and fitness" of the legislature to make the needed adjustments.[116]

This understanding followed from Dwarris's view that the legislature was a "superior power" and that the judiciary was merely a "subordinate

---

[113] William S. Holdsworth, *A History of English Law*, 17 vols. (London: Metheun & Co., 1922–72), XIII: 492–494, 493.

[114] Dwarris, *General Treatise on Statutes*, I: v.

[115] Ibid., I: vii; II: 783; II: 794.

[116] Ibid., II: 780; II: 791–792. "The truth is," Dwarris wrote, "that the legislature, and not the courts, should be driven to comply with the necessities of mankind. But this, unfortunately, had not been the practice. When rules of law have been found to work injustice, they have been evaded instead of being repealed. Obsolete or unsuitable laws, instead of being removed from the statute book, have been made to bend to modern usages and feelings. Instead of the legislature framing new provisions, as occasion has required, it has been left to able judges to invade its province, and to arrogate to themselves the lofty privilege of correcting abuses and introducing improvements. The rules are thus left in the breasts of the judges instead of being put upon a right footing by legislative enactment." Ibid., II: 792.

authority" designed to take what the legislature had created and "give it effect and put it in operation." Legislators deal with fashioning "general principles," while the judges are expected merely to "refine" those principles in order to make them fit the "individual cases"[117] that were within the legislators' intentions.

When it comes to the judicial application of the unwritten common law to particular cases and controversies, the interpretive "liberality of the judges" poses not so great a threat. But, noted Dwarris, "where the law *is* prescribed and promulgated as the declared will of the supreme power of the state, the case is wholly different."[118] There is not much room when it comes to the written law for judges to employ what Sir Edward Coke had called "the crooked cord of . . . discretion."[119] The rule was simple, in Dwarris's calculations: "Judges are bound to take the act of parliament as the legislature have made it." Thus, Dwarris insisted, "in the construction of statutes . . . the great object of the rules and maxims of interpretation is to discover the true intention of the law; and whenever that intention can be indubitably ascertained, courts are bound to give it effect, whatever may be their opinion of its wisdom or policy."[120]

Judges do not have the authority to impose upon the written law what they may "suppose" to be the intention of the legislature. To do so would in effect be to hold that the language does not really matter and, in the view of the judge, that "the legislature did not mean what it . . . expressed." This was a point worthy of great emphasis, to Dwarris's way of thinking. "The most enlightened and experienced judges," he insisted, "hold it the much safer course to adhere to the words of the statute construed in their ordinary import, than to enter into any inquiry as to the supposed intention of the parties who framed the act. They are not . . . to presume the intentions of the legislature, but to collect them from the words of the act of parliament; and they have nothing to do with the policy of the law." It was for these reasons that Dwarris argued in the strongest terms that "judges are . . . not to construe statutes by equity" but rather be limited to collecting "the sense of the legislature by a sound interpretation of the language, according to reason and grammatical correctness."[121]

Dwarris, like Story and Lieber, was an objective textualist; as a result, it was the language of a law that was the primary means of getting at the intention of the legislature. The essence of judicial power was to explore "the intention of the legislator by the commonest and most natural signs – the words and the context." There was no ambiguity here. "In the exposition of a statute," he argued, "the leading clue to the construction to be made,

---

[117]	Ibid., II: 791–92; II: 792.
[118]	Ibid., II: 791.
[119]	As quoted in ibid., II: 645.
[120]	Ibid., II: 711, 690.
[121]	Ibid., II: 703.

is the intention of the legislator, and that may be discovered from different signs. As a primary rule, it is to be collected from the words; when the words are not explicit, it is to be gathered from the occasion and necessity of the law – being the causes which moved the legislature to enact it." While Dwarris was mindful that there is always a "sense and spirit of an act," that sense and spirit cannot simply take precedence over the language; a construction rooted in the legislators' intentions must still be "warranted by, or at least not repugnant to, the words of the act." Yet neither should any effort to get at "the literal sense of the terms" be allowed to trump the intention. "The real intention," Dwarris argued, "when collected with certainty will always, in statutes, prevail over the literal sense of terms." Dwarris sought to reduce this complexity to two simple maxims. On the one hand, a thing "which is within the intention of the makers of a statute, is as much within the statute, as if it were in the letter." On the other, a thing "which is within the letter of the statute is not within the statute unless it be within the intention of the makers." This is why he insisted that great "experience and learning are . . . no less requisite for the interpretation, than for the preparation of laws." Properly undertaken, interpretation and construction require "the soundest judicial discretion."[122]

Dwarris's treatise would exert a wide influence within the law. Joseph Story, for one, would find his teachings of great value, turning to them to support his own commentaries on the law.[123] But what is most interesting about the relationship between Dwarris and Story may well be not Story's use of Dwarris but Dwarris's reliance on Story.

When the second edition of the *General Treatise on Statutes* appeared in 1848, Dwarris's debt to Story was clear. In the ninth and seminal chapter on "General Rules Relating to the Construction of Statutes," Dwarris now introduced the subject by explicit recourse to Story's authorities in his chapter on "Rules of Interpretation" in the *Commentaries on the Constitution of the United States* – Rutherforth's *Institutes of Natural Law*, Vattel's *Law of Nations*, and Domat's *Civil Law in its Natural Order*. But beyond the shared sources, Dwarris now also relied on Story himself, peppering his footnotes with references to the American jurist's *Commentaries on the Conflict of Laws*. Perhaps most telling is Dwarris's quotation of Story as authority to support the idea that, although there is indeed a "spirit of an instrument," that spirit is to be collected from the letter, thus avoiding the danger of inferences drawn from "extrinsic circumstances."[124]

---

[122] Ibid., II: 702, 693–694, 718, 702, 690, 690, 691, 692, 759 (citing Kent's *Commentaries on American Law*), 694.

[123] See, for example, Story's *Commentaries on the Law of Bailments* and *Commentaries on the Conflict of Laws*.

[124] Sir Fortunatus Dwarris, with the assistance of A. H. Amyot, *A General Treatise on Statutes: Their Rules of Construction and the Proper Boundaries of Legislation and of Judicial Interpretation* (2nd ed.; London: William Benning & Co., 1848), pp. 561–562.

Dwarris and Story shared the belief that when it came to interpretation the search for the lawmakers' intention, discerned through the language used and the context of the ills meant to be remedied, was simply the common sense of the matter. Although it might on occasion prove difficult to find that intention, the search remained the most basic obligation of the judges whose task it was to interpret the laws or the constitutions as enacted.

Eventually an American edition of "Dwarris on Statutes," as it came to be known, was prepared, a task undertaken by Platt Potter, a justice of the supreme court of New York. Potter introduced the treatise simply, as nothing less than "a standard work of the highest authority, acknowledged by all the courts of this country, as well as in England." But Justice Potter, taking his lead from Dwarris's second English edition and following Story, went further than merely editing. In the American edition he added a substantive chapter in which he sought to reduce the rules of interpretation found in Vattel, Rutherforth, Domat, Grotius, and Pufendorf to conveniently distilled lists of maxims.[125] To these he also added "American Rules," maxims taken from the likes of Chief Justice John Marshall and Francis Lieber.

Political and Legal Hermeneutics

Francis Lieber may be one of the most important and most overlooked scholars of mid–nineteenth-century America. In the 1820s he fled "Prussian oppression" for the United States, where, in a relatively short time, he made connections with many if not most of the leading intellectuals of the day.[126] Among those public men Joseph Story was of particular importance to Lieber. And in many ways, Lieber was of particular importance to him. Not only did Story write more or less as requested for Lieber's *Encyclopedia Americana*, but he constantly encouraged his foreign friend and spent a great deal of effort and time trying to secure Lieber a faculty appointment at Harvard, a post that would have thrilled Lieber, trapped as he felt he was in South Carolina and missing Boston, the city he thought of as his "American native place."[127]

---

[125] Sir Fortunatus Dwarris, *A General Treatise on Statutes: Their Rules of Construction, and the Proper Boundaries of Legislation and of Judicial Interpretation . . . with American Notes and Additions, and with Notes and Maxims of Constitutional and Statute Construction; also a Treatise on Constitutional Limitations upon the National and State Legislative Power, with a Chapter on Parliamentary Law and Parliamentary Privileges*, ed. Platt Potter (Albany, NY: William Gould and Sons, 1871), pp. 121–146.

[126] See generally Lewis R. Harley, *Francis Lieber: His Life and Political Philosophy* (New York: Columbia University Press, 1899); and Frank Freidel, *Francis Lieber: Nineteenth Century Liberal* (Baton Rouge: Louisiana State University Press, 1947). On Lieber's connections and correspondents, see Charles B. Robson, "Papers of Francis Lieber," *Huntington Library Bulletin* 3 (1933): 135–155. On his moral and political thought, especially as a reformer, see Wilson Smith, "Francis Lieber's Moral Philosophy," *Huntington Library Quarterly* 18 (1955): 395–408.

[127] As quoted in Robson, "Papers of Francis Lieber," p. 137.

Considered by many to have been the founder of the modern academic profession of political science,[128] Lieber wrote major and influential works such as the *Manual of Political Ethics*[129] and *Civil Liberty and Self-Government.*[130] And what had begun life as a chapter in the *Manual of Political Ethics* soon grew into his *Legal and Political Hermeneutics.* When William Kent, son of Chancellor James Kent, read the treatise on interpretation and construction, he could not contain himself. "'*Hermeneutics?*'" he bellowed. "Had you called your... book 'principles of interpretation,'... many an honest fellow, now frightened away, would have read and enjoyed the writings."[131] Justice Story was kinder.

Story was, he assured Lieber, "exceedingly pleased with it," finding it "full of excellent hints, and principles, and guiding rules." Moreover, the text was "written in a clear and complete style, with great force of illustration, and accuracy of statement, and withal in a spirit of candor and without partisanship." While Story confessed that there were "two or three little suggestions" he could have made, and "perhaps one or two qualifications" he might have offered, on the whole nothing he could have added would have been important to "the general scope of the dissertation."[132]

Lieber, like John Locke and Thomas Hobbes before him, understood that the problem of language and its interpretation was rooted in the facts of the human condition and man's imperfect nature. The fundamental truth was simple and straightforward: "There is no direct communication between the minds of men." Whatever "thoughts, emotions, conceptions, ideas" a person may have, they can be shared with others only through the agency of "signs." While the array of possible signs a person might use are "very various," those "by which man most frequently endeavors to convey his ideas to another, and by which in most cases he best succeeds in conveying them, are words."[133]

Because mankind's use of words has the definite purpose of conveying to others that "which moves us inwardly," there can be only one "true meaning" attached to the words that are used, and that is the meaning "those who used them were desirous of expressing." No "form of words can have more than one 'true sense'"; there can never be even "two true meanings to any text."[134] But coming to know that one "true meaning" or one "true sense" with certainty is almost always easier said than done.

---

[128] See, for example, James Farr, "Francis Lieber and the Interpretation of American Political Science," *Journal of Politics* 52 (1990): 1027–1049.

[129] 2 vols. (Boston: C. C. Little and J. Brown, 1838–39).

[130] (Philadelphia: Lippincott, Grambo, and Co., 1853).

[131] William Kent to Francis Lieber, 19 December 1843, as quoted in Freidel, *Francis Lieber*, p. 175.

[132] Joseph Story to Francis Lieber, 11 November 1837, *Life and Letters*, II: 283. One suspects Story might have objected to, or at least questioned, Lieber's willingness to dismiss Rutherforth's tripartite distinction of kinds of interpretation. Lieber, *Hermeneutics*, p. 75.

[133] Lieber, *Hermeneutics*, pp. 13, 13, 17, 21.

[134] Ibid., pp. 13, 17, 86, 66.

The great difficulty of coming to know the meaning intended to be conveyed stems from nothing less complicated than the very "nature and essence of human language." Because there is no direct communication between the minds of men, thus leaving "communication by intermediate signs only," it is "absolutely impossible" that "ambiguity can be entirely avoided." The fact is, words often mean different things according to their context; words may be used with insufficient precision; and the same words may be used to stand for different ideas by different people. Moreover, "obscurity of sense may arise either from a want of knowledge of the subject (either in the speaker or hearer, the writer or reader) or from the imperfect knowledge of the means of communication (again, either in the speaker or writer, on the one hand, or the hearer or reader on the other.)" Because of these innate difficulties, interpretation or construction becomes absolutely essential. And the "very basis of all interpretation" is the belief that a text can have only one true meaning.[135]

Because there is such a "vast variety of causes" of the ambiguity of human language, proper interpretation must proceed not "arbitrarily and whimsically" but by the rules that are "established by reason." These rules are not, by Lieber's measure, philosophically obscure or philologically intricate but are rather the dictates of "common sense." No matter how much effort has been given to detailed definition by the speaker or writer, the interpreter will inevitably have to rely on "common sense and good faith." What this means in purely practical terms is that the interpreter "must begin to give to words that meaning which . . . they ought to have,"[136] that is to say, the meaning the speaker or writer in all likelihood intended them to have.

This is not to say that such commonsense and good faith interpretation is merely a matter of "literal interpretation"; such a term Lieber held to be simply "inadmissible" in any serious discussion of interpretation. The reason is that language is more complicated than that, and the line between a literal signification and a figurative one is apt to be blurred by usage. The guide to proper interpretation cannot be the simple definitions of words but must be the intentions meant to be conveyed by those words by those who used them. The fact is that "literal interpretation is a most deceptive term" in that by an allegedly "strict adherence to the words, it wrenches them from their sense."[137]

Just as literal interpretation is to be avoided, so, too, is what Lieber calls "extravagant interpretation." Neither mode, he insists, is "genuine interpretation." The former insists on an unnatural narrowness of meaning, the latter on an unnatural expansiveness. The middle ground, the notion of a good faith interpretation, means that the interpreter is to "take the words

---

[135] Ibid., pp. 27, 27, 27, 26, 27, 34, 39, 86.
[136] Ibid., pp. 25, 21, 28, 31, 32.
[137] Ibid., pp. 66, 67, 68.

fairly as they were meant" by the user. This idea results in a "faithful interpretation" whereby the interpreter takes the words in the same sense in which he "honestly" believes they were used.[138]

This means focusing on the "most probable" sense in which they were used rather than on what might be their "original, etymological, or classical" sense. The meaning to be sought is that which "agrees most with the general and declared object of the text." When it comes to a law, for example, a knowledge of "the causes which led to its being issued . . . is of highest importance." Like Story, Lieber believed that the enterprise of interpretation properly so called can begin only with "the words themselves." Any preliminary reliance on "general principles," or "notions of public welfare," or the "supposed motives"[139] of the lawgiver will only skew the original meaning that was intended by the user.

A fundamental difficulty arises in that interpretation is itself often insufficient when it comes to determining how the "true meaning" or "true sense" of the text is to be applied at any given moment in the "complex cases of practical life." The reason, of course, is that society is not static. "Whether we rejoice in it or not," Lieber insisted, "the world moves on, and no man can run against the movement of his time." Even if a text could be drafted with "mathematical" precision, it would still suffer the assault of time for the simple reason that "things and relations change." The dilemma is that it is unrealistic to expect mankind to be "permanently fettered by laws of by-gone generations." Because "times and relations change" it may come to pass that "after a long lapse of time" the letter or the intent may have to be abandoned because, as a result of the "change in circumstances," they no longer agree. When the text proves to be "no longer directly applicable,"[140] it is at that point that interpretation must give way to construction.

The farther removed from the origin of a law the society finds itself, the more necessary it will likely be to move down the "dangerous path" of construction. But construction no less than interpretation is not merely an arbitrary imposition upon a text of meaning imported from without. While it is the necessary "drawing of conclusions respecting subjects that lie beyond the direct expression of the text," those conclusions must be drawn from elements "known from and given in the text." They are, in brief, conclusions "which are in the spirit, though not within the letter of the text."[141]

The purpose of construction going beyond the text itself is to make the text "agree and harmonize with the demands or principles of superior authority." It is, in fact, Lieber argued, "construction alone which saves us, in many instances, from sacrificing the spirit of a text, or the object, to

---

[138] Ibid., pp. 70–71, 93, 99.
[139] Ibid., pp. 99, 112, 126, 113, 114, 114, 128.
[140] Ibid., pp. 65, 135, 162–163, 135, 122 (but see Dwarris, as noted earlier), 122.
[141] Ibid., pp. 64, 56, 56.

the letter of the text, or the means by which that object was to be obtained." Without construction, laws not only might be understood in a way "fearfully destructive to the best and wisest intentions," but might even be made to "produce the very opposite of what [that intention] was purposed to effect."[142]

There is no denying that such an effort "to arrive at conclusions beyond the absolute sense of the text...is dangerous," and thus the process must be hedged round about by "safe rules" that will guide the constructor along his exegetical journey. It must be understood, at the least, that construction parallels interpretation in that each can be "close, comprehensive, transcendent, or extravagant." And one thing above all must be kept in mind, Lieber insisted, and that is that "nothing is so favorable to...the protection of individual rights, as close interpretation and construction." Thus as a matter of "constitutional hermeneutics," constitutions generally and "federal constitutions" in particular ought to be interpreted and construed closely.[143]

This is the case because constitutions consist of words that have been "well weighed" and because they form a "great contract" among the people themselves as well as between the people and their chosen rulers. There is a presumption of precision in such fundamental laws. As a general matter, it is assumed in constitutions that "the authority and power granted therein is all that is granted, and that nothing shall be considered as granted except what is mentioned."[144]

Construction, no less than interpretation, is meant to allow the interpreter to arrive at "something certain from something ambiguous and uncertain." But since the "true sense" is often "occult," the words of the text may still be so "doubtful, obscure [and] veiled" that it is quite possible that there will be "different explanations," even when sought in good faith and guarded by the rules of common sense. But it remains imperative that any interpreter or constructor never forget that the "sole legitimate office" is not to engage in the "act of bringing sense *into* the words," but rather to engage in "bringing *the* sense *out* of them."[145]

It is the temptation to import meaning rather than discern it that renders both interpretation and construction potentially dangerous, especially when it comes to constitutions and laws. The problem of "uncertainty of the law" had become, Lieber argued, "proverbial," the result of the same law being constantly subjected to a barrage of "different interpretations." No small part of the cause was the fact that all too often interpreters come to their task with such a "strong bias of mind" that it makes "the text subservient to...preconceived views." The result is that interpretation is "predestined," the manifestation of the interpreter's inclinations rather than

---

[142] Ibid., pp. 57–58, 58.
[143] Ibid., pp. 64, 77, 136, 177, 183.
[144] Ibid., pp. 183, 184.
[145] Ibid., pp. 65, 89, 87 (emphasis in the original).

the lawgiver's intentions. This is not genuine interpretation but merely "artful interpretation," a temptation every good-faith interpreter must be "watchful against being betrayed into." To avoid both "faithless" and "sinister" interpretations, those who have the power of interpretation must tirelessly "guard... against mistaking... private views and interests... passions and appetites for public virtues and demands."[146]

It is not impossible – indeed, it is quite common – that such strong biases may actually be "unknown" to the interpreter. But it is also not unlikely that such interpretive efforts that "bend laws, charters, wills [and] treaties" are not unknown and are quite intentional. Lieber was ever mindful that in politics and law whoever controls meaning controls everything. Thus, "the natural and essential character of power... will naturally lean towards extravagant constructions." Extravagant interpretation or construction becomes the handmaiden of "the natural, inherent, and necessary attribute of all power, physical or moral," which is its tendency to increase. And the use of extravagant construction or interpretation to increase power is always defended and legitimated by arguing that the case at hand "is of a peculiar character and the present time a crisis." The problem is that such extravagant constructions or interpretations are almost always "the beginning of fearful inroads" and will inevitably allow the interpreter "to defeat the object of almost any form of words."[147]

The fundamental purpose of language is communication: what did the writer or speaker mean by the language used? What were the purposes? Lieber repeatedly returns to the bedrock principle of his hermeneutics. "Every man or body of persons, making use of words, does so, in order to convey a certain meaning; and to find this precise meaning is the object of all interpretation." Yet, like Marshall and Story, Lieber denies that appeal to original motives alone is the key to that "precise meaning." In most cases the appeal to motive will prove at best "doubtful"; at worst, it may even be "dangerous." The reason is that, short of an explicit declaration of motives, recourse to them can only be a matter of supposition.[148] Such "supposed motives" will inevitably be subjective and thus probably at a far remove from the "true sense" of the text.

Again like Marshall and Story, Lieber understood that motive or intention had great interpretive weight. The question was how such motives or intentions were to be found out. "Unless motives are expressed," Lieber wrote, "it is exceedingly difficult to find them out, except by the text itself." Thus such motives "must form... a subject to be found out by the text, not the ground on which we construe it."[149] Only then will the objectivity of the text hold sway over the subjective and supposed motives that can, in

---

[146] Ibid., pp. 40, 40, 72, 72, 72, 80, 32, 182.
[147] Ibid., pp. 72, 82, 214, 137, 185, 180.
[148] Ibid., pp. 86, 114, 128.
[149] Ibid., p. 128.

fact, only be imported into the meaning of the text by a willful interpreter or constructor.

Originalism and the Tradition

Following in the path cleared by Dwarris, Story, and Lieber came a series of treatises on interpretation during the second half of the nineteenth century. In 1857, Theodore Sedgwick (1811–1859) published his *Treatise on the Rules which govern the Interpretation and Application of Statutory and Constitutional Law.* Taking his lead from Dwarris, whose treatise he found to be "a work of great soundness as well as of great originality of thought," Sedgwick undertook to do for American law what his predecessor had done for English law. After all, he argued, the "very essence" of the American constitutional order was a "government of written law." Like Dwarris, he was committed to protecting interpretation and construction from what he deemed "the mere arbitrary discretion of the judiciary." Dismissing as illegitimate any judicial reliance on "arbitrary formulae, metaphysical subtleties, [and] fanciful hypotheses," Sedgwick sought to establish a simple but compelling maxim: "The object to be obtained . . . is, as a general rule, the intention of the legislature."[150]

An English effort to bring Dwarris up to date appeared in 1875, a little over a quarter of a century after the appearance of Dwarris's second edition. As with Dwarris, Story, and Lieber, Sir Peter Benson Maxwell's treatise *On the Interpretation of Statutes* (which would run to twelve editions by 1969) took as its point of departure the most basic of all the premises of interpretation. "It is to be taken as a fundamental principle," he wrote, "standing, as it were, at the threshold of the whole subject of interpretation, that the intention of the legislature is invariably to be accepted and carried into effect, whatever may be the opinion of the judicial interpreter of its wisdom or justice." To go beyond text and intention would be to allow the judges to cast themselves adrift on "the wide sea of surmise and speculation." It is never the legitimate province of a court to "scan" a law for "its wisdom or its policy." For a court to presume to undertake "to construe an act according to its own notions of what ought to have been enacted" is to cross a boundary, and thus "not to construe the act, but to alter it."[151]

It is not simply an alternative but the "duty" of a court "not to make the law reasonable, but to expound it as it stands, according to the plain (or real)

---

[150] (New York: Voorhies [sic], 1857); see also the second edition by John Norton Pomeroy, (2nd ed.; New York: Baker and Voorhis, 1874), pp. vi, v, 228, 229. It is not without its interest that Sedgwick and Francis Lieber were friends and regular correspondents of Alexis de Tocqueville. See Aurelian Craiutu and Jeremy Jennings, eds., *Tocqueville on America after 1840: Letters and Other Writings* (Cambridge: Cambridge University Press, 2009). See especially Tocqueville's review of Sedgwick's *Treatise*, pp. 455–460.

[151] (London: William Maxwell and Sons, 1875), pp. 49, 49, 4, 6.

sense of the words." To take the law "as it stands" requires a willingness on the part of the judge to deny his own moral inclinations in order to enforce a law that may even be "absurd or mischievous." Even when such a law may be "unjust, arbitrary, or inconvenient," the judicial obligation is to give it its "full effect."[152] Legislatures may not be second-guessed.

Americans coming after Maxwell would argue similarly. Joel Prentiss Bishop, for example, never doubted that "written laws... require interpretation, the object whereof is simply to determine the meaning of the makers." Thus could he argue that "the merit of the interpretation is commensurate with its success in ascertaining what the writer meant." Like Story, Dwarris, and Lieber, Bishop in his *Commentaries on the Written Laws and their Interpretation* was a defender of textualism as the most efficacious means of arriving at the objective intention of a law or constitutional provision. The fact is, he argued, echoing Story, that "individual motives and purposes of the legislature are not judicially known." When it comes to interpretation, recourse to the language of the law is the "sole guide" to be followed by the courts. And that language and its meaning must be understood to be time-bound, and not constantly evolving. "If the statute is old, or if it is modern," Bishop insisted, "the court should transport itself back to the time when it was framed, consider the condition of things existing, and give it the meanings which the language as then used, and other considerations require." As Bishop understood, and sought to teach, "interpretation has its limits beyond which it cannot go."[153]

By the end of the nineteenth century, Henry Campbell Black, whose fame from his eponymous law dictionary was already well established, could pronounce in the preface to his *Handbook on the Construction and Interpretation of the Laws* what he considered to be the truth of legal interpretation: "It is no longer assumed to be the province of the judiciary either to quibble away or to evade the mandates of the legislature. On the contrary, the modern authorities recognize only one rule as absolutely unvarying, namely, to seek out and enforce the actual meaning and will of the law-making power." Thus could he confidently conclude that "the doctrine of equitable interpretation has become obsolete, the sanctity of the common law is no longer so jealously insisted upon, and the difference between strict and liberal construction has been reduced to a minimum." The task of the judge is limited to "discovering and expounding the intended signification of the language used, that is, the meaning which the authors of the law designed it to convey to others."[154]

---

[152] Ibid., pp. 4–5, 4, 4.

[153] Joel Prentiss Bishop, *For Civil Practice: Commentaries on the Written Laws and Their Interpretation* (Boston: Little, Brown and Co., 1882), pp. 177, 177, 60, 59, 58.

[154] (St. Paul, MN: West Publishing Co., 1896), pp. iii, iv, 1.

One had to be wary of what judges would attempt under the "pretence of interpretation" or the "guise of construction." The temptation of judges "to make a law different from what the lawmaking body intended to enact" is great indeed. By measuring a law against their personal standards of "wisdom, policy, or expediency," judges can by an interpretive sleight-of-hand transform a law from what it was intended to be into what the judge thinks it "ought" to be. But to do so is to exceed the "proper office and authority" of the judge's role.[155]

Black, more than some of the other treatise writers, was explicitly concerned, as Story had been, with interpreting the Constitution. Here, less than with statutes, the intention of the lawmaking authority is to be the guide. When it comes to the interpretation of the Constitution, Black argued, it is "a cardinal rule... that the instrument must be so construed as to give effect to the intention of the people who adopted it." This "intention is to be sought in the Constitution itself," and the text is not to be considered, to borrow Jefferson's phrase, a mere thing of wax, malleable at judicial will. As Story and Lieber had taught, there is only one correct meaning for any set of words. And by the art or craft of interpretation, the Constitution especially "cannot be made to mean different things at different times." The intention is to be ascertained by a "reasonable construction" and not left subject to the "mere arbitrary conjecture" of the judges.[156] For Black, the Constitution's meaning, in Story's words, is to be understood to be the same, "yesterday, to-day, and forever."

IV. THE PERMANENCE OF CONSTITUTIONAL MEANING

Story never failed to appreciate the inherent complexities of constitutional government. On the practical level, any scheme of government has to operate as something of a "science of adaptations – variable in its elements, dependent upon circumstances, and incapable of a rigid mathematical demonstration." On a more transcendent level, it must be understood that a "government is not a thing for an hour or a day, but is, or ought to be arranged for permanence."[157] It is through the instrumentality of a written constitution understood to be a fundamental law that the necessity of permanence is reconciled with the inevitability of change in human affairs.

The basic dilemma is that "no human government can ever be perfect." Time will always make clear certain "exigencies which may... require different adaptations and modifications of powers to suit the various necessities of the people." Because such defects and weaknesses are always likely to be exposed, it is necessary in advance "to provide means for altering and

---

[155] Ibid., p. 8.
[156] Ibid., pp. 17, 41.
[157] Story, "The Science of Government," *Miscellaneous Writings*, p. 617.

improving the fabric of government, as time and experience, or the new phases of human affairs may render proper, to promote the happiness and safety of the people."[158] But those necessary means have to avoid dangerous extremes.

It was deemed an irrefutable truth by the founding generation of Americans that any government that would be "forever changing or changeable" would soon be reduced to a state "bordering upon anarchy and confusion." Yet a constitution that provided no means of change when necessary would be dangerously viewed as "fixed and unalterable" and would likely "either degenerate into despotism, or by the pressure of its inequalities bring on a revolution." The constitutional challenge was "to make the changes practicable, but not too easy." The solution was a process at once usable and cumbersome that would "secure the deliberation, caution, and experience" of the people at the same time that it would close off the way for "experiments suggested by mere speculation or theory." Story put great stock in the fact that, in his view, the framers "knew that the besetting sin of republics is a restlessness of temperament, and a spirit of discontent at slight evils."[159] In the language of the Declaration of Independence, it was important to guard against fundamental changes being imposed for "light and transient causes."

There was simply no alternative to constitutional change by formal amendment. Most assuredly, it was not to be sought as a matter of judicial construction or interpretation. Because the Constitution was "designed for perpetuity,"[160] it was properly understood only as being "founded in permanent principles, and not dependent upon the caprice or will of particular judges." To unleash the judges in that way would prove to be nothing less than "an approach to tyranny and arbitrary power, to the exercise of mere discretion."[161] The Constitution was the result of the people operating in their truly "sovereign capacity," and the fundamental law had to be understood as having been "made by the people, made for the people, and [as] . . . responsible to the people."[162]

This theory of the "inherent sovereignty of the people"[163] means in practice that "the people themselves possess the supreme power to form, alter, amend, change and abolish at their pleasure the whole structure of their government and of course to reconstruct it in such manner, as from time to time be most agreeable to themselves."[164] Once fashioned and adopted, the language of the Constitution is thus to be understood as having a fixed and

---

[158] Story, *Commentaries on the Constitution*, II.1827.634.
[159] Ibid., pp. 634, 634–635.
[160] Ibid., I.369.251.
[161] Ibid., I.377.258.
[162] Ibid., I.415.294, I.397.282.
[163] Ibid., I.423.300.
[164] Story, "American Law," *American Journal of Comparative Law*, p. 12.

knowable meaning that can be altered only by the sober and complicated process of formal amendment. It is by this means alone that the Constitution as fundamental law can protect and preserve "the personal rights, the private property, and the public liberties of the whole people."[165] In Story's view, it is only this permanence of constitutional meaning that stands between the people and arbitrary, capricious, and unjust government.

[165] Story, "The Science of Government," *Miscellaneous Writings*, p. 620.

Epilogue

The Moral Foundations of Originalism

After Joseph Story's death on September 10, 1845, and therewith the passing of what he had called the "old race of judges,"[1] the debates over the interpretation of the Constitution only continued to intensify. Just beneath the surface of those debates lay the grave political issue of the morality of chattel slavery, what James Madison had described in the Constitutional Convention as the "most material" difference between the states. It was not their size or their mere location that put them potentially at odds, but rather the effects of "their having or not having slaves." This was what formed the "great division of interests" in the country.[2] With the passing of the founding generation – those whom Thomas Jefferson fondly recalled as "the generation of 1776" – the constitutional reconciliation of the great conflict between slavery and freedom fell to their "sons" and to what Jefferson feared would prove to be their "unwise and unworthy passions."[3]

Jefferson had immediately seen the passage of the Missouri Compromise in 1820, an agreement meant to deal with the spread of slavery into the territories, as "a fire bell in the night," an alarm that "awakened and filled [him] with terror." He was convinced that such an effort to reduce the "moral and political" principle of freedom to a mere "geographical line," as the compromise had done, only guaranteed that the "angry passions of men" would deepen the crisis. So dire was the situation that he confessed that he found his only "consolation" to be that he would not live "to weep over it." The "it" in question was what he thought would be the "useless sacrifice" of his own generation's struggle to bring "self-government and

---

[1] Joseph Story to Harriet Martineau, 7 April 1837, in William W. Story, ed., *Life and Letters of Joseph Story*, 2 vols. (Boston: C. C. Little and J. Brown, 1851), II: 277.

[2] James Madison, 30 June 1787, in Max Farrand, ed., *The Records of the Federal Convention*, 4 vols. (New Haven, CT: Yale University Press, 1937), I: 486. Hereinafter cited as *Records of the Federal Convention*.

[3] Thomas Jefferson to John Holmes, 22 April 1820, in Merrill Peterson, ed., *Jefferson: Writings* (New York: Library of America, 1988), p. 1434. Hereinafter cited as *Jefferson: Writings*.

happiness" to their beloved country. The act of "scission" to which the Missouri Compromise would likely lead would be nothing less than a great national "act of suicide."[4]

In a practical sense, the problem of slavery came to this, as Jefferson put it: "we have the wolf by the ears, and we can neither hold him, nor safely let him go. Justice is in one scale, and self-preservation in the other."[5] Yet in purely moral terms, there was no ambiguity even for some of the southerners in what John C. Calhoun had defended as their "peculiar institution."[6] Henry Clay, himself a slaveholding southerner, spoke for many when he insisted that slavery was the "deepest stain upon the character of our country." Like Jefferson, Clay feared the divide between the slave states and the free states would inevitably worsen, the passions of men being what they are. Yet he deeply believed that slavery could be perpetuated only by blowing out "the moral lights around us" and by eradicating from "the human soul...the light of reason and the love of liberty"[7] Such devices as the Missouri Compromise, Clay believed, although perhaps imperfect, would at least provide something of a working equilibrium between the states – however unsteady and impermanent that balance might eventually prove to be.

Less than a year after Justice Story's passing, the first step was taken in a legal march that would ultimately disrupt that uneasy balance between slavery and freedom. On April 6, 1846, an illiterate middle-aged black man scrawled his crude personal mark on the legal papers being filed in his name in the St. Louis circuit court. Born a slave in Virginia around the end of the eighteenth century, Dred Scott was seeking his freedom. He insisted that the fact of having traveled and resided with his master in states and territories where slavery was illegal was sufficient for him and his wife and their two children to be freed under the laws of Missouri. In June 1847, Scott lost his suit on a technicality, but was granted a right to a new trial. In 1850, he won his right to freedom – but only to see his owner successfully appeal to the Supreme Court of Missouri and have that decision overturned in 1852. In 1854, Scott appealed to the United States Court of Appeals for the district of Missouri in St. Louis; his owner again prevailed, but Scott then appealed to the Supreme Court of the United States, thus setting the judicial stage for the landmark confrontation of *Dred Scott v. Sandford.*[8]

---

[4] Ibid., pp. 1434, 1434–1435, 1434, 1435.

[5] Ibid., p. 1434.

[6] John C. Calhoun, "Speech in the Senate on the Reception of Abolition Petitions, 6 February 1837," in Richard K. Cralle, ed., *The Works of John C. Calhoun*, 6 vols. (New York: D. Appleton & Co., 1853–55), II: 626.

[7] Henry Clay, speech on African colonization, 20 January 1827, in Calvin Colton, ed., *Works of Henry Clay: Comprising his Life, Correspondence and Speeches*, 7 vols. (New York: Henry Clay Publishing Co., 1897), V: 337, 339.

[8] 60 U.S. 393 (1857). The best accounts of this sprawling and complex legal action are Don E. Fehrenbacher, *The Dred Scott Case: Its Significance in American Law and Politics*

Scott's case was only the second time in its history that the Supreme Court would strike down an act of Congress as unconstitutional; the first had been fifty-four years earlier in *Marbury v. Madison*. This time the majority of the Court invalidated the Missouri Compromise as an exercise of power by Congress to prohibit slavery in the territories, a power that the Court insisted was not granted by the Constitution. The greatest significance of the controversial decision was that it was a woefully unsuccessful political effort by Chief Justice Roger B. Taney to still once and for all the controversy over slavery. This he attempted to do by decreeing that slaves or former slaves or free blacks – indeed, any "descendants of Africans who were imported . . . and sold as slaves" – had never been, and could not be, citizens of the United States. There was nothing in the powers of Congress or the powers of the states, he insisted, that would allow that "unfortunate race" to be transformed into full members of the political community that had been created by the adoption of the Constitution.[9]

Taney insisted that his decision rested on the Constitution's "true intent and meaning when it was adopted."[10] The duty of the Court, he said, was clear:

No one, we presume, supposes that any change in public opinion or feeling, in relation to this unfortunate race, in the civilized nations of Europe or in this country, should induce the court to give to the words of the Constitution a more liberal construction in their favor than they were intended to bear when the instrument was framed and adopted. Such an argument would be altogether inadmissible in any tribunal called on to interpret it. If any of its provisions are deemed unjust, there is a mode prescribed in the instrument itself by which it may be amended; but while it remains unaltered, it must be construed now as it was understood at the time of its adoption. It is not only the same in words, but the same in meaning, and delegates the same powers to the Government, and reserves and secures the same rights and privileges to the citizen; and as long as it continues to exist in its present form, it speaks not only in the same words, but with the same meaning and intent with which it spoke when it came from the hands of its framers and was voted on and adopted by the people of the United States. Any other rule of construction would abrogate the judicial character of this court, and make it the mere reflex of the popular opinion or passion of the day. This court was not created by the Constitution for such purposes. Higher and graver trusts have been confided to it, and it must not falter in the path of duty.[11]

The chief justice then laid out in great detail what he understood to be "the history of the times" in which the colonies had won their independence and then formed their constitutions. This survey included such authorities as the Articles of Confederation, contemporary state and federal legislation,

---

(New York: Oxford University Press, 1978); and Earl M. Maltz, *Dred Scott and the Politics of Slavery* (Lawrence: University Press of Kansas, 2007).

[9] 60 U.S. 393 (1857), 403, 407, 406.
[10] Ibid., p. 405.
[11] Ibid., p. 426.

court cases both federal and within the several states, as well as Taney's own understanding of the framers' meaning in both the Declaration of Independence and the Constitution. In Taney's view, two constitutional conclusions were inevitable. First, under a proper reading of the fundamental law Dred Scott was never "a citizen of Missouri in the sense in which that is used in the Constitution." As a result, the federal court had no jurisdiction to take the case under its diversity of citizenship jurisdiction; the case should have been dismissed. As a member of that "subordinate and inferior class of beings"[12] who had always been considered property and nothing more, Scott the slave had no right to sue in the federal courts.

The second conclusion Taney reached was that the Constitution, a carefully crafted collection of limited and enumerated powers that had been delegated to the federal government by the people of the several states, had to be strictly construed in the manner of the Jeffersonian Republicans. And by such a construction it was clear that Congress was nowhere given a general power "to acquire a territory to be held and governed permanently in that character." The only power Congress had to increase the geographical territory of the country was by the formal admission of new states. Moreover, the prohibition of slavery by Congress in certain legislatively defined territories was an interference with the rights of private property of the slaveholder and thus a violation of the fundamental law – the right of the citizen not to be deprived of his property without due process of law. The Missouri Compromise was thus "not warranted by the Constitution and . . . [was] therefore void."[13] Although Taney's opinion is generally taken as that of the Court's majority, the case consisted of nine separate opinions, including two dissents by Justices John McLean and Benjamin Robbins Curtis, the latter being the more significant.

Justice Curtis, who would soon resign from the Court over Taney's administrative handling of the release to the public and the press of the written opinions in *Dred Scott*, went to the very heart of what he saw as the chief justice's faulty logic.[14] While Taney might insist that the powers of the federal courts, including those of the Supreme Court, were not so extensive as to allow the judges or justices to consider "the justice or injustice, the policy or impolicy" of the provisions crafted by "those who

---

[12] Ibid., pp. 432, 454, 404–405.

[13] Ibid., pp. 446, 450, 452.

[14] Curtis was dismayed and angered by Taney's willingness to play fast and loose with the procedures of the Court. Having prepared the first version of his opinion for circulation, Taney then withdrew it in light of Curtis's dissent in order to amend his expressed views in an effort to take into account and rebut Curtis's objections. Fehrenbacher estimates that Taney may have added as many as eighteen pages to the opinion, as Curtis had claimed. See Fehrenbacher, *The Dred Scott Case*, pp. 314–321, 389–390. See also Benjamin R. Curtis, Jr., ed., *A Memoir of Benjamin Robbins Curtis, LL.D.*, 2 vols. (Boston: Little, Brown and Co., 1879), I: 192–242. This contains the increasingly sharp correspondence on the matter between Taney and Curtis.

formed the sovereignty and framed the Constitution,"[15] he most assuredly was not practicing what he preached. In Curtis's view, Taney's construction concerning the powers of Congress to deal with slavery in the territories clearly rested not on the "true intent and meaning" of the Constitution when it was adopted, as the chief justice claimed, but upon nothing more substantial than his own personal reasons, which were "purely political." The result, as Curtis saw it, was to render a proper judicial interpretation of the fundamental law "impossible." Such political considerations and calculations cannot provide the objective foundational rules necessary for a proper judicial interpretation. There is nothing "fixed" in such political reasons, since they are more likely than not to be not only "different in different men," but often "different in the same men at different times."[16] The rule of law and true constitutional government demand more.

The most significant juridical sin committed by Chief Justice Taney, in Curtis's opinion, was his effort to transform the meaning of the Constitution by importing new meaning into old words, and by imposing exceptions to stated provisions that could be achieved only by ignoring the "clear, plain, and natural signification"[17] of the words the framers had used. Moreover, Taney's alleged "history of the times" was a masterpiece of inaccuracy and deliberate distortion. It had become a maxim in American constitutional law since the chief justiceship of John Marshall that a "practical construction, nearly contemporaneous with the adoption of the Constitution, and continued by repeated instances through a long series of years, may always influence, and in doubtful cases should determine the judicial mind on a question of interpretation of the Constitution."[18] Taney could reach his desired conclusions only by ignoring those contemporaneous constructions of the Constitution rendered by those "men intimately acquainted with its history from their personal participation in framing and adopting it"[19] that conflicted with his own views.

To Justice Curtis, Taney's opinion advocated a deeply flawed and inadequate understanding of the nature and extent of judicial power under a written and ratified constitution of limited and enumerated powers. When "a strict interpretation of the Constitution," Curtis wrote, "according to the fixed rules which govern the interpretation of the laws, is abandoned, and the theoretical opinions of individuals are allowed to control its meaning, we have no longer a Constitution; we are under the government of individual men who, for the time being have power to declare what the Constitution

---

[15] 60 U.S. 393, 405.

[16] Ibid., pp. 620, 620, 621.

[17] Ibid., p. 615.

[18] Ibid., p. 616. Curtis here cited his authorities from both the Marshall and the Taney Courts: *Stuart v. Laird*, 5 U.S. 299 (1803); *Martin v. Hunter*, 14 U.S. 304 (1816); *Cohens v. Virginia*, 19 U.S. 264 (1821); *Prigg v. Pennsylvania*, 41 U.S. 539 (1842); and *Cooley v. Board of Wardens*, 53 U.S. 299 (1852).

[19] 60 U.S. 393, 619.

is according to their own views of what it ought to mean." At a minimum, such interpretation means that there is no longer in place a true "republican government" – that is to say, a government with "limited and defined powers" – but rather a government that is either "merely an exponent of the will of Congress" or, what would be worse, "an exponent of the individual opinions of the members of this court."[20] What is lost by such a "loose and unhistorical" style of interpretation, as Curtis saw it, was nothing less than self-government properly understood.[21]

Despite his age, Justice Curtis was in many ways one of Justice Story's "old race of judges" when it came to constitutional law. And not without good reason. Graduating from Harvard College in 1829, he matriculated to the Law School and was among the first students who would sit at the feet of the newly appointed Dane Professor of Law, one Joseph Story. Receiving his law degree in 1832 (when appointed to the Supreme Court in 1851, he was the first justice ever to have such a degree)[22]; Curtis would take with him Story's appreciation for the Constitution and its proper interpretation.[23] His dissent in *Dred Scott* was a clear, powerful, and unmistakable echo of Story's own understanding of the limits of judicial construction and the necessity of judges abiding by clear rules of interpretation. The younger man had heeded well Story's admonition that in republics it is always essential to guard against the "captivations of theory"[24] lest the necessary certainty of the rule of law be supplanted by the mere arbitrariness of a judge's willful imposition of his own "theoretical opinions." To say the least, the new race of judges did not share those views.

I. THE RISE OF GOVERNMENT BY JUDICIARY

Chief Justice Taney's opinion in the case of Dred Scott helped to lay the foundation for the rise of what might properly be called government by judiciary; the decision did this in two ways.[25] In the short term, the Supreme

---

[20] Ibid., p. 621.
[21] On the dangers posed by "loose and unhistorical" interpretations, see Charles E. Shattuck, "The True Meaning of the Term 'Liberty' in those Clauses in the Federal and State Constitutions which Protect 'Life, Liberty, and Property'," *Harvard Law Review* 4 (1891): 365–392, p. 366.
[22] Henry J. Abraham, *Justices, Presidents, and Senators: A History of the United States Supreme Court Appointments from Washington to Bush II* (5th ed.; Lanham, MD: Rowman and Littlefield, 2008), p. 89.
[23] James McClellan, *Joseph Story and the American Constitution* (Norman: University of Oklahoma Press, 1971), p. 275.
[24] Joseph Story, "The Value and Importance of Legal Studies," in William W. Story, ed., *The Miscellaneous Writings of Joseph Story* (Boston: C. C. Little and J. Brown, 1852), p. 513.
[25] I borrow this phrase from the titles of two works – works, it must be said, of very different views: Louis B. Boudin, *Government by Judiciary*, 2 vols. (New York: W. Godwin, 1932); and Raoul Berger, *Government by Judiciary: The Transformation of the Fourteenth Amendment* (Cambridge, MA: Harvard University Press, 1977).

Court sharpened the moral and constitutional line between the friends and foes of slavery, thus ultimately contributing to the degeneration of the union into dissolution and civil war. So, too, did his decision lie behind the necessity of the amendments to the Constitution that would be passed in the wake of that war, not least the Fourteenth Amendment and its restatement of the Fifth Amendment's due process clause. In the longer term, Taney's new conception of what was meant constitutionally by "due process of law" that he posited in *Dred Scott v. Sandford* would eventually take root and enable the judiciary to move beyond the mere text and intention of the Constitution and embolden the judges to give voice to their personal views of justice, which they could then present as merely the requirements of what was demanded by "due process of law."

Taney expressed his new and expansive notion of what was meant by "due process of law" this way:

> the rights of property are united with the rights of person, and placed on the same ground by the fifth amendment to the Constitution, which provides that no person shall be deprived of life, liberty, and property, without due process of law. And an act of Congress which deprives a citizen of the United States of his liberty or property merely because he came himself or brought his property into a particular Territory of the United States, and who had committed no offence against the laws, could hardly be dignified with the name of due process of law.[26]

This was the first time that due process was connected to the idea of the vested rights of private property as a bar to legislation. Historically, "due process of law" was a more limited concept. "The words *due process of law*," Alexander Hamilton had occasion to explain, "have a precise technical import, and are only applicable to the process and proceedings of the courts of justice; they can never be referred to an act of the legislature."[27] In time, Taney's logic about vested rights would give rise to the more fully developed idea that there is a substantive as well as merely a procedural element in the idea of due process of law.[28]

---

[26] *Dred Scott v. Sandford*, 60 U.S. 393, 450.

[27] Alexander Hamilton in the New York Assembly commenting on the New York constitution, 6 February 1787, in Harold C. Syrett, ed., *The Papers of Alexander Hamilton*, 26 vols. (New York: Columbia University Press, 1961–79), IV: 35.

[28] Taney's reformulation of "due process of law" as relating to the substance of legislation and not merely the procedures to which one is due in the courts of law was not the first expression of the idea. The year before *Dred Scott* was handed down the New York Court of Appeals, in *Wynehamer v. New York*, for the first time held that legislation could be invalidated if its substantive provisions conflicted with what is demanded by the "due process of law." Somewhat ironically, the state court created its new theory, not to unleash the state judges to engage in moral reasoning, but precisely to keep them from it. Justice Comstock wrote that judicial reliance on "theories alleged to be found in natural reason and inalienable rights" as the grounds of a decision was "subversive of the just and necessary powers of government." 13 N.Y. 378 (1856), 391. The state law in question that sought to prohibit liquor was too arbitrary and unreasonable to stand; but it would fall not because it was "contrary to natural equity or justice" or violated "any fanciful theory of higher law

At first, the Supreme Court resisted the temptation to infuse the due process clause of the of the Fourteenth Amendment with such a substantive content. When the justices were first asked to do so, they declined, noting that in the instant case the regulation of slaughterhouses in New Orleans did not constitute "deprivation of property within the meaning of that provision."[29] In a series of cases from 1873 to 1890, the Court continued to deny that any doctrine of so-called substantive due process could be derived from the Constitution.[30] But there were ominous stirrings. As the membership of the Court was changing, there was an emerging willingness on the part of some justices to see more than mere procedural guarantees in the due process clause.[31] By 1905 the doctrine of substantive due process came into full flower in *Lochner v. New York*, in which the Court announced that the standard for constitutional adjudication under the due process clause was now whether the law in question was "a fair, reasonable, and appropriate exercise of the police power of the state" or whether it was in fact "an unreasonable, unnecessary, and arbitrary interference with the right of the individual to his personal liberty."[32] The idea that there was an unwritten but judicially enforceable "liberty of contract" implicit in the due process clause of the Fourteenth Amendment would hold sway until 1937.[33]

Taking place alongside this judicial development was a debate within the scholarly community and in the law reviews about whether the written Constitution is in fact supplemented by an unwritten constitution that consists of higher-law principles derived from the idea of natural rights.[34] There were even those willing to argue that it was not some notion of rights by nature

---

or first principles of natural rights outside the constitution." Ibid., p. 430 (Justice Selden), p. 453 (Justice Hubbard). The law was invalid, the court ruled, because such laws violated the clear text of the state constitution; they were against what was demanded by due process of law.

[29] *The Slaughterhouse Cases*, 83 U.S. 36 (1873), 81. Justice Miller insisted that to hold otherwise would have the unhappy effect of constituting the Supreme Court as a "perpetual censor" of all the legislation of the states.

[30] *Munn v. Illinois*, 94 U.S. 113 (1877); *Davidson v. New Orleans*, 96 U.S. 97 (1878); *Stone v. Farmers' Loan and Trust Co.*, 116 U.S. 307 (1886).

[31] In 1887 the Court announced that they were "under a solemn duty – to look at the substance of things whenever they enter upon the inquiry whether the legislature transcended the limits of its authority." *Mugler v. Kansas*, 123 U.S. 362 (1887), 661.

[32] 198 U.S. 45 (1905), 56.

[33] In *West Coast Hotel v. Parrish*, 300 U.S. 379 (1937), the Court refused to invalidate a state law under the doctrine of substantive due process, but it also pointedly refused to annihilate the doctrine itself. "Liberty under the Constitution," Chief Justice Hughes wrote, "is . . . necessarily subject to the restraints of due process, and regulation which is reasonable in relation to its subject and is adopted in the interests of the community is due process." Ibid., p. 391.

[34] See, for example, Thomas M. Cooley, "Comparative Merits of Written and Prescriptive Constitutions," *Harvard Law Review* 2 (1888–89): 341–357; James C. Carter, "The Provinces of the Written and the Unwritten Law," *American Law Review* 24 (1890): 1–24; William C.

that was binding but merely "social forces" that reflected what could be considered "the prevalent sense of right" of those in the community.[35] This "popular sense of right," it is important to note, was not deemed as being "stationary" but was the living "flesh and blood of the Constitution."[36] It was by this evolving "sense of right" that the judges were able to declare unconstitutional any legislative acts that might interfere with an individual's rights, "even though these acts do not violate any specific provision of the Constitution."[37]

In this view, the real lawgivers whose meaning is to be sought are not the original members of the legislature or delegates to the Constitutional Convention who passed the law or drafted the provision in question, but rather "the people of the present day who possess the political power, and whose commands give life to what otherwise is a dead letter." By rooting interpretation or construction in the "real meaning of the living lawgiver," the nation, it was argued, can free itself from being "ruled by dead men, or by the utterances of dead men." The mere written words of the legal texts are nothing more than empty vessels to be filled by those who, for the moment, wield power. The old-fashioned idea – embraced by the likes of Marshall, Story, Jefferson, and Madison – that words are signs that are meant to convey thoughts from one mind to another was dismissed as simply "altogether false."[38]

Others writing during this time were more artful in expressing their views in support of what they understood to be the innate "elasticity" of the Constitution. In a two-part article in the *Harvard Law Review* of 1900, one finds a most profound and seemingly unwavering defense of the idea that when it comes to constitutional interpretation, "the original intention must

Morey, "The Genesis of a Written Constitution," *Annals of the American Academy of Political and Social Science* (1891): 529–557; John E. Keeler, "Survival of the Theory of Natural Rights in Judicial Decisions," *Yale Law Journal* 14 (1892–96): 14–25; Thomas Thacher, "Construction," *Yale Law Journal* 6 (1896–97): 59–65; Arthur W. Machen, Jr., "The Elasticity of the Constitution," *Harvard Law Review* 14 (1900–01): 200–216, 273–285; Emlin McClain, "Unwritten Constitutions," *Harvard Law Review* 15 (1902): 531–540; Emlin McClain, "Written and Unwritten Constitutions in the United States," *Columbia Law Review* 6 (1906): 69–81; Simeon E. Baldwin, "The Courts as Conservators of Social Justice," *Columbia Law Review* 9 (1909): 567–586; Robert P. Reader, "The Due Process Clauses and the Substance of Individual Rights," *University of Pennsylvania Law Review* 58 (1910): 191–218; Herbert Pope, "The Fundamental Law and the Power of the Courts," *Harvard Law Review* 27 (1913–14): 45–67; Charles M. Hough, "Due Process of Law – Today," *Harvard Law Review* 32 (1918): 218–233; and John Dickinson, "The Law behind the Law," *Columbia Law Review* 29 (1929): 113–146, 285–319.

[35] Christopher G. Tiedeman, *The Unwritten Constitution of the United States: A Philosophical Inquiry into the Fundamentals of American Constitutional Law* (New York: G. P. Putnam's Sons, 1890), p. 9.

[36] Ibid., pp. 9, 43.

[37] Ibid., p. 81.

[38] Ibid., pp. 150, 153, 150, 146.

prevail whenever discoverable." Moreover, it is essential to keep in mind that "the intention of the framers was that their words should be applied in their reasonable and proper construction to all cases and circumstances that might in the future arise." This "intent of the framers must forever be followed, however expedient may appear a departure therefrom." This all rested upon two simple and obvious truths: first, that "the will of the framers of the Constitution . . . is sovereign"; and second, that this understanding is "the universal and cardinal rule of constitutional law."[39]

Yet all was not as simple as it seemed. Even though in theory the "law of the Constitution remains forever unchanging," in practice "the facts to which it must be applied are infinitely various." Not only that, when it comes to the Fourteenth Amendment, the true, original meaning is that "due process of law" is meant simply to forbid "arbitrary and oppressive legislation." The determination of the "constitutionality of any act of the legislature," the consideration of whether or not it is arbitrary when measured against the changing and evolving facts of the time, falls to the courts. And the constitutionality or unconstitutionality of the law in question depends only upon the judge's assessment of its "reasonableness." In making that assessment while confronting the often "novel circumstances" and "unprecedented problems" of the day, the judge must strive to deliver "a liberal and statesmanlike construction." Such a construction will be found to be that which will "prevent only what is wrong and enjoin only what is right"[40] as determined by the judge. Thus is legislative arbitrariness replaced by judicial arbitrariness.[41]

By 1937, when the Court abandoned its notion of "liberty of contract" but left in place the theoretical foundations of the doctrine of substantive due process, the ground was prepared for a new era of government by judiciary. Rather than seek to restrict government regulations that interfered with business and the free market, the justices began to take notice of the problem of personal liberties, and turned their attention to fashioning constitutional protections for "prejudice against discrete and insular minorities"[42] when it came to the fundamental rights they might see as embraced by the due process clause of the Fourteenth Amendment. The primary target of the Supreme Court would be the moral judgments of the state legislatures that would be passed into laws affecting individual liberties broadly understood rather than the previously narrower concern with economic liberties and property rights. The doctrinal strands of the Court's new thinking – that

---

[39] Machen, "The Elasticity of the Constitution," pp. 205, 203, 212. See also p. 211.

[40] Ibid., pp. 273, 277, 275, 281, 284.

[41] The author insisted, of course, that such was not the case: "The important point is to keep clearly in mind that circumstances alter cases, that a statute which on one state of facts is just and proper may on another state of facts by arbitrary and void, and that this doctrine involves no departure from the intention of the framers, nor any adoption of a shifting, variable construction of the Constitution." Ibid., p. 279.

[42] *Carolene Products Co. v. United States*, 304 U.S. 144 (1937), 152, n.4.

there are in fact rights "so rooted in the traditions and conscience of our people as to be ranked fundamental"[43] and that it is up to the Supreme Court itself to determine which rights were to be deemed fundamental and which not – would in time come together with a vengeance in the cases touching the judicially created right to privacy.

Although the right to privacy as a matter of contemporary constitutional law is of rather recent vintage,[44] the roots of the idea go back much further. Normally, it is understood to have begun with a pioneering article, "The Right to Privacy," by Samuel Warren and Louis Brandeis, which appeared in the *Harvard Law Review* in 1890.[45] In fact, there is a longer history of a developing tradition of a privacy right of which that essay was essentially a part.[46] For understanding the current constitutional right of privacy, the most important fact about the argument Warren and Brandeis presented was that it did not advocate expanding the Constitution to protect privacy. It was a more modest effort to create an action in tort law to enable the great and the good to sue for damages when beset by the "continuous ordeal of the camera" of relentless "kodakers" who made the age of yellow journalism all that it could be.[47] Their objective was to "set against the newspapers' jealously guarded first amendment rights a countervailing right on the part of individuals, an explicit 'right to privacy'."[48]

Warren and Brandeis understood that in order for such a right to be embraced by the common law "in its eternal youth" they would have to establish a principled ground for it. Thus their basic argument was that "[p]olitical, social, and economic changes entail the recognition of new rights . . . to meet the demands of society." In the instant case, those changed times demanded "a general right to privacy for thoughts, emotions, and

---

[43] *Palko v. Connecticut*, 302 U.S. 319 (1937), 324–325.

[44] *Griswold v. Connecticut*, 381 U.S. 479 (1965).

[45] Samuel D. Warren and Louis D. Brandeis, "The Right to Privacy," *Harvard Law Review* 4 (1890): 193–220.

[46] See Note, "The Right to Privacy in Nineteenth Century America," *Harvard Law Review* 94 (1981): 1892–1910.

[47] The term "kodakers" was used by the editorial writers at the *New York Times*, as quoted in Denis O'Brien, "The Right of Privacy," *Columbia Law Review* 2 (1902): 437–448. O'Brien was a member of the New York court that had bucked the state court trend and had denied the extension of the right to privacy in *Roberson v. Rochester Folding Box Co.*, 171 N.Y. 538 (1902), a holding that led to "something of a storm of professional, as well as popular, disapproval." Wilbur Larremore, "The Law of Privacy," *Columbia Law Review* 12 (1912): 694–708, p. 694. Judge O'Brien argued in his law review essay that the "right of privacy . . . is such an intangible thing and conveys such a vague idea that it is doubtful if the law can ever deal with it in any reasonable or practical way." Any court, he further warned, "that will not respect the limitations of the law upon its own powers will not long retain the respect of the people." In the law, he concluded, it is "easy enough to wander away from beaten paths that are safe, but it is not always easy to return." O'Brien, "The Right of Privacy," pp. 445, 441, 448.

[48] "The Right to Privacy in Nineteenth Century America," p. 1910.

sensations." By their common law calculus, the "general object in view [was] to protect the privacy of private life," including the "life, habits, acts, and relations of an individual."[49] The right urged by Warren and Brandeis made its way into American tort law nearly from the beginning, and by the 1960s was widely accepted.[50] But it would also prove to be an idea that would lie dormant as a matter of constitutional law and be brought to life in a way that perhaps neither Warren nor Brandeis would have expected seventy-five years earlier.

The issue that would become the focus of *Griswold v. Connecticut* had come to the Court before in *Poe v. Ullman*, but the Court had declined to reach the merits of the case.[51] Yet in the dissent of Justice John Marshall Harlan it was very clear that the doctrine of substantive due process was still lurking just around the doctrinal corner. As he insisted, "the full scope of the liberty guaranteed by the Due Process Clause cannot be found in or limited by the precise terms of the specific guarantees elsewhere provided in the Constitution. This 'liberty' is not a series of isolated points... [but] is a rational continuum which, broadly speaking, includes a freedom from all substantial arbitrary impositions and purposeless restraints."[52] The split among the justices on this question would be clearly revealed two years later – and two years before *Griswold* – in *Ferguson v. Skrupa*. In that decision for a unanimous Court, Justice Hugo Black wrote that "[t]here was a time when the Due Process Clause was used by this Court to strike down laws which were thought unreasonable, that is, unwise or incompatible with some particular economic or social philosophy." But that time had passed. "The doctrine... that due process authorizes courts to hold laws unconstitutional when they believe the legislature has acted unwisely has long since been discarded. We have returned to the original constitutional proposition that courts do not substitute their social and economic beliefs for the judgment of legislative bodies, who are elected to pass laws."[53] This was the state of doctrinal confusion when the issues in *Poe* came back to the Court for resolution in *Griswold*.

---

[49] Warren and Brandeis, "Right to Privacy;" pp. 193, 206, 215, 216.

[50] See Larremore, "The Law of Privacy" and William Prosser, "Privacy," *California Law Review* 48 (1960): 383–423. There had been firm critics, however. One had argued simply and forcefully near the beginning that "the right to privacy does not exist." And the attempt to create it was especially worrying. "That our law is a system that grows and develops in response to the demands of advancing civilization, is due to the fact that new occasions and new circumstances arise which come within the principles upon which our laws were founded; not because new principles and new rights are created to afford that protection or redress which seems to be required." Herbert Spencer Hadley, "The Right to Privacy," *Northwestern Law Review* 3 (1894): 1–21, pp. 20, 21.

[51] 367 U.S. 497 (1961).

[52] Ibid., p. 543.

[53] 372 U.S. 726 (1963), 729, 730.

In *Griswold v. Connecticut*, the Supreme Court ruled that a Connecticut statute making the use of birth control measures by married couples illegal was a violation of "a right of privacy older than the Bill of Rights – older than our political parties, older than our school system." The problem for the Court was that the law obviously violated no particular provision of the Constitution. It perhaps would not have been surprising if Justice William O. Douglas had rested his majority opinion on the discredited but not completely dead idea of substantive due process as set forth in *Lochner v. New York*; but he explicitly chose to "decline that invitation." Instead of exhuming a doctrine that many thought best left buried (and perhaps not least since he had joined Black's opinion in *Ferguson* two years earlier), Douglas held that the Connecticut law had run afoul of "penumbral rights" that were, in his view, "formed by emanations" from "specific guarantees in the Bill of Rights."[54] This sweeping opinion had been foreshadowed by Douglas in his dissent in *Poe*. There he had made clear that in his view " 'due process' as used in the Fourteenth Amendment includes all of the first eight Amendments . . . [but is not] restricted and confined to them." The idea of "[l]iberty is a conception that sometimes gains content from the emanations of other specific guarantees."[55] By any measure, this was judicial creativity of unequaled boldness.[56]

Following *Griswold*, the Court found that those penumbras were capacious enough constitutionally to protect the right of unmarried couples to use birth control[57] and the right to abortion.[58] Given the foundation of the right to privacy and the understanding of judicial power that allowed the Court to create it,[59] there was never any reason to think that it had in any meaningful

---

[54] 381 U.S. 479, 486, 482, 484.

[55] 367 U.S. 497, 516, 517.

[56] Justice Hugo Black in dissent indicted the Court's resurrection of the doctrine of substantive due process "based on subjective considerations of 'natural justice' " in order to strike down the Connecticut law as simply unacceptable. It is not the duty of the Supreme Court, he insisted, "to keep the Constitution in tune with the times." The fact was that the framers knew there would be need for change and had provided for it through the formal process of amendment. While he could agree with Justice Potter Stewart's characterization of the law as "uncommonly silly," that was not grounds enough for the Court to invalidate it. 381 U.S. 479, 522, 521, 527.

[57] *Eisenstadt v. Baird*, 405 U.S. 438 (1972).

[58] *Roe v. Wade*, 410 U.S. 113 (1973).

[59] There is no doubt that the justices involved in the drafting of the decision in *Griswold* knew that what they were doing was creating a new constitutional right. On 24 April 1965, Justice William Brennan wrote to Justice William O. Douglas with suggestions for improving the draft opinion Justice Douglas had sent to him. Douglas had initially been seeking the right of marital privacy in the notion of the freedom of association, a right earlier created by the Court by blending the rights of freedom of speech and freedom of assembly that are textually present in the First Amendment. Brennan cautioned against this approach. While insisting that Douglas was right in rejecting any approach based on the old doctrine of substantive due process, Brennan counseled that the best approach would be follow the

way reached "the limit of its logic"[60] with the abortion decision, however politically tumultuous that case would prove to be. Even more important to the idea of the right to privacy and its expansion than *Roe v. Wade* and the cases that came in its wake was the decision of the Court upholding *Roe* in *Planned Parenthood of Southeastern Pennsylvania v. Casey*. For there the justices made very clear just how truly limitless is the idea of "liberty" and just how great is their own self-proclaimed power to shape it as they might please, regardless of what the representative institutions of the federal and state governments might think.

The plurality opinion of Justices Anthony Kennedy, Sandra Day O'Connor, and David Souter in *Casey* went far beyond merely upholding *Roe*. It undertook to establish an understanding of judicial power and constitutional interpretation far more radical than what any earlier court had ever suggested. It was not enough merely to embrace, as they did, the intellectually rickety structure of substantive due process by noting once again that "a literal reading of the [Due Process] Clause might suggest that it governs only procedures by which a State may deprive persons of liberty." Such a literal reading would miss the essence of modern notions of judicial power, however. Indeed, "for at least 105 years, at least since *Mugler v. Kansas* . . . the Clause has been understood to contain a substantive component as well." And the "outer limits of that substantive sphere of liberty" was to be defined by neither "the Bill of Rights nor the specific practices of States at the time of the adoption of the Fourteenth Amendment." The fact is, when it comes

---

Court's earlier example "in *creating* a right of association . . . [from] the First Amendment to protect something not literally within its terminology of speech and assembly, because the interest protected is so closely related to speech and assembly." As he saw it, such a tack was far better: "Instead of expanding the First Amendment right of association to include marriage, why not say that what has been done for the First Amendment can also be done for some of the other fundamental guarantees of the Bill of Rights?" Brennan's goal was to see "a right to privacy *created* out of the Fourth Amendment and the self-incrimination clause of the Fifth, together with the Third, in much the same way as the right to associate has been *created* out of the First." Such a ploy would allow the Court to "hurdle" the "obstacle" posed by the fact that "the association of husband and wife is not mentioned in the Bill of Rights" and thus "effect a reversal in this case." William J. Brennan to William O. Douglas, 24 April 1965, Manuscript Division, Library of Congress. Emphasis supplied.

For a glimpse of the law office politics of the justices' chambers as they wrestled with what to do about the opinions in *Griswold*, see David J. Garrow, *Liberty and Sexuality: The Right to Privacy and the Making of Roe v. Wade* (New York: Macmillan, 1994), pp. 229–260.

60 The phrase is from Benjamin N. Cardozo, *The Nature of the Judicial Process* (New Haven, CT: Yale University Press, 1921), p. 51.

In his dissent in *Lawrence v. Texas*, Justice Scalia insisted that "[s]tate laws against bigamy, same-sex marriage, adult incest, prostitution, masturbation, adultery, fornication, bestiality, and obscenity" would be subject to invalidation since the Court had now overruled its earlier opinion in *Bowers v. Hardwick* that states have the right to pass laws "based on moral choices." 539 U.S. 558 (2003), 590.

.

to the due process clause its "boundaries are not susceptible of expression as a general rule." Any limitation on that substantive component of "liberty" depends only upon the evolving "reasoned judgment" of the Court itself.[61]

What was most shocking about the Kennedy, O'Connor, and Souter opinion in *Casey* was the seeming disdain it reflected for the idea of popular government. The Court was apparently not intended simply to be an "intermediate" institution between the people and their government "in order, among other things, to keep the latter within the limits assigned to their authority."[62] It was something far more important. Indeed, the essence of the judicial power as presented in *Casey* was that of an institution "invested with the authority to...speak before all others for [the people's] constitutional ideals." The power of the Court to declare such values – and the people's willingness to acquiesce in those declarations – was to Kennedy, O'Connor, and Souter what gave legitimacy to the people as "a nation dedicated to the rule of law."[63] It was precisely this view of its own power to "speak before all others" for the presumed constitutional ideals of the people that would in time bring the Court to the point of expanding ever further the "outer limits of the substantive sphere of liberty" in *Lawrence v. Texas.*[64]

In writing for the majority in *Lawrence* to overrule a case of only seventeen years standing that allowed the states to prohibit homosexual sodomy, Justice Anthony Kennedy insisted that the idea of liberty in the Constitution's due process clauses is not limited to protecting individuals from "unwarranted governmental intrusions into a dwelling or other private places," but has "transcendent dimensions" of a more moral sort. Properly understood, this notion of liberty "presumes an autonomy of self that includes freedom of thought, belief, expression and certain intimate conduct," whether those are mentioned in the Constitution or not. Indeed, had those who originally drafted "the Due Process Clauses of the Fifth and Fourteenth Amendments known the components of liberty in its manifold possibilities, they might have been more specific." But they could not have known, since "times can blind us to certain truths and later generations can see that laws once thought necessary and proper in fact serve only to oppress." The essence of the Constitution, for Justice Kennedy and those who joined him, is that it falls to "persons in every generation [to] invoke its principles in their own search for greater freedom."[65] Put more simply, there is nothing permanent to the Constitution, no fundamental, unalterable principles; its meaning

---

[61] 505 U.S. 833 (1992), 846, 848, 849.
[62] Jacob E. Cooke, ed., *The Federalist* (Middletown, CT: Wesleyan University Press), No. 78, p. 525.
[63] 505 U.S. 833, 868, 865.
[64] 539 U.S. 558 (2003).
[65] Ibid., pp. 562, 562, 562.

comes only from the changing moral views of successive generations of ever more enlightened justices.[66]

Justice Kennedy's understanding of the changing metaphysical contours of the right of privacy was drawn in large part from an *obiter dictum* in *Casey* where the Court had insisted that lying at the heart of the idea of liberty provided in the Constitution "is the right to define one's own concept of existence, of meaning, of the universe, and of the mystery of human life."[67] This was but something of a crude echo of a similar *dictum* by Justice Louis Brandeis in his dissent in *Olmstead v. United States*, in which he had rhapsodically insisted that the framers of the Constitution "undertook to secure conditions favorable to the pursuit of happiness. They recognized the significance of man's spiritual nature, of his feelings and of his intellect. They knew that only a part of the pain, pleasure and satisfactions of life are to be found in material things. They sought to protect Americans in their beliefs, their thoughts, their emotions and their sensations." As a result of these views, Brandeis insisted, the framers had "conferred, as against the Government, the right to be let alone – the most comprehensive of rights and the right most valued by civilized men."[68]

The problem is that this "most comprehensive of rights," these judicially discovered "transcendent dimensions" of the meaning of liberty, when embraced by the Court as a ground for judgment, are utterly at odds with the very possibility of constitutional self-government. Such understandings can only be the result of what James Madison once termed "constructive

---

[66] The underlying reason that the Court in *Lawrence* could so easily overrule *Bowers v. Hardwick* in order to extend the "outer limits" of privacy to include homosexual sodomy was that *Bowers* itself rested on the same substantive due process foundation that *Griswold* and its ancestors and heirs shared. Justice Byron White's majority opinion upholding the power of the states to prohibit homosexuality as a matter of moral choice, seeing it as "immoral and unacceptable," rested not on the fact that the Constitution was silent on such matters, thus leaving them to the states. Rather, the state statute was valid because such moral prohibitions had "ancient roots." As in *Griswold*, so in *Bowers*: such rights rest on nothing firmer or more certain than the fact that the Court found them to be "so rooted in the traditions and conscience of our people as to be ranked fundamental." All Justice Kennedy had to do in *Lawrence* was to show that Justice White's history in *Bowers* was, at the very least, "not without doubt." It certainly was not enough to sustain the "substantive validity" of the law in question. Indeed, Justice Kennedy's history, he insisted, displayed "an emerging awareness that liberty gives substantial protection to adult persons in deciding how to conduct their private lives in matters pertaining to sex." The "ethical and moral principles" that were deeply enough felt by the people of Texas to pass the law at hand were no match for the justices' confidence in their "own moral code." Such is the judicial advantage of an unwritten constitution of evolving meaning over a written one with a fixed meaning. *Bowers v. Hardwick*, 478 U.S. 186, 196, 192; *Palko v. Connecticut*, 302 U.S. 319, 324–325; *Lawrence v. Texas*, 539 U.S. 558, 571, 575, 572, 571.

[67] 505 U.S. 833, 851.

[68] *Olmstead v. United States*, 277 U.S. 438 (1928), 478.

ingenuity,"[69] an ingenuity that seeks to supplant the textual Constitution and the original intention of the framers with the justices' "own moral code"[70] – their protests to the contrary notwithstanding.

The paradox of such "constructive ingenuity" when it comes to the privacy right is that it is defended in the name of protecting new and often unheard-of individual liberties from legitimately elected majorities who have passed "laws representing essentially moral choices."[71] But by so restricting the powers of the governments (and this is almost always a restriction on the powers of the governments of the several states) to make such moral choices part of the law, the Court has greatly limited the most important right of individuals, the right to be self-governing, a right that has its roots in the very foundations of American constitutionalism.

The "constructive ingenuity" against which Madison warned is precisely the danger to which Justice Curtis pointed in his dissent in *Dred Scott*. It is a matter of reducing constitutional meaning to nothing more than what Curtis described as the "theoretical opinions of individuals... who, for the time being have power to declare what the Constitution is according to their own views of what it ought to mean."[72] The "intention of the people" is replaced by the mere intuition of the judge. The result is not a government by an "established, settled, known law" that the framers had sought, but rather that greatest of dangers which they most feared, a government by the "inconstant, uncertain, unknown, arbitrary will" of the governors. As the founding generation understood, "vague and uncertain... constitutions" could never be anything more than "the very instruments of slavery."

II. THE TYRANNY OF ARBITRARINESS

The great and unifying principle that links those whose works have contributed to the moral foundation of originalism in constitutional interpretation – a line that stretches from Hobbes to Locke to Blackstone to Jefferson, Hamilton, Marshall, Story, and Curtis – is the idea that arbitrariness in the administration of power is the greatest threat to liberty and the most likely foundation for tyranny. Justice Story, for example, clearly saw the dangers posed to the rule of law by any government that was the result of nothing more substantial than the mere "arbitrary will and caprice of rulers." The idea of "arbitrary power" – including what he condemned as the "arbitrary discretion of judges" – was, in his view, the very antithesis of

[69] James Madison to Robert S. Garnett, 11 February 1824, *Letters and Other Writings of James Madison*, 4 vols. (Philadelphia: J. P. Lippincott, 1865), III: 367.
[70] *Lawrence v. Texas*, 539 U.S. 558, 571, quoting *Planned Parenthood of Southeastern Pennsylvania v. Casey*, 505 U.S. 833, 850.
[71] *Bowers v. Hardwick*, 478 U.S. 186, 196.
[72] *Dred Scott v. Sandford*, 60 U.S. 393, 621.

constitutionalism and good government. That was true especially when those wielding the power of interpretation claimed to be imposing not their own will but rather the allegedly transcendent demands of "natural law and justice." To claim such an "unbounded jurisdiction" for the courts would be a "great mistake" in that it would create the most "formidable instrument of arbitrary power" that could be imagined.[73]

Story, of course, had come to these conclusions honestly. They were the principles of law that comprised the received tradition down to his time. The great Blackstone, as seen earlier, had argued strongly against the view that the proper interpretation of the law could ever rest simply upon the "arbitrary will" of the judges. The idea that legal meaning could be derived from the "private sentiments" of the judge deciding a cause, that the proper grounds of a decision were to be found in "the breast of the judge," the celebrated commentator pointed out, would have the effect of making "every judge a legislator" and ultimately setting the judicial power above the legislative, an act that would be, he argued, "subversive of all government." Such could not be allowed.[74]

In terms of American law and constitutional jurisprudence, this understanding of the dangers of arbitrariness in interpretation was not a view carved out to serve the political inclinations of one party or the other in the early republic. As has been suggested, the Jeffersonian Republicans and the Federalists were in complete agreement on at least this one principle. Judge Spencer Roane, that most Jeffersonian of the Jeffersonians, it will be recalled, used language that sounded much like that of Justice Story when Roane condemned what he saw as the "arbitrary discretion of the judges" being used to alter the original constitution to make it fit "the mere will and pleasure of the supreme court."[75] Ultimately, the battle over strict versus loose construction between the Jeffersonians and the Federalists was spawned by the fear on both sides about arbitrariness in the administration of power.

The common ground on which the critics of arbitrariness stood was the political philosophy of natural rights as that had begun with Hobbes and had been elaborated and refined by Locke. In Locke's estimation, arbitrariness was the greatest danger both in the state of nature and, potentially, within

---

73 Joseph Story, "The Science of Government," *Miscellaneous Writings*, p. 617; Joseph Story, "The Progress of Jurisprudence," ibid., p. 198; Joseph Story, "Law, Legislation, Codes," in *Encyclopedia Americana*, ed. Francis Lieber, 13 vols. (Philadelphia: Lea & Blanchard, 1844), VII: 576–592, p. 582; Joseph Story, *Commentaries on Equity Jurisprudence*, 2 vols. (12th ed.; Boston: Little, Brown and Co., 1877), I.2.2; I.19.15. Citations indicate volume, section, and page number.

74 Sir William Blackstone, *Commentaries on the Laws of England*, 4 vols. (8th ed.; Oxford: Clarendon Press, 1778), I: 142, 69, 62, 91.

75 Spencer Roane, "Algernon Sidney Essays on the Lottery Decision," in William E. Dodd, ed., *The John P. Branch Historical Papers of Randolph-Macon College*, 5 vols. (Richmond, VA: Taylor and Taylor, 1906), II, no. 2: 78–183, pp. 84, 80.

any civil society. Being subjected to "the inconstant, uncertain, unknown, arbitrary will of another man" was the very essence of tyranny.[76] This was a principal concern in Locke's political thought, one to which he returned again and again.[77] The "liberty of man in society" and the "[f]reedom of men under government"[78] both required a structure that would prevent arbitrariness in the way the constitution and the laws would be administered.

By the mechanics of the social contract the free, equal, and independent people in the state of nature were reduced by their own voluntary and positive agreement to "one body politick under one supreme government." But that government had to be above all else a *"lawful government,"* one in which the "ruling power" would itself be bound by "declared and received laws" and would not govern by mere "extemporary dictates and undetermined resolutions." Such dictates could only be the "exorbitant and unlimited" opinions of the governors based upon nothing more certain than their own personal "sudden thoughts, or unrestrained, and till that moment unknown wills." In Locke's view, "governing without settled standing laws" within a civil government would be no different from the "absolute arbitrary power" to which all men were subjected in the state of nature. What distinguishes life within a properly "constituted common-wealth" from the "uncertainty as . . . was in the state of nature," Locke insisted, is the rule of law. Anything less would "put a force into the magistrate's hand to execute his unlimited will arbitrarily"[79] upon the governed.

III. AN ESTABLISHED, SETTLED, KNOWN LAW

For law truly to be law, for Locke as for Hobbes, it must be known and understood by those who are to be bound by it. As Locke put it, law not only must be *"declared"* but also, more importantly, must be *"received"* by the people.[80] That is to say, its meaning must be not only "settled" but also "known" and accepted by those to be governed by it as the true "standard of right and wrong" within their society.[81] Whereas Hobbes was content to leave the matter at the level of insisting that the law be made known "by writing, or some other act,"[82] Locke hoped to be more precise. The law being made known and received depended upon what he described as

---

[76] Peter Laslett, ed., *Locke's Two Treatises of Government* (2nd ed.; Cambridge: Cambridge University Press, 1970), *Second Treatise*, 302: 22. Hereinafter cited as *Second Treatise*. Citations indicate page number followed by section number.

[77] See, for example, *Second Treatise*, sections 8, 23, 24, and 137.

[78] Ibid., 301: 22; 302: 22.

[79] Ibid., 343: 89; 351: 99; 378: 137; 378: 137; 377: 137; 387: 153; 377: 136; 377: 137.

[80] Ibid., 378: 137.

[81] Ibid., 369: 124.

[82] Thomas Hobbes, *Leviathan* (Oxford: Clarendon Press, 1909), p. 209.

its being properly *"promulgated."*[83] In his dictionary, Samuel Johnson (a great admirer of Locke, it will be recalled) would define "promulgate" not simply as "to publish" but more pointedly as "to make known by open declaration."[84] It was the necessity that the meaning of the law be "known" in order to be law in the strict sense that imposed an obligation on those in power to be bound by the original meaning or intention of the lawgivers in giving effect to the law.[85] To ignore the original intention would be to replace the meaning of the law to which the governed had consented with the extemporary will of the magistrates.

The essence of the "original constitution" of any government thus must be the understanding that "all the power of government . . . ought to be exercised by established and promulgated laws." The advantage would be twofold. First, it would enable the people to "know their duty, and be safe and secure within the limits of the law"; and second, it would serve to keep "the rulers . . . within their due bounds, and not . . . tempted, by the power they have in their hands, to imploy it to such purposes, and by such measures, as [the people] would not have known, and own not willingly." The meaning

---

[83] *Second Treatise*, 376: 136.

[84] Samuel Johnson, *A Dictionary of the English Language*, 2 vols. (London: W. Strahan, 1755), in volume two (unpaginated.) As was his habit in fleshing out his definitions, Johnson turned for one of his examples to Locke himself. As a matter of literary curiosity, it seems Dr. Johnson was a liberal editor; his Lockean example is not an accurate one. Johnson's version reads thus: "It is certain laws, by virtue of any sanction they receive from the *promulgated* will of the legislature, reach not a stranger, if by the law of nature every man hath not a power to punish offences against it." Locke's original version reads this way: "'Tis certain their laws by vertue of any sanction they receive from the promulgated will of the legislative, reach not a stranger. They speak not to him, nor if they did, is he bound to hearken to them. The legislative authority, by which they are in force over the subjects of that commonwealth, hath no power over him. Those who have the supream power of making laws in *England, France* or *Holland*, are to an *Indian*, but like the rest of the world, men without authority: and therefore if by the law of nature, every man hath not a power to punish offences against it, as he soberly judges the case to require, I see not how the magistrates of any community, can *punish an Alien* of another country, since in reference to him, they can have no more power, than what every man naturally may have over another." *Second Treatise*, 291: 9.

[85] Jeremy Bentham offered an explanation of the importance of laws being properly "promulated" that seems to take its bearings from the definition of Johnson. For Bentham, it was not enough that a law duly enacted had "the seal of the sovereign . . . set to it." More was required. "That a law may be obeyed, it is necessary that it should be known; that it may be known, it is necessary that it be promulgated. But to promulgate a law, it is not only necessary that it should be published with the sound of the trumpet in the streets; not only that it should be read to the people; not only even that it should be printed: all these means may be good, but they may be all employed without accomplishing the essential object. They may possess more of the appearance than the reality of promulgation. To promulgate a law, is to present it to the minds of those who are to be governed by it in such manner as that they may have it habitually in their memories, and may possess every facility for consulting it, if they have any doubts respecting what it prescribes." Jeremy Bentham, "Of the Promulgation of the Laws and Promulgation of the Reasons Thereof," in John Bowring, ed., *The Works of Jeremy Bentham*, 11 vols. (Edinburgh: W. Tait, 1843), I: 157.

of this fundamental original constitution depended "wholly on the people" in their sovereign capacity; as the fundamental law, it was to be understood as being "antecedent to all positive laws" the government might enact; and it was to be seen as setting down "concrete measures . . . to guide and justifie" the actions of those who would wield the powers of the government as well as to judge the legitimacy of the ordinary laws. As the expression of the sovereign will of the people, this constitution is to be deemed permanent in the sense that "no inferiour power can alter it." Thus, any attempt by the institutions of the government created by that original constitution to assume the power to rule "by extemporary arbitrary decrees"[86] would have the effect of altering the "promulgated standing laws" illegitimately. Such change can be effected legitimately only by the people in their sovereign capacity.

Because the people are sovereign, they can never cede entirely that sovereignty; they can only delegate power to be used in their interest by institutions created by their own hand for as long as they see fit to allow such arrangements to be in effect. Should the government they create prove to endanger the rights it is meant to secure and protect, the people always retain the sovereign power to "alter or abolish" whatever they have created and to start again with a government they think most likely to conduce to their "safety and happiness."

The reason the fundamental law is to restrict the government from governing by "extemporary arbitrary decrees" is that the primary purpose of any government is not to "*dispense justice*" in some abstract moral sense but rather to "decide the rights of the subject"[87] when they are the object of dispute in some concrete legal controversy. The resolution of such controversies depends upon those promulgated and known laws that have been established and received by the people as the measures of right and wrong, justice and injustice, within the civil society itself. Ultimately, justice is nothing more than the legal security of the rights and property of the people against the transgressions of both their fellow citizens and their governors.

The rule of law in the natural rights tradition is not meant to be a comprehensive moral system of the sort that would seek to transform human beings by the inculcation of some notion of virtue. Because the objective of a law-governed society is the security of individual freedom, rather than an approximation of some transcendent ideal of justice, Locke, following Hobbes, could sum it up clearly and succinctly:

Law, in its true notion, is not so much the limitation as *the direction of a free and intelligent agent* to his proper interest, and prescribes no further than is for the general good of those under that law. Could they be happier without it, the *law*, as a useless thing would of itself vanish; and that ill deserves the name of confinement

---

[86] *Second Treatise*, 389: 156; 378: 137; 378: 137; 391: 157; 378: 137; 391: 157; 376: 136.
[87] Ibid., 376: 136.

which hedges us in only from bogs and precipices. So that, however it may be mistaken, *the end of law* is not to abolish or restrain, but *to preserve and enlarge freedom*: For in all the states of created beings capable of laws, *where there is no law, there is no freedom*. For *liberty* is to be free from restraint and violence from others which cannot be, where there is no law: but freedom is not, as we are told, *a liberty for every man to do what he lists*: (For who could be free, when every other man's humour might domineer over him?) But a *liberty* to dispose, and order, as he lists, his person, actions, possessions, and his whole property within the allowance of those laws under which he is; and therein not to be subject to the arbitrary will of another, but freely follow his own.[88]

This is what Locke meant when he argued that "where-ever law ends, tyranny begins."[89]

This understanding of the power of law to secure freedom and restrain tyranny is rooted in the notion of language embraced by Hobbes and Locke that sees words as signs for the ideas in the mind of the person who uses them. In order for language to fulfill its intended function, it is essential that the reader of any words that are used make every effort to discern the ideas the writer intended to convey by so using those words. Properly interpreted, language will spawn in the mind of the reader the same idea that had been in the mind of the writer. This is no less true for the language of the law than for any other written expression. Indeed, Locke, like Hobbes before him, understood that when it came to the law, both fundamental and municipal, the search for what Hobbes called the "intendment" was indeed the "most sacred rule of interpretation."

---

[88] Ibid., 323–324: 57. Hobbes, it will be remembered, had put it very much the same way. "The use of lawes . . . is not to bind the people from all voluntary actions; but to direct and keep them in such a motion, as not to hurt themselves by their own impetuous desires, rashnesse, or indiscretion; as hedges are set, not to stop travellers, but to keep them in the way." As he saw it, "the naturall liberty of man, may by the civill law be abridged, and restrained: nay, the end of making lawes is no other, but such restraint; without the which there cannot possibly be any peace." Hobbes, *Leviathan*, pp. 268, 206.

[89] *Second Treatise*, 418: 202.

Index of Cases

Antelope, The, (1825), 333

Barron v. Baltimore (1833), 321, 336–7
Bonham's Case (1610), 43–4, 45, 46
Bowers v. Hardwick (1982), 6, 395
Brig Wilson, The, v. United States (1820), 323, 324
Brown v. Maryland (1827), 329

Carolene Products Co. v. United States (1937), 388
Charles River Bridge v. Warren Bridge (1837), 347
Cherokee Nation v. Georgia (1831), 330, 333
Chicago, Milwaukee, and St. Paul Railway Co. v. Clark (1899), 33
Coates's Executor v. Muses's Administrators (1822), 338
Cohens v. Virginia (1821), 289, 290, 294–8, 312, 313, 319, 322, 323, 324, 325, 326, 327, 330, 332, 346
Craig v. Missouri (1830), 325, 332, 339

Davidson v. New Orleans (1878), 386
Dred Scott v. Sandford (1857), 380–5, 395

Eisenstadt v. Baird (1972), 391
Ex Parte Randolph (1833), 329

Fairfax's Devisee v. Hunter's Lessee (1813), 286
Ferguson v. Skrupa (1963), 390, 391
Fletcher v. Peck (1810), 312n5, 319, 329

Gibbons v. Ogden (1824), 315, 316, 319, 321, 324, 325, 326, 327, 338, 346
Griswold v. Connecticut (1965), 2, 389, 390, 391

Huidekoper's Lessee v. Douglas (1805), 338
Hunter v. Fairfax's Devisee (1810), 286

Kamper v. Hawkins (1793), 285

Lawrence v. Texas (2003), 393, 395
Livingston v. Jefferson (1811), 322
Lochner v. New York (1905), 386

Marbury v. Madison (1803), 4, 49, 311, 317, 319, 322, 323, 326, 327, 328, 329, 330, 331, 332, 381
Martin v. Hunter's Lessee (1816), 285–9, 298, 346
Mary Ann, The, (1823), 331
McCulloch v. Maryland (1819), 270, 288–98, 319, 320–1, 326, 327, 333, 334, 337, 346
Mugler v. Kansas (1887), 386n31, 392
Munn v. Illinois (1877), 386

Nereide, The, (1815), 330

Ogden v. Saunders (1827), 314, 315, 316, 318, 324, 346
Olmstead v. United States (1928), 394
Osborn v. Bank of the United States (1824), 312, 328, 330

Palko v. Connecticut (1937), 389
Pennington v. Coxe (1804), 323, 330, 333
Planned Parenthood of Southeastern Pennsylvania v. Casey (1992), 392, 393, 394, 395
Poe v. Ullman (1961), 390
Postmaster v. Early (1827), 315, 332, 338
Prohibitions del Roy (1607), 66
Providence Bank v. Billings (1830), 316, 321

Roe v. Wade (1973), 391, 392

Slaughterhouse Cases, The, (1873), 386
Stone v. Farmers' Loan and Trust Co.
(1886), 386
Sturges v. Crowninshield (1819), 312, 322,
324, 331, 332, 333, 338

Trustees of Dartmouth College v.
Woodward (1819), 325, 335–7, 346

United States v. Burr (1807), 324, 327, 333
United States v. Fisher (1805), 332, 333

United States v. Maurice (1823), 314
United States v. Palmer (1818), 329, 330
United States v. Trans-Missouri Freight
Association (1897), 33
United States v. Wiltberger (1820), 332,
338

Ware v. Hylton (1793), 316
West Coast Hotel v. Parrish (1937), 386n33
Willson v. Blackbird-Creek Marsh Co.
(1829), 321–2
Worcester v. Georgia (1832), 330
Wynehamer v. New York (1856), 385–6n28

General Index

Adams, John, 171, 254, 256, 271, 272, 280, 281, 298, 328
Adams, John Quincy, 346
Alien and Sedition Acts, 260, 271, 272, 273, 278, 279, 281–2, 347
Ames, Fisher, 264, 265
Ames, James Barr, 11, 21, 28, 29, 30, 31, 33
"Amphictyon," 290
Anti-Federalists, 248, 249, 256
Aquinas, Thomas, 93, 107, 108
Aristotle, 41, 47, 59, 60, 61, 63, 64, 83, 101, 107
Aristotlelianism, 47, 59, 61, 63, 64, 68, 70, 83, 101, 107, 108, 199
Articles of Confederation, 225, 233, 234, 239, 242, 253, 317–19, 382

Bagshaw, Edward, 88
Bailyn, Bernard, 197–8
Baker, Sir John, ix
Barron, John, 337
Beale, Joseph, 25
Bentham, Jeremy, 204
Berger, Raoul, x, xv, 384
Berns, Walter, xv, 182
Beveridge, Albert, 346
Bible, 84, 169
bicameralism, 243, 244–6
Bill of Rights, 256
Bishop, Joel Prentiss, 364, 375
Black, Henry Campbell, 375–6
Black, Hugo, 2, 390–1
Blackstone, William Sir, ix, xi, 16, 20, 23, 26, 36, 56, 152, 169, 203–15, 250, 266, 285, 314, 339, 340, 347, 355, 357, 385
   Commentaries on the Laws of England, ix, 16, 20, 203–15, 266, 339, 347, 355

Blathwayt, William, 175
Bork, Robert H., x, xv, 1–7
   confirmation hearing of, 1–4, 6–7
Boudinot, Elias, 264, 265, 266
Bracton, Henrici de, 43, 46, 205
Bramhall, John, 93
Brandeis, Louis, 12, 389, 390, 394
Breckenridge, John, 274
Brockenbrough, William, 290
Brutus, 248
Burlamaqui, Jean Jacques, xi, 56, 169, 182, 185–8, 189, 314
Burr, Aaron, 280

Calhoun, John C., 356, 380
Cambridge University, 68, 190
canon law, see law, canon
Cardozo, Benjamin, 32, 41
Carpenter, Richard, 92, 93
Cartwright, John, 308
case method, 14, 21–7, 34, 35
cases, publication of, 26–7
Cato's Letters, 197–203
checks and balances, 221
Christianity, 59, 63, 81, 83–5, 88–9, 92, 101, 139–40, 142, 144, 199, 351
civil law, see law, civil
Clay, Henry, 380
Coke, Sir Edward, 23, 43–50, 58, 64–9, 76, 181, 285, 349, 366
   on common law, 65–9
commercial republic, 257
common law, see law, common
commonwealth by constitution, 155–62, 164, 168, 190
compact theory, 190, 272–6, 282, 293, 296, 301, 327, 360, 361
compound republic, 319–22
confederation, 239, 242, 246, 253

consent of the governed, 49, 54, 90, 103,
    105, 122, 123, 131, 150–5, 157–62,
    173, 174, 201, 208, 226, 228, 230, 231,
    232, 235, 302, 314, 317
consolidation of power, 239, 242, 259,
    275–6, 286–7, 304, 321
Constitution, 222–30, 231–2, 235–6,
    239–40, 241, 246, 247, 253, 382
  creation of, 225–51, 253
  Founders', 10, 11, 37, 39, 41, 53, 226,
    231, 232, 241, 299, 313, 317, 324, 325,
    326, 327, 342, 361, 362, 388
  as fundamental law, 249, 250, 325, 326,
    342, 362, 363, 364, 379
  higher-law background, 12, 48, 49, 53
  idea of a "living Constitution," 3, 12, 25,
    37, 38, 39, 40, 41, 42, 51, 53, 386–7,
    393–4
  ratification of, 246–7
  states, 233, 234, 240
  supremacy of, 246–7, 329
  written, 48, 49, 50, 53–4, 80–1, 187–8,
    203, 222–6, 247, 260, 314, 322, 323–4,
    329, 330, 359, 377, 386
Constitutional Convention, 225, 234, 236,
    263, 254, 255, 278, 279, 303, 313, 318,
    319, 321, 379
constitutional law, 45, 48, 50, 51, 197,
    221
  study of, 36–7, 40–1
constitutionalism, 38, 39, 41, 80–1, 203,
    222–4, 231, 251
  American, 222–4, 231, 251
construction
  constitutional, 250, 262, 263, 264–7, 274,
    299–300, 301, 302, 325, 332, 333–5,
    372–4, 376
  fair, 334–5, 325, 327, 332, 333, 336, 339,
    342, 370–1, 372, 376
  loose, 250–1, 268, 274, 292–3, 335, 396
  statutory, 357, 366–8
  strict, 9, 251, 252, 257, 258–78, 279, 283,
    288, 297, 306–10, 325, 327, 335,
    354–5, 396
Cooley, Thomas, 12
Corwin, Edward S., 7, 11, 12, 40–54
  constitutional understanding of, 41–5, 48,
    50–2
Cowell, John, 172
Culverwel, Nathaniel, 93
Curtis, Benjamin Robbins, 382–4, 395
Cushing, William, 344–5
custom, 132–44

Dane, Nathan, 17, 19, 352, 353
Darwin, Charles, 26, 38
Declaration of Independence, 226–32, 377,
    382

influence of John Locke, *see* Locke, John,
    influence on Declaration of
    Independence
De Lolme, Jean Louis, 358
dialectical reasoning, *see* scholasticism
divine law, *see* law, divine
divine right of kings, 102–5, 231
Domat, Jean, 358, 367, 368
Douglas, Stephen A., 9
Douglas, William O., 391, 391–2n.59
Duer, William Alexander, 355
Du Ponceau, Peter, 355
Dwarris, Sir Fortunatus, 364–8, 374,
    375
Dyer, Sir James, 58

Eliot, Charles W., 12, 13, 14, 20, 28, 29
Ellsworth, Oliver, 234–5
enumerated powers, 203, 241, 251, 257,
    259–60, 262, 314
epistemology, 104–6
executive power, 245–6, 248
  fear of, 233
extended republic, 240–2

faction, 235, 237, 240, 241
fair construction, *see* construction, fair
Fairfax, Lord, 285
faith, 85, 87–8, 116–17, 139, 141, 144
Federal Farmer, 249
federalism, 242–3, 255, 259, 295, 319–22
Federalist, The, 6, 218, 225–51, 255,
    257–60, 262, 286, 291, 310, 328, 356,
    357, 363
Federalists, 250, 252, 257, 261, 272, 274,
    279, 280, 311, 396
Fenno, John, 271
Filmer, Sir Robert, 99, 100–5, 145, 162,
    163, 166
  Observations on Hobbs, 163
  Patriarcha, 99, 100
Fortescue, Sir John, 43, 44, 46, 47, 68
  De Laudibus, 43, 47
Founders, American, xi, 10, 37, 53–4, 222,
    225–51, 289, 299
"Friend of the Constitution, A," *see*
    Marshall, John, as "A Friend of the
    Constitution"
"Friend of the Union, A," *see* Marshall,
    John, as "A Friend of the Union"
Freneau, Philip, 271
Fuller, Melville, 33
fundamental rights, 389

Gazette of the United States, 271
Gerry, Elbridge, 234, 243, 248, 264, 266,
    267
Glanvill, Ranulf, 46

God, 48, 81, 83, 86–8, 91–3, 95, 102–4,
    106, 109, 129, 130, 132, 137–41, 150,
    151, 165, 166, 200, 206–7, 351
Goodhart, Arthur, 31
Gordon, Thomas, xi, 56, 169, 197–203, 241
government by reflection and choice, 232–5,
    322, 357
Granger, Gideon, 279
Gratian, 59
Greenleaf, Simon, 20
Grey, John Chipman, 25
Grotius, Hugo, 36, 182, 183–5, 186, 189,
    190, 214, 250, 266, 267, 284, 314, 339,
    359, 368
    De Jure Belli ac Pacis, 182, 189
Gurney, Ephriam W., 28, 29, 30, 34

Hamilton, Alexander, 9, 15, 218, 221, 236,
    239, 242, 244, 247–50, 257, 258, 259,
    260, 261, 262, 265, 269, 270, 271,
    279, 280, 286, 322, 328, 329, 357, 385,
    395
    Report on a National Bank, 259–61
"Hampden," *see* Roane, Spencer, as
    "Hampden"
Harlan, John Marshall, 390
Harvard Law School, 11, 12–37, 352
    Dane Professor, 17–19, 20, 352, 353
    Harvard Law Review, 11, 31–5, 387
    Harvard Law School Association, 22, 29,
    30
Henry II, 43
Henry, Patrick, 204, 255, 284
higher law, *see* law, higher
Hobart, Sir Henry, 58
Hobbes, Thomas, xi, 47–9, 54, 55–81, 82,
    83–97, 98–101, 104–5, 107, 108, 118,
    129, 131, 133, 145–8, 152, 155, 161,
    162–8, 169, 170, 173, 182, 183, 184,
    185, 187, 198, 199, 200, 202, 207,
    210, 216, 217, 219, 238, 250, 314,
    315, 317, 340, 369, 370, 396, 397,
    399, 400
    *A Dialogue Between a Philosopher and a
    Student of the Common Laws of
    England*, 67–8
    influence on liberal constitutionalism,
    56–7, 80–1
    on language, 56, 69–71, 76–80, 169, 202,
    369
    on law, 56–7, 58, 66, 67, 68, 69, 74–6,
    77–80
    Leviathan, 58, 67, 82, 93, 105, 146, 163
    on religion, 63
    on sovereignty by institution, 56, 71–6,
    78, 79, 80, 81
Hoffman, David, 15, 18, 19
    A Course of Legal Study, 15, 18

Holmes, Oliver Wendell Jr., 12, 37, 40, 41
Hooker, Richard, 93
human reason, *see* reason, human
human understanding, 83, 85, 105–14,
    120–2, 144, 145, 207, 299–300
    and sensation, 87, 95, 96, 102, 112, 119,
    138, 139, 151
human will, 116, 118, 209
Hunter, Daniel, 285

ideas, 106–18, 126, 127, 139, 162, 323, 324
    innate, 95, 106, 107, 118, 127, 133, 151
    natural equality of, 105, 123–4
Independent Whig, The, 197–203
individuality of man, 105
intention of lawgiver, 78–80, 126–7, 131–2,
    183–4, 188–91, 199, 203, 211–15,
    337–40, 357–8, 359, 366–8, 372–3
intention, original, *see* original intention
interpretation, 54, 77–80, 131, 169–224,
    266, 324, 331–40, 372, 376, 400
    constitutional, ix–xii, 1–8, 9–12, 53–4,
    182, 311–30, 331–40, 376, 379–400
    of law, 169, 180, 181, 183–4, 197, 199,
    214, 219, 220, 249, 250, 266, 325, 340,
    368, 375, 376
    literal, 191, 192, 196, 325, 326, 338, 359,
    370
    mixed, 192–3, 196, 359
    rational, 194–6, 359

Jackson, Andrew, 9, 343, 344
Jacksonian Democrats, 312
Jacob, Giles, 169, 170 82
    Essays Relating to the Conduct of Life,
    175–8
    New Law Dictionary, 171, 172, 181
Jay Treaty of 1794, 285–6
Jefferson, Thomas, 9, 15, 16, 49, 171,
    226–8, 232, 250, 252–61, 268–77, 279,
    280–4, 290, 292, 293, 294, 297, 298,
    305–10, 341, 344–7, 354, 355, 361,
    376, 379, 380, 387, 395
    constitutionalism of, 252, 256, 282, 293
Jeffersonian Republicans, 261, 263, 272,
    273, 280–306, 312, 320, 354, 396
Johnson, Samuel, 173–5, 182, 398
Johnson, William, 282, 308
judges
    as policymakers, 50–2, 76, 78
    role of, 43, 47, 76, 77, 78, 219, 220–2,
    248, 376
judicial activism, 1–7, 51–2, 384–400
judicial discretion, 47, 48, 51–3, 69, 330,
    359, 367, 374
judicial power, 77, 214, 215, 217, 218, 219,
    220–2, 248–9, 283–4, 292, 295–6, 299,
    314, 326–30, 347, 367, 391–2

judicial restraint, 217–19
judicial review, 45, 50, 53, 221, 249, 311
judiciary, 245–6, 248
Judiciary Act of 1789, 294
justice, 127–8, 131, 137, 146, 148, 151,
    166, 173, 196, 216, 235–6
Justinian, 59, 60

Keener, William, 22, 23, 28
Kennedy, Anthony, 392–4
Kent, James, 15, 16, 23, 26, 36, 348, 355,
    369
Kent, William, 369
Kentucky and Virginia Resolutions, 260,
    271, 274–80, 284
Kerchival, Samuel, 308
King, Peter, 175

Langdell, Christopher Columbus, 11–37
    Cases on Contracts, 21
language, 10, 54, 56, 69, 74, 76–80, 96,
    101–2, 123–4, 127–32, 146, 162, 169,
    173, 198–9, 200–3, 323, 324, 333, 369,
    370, 374, 387
    abuse of, 70, 71, 104, 125–6, 130–2, 202,
        291, 300
    ambiguity of, 77, 192, 332, 333, 337, 370
    intention or meaning behind words used,
        76–80, 126–7, 131–2, 173, 174,
        183–4, 188–9, 191, 199, 203, 250,
        319, 323, 324, 325, 331, 340, 369,
        400
    and law, 76–80, 124–32, 162, 181, 191,
        202–3, 400
    literal meaning of, 338
    moral, 173
    speech, 73, 74, 96, 126
    words, 10, 70, 78, 80, 101, 102, 125–6,
        162, 169, 191, 202–3, 323–5, 331, 332,
        387
law
    canon, 59
    civil, 75, 80, 137, 138, 140, 142, 146,
        163, 179, 190, 221
    common, 17, 35, 42–50, 64–9, 70, 76,
        179, 204, 205, 206, 212, 213, 231, 278,
        347, 348–55, 357, 366
    Darwinian conception of, 11–12, 25–6,
        35, 37, 38
    divine, 129
    higher, 12–13, 41–5, 48, 49, 51, 81, 95,
        196
    medieval, *see* medieval law
    nature or foundation of, 26, 128, 150, 214
    and necessity of punishment, 161–2, 200,
        221, 239
    Newtonian conception of, 11–12, 37–9,
        107

positive, 35, 43, 81, 104, 149, 205, 211,
    212, 216, 314
    public understanding of, 180
    of reason, 140
    of reputation, 136–7
    as restraint, 56–7, 69, 74–6, 128–32,
        167–8, 201–2, 214, 218
    as a science, 22–4, 26, 27, 33–4, 35, 37,
        59
    statutory, 212–14
    supremacy of, 239
    written, 75, 77, 79–81, 170, 212, 223,
        226
law dictionaries, 169–82
law reviews, 31–4
Lee, Richard Henry, 232
legal education, 12–37, 41, 353
    separation of theory and practice,
        28–32
legal realism, 41, 49, 51
legal reason, *see* reason, legal
legislative power, 157–60, 170, 190, 244–8
    of Parliament and king, 209–10
liberty, 90–1, 118, 136–7, 146–9, 151, 153,
    155, 156, 166–7, 180, 218, 221, 227,
    232, 235, 316, 392, 393, 394
liberty of contract, 9, 386, 388
Lieber, Francis, 182, 364, 366, 368–76
Lincoln, Abraham, 9
Lincoln, Levi, 282, 345, 346
Littleton, Thomas, 285, 349
"living constitution," *see* Constitution, idea
    of a "living Constitution"
Livingston, Edward, 308
Locke, John, xi, 41, 44, 47–9, 54, 56, 57, 80,
    81, 82–168, 169, 170, 173–7, 182,
    183, 184, 187, 188, 197–9, 200, 202,
    206, 210, 216, 217, 219, 227, 228,
    230, 231, 232, 238, 241, 250, 284,
    314, 315, 317, 323, 369, 370,
    396–400
    and dictionaries, 173
    on education, 175–7
    *Essay Concerning Human
        Understanding*, 56, 82, 92, 97, 98,
        104, 105–44, 147, 149, 151, 152,
        162, 163, 167, 169, 173, 175, 177,
        198
    foundation of government according to,
        104–5, 144, 145, 150–5, 156, 157, 166,
        177
    influence on Declaration of Independence,
        226–32
    influence on liberal constitutionalism,
        162–8
    on knowledge and understanding, 84–8,
        95–6, 105–25, 132–6, 138–40, 144–5,
        151, 166–7, 175–7

on language, 101–2, 104, 123–32, 152,
    162, 169, 173, 174, 202, 369
on law, 129–32, 138, 152, 155–62, 167–8
on legislative power, 157–60
Letter on Toleration, A, 142
on liberty, 90–1, 118–24, 136, 137, 146,
    148, 149, 151, 153, 155, 156, 166,
    167
on natural law, 91, 102, 146–50, 159–60
on power of the sovereign, 57
Questions Concerning the Law of Nature,
    88–97, 162, 164
on religion, 84, 86, 88–9, 91, 101, 104–5,
    116, 117, 129, 137–9, 140–2, 144, 164,
    165, 166
right to revolution, 80–1, 157, 159, 165,
    210
on sovereignty, 90–1
Two Tracts on Government, 88–92, 121,
    129, 144, 162
Two Treatises of Government, 56, 82, 97,
    98, 105, 144, 162–3, 167, 169, 177,
    197, 198, 228
    First Treatise of Government, 100–5,
    134, 145
    Second Treatise of Government, 104,
    144–62, 163, 165, 397–400
on tyranny, 89, 144, 145, 160, 161, 166–7
Valedictory Address, 164–5
Lockean liberalism, Hobbesian foundation
    of, 83–97, 99–100, 104–5, 118, 129,
    141, 154–5, 161, 162–8
loose construction, *see* construction, loose

Madison, James, 6, 215, 233, 234, 237, 238,
    239, 241, 243, 245, 247, 248, 250,
    253–64, 266–8, 271, 273–9, 287,
    303–6, 316, 319–21, 345, 346, 379,
    387, 394, 395
    "Virginia Report," 277–9, 287, 291, 293
Marshall, James, 285
Marshall, John, xi, 2, 4, 8, 9, 36, 49, 221,
    250, 257, 265, 270, 280, 281, 283,
    284–6, 288–300, 309, 310, 311–42,
    343, 344, 347, 354, 356, 360, 363, 364,
    368, 373, 383, 387, 395
    as "A Friend of the Constitution," 289–93
    as "A Friend of the Union," 289–93
    constitutionalism of, 314, 317, 318,
    320–1, 324, 326, 327, 333, 344
    influence on Joseph Story, 340–4
    on judicial power, 314, 326–30
    on language, 323–5, 331–8
    and the "mind of the Convention," 313,
    317–22, 326–7, 331, 336, 364
    republicanism of, 314–17
    theory of interpretation, 310–12, 322,
    324–7, 331–40

Martin, Denny, 285
Martin, Luther, 248
Mason, George, 247, 279
Maxwell, Sir Peter Benson, 374, 375
McClellan, James, xv
McKelvey, John Jay, 32
McLean, John, 382
medieval law, 59–60, 65, 66, 85
Meese, Edwin III, xiv, xv
Missouri Compromise, 379–81
Monroe, James, 253
Montesquieu, xi, 214, 215–22, 241, 284,
    314
    on the judiciary, 217–22
    on law, 218, 219, 220
    Spirit of Laws, 214–22
morality, 140–1, 173
More, Thomas, ix
Morris, Gouverneur, 235, 248

national bank, 260–4, 267–8, 294, 326
National Gazette, 271
natural equality, 105, 146, 148, 151, 153,
    155, 201, 229, 230
natural law, 41, 43–9, 69, 71, 75–6, 79–81,
    88, 89, 91–7, 102, 104–7, 144,
    146–50, 151, 153, 154, 158–60, 178,
    186, 196, 197, 205, 207, 212, 317, 351,
    352
    Christian, 92, 93, 95
    and the Constitution, 41–5, 50, 222, 223,
    224, 228, 231
natural law theorists, 182–97
natural reason, *see* reason, natural
natural rights, xii, 44, 48, 54, 81, 90, 97,
    131, 167, 179, 190, 201, 224, 226,
    227, 228, 229, 230, 314, 316,
    386–7
    as basis of American constitutionalism,
    224–7, 228–30
    as inalienable, 229–30
New Deal, 50, 51, 52
Newton, Isaac, 38, 107, 206, 229
Nugent, Thomas, 185

O'Connor, Sandra Day, 392–3
opinion, 70, 71, 73, 85, 94, 104, 106,
    122–3, 131, 133–8, 144, 153
original constitution, *see* Constitution,
    Founders'
original intention, xi, 5, 53, 54, 78, 79, 189,
    191–4, 196, 211–12, 214, 250–1, 266,
    274, 302, 309, 312–14, 317–19, 322,
    325, 327, 330, 331, 337–8, 347, 357,
    359, 360, 387, 388, 398
originalism, *see* original intention
Oxford University, 59, 68, 82, 98, 144, 145,
    204, 358, 364

Paley, William, 359
Pinckney, Charles Cotesworth, 281
Pocock, J. G. A., 198
political jurisprudence, 51, 52
Pope, Alexander, 172
popular consent, *see* consent of the governed
popular sovereignty, 49, 54, 79, 80, 155–6,
    210, 231, 235, 246–7, 300, 301, 319,
    378, 399
positive law, *see* law, positive
Potter, Platt, 368
Powell, Lewis, xv
power, abuse of, 218, 235, 316, 395–7
Pound, Roscoe, 12
precedent, see *stare decisis*
prerogative, 210
Princeton University, 37, 40
Prior, Matthew, 175
public good, 208, 235
Pufendorf, Samuel, 35, 56, 182, 183–5,
    186–9, 214, 250, 267, 314, 339,
    368
Putnam, Samuel, 349
Pyrnne, William, 180

Randolph, Edmund, 234, 268, 269, 270, 279
Randolph, Thomas Jefferson, 307–8
Rastell, John, 58, 169–71
    *Exposiciones Terminorum Legum
        Anglorum*, 170–2
    Termes de la Ley, 58, 170–2
Rawle, William, 36, 355
Reagan, Ronald, 1
reason
    human, 48, 49, 69–70, 86, 94–6, 102,
        104, 105, 107, 115, 116, 118–20,
        123, 139, 140, 145, 146, 147, 149–50,
        151, 158–60, 167, 179, 186, 200, 206,
        207
    legal, 46–7, 50, 69
    natural, 46, 47, 48, 50, 103, 104, 151,
        352
    right, 43, 47, 48, 69, 73, 94, 151, 177,
        206
reasonable construction, *see* construction,
    fair
Reeve, Tapping Judge, 14
religion, 48, 63, 81, 83, 84, 86, 88–9, 91–3,
    95, 101–5, 109, 116, 117, 129, 130,
    132, 137–42, 144, 150, 164–6
    and civil society, 141
religious toleration, 141–4
Rehnquist, William H., xv
representation, 242–3, 255
republican government, 220, 234, 235, 236,
    239, 240, 254, 317
republicanism, 225–51, 253, 257, 258, 282,
    305

revolution of 1800, 271, 270, 280, 281, 284,
    294, 299, 320
Richmond Enquirer, 284, 290, 295, 305
Richmond Junto, 284, 290
right to abortion, 391
right to privacy, 10, 388–91, 394–5
right reason, *see* reason, right
Ritchie, Thomas, 284, 290, 291, 305
Roane, Spencer, 261, 283, 284, 285, 286,
    289–97, 306, 308, 309, 310, 396
    as "Algernon Sydney," 294–7, 396
    as "Hampden," 289–94
Robbins, Caroline, 197–8
Roosevelt, Theodore, 40
Rossiter, Clinton, 41
rule of law, 160, 161, 239, 246–51, 385,
    395–400
Rutherforth, Thomas, xi, 36, 56, 169, 182,
    189, 190–7, 250, 314, 339, 359, 367,
    369

Scalia, Antonin, xv
scholasticism, 59–65, 68–9, 82–4, 88,
    107–10, 124, 199, 202
Sedgwick, Theodore, 264, 265, 374
self-government, 238, 240, 314–17, 379–80
self-preservation, 118, 149, 154, 159, 161,
    165, 179, 201
separation of powers, 217, 218, 221, 243,
    244–6, 253
Sewall, Samuel, 349
Shaftesbury, First Earl of (Cooper, Anthony
    Ashley), 145
Sidney, Algernon, 98
    as pseudonym, 203, 241, 289, 294–7
slavery, 379–83
social contract, 80–1, 90, 97, 104, 105, 146,
    152, 190, 201, 207–8, 210, 315
Souter, David, 392–3
sovereignty, 90, 91, 300; *see also* popular
    sovereignty; sovereignty by institution
    absolute, 57, 66, 68, 71, 80–1, 207–11
    states, 233, 234, 254, 257, 297, 319
sovereignty by institution, 71–6, 78–81, 152,
    207–11, 314
speech, *see* language, speech
stare decisis, 34, 213, 295
state constitutions, *see* constitution, states
state of nature, 72, 73, 76, 104, 105,
    145–50, 152, 153, 157, 159, 161,
    164–8, 200, 207, 211, 216, 238, 314,
    315, 317
state of war, 149–50, 167–8, 200, 216
states' rights, 256, 257, 258–78, 279, 280,
    282, 297, 302–10, 320, 321, 325, 327,
    335, 354, 360
statutory construction, *see* construction,
    statutory

statutory law, *see* law, statutory
Storing, Herbert J., xiv, xv, 174
Story, Joseph, x, xi, 4, 13, 15, 17–19, 26,
    28, 36, 37, 189, 196, 288, 289,
    290, 291, 308, 309, 310, 320, 341, 342,
    343–78, 379, 380, 384, 387,
    395
  *Commentaries on the Constitution of the
    United States*, 37, 189, 309, 310, 341,
    354, 355–64, 367
  on common law, 348–55
  theory of interpretation, 361–4, 368,
    376–8
St. Germain, Christopher, 46, 47, 67–8
  *Dialogues Between a Doctor of Divinity
    and a Student of the Laws of England*,
    47, 67–8
strict construction, *see* construction, strict
Suarez, Francisco, 63, 108
substantive due process, 52, 385–6, 388,
    390–4
Supreme Court of the United States, x, 1–7,
    9–12, 248–50, 380–4, 386–95

Taney, Roger Brooke, 343, 347, 364, 381,
    382, 383, 384, 385
Taylor, John of Caroline, 261, 271, 274,
    283, 297–305, 306, 308, 310, 355
Tocqueville, Alexis de, 320
tradition, power of, 94–5
Trenchard, John, xi, 56, 169, 197–203,
    241
Tucker, John Tudor, 232

tyranny of the majority, 233, 234, 237, 239,
    240–3
Tyrrell, James, 91–2, 100, 104

Upshur, Abel, 355

Vattel, Emerich, 36, 56, 169, 182, 188–90,
    314, 367, 368

Walker, Timothy, 355
Washington, Bushrod, 287, 290
Washington, George, 16, 254, 258, 260,
    267, 268, 269, 270, 319
Warren Court, 3, 11, 51
Warren, Earl, 3
Warren, Samuel, 389–90
Webster, Noah, 174
Weightman, Roger, 229
West, John, 26
White, Byron, 6
White, Edward, 33
William of Ockham, 85, 110
Wilson, James, 5, 15, 16, 234, 242, 278
Wilson, Woodrow, 11, 12, 37–40
  *Constitutional Government in the United
    States*, 12, 38–40
  Congressional Government, 12
  Darwinian constitutional understanding,
    38–9, 40
Wolcott, Alexander, 346
Woodeson, Richard, 358
words, *see* language
Wythe, George, 14